BLACK ADOLESCENTS

BLACK ADOLESCENTS

Reginald L. Jones, Editor
University of California at Berkeley

Cobb & Henry • Publishers
Berkeley, California

Black Adolescents

Copyright © 1989 by Reginald L. Jones

All rights reserved. No portion of this book may be reproduced in any form without the written permission of the publisher.

Cobb & Henry • Publishers
P.O. Box 4900
Berkeley, California 94704–4900

Cover design by Mark van Bronkhorst

Book design and typesetting by Cragmont Publications, Oakland, California

Manufactured in the United States of America

"Black Adolescents and Youth: An Update on an Endangered Species" is a revised version of an article published by Jewelle Taylor Gibbs under the title Black Adolescents and Youth: An Endangered Species, *American Journal of Orthopsychiatry*, 1984, 54, 6-21. "Copyright © 1984 The American Orthopsychiatric Association, Inc. Reproduced by permission."

The original version of Therapeutic Interventions with Black Adolescents was published as Chapter 11 in *Minority Mental Health*, Enrico E. Jones and Sheldon J. Korchin, Eds. (Praeger Publishers, New York, 1982). "Copyright © 1982 by Praeger Publishers. Revised and reprinted with permission of the publishers."

Library of Congress Cataloging-in-Publication Data:

Black adolescents / Reginald L. Jones, editor.
    p. cm.
  Bibliography: p.
  Includes indexes.
  ISBN 0-943539-01-3 : $36.95 — ISBN 0-943539-02-1 (soft) : $25.95
   1. Afro-American teenagers—Services for.   I. Jones, Reginald Lanier, 1931- .
E185.86.B5236   1989
362.7'96'08996073—dc19   88-36427
                                                       CIP

Contributors

Iris Baly
James A. Banks
William Cavil
M.L. Clark
Halford H. Fairchild
Anderson J. Franklin
Jewelle Taylor Gibbs
Lawford Goddard
Darnell F. Hawkins
Bertha Garrett Holliday
Nolan Jones
Courtland C. Lee

Julianne Malveaux
Carolyn B. Murray
Hector F. Myers
E. Joyce Roland
Diane Scott-Jones
Edward G. Singleton
Sandra Noel Smith
Barbara Staggers
Ronald L. Taylor
Randolf Tobias
Earle H. West
Anne Bittinger White

Contents

Preface xi

I. Perspectives: Contemporary, Historical, Comparative

Black Adolescents and Youth: An Update on An Endangered Species
Jewelle Taylor Gibbs 3

Trailblazers in Black Adolescent Research: The American Council on Education's Studies on Negro Youth Personality Development
Bertha Garrett Holliday 29

Comparative Personality Development in Adolescents: A Critique
Carolyn B. Murray, Sandra Noel Smith, and
Earle H. West 49

II. Youth in Diverse Settings

Black Youth in Predominantly White Suburbs
James A. Banks 65

Rural Black Adolescents: Psychosocial Development in a Changing Environment
Courtland C. Lee 79

III. Physical and Mental Health

Health Care Issues of Black Adolescents
Barbara Staggers 99

Urban Stress and the Mental Health of Afro-American Youth: An Epidemiologic and Conceptual Update
Hector F. Myers 123

IV. Psychosocial Development and Socialization

Black Youth, Role Models and the Social Construction of Identity
Ronald L. Taylor 155

Friendships and Peer Relations in Black Adolescents
M.L. Clark 175

V. Educational Issues and Programs

Educating Black Adolescents: Issues and Programs
Randolf Tobias 207

Models of Black Adolescent Underachievement
Carolyn B. Murray and Halford H. Fairchild 229

VI. Career Development and Employment

Career and Vocational Development of Black Youth
Iris Baly 247

Transitions: The Black Adolescent and the Labor Market
Julianne Malveaux 267

VII. Counseling and Psychotherapy

Counseling Black Adolescents: Critical Roles and Functions for Counseling Professionals
Courtland C. Lee 293

Therapeutic Interventions with Black Adolescents
Anderson J. Franklin 309

VIII. Special Topics

Pregnancy and Parenting

Antecedents and Outcomes of Pregnancy in Black Adolescents
Diane Scott-Jones, E. Joyce Roland, and
Anne Bittinger White 341

Black Teenage Parenting
Lawford Goddard and William Cavil 373

Substance Use

Substance Use and Black Youth: Implications of Cultural and Ethnic
Differences in Adolescent Alcohol, Cigarette, and Illicit Drug Use
    Edward G. Singleton 385

Youth in the Criminal Justice System

Black Adolescents and the Criminal Justice System
    Darnell F. Hawkins and Nolan Jones 403

Biographical Sketches 429

Author Index 437

Subject Index 451

PREFACE

Adolescence is a developmental period, typically ages 13–21 between childhood and adulthood, during which certain physical, cognitive, non-cognitive, legal and educational events occur. The purpose of this volume is to present an overview of contemporary Black adolescents—from social, psychological, economic, educational, medical, historical, and comparative perspectives. The treatment is eclectic but most chapters share a perspective that emphasizes how race, socioeconomic status, and environmental forces shape this critical period in the development of Black youth. Even a casual perusal of the volume's content leads to the inescapable conclusion that Black adolescents share common attributes with all adolescents but, because of life and environmental circumstances, also possess characteristics that are unique to them alone. It is my hope the literature reviewed, the old theories critiqued, the new theories advanced, and the programs and interventions described, will unequivocally indicate why a volume devoted to Black adolescents is not only of signal importance, but in fact is desperately needed.

The volume consists of nineteen chapters. In Chapter 1, Gibbs presents an overview of problems facing Black adolescents, especially those in urban settings. The problems she describes and the statistics she presents to support them are chilling: one out of five Black youth are not enrolled in or completes high school; Black youth unemployed at nearly twice the rate for all teenagers; Black youth constituting more than one-fifth of all juvenile arrests in 1979 and more than one-third of those committing violent crimes; equal or higher rates (compared to White youth) in every major drug category with the exception of inhalants and hallucinogens; twice the White pregnancy rate; and an increase in the suicide rate. Gibbs' succinct overview is treated in greater detail in chapters on health care (Chapter 6), mental health (Chapter 7), education (Chapters 10 and 11), the labor market (Chapter 13), pregnancy (Chapter 16), substance use (Chapter 18), and the criminal justice system (Chapter 19).

As do her fellow contributors, Gibbs does not rest upon a mere recitation of statistics. An important section of her chapter is on strategies for intervention. Here she presents capsulized discussions of alternative secondary programs, youth employment programs, sex education and family planning interventions, approaches to delinquency prevention, and drug prevention programs. Again, many of the programs she discusses are treated in subsequent chapters. For example Tobias (Chapter 10) describes a number of alternative programs for educating Black youth, while Murray and Fairchild (Chapter 11) discuss a single program, "Winners", in detail. Lee (Chapter 14) describes comprehensive group approaches to guidance and counseling, Staggers (Chapter 6) provides valuable insights for physicians who work with Black adolescents, while Goddard and Cavil (Chapter 17) describe a comprehensive program for Black teenage parents. While most interventions are at the group level, Franklin (Chapter 15) comprehensively describes and illustrates therapeutic interventions with individual Black adolescents.

The strategies and interventions described in the various chapters are not a collection of recipes divorced from theory and the empirical literature. Quite the contrary, the suggestions proffered and the programs developed are closely tied to past research. And while statistical data have provided informative perspectives on the depth of problems faced in many areas by Black adolescents, the meaning of these data is fleshed out by constructs, models and theories that form an important part of many of the chapters. For example, Murray & Fairchild describe and critically evaluate models developed to explain Black adolescent underachievement, while Baly incisively appraises vocational development theories and their relevance for explaining certain behaviors of Black adolescents. From the perspective of a medical practitioner, Staggers looks at psychosocial theory as applied to Black adolescents. Alternative formulations designed to account for mental health problems are taken up by Myers. His discussion, like that of Singleton on substance use, Murray and Fairchild on underachievement, and Malveaux and Jones on unemployment, highlight the significance of environmental factors in helping us understand the causes of the behavior of Black adolescents. In the area of friendship and interpersonal relationships, Clark shows how research from the perspectives of interpersonal attraction theories and friendship conception theories help explain Black adolescents' close personal relationships, while Taylor shows how various theoretical perspectives help explain identity formation within Black adolescents. All of the above writings emphasize that Black adolescents are not to be blamed for their problems. The theories and models discussed not only bring coherence to empirical studies and findings, but they guide future research efforts as well. The present work will have failed miserably if it does not leave the reader with some understanding of the many areas involving Black adolescents that still require additional study and research.

The study of Black adolescents is considered in its historical context. Holliday (Chapter 2) convincingly informs us of the rich legacy of scholarship on Black adolescents in the form of the American Council on Education's studies on Negro youth personality development that were undertaken in the 1930's and 1940's. We learn that nearly 50 years ago Black youth were plagued by many of the same problems we see today— high rates of unemployment, incomplete success at school, and unequal opportunity and discrimination. Holliday draws inferences from these studies for policy and future research. Many other chapters draw implications from research for policy as well, including Gibbs' comprehensive overview, and chapters on mental health, Black youth in predominantly White suburbs and rural settings, health care, identity development, friendship, education, career and vocational development, the labor market, counseling, psychotherapy, teenage pregnancy, substance use, and youth in the criminal justice system.

Most of the literature on Black adolescents concerns a single segment of the Black adolescent population—that of urban adolescents. To be sure, problems of Black urban adolescents are numerous and severe. Indeed, the focus of many of the intervention programs and strategies presented in the present volume is expressly upon this subgroup of the Black adolescent population. Yet, it is to be regretted that generalizations about Black adolescents found in the published literature focus almost exclusively on Black urban low socioeconomic adolescents, who are virtually always characterized in narrow and pejorative terms. A comprehensive computer search of the social science literature revealed, for example, fewer than a dozen studies that had Black non–urban and/or middle and upper middle–class Black adolescents as their focus. In order to present a rounded picture, it has seemed important to present a description of Black adolescents in non–urban settings. Thus, Black adolescents in predominantly White suburbs and in rural settings are the subject of chapters by, respectively, Banks (Chapter 4) and Lee (Chapter 5). These authors forcefully remind us that Black adolescents should not be treated as a monolithic group and that unique characteristics, needs, and dynamics are associated with living in these non–urban environments.

The topics covered in individual chapters are not treated in isolation. For example, the problem of incarcerated Black adolescents is related to their reduced opportunity for employment, a point emphasized by both Hawkins and Jones and Malveaux in their discussion, respectively, of Black youth in the criminal justice system and Black youth in the labor market. Racism is yet another societal force that cuts across discrete areas. It is not surprising, therefore, that the impact of racism on the development of Black youth is discussed in relationship to educational problems, mental health, health care, counseling, psychotherapy, incarceration, friendship, and career and vocational development.

Many statistics are presented throughout this volume, most of which involve comparisons of Black adolescents with White adolescents. Such comparisons virtually always indicate—by whatever standard or index adopted—that compared to their White peers, Black adolescents are deficient. Because the comparative method is so widely used in developing descriptions of Black adolescents, a word about this method is in order. The implied rationale of comparative studies is that the behavior and functioning of Black adolescents can only be understood in relationship to a White (typically middle–class) baseline or contrast group. That is, in order to achieve an understanding of the severity or significance of a problem or behavior of Black adolescents, it is considered necessary to determine how White adolescents stand on comparable instruments or measures. Yet, it is very rarely the case that White adolescents are studied in relationship to a Black contrast group. It seems relatively clear that in order to understand the behavior of Black adolescents, Black adolescents must be studied. Study of White adolescents is quite irrelevant for such a purpose. If our objective is to understand the behavior of Black adolescents, we need to know the facts about Black adolescents, not how they are the same or different from White adolescents. Moreover, a principle or finding can have significance even if it has been established only with reference to Black adolescents. Comparative studies can be useful to legislators, human service providers, and policymakers. For example, to know that secondary school Black students are suspended more than three times as often as White students—12.8 percent vs. 4.1 percent—alerts us to a problem. Similarly, comparative studies revealing that non–White students are out of school in significantly larger proportion than White students, or studies showing that Black children—compared to White children—are more likely to live in inadequate housing, die from homicide, be arrested, raped, robbed, bear children, die in infancy, or receive inadequate medical and dental care simply confirm the existence of problems that often are well known to professional as well as lay people who are concerned about the well–being of Black youth. However, these studies do not address reasons for the differences found.

Even though data from the studies just referred to may be useful for various advocate groups, their authors often fail to address the reasons for the differences or consider how the problems can be solved. For example, the fact that 33 percent of White children ages 12–17 report ever using alcohol whereas only 23 percent of Black children report alcohol use (a statistic favorable to Black youth) misses the mark, which is that a significant number of Black as well as White children—far too many—report alcohol use. Why? And what can be done about the problem of alcohol consumption among all youth, Black or White? Similarly, comparative studies that focus upon Black–White differences in school suspensions, numbers of students out of school, or life circumstances (i.e., differences between groups in the availability of adequate housing and medical care; and group differences in the probability of being raped, robbed, arrested, etc.) fail to consider superordinate questions: why is any adolescent, Black or White, suspended from school, out of school, or the subject of reduced life circumstances? And what changes at societal, institutional and individual levels are needed to address the problems identified? Comparative studies do not address these important questions.

The perspectives advanced should not be interpreted to deny that comparative studies are often undertaken in order to understand commonalities across groups. By undertaking such work we learn about similarities as well as differences between groups. But we must remember

Preface

that observations, studies and measures on White adolescents will not inform the behavior and characteristics of Black adolescents. Indeed, it is only principles that have been discovered through direct research on Black adolescents that will lead to an understanding of the behavior of Black adolescents.

In conceptualizing this volume and bringing it to completion, I have drawn upon experiences with my own past, present, and future adolescents—Julie, Angie, Cindy, Sjaun and Leasa; and I have also drawn upon the insights of my fellow psychologists Carolyn Block and C. Diane Howell. Moreover, I was especially fortunate in having had the opportunity to teach a small seminar on Black adolescents at the University of California at Berkeley that helped to sharpen the focus of this volume. Members of that seminar were George Kinayuo, Kevin McPherson, David Scott, Naponisha Sivad, and Ronald Stevenson, Jr. I thank them for their insights and perspectives.

Next are the contributors of individual chapters who must be especially recognized for the excellence of their scholarship and a willingness to revise their chapters to make this the best book possible. I hope you, the reader, are rewarded by their knowledge, expertise, and insights.

For review of individual chapters, I am indebted to Jewelle Taylor Gibbs, Hariette McAdoo, Carolyn Murray, and Thomas Parham. Their reviews and suggestions to authors made this a far better book than it would have been without their assistance. I have also enjoyed the highly competent assistance of Sharon Ceasar and Marlene Kleinman in preparing the manuscript; Fred and Pauline Felder of Cragmont Publications in designing and typesetting the book; and Mark van Bronkhorst in designing the book cover.

Finally, I am especially indebted to my wife, Michele, who was not only understanding of my need to complete the book and who willingly shared our family time so it could happen, but who also lovingly provided many gentle nudges and prods to ensure a timely completion of this work. Michele, I am deeply appreciative.

Reginald L. Jones
Berkeley, California

Part I
Perspectives: Contemporary, Historical, Comparative

BLACK ADOLESCENTS AND YOUTH: AN UPDATE ON AN ENDANGERED SPECIES*

Jewelle Taylor Gibbs

Webster defines *species* as "a class of individuals having common attributes and designated by a common name" and *endangered* as being exposed to "... danger or peril of probable harm or loss" (Webster, 1976). Black youth in contemporary American society can aptly be described as an endangered species. Educators have written them off as unteachable, the juvenile justice system has failed to rehabilitate them, the mental health system has virtually ignored or excluded them, and social welfare institutions seem ill-equipped to respond to their multiple problems. They are, in an irretrievable sense, rejects of the affluent society.

In 1983 there were 8.4 million Black youth in the 10–24 year old age range, with nearly three million each in the 15–19 and 20–24 year old age groups (U.S. Bureau of the Census, 1981). Since this under-24 age group, in combination with over five million children under the age of 10, comprised nearly half of the total Black population, the median age for Blacks was 25.8 years, while the median age for Whites was 31.8 years. Thus, the Black population is a relatively youthful population compared to Whites and, as such, is more deeply affected by social and economic problems that have a direct impact on teenagers and young adults. Although there are currently more middle-income Black families and more Black college students than during any previous period in U.S. history, there are also more Blacks on welfare and more severe problems among the majority of Black youth who are neither middle class nor college bound.

While every other demographic group has made progress in the last 25 years in terms of the major social indicators, Black youth in the 15–24 age group have performed less well on five out of six of these social indicators. More recent data from the 1980 census and other federal government sources indicate that, compared to 1960, more Black youth are unemployed, in the juvenile justice system, involved in substance abuse, having babies out-of-wedlock, and committing suicide. The only improvement in 25 years, and that is of dubious significance, is in a reduction of high-school dropout rates. A closer look at these social indicators will underscore the negative trends for Black youth in the past two and one-half decades.[1] (See note at end of chapter.)

---

* This chapter is a revised version of a paper published in the *American Journal of Orthopsychiatry*, 1984, 54, 6–21.

Perspectives: Contemporary, Historical, Comparative

Social Indicators

Education

A surface familiarity with the statistics on the educational attainment of Black youth suggests that there has been some improvement in the past 25 years. For example, the proportion of high school dropouts among Black youth in the 14–24 age group steadily declined from 23.8% in 1960 to 13.2% in 1984 and, for 16–17 year olds, from 22.3% to 5.2% in the same period (College Entrance Examination Board, 1985). In recent years, the gap between Black and White overall dropout rates in the high school age group has reached parity, in spite of disproportionately high rates for inner city Black youth. However, these figures do not reveal the number of Black high school graduates who were functionally illiterate or barely able to fill out a job application. While an earlier survey estimated that over 20% of Black male adolescents in the 12–17 age group were unable to read at the fourth grade level (Brown, 1979), more recent statistics indicated that 21% of all 18 and 19 year old and 25% of all 20 and 21 year old Black youth had neither completed nor were presently enrolled in high school in 1980 (U.S. Bureau of the Census, 1981). Thus, more than one out of five Black youths in the 18–21 age group currently does not have the basic certificate which is necessary in our society for most entry–level jobs, apprenticeship programs, military service, or post–secondary education.

While reasons for dropping out of high school are varied, a recent Urban League Study pointed out that many Black male teenagers leave because of family economic problems, academic difficulties or disciplinary problems, while females often drop out due to pregnancy (Williams, 1982). This study also reported that nearly one–third of Black families with incomes below $6,000 had at least one child suspended from school, as well as 18% of Black families with incomes above $20,000. These figures suggest that Black students have attitudinal or behavioral problems which school administrators and teachers are either unwilling or unable to deal with effectively. Lack of communication between parents and school authorities, as well as prevailing community attitudes towards the schools, probably contribute to bureaucratic inflexibility, student alienation and hostility in a continuously escalating cycle of mistrust and maladaptive behaviors.

Whether Black teenagers drop out of school or obtain a meaningless high school diploma based on "social promotion," the consequences are higher rates of unemployment, fewer options for jobs, greater welfare dependency, and longrange limitations on their social and economic mobility.

Youth Unemployment

In December 1987, the U.S. Labor Department announced a national unemployment rate of 5.8%, but unemployment among Black youth was 33.4%, nearly twice the rate of 16.1 among all teenagers.[3] This rate was nearly three times higher than the 12.1% unemployment rate among 16–19 year old Black youth in 1960, but lower than the unemployment rates in the large metropolitan areas of the country, which have consistently ranged between 40–50% throughout the past decade. Further, a recent study found that in 1984 nearly half of the Black youth in the 16–24 age group had no work experience at all (Larson, 1986). These extremely high unemployment rates, affecting from over one–third to one–half of the nation's Black teenagers, have significant implications for Black youth and for the society at large in the next few decades. If they are unable to find jobs, they will not develop work skills, attitudes and habits which are appropriate and necessary in a competitive, highly technological economy. Moreover, recent studies have indicated that chronically unemployed Black males constitute a disproportionately high percentage of those workers who become "discouraged" and completely drop out of the job–seeking market (Auletta, 1982). Without gainful employment, they will be increasingly tempted to participate in the underground alternative economy of the urban ghettos, i.e., the illegal system of barter in stolen goods, drugs, gambling and prostitution.

Since demographers currently predict that Black and other non–Whites will constitute from 20–30% of the youth and young adult population by the year 2010, the society will be severely impacted if a large proportion of this group is not well educated, highly skilled and capable of surviving in a high technology economy (Ozawa, 1986). Further, several studies have shown that adolescent work experience is a significant predictor of adult earnings. Since Black youth are less likely than Whites to have work experience, this is viewed as a major factor in making them less competitive for later jobs and contributes to their chronic disadvantaged status in the labor market, where their average lifetime earnings will be considerably less than adult White males at all educational levels (Freeman & Wise, 1982). The prospect of a rapidly increasing cadre of unemployed and unemployable urban youth, socialized to a nonproductive lifestyle on the streets, has major implications in terms of the development of a permanent urban underclass with its attendant sociopolitical consequences.

Delinquency and Crime

The rate of delinquency among Black youth has increased from 19.6% of all juvenile arrests in 1960 to 21.4% in 1979; thus 456,638 or approximately 15% of all Black adolescents in the 15–19 age group were arrested in 1979 (Uniform Crime Reports, 1981).

Black juveniles were arrested more frequently for robbery, rape, homicide and aggravated assault than Whites. They were also more likely than White juveniles to be arrested for violent personal crimes, disorderly conduct, sexual misbehavior and handling stolen property. National data on juvenile arrests by race for Part I offenses (violent crimes against persons and property) from 1977–1982, compiled by the F.B.I., indicate that Blacks accounted for nearly one–third of all arrests, yet Blacks in this age group represent less than one–fifth of the total youth population (Krisberg, et al., 2986). Further, over half of the juvenile arrests for the most violent crimes were among Black youth in that same period.

Another perspective on Black youth crime rates is provided by the National Youth Survey, a longitudinal study of self–reported delinquency and substance use among a probability sample of 11–17 year olds in the United States. Data collected from 1976–1983 indicates that Black youth reported a slightly higher rate of general delinquency, index offenses and felony offenses than White youth, but few of these offense differences were consistent or statistically significant across age sub–groups and over the seven–year period (Krisberg, et al., 1986). Despite official statistics which indicate that Black youth are disproportionately represented among violent and high frequency offenders, Huizinga and Elliott (1985) analyzed the N.Y.S. data for 1976–1980 and found no statistically significant racial differences in high rate offenders except for one year (1976). These researchers conclude:

> Overall, these findings suggest that there are few if any substantial and consistent differences between the delinquency involvement of different racial groups. This finding is not unique. Other large scale self–report studies of delinquency have reached similar conclusions (Gold & Reimer, 1975; Elliot & Voss, 1974; Williams & Gold, 1972; Bachman et al., 1971, 1978). As a result, it does not appear that differences in delinquent behavior can provide an explanation for the observed race differential in incarceration rates. (p. 13)

Given that conclusion, it is particularly disturbing to note that a recent study conclusively demonstrated that Black youth are more likely than any other ethnic group to be incarcerated in public juvenile facilities for both overall delinquency and for Part I offenses (Krisberg, et al., 1986). Further, these authors note that, while 71% of incarcerated Black youth are confined in public facilities, only 54% of Whites are in these facilities. In 1979 Black males had the highest rate of incarceration for all sex/race subgroups (587.9 per 100,000) and Black females were highest among females incarcerated (76.9 per 100,000) in public juvenile facilities. These incarceration rates increased dramatically by 1982 to 810 per 100,000 for

Black males and 98.4 per 100,000 for Black females, more than double the rate of increase among White males and females.

By 1982, when Black males comprised about 14% of youth under the jurisdiction of the juvenile court, they represented 39% of all incarcerated male juveniles, a ratio of 44 to 1 compared to the rate of White male juvenile incarceration. Further, the rate of Black youth incarceration for Part I offenses in 1982 was 8.6 per 100, which was 69% higher than the 5.1 per 100 rate of incarceration for White youth in the same offense category (Krisberg, et al., 1986).

The proportion of minority youth in public correctional facilities increased 26% from 1977–1982, with nearly two–thirds of this increase due to Black youth. Finally, a recent report noted that, on any given day, the state prison population contains more than 5% of all Black males in their twenties. Lifetime rates predict that up to 15% of all males will spend some time in an adult prison, while only 2–3% of White males are expected to do so (Krisberg, et al., 1986).

While some studies have suggested that Black teens are more likely to be arrested, booked, remanded for trial and to receive harsher dispositions than Whites, it has also been suggested that Black youth may be arrested more frequently for minor offenses both because inner city neighborhoods are patrolled more intensively and because police overreact to the negative attitudes and "anti–authority demeanor" of Black youth (Thornton, et al., 1982). Whether or not these factors can continue to account for the widespread discrepancy between arrest rates of Black and White youth, the fact remains that Black youth are disproportionately involved in the juvenile justice system, resulting in severe limitations on their educational and occupational opportunities and creating a vicious cycle of delinquency, incarceration, recidivism, and chronic criminal careers or unemployment and marginal social adaptation in adulthood.

Moreover, the primary victims of Black juvenile crime are the juveniles themselves and the Black community. Homicide is the leading cause of death among Black youth in the 15–24 age group. In 1985 alone, more than 1,900 Black youth, ages 15–24, were murdered, over 90% by other Black youth (National Center for Health Statistics, 1986). In addition, the rate of victimization for crimes of violence is generally greater for Blacks at all income levels and the victimization rate of residents of central cities was roughly twice that of residents of urban and suburban areas (Uniform Crime Reports, 1981). In 1980, 95% of those who committed crimes against Blacks were themselves Black, and the majority of these crimes were committed by youth under the age of 24. Inner city neighborhoods are increasingly becoming brutalized by youth who burglarize stores and homes, vandalize schools and churches, and terrorize those who are old, sick and vulnerable. The major victims of these antisocial youth are Black females, age 25 and older, Black males in the 50–64 age group, and other Black male teenagers in the 12–15 age group (Uniform Crime Reports, 1981).

Substance Abuse

Recent data from the National Institute on Drug Abuse indicates that non–White youth in the 18–25 age group have higher or equal rates of drug abuse than White youth in every major drug category except for inhalants and hallucinogens (NIDA, 1979). For the younger age group 12–17, 31% of Black teens reported they had used marijuana and 29% said they had used alcohol in this 1979 NIDA Survey. While a number of recent studies have indicated that in early adolescence the overall rate of drug and alcohol use is actually lower among Black than White youth, the rates of heroin and cocaine (including the recent derivative "crack") are disproportionately high among Black male youth (Brunswick, 1979). Reliable estimates of drug use in this population are difficult to obtain due to sampling problems and other methodological issues, but selected samples of young Black, inner city males in major metropolitan areas suggest high lifetime rates of these drugs. For example, a study of drug use in a Harlem sample of Black males in the mid–1970's found that heroin and cocaine rates were three times higher than reported by a national sample of selective service registrants (Brunswick, 1979). In a second wave of the study, when the subjects were 18–23, they reported lifetime prevalence rates of 88% for marijuana and 86% for alcohol (Brunswick, Merzel, & Messeri, 1985). The mortality rate from drug–related deaths has increased dramatically in nine major metropolitan areas since 1973, with about one–third of those fatalities occurring among Black youth in the 15–24 age group (NIDA, 1980).

Drug abuse among Black youth has not only increased in the past 25 years, it has also spread from the inner cities into the suburbs and the users have become progressively involved in the use of "hard drugs" such as heroin and cocaine, which are inextricably tied to street crime. Moreover, a NIDA study has predicted an increase in drug abuse among Black and Hispanic youth through 1995 because they constitute the fastest growing segment of the population and because of their current usage patterns (NIDA, 1980). In 1980, 27% of the clients admitted to federally–funded drug–abuse treatment centers were Black and approximately 12% of these addicts were under age 18. Three out of five of this group were addicted to heroin and nearly 50% had been arrested at least once, graphically illustrating the relationship between drug abuse and delinquency (U.S. Dept. of H.H.S., 1981).

Drinking among Black teens also increased 10% in only seven years, i.e., from 20% in 1972 to 30% in 1979 (NIDA, 1979). While drinking has never been as widespread among Black youth as among Whites, nonetheless, teenage drinking is related to self-destructive behavior such as fatal accidents (75% involve alcohol), low school achievement, physical and mental health problems, and adult alcoholism (Paton & Kandel, 1978; Thornton, et al., 1982).

Again, the issue is not simply a legal or a moral issue, but our concern should be focused on the damage these young people are inflicting on themselves physically, psychologically and socially. Drug use among teens is very highly correlated to low school achievement, delinquency, and accidental deaths. Drug addiction inevitably involves teenagers in activities which will increase access to drugs, whether these involve stealing, dealing or hustling sex in order to "get high" (Gandossy, et al., 1980; Thornton, et al., 1982). Addicts lose interest in school, work, and gradually deteriorate so that "getting high" becomes the major motivation of each day and they become walking zombies, worthless to themselves, their families and their communities. Addiction among Black youth also substantially increases their risk of arrest and imprisonment, of physical and mental illness, and of death by overdosing among Black youth (Gandossy, et al., 1980; Nelson, et al., 1974).

Since 1980 when AIDS (Acquired Immunodeficiency Syndrome) diseases were first reported in the United States, drug-addicted Black youth have been particularly at risk for infection from the use of unsterilized needles. In December 1986 the Centers for Disease Control (1986b) reported that 25% of the cases of AIDS were among Blacks; among the Black male patients, 35.4% identified themselves as heterosexual intravenous drug users. The risk of AIDS infection is also increasing among the Black female partners of these men, both as a result of shared needles and through unprotected sexual intercourse.

The relationship between all forms of substance abuse and other forms of antisocial behavior has been well-documented, yet there are very few preventive programs which are specifically aimed at low-income inner city youth (Ray, 1983; Thornton, et al., 1982; Lewis, 1978). Treatment programs tend to be tailored to the young adult population and are often tied into the criminal justice system as involuntary rehabilitation programs rather than conceived as early intervention programs for novice substance abusers.

Unwed Teen-Age Pregnancy

In 1985, the Guttmacher Institute published a startling report that the pregnancy rate for American teenagers in the 15-19 year old age group was the highest of all industrialized nations at 96 per 1,000 pregnancies per year. America was also the only country where the rate was increasing and, contrary to popular stereotypes, it was increasing more rapidly among White than Black adolescent females. Despite the decreasing birth trend among Black teenagers, pregnancy rates are still twice as high among Blacks as Whites (163 per 1,000 vs. 83 per 1,000) and out-of-wedlock pregnancy is a major problem in the Black community (Children's Defense Fund, 1986). In 1980, for example, nearly one in ten Black teenage females gave birth (9.5%) compared to one in 25 White females (4.5%). Black teens are more likely to have their babies, while White teens are more likely to terminate their pregnancies by abortions. In 1983, 85.7% of babies born to Black females under age 19 were out-of-wedlock compared to 39.7% born to White teenage mothers (CDF, 1986).

These are children having children, with profound physical and psychosocial consequences for the girls themselves, as well as negative implications for their babies and their families. First, teen-age mothers are more likely to drop out of high school, more likely to go on welfare, and more likely to experience complications in pregnancy and associated physical and psychological problems than adult women who bear their first child (Chilman, 1983; Family Impact Seminar, 1979; Furstenberg, et al., 1981). Moreover, teen mothers are more likely to have larger families, to experience less occupational stability and economic mobility, and to be less competent and effective as parents.

Second, babies born to teenage mothers are more likely to have low birth-weight and other perinatal and postnatal problems, more likely to have poor health, and more likely to experience abuse or neglect. Infant mortality rates are highest among teen mothers and nearly twice as high among Blacks (21.7 per 1,000 live births in 1978) as among Whites. If they survive, these children tend to be less healthy, less academically successful in school, more likely to grow up in a single-parent, welfare-dependent family, and more likely to become single parents themselves. Third, the effects of premature fatherhood on the youthful male partners of these teenage mothers has only recently been of interest to researchers. Several studies have found that, compared to their peers who had not fathered children, these young men were more likely to attain a lower educational level and lower occupational status, to have larger families and to experience unstable marriages (Chilman, 1983; Furstenberg, et al., 1981).

Finally, the impact of these illegitimate births on Black families has yet to be fully understood and documented. However, some sociological studies suggest that children reared in single-parent homes, have fewer competent role models and fewer social supports, which, in turn, limits their ability to grow up in successfully functioning families, to develop satisfactory heterosexual relationships, and to form stable family units of their own (Ladner, 1971; Williams, 1982).

In 1983, 42% of all Black families were headed by females, but 48% of these households included children under the age of 18; half of all Black female-headed households were classified below the poverty line (CDF, 1986). Thus, the trend toward more Black teenage single mothers may have devastating long-term effects on the structure and functioning of the Black family and, ultimately, on the stability of the Black community.

Suicide

The final and most alarming social indicator of all is the increasing phenomenon of suicide among Black teens and young adults. In the 15–24 age group the suicide rate in 1960 for Black males was 4.1 per 100,000 and for Black females, it was 1.3 per 100,000. After peak rates in 1971 and 1976 in this age group, the suicide rates had declined slightly but had still nearly tripled by 1982 to 11.0 per 100,000 for Black males and nearly doubled to 2.2 per 100,000 for Black females (NCHS, 1986). While suicide rates among Black males are still lower than Whites of the same age, it has been suggested that the figures would be much higher if causes of death among Blacks, in general, were reported as reliably as causes of death among Whites. For example, if suspected cases of suicide by single-car accidents, deliberate drug overdoses, victim-precipitated homicides, and other violent accidents were included in these statistics, the suicide rates would be significantly higher, particularly since the rates of homicide and other types of violent accidents are higher among non-White youth (Holinger, 1979). In a recent analysis of long-term trends in adolescent suicide, Holinger and Offer demonstrated the correlation between adolescent population changes and adolescent suicide rates in the United States and suggested that higher rates may reflect increased peer competition—for colleges, jobs, and access to services—that occurs during periods of adolescent population growth (Holinger & Offer, 1982). Since Black adolescents are clearly in a more disadvantaged competitive position than Whites, this may very well contribute to their feelings of hopelessness and thereby increase their vulnerability to suicidal behavior.

Strategies for Intervention

This brief review of six social indicators presents a grim and depressing portrait of the plight of Black youth in contemporary American society. It also suggests that the gatekeepers and guardians of our social institutions have somehow ignored, neglected, or even colluded against the needs of these youth. In many of the largest cities, one can drive through Black ghetto neighborhoods and see dozens of unemployed youth drinking on street-corners, buying drugs in alleys, or hustling a variety of "hot goods". Many represent the second and third generation of families on welfare, both unemployed and unemployable (Auletta, 1982; Glasgow, 1981).

While our affluent society has virtually written off this group, they continue to grow and constitute a burgeoning army of alienated and angry youth. As the gap between the "haves" and the "have nots" widens, this group will be further disadvantaged by their inability to participate in an increasingly technocratic and computerized society. The riots of the 1960's and 1970's will seem pale by comparison to the potentially widespread violence which may be triggered off by an inevitable confrontation between the "haves" and the "have nots" over shrinking natural and material resources, increasingly exacerbated by conservative politicians who foster a growing public perception of these youth as welfare cheaters and antisocial parasites who are a threat to the "American Way of Life."

The current status of Black youth is one of the most severe and most challenging social problems ever to confront the helping professions, yet it is also one of the least recognized and least effectively addressed in terms of research, policy formulation, and service programs. In view of the declining commitment of the federal government and the shrinking resources of state, county, and local governments to deal with these pervasive problems, it is incumbent upon mental health and social service professionals to develop innovative and cost–efficient programs and services aimed at alleviating these problems.

One productive way to address these problems would be for persons in the helping professions to develop relationships and build coalitions with private, nonprofit organizations, civic groups and churches which serve the Black community. These groups should work collaboratively to identify problem areas, establish priorities, and develop programs and services specifically tailored to the needs of Black youth.

Programmatic Needs and Priorities

There are at least six primary areas which require the coordinated efforts of professionals and community leaders to launch a concerted attack on the massive problems of Black youth: 1) alternative secondary educational programs; 2) employment programs; 3) sex education and family planning programs; 4) comprehensive services and child care programs for teenage parents; 5) delinquency prevention and early intervention programs; 6) drug prevention and counseling programs. All of these areas have implications for the prevention of suicide and self–destructive behavior among Black youth; the need for program development is urgent. Most crucial to the current stabilization of Black youth are education, employment, and sex education/family planning programs; these are the areas that demand priority attention.

Alternative Secondary Education Programs

As Hobbs and Robinson (1982) pointed out, recent research has indicated a need for greater attention to the promotion of cognitive competence in adolescents, particularly those with a background of socioeconomic or educational disadvantage. While the government has spent millions of dollars on early childhood education programs such as Head Start, minimal attention has been paid to the needs of older youth with learning disabilities and high school dropouts. However, these authors cited a National Institute of Education report which positively evaluated several compensatory education programs which have shown promising results in increasing cognitive skills and achievement levels for these students. Flexible curricula, including work–study programs, can be designed for those students who cannot seem to benefit from the traditional curriculum, yet must develop marketable skills for entry–level employment. Street academies, such as the one sponsored by the Bay Area Urban League in Oakland, California, have been successful in reclaiming hard–core dropouts who have chronic records of failure and rejection in public schools. Since so many Black youth drop out or are forced out of school due to academic or attitudinal factors, mental health professionals can offer consultation to school personnel to institute system change regarding the reduction of truancy, school failure, classroom disruption and violence. "Project Return" in Irvington, New Jersey is an excellent example of a multidisciplinary approach to helping teenagers in a predominantly Black school district return to the regular classrooms—by modifying teacher attitudes, classroom organization, and administrative procedures, and by involving parents and students in the development of educational policies and practices (Howard, 1983). Additionally, urban secondary schools with limited financial resources and facilities must find creative ways of utilizing volunteers as teacher aides, community liaison workers, athletic coaches and performing arts specialists. Several models of such innovative programs which have been initiated in a number of urban school systems in recent years have shown early promising results (Deal, 1975; Edmonds, 1979; Hampton, 1974). As has been recently demonstrated in Chicago, appeals can also be made to local businesses to "adopt–a–school" and provide that school with tax–deductible donations of computers, technical books and supplies, employee tutors, and incentive awards for achievement in topics related to business or science.

Two other recent proposals, one advanced by a clergyman and another by an educator, may create controversy, but are worthy of consideration. The Reverend Samuel Proctor, pastor of the historic Abyssinian Baptist Church in New York's Harlem, has proposed a national youth academy to be set up for disadvantaged White and minority youth who are potential dropouts and school failures (Proctor, 1986).

These residential academies for grades 7–12 would be located in every state on abandoned military bases and supported by federal grants to the states. The educational program would be structured to accomplish three things, i.e., "...the learning of useful lifelong skills, discipline, self–respect and appreciation of accomplishment; the acquisition of basic academic tools and the mastery of subject matter at the junior and senior high school levels; and the development of the body and the cultivation of aesthetic taste" (p. 12). Rev. Proctor points out that, even though the per student cost of such a program would be about $14,000, it is still considerably cheaper than the average cost of about $30,000 for incarcerating a drug addict for one year, which may be one of the negative alternative pathways for this particular group.

The other radical proposal aimed at these potential dropouts has been advanced by Gordon McAndrew (1986), a senior research fellow at the U.S. Department of Education. He has proposed a two–tier system of high school completion, where non–college bound students would graduate with an "O" (average) diploma at the end of 10th grade and college–bound students would receive an "A" (advanced) diploma at the end of 12th grade. The high school curriculum would be revised so that basic high school requirements would all be met in grades 7–10 for an "O" diploma and a more rigorous course of college–preparatory courses would be required for the "A" diploma. While he recognizes the negative potential in this two–tiered system for tracking poor and minority youth into the lower "O" level, he defends his proposal on the grounds that it would reduce the dropout rate and would better prepare these problem students to enter the world of work upon completing high school.

Both of these proposals are radical departures from the current educational system, which seems to have failed the majority of Black youth. If current trends are not reversed by serious commitments to experiment with such innovative, daring, and even controversial programs, many Black youth will find themselves unable to compete for jobs and unable to establish economically viable families and stable households.

A recent study by the Rand Corporation found that parental satisfaction with their children's schools was directly related to their perception of their involvement and influence in the educational system (Bridge & Blackman, 1978). This suggests that it is especially important for Black parents to involve themselves in all facets of their children's education, to work in collaboration with teachers and administrators to monitor homework assignments, to establish clear and consistent academic standards, to support disciplinary practices and to assure a safe learning environment for all youth. More importantly, however, teachers, administrators and parents must continue to challenge the unfounded assumption that underachieving teenagers and high school dropouts are beyond help and doomed to a life of marginal employment but, rather, dedicate their energies to the development of appropriate remedial and experimental programs to develop the level of cognitive skills and competencies which are required for survival in a highly technological economy.

Employment

Youth employment programs are inextricably linked to educational attainment. As pointed out earlier, lack of a high school diploma, particularly among Black youth, is highly correlated to unemployment, low wages, job instability, and welfare dependency (Williams, 1982). In view of reduced state and federal funds for youth employment and training programs such as CETA, communities must make greater efforts to develop programs at the local level, which requires a cooperative effort of businesses, local government, schools and social service agencies. However, even with federal incentives in the form of wage subsidies for youth employment demonstration programs and support of the youth employment project of the National Alliance for Business, the private sector has not seemed able or willing to compensate for the jobs lost through cutbacks in government funding.

One element often missing from these youth employment programs is an understanding of the attitudes and behaviors of Black youth, which have often created unfavorable employer perceptions and lack of interest in hiring them. Social service agencies can cooperate with school counselors to develop job counseling workshops which would be designed to prepare students for the working world by discussing such basic topics as punctuality, responsibility, appropriate dress and language, office manners, positive attitudes, and bureaucratic structure and procedures. The Youth Employment Program of the Oakland, California Public School System is a good example of such interagency–community cooperation. However, greater efforts must be directed to enrolling Black professionals and small businessmen in these programs, for they can fulfill the dual purpose of providing jobs and serving as successful role models for Black youth.

Greater emphasis should be given to school–to–work transition programs for Black youth. These include a variety of programs involving a collaboration between schools and businesses to facilitate the progression from the classroom to the work setting. Two federally funded projects which have achieved favorable results with minority youth are the School–to–Work Transition Project, which provided 5–10 hours of job–related instruction weekly during the school year in 11th and 12th grades, and the Job Track Project, which consisted of two days of instruction and three days of support services, including clerical skills and counseling, to improve students' entry–level skills, attitudes, and information (Congressional Budget Office, 1982). In-school job placement services should also be expanded.

In cities like Boston and Minneapolis, a coalition of businesses have formed Private Industry Councils to collaborate with school, local governments and community leaders to develop effective minority youth employment programs. These model programs share several important characteristics, e.g., a commitment from the top leaders in the community power structure to tackle the problem, high expectations of behavior and performance from the students, and a range of support services, including counseling. In these programs employers first provide summer jobs, then full-time employment after the students successfully complete high school (Walker, 1986).

Hobbs and Robinson (1982) argue that due to demographic shifts there will be fewer young workers in the labor force in the next few decades. Thus, public policy should be geared to increasing the competence and skills of the current adolescent population in order that they will be able to maintain the nation's productive capacity in the years ahead in spite of their fewer numbers. A corollary to this argument is that Black and other non-White youth will comprise an increasing proportion of this shrinking youth population, so it is imperative that they obtain the work experience and training they will need in a highly complex economy (Williams, 1982).

Sex Education and Family Planning

Programs of sex education and family planning clinics must be modified to take into account sociocultural factors and differential attitudes toward sexuality and childbearing which exist among lower-income urban Black youth. Some studies have indicated that Black teenagers initiate heterosexual activity earlier than Whites, use birth control less frequently and feel less stigma attached to out-of-wedlock pregnancy (Chilman, 1983; Furstenberg, et al., 1981; Gibbs, 1986; Thompson, 1980; Zelnick & Kanter, 1980). Other studies suggest that the meaning of pregnancy differs in different sociocultural groups with many Black girls viewing it as an entry to adulthood and autonomy (Ladner, 1971; Stack, 1974). Thus, programs which focus on information and referral sources (and are geared to middle-class White teenagers) may be quite irrelevant and inappropriate to the needs of Black teenagers. As many experts emphasize, programs should be directed to *primary prevention*, i.e., efforts to reduce the incidence of unplanned teenage pregnancies through comprehensive programs of sex education and family planning services.

Inner city Black youth should receive sex education and have access to contraceptive services not only to prevent unwanted pregnancies but also to prevent sexually transmitted diseases. Recent surveys by the Centers for Disease Control (1986a; 1986b; 1987a) have noted an alarming increase in venereal diseases and AIDS among Black youth. Even more alarming, researchers now believe that the presence of a venereal disease weakens the immune system and increases the risk of an AIDS infection. A recent study of 400 patients being treated for venereal diseases at a Baltimore, MD clinic revealed a 5% rate of AIDS infection among teenage Black females, the highest rate for any sociodemographic group in the clinic population. Thus, sexually active Black youth who do not use barrier forms of contraception are vulnerable to sexually transmitted diseases, including the invariably fatal AIDS virus. Moreover, should a pregnancy occur, the baby of an AIDS–infected mother has a high probability of carrying the virus. As of August 1987 there were 558 cases of pediatric AIDS and nearly three of every five (60%) of these infected children were Black (Centers for Disease Control, 1987b).

In evaluating the effectiveness of these programs in the schools and the community, several studies have found that Black teenagers were less well–informed about basic facts and less effective users of contraceptives than were White (Chilman, 1983; Furstenberg, et al., 1981). However, a family planning program sponsored by the Family Planning Service at the University of Pennsylvania School of Medicine, in conjunction with several inner city high schools, offered educational and emotional support to a group of never–pregnant Black females and found that these adolescents were able to use contraceptive services effectively over a three–year period (Mudd, et al., 1978). Similarly, a model program developed by the St. Paul Maternal and Infant Care Project offered comprehensive health care and contraceptive services to inner city teens through clinics in one junior and two senior high schools, with dramatic reductions in birth rates in those schools.

Model programs aimed at preventing teenage pregnancy are proliferating throughout the country. The National Urban League, through its local affiliates initiated a program called the "Adolescent Male Responsibility Project" in 1985 with a specific appeal to teenage males as well as females to be responsible about their sexual behavior and to understand the implications of teenage pregnancy.

The Children's Defense Fund has launched an intensive campaign to reduce the rates of teen pregnancy through local community organizations as well as federal and state initiatives (CDF, 1986). Among the local programs which they have identified as effective in prevention and early intervention are comprehensive adolescent health and family planning clinics located at Johns Hopkins University in Baltimore, Presbyterian Hospital in New York City, and Grady Memorial Hospital in Atlanta.

It is also important to recognize the needs of Black adolescent males in the area of sex education and family planning. As among White males, this group tends to obtain its information about sexuality from peers and the mass media, leading to misinformation and distortion (Furstenberg, et al., 1981; Shapiro, 1980). Since multiple premarital pregnancies are a particular problem among low-income Black adolescents, sex education and pregnancy prevention programs should be designed to involve males as well as females (Beschner & Friedman, 1979; Chilman, 1983; Furstenberg, et al., 1981). Some current approaches which may prove to be effective with males and females involve the use of peer counselors in school programs, "rap" groups in community agencies, informal programs through Boys' and Girls' Clubs, youth groups and other programs which involve the use of well-trained youthful counselors who are cognizant of differing cultural values among Black youth (Shapiro, 1980).

Finally, in order to plan effective and culturally relevant family planning programs, professionals must involve Black parents and community leaders who are familiar with the deeply ingrained attitudes and social customs which have often reinforced the patterns of premarital sexuality and childbearing in the Black community.

Comprehensive Services for Teenage Parents

At the level of secondary prevention, comprehensive prenatal and postnatal services and adequate child-care services are badly needed for Black teenage parents. Evaluation studies of service programs for school-age parents have shown mixed results due to a number of factors, including lack of administrative support, poorly defined target populations and problem issues, inadequate interagency coordination, uneven quality of services, and short-term goals (Zellman, 1982). Moreover, while some of these programs produced positive short-term results in terms of improved maternal and infant health and continuing education, long-term results in terms of educational attainment, reduction of subsequent pregnancies, or achievement of economic independence were less positive (Klerman, 1979). Finally, most of these programs provide for the first-time teenage mother but not for those with higher-order pregnancies, young mothers who are particularly at risk for negative outcomes.

The Adolescent Pregnancy Program at Children's Hospital National Medical Center in Washington, D.C., though now defunct due to loss of funds, presented an excellent comprehensive, multidisciplinary approach that offered pregnancy testing, venereal disease screening, family planning and counseling services, prenatal services, labor and delivery at the university medical center, and pospartum maternal and infant care (Silber, 1982). This program had several other distinctive features such as parent education, nutrition classes, and continuity of care supervised by a primary nurse. A variety of other innovative programs have shown positive short-term results, such as New York City's Project Redirection, which offers comprehensive services to pregnant teenagers and pairs them with adult volunteer counselors.

Adequate child care services are also significantly lacking for Black teenage parents. Since these teenagers are unable to continue their education without child care, it is imperative that such services be developed in order to prevent the cycle of school leaving–lack of skills–unemployment–welfare. Further, children of teen parents are at higher risk for child abuse and neglect; relieving these parents of the full–time burden of child care will also reduce the incidence of child abuse and result in psychologically and physically healthier children. One immediate and inexpensive way to increase child care facilities for teenage parents would be for Black churches to donate their generally under–used facilities for weekday child care centers, which could be staffed by volunteers from among the retired and unemployed members of the community. This would minimize the need for paid professional staff and would maximize the use of human resources in the community, such as has been demonstrated in the Foster Grandparents Program.

Finally, it is essential that teenage fathers who have long been neglected by program planners, become involved in programs with their pregnant partners so that they can feel a closer bond and greater paternal responsibility for their babies. Since 1981, a model program, the Teenage Pregnancy and Parenting Program which offers comprehensive services to teen parents and involves the use of peer counselors, has been in operation at San Francisco General Hospital. Participants in this program are primarily Black and Hispanic and the initial results have led to cautious optimism. Similar programs have been funded in eight U.S. communities by the Ford Foundation in order to encourage involvement of teenage fathers, to improve their educational outcomes and to reduce the incidence of subsequent pregnancies.

Delinquency Prevention

Approaches to Black delinquents through the cooperative efforts of local agencies, businesses and community groups must also be conceptualized in terms of primary and secondary prevention. Evaluation studies of preventive approaches to delinquency have generally indicated that most programs are ineffective for a variety of reasons, including a failure to specify the target population, failure to match treatment to type of delinquent, and failure to control for variables such as type of offense, age, SES and community support system (Thornton, et al., 1982). Since Black delinquents tend to be overrepresented among the category of socialized or subcultural delinquents (Gibbs, 1982), primary prevention efforts should be aimed at modifying their immediate environments to provide more recreational and cultural programs and to coordinate efforts to reduce the school dropout rate and the youth unemployment rate (Lewis, 1978). It seems quite ironic that publicly funded recreational and cultural programs are usually available for youth in suburban middle-class communities, while there are few such programs or even adequate facilities for inner city youth, who are forced to play in trash-littered lots, dangerous city streets, and abandoned buildings. Again, social agency professionals could engage in some "old-fashioned" community organizing to bring together churches, civic groups and parents who can combine their facilities, resources, and volunteer energies to provide structured recreational programs in safe locations, as well as summer vacation and camp programs; classes in Black history and culture to generate in these youth a sense of history, ethnic pride and positive identity; and field trips to museums, cultural events, sports activities and to local universities, industries and government agencies. While there is no guarantee that any of these activities will actually reduce delinquency, there is some evidence that communities with extensive youth programs do have lower rates of delinquency (Thornton, et al., 1982). Similarly, any efforts that involve teenagers in productive activities will presumably reduce their energies, motivation and time for self-destructive and delinquent behavior.

Secondary prevention or early intervention efforts should focus on the establishment of more diversion programs which would be operated by youth service organizations within the community and that could prevent the premature identification and stigmatization as "delinquent" of those with first-time minor offenses. In addition, a range of comprehensive services, such as those offered by public and private agencies in Kentucky, must be available to the heterogeneous population of Black delinquents—e.g., prevention of truancy; home-based social and rehabilitative services for the delinquent and his family; day treatment programs which involve remedial education, counseling and recreation; foster care for abused or neglected children; and residential treatment facilities for the more seriously delinquent and disturbed youth (Lewis, 1978). If these approaches are going to be effective with Black delinquents, they must be planned in conjunction with Black mental health and social welfare professionals and community leaders, they must take into account the sociocultural values and structural barriers of the Black community, and they must be staffed by people who are sensitive to those values and realities.

Several comprehensive programs in Washington, D.C. have been particularly effective in addressing delinquency-prone Black youth, e.g., "City Lights" and the Junior Citizens Corps. The former program offers a range of innovative day treatment programs to disturbed and disadvantaged teens who participate in educational and therapeutic activities structured to help maintain them in the community (Tolmach, 1985). The Junior Citizens Corps is a youth agency which serves delinquent and emotionally troubled Black youth, ages 10–19, through a range of community-based programs including job counseling and referral, social rehabilitation, remedial education, social services, and youth leadership training. Inner city communities should develop a coordinated system of comprehensive services based on these models.

Finally, any programs of secondary or tertiary prevention (rehabilitation) for Black delinquents should be linked to the improvement of educational skills and vocational training, since these types of programs have generally had the most positive outcomes and, particularly for this group, are more likely to attack the underlying socioeconomic causes of their antisocial behavior.

Drug Prevention Programs

In terms of primary prevention, a recent review of evaluations of 127 drug abuse prevention programs concluded that these programs "produced only minor effects on drug use behavior and attitudes", with the eight most effective programs designed with peer or process orientations rather than an information-only approach. Moreover, current programs of drug education, like sex education, rarely take into account ethnic differences in attitudes, usage patterns, and response to treatment (Beschner & Friedman, 1979; Nelson, et al., 1974; Paton & Kandel, 1978). Such programs also must take into account the social context, the values, and the realities of the inner city teenager's lifestyle, which is very different from those of suburban White middle-class youth. Urban Black youth are exposed earlier to a variety of drugs, may be involved at an early age as "runners" or "spotters" for drug dealers, and tend to accept the pervasive presence of drugs as a fact of community life. Current high school drug education programs fail to recognize that inner city youth usually have an earlier exposure and greater level of sophistication about drugs than middle-class suburban youth. In order to be effective, drug education and prevention programs must involve the cooperation of parents and community leaders, as well as peer counselors, who will not only inform these teens about the dangers of drug abuse, but also set up supportive peer groups, who will make mutual contracts to avoid drugs and will also develop alternative forms of socializing. Parents must be willing to monitor the behavior and moods of their children, to confront them about suspicious friends and activities, and to give them positive reinforcement for staying "clean." Moreover, parents themselves must be supported and reinforced by community leaders who are willing to take a public stance against drug dealing and drug use in the Black community.

Community health centers and school-based clinics which offer comprehensive health care to Black adolescents are important in providing both education, counseling and treatment for substance abuse. In communities like Kansas City, where comprehensive health clinics are located in the public high schools, use of alcohol and marijuana decreased in the first two years of clinic operation.

Multi-service programs which combine drug and alcohol abuse education and treatment programs with health, mental health, education, employment and vocational counseling and referral services are excellent approaches to prevention and early intervention. Such programs as "The Door" in New York City offer a range of programs to low-income and minority youth from 12–20; these programs are offered after school and in the evenings and are free or low cost (CDF, 1986). These programs offer a holistic approach toward the physical, emotional, social and intellectual needs of the youth, a perspective that is often lacking in programs specifically aimed at substance abuse, but is particularly appropriate for Black youth.

With regard to secondary and tertiary prevention, most federally funded drug counseling and rehabilitation programs are aimed at older youth and at the harder drugs such as cocaine and heroin. However, Black children in the inner city are exposed to drugs at increasingly younger ages, so more locally-sponsored programs need to be developed with a focus on early intervention and prevention of long-term drug abuse. These programs could effectively utilize parents and volunteers, since the preadolescent group is a somewhat more captive audience in elementary and junior high schools, as well as through youth organizations such as Boy Scouts and Girl Scouts, Little League and other team sports, and musical and religious groups. These supervised sports, recreational, social and religious activities could also serve as a vehicle for informal drug education and prevention programs involving parents and youth leaders in approaches specifically tailored to the target group of teenagers. Such ongoing programs would be particularly effective in communities where schedules of intermittent reinforcement are necessary for many adolescents to maintain drug-free behavior. Recent attempts by the mass media to publicize the extent of adolescent drug abuse in America, through programs such as "The Chemical People," have been aimed at a middle-class audience, yet these programs have also fostered local, well-coordinated community strategies to combat drug abuse; perhaps these strategies may filter down through the widespread involvement of parents, schools, social agencies and treatment centers to low-income Black youth (Paris, 1983).

Finally, the increase in suicide rates and violent self-destructive accidents among Black youth can probably best be addressed indirectly through policies and programs of primary prevention that will reduce their feelings of helplessness, hopelessness, depression, and alienation—all of which have been related to suicidal behavior in adolescence (Grueling & DeBlassie, 1980). As noted earlier, such programs should be aimed at alleviating the social and economic conditions which have made Black adolescents, and particularly Black males, more vulnerable to school withdrawal or failure, unemployment, teenage parenthood, drug abuse and delinquency (Gibbs, 1988).

Conclusions

It is becoming increasingly clear that all of the phenomena discussed above are interrelated and, in combination, operate to reduce the life chances for Black youth, to restrict their social mobility and to move them toward a permanently disadvantaged caste status. The programs and services discussed here represent only a limited and relatively superficial approach to this complex issue. A truly effective preventive strategy must evolve from significant social and structural changes and must ultimately stem from initiatives at the federal government level to develop a comprehensive national policy for families and children that would include an adequate guaranteed income, full employment, health care services, adequate housing and recreational facilities, vocational training programs for youth, family planning services, child care services and coordinated programs to assist dysfunctional families. Since such a national family policy is the ultimate panacea and unlikely to be adopted or instituted in the foreseeable future, helping professionals must settle for limited goals and circumscribed programs to prevent future generations of Black youth from becoming permanently consigned to an underclass.

This paper has attempted to dramatize the plight of Black urban youth, who are, in several significant social dimensions, worse off vis a' vis the dominant society, than they were two and one–half decades ago. The statistics are startling and speak for themselves. But who speaks for the Black youth? The hour is late and the possibility of a permanent youthful Black "underclass" is coming closer and closer to reality. If members of the helping professions do not recognize the enormity of this situation, if we fail to develop creative solutions to this growing malignancy in our social fabric, we will share the responsibility for the inevitable outcome. If we are to avert a society split along racial and economic lines, we must expand the resources of our professional social service agencies by building collaborative relationships with local schools, churches, businesses and community organizations serving the Black community; and by recruiting and training Black parents and volunteers to assist in the planning, development and implementation of innovative and cost–effective programs of prevention and early intervention. Through these creative initiatives, professionals will be able to demonstrate a continued commitment to the process of building a society where each child will enjoy an equal opportunity to grow, to learn, to work, and to love.

Note

1. In several instances, the statistical figures from 1960 and earlier years and the more recent figures are not strictly comparable due to differences in data bases, sampling, and methods of reporting. Where these differences have not been noted in the text, it is assumed that they would not significantly alter the comparisons made and the conclusions drawn.

References

Auletta, K. (1982). *The underclass*, New York: Random House.
Barret, R., & Robinson, B. (1982). Teenage fathers: Neglected too long. *Social Work*, 27, 484–488.
Beschner, G. & Friedman, A. (Eds.). (1979). *Youth drug abuse*. Lexington, MA: Lexington Books.
Bridge, R. & Blackman, J. (1978). *A study of alternatives in American education*, Vol. IV. (Family Choice in Schooling). Santa Monica, CA: Rand Corporation.
Brown, S. (1979). The health needs of adolescents. In *Healthy people: The surgeon general's report on mental health promotion and disease prevention*. Publ. No. 79-55971A, Washington, D.C.: U.S. DHEW.
Brunswick, A. (1979). Black youths and drug-use behavior. In G. Beschner & A. Friedman (Eds.). *Youth and drug abuse*. Lexington, MA: Lexington Books.
Brunswick, A., Merzel, C., & Messeri, P. (1985). Drug use initiation among urban Black youth: A seven-year followup of developmental and secular influences. *Youth and Society*, 17, 189–216.
Centers for Disease Control (1986a). Acquired Immunodeficiency Syndrome (AIDS) among Blacks and Hispanics—United States. *Morbidity and Mortality Weekly Report*, 35, 655–666.
Centers for Disease Control (1986b). Update—Acquired Immunodeficiency Syndrome—United States. *Morbidity and Mortality Weekly Report*, 35, 757–766.
Centers for Disease Control (1987a). Increases in primary and secondary syphilis—United States. *Morbidity and Mortality Weekly Report*, 36, 393–397.
Centers for Disease Control (1987b). Update: Acquired Immunodeficiency Syndrome—United States. *Morbidity and Mortality Weekly Report*, 36, 522–526.
Children's Defense Fund (1986). *Welfare and teen pregnancy: What do we know? What do we do*. Washington, D.C.
Chilman, C. (1983). *Adolescent sexuality in a changing American society*. New York: John Wiley and Sons.
College Entrance Examination Board (1985). *Equality and excellence: The educational status of Black Americans*. New York: The College Board.
Congressional Budget Office (1981). *Improving youth employment prospects: Issues and options*. Washington, D.C.: Congress of the United States.
Deal, T. (1975). Comparison of conventional alternative secondary schools. *Educational Researcher* (April).

Edmonds, R. (1979). Effective schools for the urban poor. *Educational Leadership, 37*, 15–24.
Family Impact Seminar (1979). *Teen age pregnancy and family impact: New perspectives on policy.* Washington, D.C.: George Washington University.
Fischman, S. & Palley, H. (1978). Adolescent unwed motherhood: Implications for a national family policy. *Health and Social Work, 3*, 31–45.
Freeman, R. & Wise, D. (Eds.)(1982). *The youth labor market problem: Its nature, causes, and consequences.* Chicago: University of Chicago Press.
Furstenberg, F., Jr., Lincoln, R. & Menken, J. (1981). *Teenage sexuality, pregnancy and childbearing.* Philadelphia, PA: University of Pennsylvania Press.
Gandossy, R., Williams, J., & Harwood, H. (1980). *Drugs and crime: A survey and analysis of the literature.* Washington, D.C.: U.S. Dept. of Justice.
Gibbs, J.T. (1988). Conceptual, methodological and sociocultural issues in Black youth suicide: Implications for assessment and early intervention. *Suicide and Life–Threatening Behavior, 18* (Summer), (in press).
Gibbs, J.T. (1982). Personality patterns of delinquent females: Ethnic and sociocultural variations. *Journal of Clinical Psychology, 38*, 198–206.
Gibbs, J.T. (1982). Psychosocial factors related to substance abuse among delinquent females: Implications for prevention and treatment. *American Journal of Orthopsychiatry, 52*, 261–271.
Gibbs, J.T. (1986). Psychosocial correlates of sexual attitudes and behaviors in urban early adolescent females: Implications for intervention. *Journal of Social Work and Human Sexuality, 5*, 81–97.
Glasgow, D. (1981). *The Black underclass.* New York: Vintage Books.
Gold, M., & Petronio, R. (1980). Delinquent behavior in adolescence. In J. Adelson (Ed.). *Handbook of adolescent psychology.* New York: John Wiley and Sons.
Grueling, J. & DeBlassie, R. (1980). Adolescent suicide. *Adolescence, 15*, 89–601.
Hampton, P. (1974). Learning needs of academically disadvantaged students. *Adolescence, 9*, 555–564.
Hobbs, N. & Robinson, S. (1982). Adolescent development and public policy. *American Psychologist, 37*, 212–223.
Holinger, P. (1979). Violent deaths among the young: Recent trends in suicide, homicide, and accidents. *American Journal of Psychiatry, 136*, 1144–1147.
Holinger, P. & Offer, D. (1982). Prediction of adolescent suicide: A population model. *American Journal of Psychiatry, 139*, 302–307.
Howard, J. (1983). Systems approach to minority referrals: An alternative model of assessment and intervention. Paper presented at the Minority Assessment Conference, Arizona Conference on Applied Psychological Issues, Tucson, Arizona (November).
Huizinga, D. & Elliott, D. (1985). *Juvenile offenders' prevalence, offender incidence and arrest rates by race.* Boulder, CO: Institute of Behavioral Science.
Klerman, L. (1979). Evaluating service programs for school–age parents: Design problems. *Evaluation and the Health Professions, 2*, 55–70.
Krisberg, B., Schwartz, I., Fishman, G., Eiskovits, Z., & Guttman, E. (1986). *The incarceration of minority youth.* Minneapolis, MN: H. H. Humphrey Institute of Public Affairs, University of Minnesota.
Ladner, J. (1971). *Tomorrow's tomorrow: The Black woman.* Garden City, NY: Doubleday.
Larson, T. (1986). Employment and unemployment of young Black men. Unpublished paper, Berkeley, CA.
McAndrew, G. (1986). Turning dropouts into graduates. *Youth Policy, 9*, 3–4.

McGee, E. (1982). *Too little, too late: Services for teen-age parents* New York: Ford Foundation.

Mott, F. L. & Maxwell, N. (1981). School-age mothers: 1968 and 1979. *Family Planning Perspectives, 13*, 287–292.

Mudd, E. et al. (1978). Adolescent health services and contraceptive use. *American Journal of Orthopsychiatry, 48*, 495–503.

National Center for Health Statistics (1986). *Monthly vital statistics report.* Washington, D.C.

National Institute of Drug Abuse (1980). *Current trends and issues in drug abuse.* Washington, D.C.

National Institute of Drug Abuse (1980). *Drug abuse deaths in nine cities: A survey report.* Res. Mon. 29, Washington, D.C.

National Institute of Drug Abuse (1979). *National survey on drug abuse, 1979.* Washington, D.C.

Nelson, S., et al. (1974). A national study of the knowledge, attitudes and patterns of use of drugs by disadvantaged adolescents. *American Journal of Orthopsychiatry, 44*, 532–537.

Newsweek, (Oct. 24, 1983), p. 118.

Ozawa, M. (1986). Non-Whites and the demographic imperative in social welfare spending. *Social Work, 3*, 440–446.

Paris, B. (1983), Saving the children. *The dial.* New York: Public Broadcasting Communications, Inc., 14–16.

Paton, S., & Kandel, D. (1978). Psychological factors and adolescent illicit drug use: Ethnicity and sex differences. *Adolescence, 13*, 187–200.

Proctor, S. (1987). A national youth academy. *Youth Policy, 9*, 10–12.

Ray, O. (1983) *Drugs, society and human behavior.* St. Louis, MO: C. V. Mosby.

Shapiro, C. (1980). Sexual learning: The short-changed adolescent male. *Social Work, 25*, 489–493.

Silber, T. (1982). Adolescent pregnancy programs: A perspective for the future. *Journal of Sex Education and Therapy, 8*, 48–50.

Stack, C. (1974). *All our kin.* New York: Harper and Row.

Thompson, K. (1980). A comparison of Black and White adolescents' beliefs about having children. *Journal of Marriage and the Family, 42*, 133–139.

Thornton, W., James, J., & Doerner, W. (1982). *Delinquency and justice.* Glenview, IL: Scott, Foresman and Co.

Tolmach, J. (1985). There ain't nobody on my side, *Journal of Child Clinical Psychology, 14*, 214–219.

Uniform Crime Reports (1981). *Crime in the U.S., 1980.* F.B.I. Washington, D.C.: U.S. Dept. of Justice.

U.S. Bureau of the Census (1981). School enrollment: Social and economic characteristics of students, 1980 (Advance Report). *Current population reports,* series P–20. Washington, D.C.

U.S. Department of Health and Human Services (1981). *Statistical series, annual data, 1980,* series E, No. 21. Washington, D.C.

Walker, G. (1986). Dismissing the myths of minority youth employment. *Youth Policy, 8*, 8–11.

Webster's third new international dictionary (1976). Springfield, MA: G. & C. Merriam Co.

Williams, J. (Ed.) (1982). *The state of Black America, 1982.* New York: National Urban League, Inc.

Zelnick, M., & Kantner, J. (1980). Sexual activity, contraceptive rica, 1982. New York: National Urban League, Inc.

Zelnick, M., & Kantner, J. (1980). Sexual activity, contraceptive use and pregnancy among metropolitan–area teenagers: 1971–1979. *Family Planning Perspectives, 12,* 230–237.

TRAILBLAZERS IN BLACK ADOLESCENT RESEARCH: THE AMERICAN COUNCIL ON EDUCATION'S STUDIES ON NEGRO YOUTH PERSONALITY DEVELOPMENT

Bertha Garrett Holliday[1]

> A theory of socialization seems critical for a theory of social change.
> *Children of Bondage*, (Davis & Dollard, 1940/64, p. xv).

A Tradition of Concern for Black Adolescents

Robert Guthrie (1976), in his historical review of the psychological study of African–Americans, reveals that Black psychologists have demonstrated, for over five decades, an intense concern for developmental and socialization issues of Black adolescents. Thus for Black psychologists, the current crescendo of social policy and research interest in Black adolescents is nothing new.

Indeed, this longstanding concern of Black psychologists (and other Black social scientists) stems from historical necessity, and the realities of limited professional options. Prior to the enactment of the Community Mental Health Centers Acts of 1963 and 1967 (P.L. 88–164 and P.L. 90–574), which greatly increased employment opportunities for Black psychologists, the overwhelming majority of Black psychologists engaged in one of two professional roles. They were professors at historically Black colleges having applied missions related to the training of educators and other human service professionals for Black communities. Or they were employed as school counselors and psychologists by public school districts, which frequently were segregated either by law or custom. In both instances, Black adolescents typically were the focus of Black psychologists' day–to–day professional activities. The same can be said for most African–Americans in other social science fields.

The evidence of Black social scientists' intense concern for Black adolescents is abundant. Guthrie (1976) provides a complete listing of all of the 32 African–Americans awarded doctoral degrees in psychology and educational psychology between 1920 and 1950. The dissertations of eight of these persons relate to either classroom practices or learning issues. More significantly, dissertation titles for an additional 17 of these persons include direct reference to Black youth. Illustrative titles are: *A psychological study of delinquent and non–delinquent Negro boys* (R. P. Daniel, 1932); *Non–academic development of Negro children in mixed and segregated schools* (I. B. Prosser, 1933); *A socio–psychological study of Negro children of superior intelligence* (M. D. Jenkins, 1935); *Educational achievement and its relationship to the socio–economic status of the Negro in the high school of Philadelphia* (J. H. Brodhead, 1937); *An intensive survey of a Negro special class school* (J. Duckery, 1939); and *The measurement of adjustment of Negro college youth* (S.O. Roberts, 1944).

In addition to such research efforts, early Black psychologists engaged in significant applied efforts on behalf of Black adolescents. According to Guthrie (1976), Albert Beckham (Ph.D., New York University, 1930), during his tenure as a psychologist at Chicago's DuSable High School, established a school psychology clinic that included not only student counseling services, but also parent counseling groups and community outreach programs. Alberta Turner (Ph.D., Ohio State University, 1935) was employed for nearly 30 years in various professional psychology positions at the Ohio Bureau of Juvenile Research and Youth Commission. Carlton Goodlett (Ph.D., 1938, University of California at Berkeley; M. D., Meharry Medical College, 1944) tried valiantly but unsuccessfully to establish an Institute for the Study of the Negro Child. Later in 1948, Frederick Watts (Ph.D., University of Pennsylvania, 1941) was successful in establishing the University Counseling Service at Howard University.

Such exemplary scholarly and applied efforts suggest a unique characteristic of early involvements of Black social scientists with Black adolescents. More often than not, such involvements were distinguished by their explicit social policy thrusts and social reform intents. Thus Black social scientists' efforts with Black adolescents traditionally have been guided not only by scientific concerns, but also by social and political concerns.

This unique characteristic of early efforts of Black social scientists is best epitomized by the landmark conduct of the American Council on Education's (ACE) studies of Negro Youth Personality Development. The following is a description of this unique research effort—how and why it came to be, its procedures and results, and its past and present significance for Black adolescent research.

Overview of the ACE Studies

The Studies' Significance

The ACE studies on Negro youth personality development are of exceptional historical significance because of their scope, purpose, design, and procedures. The ACE studies are the first national research project on Black youth. The studies probably still stand as the most comprehensive such effort. The project's design encompassed large samples, multiple geographical sites, and concern with social and economic differences as observed and perceived at the levels of the individual, family, and community.

Furthermore, the ACE project is a landmark in its use of a multidisciplinary interracial research team and its unprecedented inclusion of principal investigators who were both young and Black. Indeed, the ACE studies are cornerstones of the research careers of Allison Davis, Ira DeA. Reid, E. Franklin Frazier, and Charles S. Johnson.

The ACE project is distinguished by its explicit intent to use scientific concepts and methods that would yield data appropriate for applied and policy purposes. Many of the project's findings and recommendations were used in support of the F. D. Roosevelt administration's New Deal social programs. More specifically, the studies were viewed as a major vehicle for effecting changes in both national race relations and federal policy related to Black youth and their families.

The Studies' Authorization and Objectives

The American Council on Education (ACE) is a council of national educational associations encompassing associations of universities and colleges, technical schools, secondary schools, local school districts, and state departments of education (Sutherland, 1942). Among its functions is the conduct of research.

In September of 1935, the Council authorized the establishment of its American Youth Commission (AYC). The stated purpose of the Commission was, "The encouragement of good practices and the integration of current experiences and the stimulation of new contributions in fields hitherto unexplored…in the broad area of youth welfare services" (*AYC Activities*, 1939).

In carrying out its purpose, the Commission established three major objectives: (a) compiling facts concerning the needs of youth and available resources, (b) conducting research and demonstration projects as a means for recommending solutions for youth problems, and (c) publicizing the plight of youth and advocating on their behalf as means for encouraging others to act upon its recommendations (*AYC Activities*, 1939).

The ACE studies on Negro youth personality development were conceived as the primary vehicle for addressing the needs of Black youth. The studies were financed by a $100,000 grant from the Nashville–based, Rockefeller–funded, philanthropic General Education Board (Daniel, 1938). The studies were conceived both as a series of separate community studies conducted in various regions, and as a unified research project. The separate community studies were linked by a core of common research issues (*CYP Bulletin*, 1943). All principal investigators were instructed to take "special note of the influence of segregation and isolation; the bearing upon personality stability of a narrow occupational horizon; the effects of limitation of participation in civil and social activities" (Daniel, 1938). Each study used case studies and personality inventories. In addition, two youth guidance centers were established to provide clinical resources for the study and its participants (Daniel, 1938).

The Social–Historical and Political–Economic Contexts

At the time the studies were commissioned (1938), the United States was in the midst of the Great Depression, and President Franklin Roosevelt was in his second term of office empowered by his "Grand Coalition" of liberals, small farmers, relief (welfare) recipients, and labor unions (Sitkoff, 1978).

The Great Depression had brought havoc to already socially and economically oppressed Black communities—especially in smaller northern communities and throughout the South. In addition, processes of discrimination and segregation encouraged both widespread displacement of Black workers by White labor and racial wage differentials (cf. Davis, Gardner & Gardner, 1941; Sitkoff, 1978; Wolters, 1970). The economic despair infected other areas of social life. For example, in 1933–34 in the five southern states of Alabama, Arkansas, Georgia, Louisiana, and Mississippi, less than 10% of Black youth ages 15 to 19 years were enrolled in high school (Reid, 1940, p. 40).

Such social and economic realities forced a dramatic ideological shift in the Black intellectual community. The center of Black intellectual thought shifted from the creative writers and artists to the small community of Black professionals and scholars, most of whom were trained in the then new social scientific methods. Within that community, social thought was dominated by the "class perspective"—that is, a belief that economic forces were of equal if not greater importance than race in the lives of Blacks. In contrast, the then alternative "race perspective" was distinguished by its emphases on race–specific needs and interests, and group action and protest movements (cf. Fullinwider, 1969; Sitkoff, 1978; Young, 1973).

The Studies' Theory, Methods, and Brokered Interests

In the midst of such intellectual debates, the ACE studies sought to claim an ideological middle ground. Thus although many of the ACE studies' Black researchers clearly were identified with one of the Black intellectual perspectives, the ACE studies were guided by a caste/class perspective (Warner, 1936), in which the joint effects of race and social class are emphasized.

The caste/class perspective, and its ancillary theoretical implications, are associated with the "Chicago school of Social Science". Indeed, the link between the Chicago school and the ACE studies is quite direct. Most of the ACE investigators were either faculty or graduates of the University of Chicago in the fields of anthropology, psychology, and sociology (Slaughter & McWorter, 1985).

The influence of the Chicago school also is evident in the studies' use of interdisciplinary theoretical approaches and methods. For example, in studying Black youth's personality, the ACE investigators rejected the then typical approach of seeking to classify and type personality by its various traits. Instead the investigators focused on the dynamic and natural history of personality development. Although pathological personality development was noted, emphasis was placed on those patterns of social relations and community processes that spawned such pathological development. Thus the studies investigated both the behavioral and environmental contingencies of adolescent development and socialization. Associated data collection methods ranged from structured personality inventories and psychiatric interviews to case studies, participant–observation, and archival retrieval of community characteristics information.

But despite the Chicago School's influence, the ACE studies fundamentally were a product of brokered interests among multiple parties. This is best indicated by the composition of the ACE special advisory committee, which met in 1938 to provide guidance in organizing the ACE studies and included representation from civic organizations (e.g., the Commission on Interracial Cooperation and the Progressive Education Association), private foundations (e.g., the Rockefeller–funded General Education Board and the Chicago–based Rosenwald Fund), universities (e.g. faculty of Bennington College, Howard University, and the University of Chicago) and federal government (Sutherland, 1942, pp. vi–vii).

Thus it seems that from their inception, the ACE studies represented a brokering of interests among the racially-oriented foundations, the ambitious Chicago School of social science, Black professionals and scholars with their varying ideological perspectives, the ACE and the federal government. One can infer that the deal brokered was in the coalition-building spirit of the times: Black researchers would fully participate in the ACE project on an equal status basis; the project's theories, methods, data, and recommendations would be ones that would both expose deficiencies of social and economic structures and patterns, and lend support to New Deal social reforms and Black participation therein; issues of legal segregation and social domination would not be attacked too aggressively, so as not to jeopardize the F. D. Roosevelt administration's political base.

The Studies' Findings and Conclusions

The full report of the studies' findings required the publication of seven books: (a) *Children of bondage: The personality development of Negro youth in the urban south* by Allison Davis and John Dollard (1940/1964), (b) *Negro youth at the crossways: Their personality development in the middle states* by E. Franklin Frazier (1940/1967), (c) *Growing up in the Black belt: Negro youth in the rural south* by Charles S. Johnson (1941), (d) *Color and human nature: Negro personality development in a northern city* by W. Lloyd Warner, Buford H. Junker, and Walter A. Adams (1941), (e) *In a minor key: Negro youth in story and fact* by Ira DeA. Reid (1940), (f) *Thus be their destiny* by J. Howell Atwood, Donald Wyatt, Vincent Davis, and Ira Walker (1941), and (f) *Color, Class and personality* by Robert Sutherland (1942). A summary of each of these volumes follows.

Children of Bondage

This volume, by Allison Davis and John Dollard (1940/1964), is a study of southern urban youth.

Theory and methods. The study was guided by (a) a psychoanalytic perspective of childrearing and personality, (b) a caste/class perspective of socialization with emphasis on the relation of racial (caste) and class barriers to differential social reinforcements and attainments, (c) Dollard's social learning theory (which assumes learning results from positive reinforcement of instrumental [i.e. goal–attainment] acts that occur in the context of some dilemma), and (d) a perspective of culture as a "means through which a group learns and conserves problem solutions and forces them upon new generations" (Davis & Dollard, 1940/1964, pp. 4–15).

The study actually reports findings of three interrelated investigations conducted in New Orleans and Natchez, Mississippi. One of these involves in-depth case studies of the daily lives of eight youth who were 12 thru 16 years of age and of varying social class status. These case studies included observation and interviews of not only the study participants, but also of their friends, teachers, parents, and parents' friends. The second investigation involved interviews of 74 Black youth regarding their relationships with, and attitudes towards White people. The third investigation involved interviews with 123 youth and their parents regarding childrearing practices (Davis & Dollard, 1940/1964, p. xix).

The major issues addressed by these investigations were: (a) What stereotyped forms of behavior are characteristic of Black youth? (b) How do Black SES groups differ in the behavior they demand of children? (c) What is the learning process by which children are induced or compelled to take on appropriate caste/class behaviors? The study also examined the effects of social class, family expectations, and childrearing practices on youth's social experiences and personality development (Davis & Dollard, 1940/1964, p.4).

Findings. Davis and Dollard's findings led them to propose that (a) Black youth's personality development was dominated by concerns related to adjustment to frustrations and deprivations associated with caste (i.e. racial) restrictions, and (b) the patterns of response to, or social learning associated with these restrictions are shaped by social class (i.e. by the family and its clique).

Accordingly, Davis and Dollard identified four alternative patterns of Black youth's adaptation to caste restrictions. The pattern reflecting the "reality principle" involved acceptance of caste as an inevitable frustration. The "reaction formation" pattern was defined by accommodative and deferential behavior that served as a means of defending against feelings of anger and fear. The "compensatory/displacement" pattern was guided by a need to somehow attempt to compensate for restrictions on social participation, and characterized by behavior oriented towards upward social mobility within the Black caste. The fourth adaptation involved "escaping to the North" (Davis & Dollard, 1940/1964, pp. 203-204).

The voluminous data collected by Davis and Dollard allowed them to draw numerous other conclusions, many of which address the major issues surrounding current research and policy interests in Black adolescents. For example, Davis and Dollard acknowledged the effects on their data of racial examiner effects and identified three major sources of such effects: (a) The "social gulf" and age (i.e. authority) difference between lower class Black youth and a middle class White interviewer that result in, (b) a "jolt to the self-esteem of the person with the inferior status" that causes that person to be suspicious and noncommunicative, and (c) to fear that self–disclosure might place him at either the superior status person's mercy, or some other type of emotional jeopardy (Davis & Dollard, 1940/1964, p.71).

Davis and Dollard were sensitive to the subtle variations of Black social life. They noted that the largest behavioral and social learning differences were observed between the two adjacent Black social strata of the lower class and the lower middle class (Davis & Dollard, 1940/1964, p. 264). Regrettably, in contemporary research, these two Black social groups frequently are lumped together under the rubric of "the Ghetto" (c.f. Lemann, 1986).

Davis and Dollard also discussed the sources and individual effects of downward social mobility. They found that a family's downward mobility is sparked by four major types of events: (a) A sharp decline in income or occupational status; (b) desertion by the father; (c) drunkenness or promiscuous sexual behavior by the parents; or (d) family involvement in lottery–selling, bootlegging, other "shady" enterprises. Davis and Dollard (1940/1964) observed, "The child, as well as his parents, experiences this decline in status as a series of punishments" (p. 156).

Special note also should be taken of *Children of bondage's* Chapter 13, *Social class and school learning*. It is a classic analysis of Black children's academic achievement, in which Davis and Dollard cogently argue that group differences in school learning must be considered primarily in relation to SES (socialization) training and the status controls of the school. Three major reinforcements for school learning are identified: (a) The favorable attention and opportunities for dominance which a child obtains, (b) denial of such rewards or physical punishment, and (c) avoidance of punishment and disapproval from teachers, parents and peers (Davis & Dollard, 1940/1964, pp. 280–281).

Davis and Dollard continue by noting that their data suggest that there is differential learning reinforcement of Black children (in then segregated schools) by social class. Youth of similar class status of the teacher (i.e. middle and upper–class) received more favors and status privileges from the teacher and accordingly, displayed less anxiety, and provoked additional teacher reward. On the other hand, lower class youth were punished more frequently and systematically by teachers, and displayed more anxiety and anger that served both to provoke more punishment and as a barrier to effective learning. Thus, Davis and Dollard conclude, a reciprocal pattern of reinforcement is established between teacher and child that serves to strengthen the differential achievement by social class (Davis & Dollard, 1940/1964. pp. 280–290).

Some 15 years after the conduct of the Davis and Dollard study, an interracial research team in New Orleans gained access to the raw data for *Children in bondage* and conducted a six–year follow-up study on 20 of the original New Orleans participants. The findings of this study, which probably represents the first longitudinal study of Black adolescents, were published under the title of *The Eighth Generation Grows Up* (Rohrer, 1960). The study's author noted that Davis and Dollard's emphasis on caste/class had resulted in several mispredictions of youth's later adult outcomes. The author argued that such predictions must be tempered by both recognition of the varying life trajectories available to an individual, and consideration of particularistic "social worlds"—including the behaviors and experiences of significant others, personal adaptations to critical life events, and the prioritizing of one's social roles along a value continuum.

Negro Youth at the Crossways

This study of Black youth in the border states was authored by E. Franklin Frazier (1940/1967). The study focuses on the effect on Black youth's personalities (as indicated by assessments of racial identity, motivation, and aspirations) of the youth's experiences in varying constellations of community settings. The study also examines personality effects related to race and social class status. Thus this is a rather classical social psychological analysis of personality with emphasis on social participatory patterns.

Theory and methods. According to its author, the study is based on a theoretical model wherein (a) parents' SES and life experiences shape their child socialization practices, (b) the effects of these practices on the child's personality are mediated by the child's experiences outside the home, and (c) the characteristics of such environmental experiences are related to the parents' SES and caste. This theoretical model and the study's procedures were informed by three major approaches: (a) Robert Park's (1936) ecological model which postulates relationships between social characteristics, social process (e.g. assimilation, competition), and a locale's population distribution patterns; (b) Harry Stack Sullivan's social interaction theory of self and personality, which emphasizes that the meanings of an individual's perceptions and behaviors are derived from the responses of others; and (c) the caste/class perspective.

The study was conducted in Louisville, KY and Washington, DC. An ecological sampling approach was used to ensure diverse socioeconomic representation among the study's participants who were 12 to 20 years of age. A total of seven ecological zones (i.e., concentric one mile areas around the center of the city) with concentrations of Black populations were identified. Five zones were in Washington; two were in Louisville. A qualitative methodology was used involving use of guided interview outlines (Frazier, 1940/1967, pp. x–xvii, xxxv).

Findings. Frazier found that in the border states, race relations were governed less by segregationist laws, and more by "public opinion and local folkways and mores" evidenced by racial exclusion and segregation. Frazier's major conclusion was that Black youth's adjustment to this pattern of race relations is "influenced by their family background, their position in the social organization, their group and institutional affiliations, and the social movements and ideologies in the community" (Frazier, 1940/1967, p. 38).

Frazier found that youth's socialization, personality adjustment pattern, racial identity, and behavior differed by social class. Lower–class Black youth, whose parents typically were engaged in domestic service, had early contact with the White children of their parents' employers. Of course, these contacts involved undeniable subordination for the Black youth. As these youth grew older, they frequently engaged in (menial) employment, which also involved subordination to Whites. Parents of these youth reinforced such subordination by advising their children to avoid trouble with Whites. And middle and upper class teachers often reinforced these youth's feelings of inferiority.

Consequently, Frazier found that lower–class Black youth's outward accommodation to their inferior racial status "often concealed latent conflicts...evidenced by statements of resentment toward subordination, mean and sullen dispositions" (Frazier, 1940/1967, pp. 41–53). And frequently, such behavior was exacerbated by more impulsive behavior stemming from lack of parental control associated with disorganized family circumstances. Due to their racial and economic isolation, most of these youth were influenced minimally by social movements and ideology. (Indeed Frazier claims that most had not heard of the NAACP).

Most of the lower class youth aspired to unskilled and skilled labor positions and a few aspired to traditional Black professional roles. But nearly all felt their chances of securing such employment were not equal to those of Whites.

The family socialization of Black middle class youth was distinguished by appeals to appear "respectable"—that is, to not uphold Black stereotypes, to not behave in a subordinate manner. Consequently, such youth actively sought to differentiate themselves from their lower class peers. They also tended to remain aloof from White children. But like lower class youth, they frequently were employed in menial jobs requiring subordination, were influenced minimally by social movements and ideology, and often felt discriminated against by teachers—especially if they were darkskin. These middle class youth typically aspired to rise above the semi–skilled and skilled occupations of their parents. But they also preferred Black employers.

Frazier's upper class youth, whose parents typically were professionals, present a dramatically different portrait. These youth's parents deliberately sought to avoid socializing the youth for subordination. One strategy used by Black upper class parents for accomplishing this involved invoking their economic and social status to protect their children from overt and covert forms of discrimination and prejudice. Thus these youth did not learn about the community's race relations patterns through personal experience and direct contact, but instead by means of the teachings of major community institutions. Nevertheless, the school supported the socialization goal of the upper class by allowing such youth full opportunity for success in school adjustment. Frazier observed, "Consequently, Black upper class youth are more conscious of their place in the Negro world than their status in the larger world" (Frazier, 1940/1967, p. 61–66).

Frazier found that many of these youth evidenced a defense mechanism whereby they denied any feelings of difference from, inferiority to, or insecurity in dealing with Whites. Many of these youth believed that "competence and efficiency would be recognized whatever the color of the person possessing these qualities" (Frazier, 1940/1967, pp. 158–165). Most were self-confident about their futures. Few were concerned about unequal employment opportunities. However, many were concerned about those social and civic rights that were directly related to their professional and entrepreneurial aspirations. Thus many of the upper class youth were aware of various social movements, but were unaware of their goals and activities.

Growing Up in the Black Belt

This is a study of southern rural youth by Charles S. Johnson (1941). This study examined variations in Black youth's social attitudes (e.g., aspirations and expectations) as a function of both the youth's social characteristics and those of their local communities. The study's social attitudes assessment scales represented the cutting edge of the social psychological methodology of the times.

Theory and methods. According to Johnson, the study is guided by a concern with the relation of personality to culture. (The study includes frequent reference to Harry Stack Sullivan and his social interaction theory of personality). Special emphasis is placed on investigating indices of Black youth's personal adjustment to the characteristics and mores of their communities (p. xvii).

Johnson's indices of personal adjustment were culled from life history documents, case studies, individual interviews, and attitude and psychological tests. Specifically the study included use of the following structured instruments: (a) The Kuhlman–Anderson IQ test; (b) a Personal Values Test; (c) a Personal Attitudes Test consisting of 125 true–false items assessing attitudes in the six activity spheres of home, school, church, race, social adjustment, and general emotional life; (d) a Racial

Attitudes Test, which included 14 true–false statements of attitudes toward Whites and 14 true–false statements of attitudes toward Blacks; (e) an Occupational Ratings Test; and (f) a Color Ratings Test, in which positive and negative personal characteristics are associated with various color tones. (Copies of these instruments are provided in the book's Appendix B.)

Johnson deliberately sampled for social and economic diversity. First he selected counties representative of two types of rural agricultural economies: Single crop counties where 50% of the South's Black population then lived, and diversified farming counties where another 30% of southern Blacks lived. Six single crop counties were selected: Bolivar and Coahoma Counties in Mississippi, Macon and Madison Counties in Alabama, Greene County in Georgia, and Shelby County in Tennessee. Two diversified farming counties were selected: Johnston County in North Carolina and Davidson County in Tennessee (Johnson, 1941, pp. xx–xxi).

Collectively, the sample counties tapped nearly every type of Black rural life. Thus Bolivar and Coahoma Counties were flourishing plantation areas with a small number of large landowners who were buttressed by large numbers of sharecropper tenants. Macon and Greene Counties were decaying plantation areas where the tenancy system was collapsing and the economy was in upheaval. Madison County was characterized by large numbers of White small landowners assisted by large numbers of White and Black tenants. Shelby County included both the cotton tenant culture and the urban culture of Memphis. And Davidson County included the urban center of Nashville, as well as a large Black rural nonfarm population.

From these counties, Johnson selected 931 Black youth, ages 12 through 20 years of age, and their families for his sample. These study participants represented varying social classes.

Findings. Throughout his book, Johnson repeatedly makes the point:

> One cannot comprehend the life experiences and the intimate adjustment difficulties of the rural Negro without an understanding of the physical and social worlds in which he lives. A unique environment fashions, in ways both subtle and direct, his personality and his destiny (Johnson, 1941, p. 38).

Johnson continues by observing that the plantation system, requires a specific land typology, ownership of land in large units, and authoritarian patterns of social relations where laborers are subordinate, economically dependent, and socially isolated. Johnson found that rural Blacks' social class diversity, family stability, level of education, diversity of aspirations, and racial pride increased with the economic diversity of the community. Indeed Johnson reports that the median income of the economically diverse Davidson County was over twice that of the decaying plantation Greene County. But Johnson also reports that approximately 82% of the study's 916 families were of lower class status, 18.2% included a member who voted, and only 4.4% had a family member with more than a high school education (Johnson, 1941, pp. 53–56; 77–78).

But despite this relative economic homogeneity of the families, Johnson found significant effects of social class on attitudes and child socialization. For example, upper class rural Blacks, who generally were professionals or successful landowners, actively sought to limit their children's contact with both Whites and lower status Blacks. Consequently, these youth typically had few friends. But they also had the lowest average maladjustment scores among the study's participants. They also tended not to be high academic achievers. Johnson, an early forecaster of the current concern about downward mobility among the Black middle class, observed that such relative lack of achievement is due to ceilings on Black occupational achievement in the rural south.

> For the children of these upper class families, the limits tolerated for one of the Negro race have been reached, and new occupational advances involve new racial conflicts. Further advance would be tantamount to moving the frontiers of the whole race problem (Johnson, 1941, p. 80)

Johnson also examined the role of major social institutions in Black youth's lives. Education was identified as the critical vehicle for social mobility. Consequently, schooling was an emotionally–ladened issue for many of the study's youth. Between 32% and 50% of the youth listed either "Getting an education" or "School work" as the first of their three greatest worries (Johnson, 1941, pp. 119–121). School quality and Black educational attainment were found to be directly related to a community's economic diversity. The average IQ of the study's youth also varied directly with increased economic diversity. In addition, the youth's IQ directly correlated with the intensity of their expressed respect for the church (Johnson, 1941, pp.164–169).

Johnson reported both a statistical gap between the youth's occupational aspirations and expectations and a gender effect on these attitudes. Among boys, desire to enter the professions increased with IQ; but for girls such desire varied inversely with IQ. Over 65% of the girls had professional aspirations compared to barely 39% of the boys. But only 48% of girls and 26% of boys expected to enter the professions. Johnson opined that this gap between aspirations and expectations was due to instrumental issues—that is, youth were unaware of the requirements for their desired occupations, and were unable to conceive of a means for obtaining the necessary training and education (Johnson, 1941, pp. 200–223).

The study also ventured into the territory of attitudes related to love and marriage. Johnson found an asymmetry in the preferred mate characteristics of males and females. Female youth much more so than males, expressed preference for mate characteristics associated with economic security—that is, wealth, education, and professional status. Johnson also noted the effect of a community's economic characteristics on perceptions of an ideal marriage (Johnson, 1941, pp. 224–237).

Color and Human Nature

This study of northern urban youth by W. Lloyd Warner, Buford H. Junker, and Walter A. Adams (1941) examines the effectiveness of Black youth's emotional adjustment to their social (i.e., gender and class) roles. Emotional adjustment is assumed to be indicated by expectations and attitudes towards self, Blacks, and Whites. The study is distinguished by its controversial assessments of the effects of Blacks' skin tones on their personality and social status

Theory and methods. Based on their review of earlier Black community studies, the authors identified the following underlying hypotheses of their study: Blacks' personalities are influenced by (a) racial subordination, (b) color evaluations within the group, (c) SES and occupational status, and (d) age, sex, and educational differences (Warner et al., 1941, p. 6). The study also examined the effects of the institutional processes of subjects' childhood communities on mobility, stratification, individual expectations, self perceptions, and personality development.

The study involved use of 805 life histories, which were drawn from the earlier Warner–Cayton study of the Black Chicago community. The Warner–Cayton study involved over 5000 interviews and was funded by the federal government's Depression–era WPA agency (Warner et al., 1941, p. xiii).

Analyses of case study materials were guided by psychoanalytic theory and by the caste/class perspective, which was originated by Warner. The detailed case study analyses involved both retrospective and contemporaneous data. Thus 525 of the study's subjects were 21 to 60 years of age, while 280 subjects were ages 12 to 20 years. All subjects were interviewed at least once by Black interviewers. In addition, for some cases, other information was collected from secondary sources such as psychiatric case records, autobiographies, community business surveys, and newspaper biographies (Warner et al., 1941, pp. 28–29). Case study materials were used to classify each subject along 10 criteria: sex, skin tone, age, occupation, social status, moral distinctions i.e., 'respectable' or 'shady', education, birthplace, years of residence in Chicago, and race (Warner et al., 1941, p. 4).

Findings. Through guidance provided by the study's hypotheses, the authors derived a typology of Black personality from the nine classification criteria. This typology involved classifications by gender (male, female), SES (upper, upper middle, lower middle, and lower classes), and skin color ('passable', lightskin, brownskin, darkskin). Thus the typology entailed 32 types, each of which is discussed in the study (Warner et al., 1941, pp. 27–29).

Warner, Junker, and Adams brilliantly delineated the various personal and social adjustments and compensatory behaviors necessitated at the various intersections of gender, class and color. Of course, at the time of the study, greatest status and prerogatives were associated with Blacks who were male, passable or lightskin, and of upper class status. The authors also explored how such adjustments and behaviors might be exaggerated by regional origins and childhood emotional experiences.

The authors were especially fascinated by the effects of skin color. For example, they note the following concerning the Black upper–middle class.

> In the higher ranks of the Negro society a darkskin man will compete with White and lightskin persons; he will sense their tendency to reject him on account of his Negroid appearance... He will need courage, ability, drive, and a disposition that enables him to cope with the problems of making himself socially acceptable (Warner et al., 1941, p. 81).

> A northern born darkskin man tends to expect greater opportunities and more probably has been led to regard instances of subordination of Negroes as 'prejudice'... A southern born darkskin man is aware of castelike restrictions at a much younger age...and tends to be more satisfied with his upper–middle class status...and sees the achievement and maintenance of that status as a solid and gratifying achievement (Warner et al., 1941, p. 43).

In regard to lightskin females, the authors note:

> A lightskin girl who "has what it takes" in the way of education, nimble wits, and good manners...has a better chance than a darker girl to climb socially, especially through marriage (Warner et al., 1941, p. 192).

Such analyses, which are supported by the authors' presentation of case study data, lead them to conclude:

> What a Negro has to say about his color and that of other people, together with his response to color evaluations, may often furnish a direct key to all or most of his thoughts about himself and his very existence (Warner et al., 1941, p. 293).

In a Minor Key

This volume, by Ira DeA. Reid (1940), is a statistical profile of Black

Perspectives: Contemporary, Historical, Comparative

families and youth accompanied by critical reviews of related theory and implications of the data. In the volume's introductory chapter, Reid notes that his statistical profile suggests that the characteristics of Black youth and their adjustment are related to the interracial patterns of their communities. Reid continues by identifying five such patterns:
1. Areas of relative freedom where Blacks enjoy most of the political rights and some of the social rights of the general population (e.g. New England, the Middle Atlantic and North Central states).
2. Areas of restricted social participation where the political rights of Blacks are observed, but segregated social practices are widespread (e.g. the border states).
3. Areas of subordination where Blacks do not share fully and equally in the communities' political, economic and social life (e.g. Atlanta, the East South Central states).
4. Areas of racial isolation where social participation is marked by almost complete racial separation that is not associated with racial friction (e.g. all–Black towns).
5. Areas of participation where small numbers of Blacks have lived for a long period of time and experience little racial stigma of status (e.g. in some areas in the West) (Reid, 1940, p. 7).

The study continues by providing the most sophisticated and comprehensive statistical report of the status of Negro youth published prior to 1940. Its major chapter headings include Life expectancy, Housing, Literacy and education, Farming, Employment, Black professionals, Black participation in federal Relief programs, Recreation and related facilities, The Black church, Black crime, Blacks and the criminal justice system, and Social policy.

Thus Be Their Destiny

This is a slim volume by J. Howell Atwood, Donald Wyatt, Vincent Davis, and Ira Walker (1941). The volume consists of three brief community studies of Black youth living in relatively atypical community settings (for Blacks at that time) such as small northern hamlets.

Color, Class and Personality

This volume, authored by Robert Sutherland (1942) is the project's final publication. This volume summarizes findings of the entire project and provides specific social policy recommendations.

Findings. In summarizing the studies' findings, Sutherland (1942), observed that the world of American youth is structured by "the American dream"—that is, the belief that upward social mobility is attainable by those whose individual efforts are targeted on education, economic, and social achievements. Sutherland further noted that over time the American dream had become slightly tarnished. American social class lines had tightened: Greatest opportunity was reserved for a small number and social mobility increasingly became dependent on youth's social class backgrounds. For most Black youth, the joint effects of lower class status and subordinate racial status all but foreclosed avenues to the American dream (Sutherland, 1942, pp. 9–15).

However, in examining the effects of such restrictions on Black youth's personality, the ACE researchers found:

> There is no such thing as a minority status to which all Negroes are oriented or have to adjust, but rather a hierarchical arrangement of individuals who share unequally in the goods, services, privileges, obligations, and burdens provided or imposed by the culture in which they live" (Sutherland, 1942. p. 70).

Black youth were found to differ both in their conceptions of the social significance of being Black (i.e., what it means and how it feels to be a Negro), and in their adaptations to their racial status. Their conceptions of race varied by social class, regional, and urban/rural factors.

Collectively the ACE studies found that adjustment to racial status was predicted by seven factors: (a) economic status, (b) patterns of social participation, (c) innate ability, (d) childhood experiences and childrearing practices, (e) health and emotional history and status, (f) birthorder and status in the family, and (g) gender. These factors were associated with five patterns of adjustment to racial status: (a) Dodging castelike barriers ("passing"); (b) avoidance of contact with White groups ("complacency"); (c) Black pride ("defending the race"; (d) active or vicarious aggression ("striking back at White affronts"); and (e) humility, clowning or resignation ("servility") (Sutherland, 1942, pp. 27–29; 42–58).

According to Sutherland (1942), the studies' findings suggest that improved Black youth outcomes are dependent on the expansion and equalization of family options related to employment, wages, political power, and education. Black youth's social mobility was found to be limited by economic insecurity and lack of social participation, but stimulated by economic and social security, and by parents' ability to select youth's environments.

Based on these and other study findings, Sutherland (1942) set forth numerous recommendations related to (a) development of strategies for changing racial stereotypes, (b) design of interventions upon caste and class barriers, and (c) strategies for encouraging a focus on problems of Black youth by public and private service and policy organizations.

Perspectives: Contemporary, Historical, Comparative

Implications for Future Black Adolescent Research

Although the ACE studies involved somewhat dated and simplistic techniques of assessment and analysis, their findings remain durable and visionary. This probably is due to the studies' explicit concern with not only individual characteristics (i.e., assessments of personal attributes and attitudes), but also social ecology (i.e., assessments of varying patterns of youth's social relations and participation in the spheres of the family, neighborhood, peer group, and community), and related developmental change over time. Such concern with the ecology of Black youth's lives starkly contrasts with more recent research emphases on identification of Black youth's discrete individual behavioral, cognitive, and linguistic attributes and deficiencies through use of racial comparative research designs.

The contemporaneity of the ACE studies' findings suggests the power of their research approach for dissecting complex social and developmental issues. Indeed, most of the personal issues and social predicaments of today's Black youth ring hauntingly similar to those identified in the ACE studies.

One might reasonably conclude the problems associated with the development and futures of Black youth have not significantly changed in nearly 50 years. Black youth continue to experience patterns of incomplete success at school. Black youth continue to be plagued by high rates of unemployment. They continue to confront a world of work (currently called "dual employment markets") marked by unequal opportunity and discrimination. Black youth in growing numbers come into womanhood and manhood in families where the rule is unpredictability associated with economic and social marginality. And increasingly, more often than we wish to admit, marriage is not a viable option for Black youth and young adults (Edelman, 1986).

Of course some of the ACE studies' findings (e.g. the significant effects of skin hue) may be viewed as evidence of a bygone social era. But the remnants of such effects very well may help us understand some emerging behavioral patterns among Black adolescents. For example, one might postulate that those past effects of skin hue are the cultural-historical templates for Blacks' more recent attitudes and behaviors related to varying perceptions of the significance and implications of the group's widening social class differences.

The ACE studies also suggest that the "crisis" of the Black family and the "intransigence" of its problems are not, as some would argue (e.g. Lemann, 1986), a "new" problem associated with the "dependency" spawned by welfare and poverty programs of the 1960s and 1970s. Likewise, there is nothing new about Black families' continuing resilience and upward mobility aspirations.

The ACE researchers repeatedly and doggedly tell us that effective action on Black adolescents' lives requires that we attend, simultaneously, to issues of personal attributes and attitudes, race, class, and the ecologies of varying social and physical environments. For it is within the vortex of these realities that Black adolescents live and develop their perceptions of the possibilities of their here–and–now, and future adulthoods.

The ACE researchers along with numerous other early Black social scientists negotiated innumerable professional barriers and brilliantly blazed the trail in the area of Black adolescent research. But despite this accomplishment, these researchers' findings, theories, and concepts are largely ignored in current appraisals of "the Black youth problem". Elsewhere it has been argued that such scholarly neglect is due to certain historical, economic, political, and professional issues related to the evolving epistemology of American social science and its research (Holliday, in press).

This review of the ACE studies suggests not only the historical importance of these works, but also their scientific value for conceptualizing and guiding current Black adolescent research and related social policy proposals.

Notes

1. Requests for copies of this paper should be forwarded to Bertha G. Holliday, Ph.D., Office of Mental Health System Development, DC Commission on Mental Health, St. Elizabeths' Hospital, 2700 Martin L. King Jr. Ave. S.E., Washington, DC 20032.

References

Atwood, J. H., Wyatt, D.W., Davis, V. J., & Walker, I. D. (1941). *Thus be their destiny: The personality development of Negro youth in three communities.* Washington, D.C.: American Council on Education (by AMS Press of New York).

AYC (American Youth Commission) Activities. (March, 1939).

CYP (Committee on Youth Problems of the American Council on Education) Bulletin. (February, 1943). One youth in every ten, 6(5), p. 4.

Daniel, W. G. (1938). Current trends and events of national importance in Negro education. *Journal of Negro Education*, 7(2), 220.

Davis, A. & Dollard, J. (1964). *Children of bondage: The personality development of Negro youth in the urban south.* New York: Harper & Row. (Originally published by the American Council on Education, 1940).

Davis, A., Gardner, B. G., & Gardner, M. R. (1941). *Deep south: A social anthropological study of caste and class.* Chicago: University of Chicago.

Edelman, M. W. (1987). *Families in peril: An agenda for social change*. Cambridge: Harvard University Press.

Frazier, E. F. (1967). *Negro youth at the crossways: Their personality development in the middle states*. New York: Schocken. (Originally published by the American Council on Education, 1940).

Fullinwider, S. P. (1969). *The mind and mood of Black America: 20th century thought*. Homewood, IL: Dorsey.

Guthrie, R. (1976). *Even the rat was White: A historical view* of psychology. New York: Harper & Row.

Holliday, B. G. (In press). The American Council on Education's studies on Negro youth personality development: A historical note with lessons on research, context, and social policy. In R. L. Jones (Ed.), *Advances in Black psychology*.

Johnson, C. S. (1941). *Growing up in the Black belt: Negro youth in the rural south*. Washington, D.C.: American Council on Education.

Lemann, N. (1986). The origins of the underclass. *The Atlantic Monthly* (June), 31–55, (July), 54–68.

Park, R. (1936). Human ecology. *American Journal of Sociology, 42*, 1–15.

Reid, I. DeA. (1940). *In a minor key: Negro youth in story and fact*. Washington, D.C.: American Council on Education.

Rohrer, J. H. (1960).*The eighth generation grows up*. New York: Harper & Row.

Sitkoff, H. (1978). *A new deal for Blacks: The emergence of civil rights as a national issue* (Vol. 1: The depression decade). New York: Oxford University Press.

Slaughter, D. T. & McWorter, G. A. (1985). Social origins and early features of the scientific study of Black American families and children. In M. B. Spencer, G. K. Brookins, & W. R. Allen (Eds.), *Beginnings: The social and affective development of Black children* (pp. 5–18). Hillsdale, NJ: Lawrence Erlbaum.

Sutherland, R. L. (1942). *Color, class, and personality*. Washington, D.C.: American Council on Education.

Warner, W. L. (1936). American caste and class. *American Journal of Sociology 42*, 234–237.

Warner, W. L., Junker, B. H. & Adams, W. A. (1941). *Color and human nature: Negro personality development in a northern city*. Washington, D.C.: American Council on Education.

Wolters, R. (1970). *Negroes and the great depression: The problem of economic recovery*. Westport, CT: Greenwood.

Young, J. O. (1973). *Black writers of the thirties*. Baton Rouge: Louisiana State Press.

COMPARATIVE PERSONALITY DEVELOPMENT IN ADOLESCENCE: A CRITIQUE

Carolyn B. Murray, Sandra N. Smith, Earle H. West

Introduction

Adolescence, to some extent, is a universal experience because of the rapid increase in the growth process that characteristically occurs at puberty and the impact this has on the individual's development. "Until the mid-to-late nineteenth century, the transition to adulthood in the United States was relatively fast, making for a brief adolescence" (Atwater, 1988, p. 5). However, a number of important changes took place around the turn of the century which eventually prolonged the transition to adulthood. These changes included the introduction of compulsory education, child-labor laws, and the concept of juvenile justice. These changes were imposed on youth in response to the needs of an emerging American urban-industrial society due to an increase in life expectancy, an end to the labor shortage, and a decline of apprenticeship training. "While a delayed adolescence tends to benefit youth from affluent homes who plan to continue their education in college, it often has the opposite effect on those who seek an early entry into the workplace" (Atwater, 1988, p. 8).

The traditional definition of adolescence—the period of rapid growth between childhood and adulthood—was based largely on physical changes, especially the more obvious manifestations such as increased height and weight. As a result, adolescence became synonymous with the teenage years, roughly from 13 to 18 years of age. However, the realization that adolescence pertains to a process of psychosocial development as well as physical growth implies that adolescence may begin earlier and last longer than the physical changes of puberty.

For the purposes of the present thesis, ages 13 to 18 will be used as the age criterion to delineate the period of adolescence. The present focus, however, will be on a primary aspect of the psychosocial changes which take place during this period: personality development. As previously mentioned, we recognize that to some extent adolescence is a universal experience in terms of rapid physical growth; however, we cannot overemphasize the fact that within an economically and racially stratified society such as ours, there exists diverse environmental situations (e.g., family structure, educational and career practices and opportunities, peer group activities, etc.) which influence the course of adolescent personality development. They most frequently result in psycho social development which varies qualitatively and quantitatively from individual to individual, and from group to group. The major purpose of this paper is to evaluate the empirical and theoretical comparative personality research on Black and White adolescents, two groups which are racially different, and more often than not, economically different.

Developmental Models

Currently, social scientists employ either "strong" or "weak" developmental models to describe and explain age-related changes in children's behaviors (Damon, 1983). A "strong" developmental model, such as Erik Erikson's psychosocial theory of personality development, which is specifically relevant to the present thesis, posits that developmental change will occur in a sequence of stages. These stages are qualitatively rather than quantitatively distinct from one another—that is, each new stage represents a new kind of behavior, rather than a simple increase in a behavior or an ability—and the stages describe whole systems of behavior, rather than discrete acts. The sequence of the stages are irreversible, and both the sequential order and the end point are universal, describing the development of persons in all social and cultural contexts (Damon, 1983, p. 14). Erikson's stage model is helpful in outlining the normal phases of identity development, but there are many aspects of individual variation in identity development that Erikson's model does not touch (or touches only indirectly through its potential for use in individual case studies). Furthermore, glaringly lacking are comparative investigations of Black and White adolescents.

Researchers who employ "weak" models of development describe phases of children's growth without implying that these phases are necessarily irreversible, holistic, qualitatively distinct, or universal. "Weak" model researchers may accept some of the stage characteristics but not others in order to describe the developmental changes which have been observed. In many cases, researchers employing "weak" developmental models have been able to explain developmental trends with greater accuracy than have researchers using "strong" models (Damon, 1983). There is an abundance of comparative research on Black and White adolescence using the "weak" model perspective. However, most of this research tends to treat middle-class White adolescents as the paragon of American adolescence and simultaneously views Black adolescents as a subcultural variation (Dill, 1978). The normative assumption that such models are applicable to all groups regardless of experiential factors has resulted in social scientists and educators developing a distorted view of Black adolescents. The outcome has been that Black adolescent personal attributes and behaviors are often viewed as aberrant. Further, such misperceptions have led to the conclusion that due to personality factors *alone*, the Black adolescent is primarily responsible for rising birth and crime rates, and his/her low academic achievement. And inevitably, Black adolescents are said to be major beneficiaries of the welfare system. Such views totally ignore the debilitating effects on personality of systemic prejudice and oppression.

Personality

Personality can be viewed as all behavioral predispositions that characterize a particular individual (Dill, 1978, p. 324). The individual's personality can be described as multi-dimensional, dynamic, unique, and a product of social interaction. To say that personality is multidimensional, means that skills, temperament, interests, feelings, cognitive abilities, and habits all contribute to making up an individual's personality. The dynamic nature of the personality means it is constantly changing in terms of characteristics exhibited by the person. Moreover, while there are personality similarities between individuals, differences will be found as well. Thus, every person has a unique personality. And while hereditary predisposition is the basis from which personality evolves, the resulting personality is molded by social interactions.

Due to the dearth of research on comparative personality development which employs "strong" models, the focus of the present paper is on "weak" models. The most investigated approaches in this category are the Cultural Deprivation Model and the Cultural Difference Model. Most of this research has been concerned with the lower achievement of Blacks in comparison to their White counterparts. According to cultural deprivationists, early childhood experiences in poverty environments create enduring personality formations that are inimical to effective achievement striving not only in the classroom but, indeed, in virtually all areas of life (Katz, 1968).

The Cultural Difference Model, a more recent personality approach, acknowledged that Black students brought unique socio-cultural experiences and psychological dispositions to the educational setting, but maintained that these "differences" were not "deficits." According to this view, Black American underachievement was the result of a "mis-match" between the culture of the school and the child's cultural expressions at home and in the community. However, the Cultural Difference Model has accepted the ethnocentric view propagated by the Cultural Deprivation

Model that Black children suffer from an absence of personality traits believed to be necessary for academic success (Valentine, 1971). The oldest and most fully researched tradition of this kind is the literature on adolescent self–concept. A more recent tradition, conceptually related to the self–concept research, is the study of adolescent sense of control over themselves and their lives (locus of control). A third extensively researched area is achievement motivation. All three constructs attempt to explain differences between adolescents in terms of both developmental maturity and personality characteristics, as related to educational outcomes in particular, and life accomplishments or lack of accomplishments in general. The present paper is a critical review of this literature as it pertains to cross–ethnic studies of Black and White adolescents.

Self Concept

Psychologists use the term self–concept to refer to an individual's perception of him or herself (Dill, 1978). However, a review of the relevant self–concept literature reveals the use of a wide variety of instruments, which suggests that there is no universally agreed upon definition of the self–concept construct. Self–concept has been conceived in a global, holistic sense, and also in a more limited, situation–specific sense (i.e., academic self–concept). These research difficulties are compounded by the tendency of subjects to give socially desirable responses, thus confusing ideal with actual self–concept. Moreover, where cross–ethnic comparisons are provided, cohort factors may contribute to differing and apparently conflicting results.

The cultural difference theorists agreed with the deprivation theorists that one of the most serious problems affecting the Black American child's academic achievement was his or her poor self–concept. However, they differed on the causes of this phenomenon, with the deprivation theorists suggesting that the poor self–concept of Black children was due to the distinct family style of the lower class, and the difference theorists crediting the school system and the media for the Black child's poor self–image.

Both the Cultural Deprivation and Difference Models, in attempting to explain the Black child's poor self–concept and its relationship to academic achievement, overlooked methodological errors, biased interpretations, and erroneous assumptions inherent in the self–concept literature (Banks, 1976; Brand, Ruiz & Padilla, 1974; Jones, 1972; Nobles, 1973). Moreover, most of this literature employed methodologies based on racial comparisons (Banks, 1976), exemplifying a "normative" or "neoracism" inherent in current American thought.

The self–identification of Whites was believed to be rational and a representative standard of mental health. However, research on the correlates of ethnocentrism would seem to argue against either the universality or the desirability of such evaluative sets, particularly in the case of self-concept (Banks, 1976).

While a few studies have reported results which show White adolescents scoring higher on measures of self-concept than did Black adolescents (Bridgett, 1970; and Osborne & LeGette, 1982), analyses of several large-scale nationally representative surveys of high school students, which employed relatively direct measures of self-esteem, provided little justification for the assumption that Blacks evaluated themselves less highly than did Whites (Bachman & O'Malley, 1984). Indeed, the preponderance of evidence supported the opposite conclusion, with Blacks scoring significantly higher on self-esteem scales than Whites (Harris & Stokes, 1978; Porter & Washington, 1979; Rosenberg & Simmons, 1972).

For instance, one of the most comprehensive studies was conducted by Rosenberg and Simmons (1972). These investigators collected data on the general self-concept (i.e., one's worth as a person) from 2,600 largely working class, non-Catholic youths in grades 3–12 of the Baltimore, Maryland, public schools. Three major dimensions of the self-image were studied (level of self-consciousness, level of self-esteem, and degree of instability in the self-picture). The self-concept of Black youths was found to be higher than that of Whites across all age groups both before and after controlling for socio-economic status. More disturbance was found among White adolescent females than among White males or Black females. Also, the difference in self-concept between White males and females was found to be greater than the difference between Black males and females. These findings did not disappear when social class was controlled and no class differences were found when race was held constant.

In line with Banks' (1976) criticisms of the earlier studies in which Black youths' self-esteem scores allegedly reflected self-hatred, the interpretation of the studies in which Blacks scored higher in comparison to Whites generally accused Black youth of utilizing protection mechanisms (McDill, Meyer, & Rugby, 1966), and of having a general propensity toward the extreme response category, whereas Whites tended to inhibit or qualify their responses in a more "healthy" response pattern (Bachman & O'Malley, 1984).

Earlier, Katz (1968), in an extensive review of personality approaches to Black achievement performance, made several observations in regard to the self-concept literature. His conclusions were: 1) self-concept had not been related to social class or family factors; and 2) nothing was known about its effects on school performance. Regarding Katz's prior observation, Wylie (1979) reported that 48 studies involving both well known and idiosyncratic instruments to index overall self-regard have yielded contradictory, weak, and mostly null results regarding the relationship of socioeconomic level and overall self-regard. And Hare

(1980; 1985) found that while the achievement gap between Black and White adolescents had increased, it failed to produce a similar self-esteem gap.

In terms of Katz's latter observation, self-concept appeared to be modestly correlated with academic ability, but the results depended on the specific component of self-concept, SES, or the ability level of the sample, and the level of data aggregation. For instance, Brookover and Passalacqua's (1981) study, based on a random sample of 68 schools, found that the school average academic achievement and school average academic self-concept were negatively correlated. Much of this negative relationship was apparently due to scores from seven predominantly Black schools in which self-concept was somewhat higher than average and academic achievement was markedly below average. Nevertheless, their findings demonstrated that the level of data aggregation (i.e., unit of analysis) was a critical variable. They found that individual academic achievement and individual academic self-concept were positively correlated.

In line with Brookover and Passalacqua's findings, Marsh and Parker (1984) found that within a given level of school SES, the higher the family SES, the higher the academic self-concept; but in a given level of family SES, the higher the school SES, the lower the academic self-concept. They employed the frame of reference hypothesis to interpret their findings. The underlying assumption is that the students' reference group (i.e., their classmates or their school mates) influenced academic self-concept in the sense that one's own performance is compared with that of one's reference group, and it is this relativistic perception that forms the basis of self-concept. Furthermore, they and others (Jordan, 1981) argued that while academic self- concept (self-assessment of school performance) was correlated with academic performance, global self-concept (awareness of the totality of one's self-knowledge emanating from a history of interactions with others and evaluations of how one has coped with life) may not be.

Thus, the predicted results depended on the unit of analysis, the sampling procedure, the type of analysis used, and the component of self-concept examined. This may account for the bewildering array of results found by other researchers. However, in terms of the observations made by Katz (1967), and the recent findings of large scale studies, the negative Black self-concept phenomenon is dubious at best.

Internal-External Locus of Control

The Internal-External Locus of Control construct refers to the degree to which people have a sense of efficacy or power and accept personal responsibility for what happens to them (Rotter, Liverant, &

Crowne, 1961). Comparative research in this area has consistently shown that Blacks and poor people are significantly more external than Whites or middle–class people (e.g., Coleman, et al., 1966; Lefcourt & Ladwig, 1965). Furthermore, the overwhelming majority of the Internal–External Locus of Control studies examining the relationship of the control construct and academic achievement reported a positive association between internality and achievement behavior. In line with the aforementioned personality construct (self–concept), the cultural deprivationists attributed the lower–class Black child's assumed externality to inadequate child rearing practices (e.g., Armentrout, 1971) whereas the cultural difference theorists attributed the Black child's externality to group experience with external obstacles (i.e., racism and discrimination).

The literature on Internal–External Locus of Control has been criticized on several levels (Cones, 1971). Most writers erroneously presented the locus control construct as a unitary concept. For instance, Gurin and Epps (1975) argued that the previous findings relating external control to low achievement in Blacks did not differentiate between personal–control versus control–ideology, and self–blame versus system–blame. Their results showed that high motivation and performance were positively related to both internal (i.e., personal–control) and external (i.e., system–blame) control factors among Black college students. Gurin, Gurin, Lao & Beattie (1969), and Gurin and Epps (1975), concluded that Blacks who perceived discriminating obstacles and placed blame for their problems on these systemic barriers (rather than attributing their lack of success to their own personal inadequacies) tended to be more motivated and realistic than those who categorically denied the existence of racial discrimination as a personal problem.

In line with Gurin and Epps' (1975) conclusions, Ducette and Walk (1972) reported that Black internals had lower occupational and cognitive estimations than Black externals, whereas White internals had higher occupational and cognitive estimations than White externals. In addition, Katz (1967) suggested that besides enhancing realistic social insight and strategic coping behavior, this type of external orientation also functioned to rectify the negative self–concept and identity crisis which resulted from Blacks blaming themselves for failure and racial inequalities.

With respect to the stability of this personality construct across settings, Gaa, Williams, and Johnson (1981) examined locus of control across three domains (intellectual, social, and physical), using a domain–specific measure. They found that Blacks were significantly more internal than Whites with respect to success in the intellectual domain. However, the two groups did not differ from each other in terms of the intellectual domain. The Whites were more internal than were the Blacks with respect to social failure. These findings suggest that generalized conclusions with respect to internality or externality within and between ethnic groups are probably not justified.

In summary, personality approaches like locus of control and self-esteem, which have dominated the study of Black academic achievement since Katz's (1968) review, continue to be hampered by methodological and conceptual inconsistencies. For example, recent developments in the comparative research on locus of control have clearly cast doubt on the usefulness and validity of previous research. This has been due chiefly to the recognition that locus of control is a multidimensional concept rather than a single global concept. Thus, there is a need for a fresh start which takes into consideration the demonstrated complexity of the concept, and also the possibility of social and cultural differences in the adaptiveness of various dimensions of locus of control. After reviewing a large body of research on locus of control in Black populations, Banks, Beatty, Booth, Pope, and Hart (in press) reached the conclusions that

> with respect to the status of Black populations there are three possible fundamental patterns of the evidence on locus of control. Blacks may be largely internal, largely external, or largely neither. These categories are not exclusive, and neither are they discrete as an idealized typological system. However, the evidence is clear, especially in one respect: Blacks have not been shown to be external. In fact, more than half of the explicit evidence reported for Black samples indicates a clear internal pattern of responding. Roughly 45% of the published data fail to establish Blacks as either internal or external (p. 21).

Achievement Motivation

In the McClelland–Atkinson (1961) tradition, achievement motivation was defined as an acquired, relatively stable, and general feature of personality that impelled individuals to strive for success whenever their performance at a task could be evaluated against a standard of excellence.

Past studies generally indicated that Whites tended to score higher than Blacks on trait measures of achievement motivation (Castenell, 1980). Cultural deprivation theorists (Bereiter & Engelman, 1966; Hunt, 1967; McClelland, 1961) proposed that the generally low status of Blacks was associated with a low achievement motive (Mingione, 1965; Rosen, 1969). The reasons offered by cultural deprivationists for this lack of achievement motive among Blacks have ranged from a lack of the essential tool of academic learning ability—standard English (Bereiter & Engeleman, 1966)—to the matricentric structure of the Black family (McClelland, 1961; Schroth, 1976).

In contrast to this view are the findings of a study conducted by Allen (1978), in which data were collected on the relationship of achievement orientation to family background for male adolescents and their families. He found Black and White subjects similar on indices of achievement orientation (aspiration, self–esteem, academic self–concept, achievement values, and sense of environmental control), but these indices were differentially related to the family settings. With respect to parental aspiration for the sons, no racial difference was found for fathers, but Black mothers had higher aspirations than White mothers. On the dimension of parent–child interpersonal relationships, White sons perceived their parents as more approving of them than did Black sons; White sons reported feeling closer to their parents than Black sons. Black fathers were found to be the most demanding of independence in their sons. Allen concluded that Black mothers and White fathers play the most critical roles in determining the levels of aspirations of their sons.

Proponents of the Cultural Difference Model, however, opposed this line of reasoning, suggesting that Black youths' distinctive systems of values and goals were not represented by the educational system. According to these researchers, the Black child's disinterest in classroom learning was less a matter of his or her lacking the achievement motive than of it being directed into non–intellectual pursuits (e.g., Cloward & Jones, 1963). Supporting these assumptions, Castanell (1983) found that White adolescents scored higher on a traditional achievement motivation scale that emphasized self–esteem, independence, sense of control and individualism whereas Black adolescents scored higher on an achievement scale that emphasized school, home and peer achievement motivation. In short, the cultural difference theorists proposed that the problem of motivating the minority pupil was essentially one of accommodating the educational goals of the school to the values, goals and learning styles that have been socially transmitted to the child in his or her home and neighborhood environments.

Unfortunately, the Cultural Difference Model has inherent limitations in its explanations of Black achievement difficulties. To be sure, the Cultural Difference and Deprivation Models diverged on the explanation of why Black students lack achievement motivation; however, the models were in agreement that Blacks do lack the achievement motive, and that this causes scholastic difficulties. An examination of the literature suggests that the validity of the measurement of achievement motivation with regard to Blacks has been questionable. Basic objections have ranged from the lack of the universality of achievement motive measurement (Crandall, Kathoosky, & Crandall, 1965; Kagan & Moss, 1959; and Veroff, 1966) to the fact that individuals who deemed group products and accomplishments important were not taken into consideration by the achievement motive paradigm (Castenell, 1983; Gurin & Epps, 1975; Ramirez, 1976).

A number of psychologists concluded that differences between Blacks and Whites in achievement motivation were directly related to general patterns of community oppression (e.g., Gurin & Epps, 1975). Moreover, on self report measures of achievement motivation and desire for schooling, Blacks consistently scored higher than did Whites (Ryan, 1976).

Discussion and Implications

It is all too clear from the foregoing review of the research literature that psychologists have contributed little to the understanding of comparative personality development in Black and White adolescents. More importantly, for Black adolescents, due to the practice of using the White adolescent as the ideal prototype, little is known about how personality relates to differences in academic achievement in particular, and life in general.

Much of the available literature is based on the notion that there is no real significant diversity among Black adolescents in terms of social background, educational achievement, and career goals. The Black adolescent is regularly portrayed as living in overcrowded slums in a matriarchal family that consists of too many children and too little adult guidance and supervision. This inadequate culture is then blamed for the development of yet-to-be-documented dysfunctional personality characteristics (i.e., poor self-concepts, external locus of control, and low achievement motive). First of all, there are sizeable numbers of Black adolescents who do not fit this mold. In fact, they hold allegiance to the traditional American work ethic. They study hard in school, want a good job after graduation, and hope to be loving parents of their offspring (Dill, 1978).

Secondly, even though there is a disproportionate number of Black adolescents who do indeed fit this portrait (see Gibbs, Chapter 1 of this volume), neither the causes nor the solutions lie with the supposedly deficient personality characteristics of the Black adolescent. Ogbu (1981) persuasively argues that the causes and the solutions are embedded within the structured inequality of American society, especially the caste-like stratification of unequal opportunity in the labor market. In turn this situation affects the design and process of Black education, as well as how Black youth respond to this process. Several researchers have noted that Black adolescents frequently express the view that racial discrimination and an inadequate education were major barriers to their success and, more importantly, that such barriers could not be reversed by their own actions (Elder, 1972; Ogbu, 1981). This situation is especially acute for the Black lower-class, the group that is usually hit hardest throughout educational system and then through other institutions of the society, such as the labor market.

Over forty years ago, sociologist Allison Davis (1944) aptly stated, "Our society cannot hope to educate the great masses of lower-class people in any really effective manner until it has real rewards to offer them..." (pp. 213–214). Put in the words of Ogbu (1981), for children to develop appropriate attitudes and to perform well in school, their observations of adults around them and the folklore of their community must confirm that the system works the way schools say it does. For the middle–class White adolescent this is usually the case; however, what the lower–class Black adolescent learns is that they face an automatic job ceiling, or very likely no job at all. The impact of these differential realities is that the White adolescent spends more time and effort on his or her homework than does the Black adolescent, who often develops a variety of coping responses that do not enhance success.

This view has been formalized by "adolescence as a cultural phenomenon" perspective. As articulated by Sieg (1975), adolescence is not a necessary stage of human development, despite puberty or age–related events associated with it. Instead, she defines adolescence solely in terms of the sociocultural process. According to Sieg, "adolescence is the period of development in human beings that adult privileges are due him which are not being afforded him, and that ends when the full power and social status of the adult world are accorded to the individual by his society" (p. 40). In other words, adolescence depends primarily on the discrepancy between one's actual and desired status in society, and the attainment of adulthood is the satisfactory resolution of that discrepancy. With regard to Blacks in the United States, Sieg proposes that because adult status and power have been withheld from them, it is as if our society has assigned Blacks a status of permanent adolescence, which has resulted in a characteristic reaction of frustration, rebellion, and seeming irresponsibility.

In sum, the literature has not documented specific Black–White adolescent personality differences, a situation which renders mute the assumptions that such differences are products of early family influence, and are related to differences in achievement or success in life. What has emerged consistently, however, is that while Black adolescents share with White adolescents many of the same personality traits, such as a desire for educational achievement, due to real barriers within the society–at–large to achievement for Blacks that do not exist for Whites, Blacks more frequently do not match their wish and aspirations with effort (Ogbu, 1981). Therefore, both differences in social–class and caste due to race, along with the resultant behavior patterns, must be continually considered in understanding some of the underlying factors related to adolescent psychosocial development.

Obviously, with regard to the psychosocial development of Black adolescents, further research from a cultural relativistic perspective is needed. It is clearly inappropriate to label such behaviors as deprived or pathological; instead their developmental antecedents and vital adaptational dynamics should be investigated.

References

Allen, W.R. (1978). Race, family setting, and adolescent achievement orientation. *Journal of Negro Education, 47,* 302–343.

Armentrout, J.A. (1971). Parental childrearing attitudes and preadolescents problem behaviors. *Journal of Consulting and Clinical Psychology, 37,* 279–285.

Atwater, E. (1988). *Adolescence.* 2 ed. New Jersey: Prentice Hall.

Bachman, J.G., & O'Malley, P.M. (1984). Black–White differences in self–esteem: Are they affected by response style? *American Journal of Sociology, 90(3),* 625–639.

Banks, W.C. (1976). White preference in Blacks: A pardigm in search of a phenomenon. *Psychological Bulletin, 83(6),* 1179–1186.

Banks, W.C., Beatty, L., Booth, J., Pope, J., & Hart, L. (In press). Black self–concept revisited. In R.L. Jones (Ed.), *Black Psychology* (3rd Edition), Berkeley: Cobb & Henry.

Bereiter, C., & Engleman, S. (1966). *Teaching disadvantaged children in pre–school.* Engleman Cliffs, New Jersey: Prentice Hall.

Brand, E.S., Ruiz, R.A., & Padella, A.M. (1974). Ethnic identification and preference: A review. *Psychological Bulletin, 81,* 860–890.

Bridgett, R.E. (1970). Self–esteem in Negro and White southern adolescents. Unpublished Ph.D. Dissertation, University of North Carolina at Chapel Hill.

Brookover, W.B., & Passalacqua, J. (1981). Comparison of aggregate self–concepts for populations with different reference groups. In M. Lynch. A. Noren–Hebeisen, & W. Gergen (Eds.), *Self–concept advances in theory and practice,* Cambridge, MA: Ballinger.

Castenell, Jr., L.A. (1980). Achievement motivation: An area– specific analysis. Unpublished Ph.D. Dissertation, University of Illinois at Champaign.

Castenell, L.A. (1983). Achievement motivation: An investigation of adolescents' achievement patterns. *American Educational Research Journal, 20(4),* 503–510.

Cloward, R.A., & Jones, J.A. (1963). Social class: Educational attitudes and participation. In A.M. Passow (Ed.), *Education in depressed areas,* New York: Bureau of Publications, Teachers.

Coleman, J.S., Campbell, E., Hopson, C., McPartland, J., Mood, A., Weingeld, F., & York, R. (1966). *Equality of educational opportunity,* U.S. Government Printing Office, Washington, D.C. College, Columbia University.

Cones, J.D. (1971). Locus of control and social disability. *Journal of Consulting and Clinical Psychology, 36,* 449.

Crandall, V.C., Kathoosky, W., & Crandall, V.J. (1965). Children's beliefs in their control of reinforcement in intellectual academic achievement. *Child Development, 36,* 91–109.

Damon, W. (1983). *Social and personality development.* New York: W.W. Norton & Co.

Davis, A. (1944). Socialization and adolescent personality. In *Adolescence Yearbook of the National Society for the Study of Education,* 41(Pt. 1), Chicago: University of Chicago Press.

Dill, J.R. (1978). *Child psychology in contemporary society.* Boston: Holbrook Press.

DuCette, J. & Wolk, S. (1972). Locus of control and levels of aspiration in Black and White children. *Review of Educational Research, 42,* 493–504.

Elder, G.H. (1972). Socialization and ascent in a racial minority. *Youth and Society, 2*, 74–110.
Gaa, J.P., Williams, R.E. & Johnson, S.W. (1981). Domain–specific locus of control orientations of Anglo, Black, and Chicano adolescents. *The Journal of Psychology, 107*, 185–190.
Gibbs, J.T. (in press). Black adolescent and youth: An update on an endangered species. In R. Jones (Ed.) *Black adolescents,* Berkeley: Cobb & Henry.
Gurin, P., & Epps, E. (1975). *Black consciousness, identity and achievement.* New York: John Wiley & Sons, Inc.
Gurin, P., Gurin, G., Lao, R.C., & Beattie, M. (1969). Internal– external control in the motivational dynamics of Negro youth. *Journal of Social Issues, 25(3),* 29–52.
Hare, B.B. (1985). Stability and change in self–perception and achievement among Black adolescents: A longitudinal study. *The Journal of Black Psychology, 11*, 29–42.
Hare, B.R. (1980). Self–perception and academic achievement variations in a desegregation setting. *American Journal of Psychiatry, 137*, 683–689.
Harris, A.R., & Stokes, R. (1978). Race, self–evaluation and the protestant ethic. *Social Problems, 26*, 71–85.
Hunt, J. McV. (1967). The psychological basis for preschool cultural enrichment programs. In M. Deutsch, A. Jensen, & I. Katz (Eds.), *Social class, race and psychological development.* New York: Holt, Rinehart, and Winston.
Jones, J. (1972). *Prejudice and racism.* Menlo Park, CA: Addison–Welsey Pub. Co.
Jordan, T.J. (1981). Self–concept, motivation, and academic achievement of Black adolescents. *Journal of Educational Psychology, 73(4)*, 509–517.
Kagan, J., & Moss, H.A. (1959). Stability and validity of achievement fantasy. *Journal of Abnormal and Social Psychology, 58*, 357–364.
Katz, I. (1967). The socialization of academic motivation in minority group children. In D. Devine (Ed.), *Nebraska symposium on motivation* (pp. 133–191). University of Nebraska Press.
Katz, I. (1968). Academic motivation and equal educational opportunity. *Harvard Educational review, 38*, 57–65.
Lail, S.S. (1963). A study of differences in developmental task achievement among adolescents in grades seven, nine and eleven. Unpublished Ed.D. Dissertation, University of Kentucky.
Lefcourt, H.M., & Ladwig, G.W. (1965). The effects of reference group upon Negroes task persistence in a biracial competitive game. *Journal of Personality and Social Psychology, 1(6),* 671–675.
McClelland, D.C. (1961). *The achieving society.* New York: Van Nostrand.
McDill, E., Meyer, E., & Rugby, L. (1966). *Sources of educational climate in high schools.* Baltimore, MD: John Hopkins University.
Marsh, H.W., & Parker, J.W. (1984). Determinants of student self– concept: Is it better to be a relatively large fish in a small pond even if you don't learn to swim as well? *Journal of Personality and Social Psychology, 47(1)*, 213–231.
Mingione, A. (1966). Need for achievement in Negro and White children. *Journal of Consulting Psychology, 3*, 45–53.
Nobles, W. (1973). Psychological research and the Black self– concept: A critical review. *Journal of Social Issues, 29(1)*, 11–31.
Obgu, J.U. (1981). Black education: A cultural–ecological perspective. In H.P. McAdoo (Ed.), *Black Families,* Beverly Hills: Sage Publications.

Osborne, W.L. & LeGette, H.R. (1982). Sex, race, grade level, and social class differences in self–concept. *Measurement and Evaluation in Guidance, 14,* 195–201.

Porter, J.R., & Washington, R.E. (1979). Black identity and self– esteem: A review of studies on Black self–concept 1968–1978. *Annual Review of Sociology, 5,* 53–74.

Ramirez, M., & Price–Williams, D.R. (1976). Achievement motivation in children of three ethnic groups in the United States. *Journal of Cross–Cultural Psychology. 7(1),* 49–60.

Rosen, B. (1969). Race, ethnicity and the achievement syndrome. *American Sociological Review, 24,* 417–460.

Rosenberg, M., & Simmons, R.G. (1972). *Black and White self– esteem: The urban school child.* Washington, D.C.: American Sociological Association.

Rotter, J.B., Liverant, S., & Crowne, D.P. 91961). The growth and extinction of expectancies in change controlled and skilled tests. *Journal of Psychology, 52,* 161–177.

Ryan, W. (1976). *Blaming the victim.* (2nd ed.). New York: Vintage Books.

Schroth, M.L. (1976). Sex and grade–level differences in need achievement among Black college students. *Perceptual and Motor Skills, 43(1),* 135–140.

Sieg, A. (1975). Why adolescence occurs. In H.D. Thornberg (Ed.), *Contemporary adolescence: Readings, 2nd. ed.,* Monterey, CA: Brooks/Cole Publishing Company.

Valentine, C.A. (1971). Deficit, difference, bi–cultural models of Afro–American behavior. *Harvard Educational Review,* 41(2), 137–157.

Veroff, J. (1966). Measuring the achievement motive in young boys and girls. Unpublished manuscript. Ann Arbor: University of Michigan.

Wylie, R.C. (1979). *The self–concept: Theory and research on selected topics* (Vol. 2). Lincoln: University of Nebraska Press.

Part II
Youth in Diverse Settings

BLACK YOUTH IN
PREDOMINANTLY WHITE SUBURBS[1]

James A. Banks

The number of middle class Blacks has increased significantly since the civil rights movement of the 1960s. When Blacks become middle class, they frequently move from the central area of the city to the suburbs. Between 1960 and 1977, the number of Black suburban residents increased 71.8%. In 1977, 18.8% of Blacks were suburban residents (Lake, 1981). In 1981, one out of every five Blacks lived in the suburbs (Carlson, 1981).

Black suburban residents are highly diversified. Many Black suburban residents live in predominantly Black working class spillover communities. Others live in predominantly Black middle class spillover communities. Still others live in predominantly Black middle class suburbs. However, a significant number of Black suburban residents live in predominantly White middle class suburban communities. They are a small but increasingly significant minority within their communities.

Blacks who live in the nation's predominantly White suburban communities have been largely neglected by social science theorists and researchers. Most of the existing studies focus on lower status Blacks who are residents of central cities (Ladner, 1973). This is the case, in part, because lower class Blacks make up the largest subgroup of Blacks. Yet, the Black community is becoming more and more diversified in terms of values, behaviors, and attitudes because of increasing social class variation within the group (Willie, 1974; Wilson, 1978). One of the most important characteristics of Blacks today is their intra-group variation. Unless more research is done that contributes to a description of the intra-group variation within the Black population, we run the risk of perpetuating the inaccurate notion that Blacks are a monolithic, lower class ethnic group.

Since the 1960s, a number of important studies have been done on Black suburban residents. However, most have described migration and dispersal patterns and not the social and psychological world of the Black suburbanite. None of the studies reviewed was exclusively concerned with the lives of Black families who were residents of predominantly White suburbs. Among the studies that focus on migration patterns and the qualities and characteristics of the suburbs in which Blacks live are those by Blumberg and Lalli (1966), Farley (1970), Downs (1973), Rabinovitz (1975), Rose (1976), Frey (1978), Clark (1979), Connolly (1979), Marshall and Stahura (1979), and Lake 1981). Pettigrew (1973) is one of the few researchers to examine psychological factors related to Black suburbanization. He studied the attitudes of Whites, income levels, and the willingness of Blacks to move to the suburbs. In an earlier investigation, Northwood and Barth (1965) studied the attitudes of Black and White families who lived in selected predominantly White neighborhoods of a large city in the Northwest.

The Study of Black Suburban Youths

There is a dearth of research that describes and interprets the social, psychological, and educational experiences of Black suburban youth. Indeed, a comprehensive search of seven computerized databases (Psychological Abstracts, ERIC, Dissertation Abstracts, Sociological Abstracts, Family Resources/Family Relations Population Bibliography, and Mental Health Abstracts) for the period 1970–1987 yielded only four entries, three (Cloud, 1980; Katzman, 1983; and Randolph, 1970) of which were related to the impact of Black suburbanization on the schools, and one (Zschock, 1971) that looked at low socioeconomic status Black youth in predominantly White suburbs. Of the four studies, only Zschock actually interviewed the youth, and his concern was problems of employment and community needs. A study of factors influencing the psychosocial development of Black youth in predominantly White suburbs, then, is timely and needed. The present chapter is written to help fill this void. It draws upon and interprets data from a larger study of Black families who lived in selected, predominantly White suburban communities of a large metropolitan area in the Pacific Northwest, the population of which exceeds one million. The major purpose of the larger study was to describe family socialization practices related to the acquisition of racial attitudes and ethnic behavior. The work presented herein describes the self–concepts of ability, general self–concepts, level of externality, and attitudes toward physical characteristics, neighborhoods, and schools of the children in the larger study and integrates the findings into an ethnicity typology the author developed (Banks, 1976, 1981) (see Figure 1).

The subjects were 98 youths who were members of the 57 families who participated in the larger study. Fifty (78%) of the 64 families participating in the larger investigation (64 families, of whom 57 are included in results reported herein) were headed by two parents; 14 (22%) were single–parent families. All but one of the single–parent families were headed by a female. The parents had high incomes and high levels of educational attainment. Fifty–one percent of the families had 1982 incomes of $40,000 or above. Fifty–five percent of the parents had either some graduate or professional school training or had finished graduate or professional school. The participants ranged in age from 8 to 18, with a mean age of 12.8.

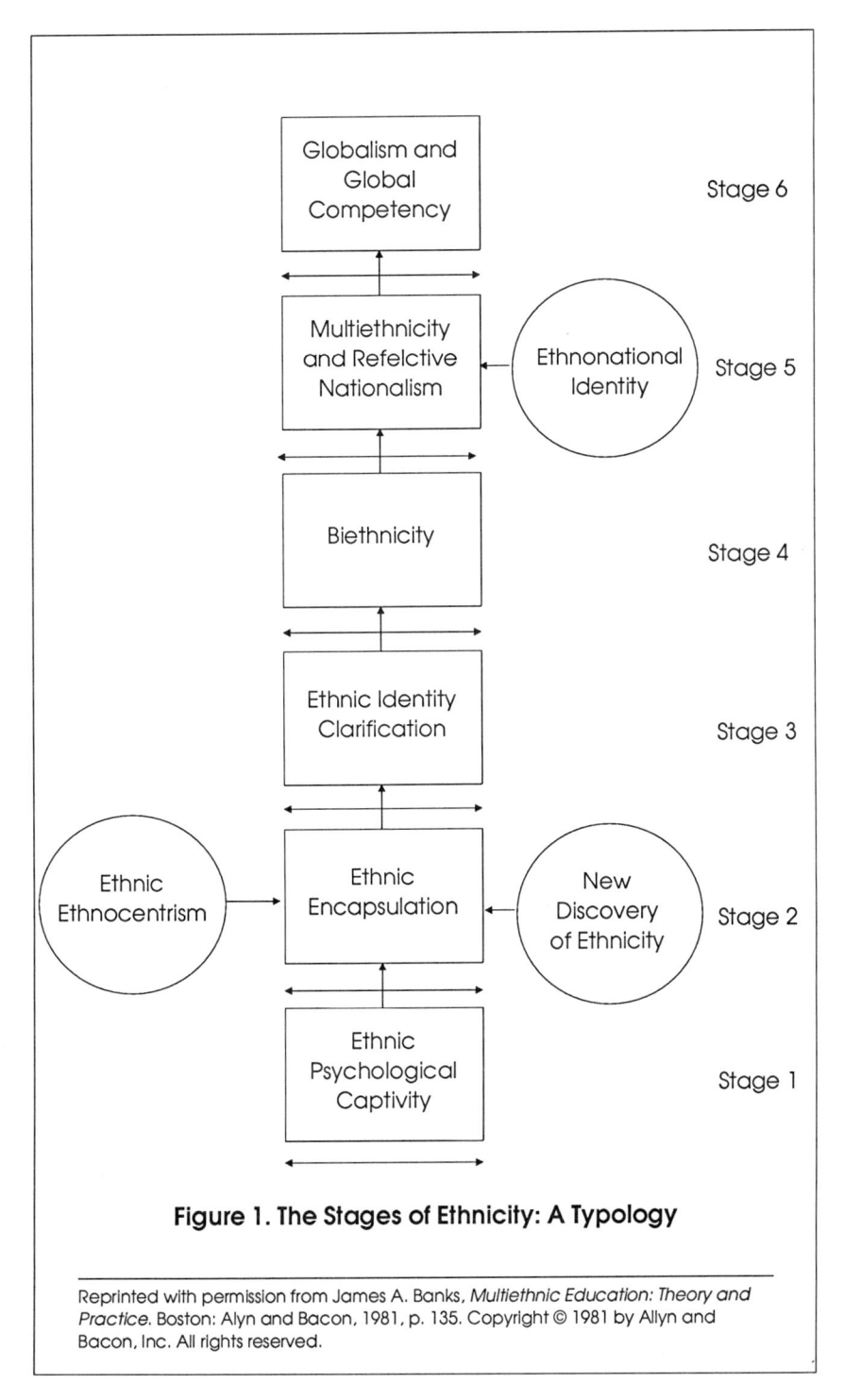

Black Youth in Predominantly White Suburbs

- **Stage 6**: Globalism and Global Competency
- **Stage 5**: Multiethnicity and Refelctive Nationalism ← Ethnonational Identity
- **Stage 4**: Biethnicity
- **Stage 3**: Ethnic Identity Clarification
- **Stage 2**: Ethnic Ethnocentrism → Ethnic Encapsulation ← New Discovery of Ethnicity
- **Stage 1**: Ethnic Psychological Captivity

Figure 1. The Stages of Ethnicity: A Typology

Reprinted with permission from James A. Banks, *Multiethnic Education: Theory and Practice.* Boston: Alyn and Bacon, 1981, p. 135. Copyright © 1981 by Allyn and Bacon, Inc. All rights reserved.

The participants were administered the following scales: the Brookover Self–Concept of Ability Scale (Brookover, 1962), the Rosenberg Self–Esteem Scale (Rosenberg, 1965), the Stephan–Rosenfield (1979) Racial Attitude Scales, the Nowicki–Strickland (1973) Locus of Control Scale, and a 45–item questionnaire developed by the author with subscales that measure Attitudes Toward School, Physical Self–Concept, Attitudes Toward Blacks, Attitudes Toward Whites, and Attitudes Toward Neighborhood. Two measures of ethnocentrism (pro–Blackness) were derived from the differences between the subjects' attitudes toward Whites mean scores and their attitudes toward Blacks mean scores on the Banks racial attitudes subscales and the Stephan–Rosenfield subscales.

In sections following, a stages of ethnicity typology will be presented and the results of the present investigation will be discussed in the context of the typology. The findings will then be summarized and discussed in the light of larger issues surrounding the socialization of Black youth who live in predominantly White suburbs.

The Stages of Ethnicity Typology

Stage 1: Psychological Captivity. During this stage the individual inculcates the negative ideologies and beliefs about his/her ethnic group that are institutionalized within the society. Consequently, he/she exemplifies ethnic self–rejection and low self–esteem. The individual is ashamed of his/her ethnic identity during this stage and may respond in a number of ways, including avoiding situations that bring him/her into contact with other ethnic groups, or striving aggressively to become highly culturally assimilated.

Stage 2: Ethnic Encapsulation. Stage Two is characterized by ethnic encapsulation and exclusiveness, including voluntary separatism. The individual participates primarily within his/her own ethnic community and believes that his/her ethnic group is superior to that of others. Many individuals within Stage 2, such as many Anglo–Americans, have internalized the dominant societal myths about the superiority of their ethnic or racial group and the innate inferiority of other ethnic groups and races.

Stage 3: Ethnic Identity Clarification. At this stage the individual is able to clarify his/her attitudes and ethnic identity, to reduce intrapsychic conflict, and to develop clarified positive attitudes toward his/her ethnic group. The individual learns to accept self, thus developing the characteristics needed to accept and respond more positively to outside ethnic groups. During this stage, ethnic pride is genuine rather than contrived.

Stage 4: Biethnicity. During this stage individuals have both a healthy sense of ethnic identity and the psychological characteristics and skills needed to participate successfully in their own ethnic culture as well as in another ethnic culture. The individual also has a strong desire to function effectively in two ethnic cultures. We may describe individuals within this stage as *biethnic* or *bicultural*.

Stage 5: Multiethnicity and Reflective Nationalism. The Stage 5 individual has clarified, reflective, and positive personal, ethnic and national identifications, positive attitudes toward other ethnic and racial groups, and is self-actualized. The individual is able to function, at least beyond superficial levels, within several ethnic cultures within his or her nation, and to understand, appreciate, and share the values, symbols, and institutions of several ethnic cultures within his or her nation.

Individuals within this stage have a commitment to their ethnic groups, an empathy and concern for other ethnic groups, and a strong but reflective commitment and allegiance to the nation state and its idealized values, such as human dignity and justice.

Stage 6: Globalism and Global Competency. The individual within Stage 6 has clarified, reflective, and positive ethnic, national, and global identifications and the knowledge, skills, attitudes, and abilities needed to function within ethnic cultures within his or her own nation as well as within cultures outside his or her nation in other parts of the world. The Stage 6 individual has the ideal delicate balance of ethnic, national, and global identifications, commitments, literacy and behaviors.

Characteristics of the Stages of Ethnicity Typology

This typology is an ideal type construct and should be viewed as dynamic and multidimensional rather than as static and linear (see Taylor (in press), and Cross, Parham and Helms (in press) for a discussion of related typologies. The characteristics within the stages exist on a continuum. Thus, within Stage 1, individuals are more or less ethnically psychologically captive; some individuals are more ethnically psychologically captive than others.

The division between the stages is blurred rather than sharp. Thus a continuum also exists between as well as within the stages. The ethnically encapsulated individual (Stage 3) does not suddenly attain clarification and acceptance of his/her ethnic identity (Stage 4). This is a gradual and developmental process. Also, the stages should not be viewed as strictly sequential and linear. I am hypothesizing that some individuals may never experience a particular stage. However, I hypothesize that once an individual experiences a particular stage, he/she is likely to experience the stages above it sequentially and developmentally. I believe, however, that individuals may experience the stages upward, downward, or in a zigzag pattern. Under certain conditions, for example, the biethnic (Stage 4) individual may become multiethnic (Stage 5); under new conditions the same individual may become again biethnic (Stage 4), ethnically identified (Stage 3), and ethnically encapsulated (Stage 2).

Stages of Ethnicity of Black Suburban Youth

Stage 1 individuals have negative beliefs and attitudes toward their own ethnic group and have internalized the negative images of themselves that are perpetuated by the larger society. Black children who are socialized within a predominantly White suburban community, and who attend predominantly White schools, such as the children in this study, may run the risk of internalizing the negative images of Blacks and the White standards of beauty that are institutionalized within most predominantly White communities. Previous research on children's racial attitudes suggests that this may be the case (Williams and Morland, 1976).

However, there is little evidence in this study that these children have internalized negative images toward Blackness, White standards of physical beauty, or negative racial attitudes toward Blacks as a group. The ten–item Physical Self–Concept subscale in this study was designed to measure how Black youths evaluated their physical characteristics and race and to determine how physical self–evaluation was related to other variables. These children evaluated their physical characteristics and Blackness positively. The mean physical–self score was 33.14 out of a possible score of 40. Over 90% of the children agreed with this statement: "I like the way I look"; 98% agreed with the statement, "I like the color of my skin." Only 8.2% of the children agreed with the statement "My looks bother me."

Most of the children in this study had positive attitudes toward Blacks as a group. On the Stephan–Rosenfield scale (the lower the score on this scale, the more positive the attitudes), the mean score on the Attitudes Toward Blacks subscale obtained by the children in this study was 22.86. In an earlier study conducted by Stephan and Rosenfield (1979), White students had a mean score on the Attitudes Toward Whites subscale of 23.1. The Black students in the present study were slightly more positive toward their racial group than the White students in the Stephan–Rosenfield study.

Stage 2 is characterized by ethnic encapsulation and ethnic exclusiveness, including voluntary separatism. Individuals within this stage also tend to evaluate their ethnic group much more positively than outside ethnic groups. Given the sociocultural environment in which the children in this study were being socialized, it is not surprising that the results of this study indicate that they had few Stage 2 characteristics. Most respondents had highly positive attitudes towards Blacks as well as toward Whites. They had very low ethnocentrism scores, when ethnocentrism was determined both by using means from the Banks and Stephan–Rosenfield subscales (Banks subscale: Ethnocentrism mean = 4.1; highest possible score = 32) (Stephan–Rosenfield subscale: Ethnocentrism mean = 3.32, highest possible score = 40).

At Stage 3, the individual is able to clarify his/her ethnic identity and to develop positive and clear attitudes toward his/her ethnic group. At Stage 4, the individual has a healthy sense of ethnic identity, positive attitudes toward another ethnic group, and is able to participate successfully in his/her ethnic culture as well as in another ethnic culture. Individuals within this stage also have a strong desire to function effectively within two ethnic cultures.

The data indicate that most of the children in this study have clarified ethnic identities (Stage 3) and are biethnic in their racial attitudes, perceptions and behavior (Stage 4). Responses to a number of items in the questionnaire indicate that the children have positive racial attitudes toward both Blacks and Whites, that they enjoy interacting with both their Black and White friends, and wish that more Black children and teachers were in their social environments.

On the Stephan–Rosenfield subscales, the mean score for attitudes toward Whites was 25.8; the mean score for attitudes toward Blacks was 22.86. On the Banks racial attitudes subscales, the mean scores for attitudes towards Whites was 22.20; the mean score for attitudes toward Blacks was 26.15. The findings from both sets of subscales indicate that the children were biracial in their racial attitudes, i.e., they had positive attitudes toward both Blacks and Whites, although they had slightly more positive attitudes toward Blacks than toward Whites on both sets of scales.

Virtually all (98%) of the children agreed with the statement: "I am proud to be Black." Most (88.8%) agreed with the statement, "I wish more Black students were at my school"; 87.8% agreed with the statement "I wish more Black people lived in my neighborhood." A majority (88.8%) of the children agreed with the statement: "I like to spend a lot of time with my Black friends"; 86.9% agreed with the statement, "I wish I had more Black friends."

The fact that most of the children in this study had highly positive attitudes toward Blacks did not cause them to have negative attitudes toward Whites. They also had highly positive attitudes toward Whites and indicated that they enjoyed their White friends. Most of the children (84.7%) disagreed with the statement "I spend as little time with Whites as possible." A large majority (87.8%) agreed with the statement "I get along well with other kids in my neighborhood." Most of the subjects not only had highly positive attitudes toward Whites and their White friends, but believed that their White friends and neighbors had positive attitudes toward them. Most agreed with these statements: "The kids in my neighborhood like to do things with me" (81.6%); and "The kids in my neighborhood think I am important" (63.3%). Most (74.5%) disagreed with the statement, "The kids in my neighborhood leave me out of things."

Almost 89% of the subjects disagreed with the statement, "The students at school leave me out of things"; 74.5% disagreed with the statement, "The teachers at school make me feel different." However, it is interesting to note that 25.5% of the students agreed with the statement that teachers make them feel different. This finding suggests that the students may feel slightly more accepted by their peers than their teachers.

Most of the children in this study not only had highly positive attitudes toward Whites, but felt that their White peers and teachers treated them in a nondiscriminatory way. However, while these statements accurately describe the responses of most of the children in this study, the reader should keep in mind that on each of the items discussed above, a percentage of the children responded differently from most of the others. Because researchers should remain sensitive to intraethnic differences, it is important that we study closely the responses and profiles of those who respond differently from most other subjects. At some future time, there should be careful study of the responses of divergent responders, for example, of the 25.5% of students who agreed with the statement, "The teachers at school make me feel different."

Some Questions Raised by Biethnicity (Biculturation)

While most of the findings in this study give us reason to be optimistic about the experiences of Black children socialized within a predominantly White suburban community, several of our results raise questions about individuals who function biculturally, especially when they are part of a small minority within a dominant or mainstream culture.

As previously stated, the children in this study had positive attitudes toward Blacks. However, age correlated negatively with attitudes toward Blacks when racial attitudes were measured with the Stephan-Rosenfield scale. This indicates that, for this population, older children had slightly more negative attitudes toward Blacks than younger children. There was a moderate but significant *negative* relationship between attitudes toward school and attitudes toward Blacks, when attitudes toward Blacks were measured with the Banks subscale. (This finding may be an artifact of the Banks scale which included several questions related to attitudes toward Blacks in the school setting.) There was also a moderate but significant negative relationship between attitudes toward Blacks (Banks scale) and attitudes toward neighborhood. This indicates that the more the children liked their neighborhoods the more negatively they felt toward Blacks.

Stage 5 individuals have positive attitudes toward more than two ethnic groups and the skills and desire to function with them. Stage 6 individuals not only have positive attitudes toward a range of ethnic groups within the United States but also the kind of identity, attitudes, skills, and abilities needed to function successfully within cultures outside of the United States. The present study does not provide data which shed light on these two stages since it was a study of Black children and their attitudes toward only one other ethnic cultural group: Anglo and/or Mainstream Americans.

Summary

In this brief chapter, I have presented a stages of ethnicity typology and interpreted findings from a study of Black suburban youths within the context of the typology. The research findings suggest that few individuals who participated in the study can be characterized as Stage 1 (ethnic psychological captives) individuals since most of them had highly positive attitudes toward Blacks. Few may be described as Stage 2 individuals (ethnically encapsulated) since they had positive attitudes toward both Blacks and Whites and enjoyed social contacts with both Black and White peers.

The data suggest that most of the students in the suburban study can be characterized both as Stage 3 (Ethnically clarified) and Stage 4 (Bicultural) individuals. While these two stages are conceptually distinct, in reality individuals are likely to retain their Stage 3 (Ethnic clarification) characteristics as they function biculturally (Stage 4). Individuals are also likely to remain ethnically clarified (Stage 3), bicultural (Stage 4), and multiethnic (Stage 5) as they function at Stage 6 (globalism). The results further suggest that individuals who function at Stages 3 through 6 will usually retain the characteristics obtained in each of the earlier stages as they acquire the characteristics of the next higher stage. While this is true of Stages 3 through 6, as individuals move from Stages 1 and 2 to Stage 3, they are likely to retain few of the characteristics of the first two stages. This is because Stages 1 and 2 differ substantially from Stages 3 through 6.

Some of the intercorrelations of the variables in the study (such as the relationship between age and attitudes toward Blacks, attitudes toward Blacks and attitudes toward school, and attitudes toward Blacks and attitudes toward neighborhood) suggest that bicultural functioning may have complex effects on the attitudes of individuals toward their own racial group, especially if they are part of a small minority group in the bicultural environment. These intercorrelations indicate that bicultural functioning is a complex phenomenon that merits further study and analysis.

The predominantly White suburban communities in which the children in this study were being socialized have not prevented them from developing positive attitudes toward themselves, their communities, and their schools. These children were biracial in their attitudes—they had positive attitudes toward both Blacks and Whites—although they were slightly more positive toward Blacks (mean = 26.15) than toward Whites (mean = 22.20). The findings suggest that Black children socialized within predominantly White suburban communities are likely to become highly attitudinally assimilated into White society and that this kind of assimilation may have complex effects on their racial attitudes toward Blacks and their levels of ethnocentrism. As attitudinal assimilation increased, these children became increasingly more positive toward their schools and neighborhoods and more positive toward Whites, but less positive toward Blacks.

The findings of this study suggest, however, that attitudinal assimilation may have some desirable educational consequences: The children in this study who had highly positive attitudes toward Whites and toward their schools and neighborhoods were also more internal. Internality is positively related to academic achievement and to other success–related behavior. Internality was negatively related to positive attitudes towards Blacks and to ethnocentrism. This latter finding raises a question about whether Black children can remain ethnic in their racial attitudes and attain high levels of internality. This question warrants study within a wide range of populations in which Black youths are socialized. (A summary of studies of internality and Black youth can be found in Banks, Ward, McQuater, and DeBritto, in press).

Several findings in this study suggest that the experiences of Black females in predominantly White suburban communities may be slightly more difficult than those of Black males. Girls not only liked their neighborhoods less than boys did but had slightly more negative attitudes toward Blacks. This study also suggests that life in White suburbia may be a bit more difficult for children as they grow older. The older children (adolescents) in this study had significantly more negative attitudes toward their neighborhoods and toward Blacks. These two findings, which must be interpreted cautiously because of the limitations of this study, merit further study and investigation.

Many of the findings of this exploratory study are consistent with those of other researchers. However, the findings must be interpreted with caution because of the sample size (N=98), the nonrandom selection of the subjects, and because the study was conducted in only one geographic region. However, the design enabled us to study a population that is extremely difficult to identify and convince to participate in social research. While this study has limitations, it raises important questions about the relationship between race, social class, and sociocultural environment, and provides fruitful hypotheses that merit further study by researchers.

Notes

1. This chapter describes findings from a larger study of Black families in predominantly White suburbs. I wish to thank the Rockefeller Foundation for supporting the research study described in this chapter through its Research Fellowship Program, the families who participated, Cherry McGee Banks for help with the procedures, and Percy D. Peckham for help with the data analysis. Additional details of the methods, procedures, instruments, and findings of this study can be found in Banks (1982, 1984a, 1984b).

References

Banks, J. A. (1976). The Emerging stages of ethnicity: Implications for staff development. *Educational leadership, 34,* 190–193.

Banks, J. A. (1982). A study of Black suburban youths: Implications of the major findings for the stages of ethnicity typology. Paper presented at the Annual Meeting of the American Educational Research Association, New York, New York, March 19–23. ERIC Document Number: ED 226–095.

Banks, J. A. (1981). *Multiethnic education: Theory and practice.* Boston: Allyn and Bacon.

Banks, J. A. (1984a). Black youths in predominantly White suburbs: An exploratory study of their attitudes and self–concepts. *Journal of Negro Education, 53,* 3–17.

Banks, J. A. (1984b). An exploratory study of assimilation, pluralism, and marginality: Black families in predominantly White suburbs. Paper presented at the Annual Meeting of the American Educational Research Association, New Orleans, April 23–27. ERIC Document Number: ED 247–157.

Banks, W. C., Ward, W. E., McQuater, G. V., & DeBritto, A. M. (In press). Are Blacks external: On the status of locus of control in Black populations. In R. L. Jones (Ed.). *Black psychology* (Third Edition). Richmond, CA: Cobb & Henry.

Blumberg, L., & Lalli, M. (1966). Little ghettos: A study of Negroes in the suburbs. *Phylon, 27,* 117–131.

Brookover, W. B., Paterson, A. & Thomas, S. (1962). *Self–concept of ability and school achievement* (U.S.O.E. Cooperative Research Report, Project. No. 845). East Lansing: Michigan State University.

Carlson, E. (October 20, 1981). Blacks increasingly head to suburbs. *The Wall Street Journal*, Section 2, 25.
Clark, T. A. (1979). *Blacks in suburbs: A national perspective*. New Brunswick, NJ: Rutgers University Center for Urban Policy Research.
Cloud, O. M. (1980). Blacks moving to suburban apartments: Changes in formerly all–White areas aid school desegregation. Kentucky Commission on Human Rights, Staff Report 80-6. 32 pp.
Connolly, H. X. (1979). Black movement in the suburbs: Suburbs doubling their Black populations during the 1960's. *Urban Affairs Quarterly, 14*, 91–111.
Cross, W., Parham, T., & Helms, J. (In press). Nigrescence: A literature review. In R. L. Jones (Ed.). *Black psychology* (Third Edition). Richmond, CA: Cobb & Henry.
Downs, A. (1973). *Opening up the suburbs: An urban strategy for America*. New Haven, Yale University Press.
Farley, R. (1970). The changing distribution of Negroes within metropolitan areas: The emergence of Black suburbs. *American Journal of Sociology, 75*, 512–529.
Ford, M. (1979). The development of an instrument for assessing levels of ethnicity in public school teachers. Unpublished doctoral thesis, University of Houston, 1979.
Frey, W. H. (1978). Black movement to the suburbs: Potentials and prospects. In F. D. Bean & W. P. Frisbie (Eds.), *The demography of racial and ethnic groups*. New York, Academic Press, pp. 78–117.
Gordon, M. M. (1964). *Assimilation in American life: The role of race, religion, and national origins*. New York, Oxford University Press.
Jones, L. N. (1982). The Black churches in historical perspectives. *The crisis: A record of the darker races, 89*, 6–10.
Katzman, M. T. (1983). The flight of Blacks from central–city public schools. *Urban Education, 18*, 259–283.
Ladner, J. A. (Ed.), (1973). *The death of White sociology*. New York, Vintage.
Lake, R. W. (1981). *The new suburbanites: Race and housing in the suburbs*. New Brunswick, Center for Urban Policy Research, Rutgers University.
Marshall, H. H., & Stahura, J. M. (1979). Determinants of Black suburbanization: Regional and suburban size category patterns. The *The Sociological Quarterly, 20*: 237–253
Northwood, L. K. and Barth, E.A.T. (1965). *Urban desegregation: Negro pioneers and their White neighbors*. Seattle, University of Washington Press.
Nowicki, S., Jr., & Strickland, B. R. (1973). A locus of control scale for children. *Journal of Consulting and Clinical Psychology, 40*, 148–154.
Pettigrew, T. F. (1973). Attitudes on race and housing: A socio–psychological view. In H. Hawley & V. P. Rock, (Eds.), *Segregation in residential areas*. Washington, D.C., National Academy of Sciences, pp. 21–84.
Rabinovitz, F. F. (1975).*Minorities in suburbs: The Los Angeles experience*. Joint Center of Urban Studies of the Massachusetts Institute of Technology and Harvard University, Working paper No. 31.
Rose, H. M. (1976). *Black suburbanization: Access to improved quality of life or maintenance of the status quo?* Cambridge, Ballinger Publishing Co.
Randolph, H. (1970). The Black suburbanite and his schools. An interim report on a study of the impact of Black suburbanization on the school system. New York: Center for Urban Education, 93 pp.
Rosenberg, M. (1965). *Society and the adolescent self–image*. Princeton: Princeton University Press, 1965.

Stephan, W. G., & Rosenfield, D. (1979). Black self-rejection: Another look. *Journal of Educational Psychology, 71*, 708–816.

Taylor, J. (In press). Cultural conversion experiences: Implications for mental health research and treatment. In R. L. Jones (Editor). *Advances in Black psychology*. Richmond, CA: Cobb & Henry.

Williams, J. E. & Morland, K. (1976). *Race, color and the young child*. Chapel Hill: University of North Carolina Press.

Willie, C. V. (1974). The Black family and social class. *American Journal of Orthopsychiatry, 44*, 50–60.

Wilson, W. J. (1978). *The declining significance of race: Blacks and changing American institutions*. Chicago: University of Chicago Press.

Zschock, D. K. (1971). Black youth in suburbia. *Urban Affairs Quarterly, 7*, 61–74.

RURAL BLACK ADOLESCENTS: PSYCHOSOCIAL DEVELOPMENT IN A CHANGING ENVIRONMENT

Courtland C. Lee

Introduction

The challenges associated with Black adolescent development have been examined extensively in recent years. Social scientists have discussed the stresses confronting Black youth as they make the transition from childhood to adulthood, pointing to a serious stifling of academic, vocational and social development (Gordon, 1978; Staples, 1975). Such discussion has tended to focus primarily on the developmental challenges of Black adolescents living in urban settings, because of the mistaken notion that the Black population has become almost totally urban. Extensive analysis of developmental issues for Black youth in contemporary rural America has generally been lacking, despite the fact that census data indicate that approximately one-quarter of the Black population of the United States lives in rural areas (U.S. Bureau of the Census, 1983). As with life in an urban setting, Blacks in rural areas generally face significant social and economic challenges.

It is apparent that rural Blacks constitute a large group with social problems that in many ways are distinct from urban realities. These distinctions raise important questions concerning adolescent psychosocial development in rural Black America. Among these is the important question of how rural Black adolescents adapt to a challenging environment in their childhood-to-adulthood transition. Within this context, this chapter analyzes important aspects of the psychosocial development of Black adolescents in the contemporary rural environment. The basis for the discussion is the idea that human beings live in a reciprocal interaction with their environment. Rural Black youth change and are changed by environmental conditions in their psychosocial development. Such interactional processes between Black adolescents and the rural environment promote identity development. Psychosocial development for rural Black adolescents can be better understood by examining factors that impact upon the process by which young people develop a view of self in relation to the world.

Characteristics of Rural Black America

In order to understand aspects of rural Black adolescent psychosocial development, an overview of some important characteristics of rural Black America is necessary. This will help to delineate the social environment with which many rural Black youth must interact in developing an identity.

Before World War I, about three–fourths of all Blacks in the United States lived in rural areas, almost exclusively in the South (Havighurst & Neugarten, 1975). However, after the war, mechanization came to southern agriculture and traditional job opportunities for Black sharecroppers and farm laborers declined. As a result, thousands of Blacks were attracted to occupational and social opportunities in urban areas in the northern and western parts of the country. This migration basically transformed Blacks from a rural to an urban ethnic group. However, over 6 million Blacks, or 24% of the total Black population, currently reside in nonmetropolitan areas of the United States (U.S. Bureau of the Census, 1983). The majority of rural Blacks (at least 90%) live in the South, whereas their urban counterparts are more evenly distributed throughout all the regions of the United States.

Rural southern Blacks, not unlike those in urban centers throughout the country, continue to be burdened by socioeconomic disadvantage. This, in spite of the fact that rural America has recently undergone an important social, economic and cultural transformation. Within the last two decades more new industrial and technological jobs have been created in rural areas than in urban centers, which reverses the previous historical trend of concentrating industrial expansion in or near cities (Lonsdale & Seyler, 1977). This industrial growth has tended to bring greater opportunities to local rural communities whose previous economic life relied almost exclusively on agricultural production. As the economy has become more diversified, the labor market has expanded and has created more options for rural workers.

However, much of this rural economic growth has failed to directly benefit Black people and their contributions to southern rural development, in large measure, have been underutilized. Many rural Blacks lack the general education and requisite job skills necessary for employment in new industrial and technological fields (Godwin, 1977). Significantly, industrial growth has tended to avoid poor southern rural counties with high concentrations of underemployed Blacks. Some portion of this is, no doubt, due to discrimination, but more likely it is because the Black labor force is perceived as being less productive (Seyler, 1979; Walker, 1977). Even when new technological industries do locate in rural areas with large Black populations, the local residents are usually hired for low–paying unskilled or semi–skilled jobs, while better paying positions have gone to immigrants (Marshall, 1977; Till, 1974).

The failure to be fully included in the new rural socioeconomic growth, coupled with the age–old southern traditions of segregation, discrimination and social isolation have resulted in many Blacks residing in poor and predominantly Black southern rural counties. Many of these counties are identified as "persistently poor" by the federal government because of their chronically high levels of poverty (Davis, 1979; Deavers & Brown, 1979).

Chronic underinvestment in both human and community development therefore, has resulted in a plethora of social stresses for rural Blacks. These include such problems as poor housing, inadequate health services and educational underattainment. It is important to note that rural Blacks lag behind all other groups in educational characteristics such as school enrollment, enrollment in preprimary programs, high school graduation, college completion, adult education, and functional illiteracy (Fratoe, 1980).

It is within the context of these environmental characteristics that the contemporary Black adolescent in southern rural America must develop academic, career and personal–social skills. Given this description of a social environment characterized by poverty, inadequate services and limited job opportunities, how do Black adolescents come to terms with their surroundings and develop a sense of self?

Characteristics of Rural Black Youth

Erik Erikson in his landmark book, *Childhood and Society* (1950) constructed an eight-stage epigenetic model of human psychosocial development that encompasses the life–span. Each stage of life, according to Erikson, is strongly influenced by intrapsychic as well as environmental factors that impact upon the resolution of certain life–tasks. For Erikson, adolescence is the transitional stage between childhood and adulthood where internal psychodynamic and external environmental forces combine to help young people complete the task of developing identity, or knowledge of self, in relation to the world.

Erikson's notions are important to consider when examining the psychosocial development of rural Black adolescents. These young people in many cases are attempting to develop an identity within the context of extreme environmental stress, often related to economic and social pressure. A crucial key to understanding how rural Black adolescents develop an identity and learn to adapt lies in exploring the person–environment interaction between these young people and significant aspects of rural society.

A review of the literature on the person–environment interaction of rural Black adolescents reveals several studies of psychosocial development from different social eras that seem to fall within Erikson's theoretical framework. In 1941, Charles S. Johnson conducted a landmark study for the American Youth Commission of the American Council on Education (ACE), titled *Growing Up in the Black Belt: Negro Youth in the Rural South*. (For further discussion of this and other ACE studies, see chapter by Holliday in the present volume). Johnson investigated Black adolescent personality development in the rural South. Against the backdrop of segregation and economic hardship which characterized the time–period, Johnson examined the lifestyles, attitudes, values, and behaviors of Black youth in eight southern rural counties, in an attempt to develop indices of coping and adjustment. What emerges from Johnson's work is a psychosocial profile of rural Black adolescents of that time. Johnson was able to identify important variables in the person–environment transaction of Black youth which appeared to be related to their personality development.

Johnson's work was expanded upon, to some extent, by Robert Coles in *Children of Crisis: A Study of Courage and Fear* (1964). From the perspective of a child psychiatrist, Coles studied psychosocial issues of youth dealing with the stress of facing desegregation in the South. Through observation and participation in the lives of southern people, many of them Black teenagers from rural areas, he was able to bring into focus important aspects of their attitudes and behaviors as they learned to cope with, and adapt to, the profound social changes wrought by desegregation in the 1960's. As with the earlier work of Johnson, a rudimentary profile of rural Black adolescents emerges from Coles' observations. From this profile can be discerned important factors that appear to be associated with Black adolescent adaptation in a difficult time of change and conflict in the southern rural environment.

In a series of studies that continue the research efforts initiated by Johnson and Coles, this author has investigated the psychosocial development of Black adolescents in contemporary rural America. These investigations, conducted against the background of social and economic disadvantage for Black people amidst rapid rural industrial and technological expansion, have focused on factors related to academic, career and social development. A primary aim of this research has been to better understand the person–environment interaction process that facilitates the building of a knowledge of self among rural Black adolescents.

An important feature of this research has been to examine psychosocial variables that appear to successfully influence that interaction process. From a comprehensive study that investigated the existence of possible factors associated with educational and social development for Black youth in a poor, predominantly Black rural region in the Southeast, a profile of successful teenagers emerged (Lee, 1984a). This profile revealed the existence of intrapersonal and environmental variables that may indeed positively impact upon the person–environment interaction of Black adolescents and lead to academic and social competence. Further analysis suggested that a number of these variables had significant relationships with important aspects of their success, often despite socioeconomic hardship (Lee, 1984b).

Interestingly, the data from this research suggested concepts and notions that are, in large measure, consistent with the classic findings of Johnson and Coles. It might be conjectured that there may be a degree of consistency over time in many of the psychosocial variables contributing to adaptation styles associated with identity development among rural Black adolescents—this, in spite of major social, economic and cultural changes in the rural South within the last 50 years.

What, then, are these variables which appear to be important in facilitating identity development among rural Black adolescents? What factors appear to successfully influence the transaction between rural Black youth and their environment?

Both past and present research evidence would seem to suggest that answers to these questions lie in several major areas: Home and Family Life, School Experiences, Social Relationships, Activities, Aspirations, Attitudes and Values, and Self–Concept. Of particular interest is how family life, school experiences, social interactions and free–time activities impact upon the aspirations, values and self–concept of rural Black adolescents.

Home and Family Life

The family has been a traditional bastion of strength for Black people (Billingsley, 1968; Hill, 1971; Nobles, 1974). However, contemporary social forces have done much to undermine the integrity of Black family life. This has been especially evident in urban areas where Black families struggle to maintain a sense of cohesiveness against often overwhelming social and economic odds. Indeed, the environmental press on urban Black families has often blunted their effectiveness as a socializing institution for young people (Staples, 1978).

Although present–day rural Black families face systemic threats to their well–being, the traditional strengths that have been the hallmark of Black family life appear to prevail in their structure and functioning. A consistent theme throughout past and present research related to rural Black adolescent development is the importance of home and family life to identity formation. My speculation is that in the rural person–environment interaction process of Black youth, the family is the dominant socializing environment.

It might also be conjectured that because of the physical distance that often separates people in rural areas along with the limiting nature of rural poverty, young people are often forced to spend a great deal of time in a family setting. While this may be true to some extent, there also appears to be a quality to the time spent in the home with family members that, upon repeated scrutiny, reveals important and seemingly enduring socializing factors.

Explorations into the dynamics of the healthy adolescent personality, both past and present, suggest the existence of closely knit, multigenerational family structures among rural Blacks. Family members appear to share in most life–activities. Family structure is perhaps best seen in the high degree of parental control exerted over children. Parents can generally be described as strict in child–rearing practices, that include enforcing established family rules and household procedures.

An important part of the parenting process involves instilling a set of values in children. These values appear deeply rooted in the African, African–American and rural traditions of parents and include respect for other people (particularly elders) and honesty. Two other noteworthy values stressed are the importance of education and strong religious faith. Despite problems associated with rural Black educational attainment, parents strongly promote education as the vehicle for social and economic advancement. In addition, parents instill religious values by generally enforcing a policy of regular family church attendance.

Within the family structure, siblings and extended family members often play important roles in adolescent development. Given the generally isolated nature of rural family units, siblings become ready companions for recreational activities. This close sibling interaction serves to enhance a sense of family commitment among young people. Older siblings, for the most part, serve as important role models to adolescents, while young siblings provide teenagers with the opportunity to develop a sense of responsibility through the babysitting experience.

With respect to extended family members, it is not uncommon to find several generations of the same family living in geographical proximity to one another in rural districts and counties. Because of this, the influence of parents on adolescent development is greatly enhanced by that of grandparents, aunts and uncles. Grandparents appear to be especially important as extended family members. They often serve as surrogate parents, give strong educational encouragement and dispense sage advice concerning problems and challenges.

A pervasive theme in rural Black homes is that children, from an early age, have a major role to play in the continued functioning of family life. As such, young people are expected to assume a major share of family responsibilities. By adolescence, most young people have an extensive list of domestic chores for which they are responsible. Many of these continue to center around helping with agricultural activities (e.g., picking cotton or tobacco). It is highly unusual, therefore, to find a Black child in a rural area who has reached adolescence without a strong sense of responsibility to family.

Home and family life provide young people with a support–base and environment deeply rooted in the traditional strengths of Black families. Importantly, in rural areas these strengths seem to be perpetuated in spite of hardship or environmental changes. Identity development for rural Black youth seems, in part, to be a function of closely knit, multigenerational families exercising parental control. These families promote values and foster a sense of responsibility for self and others.

It is interesting to note that often when family situations in urban centers become chaotic, Black parents will send their children for a period of time to live with extended family members in the rural South. It is anticipated that in a southern rural family environment, young people will experience order, stability and a sense of tradition.

School Experiences

Contemporary education in rural America still suffers from the legacy of segregation. In those economically disadvantaged counties in the rural South where Black people comprise the majority of the population, there is generally a chronic underinvestment in educational development, leading to significant educational underattainment (Fratoe, 1980). These counties, unlike more prosperous ones, do not have the financial resources to provide comprehensive educational programs and services. There is evidence to suggest that differences in the level of financial support among school districts leads to differences in the level of student achievement. Rural school systems with large concentrations of low–achieving Black students, tend to get fewer educational resources than systems with higher–achieving (usually White) students (Levitan, 1975).

In another vein, the quality of education can be affected by the very nature of the rural environment. The seasonal nature of agricultural work often requires that young people miss significant amounts of time from school to assist with family farming. Additionally, long school bus rides in rural areas are often the norm for many students due to the vast distances that often separate home and school, coupled with the inaccessibility of many roads.

Despite indications of stifled educational progress, school remains an important institution of socialization for rural Black adolescents. Indeed the school, along with the church, occupies a level of dominance just below the home and family in its socializing influence. Because of isolation and limited outside activities in many rural areas, the school becomes a primary center of social activity outside of the home. Unlike their urban counterparts who have the varied enticements of the city streets to offer social diversions, rural youth gravitate to the local junior or senior high school for many activities.

Curricular and extracurricular activities, such as the 4–H Club, Future Farmers of America and Future Business Leaders of America, provide important forums for peer socialization. Significantly, in many rural areas, high school activities such as athletic events provide a major social diversion for the total community.

Serving as a miniature social system, and as a major social setting for community activities, the school helps rural Black youth to strengthen their identities and learn to function within their peer culture. Despite limited resources to fund schooling, the rural Black community stresses the value of education among its young people. Rather than a negative experience, school is a strong influence on adolescents' attitudes and social behavior.

Social Relationships

Social scientists have noted the importance of social relationships to adolescent development (Coleman, 1961; Eitzen, 1975; Friesen, 1967). It is the formation of social relationships outside of home and family that helps young people develop a sense of self in relation to the rest of the world. This is no different for contemporary rural Black youth. The isolation and family interconnections that often form cohesive Black communities in many rural areas make social relationships an integral part of the lives of young people. The building of social networks helps adolescents extend the rural kinship principle beyond the home to the total Black community.

Peer relationships are fostered through activities in the two most important social centers in rural communities, the school and the church. Often friendships become sibling-like relationships for young people. Besides a nice personality and the ability to relate, dependability and honesty seem to be major qualities desired in friends.

In addition to highly developed social networks among peers, young people often establish bonds with elders who are highly respected within the community. Many of these relationships are formed with individuals associated with the church, such as ministers or deacons. Others are developed with godparents and family friends. These significant other people offer encouragement and guidance, especially in the area of education. Such direction is an important supplement to that received in the home. In addition, these respected elders often model accepted community attitudes, behavior and values.

Activities

Activities that occupy the free-time of adolescents are an important aspect of their identity development. Such activities provide a forum for social participation, that is so important in developing a sense of self in relation to others. They also help in fostering an attitude of competence with respect to self in relation to abilities and interest.

The free-time activities of rural Black youth do not appear much different than those of young people in any contemporary environment. Free-time is generally occupied with activities such as watching television, participating in sports, babysitting, listening to music, and playing video games.

However, as indicated earlier, unlike adolescents in other environments, the relative dearth of social arenas in many rural areas often limits free-time activities to the home, the school and the other primary agent of rural socialization, the church. A significant portion of the lives of many Black teenagers in rural areas is spent in church–related activities. These generally include singing in choirs, ushering and participating in comprehensive church–sponsored youth groups. Importantly, these activities are not merely confined to Sunday worship services, but take place on a continuous basis through the week. It must be considered, as will be discussed later, that the pervasive influence of the church on many free-time activities has an affect on identity development. The attitudes and values of rural Black youth are often profoundly affected by extensive involvement in church–sponsored activities.

What emerges from this look at home and community life is an indication of important influences on identity development. Several aspects related to this development will now be considered in terms of how they are influenced by the interaction process that occurs between rural Black youth and their environment.

Aspirations

Until the 1960's, little research had been conducted on the future orientation of rural Black adolescents. However, since that time, social scientists have accumulated data on the aspirations of Black youth in rural areas (Cosby & Ohlendorf, 1973; Lee, 1984c; McNair & Brown, 1983). The evidence seems to suggest that within the context of rural Black educational underattainment and the socioeconomic mobility that goal attainment can potentially produce, the occupational goals that develop among contemporary Black youth in rural areas are relatively pragmatic in nature.

Research on educational goals (Hernandez & Picou, 1969; Lee, 1986; Thomas, 1970) suggests that significant numbers of rural Black adolescents plan to attend institutions that emphasize vocational or technical training upon completion of high school. In connection with this, evidence from career development studies suggest that many of these young people plan to enter skilled craft or technical occupations (Cosby, 1973; Lee, 1984c).

It is perhaps not surprising to find many of these young people aspiring to educational training that will lead to future employment in skilled craft occupations. In rural regions where the occupational traditions have centered around the skilled crafts often associated with agricultural work, such aspirations among young people appear logical. On the other hand, plans to prepare for and enter technical occupations are no doubt influenced by the widespread social and economic changes occurring in the rural South brought on by "high–tech" industrial growth. It is apparent that adolescents perceive future job opportunities in newly emerging rural technical enterprises and desire to prepare themselves accordingly.

Despite growing socioeconomic opportunity in many areas of the rural South, plans for future urban migration are still common among Black youth. Adolescents in those poor and predominantly Black rural communities, like thousands of their predecessors during this century, often concede the lack of opportunity for educational, economic or social advancement in local areas and aspire to greater gains in urban centers.

As mentioned previously, rural Black parents strongly promote the values of education among these children. Given the limits of their own educational background in many cases as well as their perceptions of new options for advancement, parental expectations are that young people will acquire the education that will prepare them for greater social and economic opportunity. Significantly, much of the recent research on Black youth in rural areas (Lee, 1984c; McNair & Brown, 1983) points to the influence of parents as perhaps the most significant variable to be considered in the adolescent goal–setting process.

Extant evidence suggests a degree of pragmatism in the aspirations of rural Black youth, fostered by strong parental influence. The educational and occupational goals frequently expressed by Black adolescents in recent rural studies, attest to the fact that they are cognizant of where future occupational opportunities will be found. They also understand the nature of educational attainment that will prepare them for such opportunity and its accompanying socioeconomic mobility.

Attitudes and Values

The attitudes and values of rural Black youth are learned in the socialization process and determined by socio–cultural factors indigenous to the rural Black home, church and community. The legacies of isolation and socioeconomic hardship among rural Black people have made the home, church and community relatively conservative institutions that perpetuate traditional attitudes and values. Even a casual comparison of attitudes and value systems between rural and urban areas would lead to the conclusion that rural Black youth are more conservative and traditional than their urban peers.

As has been noted, experiences with significant others in the home and community support the formation of traditional values such as honesty and respect for other people. The value of education is also widely promoted and generally accepted by young people as the major vehicle for Black socioecomic advancement.

Another set of traditional values that is promoted through home and community experiences is associated with the world of work. The value of hard work is important to Black adolescents in rural areas. Concomitantly, being well-paid for work and having a job from which one is unlikely to be fired are important values (Lee. 1984d). Given rural Black traditions, parents and significant other people in the community who are often in low skilled or semi-skilled occupations, impart the notion of hard work, a good salary and a steady job as being crucial to Black survival.

Traditional religious values provide a major focus to the lives of these young people. These values are fostered through regular family church attendance and having the church serve as a major center of adolescent social activity.

The influence of the Black church and its theology on Black culture and history is widely recognized (Cone, 1970; Frazier, 1964; Lincoln, 1974). Indeed, the Black church emerged as an institution from the southern rural traditions of Black people and in scores of communities throughout the region, was and continues to be, the center of religious as well as cultural and social life.

Within this context, religion and serving God are major priorities in young Black lives. It is not uncommon to find young people undergoing religious rebirths and having salvation experiences that provide important philosophical direction to their lives.

It is perhaps not surprising to find that for many rural Black adolescents, the Reverend Dr. Martin Luther King, Jr. is the most admired Black historical figure (Lee, 1984a). While not a product of a rural environment, Dr. King was a southern religious leader with traditional values who many young people perceive as using his deep religious faith to fight for Black dignity.

As might be expected, the development of traditional values fosters a degree of conservatism in attitudes associated with important social issues that confront adolescents. Despite the liberalizing forces of social change which have transformed youthful attitudes in recent decades, rural Black youth often express conservative views regarding activities such as teenage drinking and drug abuse. For many, such activities are seen as being counter to the dictates of family and church.

Attitudes regarding adolescent sexual activity, however, are often more moderate. While engaging in sexual activity is often disapproved of for self, there is a general tolerance of such activity among peers.

Self-Concept

The self-concept of Black youth has been the subject of much discussion and investigation (Ausubel & Ausubel, 1963; Clark & Clark, 1947; Rainwater, 1967). Prevalent in much of this work have been notions of low self-esteem, self-hatred and confused self-identity among Black adolescents and children (Clark & Clark, 1947; Coles, 1967). Unfortunately, the bulk of the work on Black self-concept has been comparative in nature, focusing on Black self-identity in relation to that of Whites. The conceptions and research on Black self-concept, therefore, have been controlled by forces outside the Black community. The consequence of this has been erroneous assumptions about Black self-identity emerging from a White frame of reference (Nobles, 1980).

Often neglected is the notion that within the Black community are factors that account for the development of a positive self-concept among young people (Barnes, 1980). This present examination of the rural Black community has revealed variables important to the development of a positive adolescent self-concept.

The positive nature of adolescent self-identity appears deeply rooted in the culture of rural Black communities. The continued isolated and segregated nature of many of these communities provides a social environment in which adolescents develop self-perceptions in relation to Black, as opposed to White, culture. It has been found that for many rural Black teenagers, interactions with Whites are limited. They spend significant amounts of time with family members, attend predominantly Black schools or socialize primarily with Black peers at integrated schools, and attend church and participate in activities primarily within the Black community. Consequently, they neither compare themselves with Whites nor do they harbor desires to be White. Conversely, they do not consciously acknowledge their Blackness, rather, it is merely a natural and unconsciously accepted part of their identity (Lee, 1984a).

Growing out of this natural acceptance of Blackness is an important view of self in relation to family and community. As was alluded to earlier, adolescent self-concept is tied to the kinship principle that is deeply rooted in rural Black families and communities. Black people in rural areas share a sense of collective unity for accomplishing life tasks and meeting life challenges. This kinship principle is embedded in the African heritage of Black people (Nobles, 1980). Self-concept formation is strongly influenced by this kinship notion. The self-concept of rural Black youth appears to develop around a traditional African philosophy of Self, "I am because we are; and because we are, therefore I am" (Mbiti, 1970). Adolescent self-perception, therefore, is an extended view of self-in-relation-to-others.

Summary and Conclusions

Summary

The available evidence suggests that Black adolescents in rural America constitute a group of young people whose psychosocial development is distinct from that of their urban counterparts. While they face many of the same social and economic challenges that confront urban youth, the nature of the rural Black environment serves to alter the impact of these stresses for rural adolescents.

The profile that emerges of the contemporary southern rural Black adolescent is one of an individual making the childhood-to-adulthood transition against the background of tradition and change. In exploring identity formation, key factors in youthful person–environment transactions appear to contribute to successful adaptation amidst the socioeconomic challenges that confront rural Black people.

The psychosocial development of rural Black adolescents appears to be strongly influenced by close and supportive family networks. In addition, well-developed community networks that include the church and the school contribute to this development. Socialization within these networks produces important personality characteristics that provide the basis for adolescent identity formation. Rural Black adolescents generally develop positive self-concepts linked to an extended view of self as a member of a collective family and community social system. They tend to possess traditional values associated with religious faith, the nature of work, and interpersonal relationships. Their views regarding adolescent social issues are often conservative in nature, reflecting the traditions of their family and community. Finally, they appear to set their future educational and occupational goals in a pragmatic manner.

Implications for Psychoeducational Intervention. The profile of the rural Black adolescent presented in the present chapter has clear implications for psychoeducational policy and programming implications. The factors that appear to contribute to identity formation provide rural educators and other professionals with a basis for psychoeducational intervention with Black youth. Having an understanding of important psychosocial factors, how can teachers, counselors, administrators, and other professionals address the educational and social challenges facing these young people? How can these professionals promote optimal academic, career and personal–social development among rural Black youth?

Answers to these questions lie in understanding the relationship between the rural Black adolescent and his or her community, and capitalizing on factors such as family influence, social relationships or attitudinal orientations, to achieve specific results in the realm of psychosocial development. Some examples may illustrate this, first, it may be incumbent upon professionals to incorporate the inherent strength and structure of the rural Black family into psychoeducational intervention. The ultimate goal of any family intervention strategy should be maximizing family influence on all aspects of adolescent development. This could be achieved by consulting with parents and other family members about enhancing attitudes and skills in the home that promote educational progress. With respect to occupational aspirations, consultation with rural Black families could result in strategies for improving their impact on adolescent career focus. Such strategies might include assisting parents in helping young people use occupational information or in facilitating adolescent aptitudes and interests consistent with emerging rural technological occupational opportunities.

Second, educational professionals should exploit the spirit of collective unity among rural Black people by promoting the notion of shared responsibility for adolescent development. It is important that instructional strategies promote cooperation as opposed to competition. Friends should be assisted in helping friends face academic or social challenges through tutorial or peer counseling efforts. In addition, volunteer efforts might be coordinated that involve community people in psychoeducational service delivery. Significant people such as ministers and other church leaders might be enlisted in establishing supplemental educational programs and activities in the church.

Third, the attitudes and values fostered in the rural Black home and community might provide the basis for the development of educational programs and the refinement of cognitive–behavioral strategies for proactive teaching in junior and senior high schools. Further, in the important area of school counseling, incorporating the traditional attitudinal orientation and values of Black youth into the helping process might stimulate the development of individual and group interventions for facilitating academic, career and personal skills.

Conclusions

Whatever the limitations of focus, or of the empirical findings examined within it, this chapter has attempted to advance a general understanding of the psychosocial development of rural Black adolescents. It has built upon research efforts on the personality development of rural Black youth conducted over the last several decades, culminating in a contemporary psychosocial profile. Rural Black youth are making an important life transition against the background of change in a traditional environment. It is incumbent upon psychoeducational policymakers and program developers to understand the rural environment and its impact on the identity development of Black youth. Such understanding can provide the impetus for meeting the challenges of improving the quality of life for rural Black adolescents.

References

Ausubel, D., & Ausubel, P. (1963). Ego development among segregated Negro children. In A. H. Passon (Ed.), *Education in depressed areas*. New York: Bureau of Publications, Teachers College, Columbia University.

Barnes, E. J. (1980). The Black community as the source of positive self–concept for Black children: A theoretical perspective. In R. L. Jones (Ed.), *Black psychology* (2nd edition). New York: Harper & Row.

Billingsley, A. (1968). *Black families in White America*. Englewood Cliffs, NJ: Prentice–Hall.

Clark, K. B., & Clark, M. (1947). Racial identification and preferences in Negro children. In T. M. Newcomb & E. L. Hartley (Eds.), *Readings in social psychology*. New York: Holt, Rinehart & Winston.

Coleman, J. S. (1961). *The adolescent society*. NY: Free Press.

Coles, R (1960). *Children of crisis: A study of courage and fear*. Boston: Little, Brown & Co.

Coles, R. (1967). It's the same but it's different. In T. Parsons & K. B. Clark (Eds.), *The Negro American*. Boston: Beacon Press.

Cone, J. H. (1970). *A Black theology of religion*, Philadelphia, PA: J. B. Lippincott Co.

Cosby, A. G., & Ohlendorf, G. (1973). Educational and Occupational status projections: Stability and reciprocal linkages. Paper presented at the annual meeting of the Rural Sociological Society, University of Maryland, College Park.

Davis, T. F. (1979). *Persistent low–income counties in nonmetro America*. U.S. Dept. of Agriculture: Economics, Statistics, and Cooperatives Service, RDRR–21.

Deavers, K. L., & Brown, D. L. (1979). Social and economic trends in rural America. White House Rural Development Background Paper.

Eitzen, D. S. (1975). Athletics in the status system of male adolescents: A replication of Coleman's "The Adolescent Society." *Adolescence, 10*, 267–276.

Erikson, E. (1950). *Childhood and society*. New York: W. W. Norton & Co., Inc.

Frazier, E. F. (1963). *The Negro church in America*. Liverpool: The University of Liverpool.

Fratoe, F. A. (1980). *The education of nonmetro Blacks*. Economics, Statistics, and Cooperatives Service, U.S. Dept. of Agriculture, RDRR–21.

Friesen, D. (1967). Academic–athletic–popularity syndrome in the Canadian high school society. *Adolescence, 3*, 39–52.

Godwin, L. (1977). *Rural jobs from public works: A rural employment outreach experimental and demonstration project, Phase I*. National Rural Center.

Gordon, T. A. (1978). The Black adolescent. In L. E. Gary (Ed.), *Mental health: A challenge to the Black community*. Philadelphia, PA: Dorrance & Co.

Havighurst, R. J., & Neugarten, B. L. (1975). *Society and education*. New Jersey: Allyn & Bacon, Inc.

Hernandez, P. F., & Picou, J. S. (1969). *Rural youth plan ahead: A study of the occupational, educational, residential and marital expectations of rural youth in Louisiana*. Louisiana State University, Agricultural Experiment Station, Bulletin No. 640.
Hill, R. (1971). *The strengths of Black families*. New York: Emerson Hall.
Johnson, C. S. (1941). *Growing up in the Black belt: Negro youth in the rural south*. Washington, D.C.: American Council on Education.
Lee, C. C. (1984). Successful rural Black adolescents: A psychosocial profile. *Adolescence, 20,* 129–142. (a)
Lee, C. C. (1984). An investigation of the psychosocial variables related to academic success for rural Black adolescents. *Journal of Negro education, 53,* 424–434. (b)
Lee, C. C. (1984). An investigation of the psychosocial variables in the occupational aspirations and expectations of rural Black and White adolescents: Implications for vocational education. *Journal of Research and Development in Education, 17,* 28–34. (c)
Lee, C. C. (1984). Work values of rural Black, White, and Native American adolescents: Implications for contemporary rural school counselors. *Counseling and Values, 28,* 63–71. (d)
Lee, C. C. (1986). A study of the psychosocial factors in the educational goals of rural and urban Black adolescents. Unpublished manuscript.
Levitan, S. A. (1975). *Still a dream: The changing status of Blacks since 1960.* Cambridge, MA: Harvard University Press.
Lincoln, C. E. (1974). *The Black church since Frazier.* NY: Schocken Books.
Lonsdale, R., & Seyler, H. L. (Eds.) (1979). *Nonmetropolitan industrialization.* New York: U. H. Winston & Sons.
McNair, D., & Brown, D. (1983). Predicting the occupational aspirations, occupational expectations and career maturity of Black and White male and female tenth graders. *Vocational Guidance Quarterly, 32,* 29–36.
Marshall, R. (Ed.) (1977). *Human resource dimensions of rural development.* University of Texas: Center for the Study of Human Resources.
Mbiti, J. S. (1970). *African religions and philosophies.* Garden City, NY: Anchor Books, Doubleday.
Nobles, W. (1974). African root and American fruit: The Black family. *Journal of Social and Behavioral Sciences, 20,* 66–77.
Nobles, W. W. (1980). Extended self: Rethinking the so-called Negro self-concept. In R. L. Jones (Ed.), *Black psychology* (2nd edition). New York: Harper & Row.
Nobles, W. W. (1980). African philosophy: Foundations for Black psychology. In R. L. Jones (Ed.), *Black psychology* (2nd edition). New York: Harper & Row.
Rainwater, L. (1967). Crucible of identity: The Negro lower-class family. In T. Parsons and K. B. Clark (Eds.), *The Negro American.* Boston: Beacon Press.
Seyler, H. L. (1979). Contemporary research emphasis in the United States, in *Nonmetropolitan industrial growth and community change.* Boston: Lexington Books.
Staples, R. (1975). To be young, Black, and oppressed. *Black Scholar, 7,* 2–9.
Staples, R. (1978). Black family life and development. In L. E. Gary (Ed.), *Mental health: A challenge to the Black community.* Philadelphia, PA: Dorrance & Co.
Thomas, K. A. (1970). *Educational orientations of southern rural youth: An analysis of socioeconomic status and racial differences.* Unpublished Master's Thesis, University of Kentucky.

Till, T. (1974). Industrialization and poverty in southern nonmetro labor markets. *Growth and Change, 5,* 18–24.

U.S. Bureau of the Census (1983). Current Population Reports. Series P–23, No. 130, *Population Profile of the United States: 1982.*

Walker, J. L. (1977). *Economic development and Black employment in the nonmetropolitan south.* University of Texas: Center for the Study of Human Resources.

Part III
Physical and Mental Health

HEALTH CARE ISSUES OF BLACK ADOLESCENTS

Barbara Staggers

What I planned to do with the rest of my life?
Not–a–thing. Ha, Ha, Ha

What I planned to do with the rest of my life? Finish what I already started.
Rappin!

Life at my age is hard as hell. I never know what's next, until it's revealed.

I always have to ask why I got it so hard living my life behind my guard.

See I'm dammed if I do and dammed if I don't and notice'n people livin their life as a joke.

Playing with dope each and every day and if they end up dead its just that way,

Because you're on your own, and own is alone, and life gets harder as I grow.

—5/16/88 C.G., age 16

Sometimes I have to laugh when I'm told to go to the doctor to get a check–up. Who cares about my health? I just feel like I want to explode. Explode into a million little pieces that can be rearranged and changed so that I can deal with life... I deserve to be happy. I deserve to learn how to live a happy, healthy life. I deserve to have a chance to really find out how happy and healthy I can be... I'm supposed to be in the prime of my life. But who looks out for me? Who cares about me, my life, my health? I see so much sickness, so much death. I just want to explode.
—The voice of a Black male youth, age 15.

For Black adolescents, the process of living a healthy and productive life is in jeopardy. Jewelle Taylor Gibbs terms the Black adolescent "an endangered species" (see Chapter 1, this volume). If Black adolescents are endangered, the community is at risk as well, for the Black population of America is a youthful one; fifty percent of Blacks in America are less than 24 years old. In 1980, 10.5 million Black youths were younger than 19 and three million Black youths were in the 15–19 age range. The provision of adequate health care for Black youths is critical to their development as healthy and happy human beings. Yet, within the framework of contemporary American society, the Black adolescent population has critical

Physical and Mental Health

Table 1
Major Areas of Mortality and Morbidity for Black Adolescents

Mortality

1. Homicide

2. Accidents

3. Suicide

Morbidity

1. Substance Abuse

2. Sexual Behavior and Contraception

3. Pregnancy and Abortion

4. Academic Performance

5. Depression and Stress

6. General health care issues
    dental care
    nutrition related disorders
    hypertension
    inherited diseases

---

health care needs that are inadequately addressed (Gibbs, 1984; National Data Book and Guide to Sources, 1983).

This chapter will address the major areas of morbidity (relative incidence of disease) and mortality (death rate) for the Black adolescent population. (See Table 1) It will also describe and critically evaluate current theories of adolescence as they pertain to medical intervention for Black adolescents.

The provision of adequate health care to the adolescent population in the 1980's is no easy task. Seventy percent of deaths in the adolescent age group can be attributed to accidents, homicides, and suicides. For Black adolescents, violence seems to have become a central thread woven into the fabric of their lives. The impact of violence cannot be ignored.

Case 1

My friend was stabbed to death last week trying to break up a fight. He didn't know either guy... They just killed him.

This morning another of my buddies shot himself in the head. He was playing Russian roulette. Why would he do that?... I keep wondering, am I next? —I.C., age 17

Homicide, accidents, and suicide (in that order) are the leading causes of death for Black adolescents. These major areas of mortality are intricately connected to violence perpetrated by others or self that end in a termination of life (National Data Book and Guide to Sources, 1983; Morbidity and Mortality Weekly Report, 1985a; Morbidity and Mortality Weekly Report, 1985b). All three of these areas are associated with unique circumstances and thus each will be examined independently and in more detail below.

Homicide is the leading cause of death among Black adolescents both male and female. However, the greatest toll is found in the loss of lives in Black males age 15–24 years. Within this age range the homicide rate is 6–10 times that of White males. In 1980 alone 2,000 10–19 year old Black males were murdered (U.S. Department of Justice, 1981; Jones, 1986). These homicide rates were highest in large urban areas where housing was inadequate, unemployment rates high, and the majority of the population lived on limited economic resources (Morbidity and Mortality Weekly Report, 1985a). In addition, most Black adolescent homicides were committed by an acquaintance (non–family member) of the victim, and a large percentage of those homicides were drug–related (Morbidity and Mortality Weekly Report, 1985a; U.S. Department of Justice, 1981; Tardiff, Gross, & Messner, 1986; Randolph, & Rivers, 1985).

While violence perpetrated by others is the leading cause of death among Black adolescents, suicide is the third leading cause of death for Black male adolescents and the sixth leading cause of death for Black female adolescents (National Data Book and Guide to Sources, 1983; U.S. Government Printing Office, 1975; Morbidity and Mortality Weekly Report, 1985b). The 15–20 year old Black male adolescent seems to be at highest risk. At one time, the suicide rate for this age group was higher than for any other age population group (Vital Statistics of the United States, 1970–1975). The suicides appear to be associated with increased stress, decreased job availability, decreased accessibility to educational opportunities, and the stress of peer competition. There also are increased feelings of vulnerability, frustration, hopelessness and anger, all of which can lead to suicide or other acting–out behaviors (Holinger, & Offer, 1982; Seiden, 1970; Staples, 1982).

Although accidents are considered the second leading cause of death, the statistics may underrepresent the true data because most deaths by accidents are associated with automobiles. Thus, the data may

Physical and Mental Health

be biased because private automobiles are often less accessible to Black adolescents than to White adolescents (Randolph, & Rivers, 1985). In all these major areas of mortality (homicide, suicide, accidents) the loss of potential years of life and loss of sheer numbers of lives of Black youth demonstrate the impact of violence on health and health care. If there is no life, there can be no hope, no change, no chance to grow and build. Health within the Black adolescent community is nonexistent if their lives are in grave jeopardy. The health care system must learn to address and meet this overwhelming loss of a most valuable resource—the lives of Black youth.

Like the major causes of mortality in the Black adolescent population, the major areas of morbidity are a reflection of the high risk lifestyle of many Black youths. These lifestyle related health care problems include substance abuse, sexuality related health issues (sexual behavior and contraception, pregnancy and abortion, sexually transmitted diseases), academic problems, and mental health disorders (stress, depression, and psychosomatic illness).

Case 2

> *I tried cocaine. Everyone else was using it... I needed a lift... Sometimes I think I want to get off. I know I can. I just have to make up my mind to stop. Its not really a problem...* —R. H., age 16

Drug abuse has been termed the self–inflicted use of excessive alcohol, marijuana, cigarettes, angel dust, and narcotic use (Johnson, 1985). Over the past twenty years, in comparison with their White counterparts, Black adolescents have increased in their rate of drug use in every category except inhalants and hallucinogens. This includes increases in the use of marijuana, heroin, cocaine, alcohol, and amphetamines (Gibbs, 1984; Staples, 1982; National Institute of Drug Abuse, 1980; Johnson, 1985; Drug Abuse Deaths in Nine Cities, 1980).

The impact of increased drug usage is reflected in statistics that indicate an increase in deaths due to narcotic use in large urban areas for Black youths aged 15–24 (Staples, 1982; National Institute of Drug Abuse, 1980b), the high percentage of Black adolescents in drug detoxification and rehabilitation programs (Gibbs, 1984; U.S. Department of Health and Human Services, 1981), increased adolescent addiction to drugs (Staples, 1982; National Institute of Drug Abuse, 1979; National Institute of Drug Abuse, 1980b; U.S. Department of Health and Human Services, 1981), and changes in health reflected in increased problems associated with drug use (such as diseases of the kidney, lungs and heart, nerve and brain damage that can lead to personality changes, poor school performance, and antisocial behavior) (Brunswick, & Nessin, 1986; Caton, & Kandel,

Health Care Issues of Black Adolescents

1978; Thornton, James, & Doerner, 1982). Drug abuse (and the lifestyle associated with it) are a major health risk for Black adolescents. Therefore drug abuse in the Black community is a two pronged problem. There is a medical aspect which includes the direct affects of the drug and there is the aspect of rampant terrorism in the associated drug trafficking. (This terrorism and violence is much more prevalent in the Black community).

Some examples of the impact of increased drug usage and its associated lifestyle can be seen in the following examples.

> **Example #1.** In an urban area during the space of one month in three community high schools there were three murders on school campuses during school hours. All were drug related. Students were pouring into the adolescent health clinics out of fear for their lives, emotional stress and need for psychosocial support. The school district's response was to increase security by adding armed guards in hallways, frisking students, and searching lockers. One student commented, "going into school now is like going into a maximum security prison".

> **Example #2.** A 16 year old male presents himself to the hospital emergency room with a gunshot wound in his thigh. The wound is 2–3 days old. Upon initial questioning the youth states he shot himself accidentally. Later it is found he was involved in a drug related shootout where three of his closest friends were killed and a neighborhood terrorized. He reports at the time he was shot and shooting at others, he doesn't remember much because he was so high.

These are examples of the direct impact the adolescent drug abusers' violence has upon other adolescents and members of the Black community.

In the area of sexuality–related health care (which includes sexual behavior and contraception, pregnancy and abortion, and sexually transmitted diseases) the Black adolescent is also at risk.

Case 3

> I started my period at 9. Started having sex when I was 11 or 12. I'm 14 now...
>
> No, I don't use any birth control. I've only been pregnant once. That happened when I was 12. I lost the baby. I haven't used anything since then and I haven't gotten pregnant. So why bother to use anything...
>
> Sure I had one of those infections. But I'm cured now. I don't see that guy anymore...

Sexual Behavior and Contraception

Black females tend to have an earlier menarche than their White female counterparts, thus demonstrating an earlier physiological developmental timetable. Black males, on the other hand, have a similar physiological developmental timetable compared to their White male counterparts (William, 1975; Harlan, Grillo, Cornone–Huntley, & Leaverton, 1979; Westney, Jenkins, Butts, & Williams, 1984). Recent data suggest that Black adolescents are more likely to initiate sexual intercourse at an earlier age (the average age of first intercourse for Black adolescents is 15.5, for White adolescents, the age is 16.4) than their White counterparts. Why Black adolescents tend to initiate sexual intercourse at an earlier age is unclear, but the explanations are believed to be multifactorial. Intercourse appears to be important as a symbol of peer acceptance, partner commitment, or evidence of maturation of males and females into adulthood (Smith & Udry, 1985; Staples, 1972; Rainwater, 1970; Furstenbery, 1976). Some scholars believe the primary motivation for this sexual activity comes from a psychosocial need for acceptance love, autonomy, and the need for experimentation (O'Reilly, & Aral, 1985; Gabriel, & Mefinarney, 1983). Other scholars postulate Black adolescents engage in less precoital activity (i.e., necking only prior to the initiation of sexual intercourse) and follow a less sequential graduation of sexual behaviors prior to the initiation of intercourse (i.e., they do not move from necking to petting to heavy petting clothed, then petting unclothed, then sexual intercourse) (Smith & Udry, 1985).

Whatever the reason, Black adolescents, like other adolescents, appear to be at risk for complications associated with sexual behavior (i.e. intercourse) including increased pregnancy rates and increased rates of sexually transmitted diseases resulting from decreased contraceptive usage. The reasons for this decreased contraceptive use are unclear. One survey estimated that approximately 28% of Black females and 18% of Black males used contraception at first intercourse (Hogan, Astone, & Kitagawa, 1985).

Socioenvironmental factors influencing contraception use are varied but most appear to affect contraception use only at first intercourse and not subsequent initiation of more effective contraception practice (Zelnik, & Kantner, 1980; Hogan, Astore, & Kitagawa, 1985). Therefore, as the Black adolescent becomes more sexually experienced, there is increased contraception use (Zelnik, & Kantner, 1980; Hogan, Astore, & Kitagawa, 1985). Yet in 1980, Zelnik and Kantner reported only 31% of 15–19 year old Black adolescents reported always using contraceptives, and 40% stated that they never used contraception.

Major problems of Black adolescents who use contraceptives include:

1. Decreased effectiveness of method used (i.e., condom only or

withdrawal, reliance on nonmedical methods) (Zelnik, & Kantner, 1980; Clark, Zabin, & Hardy, 1984; Zelnik, Kim, & Kantner, 1979).
2. Possible misconceptions surrounding the availability of contraception (e.g., in one study, more than 50% of Black males thought they had to have parental consent to get a nonprescription contraceptive at a drug store, 40% thought they needed parental permission to attend a Family Planning Clinic (Clark, Zabin, & Hardy, 1984).
3. Misinformation and distortion of information surrounding sexuality (information coming from peers and mass media rather than parents) (Morbidity and Mortality Weekly Report, 1985a). (This is very similar to problems found with White adolescent contraceptive practices).
4. Conflicting beliefs surrounding teenage parenting and parenthood (e.g., best age to have a child is younger than the best age to get married; feeling of little risk attached to teen pregnancy; not being encouraged to get pregnant but seeing parenting as an important viable adult role.) (Gibbs, 1984; Zelnik, & Kantner, 1980; Clark, Zabin, & Hardy, 1984; Furstenberg, Lincoln, & Menken, 1981; Thompson, 1980).

Thus, the initiation of early sexual activity combined with less effective contraceptive use and conflicting attitudes about the possibility of pregnancy set the stage for increased Black adolescent teenage pregnancy.

Pregnancy and Abortion

Current statistics on Black adolescent pregnancy reveal the following:

1. Like most adolescents, Black adolescents tend not to use contraception until after the initiation of sexual intercourse. Half of all pregnancies occur within six months after initiation of intercourse and one fifth within one month after initiation of intercourse (Zelnik, & Shah, 1985).
2. Eighty–three percent of babies born to Black adolescents are born out of wedlock compared to 33% to White adolescents' babies (Gibbs, 1984; U.S. Bureau of the Census, 1983).
3. During 1981, the age specific fertility rate of Black adolescents age 10–14 years was 8.2 times greater than that of Whites (Morbidity and Mortality Weekly Report, 1985d; National Center for Health Statistics, 1981).
4. Black and non–White females accounted for approximately 50% of the abortions given to females under the age of 15 (Center for Disease Control, 1983).

Physical and Mental Health

Reasons for the high number of Black adolescent pregnancies (demonstrated in the high fertility rates, etc.,) is unclear. The pregnancies appear to be related to a variety of socioenvironmental factors, including perception of pregnancy as an acceptable life choice (Furstenberg, Lincoln, & Menken, 1981; Thompson, 1980; Ladner, 1971; Stuck, 1974), decreased communication at home on sexuality related topics (Freeman, Rickels, Huggins, & Garcia, 1984; Zelnik, & Kim, 1982), limited education, information, and awareness surrounding the effects of pregnancy (Hogan, Astore, & Kitagawa, 1985; Furstenberg, Lincoln, & Menken, 1981; Chilman, 1983; Family Impact Seminar, 1979; Zelnik, & Kim 1982), patterns of inconsistent contraception practices (Zelnik, & Kantner, 1980; Zelnik, Kantner, & Ford, 1981), and personal motivation for the Black adolescent (e.g. establishment of autonomy, identification, maturation, peer acceptance) (Thompson, 1980; Ladner, 1971; Stuck, 1974).

Increased pregnancy rates are but one possible outcome of irregular contraceptive usage. Black adolescents are also at risk for exposure to sexually transmitted diseases (Zelnik, & Kantern, 1980; O'Reilly, & Aral, 1985). The medical risk of sexually transmitted diseases is an important one for Black adolescents because one complication of these diseases is infection of the female reproductive system (Pelvic inflammatory disease), which can leave a female infertile or sterile and also increase risk of tubal pregnancies and abcesses. For Black and non–White adolescents in 1975–81, the hospitalization rate for pelvic inflammatory disease was 2.3 times the rate for White adolescents (Washington, Sweet, & Shafer, 1985). Although multifaceted and complicated, the impact of sexuality–related problems on the overall health care of Black adolescents cannot be ignored especially in the light of the recent AIDS (Acquired Immunodeficiencey Syndrome) epidemic. Since AIDS is a fatal disease without any known cure, this elevates the consequences of sexually transmitted diseases to an unparalleled level. Black adolescents like all adolescents in America are experiencing the consequences of initiation of sexual activity during their formative developmental years.

No discussion of health care is complete without a discussion of mental health issues that are closely intertwined with general health care concerns. For Black adolescents critical areas that are closely related and impact upon health status include – academic performance, depression, and stress.

Case 4

I don't go to school any more. I used to get straight A's. My friends called me a nerd and I din't fit in. So, I purposefully cut class. Of course that's caused problems at home. But I'm not here to talk about school. I want you to do

something about these stomachaches I have. They started in September.
Female youth, age 14

Academic Performance, Depression and Stress

For Black adolescents, school problems (poor school performance, poor grades, attitudinal problems, etc.,) are high life stressors which can manifest themselves in medical complaints such as headaches, stomachaches, and chest pain (Greene, Walker, Hickson, & Thompson, 1985). Greene et al., also report that negative life events are stressors that can cause recurrent nonorganically based (psychosomatic pain). Thus complaints of headaches, stomachaches or chest pains can be seen as a result of school changes, poor grades, bad report cards and a variety of other school problems. These school stresses can incorporate a variety of problems including functional illiteracy, learning disabilities, socialization patterns and negative or difficult school encounters secondary to biases that exist within the current socioeconomic and political systems of the United States.

> An 18 year old Black male came to the clinic with a chief complaint of headaches. Upon close questioning the physician learned the boy's headaches began two months ago. He denies any stresses or changes in his life. A complete physical exam yielded entirely normal results. Reopening the possibility of stress–related headaches, the youth reported that he had three close friends who had been murdered within the past two months. The most recent to die had been a childhood friend killed at school one week previously. The youth was to have gone to school with his friend the morning of his death as part of a usual routine but had been delayed. He then admits that he had been threatened by a gang and had cut school the past week. Yet he still does not feel he has any stress and reports all of this with a flat, unemotional affect.

Besides being linked to school problems, additional stresses in the life of Black adolescents can include encounter with socioeconomic stressors like decreased income, racism, unemployment and decreased job opportunity, home and family stress, and the need to establish a positive self–image and personal identity in an environment that perceives them negatively (i.e., sees being Black as being disadvantaged, culturally deprived, and undesirable) (Comer, 1985; Carter, 1972; Spurlock, & Lawrence, 1979). Just as with school problems, socioeconomic stressors can cause psychosomatic illness and depression.

> A young Black female previously a straight A student, comes to the clinic with a complaint of chest pain, abdominal pain, and backaches. She has an entirely normal physical exam. With additional question-

ing she reports she is enrolled in an exclusive private all girl's school with only two other Black students. Over the past 6 months the teachers have been confusing the students, calling them by each other's names, and mistaking their tests. She states she is not motivated to do any work in school, because she is angry about being called someone else's name and about being confused with someone she does not resemble in appearance, speech, or dress. She also had trouble understanding why the same teacher never confuses the 400 non–Black students.

Depression among Black adolescents can contribute to increasing suicide rates, poor school performance or change in school performance, and increased risk taking and acting out behavior including increased violence (homicide, delinquency), drug usage, and sexual acting out such as pregnancy (Gibbs, 1985; Schouenbach, Kaplan, Wagner, Grimson, & Miller, 1983).

Schouenbach, et al., (1983) estimate that 41–85% of Black adolescent males and 34–76% of Black adolescent females suffer from depression, with Black males at higher risk and less able to report their depression. Depression in Black adolescents appears to be linked to a constellation of psychoemotional–environmental factors, including 1) problems with the development of a sense of identity and feelings of personal inefficacy within an often insidiously oppressive social system, 2) adaptability and an inability to cope with environmental stressors, and 3) a lack of and/or breakdown of traditional psychoemotional support in the family, school, and community (Gibbs, 1985; Schouenbach, Kaplan, Wagner, Grimson, & Miller, 1983; Earls, 1984; Beardski, 1984). (For additional information, please refer to the Myers chapter, this volume.)

In the area of general health care, Black adolescents are at risk for increased dental disease, nutrition–related disorders, hypertension, and inherited diseases. There is increased prevalence of dental disease, e.g., caries (cavities), gingivitis, etc. (William, 1975; Cipes, Kejaks, Lund, & Otradovic, 1983; Fieldking, & Nelson, 1973). These problems may be related either to decreased dental accessibility or ignorance of proper dental hygiene. Like other disorders, the problem may also stem from nutrition–related diseases, such as iron deficiency anemia, that are most prevalent in the Black adolescent (Fitzpatrick, Chacko, & Heald, 1984; Garn, Smith, & Clark, 1975; Heald, 1975; Pearson, McLean, & Brigetz, 1971; Yip, Schwartz, & Deinard, 1984), obesity (Johnson, & Mack, 1978; Stunkard, et al., 1972) and, recently, the adolescent eating disorders of anorexia and bulimia.

Nutrition and obesity combine with a variety of genetic and environmental factors, e.g., increased stress, to place Black adolescents at risk for hypertension or high blood pressure. Both Black adolescent males and females are at greater risk to develop hypertension (primary diastolic hypertension) than their white counterparts (Hediger, Schell, Katz,

Gruskin, & Eveleth, 1984). Approximately 25% of Black adolescents at age 17 have hypertension (William, 1975; Webb, 1984). The Black male is at greatest risk.

Hypertension, which may have a hereditary component, can cause major health problems. Sickle cell disease and Glucose–6–phosphate–dehydrogenase deficiency (G–6PD) are also inherited (William, 1975; Fieldling, & Nelson, 1973). The latter two, manifested in early childhood, affect the blood. A Black youth who reaches adolescence with sickle cell disease is at risk for a variety of medical and psychosocial complications, including:
1. Need for chronic pain management
2. Development of possible drug dependency
3. Loss of spleen, requiring continuous antibiotic medication
4. Numerous bone, lung, or brain infarcts (damage)
5. Congestive heart failure
6. Repeated hospitalization
7. Delay in physical maturation
8. Loss of school time
9. Lack of peer socialization
10. Problems with issues surrounding independence, dependence, and autonomy, and shortened life expectancy (William, 1975; Vichinsky, & Lubin, 1980; Fieldling, & Nelson, 1973).

Less critical health care issues can arise with G6PD if Black adolescents avoid exposure or ingestion of certain damaging drugs, chemicals, and food (William, R., 1975).

Problems of Current Adolescent Medical and Psychosocial Theory

Adolescence is the period when rapid physical, psychosocial and emotional changes occur. The physical changes include rapid growth, development of secondary sex characteristics, and the emerging capacity for reproduction. The major psychosocial changes involve the transition from childhood to adulthood and include heightened sexual impulses, establishment of a stable identity, emancipation or establishment of independence from the family, acceptance of sexuality and adjustment to an adult sexual role, and determination of a role in society through choosing a career or vocation (Johnson, 1985; William, 1975; Irwin, 1982).

Current adolescent medical theory postulates three stages of psychosocial development (see Table 2), and five stages of physiological development (Table 3) (Irwin, 1982; Tanner, 1962). These stages constitute guidelines by which the health care provider can determine the developmental

Physical and Mental Health

level of the adolescent. For Black adolescents, this developmental framework is fraught with inadequacies and cultural biases.

Table 2
Psychosocial Development of Adolescents

Early Adolescence (Age: Females, 11–13 Years; Males, 12–14 Years)

Characteristics	Impact
Begins to leave family and concentrate on relationships with peers	Begins to encourage adolescent to come alone for visit
With the onset of puberty, becomes concerned with developing body	Adolescent has major questions throughout physical examination, "Am I normal?"
Compares own normality with peers of same sex	Continually concerned about the developmental stages of sexual characteristics
Exploration of new found ability to abstract with onset of formal operations	As described by Piaget, the adolescent can think abstractly and begins to consider the full range of possibilities for his/her life

Middle Adolescence (Age: Females, 13–16 Years; Males, 14–17 Years)

Characteristics	Impact
Has major conflicts over independence	Anything to foster independence; the physician should encourage this process
Explores ability to attract opposites	Sexual behavior and experimentation begin
Peer group sets behavioral standards	The peer group will determine whether the young person will comply or not with certain regimens; peer may accompany patient to visit
Cognitive growth increased	Able to formulate goals for future which may not be realistic because ego identity is not fully formed

Late Adolescence (Age: Females, 16–21 Years; Males, 17–21 Years)

Characteristics	Impact
Emancipation is nearly secured; can take or leave advice	With emancipation, the young person begins to recognize the consequences of his/her actions

(Table 2, continued)

Characteristics	Impact
Body image and gender role definition is secured	A moral code has been established and the adolescent feels comfortable with sexual relationships and decisions
Relationships are no longer narcissistic; there is a process of giving and sharing	This enables both physician and patient to be more direct in their questions and responses in the clinical setting
Cognitive development, formal operations have continued to mature	The physician can share the options with the patient who can grasp the full range of options
Functional role begins to be defined	Life goals can be significantly discussed because the adolescent is committing his/her energies to achieving a goal

Adapted from: Irwin, C. *Pediatrics* (11th Ed.) Rudolph, A., ed. Norwalk, CT: Appleton–Century Crofts, 1982, p. 39

No Black adolescents were used in the sample population from which Tanner's measures of physiological development were derived (Harlan, Grillo, Cornone–Huntley, & Leaverton, 1980; 1979; Westney, Jenkins, Butts, & Wiilliams, 1984; Tanner, 1962). Further, although the progression of events is similar among Black youth, for Black adolescent females, the onset of physiological development and maturation is earlier than for her White female counterpart (Harlan, W., et al., 1980). Cultural bias may be reflected in the data because of the possibility that an examiner who is unfamiliar with the norm for adolescent female development might deem physiological maturation which is normal as, in fact, abnormal or precocious.

Cultural bias within the physiological stages is also evident. A classical example can be seen in the description of male genital maturity ratings. Here, the description of testicular growth includes "enlarged scrotum, *pink*, texture". How many Black adolescents will have pink scrotums?

Although general information about stages of physiological development may hold true, terminology and samples are racially and culturally biased; and the Black adolescent population has been left out of the sampling for a measure held as the *gold standard* for physiological development of adolescents.

Psychosocial development theory has three major pitfalls when applied to Black adolescents: (1) it operates primarily from a deficit orientation; (2) it does not include tasks critical to Black adolescent

Physical and Mental Health

Table 3
Sex Maturity Ratings

Boys

Stage	Pubic Hair	Penis	Testes
1	None	Preadolescent	Preadolescent
2	Scanty, long, slightly pigmented	Slight enlargement	Enlarged scrotum, pink texture altered
3	Darker, starts to curl, small amount	Penis longer	Larger
4	Resembles adult type, but less in quantity; coarse, curly	Larger; glans and breadth increase in size	Larger, scrotum dark
5	Adult distribution, spread to medial surface of thighs	Adult	Adult

Girls

Stage	Pubic Hair	Breasts
1	Preadolescent	Preadolescent
2	Sparse, lightly pigmented, straight, medial border of labia	Breast and papilla elevated as small mound; areolar diameter increased
3	Darker, beginning to curl, increased amount	Breast and areola enlarged, no contour separation
4	Coarse, curly, abundant, but amount less than in adult	Areola and papilla form secondary mound
5	Adult feminine triangle spread to medial surface of thighs	Mature; nipple projects, areola part of general breast contour

Adapted from: Tanner, J.M.: *Growth at Adolescence*, ed. 2, Oxford, England, Blackwell Scientific Publications, 1962.

Health Care Issues of Black Adolescents

development (culturally relevant tasks); and (3) it includes tasks that are culturally irrelevant. Most psychosocial literature gives more attention to problems of adolescents and their families than to examples of successful adjustment. The approach also appears to be individualistic; it focuses on personal tasks that the adolescent must accomplish. If the tasks are not accomplished, deficits in the adolescent, the family or the community are alleged to exist. Often, adolescent developmental theories attribute to Black youth deficits that in fact may be due to their "limited opportunities". Black adolescents are also portrayed as unable to complete developmental tasks due to socioenvironmental stressors, i.e., high unemployment, lower economic status, and lack of educational opportunity.

New research has demonstrated that contrary to the conventional medical model, Black adolescents undergo a psychosocial developmental process that is adaptable to the constraints placed upon them (Comer, 1975; Carter, 1972; Comer, & Hill, 1985; Jackson, McCullough, & Gurin, 1981).

Critical issues important to the development of psychological well-being of the Black adolescent include positive self-concept, positive self-image, increased personal efficacy, acceptance of some form of cultural/ethnic identification, and motivation. The psychological literature demonstrates proactive orientations toward racial barriers transmitted by parents to children, can lead to an increased sense of personal efficacy, and increased academic performance. Although slight gender differences are transmitted to males and females, the message includes a sense of ethnic pride, self-development, racial barrier awareness, and egalitarianism. These proactive intergenerational transmissions were associated with increased personal efficacy, effective motivation, achievement and perceived prospects for upward mobility (Bowman, & Howard, 1985). If school, family and community all operated from the same cultural frame of reference, there was increased school performance, decreased depression, a positive self-image, and mastery of tasks (Bowman, & Howard, 1985; Barnes, 1980; Billingsley, 1968; Comer, & Poussaint, 1975; Gurin, & Epps, 1974; Jackson, McCullough, & Gurin, 1981; Spurlock, 1985). This sense of cultural continuity allowed Black adolescents a chance to develop dualism, a healthy flexible dual identity which allowed them to cope effectively with racial inequalities, maintain a personal sense of achievement and efficacy while having an appropriate external orientation toward racial barriers and opportunities (Bowman, & Howard, 1985; Gurin, & Epps, 1974).

Thus, despite psychosocial obstacles, Black adolescents can have healthy psychosocial development, although strategies for achieving this objective may vary from those proposed in the current medical model. A more social-ecological or interactionist model is needed. Such a model would assess the effects of individual, group, and institution interactions over time, and would explore mechanisms of and obstacles to adjustment

Physical and Mental Health

of the individual. Although the development of racial, cultural or ethnic identity is critical during adolescence, it is rarely dealt with within current adolescent medical model psychosocial literature (Gurin, & Epps, 1974; Jackson, McCullough, & Gurin, 1981; Spurlock, 1985; White, 1984; Jones, 1972; Jones, 1980).

The major data on racial identification comes from work being done by prominent Black psychologists,educators, and physicians. When normative adolescent development is discussed in standard medical textbooks, there is little mention of the fact that Black adolescents must face the additional task of establishing some form of racial, ethnic, or cultural identification. If this culturally relevant task is not appropriately completed, or if the adolescent is not supported by the environment, major stresses such as depression, acting–out behavior including anger, violence or sexual promiscuity may result (Comer, 1985; Carter, 1972; Comer, & Hill, 1985; Barnes, 1980; Spurlock, 1985; Jones, 1980). Because the Black adolescent must deal with the reality of what it means to be Black in America, the struggle to complete the task may translate into headaches, stomachaches and chest pains. If the health care provider is not sensitive to the possibility that the process of racial identity formation may be a potential cause of stress, then the diagnosis may be incorrect or only partially correct. Two examples may be seen in the following:

A 15 year old female comes in with a complaint of recurrent headaches. Upon closer questioning the clinician discerned the headaches began at the time she entered high school. Associated with the entrance to high school the youth has also experienced for the first time racial prejudice. She was told by some teachers she was to dark to ever amount to anything. Her White peers were calling her "nigger" or "Blackie". Some of her Black peers were telling her she was "too dark" to ever date or be successful socially. Her physical exam is normal.

Many clinicians would diagnose this patient as having stress–related headaches. However, how many would gain the information or even address the racial issues that are critical to this youth's stress. Clinicians who are not sensitive to ethnic diversity would limit their diagnosis to stress–related headaches and fail to explore the critical racial issues which actually underly those headaches. This youth was struggling to deal with issues around her own skin color as well as the social consequences of being Black. Therapy focused solely on relieving stress–related headaches would be extremely superficial and of limited value. In this case what is needed is exploration of racial identity and reinforcement of coping mechanisms to deal with racism.

A seventeen year old male comes in complaining of stomachaches. He is president of his class, a star athlete and an honor student. The stomach pain began when the youth started to plan for his Junior Prom. His physical exam is negative.

When questioned about his school, home and community environment the youth reports he is the only Black in his class and that there are only four Blacks in his entire High School of 1,300 students. He has been unable to find a prom date because everyone is "unavailable". All the females he thought he was close to "can't go out, can't be seen with him, or can't date him". Some examples of his experiences: One mom– "My daughter's not home" even though he sees and hears her in the house and "don't ever come back"; female classmate "You know I like you but I can't be seen with you...well anyways not on a date."; male classmate, "Just who do you think you are. Don't you know your place"; female classmate, "I'd like to go out with you but my parents and friends say I'll be an embarrassment or shame to the White race".

This youth was upset about these and other statements made by people he had grown up with and known all his life. He stated that now that he is a young Black male people perceive and respond to him differently in school and in the community.

Again this youth might accurately be diagnosed as having a stress–related stomachache. Yet, the impact of racial prejudice on this youth's socialization process is paramount. It is important to note that this youth's perception of his community's changing views about him are probably accurate. It is not uncommon for Black youths who have grown up in predominantly White neighborhoods to experience a virtual desertion of their White friends and peers when they reach puberty. Sometimes this desertion may not be precipitated by the White peers themselves but by parental or community pressure.

The message this youth received was that he was good enough to be in class, good enough to win the games, and good enough to be a leader, but not good enough to date a White female. This youth was confronted with the community's phobia about Black males dating White females. Therefore, appropriate therapy would focus on getting the youth to recognize prejudice and not internalize the experience of being socially rejected. Therapy should also focus on appropriate alternatives within the Black cultural framework for the youth to be able to complete his socialization process. For example, he could go outside his community to find a date, his interaction within Black social networks should be increased with peers his own age and he, his family and support counselors could confront members of the community around issues of racial prejudice and cultural tolerance.

The last area of difficulty within the current psychosocial model is the presence of culturally irrelevant and culturally biased tasks. How realistic is it to expect the Black adolescent to find a job to complete his development when there is 50 to 60% unemployment (and greater) in some cities? It may be very realistic if the effects of racism, decreased job and economic opportunity, and increased societal constraints on job advancement are taken into account, weighed and the probabilities examined. If this interaction process does not take place, is the interpreta-

Physical and Mental Health

tion valid? Do the tasks set up by the theories as evidence of normal development set the Black adolescent up for failure? To a certain extent, yes. Often, the theoretical models used are not based on the Black adolescent's experience or Black adolescent norms.

The tasks often involve stereotyping behaviors. For example, individuation from the family and independence are considered tasks to be completed by the adolescent. This places Black adolescents in opposition to their greatest support system—their families. Extended family structure, cohesiveness within the family, and community have been demonstrated to be maximally important in the establishment and maintenance of physical and mental health for Black adolescents. The family structure acts as a buffer against and conduit through an often hostile environment; independence can put Black adolescents at risk for major stress and associated health problems.

For the Black adolescent, the issue then becomes why the rocketing medical problems? The problems are fueled by poverty, racism, limited employment, limited opportunity, cultural bias in theoretical frameworks, and the fact that professionals who plan interventions often lack education and information about Black culture. The problems are also fueled by an insensitivity within the medical system and by health care providers. For example, in a major national medical center, a Black adolescent male was inappropriately diagnosed as being psychotic because he was acting bizarre. No one bothered to consider that this patient's bizarre behavior might possibly be due to his longstanding severe seizure disorder. He was perceived as a large potentially *dangerous* Black male. Consequently, the treatment of this patient was inappropriate.

In another example, a Black male adolescent was labelled by his doctors as having a phobia because he was afraid to leave the house. The doctors had not considered the fact that this Black male adolescent had undergone the horrifying experience of being pulled off a bus and having the police put a gun to his head, simply because he happened to "look like" a wanted criminal. The impact of this terrible event upon his psyche had not been explored. Neither had his rather accurate perception that the possibility of his being an "accidental casualty" in a police investigation was very real. He was a large, easily visible Black male who could easily be "confused" with some "criminal". He had accurately perceived that when he was pulled off that bus he was at risk for harassment and or incarceration because he "looked like someone".

To solve health care problems of Black adolescents, the focus must not be on individual change but on socio–political–economic changes that will impact major environmental stressors. There must also be an increase in the observance, evaluation and documentation of the strengths, positive outcomes, and factors that make a difference in the lives of Black adolescents. For example, why isn't it widely known that the Black Bishops, an all Black secondary class team from a socially disadvantaged area in Philadelphia, holds more recent national chess championships than any secondary school in the history of the country?

In order to address medical problems of Black adolescents there must be an implosion of beliefs, ideas, and strategies that are culturally relevant, culturally appropriate and culturally mediated. No one easy answer exists; there is no one solution. Black adolescents health care problems are, sadly, a reflection of the face of the Black community. Many of the problems, and the solutions, are those facing Black Americans in contemporary society.

References

Barnes, E. (1980). The Black community as the source of positive self–concept for Black children: A theoretical perspective. In R. Jones (Ed.), *Black psychology*, (2nd edition), New York: Harper and Row.

Beardslee, W. (1984). Familial influence in childhood depression. *Pediatric Annals*, 1984, 13; 1:32–36.

Billingsley, A. (1968). *Black families in White America*. Englewood Cliffs, N.J.: Prentice Hall.

Bowman, P., & Howard, C. (1985). Race related socialization, motivation, and academic achievement: A study of Black youths in three–generation families. *Journal of American Academy of Child Psychiatry*, 24, 134–141.

Brunswick, A., & Messin, P. (1986). Drugs, Lifestyle, and health: A longitudinal study of urban Black youth. *American Journal of Public Health*, 75, 52–57.

Carter, J. H. (1972). The Black struggle for identity. *Journal of National Medical Association*, 64, 236–238.

Caton, S., & Kandel, D. (1978). Psychological factors and adolescent illicit drug use: Ethnicity and sex differences. *Adolescence*, 13, 182–200.

Center for Disease Control (1983). *Abortion surveillance report 1979–1980*.

Chilman, C. (1983). *Advanced sexuality in a changing American society*. New York: John Wiley.

Cipe, S. M., Kejaks, S., Lund, A., & Otradovic, C. (1983).

Differences in dental experiences, practices, and beliefs of inner city and suburban adolescents. *American Journal of Public Health*, 73, 1305–1307.

Clark, S., Zabin, L., & Hardy, J. (1984). Sex, contraception and parenthood: Experience and attitudes among urban Black young men. *Family Planning Perspectives*, 16, 2:77–82.

Comer, J. (1985. Black children and child psychiatry. *Journal of American Academy of Child Psychiatry*, 24, 2129–133.

Comer, J., & Hill, H. (1985). Social policy and the mental health of Black children. *Journal of American Academy of Child Psychiatry*, 24, 175–181.

Comer, J., & Poussaint, A. (1975). *Black child care: How to bring up a healthy Black child in America*. New York: Simon and Schuster.

Earls, F. (1984). The epidemiology of depression in children and adolescents. *Pediatric Annals*, 13, 47–53.

Eisenberg, L. (1984). The epidemiology of suicide in adolescents. *Pediatric Annals*, 13, 47-53.

Family Impact Seminar, (1979). *Teen age pregnancy and family impact: New perspectives on policy*. Washington, D.C.: George Washington University.

Fieldling, J., & Nelson, S. (1973). Health care for the economically disadvantaged adolescent. *Pediatric clinics of North America*, 975–988.

Fitzpatrick, S., Chacko, M. & Heald, F. (1984). Iron deficiency in Black females during late adolescence. *Journal of Adolescent Health Care*, 5, 71–74.

Freeman, E., Rickels, K., Huggins, G., & Garcia, C. (1984). Urban Black adolescents who obtain contraception services before or after their first pregnancy. *Journal of Adolescent Health Care*, 5, 183–190.

Furstenberg, F. (1976). *Unplanned parenthood*. New York: Free Press, 37–60.

Furstenberg, F., Lincoln, R., & Menken, J. (1981). *Teenage sexuality and childbearing*. Philadelphia: University of Pennsylvania Press.

Gabriel, A., McAnarney, E. (1983). Parenthood in two subcultures: White middle class couples and Black low–income adolescents in Rochester, New York, *Adolescence*, 8:595–608.

Garn, S., Smith, F., & Clark, D. (1975). Lifelong differences in hemoglobin levels between Blacks and Whites. *Journal of National Medical Association*, 67, 91–96.

Gibbs, J. (1985, April). Assessment of depression in urban adolescent females: Implications for early intervention strategies. *The Black family: Mental health perspectives*. San Francisco: Rosenberg Foundation. pp. 67–79.

Gibbs, J. T. (1984). Black adolescents and youth: An endangered species. *American Journal of Orthopsychiatry*, 54, 6–21.

Greene, J., Walker, L. Hickson, G., Thompson, J. (1985). Stressful life events and somatic complaints in adolescents. *Pediatrics*, 75, 19–22.

Gurin, P., & Epps, E. (1974). *Black consciousness, identity, and achievement*. New York: John Wiley and Sons.

Harlan, W., Grillo, G., Cornoi–Huntley, J., & Leaverton, P. (1979). Secondary sex characteristics of girls 12–17 years of age: The U.S. Health Examination Survey. *The Journal of Pediatrics*, 96, 1074–1078.

Harlan, W., Grillo, G., Corone–Huntley, J., & Leaverton, P. (1979). Secondary sex characteristics of boys 12–17 years of age: The U.S. Health Examination Survey. *The Journal of Pediatrics*, 95, 293–297.

Heald, F. (1975). Adolescent nutrition. *Medical Clinics of North America*, 59, 1329–1336.

Hediger, M., Schell, J., Katz, S., Gruskin, A., & Eveleth, P. (1984). Resting blood pressure and pulse rate distribution in Black adolescents: The Philadelphia blood pressure project. *Pediatrics*, 74, 1016–1021.

Hogan, D., Astore, H., & Kitagawa, E. (1985). Social and environmental factors influencing contraceptive use among Black adolescents. *Family Planning Perspectives*, 17, 165–169.

Holinger, P. & Offer, D. (1982). Prediction of adolescent suicides: A population model. *American Journal of Psychiatry*, 139, 302–307.

Irwin, C. (1982). Approach to the adolescent patient: Health maintenance assessment. In A. Rudolph (Ed.), *Textbook of pediatrics*, 11th Edition. Norwalk, CT:Appleton, Century, Crofts.

Jackson, J., McCullough, W., & Gurin, G. (1981). Group identity within Black families. In H. McAdoo (Ed.), *Black families*. Beverly Hills, CA: Sage Publications.

Johnson, F. & Mack, R. (1978). Obesity in urban Black adolescents of high and low relative weight at 1 year of age. *American Journal of Diseases of Childhood, 131,* 862–864.
Johnson, R. L. (1985). Black adolescents: Issues critical to their survival. *Journal of the National Medical Association, 77,* 447–449.
Jones, K. (1986). A crisis report on the status of the Black American male. *The Crisis, 93,* 17–21, 44.
Jones, R. (1972). *Black psychology.* New York: Harper & Row.
Ladner, J. (1971). *Tomorrow's tomorrow: The Black woman.* Garden City, N.J.: Doubleday.
Morbidity and Mortality Weekly Report. (1985a). Homicide among young Black males—United States 1970–1982. *Morbidity and Mortality Weekly Report, 34,* 629–633.
Morbidity and Mortality Weekly Report. (1985b). Suicide–United States, 1970–1980. *Morbidity and Mortality Weekly Report, 34,* 353–357.
Morbidity and Mortality Weekly Report. (1985c). Teenage pregnancy and fertility trends—United States 1974–1980. *Morbidity and Mortality Weekly Report, 34,* 277–280.
Morbidity and Mortality Weekly Report. (1985d). Abortions in adolescents. *Morbidity and Mortality Weekly Reports, 33.*
Morgan, M., Wingard, D., & Felice, M. (1984). Subcultural differences in alcohol use among youth. *Journal of Adolescent Health Care, 5,* 191–195.
National Center for Health Statistics. (1981). Advance Report of Final Natality Statistics: *Monthly Vital Statistics Report. 32,* 84–1120.
National Institute of Drug Abuse. (1979). *National survey on drug abuse.* Washington, D.C.: National Institute of Drug Abuse.
National Institute of Drug Abuse. (1980a). *Current trends and issues in drug abuse.* Washington, D.C.: National Institute of drug Abuse.
National Institute of Drug Abuse. (1980b). Drug abuse deaths in nine cities: A survey report. *Research Monograph, 29.* Washington, D.C.: National Institute of Drug Abuse.
O'Reilly, K. & Aral, S. (1985). Adolescence and sexual behavior, trends and implications for STD. *Journal of Adolescent Health Care, 6,* 262–270.
Paton, S. and Kandel, D. (1978). Psychological factors and adolescent illicit drug use: ethnicity and sex differences. *Adolescence, 13,* 187–200.
Pearson, H., McLean, F., & Brigetz, R. (1971). Anemia related to age: A study of a community of young Black Americans. *Journal of the American Medical Association, 215,* 1982–1984.
Powell, G. (1985). Self–concepts among Afro–American Students in racially isolated minority schools: Some regional differences. *Journal of American Academy of Child Psychiatry, 24,* 142–149.
Pumariega, A., Edwards, P. & Mitchell, C. (1984, January). Anorexia nervosa in Black adolescents: Case reports. *Journal of the American Academy of Child Psychiatry, 23,* 111.
Rainwater, L. (1970). *Behind ghetto walls: Black families in a federal slum.* Chicago: Aldine Publishing.
Randolph, L., & Rivers, S. (1985). A comparison of selected health indicators for Black and White children in New York State. *New York State Journal of Medicine,* 131–134.
Riley, M. (1986). Footnotes of a culture at risk. *The Crisis, 93,* 23–27, 44.

Seiden, R. (1970). We're driving young Blacks to suicide. *Psychology Today, 4,* 24–28.
Schoenbach, V., Kaplan, B., Wagne, E., Grimson, R., & Miller, F. (1983). Prevalence of self–reported depression symptoms in young adolescents. *American Journal of Public Health, 83,* 1281–1287.
Smith, E., & Udry, J. (1985). Coital and non–coital sexual behaviors of White and Black adolescents. *American Journal of Public Health, 75,* 1200–1203.
Spurlock, J. (1985). Assessment and therapeutic intervention of Black children. *Journal of the American Academy of Child Psychiatry, 24,* 2: 168–174.
Spurlock, J., & Lawrence, L. (1979). The Black child. In *Basic handbook of child psychiatry, 1,* 243–257. New York: Basic Books.
Stack, C. (1974). *All our kin.* New York: Harper and Row.
Staples, R. (1982). Black masculinity, the Black male's role in American society. In *To be young, Black and male* (pp. 21–39). San Francisco, CA: The Black Scholar Press.
Staples, R. (1972). The sexuality of Black women. In L. Gross (Ed.), *Sexual behavior, current issues: An interdisciplinary perspective* (pp. 4–15). Flushing: Spectrum Publishing.
Statistical series, annual data (1980, 1981). Series E., No. 21. Washington, D.C.: U.S. Dept. of Health and Human Services.
Stunkard, A., (1972). Influence of social class on obesity and thinness in children. *Journal of the American Medical Association,* 116: 579–584.
Tanner, J. Growth at adolescence. (1962). Oxford: Blackwell.
Tardiff, KI., Gross, E. & Messner, S. (1986). A study of homicides in Manhattan, 1981. *American Journal of Public Health, 72,* 139–143.
Thompson, K. (1980). A comparison of Black and White adolescents' beliefs about having children. *Journal of Marriage and the Family, 42,* 133–139.
Thornton, W., James J., & Doerner, W. (1982). *Delinquency and justice.* Glenview, Ill.: Scott, Foresman.
U.S. Bureau of the Census. (1981). School enrollment: Social and economic characteristics of students, 1980. Advance report. *Current population reports, Services, P–20.* Washington, D.C.: U.S. Bureau of the Census.
U.S. Bureau of Census. (1983). *National data book and guide to sources: Statistical abstract of the United States, 1982–1983, 103rd edition.* Washington, D.C.: U.S. Bureau of the Census.
U.S. Department of Health and Human Services. (1981). Series E., No. 21. Washington, D.C.: U.S. Department of Health and Human Services.
U.S. Department of Justice. (1981). Uniform crime reports: Crimes in the U.S. Washington, D.C.: F.B.I., U.S. Department of Justice.
U.S. Government Printing Office (1975). Vital statistics of the United States, 1970–1975 (1975). Tables 1–26. Washington, D.C.: U.S. Government Printing Office.
Vichinsky, E., & Lubin B. (1980). Sickle cell anemia and related hemoglobinopathies. *Pediatric Clinics of North America, 27,* 429–447.
Washington, A., Sweet, R., & Shafer, N. (1985). Pelvic inflammatory disease and its seguelae in adolescents. *Journal of Adolescent Health Care, 6,* 298–311.
Webb, H. (1984). Health care problems in the 1980s. Community health centers providing care for urban Blacks. *Journal of the American Medical Association, 76,* 1063–1067.
Westney, O., Jenkins, R., Butts, S., & Williams, I. (1984). Several development behaviors in Black preadolescents. *Adolescence, 19,* 558–568.

Westoff, C., Calot, G., & Foster, A. (1983). Fertility in developed nations: 1971–1980 *Family Planning Perspectives, 15,* 105–110.
White, J. (1984). *The psychology of Blacks.* Englewood Cliffs, New Jersey: Prentice Hall.
William, R. (1975). *Textbook of Black–related diseases.* New York, McGraw–Hill, Inc.
Yip, R., Schwartz, S., & Deihard, A. (1984). Hematocrit values in White, Black and American Indian children with comparable iron status: Evidence to support uniform diagnostic criteria for anemia among all races. *American Journal of Diseases of Childhood, 138,* 824.
Zelnik, M., & Kantner, J. F. (1980). Sexual activity, contraceptive use and pregnancy among metropolitan–area teenagers, 1971–1979. *Family Planning Perspectives, 12,* 230–237.
Zelnik, M., & Kantner, J. F. (1977). Sexual and contraceptive experience of young unmarried women in the United States, 1976 and 1971. *Family Planning Perspectives, 9,* 55–71.
Zelnik, M., & Kim, Y. (1982). Sex education and its association with teenage sexual activity, pregnancy, and contraceptive use. *Family Planning Perspectives, 14,* 117–126.
Zelnik, M., Kantner, J., & Ford, K. (1981). *Sex and pregnancy in adolescence.* Beverly Hills: Sage Publications.
Zelnik, M., Kim, Y., & Kantner, J. (1979). Probabilities of intercourse and conception among U.S. teenage women, 1971 and 1976. *Family Planning Perspectives, 11,* 177.
Zelnik, M., & Shah, F. (1985). First intercourse among young Americans. *Family Planning Perspectives, 15,* 64–70.

URBAN STRESS AND MENTAL HEALTH IN BLACK YOUTH: AN EPIDEMIOLOGIC AND CONCEPTUAL UPDATE

Hector F. Myers

> Black youth in contemporary American society can aptly be described as an endangered species. Educators have written them off as unteachable, the juvenile justice system has failed to rehabilitate them, the mental health system has virtually ignored or excluded them, and social and welfare (agencies) seem ill–equipped to respond to their multiple (needs).
>
> Jewelle T. Gibbs, 1984, p. 6

Introduction

Gibbs' poignant statement aptly characterizes the current social status of a significant plurality of Black youths, especially youths of the Black underclass. Inherent in this indictment is the conviction that the problems of Black youth as a group emerge out of the structure of society. They are the predictable products of a pattern of social relations between these youths, their proximal communities (i.e. families, neighborhoods), and the social, political and economic processes extant in the broader distal community (i.e. social agencies, institutions, social policies, etc.). This statement also implies a pattern of social responses to the expressed problems and needs of Black youth which are characterized by misunderstanding, neglect, confusion and ultimately rejection.

The evidence indicates that we have thousands of Black youth increasingly less capable of negotiating the rough waters of modern American society. We argue that this "underpreparedness" is a product of the social structure. The problems of children are not ordained by fate and cannot be adequately explained by analyses that focus simplistically on individual personality, intellectual or social deficits. Rather, the mental health problems of Black youth can be more accurately described as resulting from the peculiar relationships between these youth and the system of social and economic relationships of which they are a part. Many of their difficulties may be viewed as "problems of adaptation", i.e. the predictable products of efforts to adapt to oppressive social processes that result in the "manufacture of illness, disability and social marginality" (Myers, 1979; Myers & King, 1980).

In this chapter, I will first examine the available epidemiologic evidence of the mental health status of urban Black youth, with specific attention focused on the prevalence of psychiatric disorders and on disorders of social adjustment (i.e. delinquency and violence, suicide, and substance abuse). There are currently no known epidemiologic surveys of mental health that include adequate samples of Blacks and that also use sound assessment and diagnostic techniques (Williams, 1986). The two most recent such surveys, the NIMH Epidemiologic Catchment Area study (ECA) (Regier et al., 1984; Eaton et al., 1984; Robins et al., 1984) and the National Survey of Black Americans study (NSBA) (Jackson, 1980; Neighbors et al., 1983) can be criticized either because of inadequate Black samples (ECA) or because of inadequate assessment and diagnostic procedures (NSBA). Therefore, we must rely on available data from published reports of treated or identified cases that are included in national data base reports from the National Institute of Mental Health (NIMH) and the Center for Disease Control (CDC). Data from these sources provide useful indications of gross trends, but typically underestimate the true population prevalence of major mental health status indicators. Therefore, these data are presented as indication of the "relative status of Black youth" rather than as precise statements of the "actual status" of these youth.

In the second part of this article I will conceptualize this evidence of increased marginalization of urban Black youth from the perspective of a model of urban stress. This model does not examine the contradictions endemic to the social structure which contribute to the creation and maintenance of social stresses, but rather on how these stresses are mediated by the attributes of Black youth, their families, communities and the primary social agencies that intersect their lives (i.e. the schools, welfare system, the judicial system, and the health and mental health systems). These factors can either exacerbate or ameliorate the detrimental impact of social stresses and vulnerabilities, and as such, can be useful in our analyses and intervention efforts.

Epidemiologic Evidence

Psychiatric Disorders

Data from the National Institute of Mental Health cited in Myers & King (1980) Indicates that there has been a recent increase in psychiatric services for persons under age 18. It is not clear why this increase in youth mental health services has occurred. Is it because of earlier detection of symptoms, increased prevalence of psychiatric disorders in American youth, or because of greater awareness, availability and acceptance of such services? An early report on the rate of admissions to psychiatric hospitals in New York for youth under age 15 per 100,000 population showed that nonWhite youth are hospitalized at almost three times the rate for White youth, and that the rate for nonWhite males was almost five times that for White males (Shiloh & Selavan, 1974). A concurrent report on a similar population between the ages of 11–24 who were hospitalized with a diagnosis of schizophrenia in 1969 showed that non-White males and females were hospitalized at almost twice the rate as were Whites with this diagnosis (i.e. 258.8 vs 120.3/100,000 pop. for males, and 142.0 vs 84.4/100,000 pop. for females). These data provide early indication of significant differences by race and gender in the rate of hospitalization and in the severity of the diagnosis given to nonWhite youth.

This mental health trend is even more striking when we examine the pattern of institutionalization of youth as a function of both race and social class. Comparing the rates of institutionalization of Blacks under the age of 18 from 1966 to 1971 as reported in a 1977 HEW report (DHEW Publication No. (ADM) 77–433, 1977) we find that in 1966 the rate of institutionalization was 696/100,000 population. By 1971, this rate almost doubled to 1,091. Furthermore, if we look at the types of institutions to which these youngsters have increasingly been referred, we find that despite a significant decrease of 47% between 1966 and 1971 in the rate of psychiatric hospitalization, there was a compensatory increase of 38% in the number of Black youth in juvenile institutions, and an 11% increase in the number of Black youth in homes and schools for the mentally retarded. This indicates a shift away from defining the problems of these youth as mental health problems and providing mental health services towards defining the problems as due either to developmental deficits or to deficits in social control. This shift is evident in the data from the same source which indicates that while White male and female institutionalization rates were decreasing by 21% and 39% respectively, the rates from Black males and females were increasing by 56% and 14% respectively. These changes are also evident in the data reported in the recent report from the Childrens' Defense Fund (1985) which noted that Black youth ages 15–19 are 4 times more likely to be incarcerated today than White youth.

More recent data on inpatient psychiatric rates for youth (under age 18) by gender and race (Whites vs nonWhites) in 1980 confirm some of the earlier hospitalization trends. Using data from three sample surveys of inpatient services at State and County mental hospitals, private psychiatric hospitals and non– federal general hospitals, Milazzo–Sayre et al. (1986) note that the number of hospitalized youth in general has dropped significantly in the last decade. The majority of those youth who were hospitalized were males (53% vs 47%) and Whites (82.1% and 17.9%).

Physical and Mental Health

Table 1
Youths Incarcerated in Correctional Institutions, by Sex, Age, and Race, 1980

Age and Sex	Black	White	Total
Under 15			
Number	540	1,085	1,733
Rate per 1,000	0.1	0.0	0.0
15–19			
Male			
Number	17,730	23,734	45,669
Rate per 1,000	11.8	2.7	4.2
Female			
Number	782	1,367	2,363
Rate per 1,000	0.5	0.2	0.2
Total			
Number	18,512	25,101	48,032
Rate per 1,000	6.2	1.5	2.3
20–24			
Male			
Number	56,439	64,860	132,937
Rate per 1,000	44.0	7.4	12.5
Female			
Number	3,202	3,477	7,329
Rate per 1,000	2.2	0.4	0.7
Total			
Number	59,641	68,337	140,266
Rate per 1,000	22.0	3.9	6.6

Source: U.S. Department of Commerce, Bureau of the Census, *1980 Census of Population, Volume 1, Characteristics of the Population, Chapter D. Detailed Population Characteristics, Part I, United States Summary*, PC80-1-D1-A (Washington, D.C., May 1984), table 266. Calculations by Children's Defense Fund.

Source: Black & White Children in America: Key Facts. Children's Defense Fund. Washington, D.C., 1985.

Urban Stress and the Mental Health of Black Youth

However, the rate of hospitalization per 100,000 pop. was actually greater for nonWhites (mainly Blacks (i.e. 131/100,000 for nonWhites vs 128/100,000 for Whites). Thus, while the number of hospitalized non-White youth is significantly lower than for White youth, the rate of hospitalization for nonWhite White youth is actually greater than their representation in the population. This suggests that great care must be exercised in interpreting the significance of data indicating reduction in the numbers of Black or nonWhite youth receiving mental health services.

In addition to questions about differences in the numbers and rate of hospitalization, we also need to investigate differences in the types of disorders for which these youth may be hospitalized. Data comparing White and nonWhite youth in inpatient psychiatric facilities by predominant psychiatric diagnoses indicate a continuation of the earlier trend towards more severe disorders and more "conduct and socialization disorders" among older, males and nonWhite youth. NonWhite youth were overrepresented among those diagnosed as suffering from Affective disorders (19.6% vs 17.6%), Schizophrenia (20.5% vs 10,0%), Personality disorders (7.9% vs 6.9%) and Other disorders (11.7% vs 8.3%). White youth, on the other hand, were more represented in the Preadult disorders (23.5% vs 17.1%) and in the Other Non–psychotic disorders (26.3% vs 14.8%). These overall differences varied by age, gender, and by the type of psychiatric facility. NonWhite males in public psychiatric facilities were almost 6 times as likely as White youth to have a diagnosis of Schizophrenia and related disorders.

On the whole, Black youth do not appear to be hospitalized for diagnosable psychiatric impairment as much as White youth, but when they are hospitalized, their disorders are typically more severe. This conclusion must be treated with considerable caution, however, because it is not clear whether this difference reflects greater psychological hardiness on the part of Black youth, or lower tolerance for psychiatric symptomatology in Whites, or to the fact that inner–city Black youth often express their distress in more confrontive, "acting–out" behaviors which are more likely to bring them to the attention of the police and the courts rather than to mental health providers.

There is also the perception of many that a variety of behaviors of inner–city youth, which would be considered clinically meaningful in Whites, are thought to be normative to the subculture of inner–city Black youth and are, therefore, not indicative of true psychiatric disorders (e.g. socialized delinquency). Lopez (1983) suggests that such a perception might indicate an "underpathologizing bias" which may result in failure to recognize and treat clinically impaired Black youngsters before their mental health problem deteriorates into more severe, chronic disability.

Others have argued, however, that this point of view reflects genuine concerns over the appropriate interpretation of clinically relevant behaviors across ethnic groups. Many of the assumptions and inferences

Table 2
Number, percent distribution, and rate per 100,000 civilian population[1] of admissions under age 18 to selected inpatient psychiatric services, by age, sex, and race: United States, 1980

Age, sex, and race	Total	State and county mental hospitals	Private psychiatric hospitals	Non-Federal general hospitals Total	Public	Nonpublic	Multiservice
Number							
Total, under 18	81,532	16,612	16,735	48,185	10,420	33,175	4,590
Age							
Under 10	3,883	829	720	2,334	1,148	987	*
10-14	22,885	4,955	4,893	13,037	3,215	8,923	899
15-17	54,764	10,828	11,122	32,814	6,057	23,265	3,492
Sex							
Male	43,222	11,498	9,386	22,338	4,957	15,401	1,980
Female	38,310	5,114	7,349	25,847	5,463	17,774	2,610
Race							
White	66,938	12,432	14,735	39,771	7,824	28,000	3,947
All other races	14,594	4,180	2,000	8,414	2,596	5,175	643
Percent distribution							
Total, under 18	100.0%	100.0%	100.0%	100.0%	100.0%	100.0%	100.0%
Age							
Under 10	4.8	5.0	4.3	4.8	11.0	3.0	*
10-14	28.1	29.8	29.2	27.1	30.9	26.9	19.6
15-17	67.2	655.2	66.5	68.1	58.1	70.1	76.1
Sex							
Male	53.0	69.2	56.1	46.4	47.6	46.4	43.1
Female	47.0	30.8	43.9	53.6	52.4	53.6	56.9
Race							
White	82.1	74.8	88.0	82.5	75.1	84.4	86.0
All other races	17.9	25.2	12.0	17.5	24.9	15.6	14.0
Rate per 100,000 civilian population							
Total, under 18	128.1	26.1	26.3	75.7	16.4	52.1	7.2
Age							
Under 10	11.7	2.5	2.2	7.1	3.5	3.0	*
10-14	125.5	27.2	26.8	71.5	17.6	48.9	4.9
15-17	442.8	87.6	89.9	265.3	49.0	188.1	28.2
Sex							
Male	132.9	35.4	28.9	68.7	15.2	47.4	6.1
Female	123.1	16.4	23.6	83.0	17.5	57.1	8.4
Race							
White	127.5	23.7	28.1	75.8	14.9	53.3	7.5
All other races	130.9	37.5	17.9	75.5	23.3	46.4	5.8

[1] Population estimates used as denominators for rate computations are from the *Current Population Reports* of the U.S. Bureau of the Census, Series P-25, No. 929, table 3, p. 19.

* Five or fewer sample cases; estimate not shown because it dos not meet standards of reliability

Note: Percentages may not add to 100% due to rounding.

Table 3

Percent distribution of admissions under age 18 to selected inpatient psychiatric services, by race and selected primary diagnoses: United States, 1980

Race and selected primary diagnoses	Total	State and county mental hospitals	Private psychiatric hospitals	Non-Federal general hospitals
White	66,938	12,432	14,735	39,771
Alcohol-related disorders	2.7%	8.4%	2.3%	1.1%
Drug-related disorders	4.6	11.5	2.8	3.2
Affective disorders	17.6	9.4	29.7	15.6
Schizophrenia and related disorders	10.0	6.4	10.9	10.8
Personality disorders	6.9	12.2	8.4	4.6
Pre-adult disorders	23.5	28.4	27.1	20.7
Other nonpsychotic disorders	26.3	14.3	14.3	34.6
Other	8.3	9.3	4.6	9.4
All other races	14,594	4,180	2,000	8,414
Alcohol-related disorders		*	*	* *
Drug-related disorders	*	*	*	*
Affective disorders	19.6	9.8	29.1	22.2
Schizophrenia and related disorders	20.5	33.7	25.2	12.7
Personality disorders	7.9	*	7.2	10.0
Pre-adult disorders	17.1	20.9	24.6	13.4
Other nonpsychotic disorders	14.8	10.6	7.4	18.6
Other	11.7	12.5	5.6	12.8

* Five or fewer sample cases; estimate not shown because it does not meet standards of reliability.

Note: Percentages may not add to 100% due to rounding.

Source: Use of Inpatient Psychiatric Services by Children & Youth under age 18, U.S., 1980. *Mental Health Statistical Note, No. 175,* pp. 12, 17.

drawn about the clinical significance of some behaviors as expressions of psychiatric disorders are not always appropriate or valid in diagnosing the behaviors of Blacks and other minorities (Jones & Korchin, 1982; Franklin, 1982; Banks, 1982). Many of these behaviors, such as anger, suspiciousness, challenges to authority, etc., may well be healthy, and appropriate responses to the insidious ego–insults to which many youth are subjected to on a daily basis. Consequently, valid clinical judgements of the meaning of behaviors should not be based on assumptions about singular norms, but should be tempered by an awareness of the contextual demands that shape and reinforce those behaviors.

On the other side of the coin, however, it can also be argued that while behaviors and coping styles may evolve quite appropriately from the peculiar demands of particular settings (e.g. inner–city communities), those behaviors may still be deemed maladaptive and clinically significant if they clearly interfere with the development and functioning of the person or group. It is important, therefore, that the assessment of the behavior of Black youth include not only consideration of their potential adaptiveness, but also of their current and long–term impact on the functional well–being of these youth.

To further complicate the issue of making valid decisions about Black behavior, several challenges have also been raised about the accuracy of the diagnosis of psychopathology in Blacks. These challenges have been based on questions about diagnostic biases of clinicians, as well as about possible differences in symptom expression across ethnic groups, and between children, adolescents and adults. This issue is particularly relevant to our interpretation of the distribution of White and nonWhite youth in the various diagnostic categories. Do these data reflect real differences, or differences in diagnostic accuracy? Several investigators have demonstrated that there is a tendency among clinicians to give more severe diagnoses to Black patients which are independent of the symptom picture presented (Thomas & Sillen, 1972; Bloombaum, Yamamoto & James, 1968; Bulhan, 1985). This "overpathologizing bias" among clinicians may account for some of the overrepresentation of Blacks among the patients with the more severe diagnoses.

Others have also argued that some of the misdiagnosis of Blacks may well be due to observed differences in symptom expression. For example, in the case of Depression, several studies have indicated that depressed Black patients report more worry, muscular tension, general anxiety and autonomic symptomatology than White depressed patients (Uhlenhuth & Paykel, 1973); they tend to show more negativity, to both internalize and express more anger and hostility, and to express less feelings of helplessness (Raskin et al., 1975). Depressed Blacks have also been described as recovering faster than Whites, and showing different gender–specific responses to anti–depressant medications (Raskin & Crook, 1975). Excessive use of alcohol and other substances, perhaps in an effort to control symptoms, also tend to complicate the clinical picture of depression in Blacks.

These differences were observed in adults and not in adolescents, and therefore, may not be relevant. However, given the overrepresentation of young Black males among those diagnosed as suffering from disorders of adjustment, socialization and impulse control, many of these youngsters may well be suffering from depression, and anger is a salient feature in their symptom profile. Partial support for this hypothesis is provided by the formulators of the present psychiatric diagnostic system which treats disorders such as Depression as the same syndrome in adolescents and in adults. Therefore, it is reasonable to suspect that the anger and hostility frequently observed in depressed Black adults is also likely to be part of the syndrome of Depression in Black youth.

Juvenile Delinquency and Violence

The most socially distressing indicators of the negative trajectory of the mental health and social adjustment of urban Black youth are the startling statistics of the extent that juvenile delinquency and violence have become a part of life for this population. The Children Defense Fund report (1985) cites national data on crimes for youth under age 18 and noted that while Black youth comprised about 15% of the youth population in 1983, they accounted for almost half of the youth arrests for violent crimes, 1/4 of the youth arrests for property crimes, over half of the arrests for murder and aggravated assault, and over 2/3 of the youth arrests for rape.

In another recent special report from the Center for Disease Control (CDC) entitled "Homicide among Young Black Males, U.S., 1970–1982 (MMWR, 1985), it was noted that homicide is the leading cause of death for young Black males 15–24 years old. The Black male homicide rate was almost six times that for their White male cohorts in 1982 (i.e. 72.0 vs 13.1/100,000 pop.), with most of this violence perpetrated by Black youth in the Northeastern and Northcentral states, and among those living within standard metropolitan statistical areas (SMSAs).

One glimmer of encouragement can be seen in these data, and that is that there was an overall decrease of 33.5% in the homicide rate for young Black males between 1970–1982. However, I am afraid that some of that progress might have been reversed between 1982 and 1986 when we experienced what appeared to have been a resurgence of Black gangs in most major cities, greater penetration of drugs such as PCP and rock cocaine into inner–city neighborhoods, and the subsequent professionalization of Black youth gang–related violence.

An analysis of the particular features of Black youth violence is also instructive. In 1982, according to the MMWR (1985) most young Black

Physical and Mental Health

Table 4a
Arrests for Violent and Property Crimes, by Race and Age, 1983

	Underage 18			Age 18+		
		Percentage of Arrests			Percentage of Arrests	
	Total	Black	White	Total	Black	White
Violent crime	74,604	48.8%	49.6%	368,096	46.0%	52.6%
Murder	1,345	57.4	41.5	16,682	49.6	49.0
Forcible rape	4,373	69.3	29.5	25,741	47.4	51.2
Robbery	35,195	39.4	59.4	98,673	60.1	38.7
Aggravated assault	33,691	54.7	44.0	227,000	39.4	59.1
Property crime	577,844	28.6	69.5	1,124,867	34.8	63.6
Burglary	158,842	26.5	72.1	255,762	34.5	64.4
Larceny–theft	376,152	29.9	68.1	789,493	34.9	63.3
Motor vehicle theft	36,403	26.9	70.9	68,892	35.1	63.3
Arson	6,447	15.9	82.8	10,720	27.7	71.1
Violent and property crimes	652,448	31.6	66.6	1,492,963	37.5	60.9

Source: U.S. Department of Justice, Federal Bureau of Investigation, *Uniform Crime Reports, Crimes in the United States, 1983*, (Washington, D.C., 1984), table 36.

Table 4b
Criminal Victimization Rates for Adolescents, by Race, 1982
(victims per 1,000 persons per year)

Age and Crime	Black	White	Total
12–15			
All personal crimes of violence	59.4	51.5	52.0
Rape	2.0	1.3	1.4
Robbery	21.3	8.3	10.2
Assault	36.1	42.0	40.5
All personal crimes of theft	115.4	131.7	127.4
16–19			
All personal crimes of violence	76.4	70.7	71.2
Rape	1.4	2.2	2.0
Robbery	25.0	9.4	11.9
Assault	49.9	59.2	57.3
All personal crimes of theft	106.7	131.5	127.9

Source: U.S. Department of Commerce, Bureau of the Census, unpublished data from the 1982 Criminal Victimization Survey.

Table 4c
Homicide Deaths, by Age and Race, 1980
(deaths per 100,000 population)

Age	Black	White	Total
Under 1 year	15.7	4.3	5.9
1–4	6.8	1.7	2.5
5–9	2.0	0.7	0.9
10–15	3.2	1.1	1.4
15–19	29.9	7.5	10.6

Source: U.S. Department of Health and Human Services, National Center for Health Statistics, unpublished data. Calculations by Children's Defense Fund.

Source: *Black & White Children In America: Key Facts.* Children's Defense Found. Washington, D.C., 1985, page 106.

male homicide victims were killed during or after arguments or other nonfelony circumstances (65%) and were killed by persons known to them (i.e. 46.2% by acquaintances and 7.7% by relatives). This higher risks of participation and victimization was also evident in two reports from two major metropolitan areas: Los Angeles (MMWR, 1986), and Metropolitan Dade County, Florida (Copeland, 1984). In Los Angeles, between 1970–1979, Black and Hispanic youth were 5.6 and 2.3 times more likely than their White cohorts to be victimized by homicide. Blacks were at the greatest risk of victimization (45.6/100,000 pop.), and they evi-

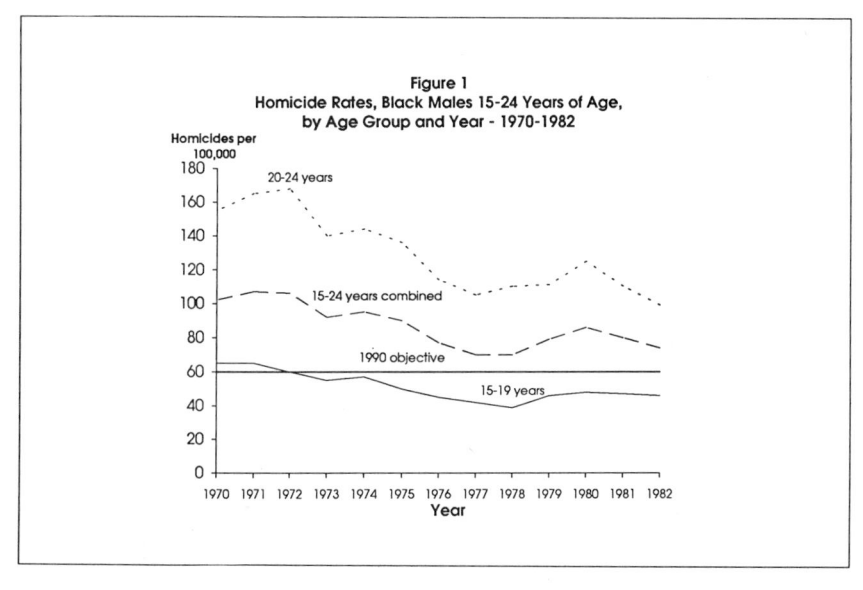

Figure 1
Homicide Rates, Black Males 15-24 Years of Age, by Age Group and Year - 1970-1982

Physical and Mental Health

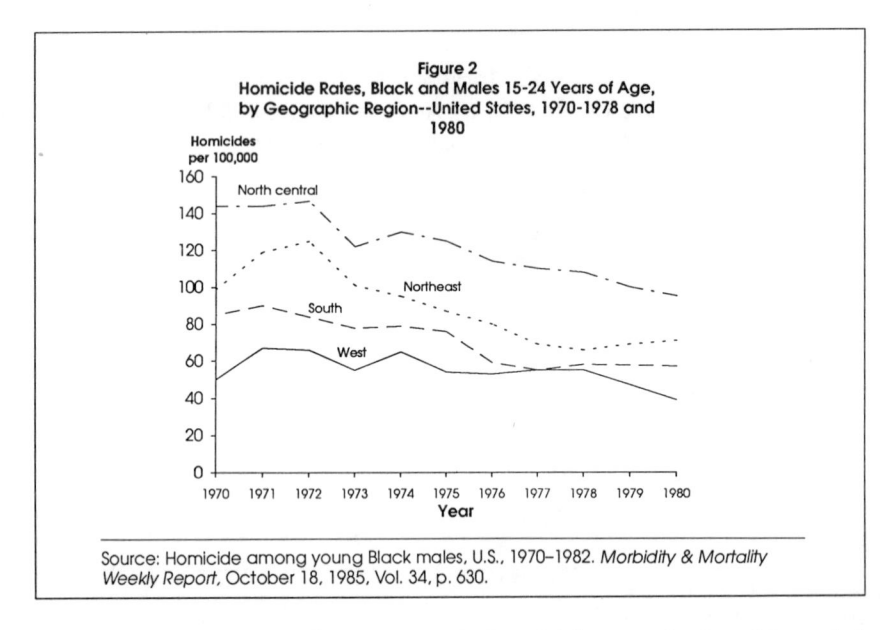

Figure 2
Homicide Rates, Black and Males 15-24 Years of Age, by Geographic Region--United States, 1970-1978 and 1980

Source: Homicide among young Black males, U.S., 1970–1982. *Morbidity & Mortality Weekly Report*, October 18, 1985, Vol. 34, p. 630.

denced the greatest absolute increase in homicide rates during this period (35.7/100,000 in 1978) to 61.3/100,000 in 1979). Alcohol, drugs and intra-familial conflicts were frequent contributing factors. Similar trends were found in the Dade County study, although a slightly higher proportion of youth deaths was crime–related.

National data reported in the CDF report (1985) also noted that Black youth ages 12–19 were 1.12 times more likely to be victims of robbery than White youth. On the other hand, White youth were 1.18

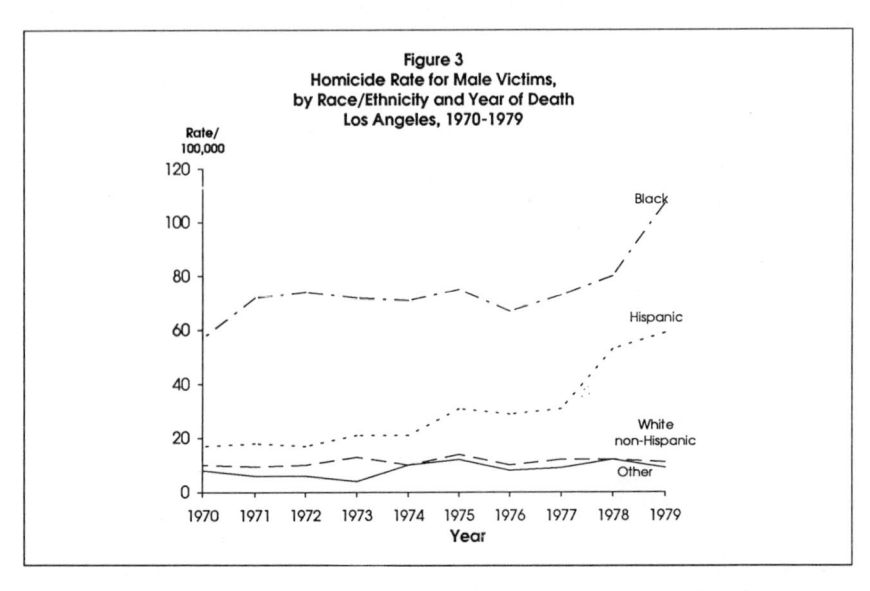

Figure 3
**Homicide Rate for Male Victims, by Race/Ethnicity and Year of Death
Los Angeles, 1970-1979**

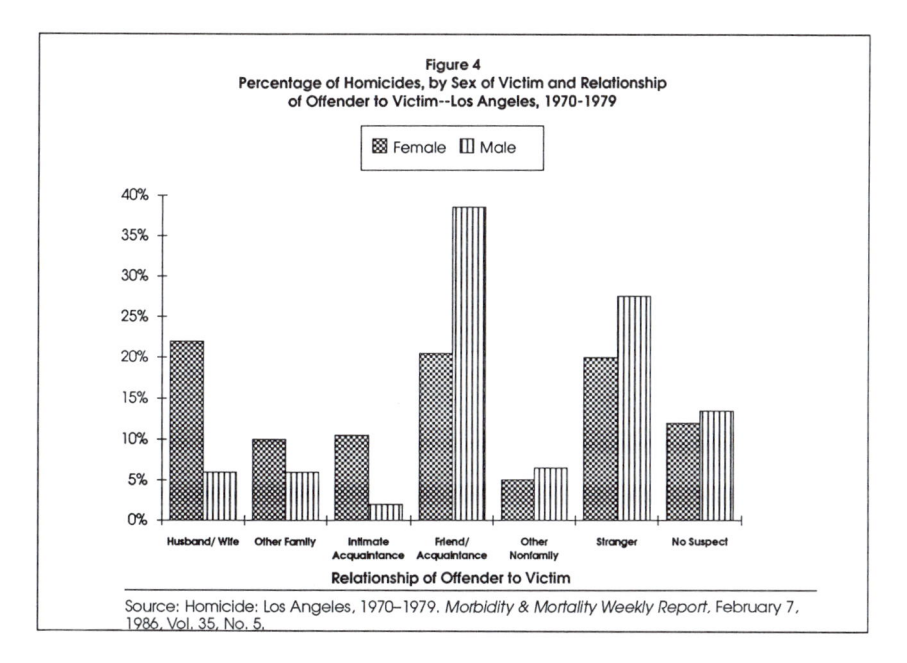

Figure 4
Percentage of Homicides, by Sex of Victim and Relationship of Offender to Victim--Los Angeles, 1970-1979

Source: Homicide: Los Angeles, 1970–1979. *Morbidity & Mortality Weekly Report*, February 7, 1986, Vol. 35, No. 5.

times more likely to be assaulted and 1.19 times more likely to be victims of theft than Black youth (See Table 4).

Several comparison studies of juvenile delinquency have been conducted that included Black subsamples (Kashani, Horowitz & Daniel, 1982; Calhoun, Connley & Bolton, 1984). Many of these studies point to differences in the presence of diagnosable character disorders in Black delinquents, which have led several investigators to make a distinction between delinquency that is associated with adolescent psychopathology vs socio–cultural delinquency (Weiner, 1982). The latter, which is presumably more applicable to Black juvenile delinquents is considered to be consistent with and the product of culturally–defined or situationally determined processes and norms of behavior. A major implication of this distinction is that a significant amount of Black delinquent behavior is caused by patterns of relationships within the proximal community, rather than by underlying psychopathology. As such, therefore, much of it is contextually circumscribed. Theoretically, changing these undesirable behaviors will require either changing the behavioral norms in the community, changing the degree to which these youth adopt those behavioral norms, or removing these adolescent delinquents from the community.

Empirical evidence that either of these approaches work is still lacking, perhaps because some are politically controversial or practically unfeasible or because a very complex set of issues have been oversimplified. Making the types of superficial changes in the settings which are often attempted (e.g. employing a few inner–city youth during the summer) may actually create more problems than they solve because they

Physical and Mental Health

fail to address the core problems associated with chronic unemployment and underemployment in the community, but they create the expectation of change. Removal of the offending youth via incarceration or hospitalization rarely benefits the individual delinquent because the settings in which they are confined actually exacerbate their delinquency. More importantly, the situations from which they have been removed remain unchanged, and therefore, continue to produce more frustrated, delinquent youth. For a more detailed analysis of these issues please see the paper by Hawkins & Jones in this volume.

Suicide and Related Self-Destructive Behaviors

Violence directed against the self as a response to overwhelming feelings of hopelessness and helplessness is another significant indicator of the mental health status of a population. Accurate data on adolescent suicide are spotty, but recent attention to childhood suicide may indicate increasing rates. The groups at greatest suicide risk have consistently been identified as White males between the ages of 25–34, those over 65 and those between 15–24 years. Recent data from CDC (MMWR, 1985) indicate the age-adjusted suicide rate for Whites in 1980 (12.1) was almost twice that for Blacks and other races (6.7). Of all suicides committed in that year, 70% were committed by White males, 22% by White females, 6% by Black and other males, and 2% by Black and other females. In addition, the decade of 1970–1980 was marked by a dramatic 50% increase in suicides among persons 15–24 years, most of which was due to increases in the rates for White males.

While these data are encouraging with respect to the mental health of Black youth, we perceive a less encouraging picture when we consider suicide in terms of the number of "years of potential life lost before age 65" (YPLL). The crude YPLL attributable to suicide increased for both Black and White males between 1968 to 1983. For White males, the YPLL rate increased 52.7%, while for Black males it increased 65.5%. For both Black and White females, suicide attributable YPLL did not change appreciably during this time. Thus, while the total numbers and rate/100,000 pop. of suicides among males 15–24 years is primarily accounted for by White males, Black male suicide is accounting for more years of life lost at a faster rate than for Whites.

Significant information can also be obtained from an analysis of suicide among Blacks. According to Seiden (1972), Blacks between the ages of 15–24 commit suicide at a rate higher than that of the total Black population of all ages. This is especially true for young Black females. Mars (1969) notes that the suicide rate among U.S. Black women is the 14th highest in the world and it had risen 80% in the two decades prior to his report. Allen (1973) reports that in California, the rate of Black female sui-

Table 5a
Age-adjusted suicide rates,* by race, sex, and year United States, 1970-1980

Year	White Male	White Female	White Total	Black and other Male	Black and other Female	Black and other Total	All races Male	All races Female	All races Total	Unadjusted Rate
1970	18.2	7.2	12.4	10.3	3.3	6.5	17.3	6.8	11.8	11.6
1971	18.0	7.4	12.4	10.1	3.8	6.7	17.2	7.0	11.8	11.6
1972	18.4	7.3	12.6	11.8	3.6	7.4	17.8	6.9	12.1	11.9
1973	18.6	7.0	12.5	11.5	3.3	7.1	17.8	6.6	11.9	11.9
1974	18.9	7.0	12.7	11.6	3.2	7.1	18.1	6.6	12.1	12.0
1975	19.6	7.3	13.2	11.9	3.5	7.4	18.8	6.8	12.5	12.6
1976	19.0	7.0	12.7	12.1	3.4	7.4	18.3	6.6	12.1	12.3
1977	20.3	7.1	13.5	12.2	3.6	7.6	19.4	6.7	12.8	13.8
1978	19.0	6.6	12.5	11.9	3.2	7.2	18.2	6.1	11.9	12.3
1979	18.6	6.3	12.1	12.7	3.3	7.7	17.9	5.9	11.7	12.1
1980	18.9	5.7	12.1	11.3	2.8	6.7	18.0	5.4	11.4	11.9

* Age-adjusted rates per 100,000 population computed by the direct method of standardization using the total population for 1940 as the standard population

Source: Suicide, U.S., 1970-1980. *Morbidity & Mortality Weekly Report*, June 21, 1985, Vol. 34, No. 24, p. 353.

Table 5b
Suicides among 15 to 19 Year Olds, by Sex and Race, 1973 and 1980 (deaths per 100,000 population)

Sex and Year	Black	White	Total
Male			
1980	5.6	15.0	13.8
1973	5.7	11.4	10.7
Female			
1980	1.6	3.3	3.0
1973	2.1	3.2	3.1
Total			
1980	3.6	9.2	8.5
1973	3.9	7.4	7.0

Source: U.S. Department of Health and Human Services, National Center for Health Statistics, unpublished data. Calculations by Children's Defense Fund.

Table 6

Years of potential life lost before age 65 years (YPLL) due to intentional injuries, by sex and race—United States, 1983

		Suicide YPLL			Homicide YPLL	
Sex and race	Total	(%)	Rate*	Total	(%)	Rate*
Males						
White	445,890	(70.6)	458.1	245,139	40.2	251.9
Black	37,524	5.9	282.6	212,985	(35.0)	1,603.9
Other	11,485	(1.8)	368.7	10,408	(1.7	334.1
All	494,899	(78.3)	435.2	468,532	(76.9)	412.0
Females						
White	124,475	(19.7)	121.7	81,193	(13.3)	79.4
Black	9,085	(1.4)	61.4	55,186	(9.1)	373.1
Other	3,531	0.6	108.9	4,333	(0.7)	133.6
All	137,091	(21.7)	114.0	140,712	(23.1)	117.0
Total	631,990	(100.0)	270.1	609,244	(100.0)	260.3

* Per 100,000 persons

cides during 1970 was 30.1/100,000 pop. as compared with 13.6/100,000 pop. for White females ages 20–24. These data are consistent with the conclusion noted by Kiev & Anumonye (1976) that suicide is the most common cause of death among young Black women, at least in the mid 70s.

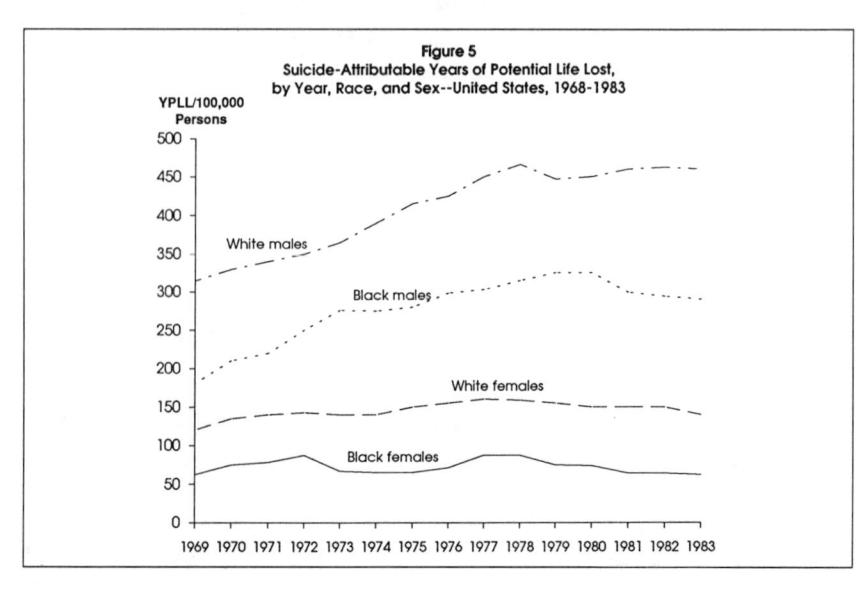

Figure 5
Suicide-Attributable Years of Potential Life Lost, by Year, Race, and Sex--United States, 1968-1983

There are some problems with these data, however, because we are not sure what lethal actions are subsumable under this heading for adolescents. Our traditional concepts of suicide which include self–inflicted gun shot wounds, poisoning, hanging, jumping from buildings, slashing wrists, which are the most common methods used may need to be modified to include some cases of drug overdose, victim–precipitated homicide, drunken driving and driving under the influence of drugs, and other high risk habits. When deaths from all of these causes are considered, suicide appears to be increasing among Black youth, especially among young male substance abusers.

Substance Use and Abuse

The problem of substance use and abuse has reached epidemic proportions in American society. According to annual estimates of substance use in the U.S., 30% of all Americans smoke cigarettes, and 20% of adolescents smoke (USPHS, 1980; Johnson et al., 1984); 60% consume alcohol, and a comparable percentage of American youth drink (NIAAA, 1983; Johnson et al., 1984); and, between 25% and 30% of all Americans are occasional users of marijuana, cocaine and nonprescription stimulants or sedatives, with slightly larger numbers of youth using marijuana, stimulants and inhalants (NIDA, 1979a, b).

These general population trends appear to be somewhat more striking among inner–city Black youth among whom substance use may well have reached epidemic proportions. While the evidence is not conclusive that significantly more Black youth than Whites are using chemical substances, there is evidence suggesting that the pattern of use, the types of substances used, and the prevalence of chronic substance abuse may be different (Brunswick, 1979, 1980; Gibbs, 1984; Maddahian et al., 1985). Data cited in the CDF report (1985) on the percentage of youth using drugs in 1982 indicate that contrary to popular belief, Black youth are less likely to report using drugs than White youth. The report also indicates that marijuana is the most popular drug of abuse among youth, with younger adolescents reporting lower use than young adults. The report also notes that White youth and young adults are twice as likely to abuse psychotropic medications than Black youth and young adults. Unfortunately, this report did not provide any data on drugs such as cocaine, PCP, heroin, or even alcohol, all of which previous studies have suggested are somewhat more likely to be used by inner–city Black youth. In fact, reports in both the popular and scientific literatures indicate that substances such as PCP and rock cocaine have reached epidemic proportions in inner–city communities, and have become integral to the underground economy of those communities. This means that inner–city Black children and youth are probably exposed to these substances and to the associated

Physical and Mental Health

Table 7
Percentage of Youths Who Have Used Drugs of Abuse, by Drug, Age, and Race, 1982

Drug and Age	Black	White	Total
Marijuana			
12–17	23%	27%	27%
18–25	61	65	64
Cocaine			
12–17	n.a.	n.a.	n.a.
18–25	18	30	28
Non-medical use of prescription-type psychotherapeutic drugs*			
12–17	5	11	10
18–25	14	31	28

Source: U.S. Department of Health and Human Services, Alcohol, Drug Abuse, and Mental Health Adinistration, *National Survey on Drug Abuse; Main Findings 1982* (Washington, D.C., 1983), tables 21, 11, 23, 39 and 40.

*Stimulants, sedatives, tranquilizers, and analgesics.

Source: *Black & White Children in America: Key Factors.* Children's Defense Fund Washington, D.C., 1985, page 84.

lifestyle at an earlier age and to a greater extent than their White cohorts. This observational and anecdotal evidence do not constitute prima facie evidence of greater drug use among Black youth, but they cast considerable doubt on any report which suggests that these youth are using significantly less drugs than White youth, or that Black youth are at lower risk of becoming involved in drug use.

We have thus far focused our attention on some of the major "hard signs" of psychosocial disability, but these data do not exhaust the picture of the problems of living faced by the significant plurality of Black children and youth of the underclass. The "softer" socio–demographic signs are even more alarming because they portend dramatic increases in mental health problems for the next several generation of Black youth. The latest statistics compiled in the Childrens Defense Fund report (1985) and in the Urban League's State of Black America report (1985) are quite alarming. Both reports note that despite periods of increased allocations for urban education, health, social welfare, and mental health in the 1970s, increasing numbers of Black children and youth are worst off today than their older siblings were just a decade ago. More Black children are doing poorly in school; more are dropping out of school; while fewer are getting pregnant, those that get pregnant are less likely to marry, are more likely not to finish school, and are more likely to become heads of poverty–stricken, multi–problem families; many are being diagnosed (and perhaps midsdiagnosed) as emotionally disturbed or mentally retarded; and a significantly greater number of them are becoming involved in gangs, violence and substance abuse.

Taken as a whole, these data underscore a negative social and mental health trajectory for Black children and youth in America. This does not apply to all Black children and youth in America, because despite some important reversals in the gains afforded by the civil rights movement, the stable Black working and middle classes are continuing to make small and steady progress. In fact, current evidence seems to suggest the development of two separate Black societies, one that is beginning to show some gains from increased opportunities in higher education, business and the professions, and a larger, growing majority of Blacks who are getting poorer and more socially marginal with each generation. It is to this segment of Black youth, the urban underclass that we must continue to direct our attention, concern, resources and energies.

Theoretical Framework for an Alternative Formulation

The Environment of the Black Adolescent of the Underclass

It is axiomatic that all youth live and interact within a social context. If we are to develop critical analyses of the mental health condition of Black youth, we must begin with an analysis of the nature and quality of interactions between these youth and their social environment. Human development is dependent upon this reciprocal interaction. The average inner–city Black adolescent develops in a social context (i.e. familial, community, fluctuations in the economy, political climate, etc.) which is characterized by substandard housing, chronic unemployment and underemployment, and higher risk for a variety of physical illnesses and disabilities, injuries, socio– emotional maladjustments, and death than most other American youth. From all objective indications, Black youth face both normal and extraordinary developmental tasks, with much of the latter determined by the severely disadvantaged and oppressed social contexts in which most live.

This social context must serve as the basis and point of departure for a truly scientific explanation of the mental health of Black urban youth. Understanding the conditions of the community implicitly raises questions of how and why these conditions prevail.

There can be no question that Black children and youth are being devastated. One of the major issues raised by King (1980) concerns a deep structure coterminous with the capitalistic social order that maintains these social conditions. That is, a history of economic and social exploitation that is designed to benefit a few and which result in the data previously described. The adolescent who is part of these conditions interacts with, changes, and is changed by these conditions. The influence of this larger social context we label a social stress condition, which is mediated internally by the Black adolescent in an interaction that results in coping strategies that contribute to determining what mental health state will be achieved by these youth. We argue that our understanding of the mental health and social status realities of urban Black youth can be enhanced by an analysis of the significance of stress in mental health and the nature of the relationship between social stresses and the coping efforts used by Black adolescents.

An Urban Stress and Mental Health Model

The model we propose for understanding the relationship between stress factors and their influence on the development of Black youth is an urban stress model (Myers, 1982). The model draws upon the theory and research on social stress and its effects. The emphasis is on the dialectic between the appraisal and adaptive process within the person, and the transactional processes between the person and the social context to predict mental health outcomes (Lazarus & Launier, 1978).

The basic paradigm of the proposed model consists of an elaboration of Selye's (1950, 1976) and Lazarus' (1967, 1974) stress–adaptation models which propose adaptation as a precursor to disease and system malfunctions. The basic paradigm contains six components: (1) exogenic and endogenic antecedents which define the basal operating state of the person or group, which is determined by their biological and experiential histories, and by the sociopolitical context in which they have developed and continue to function (i.e. basal stress load); 2) the internal and external mediators, which are the individual attributes of the person and the attributes of the social network that can increase or decrease the experience and relative impact of social stressors; (3) the social stressors, which are the objective social events and factors that require some adaptation or adjustment in the usual level and pattern of functioning; (4) the stress state, which is the generalized reaction to tension created by the disruption of the pattern of usual function which may vary from a state of mild discomfort to a state of significant distress, dysfunction and disease; (5) the coping and adaptation process, which is the complex physiological, cognitive–affective and behavioral response process of coping with the stressors, and finally, (6) the health and mental health outcomes resultant from the stress–coping process. This model is diagrammed in Figure 6.

Several empirically validated assumptions are made in this model. First, we assume that the greater the amount, intensity, duration and meaningfulness of the stress experienced, the greater the likelihood of illness and the greater the severity of the resultant disorder (Lazarus & Folkman, 1982). Second, we also assume that the amount of stress experienced and the severity of the impact of stress are related to factors of social class and race (Dohrenwend & Dohrenwend, 1970; Myers, 1982). Third, that the impact and meaning of any stressor or class of stressor is influenced by internal and external mediating factors that are at least in part related to the person's social class, ethnic background and gender (Kessler, 1979; Kessler & Cleary, 1980; Neighbors et al, 1983). Fourth, we assume that the person's or group's state of relative health can be meaningfully predicted from their race x social class stress dynamics (Myers, 1976, 1982).

The Antecedent Stress State or Stress Load. Dohrenwend & Dohrenwend (1970) and Myers (1976) argued that the negative interaction of two factors, race and social class, serves to create a cross–generational pattern of stress induction and stress accumulation in the urban Black poor. This pattern is created by the cumulative effect of greater exigencies of daily living and greater risks of facing troubles that place increasing demands on already taxed resources (Brenner, 1973). It is on this basis that we assert that the Black urban poor can be reasonably characterized as likely to be functioning under a higher stress load than the norm. This means that they may well be psychologically and perhaps even physiologically primed to perceive and react to stimuli as more stressful than nonBlacks and the more affluent (i.e. stress–primed). Socioecological evidence of increased risk for hypertension in this group lends some credence to this contention (Harburg et al., 1978). Evidence of differences in the perception of life stresses between Blacks and Whites has also been provided by several studies (Askenasy et al., 1977; Wyatt, 1978).

Further, we also suggest that children in poverty environments begin to develop, even in utero, in insidiously stressful environments which increase significantly their risks for a variety of disorders. The available evidence of significant race x SES trends in prematurity, infant mortality, and birth defects may be the outcomes of a state of greater stress vulnerability and sensitivity in Black parents (CDF report, 1985). The report of higher mean neonatal heart rates in low SES Black infants compared to Whites provides additional partial support for this hypothesis (Schacter et al., 1974). Thus, we suggest that a critical antecedent in the stress dynamics of Black low income youth is the higher basal stress level at which many must function even before birth.

Mediating Factors. In addition to the fact of being exposed to insidiously stressful environments, we also recognize that there are important internal and external factors that influence the degree to which specific stressors or stress conditions will impact on each Black child or adolescent. These factors mediate (i.e. increase or decrease) the effects stressors have and help to account for individual differences in vulnerability to stress and risk for disease, disability and disfunction.

External mediating factors would include a host of historical experiences and exigencies associated with low income and ethnic status. Included among these are the many negative attributes of the inner–city, poverty ecology, all of which serve to exacerbate the impact of other social stressors. Myers (1976) and Cheek (1976) also identify the important role that institutionalized racism plays by manipulating the response options and rewards obtainable by Blacks. Behaviors often rewarded and held in high esteem for some (e.g. assertiveness) are either severely punished or inconsistently rewarded in Blacks (e.g. assertiveness by Black males). A recent study by Dressler (1985) found that while an active coping style buffered the effects of stressors for Black women, such an active style exacerbated the effects of stressors for Black men. These factors also operate by changing the assumptions and expectations faced by Blacks and Whites. While Whites are assumed and expected to be competent, Blacks are often expected to be incompetent, and to be passive and compliant when those expectations are imposed on them. Thus, many behaviors that are socially devalued are considered normative for Blacks. Unfortunately, many Black youth adopt those behaviors and lifestyles without fully understanding how they are participating in their own oppression.

On the positive side, many of the attributes considered typical of Black communities and social networks such as the extended family networks, the activist church, etc. have historically served as sources of support to mediate stressors and to provide a foundation for survival and social mobility (McAdoo, 1978). Many have argued that much of the frustration, resentment and feelings of impotence and worthlessness observed in many Black children and youth can be attributed to conflict between their natural strivings for competency and control and the myriad of ego–deflating experiences which they confront. The social networks and resources of the traditional Black family and community evolved in an effort to mediate this conflict and to bolster the self–esteem and sense of personal control of these young people. As these support networks are undermined by dissention, substance abuse and individualism, they become less effective in fulfilling their buffering function.

People as acting and transacting beings are continuously assessing themselves and the social context, and then elaborating transactional strategies to maximize personal odds. Urban Black children and youth appear to be operating in a social order in which the rules appear to be stacked against them. The degree to which they perceive the odds against them as manageable or overwhelming will depend on their transactional competency, the coping competency and success of their parents and other adult models, and on the availability of effective resources and supports. It is not surprising that the "streets" and the "playgrounds" have always had a strong appeal for Black youth. Money and reputations can be made by those with the skills and courage to do so. Success is not determined by the usual sources of power in society, but by the rules and methods of the Black underclass.

A host of internal mediating factors also play important roles in the relative success or failure of efforts to cope with social stress. Central among these are such factors as individual temperaments (e.g. the tendency to remain calm under pressure), one's repertoire of coping behaviors and skills (Watts, 1974; Sewell & Severson, 1975); past successful coping experiences (Lazarus, 1967; Antonovsky, 1979); accuracy and sophistication of assessment and problem–solving skills (e.g. the ability to read situations, to think through problems), and finally, stable ethnic identity, self- and group–perception of efficacy in manipulating and controlling environments and one's self (Antonovsky, 1979; Akbar, 1974; Epstein & Komorita 1970; Gurin et al., 1969; Nobles & Goddard, 1977; Guttentag & Klein, 1976; McAdoo, 1973, 1976). This last factor, personal effectance, subsumes under it the attributes of self–and group– esteem and locus of control.

On the basis of this formulation, urban Black youth can be said to be highly stress vulnerable because of mediating external stress–inducing factors, but also because of the existence of internal factors that may reduce their stress coping effectiveness. The latter are part of the legacy of oppression and racism, and they are still being reinforced by the social processes that condemn many Black youth to a condition of social marginality (e.g. class oppression, the remediation mentality in education, the graduation of functional illiterates, the proliferation of drugs and other substances, the increasing tendency to use violence in the solution of interpersonal conflict, etc).

Social Stressors. Much of the research on psychosocial stress effects on health emphasizes the importance of episodic, life crises that disrupt daily functioning (e.g. death of a relative, economic reversal, etc,.) (Holmes & Masuda, 1974; Dohrenwend & Dohrenwend, 1974). The literature consistently reports that individuals from low income backgrounds not only experience more major stresses in their lives, but also that these events are more disruptive for them than for their more affluent counterparts (Eaton et al., 1978; Liem & Liem, 1978; Kessler & Cleary, 1980).

This emphasis on major stressful experiences is, however, only one small part of the stress picture. For the poor, and particularly urban Black children and youth, the fact of greatest significance is the insidiousness and pervasiveness of stress in their everyday lives (Ilfeld, 1978; Myers,

1982; Belle, 1982). It is this insidious pattern of stress that contributes to the reported high incidence of mental health casualties among the lower social classes (Brown & Harris, 1978).

The Coping and Adaptation Process. Selye (1977), Lazarus (1977) and Folkman, et al. (1986) have consistently affirmed that health outcomes are more the products of efforts to cope with stress than the direct results of the stressors themselves. This suggests, therefore, that a useful approach to the analysis of the mental health needs and problems of Black children and youth should include an analysis of their stress–coping processes. Unfortunately, very little systematic work has been done in this area. We do not know, for example, what coping strategies are used by urban Black youth to adapt to the myriad of stresses they must face daily. Inferences from the outcomes of those coping efforts suggest that most are not very effective. We do have some information on the adjustment strategies that Black college students and young adults use in coping with the demands of predominantly White universities, and these different coping patterns have been associated with different possible outcomes (Gibbs, 1974; Harrell, 1979).

It is important in our thinking not to fall prey to the practice of blaming the victim, but to go beyond that and include an assessment of the constraints and opportunities for coping. We know that how one copes with stress is influenced by the nature of the stresses, by prior experiences with similar stresses, and by the availability of adequate coping resources. When we analyze the reality of urban Black youth several relevant factors are apparent. First, they grow up in an insidiously stressful environment. Second, they must develop a repertoire of coping behaviors for a variety of stressors but in a context of severely restricted resources for coping, and they face various social barriers of access to additional coping resources. Third, they have access to fewer models of competent coping, and many of those have distanced themselves from the daily hassles of living in inner–city communities. Thus, the coping task facing these youth is not simply to develop effective means of coping with overwhelming odds, but also to develop a "social stance" capable of both overcoming the odds and transforming the extant social processes. To evolve only an adaptational strategy permits only survival, and the evidence clearly suggests that this survival is rather tenuous and it is occurring at great personal and collective costs. What appears to be necessary for urban Black youth is the elaboration of stress–innoculating, mastery–oriented coping strategies than can radically transform the essentially negative personal–social transactions in which many are currently trapped.

The urban stress model suggests a way to begin to account for the differential prevalence of psychiatric and social disability among the youth of the Black underclass. Primary emphasis in the analysis is placed on the interaction between the child or youth and the environment. The degree to which the individual is affected by the stresses endemic to the environment is a function of an interaction mediated by his or her personal and collective assets and coping styles. External sociopolitical factors operate to either enhance or to impede coping by determining the level of stress exposure, the options for coping available, and the impact those stresses can have on these youth.

A stress model of this type stops short of articulating precisely how the external context influences degree of vulnerability to psychiatric disorders. Rather, it promotes a framework for analysis that underscores the connectedness between contextual predisposing and mediating factors and internal adaptational strategies that evolve over time. Psychological and social disorders in these groups can be viewed as "predictable" by-products of the oppressive psychosocial conditions extant at any point in the history of the group.

Conclusions

This conceptual model argues for a shift in the thrust of mental health thinking, research and interventions with urban Black youth. The questions asked, the assumptions made, the conceptualization of the relationships between the major variables of interest, and the research and intervention models require reconsideration. New research efforts need to be mounted based on questions about the coping styles, the pressures and demands faced, the pattern of life span development and the crises and conflicts faced by these youth. Research is also needed to define what it takes to succeed under these conditions of insidious stress, and to define what are the specific stressors created by the social structure and their specific mechanism of effects. We should be able to use models such as King's (1980) to develop a multidimensional taxonomy of stress conditions that is meaningful to Black children and youth.

Specific studies are also needed to identify mental health outcomes as products of social processes impacting on a community or group over time. An example of such an effort is the research by Brenner (1973) which looked at the relationship between economic downturns, social class, ethnicity, and psychiatric hospitalization rates. This study defined the context of economic reality and traced its effects historically on the mental health of different groups. This study stopped short, however, of assessing the true prevalence of psychiatric disorders in the target populations, nor did it address the process of demands and coping efforts made in response to the economic downturns which were pathogenic.

Research is also needed that is multidisciplinary and multifactorial in focus. Such studies would approach specific problems from various disciplinary perspectives simultaneously. For example, studies of Black youth violence might investigate the interplay of economic forces, family and community climate, the degree of involvement of youth in the local underground economy, the attitudes and practices of the police and the judicial system and any changes in those, and the availability and utility of mental health resources to meet the needs of the community.

Similarly, mental health training and services will eventually have to be reconceptualized and made consistent with any new knowledge obtained. The training of mental health caregivers will soon have to reflect perspectives and competencies that go beyond the assessment and treatment of disorders in individuals to include the effective assessment of and intervention in environments and social systems. This will require a revision of our current diagnostic practices and nomenclature to reflect the basic premise that individual disorders result from disordered transactions between persons and environments (Barker, 1964, 1973; Rappaport, 1977).

Mental health services will also need to be reconceptualized away from the individual disease models to more social action, preventive models. The primary thrust should be to alleviate and prevent individual pain and disorder by assessing and removing the social sources of distress. The mental health needs of urban Black children and youth are intimately tied to basic societal structures and processes. Efforts to address and to correct the problems of these youth require direct confrontation with the policies and practices in society that create and maintain our existing social order. Treating the individual casualty is folly if we ignore the policy decisions that result in high unemployment, inadequate education, poor nutrition, and the poor quality of life that has become synonymous with urban ghetto living. A radical change in the current mental health status of urban Black children and youth will require radical changes in our economic policies, in our social policies, and in our health, education and welfare policies.

In closing, it is instructive that we be reminded of the sage observations of Aimee Cesaire, who stated that...

> A (nation) that proves incapable of solving the problems it creates is a decadent (nation). A (nation) that chooses to close its eyes to its most crucial problems is a stricken (nation). A (nation) that uses its principles for trickery and deceit is a dying (nation).
>
> Aimee Cesaire, Discourse on Colonialism, 1972

The plight of the mental health of Black youth of the underclass demand that we turn over a new leaf and set afoot new conceptual and intervention models that are up to the challenge posed by the data we have reviewed here. The survival of this country depends on it, for we are only as strong as the weakest and most oppressed among us.

References

Akbar, N. L. (1974). Awareness: The key to Black mental health. *Journal of Black Psychology, 1*, 30–37.

Allen, N. H. (1973). *Suicide in California 1960–1970*. Monograph. Sacramento: State of California, Department of Public Health.

Antonovsky, A. (1979). *Health, stress and coping*. San Francisco: Jossey-Bass.

Askenasy, A. R., Dohrenwend, B. P., & Dohrenwend, B. S. (1977). Some effects of social and ethnic group membership on judgements of the magnitude of stressful life events: A research note. *Journal of Health & Social Behavior, 18*, 432–439.

Baker, E. G., & Schoggen, P. (1973). *Qualities of community life*. San Francisco: Jossey-Bass.

Banks, C. W. (1982). Deconstructive falsification: Foundations of critical method in Black psychology. In E. E. Jones & S. J. Korchin (Eds.), *Minority mental health*. NY: Praeger Press, 59–73.

Barker, R. G. (1964). *Ecological psychology: Concepts and methods for studying the environment of human behavior*. Stanford, CA: Stanford University.

Belle, D. (Ed.). *Lives in stress: Women and depression*. Beverly Hills, CA: Sage Publications.

Brenner, H. (1973). *Mental illness and the economy*. Cambridge, MA: Harvard University.

Brown, G. & Harris, T. (1978). *Social origins of depression: A study of psychiatric disorder in women*. NY: Free Press.

Brunswick, A. F. (1980). Social meanings and developmental needs: Perspectives on Black youths drug use. *Youth & Society, 11(4)*, 449–473.

Brunswick, A. F. (1979). Black youths and drug–use behavior. In G. Beschner & A. Friedman (Eds.), *Youth & drug abuse: Problems, issues and treatment*. Lexington, MA: Lexington Brooks.

Cesaire, A. (1972). *Discourse on colonialism*. New York: Monthly Review Press.

Cheek, D. K. (1976). *Assertive Black, puzzled White: A Black perspective on assertive behavior*. San Luis Obispo, CA: Impact Publishers.

Copeland, A. R. (1984). *Homicide during teenage years—The ten year Metropolitan Dade County experience from 1973–1982*.

Dohrenwend, B. S., & Dohrenwend, B. P. (1970). Class and race as status-related sources of stress. In S. Levine & N. A. Scotch (Eds.). *Social stress* (pp. 111–140). Chicago: Aldine.

Dohrenwend, B. P., & Dohrenwend, B. S. (1974). *Stressful life events: Their nature and effects*. NY: John Wiley & Sons.

Dressler, W. W. (1985). The social and cultural context of coping: Action, gender and symptoms in a southern Black community. *Social Science & Medicine, 21(5)*, 499–506.

Eaton, W. W., Holzer, C. E., Von Korff, M. et al. (1984). The design of the epidemiologic catchment area surveys. *Archives of General Psychiatry, 41*, 942–948.

Epstein, R., & Komorita, S. (1970). Self-esteem, success, failure, and locus of control in Negro children. *Developmental Psychology (Part I), 1(4)*, 2–8.

Folkman, S., Lazarus, R. S., Gruen, R. J., & DeLongis, A. (1986). Appraisal, coping, health status, and psychological symptoms. *Journal of Personality & Social Psychology, 50*, 571–579.

Franklin, A. J. (1982). Therapeutic interventions with urban Black adolescents. In E. E. Jones & S. J. Korchin (Eds.), *Minority mental health*. NY: Praeger Press, 267–195.

Gibbs, J. T. (1974). Patterns of adaptation among Black students at a predominantly White university: Selected case studies. *American Journal of Orthopsychiatry, 44*, 728–740.

Gibbs, J. T. (1984). Black adolescents and youth: An endangered species. *American Journal of Orthopsychiatry, 6*(1), 6–21.

Gurin, P., Gurin, G., Lao, R. C., & Beattie, M. (1969). Internal- external control in the motivational dynamics of Negro youth, *Journal of Social Issues, 24*(3), 29–53.

Guttentag, M., & Klein, I. (1976). The relationships between inner vs. outer locus of control and achievement in Black middle–school children. *Educational and Psychological Measurement, 36*(4), 1101–1109.

Harrell, J. P. (1979). Analyzing Black coping styles: A supplemental diagnostic system. *Journal of Black Psychology, 5*, 99–108.

Holmes, T., & Masuda, M. (1974). Life change and illness susceptibility. In B. P. Dohrenwend & B. S. Dohrenwend (Eds.), *Stressful life events: Their nature and effect*. NY: J. Wiley & Sons.

Ilfeld, F. W. (1978). Psychological status of community residents along major demographic dimensions. *Archives of General Psychiatry, 35*, 716–724.

Jackson, J. (March, 1980). Summary and description of the national survey of Black Americans. Technical Report, Institute for Social Research, University of Michigan.

Johnson, L. D., O'Malley, P. M. & Bachman, J. G. (1984). *Highlights from drugs and American high school students, 1975–1983*. Washington, D.C.: U.S. Government Printing Office.

Jones, E. E., & Korchin, S. J. (1981). Minority mental health: Perspectives. In E. E. Jones & S. J. Korchin (Eds.), *Minority mental health*. NY: Praeger Press. 3–36.

Kessler, R. C. (1979). Stress, social status and psychological distress. *Journal of Health & Social Behavior, 20*, 259–272.

Kessler, R. C., & Cleary, P. D. (1980). Social class and psychological distress. *American Sociological Review, 45*, 463–478.

Kiev, A., & Anumonye, A. (1976). Suicidal behavior in a Black ghetto, a comparative study. *International Journal of Mental Health, 5*(2), 50–59.

King, L. M. (1978). Social and cultural influences on psychopathology. *Annual Review of Psychology, 29*, 405–433.

King, L. M. (1980). Models of meanings in mental health: Model eight—the transformation of the oppressed. *Perspectives on Individual and Social Transformation, 1*(1).

Lazarus, R. S. (1967). Cognitive and personality factors underlying threat and coping. In M. H. Appley & R. Trumbull (Eds.), *Psychological stress: issues and research*. NY: Appleton–Century–Crofts, 151–181.

Lazarus, R. S. (1974, 1977). Psychological stress and coping in adaptation and illness. *International Journal of Psychiatry in Medicine, 5*(4), 321–333. In Z. J. Lipowski, D. R. Lipsitt, & P. C. Whybrow (Eds.), *Psychosomatic medicine: Current trends and clinical applications* (pp. 14–26). New York: Oxford University Press.

Lazarus, R. S., & Folkman, S. (1982). Coping and adaptation. In W. D. Gentry (Ed.), *The handbook of behavioral medicine*. NY: Guilford Press, 282–325.

Lazarus, R. S., & Launier, R. (1978). Stress-related transactions between person and environment. In L. A. Pervin & M. Lewis (Eds.), *Perspectives in international psychology*. NY: Plenum Press, 287–327.

Liem, R., & Liem, J. (1978). Social Class and mental illness reconsidered: The role of economic stress and social support. *Journal of Health & social behavior, 19*, 239–156.

Maddahian, E., Newcomb, M. D., & Bentler, P. M. (1985). Single and multiple patterns of adolescent substance use: Longitudinal comparisons of four ethnic groups. *Journal of Drug Education, 15*, 311–327.

McAdoo, H. P. (1973). *An assessment of racial attitudes and self-concepts in urban Black children*. Final Report, Washington, D.C.: Children's Bureau (DHEW).

McAdoo, H. P. (1976, March 25). A re-examination of the relationships between self-concept and race attitudes of young Black children. Paper presented at the Demythologizing of the Inner City Black Child Conference, Atlanta, GA.

Milazzo-Sayre, L., Benson, P. R., Rosenstein, M. J., & Manderscheid, R. W. (April, 1986). *Use of inpatient psychiatric services by children and youth under age 18, United States, 1980. Mental Health Statistical Note, No. 175.*, Washington, D.C.: U.S. DHHS Publishing.

Morbidity and Mortality Weekly Report (1985). Homicide among young Black males—U.S., 1970–1982. *Morbidity and Mortality Weekly Report, 34(41)*.

Morbidity and Mortality Weekly Report (1986). Homicide—Los Angeles, 1970–1979. *Morbidity and Mortality Weekly Report, 35(5)*.

Myers, H. F. (1976). Holistic definition and measurement of states of non-health. In L. M. King, V. Dixon, & W. Nobles (Eds.), *African philosophy: Assumptions and paradigms of research on Black persons* (pp. 139–153). Los Angeles: Fanon Center.

Myers, H. F. (1982). Stress, ethnicity and social class: A model for research with Black populations. In E. E. Jones & S. J. Korchin (Eds.), *Minority mental health*. NY: Praeger Press, 118–148.

Myers, H. F., & King, L. M. (1980). Youth of the Black underclass: Urban stress and mental health. Notes for an alternative formulation. *Fanon Center Journal, 1(1)*, 1–27.

National Institute of Mental Health (1977). *Psychiatric services and the changing institutional scene, 1950–1985*. DHEW Publication No. (ADM) 717–433, Series B., 12, 17.

National Urban League (1986). *The State of Black America*. National Urban League Report, New York.

Neighbors, H. W., Jackson, J. S., Bowman, P., & Gurin, G. (1983). Stress, coping and Black mental health: Preliminary findings from a national study. *Prevention in Human Services, 2*, 5–28.

NIAAA (1982). Physiological effects of alcohol. *Alcohol topics in brief*. Rockville, MD.

NIDA (1979a). *National survey on drug abuse*. Washington, D.C.: U.S. Government Printing Office.

NIDA (1979b). Drug abuse prevention for your community. *Washington, D.C.: U.S. Government Printing Office*.

Nobles, W. W., & Goddard, L. (1977). Consciousness, adaptability and coping strategies: Socieconomic and ecological issues in Black families. *Western Journal of Black Studies, 1*, 105–113.

Premature mortality due to suidcide and homicide – U.S, 1983. *Mortality and Morbidity Weekly Report*, June 6, 1986, 35(22).

Rappaport, J. (1977). *Community psychology: Values, research, and action*. New York: Holt, Rinehart & Winston.

Raskin, A. & Crook, T.H. (1975). Antidepressants in Black and White patients. *Archives of General Psychiatry*, 32(5), 643–649.

Raskin, A., Crook, T., & Herman, K. (1975). Psychiatric history and symptom differences in Black and White depressed inpatients. *Journal of Consulting*, 43(1), 73–80.

Regier, D. A., Myers, J. K., & Krammer, M. et al. (1984). The NIMH epidemiologic catchment area program. *Archive of General Psychiatry*, 41, 934–941.

Robins, L. N., Helzer, J. E., & Weissman, M. M. et al. (1984). Lifetime prevalence of specific psychiatric disorders in three sites. *Archive of General Psychiatry*, 41, 949–958.

Seiden, R. H. (1972). Why are suicides of young Blacks increasing? HSMHA, *Health Reports*, 87(1), 3–8.

Selye, H. (1950). *The psychology and pathology of exposure to stress*. Montreal: Acta.

Sewell, T. W., & Severson, R. A. (1975). Intelligence achievement in first grade Black children. *Journal of Consulting and Clinical Psychology*, 43(1), 112.

Shiloh, A., & Selavan, I. C. (Eds.) (1974). *Ethnic groups in America: Their morbidity, mortality, and behavior disorders*.

Suicide – U.S., 1970–1980. *Mortality and Morbidity Weekly Report*, June 21, 1985, 32(24).

Thomas, A., & Sillen, A. (1972). *Racism & psychiatry*. NY: Brunner/Mazel, Inc.

USPHS (1980). *Smoking, tobacco & health: A fact book*. Washington, D.C.: U.S. Government Printing Office.

Watts, G. (1974). New evidence in the argument about race and intelligence: How about it, Jensen? *World Medicine*, 9(13), 77.

Weiner, I. B. (1982). Delinquent behavior. In *Child & adolescent psychopathology*. NY: J. Wiley & Sons, 329–432.

Williams, D. H. (1986). The epidemiology of mental illness in Afro–Americans. *Hospital and Community Psychiatry*, 37(1), 42–49.

Wyatt, G. E. ()1977). A comparison of the scaling of Afro– American life change events. *Journal of Human Stress*, 3, 13–18.

Part IV
Psychosocial Development and Socialization

BLACK YOUTH, ROLE MODELS AND THE SOCIAL CONSTRUCTION OF IDENTITY

Ronald L. Taylor

The past two decades have witnessed important revisions in conventional approaches to and assessments of Black psychosocial development. While earlier research and writings were characterized by an emphasis on Black psychological deficits (i.e., negative self–concept, low self–esteem, low motivation and intelligence) presumed to flow from such experiences as caste victimization, racial isolation, and negative group identifications, more recent work is marked by a decided shift away from such deficit-based formulations and toward the utilization of theoretical constructs and approaches which highlight Black psychological strengths, competencies and adaptive capacities (Taylor, 1976a; Jones, 1980; Jones & Korchin, 1982; Spencer, 1982; Spencer, Brookins, and Allen, 1985). These newer perspectives attempt to advance a more dynamic and complex view of Black psychological development than earlier conceptualizations which largely assumed an isomorphic relationship between the disadvantaged position of Afro–Americans and the character and quality of their psychosocial functioning (Cross, 1978; Jenkins, 1982; White, 1984). From the new perspective, Black children and youth are presented not as passive recipients of environmental inputs but as individuals with "dialectical capacities to alter, adjust to, or resist (however subtly) these environmental 'determinants'" (Rychlak, 1982, p. vii).

Consistent with this new orientation is the focus on identity or identity–formation in recent work on Black children and youth (Spencer, et al., 1985), a theoretical construct more inclusive of the developmental process than self–concept or self–esteem (Erikson, 1968; Goethals & Klos, 1970; Hauser, 1971). Identity–formation is a complex developmental process, involving a synthesis of multiple psychosocial and intrapsychic components. It is first and foremost a constructive process and calls attention to individual choice and decision in the elements internalized as self–referential (Furth, 1978). Among its most important components are those role models and significant others with whom the individual identifies. While the significance of such critical identifications in the psychosocial economy of children and youth has long been acknowledged in the literature on human development, the relative influence and importance of these significant referents in the psychological development of Black children and youth has received only cursory attention (Taylor, 1976a; 1976b; Oberle, Stowers, & Falk, 1978; Hare & Castenell, 1985; Rosenthal, 1971).

In an earlier study of Black youth and role model identifications, the author (Taylor, 1976a) sought to demonstrate the heuristic value in conceptualizing psychosocial identity- formation as a process in which youth, through their selection and identification with various role models, seek to "construct" or cultivate features of their personal and social identities. That study, involving thirty Black male college youth (ranging in age from 18 to 21), revealed that the role model identifications of these youths were significantly related to the quality of integration of their psychosocial organization. This paper reports the results of a more recent study, conducted in 1984–85, of role model identifications among twenty-two Black male youths (ranging in age from 17–20) from inner–city, low–income families (See methodological note for details of the study). As in the previous study, the technique of investigation involved the use of intensive interviews and autobiographical reports, organized around topics empirically shown to be relevant to psychosocial development. Such topics included the youth's early and more recent experiences in the family and community, conceptions of the future as reflected in aspirations and plans, value orientations and self–definitions. These data in turn provided the general context within which role models and their functions in the evolving identity–formations of these youths was investigated. The psychoanalytic theory of development as enunciated by Erikson (1964; 1968) and social learning theory as presented in the work of Bandura and his associates (1963; 1969; 1971), provided the general conceptual framework for these investigations.

Youth and Identity–Formation: An Overview

Psychoanalytic Perspective

Central to the psychoanalytic theory of development, as reformulated by Erikson (1950; 1964; 1968), is the concept of identity or identity–formation. For Erikson, the quintessential task of adolescence is the formation of identity, i.e., the establishment of a sense of one's uniqueness as a person. Identity denotes certain comprehensive gains derived from preadult experiences, which prepare the youth for the tasks of adulthood. It emerges as a configuration gradually established through successive synthesis and resynthesis of psychosocial components, involving the articulation of personal capacities, values, significant identifications, and fantasies with plans, ideals, expectations, and opportunities. It is the formation and integration of this configuration which Erikson views as the source of psychosocial crisis and strain during late adolescence. During this period, the youth is exposed to a "combination

Black Youth, Role Models and the Social Construction of Identity

of experiences which demand his simultaneous commitment to physical intimacy, to decisive occupational choice, to energetic competition, and to psychosocial self–definition" (Erikson, 1959, p. 123). Thus the task becomes one of consolidation and continuity, selective repudiation and mutual assimilation of childhood identifications, and their integration into a new configuration.

Although differing in the emphasis they give to intrapsychic and sociocultural factors as sources of stress and strain during this period, students of development are generally agreed that the youth stage of the life cycle is rendered ever more problematic by changes occurring at all levels of integration: social, psychological, and physiological. Having lost their former childhood status but not yet having acquired the full status of the adult, youth find themselves in a transitional period between statuses and affiliations, characterized by rootlessness and a high degree of change. The experience of status discontinuity confronts the youth with few norms and clearly defined role expectations to guide behavior, which helps to account for the primacy of the youth subculture as a source of interim status and support during this period (Coleman, 1965; Keniston, 1968). At the psychological level, late adolescence is perhaps the first time that the individual consciously attempts to conceptualize the self, to assess what one has been as a child, is now, and would like to be in the future. The necessity of status and role transition inspires a substantial reassessment of the self and a corresponding change in sense of identity. That serious attempts at conscious conceptualization do occur at late adolescence is revealed in a study of 3,500 adolescents conducted by Douvan and Adelson (1966), who concluded that: "childhood [for these youths] is felt to be pre– history, pre–identity. The autobiographical fiction, the myth of the self in time, the narrative of what we were and then became are all, in some distinctive sense, dated from adolescence. We view childhood as a preparation" (p. 3).

There is little evidence that Black adolescents are any less affected by the stress and strain of the period than are other youths. On the contrary, there is evidence that minority group status and associated disadvantages generate experiences and identity conflicts specific to Black adolescents (Hauser, 1971; Ianni, 1983; Spencer, 1985). As a consequence, Black and White youths may be observed to differ with respect to the nature and types of problems they confront and in the pattern and pace of identity–formation (Silverstein & Krate, 1975; Hunt & Hunt, 1977; Spencer, 1982).

As Keniston (1968; 1971), Erikson (1959) and others (Goethal & Klos, 1970; Konopka, 1973) have noted, *choice* and *commitment* become dominant themes in the struggle for relative identity–formation during late adolescence. Indeed, "[the] move toward commitment is so serious and so significant that providing healthy conditions to let it unfold becomes just as crucial for human development as providing healthy conditions for growth in early childhood" (Konopka, 1973, p. 302). Erikson concurs when he writes that the development of a healthy identity "depends on a certain degree of *choice*, a certain hope for our individual *chance*, a conviction in freedom of self–determination" (1959, p. 93). The need to develop a sense of identity from among all past, current, and potential relations compels the youth to make a series of increasingly more circumscribed selections of personal, vocational, and ideological commitments, which signify "the emotional, intellectual, and sometimes physical reach for other people as well as ideals, ideologies, causes, and work choices" (Konopka, 1973, p. 307). The range of possibilities are not unlimited, however, and are likely to be greatly influenced by the institutional or sociocultural contexts within which youth find themselves. Moreover, such variables as race, sex, class, and community of residence may effectively delimit the range of options available to youth, and have a decided effect on the content, duration, and stressfulness of the period (Ianni, 1983; Smith, 1976).

Faced with the prospect of choice and decision, of preparing for adult status and responsibilities, youth are likely to be shopping around for useful behavioral models, i.e., individuals who would serve as objects of experimentation and guidance into an identity not yet clearly defined. Thus the dominant mode of psychosocial functioning becomes to "lose and find themselves in others", i.e., to learn through identification how to become or achieve those identity elements most desired or, as is more often the case, learning through observation what identity features are worth cultivating. Perhaps at no other time is the tendency to rely on role models more open to observation than during late adolescence. It is seen, for example, in teenage fads, hero worship, and teen cliques (Sebald & White, 1980; Tanner, 1978). Youth desperately seek someone to have faith in, to look up to, someone to serve as a reliable and trustworthy model for experimentation and guidance into their new identities. As Erikson (1956) observes, "[to] such a person the late adolescent wants to be an apprentice or disciple, a follower...a patient" (p. 76). The phrase "in search of identity" appropriately describes the youth's experimentation with different models and value systems to find the ones of best fit. Since psychosocial identity is something to be constructed and not merely a function of social inheritance, there is the necessity of experimenting and choosing, and the possibility of making incorrect or inappropriate choices.

Social Learning Theory and Processes

As the research of Bandura and Walter (1963) and Bandura (1969; 1971) has shown, the selection and identification with role models do not occur at random but are a function of the personal and social characteristics of the identifier, and the functional utility, attributes, and resources of the model. Such model attributes as age, gender, race, and ethnic status are important determinants of role model identifications, as are the youth's own preferences and aspirations for the future. Thus, in their choice of role models, youth are likely to choose these attributes or qualities that have functional utility, i.e., qualities that fit them, become them, properties that enhance their other qualities. It may be assumed that most youths have some knowledge about those relevant aspects of role models that are likely to be instrumental in achieving their own goals. Whether such "knowledge" is accurate or valid seems irrelevant; it will, in any case, be organized in a relatively well-ordered set of preferences, and such preferences, in turn, will determine the types of models chosen for observation and emulation (Hauser, 1971; Rochberg-Halton, 1984).

Given youths' preoccupation with vocational and value related issues during this period of development, i.e., developing instrumental competence and "fidelity" to some belief or ideological system (Keniston, 1971; Adelson, 1975), the dominant theme in their choice of role models is likely to be work and value relevant. The active search for acceptable roles more or less congenial to one's talents, aspirations, and identity goals, and offering new opportunities to develop personal capacities while giving freer scope to one's established style, are likely to be seized upon by the youth—a fact undoubtedly related to the youth's selection of an occupation (Havighurst & Gottlieb, 1975). With the heightened sense of self awareness and the emergence of strong vocational interests, the tendency toward a "personalization" of values seems an almost necessary occurrence. By personalization of values is meant the tendency among youth to bring their own experiences to bear in affirming and promoting a value system (Smith, Bruner, & White, 1956; Keniston, 1968; Adelson, 1975). The trend implies the beginning of the formation of a system of values which serves as a guide to conduct and valuation appropriate to the youth's circumstances. Thus the particular values and beliefs embraced by youths are not simply carbon copies of parental values but are a function of experiential confirmation gained through observation of relevant role models and day to day encounters with the social world.

On the basis of the preceding discussion, youth may be observed to rely upon two types of role models in cultivating features of their identities, and in accomplishing the various tasks involved in its formation. Such models may be conceived as: 1) specific persons who serve as examples by means of which specific skills and behavior patterns are acquired, and; 2) a set of attributes or ideal qualities which may or may not be linked directly with any one particular person as such, in which case the model is symbolic, representing a synthesis of diffuse and discrete phenomena. In the first case, we may refer to such models as *exemplary*; in the second, as *symbolic* models. Each serves a different function and is invested with different meaning by youth engaged in the process of identity- formation.

Exemplary models may be seen as persons who provide the technical knowledge, skills, or behavioral patterns which may be utilized by the youth for developing behavioral competence; in effect, they demonstrate for the youth how something is done. Such models may be utilized by the youth when convenient without seeing in them the embodiment of all that he or she aspires to become. A variety of exemplary models may be utilized for cultivating different features of identity and may reflect more clearly the achievement strivings and identity goals of the youth. Symbolic models, on the other hand, may be conceived as representing particular values, ideals, or ideological systems. We have in mind the tendency of societies to embody their precepts, ideals, or other collective representations, in mythical, historical, and/or living figures (i.e., heroes), and the inclination of individuals to view certain figures as repositories of particular virtues, beliefs, or esteemed attributes. As persons, symbolic models have the power to move individuals psychologically, to inspire or motivate the youth toward the achievement of certain goals or the acceptance of certain values and beliefs. In short, such models are personages with whom the youth may feel a certain unity and pride (Klapp, 1971).

Since the nature and extent of a particular model's influence on the emerging psychosocial identity of youth may vary, such a possibility must be taken into account. It is possible to conceptualize the relationship between the youth and his or her models on several levels. We might distinguish between *type*, *content*, and *scope* of the relationship. *Type* refers to the quality or tone of the relationship, and may be defined as *positive*, *neutral*, or *negative*. The quality of the relationship between the subject and the model can be established largely through an analysis of the content of their relationship. By *content* is meant the nature of the model's influence as this is defined or described by the subject. Such influence may be described as having occurred on the level of overt behavior or conscious orientations, with respect to values, aspirations, beliefs or goals. In addition, the influence of the model may be seen as general or specific, in which case we refer to the *scope* of the model's influence, i.e., whether the youth is inclined toward appropriating specific behaviors or orientations of the model, or whether the desire is generally to "be like" the model in most respects. In these terms, the scope of the model's influence would indicate whether he or she functions in the capacity of exemplary or symbolic model.

Such, then, is the conceptual framework we applied in organizing and evaluating the data from our investigations of Black youth and role modeling behavior. Below we compare the findings from an earlier study of role model identifications among Black male college youth with the results of a more recent study of role model identifications among inner–city Black male youths.

Black Youths, Role Models, and the Social Construction of Identity

As we noted at the beginning of this paper, our study of Black youth was designed to discover the nature and types of role models with whom these youths had an opportunity to observe and interact with, those they appropriated for themselves and presented to others, how they conceptualized such models and their importance in life, and how the selection and characteristics of their role models changed or remained constant with growth and maturity. Comparing the results of our study of Black male college youth with the findings from our sample of inner–city youth revealed significant variations between these groups in patterns of role–model identifications and in the quality of integration of their psychosocial organization.

The College Sample

In our analysis of the data from the college sample of Black youth we found that patterns of role model identification centered primarily, though not exclusively, in the family. Parental models were observed to play a far more decisive role in the psychosocial development of these youth than other figures, functioning in both the exemplary and symbolic capacities. The influence of parents as role models was more varied than this simple dichotomy would suggest, however. While other individuals were identified by these youths as significant sources of influence on their lives, their impact on the evolving identity of these youths, on the whole, tended to be more goal–specific. Indeed, it has been noted that the influence of one parent or the other tends to exceed the influence of any one or two persons in our lives (Winch, 1962; Scanzoni, 1971; Rochberg–Halton, 1984). In childhood, the more formative and influential role is assigned to the mother whose early and frequent interactions with the child are shown to be critically important in the child's subsequent development (Knoff, 1986). A different pattern of influence, however, may emerge during later stages of development. For male adolescents, the mother may continue to serve as a source of moral and emotional support while others, including the father, may serve as models through whom they seek to cultivate other features of their personal and social identities. In fact, this was precisely the pattern which emerged from the accounts of our subjects. The model who figured most prominently in their accounts of their more recent development was clearly the father or father surrogate.

It was apparent from the various accounts of our college youth that considerable changes had occurred over the years in their relationship with their fathers, growing stronger or weaker, as the case may be, as each youth gained in the capacity and knowledge to make critical judgments of the father's personal qualities, competences, and limitations. Changes at both the conceptual and perceptual levels apparently resulted in changes in valuing and behaving toward the father as role model. In short, as these youth experienced change, both physically and psychologically, their perceptions and evaluations of their fathers also changed.

For the majority of these youths, the father's influence as a model was often a function of his ability to provide crucial resources, i.e., pertinent behavior patterns, value orientations, and the like, which the youth found through experience to be effective in coping with developmental problems. Thus the father's role as a model was often contingent upon and expressed in terms of what he did or failed to do for the youth at various critical stages in life, especially during more recent years. What emerged was a general principle of reciprocity, i.e., an exchange of resources for identification, between father and son. On the level of value orientations and behavior, some sample comments included the following:

> My father taught me never to think of myself in negative terms, to always believe I could do anything I put my mind to.

> He taught me how to take life, to handle things, and to deal with the problems Black men have to face in this society.

> By the way he was able to rise above problems and deal with them, he inspired me to adopt the same attitude toward things in life.

> The way he carried himself, his style and ways of acting in situations really inspired me to strive to be like that, to have these qualities.

In short, the more useful or valuable the sources (i.e., behavior patterns and orientations) provided by the father in the past were perceived to be, the more the youth was inclined to identity with the father as a positive role model, and to look to him for guidance in coping with current problems and concerns.

In many cases, the father served as an exemplary rather than as a symbolic model for these youths, i.e., few choose him as their identity ideal. Yet, a strong emotional attachment was shared among those youth who identified the father as their primary object of emulation, with important consequences in some cases, for their perceptions and attitudes toward other available or potential models. In some instances, early and continuing strong identification with the father involved a degree of fidelity that severely restricted, if not totally precluded, the youth's selection of others as objects of identification. At minimum, such emotional attachments created a degree of ambivalence toward other potential role models. The son's strong allegiance to the father as model was often expressed following the formula, "I can't think of anyone who is as good as my father in any respect." Such cases were not numerous, however, and were distinguished by fathers who had achieved considerable professional and/or material success.

For some college Black youth, the father emerged not as an object of positive identification, but as an object of disdain and hostility, i.e., as a negative model or prototype of identity features, the youth sought actively to avoid. The youth's perception of the father's shortcomings, his poverty of resources and power in the home, his failure to live up to professed values and beliefs, and the generally impersonal (or hostile) relationship between father and son, were among the principal factors accounting for the father's role as negative role model. Yet even in this capacity, the father tended to exert a considerable influence on the youth. The repudiation of the father as a positive role model tended to go beyond rejection of him at the level of attitudes and values, but frequently moved the youth to action in opposition to the father, involving the formation of counter behaviors and values. Thus the father's role as negative role model was often just as influential in shaping the behavior, values, and identity aspirations of the youth as was his function in a more positive capacity.

In addition to their fathers, a number of other individuals in the family, community, and the broader society, were observed to play important roles in the emergent identities of these youths. In general, the functions of such individuals fell roughly into two main categories: as work relevant and value relevant role models. Both, of course, are essential in the youth's ability to evolve an identity ideal, i.e., an interrelated set of images which have psychological meaning for him. Almost all youth had strong work models, i.e., identified closely with someone in a vocational area in which they were seriously interested, and such models were often credited with having deepened their vocational interests and commitment to career attainment in some area. Moreover, as these youth moved toward setting priorities among their interests and preferences, and sought to give a certain structure and meaning to life, their value relevant models were seen to emerge. Such value relevant models were both living and dead, and were chosen largely on the basis of their manifest courage, achievements, and convictions. In short, such models supplied the youth with values and beliefs about what is worthwhile in life, inspired hope in the future, and the youth's individual chance for success.

How various traits or characteristics of individuals were brought together to form an identity ideal which, in turn, gave both shape and direction to personal organization, was perhaps the single most important result to emerge from our analysis. In the process of evolving an identity ideal, early experiences with àdults felt to be psychologically significant helped to define the general range within which these youths could elaborate a personal ideal that had some degree of consistency. The molding of the general design and the embellishment of details of such an image is a process that goes on through time, and may be compared to the method of successive approximation for obtaining the characteristics of best fit. Failing to find a specific role model that epitomizes his identity ideal, the youth attempts to create the ideal by borrowing a single trait or several such traits from a host of available models. As one youth responded: "You take Martin Luther King's articulateness, Malcolm X's convictions and courage, and my father's physical strength and imagination, and that's what I want to be, that's my ideal."

While the value orientations, career aspirations, and self- definitions of most of our college youth were observed to crystallize around those role models or significant others with whom these youth identified, indicating progressive identity- formation during their college years, it was apparent that a number of these youths were in the midst of resolving what White (1984) has called the "inclusion–exclusion identity dilemma", characterized by "a set of dualities defined by being part of, yet apart from, American society, in it but not of it, included at some levels and excluded at others" (p. 96). As White observes, such a dilemma, complicated by the Black youth's exposure to two different value systems (i.e., Afro- American and Euro–American), tends to generate strong feelings of indignation and rage among these youths and frequently delays or interferes with the process of consolidating values, selecting appropriate role models, and defining career aspirations. Indeed, for those youth in our sample whose responses yielded evidence of such a dilemma, their role model identifications and general value orientations tended to be more tentative and less definitive than for youth who were less preoccupied with or aware of the dilemma, or who had succeeded in resolving it.

In sum, the establishment of significant role model identifications was found to be intimately related to the stage of identity development achieved, and to the quality of integration of psychosocial organization among Black college youth involved in the study. Our findings suggest that the establishment of primary or significant role model identifications is an essential aspect of the maturational and organization effort of youth implying an ordering, in terms of their relative importance for each youth, of an interrelated set of values that have psychological significance for him.

The Inner–City Youth Sample

In contrast to college youth, our sample of inner–city youth experienced more difficulty in identifying individuals they regarded as significant models in their lives, a problem reported to be common among low–income youths (Hauser, 1971; Silverstein & Krate, 1975). Nearly half (10) of these youths reported no significant role model identifications in their lives, though some expressed strong affection for various family members and friends. The reason most frequently given for the lack of

Black Youth, Role Models and the Social Construction of Identity

role models was the desire to "be myself." In their desire to be themselves, identification with and emulation of various role models were felt to be "phony", "childish", and "unrealistic". As a consequence, they expressed little interest in individuals currently accessible to them as role models, and a tenuous attachment to role models appropriated in the past. Indeed, a dominant theme in the accounts of these youth was one of mistrust of others as potential resources for knowledge, skills, and social support, an attitude that undoubtedly has its origin in their experiences in the home and community. A lack of trust and confidence in their social environment (a legacy of an often precarious existence), combined with the experience of actual or the threat of loss of support from significant others (e.g., through death, incarceration, desertion, or illness) apparently convinced not a few of these youths, that life is capricious and unpredictable, and that individuals, including significant others are often "untrustworthy" and "unreliable."

What many of these youths share in common is the experience of failure and disappointment, in themselves and in others, which has profoundly affected their sense of self–determination, confidence, and willingness to explore alternative possibilities for self–actualization. A major source of frustration for many of these youths was school. For a variety of reasons most of these youth found school an unpleasant experience, made difficult in part by their inability to perform well in scholastic work. Efforts to do well were often thwarted by the necessity to work after school because of family obligations or the need to support themselves. Moreover, parents and teachers were frequently reported to have offered little encouragement or support for their efforts. In addition, family conflict and instability, a frequent lack of family resources and privacy were reported to have contributed to frustration and difficulties in school. As a result, more than half of these youths had dropped out of school and found employment in unstable jobs.

One of the most striking results to emerge from this study was the general lack of identification by these youth with their fathers. Fewer than a third mentioned the father as a positive source of influence on their lives, while an almost equal number characterized the father's influence as largely negative, or expressed an attitude of indifference toward him. For youth whose fathers were present in the home, or who maintained frequent contact with their fathers despite his absence from the home due to marital separation or divorce, it was observed that those critical variables determinative of the son's identification with the father were essentially the same for these youths as for youth in general. That is, what fathers do or fail to do for their sons, the resources they provide in the form of information and training for coping with the problems of the social environment, for future role performance, and in emotional support and guidance, tends to precede and greatly influence identification by the son with the father (Winch, 1962; Scanzoni, 1971; Cummings, 1977). Thus those youths whose early and continuing relationship with their fathers was on the whole positive, and who credited their fathers with having provided resources which they perceive to have facilitated their psychosocial development, were more likely to mention the father as a positive role model in their lives. Conversely, those youth whose relationship with their fathers was characterized as cold and distant, quarrelsome and punitive, and who perceived their fathers as lacking in ability to provide resources in support of the family, were more likely to reject the father as a significant other or to see him as a negative role model in their lives. Where youth have had limited opportunities to observe and interact with their fathers, as in the case where the father is absent from the home as a result of incarceration, divorce, or death, their attitudes toward the father as role model were more likely to be ambivalent, vacillating between idealizing certain of the father's putative qualities while repudiating others.

While nearly a third of these youth identified their mothers and relatives as significant others in their lives, a major source of influence and identification for a preponderance of these youths was the peer group. The tendency among low-income youth to become deeply involved in their peer group societies has been noted by a number of writers (Coleman, 1965; Bronfenbrenner, 1970; Williams & Kornblum, 1985). The development of such strong peer group affiliations and orientations has been attributed to a breakdown in parental authority, early dependency on siblings and peers (rather than adults) as caretakers, and conflicting normative expectations from adults in low-income communities (Ianni, 1983; Silverstein & Krate, 1975). For our sample, peer group affiliations were not only important sources of security and achievement, but of social status, value orientations, and self-definitions. Many youths spoke with considerable pride about their reputation among peers in the community, and their own function as a role model for others. To be sure, the psychological benefits of such peer group involvements may be short-lived and limited, but serve a critically important compensatory function for youth who feel estranged from major social institutions, who find positive adult role models in short supply, and whose opportunities for self-actualization through achievement, employment, or other conventional avenues are severely restricted.

Few of our inner-city youths had strong work or value relevant role models, though many expressed interest in a wide variety of such models in the larger society. Such individuals included well known Black entertainers (e.g., athletes, singers, T.V. and movie personalities), politicians, and leaders of national religious organizations, but few such individuals became the object of much serious consideration, i.e., as figures with whom the youth sought to model himse'f or from whom he appropriated identity features for cultivating his identity ideal. Rather, these youths interest in such figures was often shallow and temporary, serving perhaps as a protective maneuver by which these youths sought to shield the self against the threat of identity diffusion. While some youth had chosen an occupation or mentioned a preferred one, they often lacked the knowledge of its major requirements, tended to exaggerate their personal qualifications for pursuing the occupation, and gave the impression that their occupational choice or preference would easily be abandoned should some other more attractive alternative (legitimate or illegitimate) became available. In sum, to the extent that role models were important in the lives of our inner– city youths, they were often employed in a normative and comparative capacity, i.e., as a means through which these youths learned to display appropriate conduct as defined largely by their peers in social situations of short duration, and as standards of comparison by which they sought to gauge the adequacy of their actions vis–a–vis significant others (e.g., peers). These rather circumscribed functions of role models seem consistent with these youths general mistrust or ambivalence toward others as objects of strong identification.

It may be argued that the manner in which role models function in the lives of many of our inner–city youths reflects the extent to which some of the more important psychosocial issues associated with identity formation have failed to be engaged by these youths. For example, the tendency among some inner–city youths to define themselves almost exclusively along the lines of some special but narrow skill or set of identifications, may be interpreted as evidence of what Erikson (1959) refers to as "identity foreclosure", i.e., a premature crystallization of identity. The etiology of this pattern may be found in the youth's perception or experience of restricted alternatives, role model deprivation, and limited opportunities for assuming responsible adult roles and status by way of work roles, either now or in the future. Lacking is a sense of anticipation of achievement or what Erikson calls "a certain hope in one's individual chance." The result is constriction of wishes and goals, impoverished role model identifications, and total commitment to role fixation. A more apt description of the psychosocial status of other inner–city youths may be "identity–diffusion", characterized by a lack of commitment to a set of self–definitions, values, and plans for the future. Their approach to life tends to be haphazard and disorganized, their role model identifications conflicting and tenuous. The general pattern here is one of varying degrees of confusion and a lack of integration and wholeness in personal organization. In their study of self– attitudes and identity patterns among Black and White male youths, Hunt and Hunt (1977) observed that while White males in their study developed highly integrated and focused identities by their senior year in high school, the identities of their Black male subjects coalesced increasingly around differentiated terms of selfhood. Like White (1984), they note that the weaker commitments to potential terms of psychosocial identity among low–income Black youths are a function of their environment, where subcultural or "'shadow values' emerge to provide symbols of accommodation to the reality of structural barriers to achievement, creating—in conjunction with the dominant values—a world of cultural dualities. In light of these considerations the diffused or loosely integrated identity structure of the Black boys in our sample would appear to be structurally-imposed adaptation to their circumstances" (p. 556). In short, whether because of anxieties created by their immediate social environment and delimited life chances, or because available alternatives do not engage their true talents or gratify their need–linked capacities, these youths remain committed to a bachelorhood of pre–identity.

The apparent differences between our college and inner–city youths in their choice and identification with various role models are undoubtedly related to differences in actual and perceived access to opportunities and resources, as well as to variations in the conditions of familial and community life. Indeed many regard as unrealistic the expectation that youths growing up under conditions of family instability, economic insecurity, and relative social isolation, can develop the motivation, competence, and other personal resources that culminate in a strong sense of personal identity (Kilson, 1981; Ogbu, 1985; Hare & Castenell, 1985). As Spencer (1982) has observed, Black low–income children are likely to experience greater discordant information as it relates to their self–attitudes and identity than their Black middle–income counterparts, and the former may be expected to experience "identity imbalance" in the absence of psychological or sociocultural interventions. Even so, the problems posed by social and economic deprivation are met in different ways and with differing degrees of resourcefulness by different youths depending upon the social contexts within which they find themselves. In the face of seemingly insurmountable personal and social barriers, some inner–city youths do manage to surmount them. Who manages, and how, is not at all clear, but much can be learned from the work of such researchers as MacLeod (1987), William and Kornblum (1985), Clark (1983), and Perkins (1975) on low–income youths, and from the autobiographical accounts of a number of Black writers (e.g., James Baldwin, Claude Brown, Malcolm X) whose rich descriptions of their life and development in the inner–city offer many useful clues.

Summary and Conclusions

It has been argued that the establishment of primary role mode identifications is an essential aspect of the developmental and maturational process, a principal means through which psychosocial identity grows in ever more mature interplay with the identities of the youth's role models. As such, the cultivation of identity through the process of identification inevitably gives to the youth's identity features which are common to the identities of others. Thus the youth identifies with others and these others become extensions of his or her identity, i.e., features or symbols of its content. Most youth may be observed to hold a more or less organized set of preferences which influence their perceptions and identifications with others. Such preferences, together with values, beliefs, and aspirations, are shaped to a substantial degree by the sociocultural contexts in which these youths grow up, their experiences of success and failure, and their subjective assessment of talents, skills, and opportunities. It may be observed, and data from our research supports the observation, that youths become oriented toward or identify with others whom they perceive as having the ability or resources to assist them in cultivating their preferred styles of conduct or behavior, and tend to reject or ignore individuals whom they perceive as lacking in these resources. Since identification with another implies a state of affairs yet to be realized, it may be assumed that in their selection and identification with particular role models, youths sense some meaningful "pay–off" between involvement with the model and their short or long–term goals. In addition, it may be observed that most youths are likely to have some knowledge about the relevant aspects of others in their social environment who are in a position to facilitate the attainment of their goals; and while such knowledge may or may not be objectively valid, it is likely to be organized in a relatively well–ordered set of preferences which serves as a source of reference for role model identifications.

In general, data from both samples of Black youths indicate that the personal attributes of these youths are major determining factors in their choice of role models and that the functions of such models in the evolving psychosocial economy of these youths cannot be meaningfully interpreted apart from the context of their personal histories, including their belief systems, basic value orientations, and aspirations. But such beliefs, aspirations and values are often influenced by significant identifications extending back to childhood and leads us to the fundamental observation that early identification often influence and limit the range of present objects of identification.

Within this context, the conclusion is strongly urged that role models have no unity of their own but function within the definition of their status provided by the subject. That is, the youth acts toward the model and is influenced by it in terms of those properties ascribed to it. How attractive or relevant a given model is perceived to be depends largely upon the dominant concerns of the youth at some given point in time. The youth, for example, who is preoccupied with the problem of choosing and preparing for a career, developing interpersonal or "survival" skills, or in the midst of a dilemma over his or her sexual identity or social status, is likely to the drawn toward those environmental models perceived to be relevant and useful in resolving these concerns. The tendency is to appropriate those part aspects of the model with which the youth is most immediately concerned, whether in fantasy or in actuality, sometimes borrowing a single trait from the model while ignoring other qualities judged to be irrelevant for the issue or problem at hand. While the function of the model under these conditions may be limited, its influence may broaden in scope as the appropriated element or quality is discovered to have more general application in synthesizing a number of existing behavioral traits. In sum, the function of a given role model depends in large measure upon the way in which it meets the needs of the youth's stage of development, the youth's established or preferred style of conduct, and the youth's dominant concerns at some point in time. It should be noted, however, that the interrelationship between primary role model identifications and identity–formation is not a matter of simple cause and effect, of independent and dependent variables. Rather, each is influenced by the other. As youth move through the life cycle, and as their abilities change, as they accumulate a record of achievements and failures, their interests in and evaluations of one or another role model and, consequently, the nature of the model's function or influence, are also observed to change.

Although our aim in the investigation of Black youth and role model identifications has been analytical and descriptive rather than prescriptive, several practical implications emerge from our data. The finding that many Black male youths in the inner–city are reluctant or unwilling to invest themselves, i.e., their aspirations and trust, in any and all role models calls attention to the need for concerted efforts to restore their sense of confidence and trust in themselves and in others in their social environment. As Erikson (1968) has noted, the lack of confidence and trust is often the result of the youth's sense of "having been deprived...and of having been abandoned" by significant others and the society at large. While family experiences are clearly implicated in the development of such attitudes, so too are youths' experiences in school and their involvement with peers. Indeed, there is some evidence that peers, neighborhood, and school experiences play a greater role than family experiences in shaping the personal attitudes and characteristics among Black male youths in the inner–city (Cummings, 1977; Glasgow, 1980). Thus considerably more attention must be given to reducing the effects of what Allen, Spencer, and Brookins (1985) have termed the "ecologies of deprivation", characterized by poverty, substandard education, and limited employment opportunities, which diminish the ambition and drive of these youths and undermine their self– confidence. While the emotional support, encouragement, and guidance of parents and others in the community are essential in any strategy directed toward improving the life chances of inner– city youths, such efforts are likely to be insufficient in the absence of well–conceived social programs designed to increase these youths prospects for employment and self–sufficiency through better education and training. The role of the school is particularly important in this regard, since there is evidence that negative school experiences, i.e., negative teacher attitudes and evaluations, severe disciplinary actions, and poor scholastic performance, are powerful determinants of feelings of fate control among Black male youths (Hunt & Hunt, 1977; Hare & Castenell, 1985). Unless teachers and other school personnel become far more sensitive to the unique problems of Black male youths, these youths will continue to feel estranged from the school environment and find distancing strategies which enable them to maintain positive efficacy and self–esteem.

While a variety of social programs and a greater abundance of positive adult role models (i.e., men and women who have successfully surmounted the obstacles to achievement and self– sufficiency) would undoubtedly inspire a greater sense of hope and confidence in the future among these inner–city youths, nothing seems more essential, as Kenneth Clark (1965) observed more than twenty years ago, than "evidence that some one cares enough and consistently enough really to help them. Their experience, their lives, give substance to a persistent doubt that this is so" (p. 98–99). What is important here is not just the presence of role models or significant others, but individuals committed to a sustained effort to secure a brighter future for these youths.

Methodological Note

The thirty Black male subjects involved in the original study were drawn at random from a partial list (a complete list was not available) of all full–time Black male students enrolled at a major private university in Boston, Massachusetts. In return for preparing an autobiography and completing a personal interview, each participant was paid a nominal sum. Based on information regarding the socioeconomic status of their parents (i.e., occupation, education, and income), it was established that the majority of the subjects came from middle and working– class families. Geographically, subjects came from all regions of the country, though most were born in the Northeast. As noted, subjects were requested to write an autobiography according to a topical outline provided by the author concerning early childhood experiences, family relations, adolescent experiences and interactions with adults in their communities, and their aspirations and goals. The interviews were guided by a similar list of topics, were recorded on tape, and later transcribed. The length of the interviews ranged from one and a half to three hours, and were usually conducted in the subject's dormitory quarters.

The sample of inner–city youth, all residents of the city of Hartford, Connecticut, was obtained through various contacts with local adults and recruiting on the high school playgrounds and other popular teenage hangouts in the city. Although many of these youth were eager to talk about their life's experiences, only a limited number (twenty-two) were willing to describe their experiences in written form. Nearly all of these youths came from low-income families, with more than half (fourteen) from families on welfare. As expected, many of these youths were less articulate than our college sample, and their autobiographies had frequently to be supplemented by requests for additional information during the personal interviews. Interviews were normally conducted in a meeting room of a local fraternal organization, and ranged from one to two and one half hours. Identical topics covered in our study of Black male college youth were covered in our investigation of inner-city youths as well. Each subject was paid a nominal sum for participation in the study.

References

Adelson, J. (1975). The development of ideology in adolescence. In S. Dragastin & G. Elder (Eds.), *Adolescence in the life cycle* (pp. 63–78). Washington, D.C.: Hemisphere Publishing Corp.

Bandura, A. (1969). Social learning theory of identificatory processes. In David Goslin (Ed.), *Handbook of socialization theory and research* (pp. 213–262). Chicago: Rand McNally.

Bandura, A. (1971). Analysis of modelling processes. *Psychological modelling: Conflicting theories.* Chicago: Aldine-Atherton.

Bandura, A. (1978). Self-system in reciprocal determinism. *American Psychologist, 33,* 344–358.

Bandura, A., & Walters, R. (1963). *Social learning and personality development.* New York: Holt, Rinehart & Winston.

Bronfenbrenner, U. (1970). *Two worlds of childhood: U.S. and U.S.S.R.* New York: Simon and Schuster.

Clark, K. (1965). *Dark ghetto: Dilemmas of social power.* New York: Harper & Row.

Clark, R. (1983). *Family life and school achievement: Why poor Black children succeed or fail.* Chicago: University of Chicago Press.

Coleman, J. (1965). *Adolescents and the schools.* New York: Basic Books.

Cross, W. (1978). Black Families and Black identity: A literature review. *Western Journal of Black Studies, 2,* 111–124.

Cummings, S. (1977). Family socialization and fatalism among Black adolescents. *Journal of Negro Education, 46,* 62–75.

Douvan, E., & Adelson, J. (1966). *The adolescent experience.* New York: Wiley.

Erikson, E. (1950). *Childhood and society.* New York: Norton.

Erikson, E. (1956). The problem of ego identity. *Journal of the American Psychological Association, 4,* 58–121.

Erikson, E. (1959). Identity and the life cycle. *Psychological Issues, 1,* 1–171.

Erikson, E. (1964). A memorandum on identity and the Negro youth. *Journal of Social Issues, 20,* 29–42.

Erikson, E. (1968). *Identity: Youth in crisis*. New York: Norton.
Furth. H. (1978). Young children's understanding of society. In H. McGurk (Ed.), *Issues in childhood social development* (pp. 228–256). London: Methuen.
Glasgow, D. (1980). *The Black underclass*. New York: Vintage Books.
Goethals, G., & Klos, D. (Eds.), 1970. *Experiencing youth: First person accounts*. Boston: Little, Brown.
Hare, B., & Castenell, L. (1985). No place to run, no place to hide: Comparative status and future prospects of Black boys. In M. Spencer, G. Brookins, & W. Allen (Eds.), *Beginnings: The social and affective development of Black children* (pp. 201– 214). Hillsdale, NJ: Lawrence Erlbaum.
Hauser, S. (1971). *Black and White identity formation*. New York: Wiley.
Havighurst, R., & Gottlieb, D. (1975). Youth and the meaning of work. In N.S.S.E. Committee on Youth, *Youth: The 74th yearbook of the national society for the study of education* (pp. 145– 160). Chicago: University of Chicago Press.
Hunt, J., & Hunt, L. (1977). Racial inequality and self–image: Identity maintenance as identity diffusion. *Sociology and Social Research, 61,* 539–559.
Ianni, F. (1983). *Home, school and community in adolescent education*. New York: Columbia University, Institute for Urban and Minority Education. (ERIC Document Reproduction Service No. Ed. 336 300).
Jenkins, A. (1982). *The psychology of the Afro–American*. New York: Pergamon.
Jones, E., & Korchin, S. (Eds.), 1982. *Minority mental health*. New York: Praeger.
Jones, R. (Ed.), (1980). *Black psychology*. New York: Harper & Row.
Keniston, K. (1971). *Youth and dissent*. New York: Harcourt.
Keniston, K. (1968). *The young radicals*. New York: Harcourt.
Kilson, M. (1981). Black social classes and intergenerational poverty. *The Public Interest, 64,* 58–78.
Klapr, O. (1971). *Social types: Process, structure and ethos*. San Diego, CA: Aegis Publishers.
Knoff, H. (Ed.), 1986. *The assessment of child and adolescent personality*. New York: Guilford Press.
Konopka, G. (1973). Requirements for healthy development of adolescent youth. *Adolescence, 8,* 302–316.
MacLeod, J. (1987). *Ain't no makin' it*. Boulder, CO: Westview Press.
Oberle, W., Stowers, K., & Falk, W. (1978). Place of residence and the role model preferences of Black boys and girls. *Adolescence, 13* 13–20.
Ogbu, J. (1985). A cultural ecology of competence among inner– city Blacks. In M. Spencer, G. Brookins, & W. Allen (Eds.), *Beginnings: The social and affective development of Black children* (pp. 45–66). Hillsdale, NJ: Lawrence Erlbaum.
Perkins, E. (1975). *Home is a dirty street*. Chicago: Third World Press.
Rochberg–Halton, E. (1984). Object relations, role models and cultivation of the self. *Environment and Behavior, 16,* 335–368.
Rosenberg, M. (1957). *Occupations and values*. Glencoe: Free Press.
Rosenthal, R. (1971). *Pathways to identity: Aspects of the experience of Black youth*. Cambridge, MA: Final Report, Harvard University, 1971, ERIC, ED 053.
Rychlak, J. (1982). Forward. In A. Jenkins, *The psychology of the Afro–American*, (pp. vii–viii). New York: Pergamon.
Scanzoni, J. (1971). *The Black family in modern society*. Boston: Allyn & Bacon.
Sebald, H., & White, B. (1980). Teenagers divided reference groups: Uncover alignment with parents and peers. *Adolescence, 60,* 979–984.
Silverstein, B., & Krate, R. (1975). *Children of the dark ghetto*. New York: Praeger.

Smith, E. (1976). Reference group perspectives and the vocational maturity of lower socioeconomic Black youth. *Journal of Vocational Behavior, 8*, 321–336.

Smith, M., Bruner, J., & White, R. (1956). *Opinions and personality*. New York: Wiley.

Spencer, M. (1982). Personal and group identity of Black children: An alternative synthesis. *Genetic Psychology Monographs, 106*, 59–84.

Spencer, M. (1985). Cultural cognition and social cognition as identity correlates of Black children's personal–social development. In M. Spencer, G. Brookins, & W. Allen (Eds.), *Beginnings: The social and affective development of Black children* (pp. 215–230). Hillsdale, NJ: Lawrence Erlbaum.

Tanner, J. (1978). Pop, punk and subcultural solutions. *Popular Music and Society, 1*, 68–71.

Taylor, R. (1976a). Psychosocial development among Black children and youth: A reexamination. *American Journal of Orthopsychiatry, 46*, 4–19.

Taylor, R. (1976b). Black youth and psychosocial development: A conceptual framework. *Journal of Black Studies, 6*, 353–372.

Taylor, R. (1977). The orientational others and value preferences of Black college youth. *Social Science Quarterly, 57*, 797–810.

White, J. (1984). *The psychology of Blacks: An Afro–American perspective*. Englewood Cliffs, NJ: Prentice–Hall.

Williams, T., & Kornblum, W. (1985). *Growing up poor*. Lexington, MA: Lexington Books.

Winch, R. (1962). *Identification and its familial determinants*. New York: Bobbs–Merrill.

FRIENDSHIPS AND PEER RELATIONS OF BLACK ADOLESCENTS

M.L. Clark

Adolescence is a developmental stage marked by rapid changes in the areas of physical, emotional, social and sexual development. During this stage a child must make the gradual transition from one who is totally dependent on parents to an independently functioning adult. Peers and friends become more influential during adolescence than at previous stages and function as powerful agents of socialization (Douvan & Adelson, 1966; Fine, 1980). Peers serve as a baseline for social comparison and thus are able to either strengthen or weaken the developing self–concept (Fine, 1981; Mannarino, 1978). The behaviors, attitudes, and perceptions that evolve are unique to this developmental age group, although peer norms do not necessarily conflict with parental norms (Maccoby & Martin, 1983).

Close friends (i.e., voluntary associates) are more influential than the overall peer group (i.e., the involuntary group from which friends are chosen) in bringing about changes in adolescent behaviors and attitudes (Campbell & Alexander, 1965; Epstein, 1983b). Through close relationships, adolescents are able to test out their value system and enhance their social development (Hallinan, 1980). Fine (1981) described friendship as functioning in three capacities: an arena for social interaction, a cultural institution that transmits knowledge, and a shaper of the social self–concept.

Peer relations and friendships are important for male and female adolescents of all ethnic and racial groups (Fine, 1980; Savin–Williams, 1980). The degree of influence that peers have on the adolescent's overall social development, however, is directly related to cultural variables. The role that the family plays in adolescent socialization and the quality of parent–child interactions will have an impact on the nature and influence of peer and friendship relations (Douvan & Adelson, 1966; Epstein, 1983e; Hunter & Youniss, 1982; Maccoby & Martin, 1983).

Ethnic differences in family structures and socialization patterns may lead to ethnic variations in the level of influence that friends and family have on adolescents. Although the influence of peers increases during adolescence for both Blacks and Whites, the family is perceived as a stronger source of support by Black than White adolescents. Cauce, Felner, and Primavera (1982) assessed the structure of social support for Black, White, and Hispanic adolescents. Black adolescents rated family as more supportive and perceived that more total support was available to them than either White or Hispanic students. Consistent with this finding, Black high schoolers were found to be more parent–oriented than their White peers by Di Cindio, Floyd, Wilcox, and McSeveney (1983).

Although adolescents share many commonalities, there are unique cultural experiences that may lead to differences in the social development of minority and majority adolescents. Theories of adolescence that have been built upon data collected from middle class, White samples cannot be totally generalized to minority groups. Without including the effect of social class and taking into account the impact of racism, it is impossible to understand the social environment of Black adolescents.

The purpose of this chapter is to review the current literature on the intragroup relationships of Black adolescents. First, theories of friendship or peer relations are summarized and their explanatory power for Black adolescent relationships evaluated. Second, research that has assessed the nature of Black friendships is reviewed, focusing on those studies that have information pertinent to understanding close relationships. Although popularity (Asher, Oden, & Gottman, 1977; Hartup, 1983) and social competence (Putallaz & Gottman, 1981) are topics covered in the friendship literature they will not be discussed because of insufficient information for Black adolescents. Third, the review of intergroup relationships centers around Black–White interracial acceptance, interracial contact and interracial dating. Finally, the chapter concludes with a summary and suggestions for future research.

Theories of Friendship Relations

Interpersonal Attraction Theories

Theories of adolescent friendship relations have their origins in the interpersonal attraction literature. The reinforcement, cognitive consistency, equity, and social comparison theories dominate present thinking about the relationships of children and adolescents. The reinforcement– affect model (Byrne, 1971; Byrne & Clore, 1970) and the social exchange theory (Homans, 1974; Thibaut & Kelley, 1959) are two reinforcement models of interpersonal attraction. They explain social relationships by assessing the nature of rewards and costs that exist in close relationships.

The reinforcement–affect model states simply that we are attracted to and like people who reward us and dislike those whom we perceive to treat us in negative ways. We can develop a liking for people, however, based solely on their association with a rewarding experience (Lott &

Lott, 1974). The basic premise of the social exchange theory is that friendship selection and rejection depend upon one's perception of the rewards and costs that exist in a relationship. Friendships are maintained as long as the rewards outweigh the costs (i.e., time, energy, financial and psychological commitment) of staying in the relationship. In addition, people may stay in relationships with those they are not attracted to because they lack alternatives, which would be characterized as an association and not a friendship (Berscheid & Walster, 1983).

Balance theory is the most popular of the cognitive consistency theories of interpersonal attraction. Heider (1958) identified "unit relationship and "sentiment relationship" as basic components of interpersonal attraction. "Unit relationships" occur anytime people feel that they are part of a group because they perceive some similarity to the group members. In some cases close proximity is enough for people to perceive a unit relationship between themselves and others that they frequently come into contact with. The "sentiment relationship" refers to the degree of liking we have toward another person. According to Heider, people try to maintain balance between their unit and sentiment relationships. Stress results from imbalance and people try to change stressful relationships to bring about balance.

Equity theory (Walster, Walster, & Berscheid, 1977) incorporates principles from the balance theory and the reinforcement models. The theory states that people are attracted to and try to stay in relationships perceived to have the greatest outcomes (i.e., rewards minus costs), which they try to increase. Rules are established so that each person can receive an equitable proportion of rewards and there is some attempt to maintain reward–cost balance on an individual and group level. Whenever inequity occurs distress results, followed by an attempt to reinstate equity rules to restore balance (see Berscheid & Walster, 1983).

According to the theory of social comparison processes (Festinger, 1954) people possess a drive for self evaluation and when objective means are not available, they evaluate their own opinions and abilities by comparing them to those of others. The source of comparison will generally be someone who is perceived to have similar opinions or abilities. People will cease to compare themselves with those whom they begin to view as dissimilar. In addition, a strong attraction may result in pressure to conform to the abilities and opinions of the source of one's attraction.

Interpersonal Attraction and Black Adolescents

Three factors from the adult interpersonal attraction theories appear to have applicability for explaining the friendships and peer relations of Black and White adolescents: similarity, reciprocity, and proximity. Problems occur, however, in the indiscriminate application of adult theories to explain the behavior of children and adolescents. There are many unique qualities of adolescent social behavior, although some similarities to adult relationships do exist (Epstein, 1983a; Reisman & Shorr, 1978). The majority of data on adolescent friendships have been gathered in school settings. Therefore, school structure will influence the degree to which similarity, reciprocity, and proximity guide the friendships of adolescents.

Interpersonal attraction theories suggest that social interaction is enhanced by similarity of the interactors (Newcomb, 1961; Thibaut & Kelley, 1959). If friends help to validate the adolescent's self-concept, one must be capable of selecting friends that have similar characteristics and attitudes who can give feedback consistent with one's own self-concept. In racially homogeneous settings both Black and White adolescents have a variety of peers from which to select best friends. In predominantly White classes Black students may have only a small pool of same–race peers from which to make friendship choices. Consequently, Black adolescents cannot use similarity in race as a criteria for friendship selection and may have to use similarity in other attributes for their friendship selections.

There are several possible outcomes of not having an adequate number of desirable alternatives for friends. First, Black students can select best friends from among the limited number of Black classmates. They may not share a great degree of similarity, however, with these same-race peers on other factors such as attitudes, values, interests, and school ability. The lack of alternatives may cause Black adolescents to associate with those whom they have no attraction, supporting elements of the social exchange theory. Second, Black adolescents may seek out cross–race peers who are perceived to be similar on attributes other than race. These White peers, however, may perceive the Black students as dissimilar to them. Black students may be disliked by White peers because of this perceived dissimilarity. Finally, Black students may give up developing friendships within their school and have best friends who attend other schools. All of these alternatives would leave the Black adolescent without an adequate peer support network to help reduce the stress associated with school-related problems. Miller (1983) has suggested that minority students need an adequate support group of same–race peers in school to avoid feeling threatened and experiencing adjustment problems.

Minority adolescents may experience more imbalance in school settings than majority adolescents. Their relationships in predominantly White classrooms are likely to be nonreciprocal or unstable (Clark & Ayers, 1985; Epstein, 1983d; Hallinan, 1982) which suggest that the rewards in these relationships do not outweigh the costs and equity may not exist. The outcome, according to balance and equity theories, should be more stress experienced by Black adolescents than White students.

Although imbalance or asymmetry occurs in the friendships of children and adolescents, it may not result in the level of stress associated with adult relationships. Children (Hallinan & Tuma, 1978) and adolescents (Epstein, 1983d) change friendships frequently although stability increases with age. The lack of friendship reciprocity and stability may be a necessary component of personal and social development (Epstein, 1983a). Through changing friends children are able to learn about the maintenance and dissolution of friendship and thus their knowledge about the friendship process is enhanced. In addition, it is possible that children must learn to function in nonreciprocal (i.e., asymmetric) relationships to be well adjusted. Unit relationships are forced to change because students must change classes, especially during high school. Thus, asymmetry in relationships is tolerated to maintain a healthy level of adjustment (Epstein, 1983a); however, Black adolescents in predominantly White classrooms must learn to tolerate more imbalance and stress than their White peers.

There are other ways in which school structure impacts on the friendships of Black adolescents. The teacher's perception of each child can influence peer perceptions and interactions (Miller & Gentry, 1980). Teachers are more likely to have negative expectations of Black than White students' academic performance and behavior (Baron, Tom, & Cooper, 1985). The teachers' attitudes toward these Black students may be internalized by class members, resulting in few positive peer interactions for Black students. According to Gerard, Jackson & Conolley (1975) the more teachers underestimate the academic performance of their minority students, the fewer friendship choices these students receive from their White peers. In addition, school structure may "impose rewards and costs on particular types of associations, despite the student's personal preferences or decisions" (Epstein, 1983a, p. 42). Cross– race friendships may be discouraged especially if they occur between Blacks and Whites of different gender. Classroom environments may encourage children to dissolve present friendships or to develop new friendships. Thus, associations or friendships may persist even when rewards are low only because associations have been forced.

The social climate of the classroom may affect the level of friendliness within a class. The reinforcement–affect model (Lott & Lott, 1974) implies that in classrooms where students have adequate success experiences or receive ample positive reinforcement from either the teacher or their learning experiences, high levels of peer compatibility should exist. Research does support the notion that friendship selection is greatest in high participatory (i.e., high peer interaction) and open classrooms (Epstein, 1983d; Hallinan & Tuma, 1978), environments which encourage peer contact. According to balance theory, people tend to like those who are in close proximity because these people are perceived as part of a unit. Proximity results in familiarity which is a necessary precursor for interpersonal attraction (see Zajonc, 1968). Segregation of students within classes by either gender, race, or academic performance, however, reduces peer contact and may have the most detrimental effect on Black adolescents in predominantly White classrooms.

Some additional problems encountered when trying to apply interpersonal attraction theories to Black adolescent relationships are common to majority adolescents as well. For example, children and adolescents may not have achieved the level of social cognition needed to make proportionate assessments of rewards and costs in a relationship. The costs of time, energy, financial and psychological commitment, identified by the social exchange theory, may not be considered in the relationships of adolescents and certainly not younger children. While adults invest time and energy into their friendships, children invest more in activities than in relationships (Epstein, 1983a). In addition, social knowledge and expectations of friends may account for marked differences in adult versus childhood friendship patterns. Developmental models support the notion that with increasing age, criteria for friendship selection and the general structure of relationships change (Bigelow & La Gaipa, 1980; Selman & Selman, 1979; Smollar & Youniss, 1982). In conclusion, interpersonal attraction theories do have relevance for explaining the close relationships of Black adolescents. Nevertheless, their applicability is limited by the effects of age, race, and school structure.

Cognitive-Developmental Theories

Instead of focusing on the dynamics of interpersonal attraction, the cognitive-developmental theories attempt to explain the changes in children's thinking about friendships (Bigelow & La Gaipa, 1980; Selman, 1977; Smollar & Youniss, 1982). The theories suggest that as children increase in age their friendship conceptions become less egocentric and concrete and more empathic and abstract. Young children view friendship as a surface relationship in which friends participate in mutual activities and share their goods. They seek self-satisfaction from their friendships and believe that friendships are transient, require positive interactions, and cannot endure conflicts. In adolescence, friendships are described as internal, dispositional relationships which are expected to possess loyalty, commitment and empathy, bring mutual satisfaction, and endure over time (Shantz, 1983).

The cognitive-developmental theories have all taken a stage approach to explaining friendship conceptions. The theories seem to follow an additive developmental model, that is, as age increases children do not discard earlier friendship conceptions but instead acquire new ideas that begin to dominate their thinking about friendships. Theorists have either used some form of a semi-structured interview to ask children about their friendship conceptions or analyzed essays children have written about friendships. Damon (1977) identified three stages of friendship conceptions. To the 5– to 7–year–old a friend is someone with whom one can play, share goods and have fun; nevertheless, the relationship is viewed as transient. From middle to late childhhood, friends are expected to be helpful and trustworthy. By age 11 children believe that friends should understand and help each other, and share similar thoughts and feelings.

Youniss and associates (Smollar & Youniss, 1982; Youniss & Volpe, 1978) have studied children's conceptions of how friendships are established and dissolved and the type of friendship interaction rules that children have established. They have proposed three stages of friendship conceptions. During the first stage, preadolescents think that one must share material goods and play with prospective friends in order to establish friendships; the emphasis is on evaluating peer behaviors. They expect that one must interact cooperatively in order to obtain rewards from and maintain their friendships. During the second stage, early adolescents evaluate the personal qualities of their peers when developing friendships. Those who are perceived to have attitudes and a personality similar to the adolescent are viewed as friends. In addition, there is the belief that friends should contribute equally to the friendship and receive equal rewards from the relationship. Mutual respect is an essential element in developing friendships at this level. Stage three is reached by mid to late adolescence. At this point friends are expected to exchange intimate information and offer emotional support. In addition, adolescents develop interpersonal sensitivity as they learn to accept and respect the individuality of friends. Thus by adolescence the rules for developing a friendship involve cooperation, mutual respect, and interpersonal sensitivity.

Children's knowledge about formation, intimacy, trust, reciprocity, jealousy, conflict resolution and termination in friendship relations was examined by Selman and associates (Selman, 1980; Selman & Selman, 1979). They presented children with a dilemma that might occur in a friendship and asked them to explain how the dilemma would affect the friendship. Selman and Selman (1979) identified five stages of friendship conceptions. From age 3 to 7 children are at the stage of "momentary playmateship". Friends are selected from peers who live in close proximity, share activities and material possessions. Friendship is defined as "momentary or repeated incidents of interaction between two persons who come together to play" (Selman, 1980, p. 136). Somewhere between 4 to 9 years of age children reach the stage of "one–way assistance". At this point friendships are thought to be self–satisfying and friends are peers who satisfy the child's needs and desires. During these first two stages children have egocentric friendship conceptions and focus on the physical rewards they receive from a relationship as a major determinant of friendship.

In the remaining stages of children's friendship conceptions a realization that friendships are mutual relationships exists. From the ages of 6 to 12, the stage of "two–way fair weather cooperation" emerges, when children recognize the reciprocal nature of friendships and attempt to select friends who have similar likes and dislikes. Friendships are readily dissolved when dissimilarity in likes and dislikes becomes apparent. From 9 to 15 years of age children evolve to the stage of "intimate, mutually shared relationships". Friendships are thought to provide mutual support and intimacy in an atmosphere where friends share feelings, secrets, problems and future plans. By age 12 many children arrive at the stage of "autonomous interdependent friendships" in which they begin to realize that friends can have independent relations that need not threaten the friendship. In addition, they become more adept at trying to satisfy the psychological needs and desires of both people involved in a friendship.

Bigelow (1977) and Bigelow and La Gaipa (1975) have studied the developmental changes in what children expect from their friends (friendship expectations). By doing content analyses of essays that children wrote about friendships they were able to identify dimensions of friendship expectations that appeared to emerge at different ages. These dimensions were loosely grouped into 3 stages that progressed from an emphasis on common activities, and propinquity (second and third grades) to character admiration and conventional morality (fourth and fifth grades) to a concern with loyalty and commitment, empathy, and intimacy potential (sixth and seventh grades. Young children expect friends to participate in mutual activities, older children expect friends to be nice and kind and adolescents expect loyalty, commitment and empathy from friends.

Cognitive–Developmental Theories and Black Adolescents

Although the friendship conception theories provide valuable insight into the friendships of children and adolescents, there are some limitations in applying these theories to Black adolescents. Most theorists have provided some normative– developmental data to validate their friendship stages (Bigelow & La Gaipa, 1980; Selman, 1981; Smollar & Youniss, 1982). Nevertheless, these data have been gathered on White, middle class children and adolescents. The extent to which these friendship conceptions are reflective of minority children and adolescents has rarely been explored.

The friendship conceptions that children and adolescents develop will depend upon the cultural values prevalent in their immediate environment. One might expect that those who vary in their cultural orientations or socialization patterns may also vary in the qualities they find important in friends. For example, gender differences in friendship expectations have been found during late adolescence. Girls expect more intimacy and emotional support from their friendships than boys (Hunter & Youniss, 1982; Smollar & Youniss, 1982). Attempts to assess ethnic differences in friendship conceptions have been sparse. Only one study has compared the friendship expectations of Black and White early adolescents and no significant racial differences were found (Clark & Ayers, 1986b). Additional studies are necessary to investigate gender, racial, and SES patterns of friendship conceptions. In addition, studies must explore whether children and adolescents have a different set of friendship conceptions for cross–gender and cross–race friendships than they have for same–gender and same–race friendships.

A general imitation of the friendship conception research is that little data have been collected to examine the relationship between friendship conceptions and behaviors toward friends. A few studies have found a relationship between friendship expectations and adolescents' evaluations of their present friendships (Clark & Ayers, 1986b) for Black and White early adolescents; nevertheless, too few studies exist to make any conclusive statements. Finally, several theorists have suggested that at all ages children select friends who have friendship conceptions that are similar to their own (Bigelow & La Gaipa, 1980; Selman, 1981). Nevertheless, Bigelow and La Gaipa (1980) found that only 44% of their children named as their best friend a child who was at a similar friendship expectancy level. Clark and Ayers (1986b), however, found racial differences in the extent to which friends had similar friendship expectations; White friendship dyads had more similar friendship expectations in the areas of conventional morality and empathic understanding than the Black dyads. An understanding of how friendship conceptions influence friendship selection, maintenance, and dissolution for White and/or nonWhite adolescents awaits further investigation.

To understand the friendships of Black adolescents one must integrate theory from the interpersonal attraction and cognitive–developmental areas. Adequate models that incorporate these two approaches and also include information on how environmental restrictions (e.g., racial concentration of a school) influence the process of friendship development, maintenance, and dissolution of Black adolescents are presently not available but the construction and validation of such models should be a future goal.

Factors Influencing Friendships

The friendship literature is replete with terminology that must be clarified. Popularity, friendliness, and friendship are not synonyms; each concept has its own methodology within the sociometric technique used so frequently in friendship studies. "Popularity" refers to one's status within a designated peer group and is measured by the number of friendship choices received. The number of friendship choices made assesses an individual's "friendliness."

"Friendship" is determined by mutual friendship choices. Further distinction is made regarding the degree of mutuality or reciprocity in friendships. Mutual or reciprocal friends exist whenever bilateral liking occurs, i.e., both members of a relationship share similar degrees of liking for each other. Unilateral relationships, sometimes referred to as nonmutual or nonreciprocal friends, occur when only one member of a pair expresses a liking for the other. In addition, some studies try to qualify friendships by distinguishing between acquaintances, friends, and best friends (for further information, see Epstein, 1983b; Hallinan, 1980; Mannarino, 1980). When friendship conception theorists use the term reciprocity they are referring to more than just mutual liking. They regard reciprocity as a quality that emerges in friendships during early adolescence. Reciprocity in friendships is characterized by mutual respect and the realization by each friend that mutual needs must be met to maintain the friendship (Smollar & Youniss, 1982; Youniss, 1980). These differences in terminology and methodology must be kept at the forefront in order to accurately evaluate friendship research.

The present section examines existing knowledge about the intragroup close relationships of Black adolescents. Studies that can add some insight into the degree to which similarity, reciprocity, and proximity influence either the formation or stability of Black adolescent friendships are reviewed. Few studies have measured dimensions of Black friendships, therefore, much of the data covered in this section comes from friendship studies that have included race as a secondary variable of interest. When deemed appropriate, data from Black preadolescent samples are included. The following literature review is also limited by covering only studies assessing the nature of friendships. Because of inadequate information, popularity (i.e., status within the peer group) of Black students is not covered.

Friendship Similarity

Similarity in physical characteristics, attitudes, personality, ability and behavior are thought to be necessary components of friendships. Hartup (1983) identified three ways in which similarity can influence the friendship process. First, similarity may determine friendship selection because there is a greater attraction to peers who are perceived as similar. Second, similarity strengthens social identity and is necessary for friendship stability. Third, similarity may be an outcome of friendship. Through increased associations mutual friends become more similar in attitudes and behaviors. Similarity in physical characteristics (i.e., race, gender, age) are important throughout the life span, however, personality and attitudinal similarity become increasingly important during the adolescent years.

Race. Both Black and White children of all ages prefer friends that are of the same race (Clark & Drewry, 1985; Hansell, 1981; Taylor & Rickel, 1981; Tuma & Hallinan, 1979). Clark and Ayers (1985) found that 80% of their junior high school sample selected best friends that were of the same race; a finding which supports previous research (e.g., Schofield, 1981). Although Black and White students prefer same–race peers, White students appear to be more ethnocentric than Blacks. In majority–White classrooms Black students make more cross–race friendship choices than their White peers (Asher, Oden, & Gottman, 1977; Hallinan, 1982; Hartup, 1978). Hallinan (1983) suggested that the prevalence for same–race friends may result from Black–White differences in academic achievement. White students have more minority friends when social class and achievement levels are equal (Rosenfield, Sheehan, Marcus, & Stephen, 1981).

The preference for same–race friends appears to steadily increase from elementary to high school. Greater segregation in both high school courses and activities were cited by Epstein (1983d) as reasons for greater race cleavage during the high school than junior high school years. It may also be that increased racial cleavage is influenced by the onset of dating and adolescent conformity to society's expectations that dating, marriage and even social mingling should be intraracial. Thus, peer contact becomes restricted to those who are perceived as appropriate partners for dating or socializing with outside of school.

Some data suggest that Black friendships may differ from White friendships. Clark and Ayers (1986b) measured the qualities adolescents find important in a friend (friendship expectations), the evaluation of present friendships, and the level of satisfaction with friends for a sample of Black and White eighth graders. The Black and White adolescents had similar friendship expectations; they expected the same levels of mutual activity, conventional morality, loyalty and commitment, and empathic understanding from their friends. Nevertheless, White friendship dyads had more similar beliefs regarding the importance of empathic understanding and conventional morality in friendships than Black friendship dyads. Finally, the variables that predicted satisfaction with friends differed for Black and White adolescents. For the White students, friendship satisfaction was best predicted from their evaluation of the quality of mutual activities in their friendships. The level of empathic understanding was the best predictor of satisfaction with friends for the Black adolescents. In general, there were more similarities than differences in the friendship expectations and friendship evaluations of the Black and

White adolescents; nevertheless, the differences deserve further investigation. In addition, this study focused on in-school friendships and the nature of friendships that develop in nonschool settings may differ.

Gender. Hartup (1978) stated that "except for chronological age, no characteristic is more extensively shared by friends than gender" (p. 158). A sex cleavage in friendships is evident from the preschool years and persists throughout adolescence. Findings are similar for the few studies with predominantly Black samples (Eisenhart & Holland, 1983; Tuma & Hallinan, 1979). Eisenhart and Holland (1983) found student-controlled activities to be more gender segregated than teacher-controlled activities for a predominantly Black sample of preadolescents. In addition, Sagar, Schofield, and Snyder (1983) found that gender segregation was more pronounced among White than Black preadolescents.

Numerous studies have found that same-sex friendships prevail in junior high, and high school (Clark & Ayers, 1985; Epstein, 1983d; Hallinan, 1979; Hallinan & Tuma, 1979; Schofield & Sagar, 1977; Singleton & Asher, 1979). When cross-sex choices are made they are likely to be nonreciprocated or unstable (Asher, Oden, & Gottman, 1977; Clark & Ayers, 1985; Kandel, 1978b). Cross-sex friendships do not begin to increase until late adolescence. Epstein (1983d) found more cross-sex friendships in the twelfth than ninth grade and concluded that the onset of dating was responsible for the increase.

In an effort to explain the high frequency of same-sex friendships Dweck (1981) and others (Eisenhart & Holland, 1983) have suggested that the differential socialization of boys and girls results in gender differences in interests, values, and interaction styles. Dweck concluded that through exposure to different experiences, males and females eventually develop different views of the world and areas of competence. Eisenhart and Holland (1983) identified the peer group as the primary agent for transmission of gender identity during preadolescence. Consistent with these views Schofield (1981) presented interview data from Black and White preadolescents supporting the view that boys and girls perceive themselves as possessing greater similarity with their same-sex peers.

Frequently race and gender interact to determine friendship selection but findings are not always consistent. Eisenhart and Holland (1983) reported that preadolescents selected as best friends those with similar gender and racial identities. Black females were more likely to select peers of their gender-race group as work partners or desired classmates than White females or White males. A similar pattern existed for Black males. Sagar et al. (1983), however, found that White girls had the strongest preference for peers of the same race and sex.

In addition to the obvious sex cleavage in friendships, some evidence suggests that males and females have different expectations of their friends. Clark and Ayers (1986b) found that Black and White females expected more conventional morality (e.g., truthfulness, kindness) and empathic understanding from their friends than Black and White males. In addition, females reported these qualities as present in their actual friendships more often than males. Nevertheless, the Black males reported more loyalty and commitment in their friendships than the Black females or White males.

The structure of male and female friendships also differs. During adolescence the intimacy level within female friendships exceeds that of male friendships (Berndt, 1982; Crockett, Losoff, & Petersen, 1984). Adolescent girls more often than do boys refer to intimate conversations with friends (Bigelow & La Gaipa, 1980), are more likely to assume that a person will confide in a friend (Mark & Alper, 1980), expect more intimacy and emotional support from friends (Smollar & Youniss, 1982), and report more intimate self-disclosure in general. Female friendships are thought to be oriented toward issues of loyalty, intimacy, and commitment whereas male friendships are dominated by achievement and status issues. The relationships of boys are centered around sharing activities instead of disclosing feelings (Berndt, 1982; Karweit & Hansell, 1983b).

Adolescent girls have smaller, more exclusive friendships than adolescent boys who tend to have looser social networks (Berndt. 1982). Coates (in press) found that Black males reported having a larger number of best friends than Black females although the overall size of their social networks (i.e., the number of persons with whom they did have contact) did not differ. Girls intentionally keep their number of intimate friends small. For example, Eder and Hallinan (1978) found that girls in mutual dyadic friendships were less likely than boys to accept the friendship advances from another same–sex peer. According to Karweit and Hansell (1983b) "Females are concerned with developing interpersonal skills which are best practiced in dyadic relationships. Males, however, are more concerned with developing autonomy and independence, best worked out in a larger group context" (p. 119). These findings suggest that female friends should be more similar in attitudes, interests and personality than male friends because similarity may be necessary before intimate self–disclosure can occur.

Age. Adolescents tend to select friends that are in their age group. Kandel (1978a) found high similarity estimates for age and grade level between high school friends. Karweit and Hansell (1983a), in their attempt to explain age segregation, have reasoned that school structure limits the contact of heterogeneous age groups. In most schools, students take classes with those who are in the same grade. Many extracurricular activities are structured by grade level. In addition, older adolescents have higher status and are not likely to seek out friendships with the younger students who are perceived as having a lower status (Karweit & Hansell, 1983a). Thus, heterogeneous age groups are rare in school settings but do exist more frequently in neighborhoods where age mixing is more likely (see Montemayor & Van Komen, 1980).

Personality and Attitudes. Some studies have assessed the degree of personality and attitudinal similarity that exists between adolescent friends. Best friends appear to be more similar in sex, age, and race than in personality or attitudes. Most studies have not been able to provide strong evidence that friends have more similar attitudes and personalities than acquaintances (for reviews, see Berndt, 1982; Hartup, 1983). In addition, studies have not included Black samples or race as a variable in their analyses. A widely cited study by Kandel (1978b) included 1879 friendship dyads; however, 92% were White dyads and because of possible sampling bias the data were not analyzed by race. One study has assessed differences in the personality similarity of Black and White friendship dyads. Within Black dyads there was greater friendship similarity than within White dyads for levels of anxiety, school achievement, and happiness (Clark & Ayers, 1985). White friends, however, were more similar than Black friends in the areas of intelligence, assertiveness, and mental alertness. Black friends were also more likely than White friends to have similar levels of physical attractiveness.

Males and females differ in the degree to which their personalities and attitudes are similar to their best friends. Females were found to be more similar to their friends than males in degree of extraversion (Wellman, 1926); values, attitudes, and behaviors (Cohen, 1977); personality and intelligence (Clark & Ayers, 1985). On the other hand, males were more similar to their friends than females on several status variables (i.e., classroom nominations for neatness and nicest clothes) (Clark & Ayers, 1985). Race by sex interactions have also been found with White female dyads more similar in intelligence and personality than the other race–gender groups (Clark & Ayers, 1985).

A few studies have tried to determine if friendship similarity is more a function of association than initial attraction to similar peers (Cohen, 1977, 1983; Epstein, 1983e; Kandel, 1978a). Results indicate that initial similarity is a strong factor in friendship formation and maintenance; however, friends become more similar as their relationship proceeds (Cohen, 1977; Epstein, 1983e). These data are limited to White samples and thus may not be descriptive of nonWhite adolescents. In addition, Duck and Craig (1978) have suggested that researchers should go beyond trying to determine if "friends start similar or become similar through association" (p. 242). According to these researchers, personality similarity is important for adolescent and adult friendship formation and maintenance. Nevertheless, the kind of similarities that are responsible for interpersonal attraction may differ from the type of similarities needed to maintain relationships.

Adolescents may perceive their friends to be more similar to them than they actually are. Perceived personality or attitudinal similarity may therefore be a greater determinant of interpersonal attraction than actual similarity. Some studies have found a relationship between interpersonal attraction and perceived attitudinal similarity (La Gaipa & Werner, 1971; Spurgeon, Hicks, & Terry, 1983) or actual attitudinal similarity (Duck, 1983); nevertheless, other findings are inconsistent (see Hartup, 1983). Future researchers should explore the different types of personality similarity that exist throughout the course of a friendship, and further investigate the relationship between perceived similarity, actual similarity and friendship formation and maintenance.

Friendship Reciprocity

Reciprocity or mutuality is considered an essential component of friendship. Relationships with reciprocity–of–liking are necessary for normal social development and personal adjustment (Fine, 1980; Hartup, 1983). Adolescent friendships are characterized by intimacy and self–disclosure (La Gaipa, 1979). These qualities can only develop, however, in relationships where mutual liking exists.

Reciprocal friendships are formed more often between peers who share similar characteristics. For example, reciprocal friends were found to be more similar in interpersonal understanding and social self–competence and they expressed more reciprocal interaction in communicative, affective, and task– oriented behaviors than nonmutual friends, acquaintances, or non– friends (Kurdek & Krile, 1982; Newcomb & Brady, 1982; Newcomb, Brady, & Hartup, 1979). Karweit and Hansell (1983a) found that reciprocated adolescent friendship pairs were more likely than nonreciprocated pairs to be similar in college plans, curriculum father's education and occupation, and school status. Kandel (1978b) reported the same trend when assessing behavioral, attitudinal, and sociodemographic similarity of high school students. Reciprocal friendships are also more stable than nonreciprocal friendships (Epstein, 1983d) and students without reciprocated or stable friendships are likely to experience a greater than normal degree of school stress (Epstein, 1983a).

Mutual friendships are more common among girls than boys. Girls have more cliques (i.e., a group of four or more persons in which at least two are involved in mutual choice relationship) (Cohen, 1977), and adolescent and preadolescent females have more reciprocated friendships than do boys (Eder & Hallinan, 1978; Epstein, 1983a; Hansell, 1981; Spurgeon, Hicks, & Terry, 1983). In addition, the number of female reciprocal relationships increases with age (Epstein, 1983a).

Black children who are the minority in desegregated classrooms may have some difficulty in finding peers who will reciprocate their friendship choices. Based on the data of Hallinan (1982), in majority White classes Black children made 70% cross–race choices but White children made only 15% cross– race choices. Thus, Black children are likely to have nonreciprocal relationships if they are attending predominantly White schools (i.e., less than 38% Black population). Ayers and Clark (1985) found that 40% of the Black students and only 14% of the White students in their predominantly White classrooms had no reciprocated best friends. In addition, Sagar et al. (1983) found that when Black students selected White peers for work partners their choices were not generally reciprocated by their White peers.

Friendship Proximity

Children and adolescents tend to select close friends from peers who are in their classrooms, live in the same neighborhood, or those who are involved in similar extracurricular activities. Neighborhoods and schools possess characteristics that can either enhance or prevent peer interaction (see Allen, 1981; Epstein, 1983c; Karweit, 1983). Past researchers have proposed that proximity helps to facilitate friendship formation by increasing contact (Festinger, Schacter, & Back, 1950) or that proximity increases familiarity which in turn generates attraction (Berscheid & Walster, 1983). Adolescent girls spend more time than boys talking on the phone to their best friends each day (Crockett, Losoff, & Petersen, 1984) and their time spent talking to friends increases from sixth to eighth grade. Boys come into more contact with their good friends at nonschool activities. Girls have more in–school contact with friends in student government and service clubs while boys have their greatest contact with close friends through involvement in sports (Karweit, 1983). Females were found to participate in more extracurricular activities than males by Hansell and Karweit (1983). Males and females in the college curriculum however, were involved in a number of extracurricular activities, which increased their opportunities to meet new friends.

There also are racial differences in the amount of contact among adolescent friends. Ayers and Clark (1985) found that Black adolescents were more likely to live in walking distance of their selected best friends and spent more time outside of school with their friends than White adolescents. White friends saw each other more often than Black friends in class or at church. Black students spent more time than White students each week with their best friends; Black males spent significantly more time with their best friends than Black females or White students. Coates (in press) also found that Black male adolescents saw their friends more frequently than Black females. The males' contact with friends was often in public settings; whereas, the females were more likely to see their friends in private settings.

School organization (i.e., type of courses, classroom assignments, seating arrangements, or extracurricular activities) determines the degree of student homogeneity and directly affects which students come into contact, whom they select as friends, and who they can be influenced by in school (Epstein, 1983c). School size, age segregation and curriculum tracking are additional characteristics of schools that influence peer interaction and thus friendship selection. Greater peer interaction occurs in small schools, within grades and within programs designed for students at different ability levels (Karweit & Hansell, 1983a).

The formation of interracial friendships depends upon the ethnic mixture within a school or classroom. Hallinan (1982) studied classroom racial composition and friendship selection in classrooms that were majority White (67% to 88% White), majority Black (67% to 89% Black), and racially balanced (38% to 60% Black). In majority Black classrooms 30% of the White choices were same–race and 70% were interracial. In majority White classrooms the figures are identical for Black choices (30% same race, 70% interracial). In racially balanced classrooms more same–race friendships were selected by both Black and White children (Black children: 70% Black & 30% White; White children: 61% White, 39% Black). Thus, Black and White children make more cross–race friendship choices when they are in classrooms where their racial group is in the minority. In racially balanced classrooms more same–race choices are made.

Although McPartland (1986) suggested that "as the proportion of students from other races increases in a student's classes, the proportion of those who have close friends outside their own race increases" (p.236), the implied linear relationship between racial composition and cross–race choices may be inaccurate. Longshore (1982) found a curvilinear relationship between cross–race friendliness and the racial composition of a school. White hostility toward Black peers was greater in schools with 40% to 60% Black populations, thus, supporting the findings of Hallinan (1982). Longshore concluded that intergroup hostility is most frequent in schools where no racial group is perceived as being in control. Despite these findings no conclusive statements can be made about cross–race friendliness and the racial composition of the school without considering the students' social class, which has not been done in previous studies.

Black students who are in classrooms that offer them considerable contact with same–race peers (i.e., predominantly Black and racially balanced classrooms) form and maintain friendships more readily than their White peers (Hallinan, 1982; Tuma & Hallinan, 1979). This environment offers the elements that are necessary for Black adolescents to develop close friendships. Nevertheless, Black students attending predominantly White schools do find ways to adjust, such as seeing their close friends more often than White students outside of school, or choosing their best friends outside of their school contacts.

Intergoup Relations

A more comprehensive body of literature is available for intergroup relations than for intragroup relations of Black adolescents. Many studies have assessed the change in racial attitudes or prejudice following desegregation; however, they are not the subject of this review (For review, see Rosenfield & Stephan, 1981). This review is limited to studies that have assessed either interracial acceptance, interracial contact, or interracial dating for adolescent populations.

Interracial Acceptance

Minority children are often not accepted as equal status peers by their White classmates. The explanations for the lack of interracial acceptance in desegregation classrooms vary. The perception of cross–race aggression has commonly been identified as a barrier to interracial acceptance. Several studies have reported that Whites in desegregated schools view their Black peers as aggressive (Carter, DeTine–Carter, & Benson, 1980; Schofield, 1981). These studies have rarely controlled for the differential social class levels of Black and White students. For example, Schofield (1981) included White students from middle–or upper–middle-class homes and Black students from mainly poor or working–class homes in her ethnographic study of intergroup relations. The data cannot be generalized, however, to interactions between Black and White students of similar social class levels.

Differential academic achievement of Black and White adolescents has been designated as the greatest deterrent to interracial acceptance in the school setting. Some researchers suggested that Black children's low classroom status resulted from their poor academic performance (Glidewell, Kantor, Smith, & Stringer, 1966; Pettigrew, 1969). The students' perception of the academic competence of their cross–race peers may have a limited influence on interracial acceptance. Carter, DeTine, Spero, and Benson (1975) found that Black junior high school students selected both Black and White peers to satisfy their needs for achievement recognition (academic acceptance); White adolescents preferred White peers to fulfill this need. Both Black and White students preferred same–race peers to satisfy their needs for social acceptance. Sex and grade point average, however, were better predictors of academic and social acceptance than race for the Black and White adolescents.

The lack of interracial acceptance of minority students has also been associated with parental interracial contacts. It has been suggested that minority children who have parents experienced in interracial interactions are more readily accepted by their White peers than minority children whose parents live a more racially segregated existence (Miller &

Gentry, 1980; Orive & Gerard, 1975). Minority parents with White contacts are thought to provide better models of appropriate interracial behavior for their children than parents with limited White contact (Miller & Gentry, 1980). One fallacy in this line of thinking is that it places the burden of interracial acceptance on Black and other ethnic minority students. The assumption that Black students, whose parents have limited interracial contacts, lack the social skills needed to become socially competent in a racially integrated setting is without empirical validation. Any attempt to understand the nature of interracial acceptance must begin with the acknowledgement of reciprocal causality. The presence or absence of interracial acceptance depends on the racial attitudes and behaviors of both Black and White students.

Interracial Contact

Desegregation has placed together Black and White children with different social backgrounds and thus different values, attitudes, likes and dislikes (St. John, 1975). According to Allport (1954) contact between ethnic groups would reduce racial prejudice and promote interracial friendships if the contact was prolonged, between those of equal status, and sanctioned by those in authority roles. In desegregated schools racial contact is not always prolonged because ability grouping within schools and classrooms can artificially separate students by race. Black and White students are rarely matched in social backgrounds because a disproportionate number of Black Americans are located in the lower social class. In addition, school teachers and principals may practice differential treatment of Black and White students (Baron, Tom, & Cooper, 1985). Finally, before positive interethnic interactions can occur, contact should be informal instead of formal as it often is in desegregated schools (Rosenfield & Stephan, 1981).

The term "resegregation" refers to the "separation of children by race or ethnicity within the walls of desegregated schools" (Eyler, Cook, & Ward, 1983). Many practices and programs implemented by schools to manage diversity in students, such as academic tracking, compensatory education, special education and bilingual education, result in resegregation. For example, when students are sorted into homogeneous ability groups a disproportionate number of Black students are placed in the low ability group. Black students are overrepresented in compensatory education programs and classes for the educable mentally handicapped and underrepresented in classes for the gifted and talented. Black students often spend less time in school than their White peers because Black students have higher suspension rates (Eyler, Cook, & Ward, 1983). In addition, many extracurricular activities are either limited to (e.g., Honor Societies) or attract (e.g., Student Council) students in the high ability groups (Karweit, 1983; Schofield & Sagar, 1982). Finally, the interethnic attitudes of teachers and other school officials influence the use of resegregation practices and therefore the opportunities for interaction between Black and White students (Epstein, 1985).

Desegregation has had little effect on reducing ethnocentric peer interactions. Black and White students elect to sit next to same–sex peers when voluntary seating arrangements are employed. Black children are twice as likely as White students to initiate interracial interaction (Sagar, Schofield, & Snyder, 1983). When cross–race interactions occur they are more task related than same–race interactions (Schofield & Francis, 1982). Black and White students interact when necessary to complete assigned tasks.

Black males interact more cross–racially than Black females (Schofield, 1982). In some cases Black females have been described as social isolates in desegregated classrooms, having less interactions with teachers and peers (Carithers, 1970; DeVries & Edwards, 1974; Patchen, 1982; Schofield, 1982) and less social power (Cohen, Lockheed, & Lohman, 1976) than Black males. Participation in team sports encourages informal equal status interaction and consequently increases interracial acceptance for Black and White boys (Miracle, 1981). Schools provide few opportunities for Black and White girls to develop equal status relationships, especially when social class and academic performance differences exist.

Patchen, Davidson, Hofmann, and Brown (1977) conducted a large scale study of factors that influence interracial behavior and attitudinal changes for high school students. Black and White adolescents with positive cross–race attitudes reported more positive interracial contact than adolescents with negative attitudes. Aggressive students (Black and White) reported more negative cross–race interactions and attitudes than less aggressive students. White students who experienced positive interracial interactions in elementary school and had family and peers with positive attitudes had more positive interracial interactions in high school than the other students. Proximity to other–race students and participation in school activities increased interracial contact and friendships. Black students who possessed similar values to those held by White students were more likely to get along with Whites. Patchen et al. (1977) concluded that negative interracial behavior resulted from aggressive behavioral patterns, prior racial attitudes, and the racial attitudes of family and peers. Positive interracial behavior depended upon prior racial attitudes and the opportunity for cross–race interactions.

Cooperative learning teams have been used to increase the number of cross–race friendships in school settings. These teams consist of ethnically mixed learning groups who study together within school and are rewarded for the group's performance (Slavin, 1985). Many studies have reported increased cross–race acceptance and interaction as a result of cooperative learning teams (see reviews by Sharan, 1980; Slavin, 1985).

Hansell and Slavin (1981) found that students who worked in cooperative interracial teams made and received more cross-race friendship choices than those without interracial team contact. Slavin and Hansell (1983) attributed the success of cooperative learning team to its ability to create a perception of similarity among Black and White students who originally perceived themselves to be dissimilar.

Sometimes the interracial friendships that develop as a result of cooperative learning teams are not close relationships. For example, Hansell (1984) found that friendships between races and sexes were often weak instead of strong relationships. By using cooperative-group intervention strategies, he was able to increase the number of weak relationships between Black and White students but could not bring about close cross-race friendships. Hansell noted, however, that any intervention that can establish weak interracial ties can potentially improve intergroup relations because these weak cross-race ties may help to bring together White and Black peer groups who previously had little contact.

Cooperative learning teams do not always result in greater cross-race friendships or more positive cross-race attitudes. Weigl, Wiser, and Cook (1975) compared classrooms using the whole-class method of instruction to classes using a small-group method, consisting of interracial teams of 4 to 6 students. Classes taught by the small-group method had less cross-race conflict and more cross-race helping than the traditional classrooms. White students in cooperative interracial teams gave Mexican-American peers more desirable ratings than Whites in the traditional classrooms. The White ratings of Black peers, however, were not increased by contact in the cooperative teams. In addition, the Black-White, Black-Hispanic, Hispanic-Black and Hispanic-White attitudes were not affected by the cooperative methods. Sharan (1980) cautioned that any increase in interethnic relations as a result of cooperative learning teams may be unilateral with a positive change occurring only in the minority group's attitude toward the majority group. Regardless, cooperative intervention techniques may still be useful strategies to increase interracial contact and acceptance.

It was once assumed that school desegregation would increase interracial contact and result in achievement gains for Black children. This expectation was based on the "lateral transmission of values hypothesis" which makes the following assumptions: Black and White children have different value systems regarding education; the value system of Black students is less desirable than that of White students; in desegregated classrooms sufficient social contact will occur for transmission of values; Black children will desire to emulate their White peers; and social influence will be unidirectional—White children will influence Black children because those in the minority will adjust their values and behaviors to resemble those in the majority (Gerard, 1983; Miller & Gentry, 1980).

The empirical data regarding the relationship between desegregation and academic achievement of Black children are inconsistent. Many of the studies show that desegregation has neither increased nor decreased the academic performance of Black children (Cook, 1984; Stephen, 1978). Research that focuses on the short-term achievement gains of minority children following desegregation do not often report significant increases. Achievement gains occur more frequently when cumulative gains are assessed in long-term longitudinal studies. The longer minority children attend desegregated schools, the more likely they are to experience an increase in achievement scores. For example, Black children who began desegregation in kindergarten or first grade had significant increases in their academic achievement; whereas, those who did not begin desegregation until late elementary or junior high school showed no achievement gains (Crain, Mahard, & Narot, 1982). Whenever significant gains were found it has not been clear why they occurred. Miller and Gentry (1980) concluded from their literature review, however, that peer acceptance was not "an antecedent of the minority child's academic achievement in the predominantly White classroom" (p. 168).

Interracial Dating

Interracial dating is another dimension of intergroup relations. Understanding interracial dating requires integrating information about cross-sex and cross-race relationships. Although there is adequate information on dating, there have been few attempts to understand the factors motivating interracial dating. The interracial dating literature that does exist is a theoretical and does not try to incorporate basic information from the interracial contact and interracial acceptance areas. An additional limitation is that most studies focus on college students who are a select group of adolescents. High school populations are more representative and data taken from this group have a greater potential for generalizability.

Black–White contact may increase the incidence of interracial dating. Willie and Levy (1972) found that Black high school students who attended integrated high schools reported more interracial dating than those who attended predominantly Black schools. More recent data support the notion that interracial dating is accepted on predominantly White campuses; a number of students express a desire to date interracially (Clark et al., 1986; Lampe, 1981; Stimson, Stimson, Kelton, & Carmon, 1979). Black males are more willing to date and marry interracially than Black females (Clark et al., 1986; Stimson et al., 1979). Black females more than Black males expressed concern about peer acceptance of their interracial dating (Stimson et al., 1979).

Although several previous studies have identified interracial sex as the motivating force behind interracial dating (Day, 1972; Sebald, 1974; Willie & Levy, 1972), Lampe (1982) found that the motives for interracial dating were the same as for intraracial dating. Very few students indicated that they interracially dated for sex, curiosity, or to prove a lack of prejudice. The majority of interracial daters said that when they dated a person of another race it was because they liked the person. When asked if interracial dating had changed their interethnic attitudes, most students indicated that their attitudes had remained unchanged.

Black students are willing to interracially date, but the majority prefer and date other Blacks, including those who interracially date. Clark et al. (1986) found few Black males who admitted to seriously dating White females and none who dated only Whites. These findings suggest that Black males who interracially date may not prefer to date White females but will in cases where the cross–race alternatives greatly outnumber the same–race alternatives.

Conclusions

This chapter has used the interpersonal attraction theories and the friendship conception theories as the foundation for understanding the close relationships of Black adolescents. In addition, it reviewed and evaluated the current literature on the intragroup and intergroup relations of Black adolescents. One major conclusion to be drawn is that the predominantly White school environment may significantly influence the pattern of peer and friendship relations for Black adolescents. School is a microcosm of the social status system in our society. Similarity, reciprocity and proximity are important for the formation and stability of close relationships, however, the predominantly White school may create an environment characterized by dissimilarity and imbalance for Black adolescents. Isolation in school for Black students may not be a function of deficient social skills, but instead an outcome of structural factors such as the lack of desirable friendship alternatives. Black females may have fewer friendship alternatives than Black males because they are less likely to be accepted by their White peers. In addition, biased teachers can hinder the friendship formation and peer relations of Black students which is especially detrimental in predominantly White classrooms.

Currently, information on the intragroup relations of Black adolescents is sketchy. A new body of research is needed with the major purpose of assessing the unique qualities of Black friendships. This research should study both static (i.e., selection variables) and dynamic (i.e., interaction styles) variables with an attempt to assess, gender, social class, and achievement differences. Additional research should further explore the friendship conceptions of Black adolescents and determine how these conceptions influence the selection and maintenance of friendships. It is essential to assess cross-sex friendships so that this information can be used as a foundation for understanding Black dating patterns, another area that has been grossly overlooked. In addition, nonschool friendships should be studied, especially in light of the fact that Black students select close friends outside of their school contact more frequently than their White peers. Finally, future research should determine the qualities that exist in successful cross- race friendships.

References

Allen, V. (1981). Self, social group, and social structure. In S. R. Asher & J. M. Gottman (Eds.), *The development of children's friendships* (pp. 182–203). New York; Cambridge University Press.

Allport, G. (1954). *The nature of prejudice*. Cambridge, MA: Addison–Wesley.

Asher, S., Oden, S., & Gottman, J. (1977). Children's friendships in school settings. In L. Katz (Ed.), *Current topics in early childhood education* (Vol. 1; pp. 33–61), Norwood, NJ: Ablex.

Ayers, M., & Clark, M. (1985, March). Reciprocity and junior high school friendships. Paper presented at the annual meeting of the Southeastern Psychological Association, Atlanta.

Baron, R., Tom, D., & Cooper, H. (1985). Social class, race and teacher expectations. In J. Dusek (Ed.), *Teacher expectancies* (pp. 251–269). Hillsdale, NJ: Lawrence, Erlbaum.

Berndt, T. (1982). The features and effects of friendship in early adolescence. *Child Development, 53,* 1447–1460.

Berscheid, E., & Walster, E. (1983). *Interpersonal attraction*. MA: Addison–Wesley Publishing Company.

Bigelow, B. (1977). Children's friendship expectations: A cognitive developmental study. *Child Development, 48,* 246–253.

Bigelow, B., & La Gaipa, J. (1975). Children's written descriptions of friendship: A multidimensional analysis. *Developmental Psychology, 11,* 857–858.

Bigelow, B., & La Gaipa, J. (1980). The development of friendship values and choice. In H. Foot, A. Chapman, & J. Smith (Eds.), *Friendship and Social Relations in Children* (pp. 15–44). New York: Wiley.

Byrne, D. (1971). *The attraction paradigm*. New York: Academic Press.

Byrne, D., & Clore, G. (1970). A reinforcement model of evaluative responses. *Personality: An International Journal,* 103–128.

Campbell, E., & Alexander, G. (1965). Structural effects and interpersonal relationships. *American Journal of Sociology. 71,* 284–289.

Carithers, M. (1970). School desegregation and racial cleavage 1954–1970: A review of the literature. *The Journal of Social Issues, 26,* 25–48.

Carter, C., DeTine, S., Spero, J., & Benson, F. (1975). Peer acceptance and school-related variables in an integrated junior high school. *Journal of Educational Psychology, 67,* 267–273.

Carter, D., DeTine–Carter, S., & Benson, F. (1980). Interracial acceptance in the classroom. In H. Foot, A. Chapman, & J. Smith (Eds.), *Friendship and social relationships in children* (pp. 117–143). New York: Wiley.

Cauce, A., Felner, R., & Primavera, J. (1982). Social support in high-risk adolescents: Structural components and adaptive impact. *American Journal of Community Psychology, 10,* 417–428.

Clark, M., & Ayers, M. (1985, April). Race, gender and reciprocity effects on friendship similarity during early adolescence. Paper presented at annual meeting of the American Educational Research Association, Chicago.

Clark, M., & Ayers, M. (1986a, August). Early adolescents' friendship expectations and friendship evaluations. Paper presented at the annual meeting of the American Psychological Association, Washington, D.C.

Clark, M., & Ayers, M. (1986b, April). Friendship expectations and the evaluation of present friendships: Effects of reciprocity, gender and race. Paper presented at the annual meeting of the American Educational Research Association, San Francisco.

Clark, M., & Drewry, D. (1985). Similarity and reciprocity in the friendships of elementary school children. *Child Study Journal, 15,* 251–264.

Clark, M., Windley, L., Jones, L., & Ellis, S. (1986). Dating patterns of Black students on White Southern campuses. *Journal of Multicultural Counseling and Development,14,* 85–93.

Coates, D. (in press). Gender differences in the structure and support characteristics of Black adolescents' social networks. In C. Feiring, D. Coates, & M. Lewis (Eds.). *The social networks of females and males: A life-span perspective.*

Cohen, E., Lockheed, M., & Lohman, M. (1976). The center for interracial cooperation: A field experiment. *Sociology of Education, 49,* 47–58.

Cohen, J. (1977). Sources of peer group homogeneity. *Sociology of Education, 50,* 227–241.

Cook, S. (1984). The 1954 social science statement and school desegregation: A reply. *American Psychologist, 39,* 819–832.

Crain, R., Mahard, R., & Narot, R. (1982). *Making desegregation work: How schools create social climates.* Cambridge, MA: Ballinger Publishing Company.

Crockett, L., Losoff, M., & Petersen, A. (1984). Perceptions of the peer group and friendship in early adolescence. *Journal of Early Adolescence, 4,* 155–181.

Damon, W. (1977). *The social world of the child.* San Francisco: Jossey–Bass.

Day, B. (1972). *Sexual life between Blacks and Whites: The roots of racism.* New York: World Publishing.

DeVries, D., Edwards, K., & Slavin, R. (1974). Student teams and learning games: Their effects on cross–race and cross–sex interaction. *Journal of Educational Psychology, 66,* 741–749.

Di Cindio, L., Floyd, H., Wilcox, J., & McSeveney, D. (1983). Race effects in a model of parent–peer orientation. *Adolescence, 18,* 369–379.

Douvan, E., & Adelson, J. (1966). *The adolescent experience.* New York: Wiley.

Duck, S. (1983). *Friends for life: The psychology of close relationships.* New York: St. Martin's Press.

Duck, S., & Craig, G. (1978). Personality similarity and the development of friendship: A longitudinal study. *British Journal of Social and Clinical Psychology, 17,* 237–242.

Dweck, C. (1981). Social–cognitive processes in children's friendships. In S. R. Asher & J. M. Gottman (Eds.). *The development of children's friendships* (pp. 322–333). New York: Cambridge University Press.

Eder, D., & Hallinan, M. (1978). Sex differences in children's friendships. *American Sociological Review, 43,* 237– 250.

Eisenhart, M., & Holland, D. (1983). Learning gender from peers: The role of peer groups in the cultural transmission of gender. *Human Organization, 42,* 321–332.

Epstein, J. (1983a). Examining theories of adolescent friendships. In J. Epstein & N. Karweit (Eds.), *Friends in school: Patterns of selection and influence in secondary schools,* (pp. 39–61). New York: Academic Press.

Epstein, J. (1983b). Friends among students in schools: Environmental and developmental factors. In J. Epstein & N. Karweit (Eds.), *Friends in school: Patterns of selection and influence in secondary schools* (pp. 3–25). New York: Academic Press.

Epstein, J. (1983c). School environment and student friendships: Issues, implications, and intervention. In J. Epstein & N. Karweit (Eds.), *Friends in school: Patterns of selection and influence in secondary schools* (pp. 235–253). New York: Academic Press.

Epstein, J. (1983d). Selection of friends in differently organized schools and classrooms. In J. Epstein & N. Karweit (Eds.), *Friends in school: Patterns of selection and influence in secondary schools* (pp. 73–92). New York: Academic Press.

Epstein, J. (1983e). The influence of friends on achievement and affective outcomes. In J. Epstein & N. Karweit (Eds.), *Friends in school: patterns of selection and influence in secondary schools* (pp. 177–200). New York: Academic Press.

Epstein, J. (1985). After the bus arrives: Resegregation in desegregated schools. *Journal of Social Issues, 41,* 23–43.

Eyler, T., Cook, V., & Ward, L. (1983). Resegregation: Segregation within desegregated schools. In C. Rossell & W. Hawley (Eds.), *The consequences of school desegregation* (pp. 126–162). Philadelphia: Temple University Press.

Festinger, L. (1954). A theory of social comparison processes. *Human Relations, 7,* 117–140.

Festinger, L., Schachter, S., & Back, K. (1950). *Social pressure in informal groups.* New York: Harper.

Fine, G. (1980). The natural history of preadolescent male friendship groups. In H. Foot, A. Chapman, & J. Smith (Eds.), *Friendship and social relations in children* (pp. 293–320). New York: Wiley.

Fine, G. (1981). Friends, impression management, and preadolescent behavior. In S. Asher & J. Gottman (Eds.,), *The development of children's friendships* (pp. 29–52). New York: Cambridge University Press.

Gerard, H. (1983). School desegregation: The social science role. *American Psychologist, 38,* 869–877.

Gerard, H., Jackson, T., & Conolley, E. (1975). Social contact in the desegregated classroom. In H. B. Gerard & N. Miller (Eds.), *School desegregation* (pp. 211–242). New York: Plenum Press.

Glidewell, J. C., Kantor, M. D., Smith, L. M., & Stringer, L. A. (1966). Socialization and social structure in the classroom. In L. W. Hoffman & M. L. Hoffman (Eds.), *Review of child development research* (Vol. 2; pp. 221–256). New York: Russell Sage Foundation.

Hallinan, M. (1979). Structural effects on children's friendships and cliques. *Social Psychological Quarterly, 42,* 43– 54.
Hallinan, M. (1980). Patterns of cliquing among youth. In H. C. Foot, A. J. Chapman, & J. R. Smith (Eds.), *Friendship and social relations in children* (pp. 321–342). New York: John Wiley & Sons.
Hallinan, M. (1982). Classroom racial composition and children's friendships. *Social Forces, 61,* 56–72.
Hallinan, M. (1983). Commentary: New directions for research on peer influence. In J. Epstein & N. Karweit (Eds.), *Friends in school: Patterns of selection and influence in secondary schools* (pp. 219–231). New York: Academic Press.
Hallinan, M., & Tuma, N. (1978). Classroom effects on change in children's friendships. *Sociology of Education, 51,* 270–282.
Hansell, S. (1981). Ego development and peer friendship networks. *Sociology of Education, 54,* 51–63.
Hansell, S. (1984). Cooperative groups, weak ties, and the integration of peer friendships. *Social Psychology Quarterly, 47,* 316–328.
Hansell, S., & Karweit, N. (1983). Curricular placement, friendship networks and status attainment. In J. Epstein & N. Karweit (Eds.), *Friends in school: Patterns of selection and influence in secondary schools (pp. 141–161). New York: Academic Press.*
Hansell, S., & Slavin, R. (1981). Cooperative learning and the structure of interracial friendships. *Sociology of Education, 54,* 98–106.
Harrison, A., Serafica, F., & McAdoo, H. (1984). Ethnic families of color. In R. Parke (Ed.), *Review of child development research* (pp.329–371). Chicago: University of Chicago Press.
Hartup, W. (1978). Children and their friends. In H. McGurk (Ed), *Issues in childhood social development.* London: Metheun.
Hartup, W. (1983). Peer relations. In P. H. Mussen & E. M. Hetherington (Eds.), *Handbook of child psychology. Socialization, personality, and social development* (Vol. IV; pp. 103–196). New York: Wiley.
Heider, F. (1958). *The psychology of interpersonal relations.* New York: Wiley
Homans, G. (1974). *Social behavior: Its elementary forms* (Rev. ed.). New York: Harcourt Brace Jovanovich.
Hunter, F., & Youniss, J. (1982). Changes in functions of three relations during adolescence. *Developmental Psychology, 18,* 800–811.
Kandel, D. (1978a). Homophily, selection, and socialization in adolescent friendships. *American Journal of Sociology, 84,* 427–436.
Kandel, D. (1978b). Similarity in real–life adolescent friendship pairs. *Journal of Personality and Social Psychology, 36* 306–312.
Karweit, N. (1983). Extracurricular activities and friendship selection. In J. Epstein & N. Karweit (Eds.), *Friends in school: Patterns of selection and influence in secondary schools* (pp. 131–139). New York: Academic Press.
Karweit, N., & Hansell, S. (1983a). School organization and friendship selection. In J. Epstein & N. Karweit (Eds.), *Friends in school: Patterns of selection and influence in secondary schools* (pp. 29–38). New York: Academic Press.
Karweit, N., & Hansell, S. (1983b). Sex differences in adolescent relationships: Friendship and status. In J. Epstein & N. Karweit (Eds.), *Friends in school: Patterns of selection and influence in secondary schools* (pp. 115–130). New York: Academic Press.

Kurdek, L., & Krile, D. (1982). A developmental analysis of the relationship between peer acceptance and both interpersonal understanding and perceived social self–competence. *Child Development, 53*, 1485–1491.

La Gaipa, J. (1979). A developmental study of the meaning of friendship in adolescence. *Journal of Adolescence, 2*, 201–213.

La Gaipa, J., & Werner, R. (1971). Attraction and relevancy of attitude similarity–dissimilarity: Impersonal topics and friendship beliefs. *Psychonomic Science, 22*, 83–84.

Lampe, P. (1982). Interethnic dating. *International Journal of Intercultural Relations, 6*, 115–126.

Lampe, P. (1981). Towards amalgamation: Interethnic dating among Blacks, Mexican Americans and Anglos. *Ethnic Groups, 3*, 97–109.

Longshore, D. (1982). Race composition and White hostility: A research note on the problem on control in desegregated schools. *Social Forces, 61*, 73–78.

Lott, A., & Lott, B. (1974). Group cohesiveness communication level, and conformity. *Journal of Abnormal and Social Psychology, 62*, 408–412.

Maccoby, E., & Martin, J. (1983). Socialization in the context of the family: Parent–child interaction. In P. H. Mussen & E. M. Hetherington (Eds.), *Handbook of child psychology: Socialization, personality, and social development* (Vol. IV, pp. 1–101). New York: John Wiley & Sons.

Mannarino, A. (1980). The development of children's friendships. In H.C. Foot, A.J. Chapman, & J.R. Smith (Eds.), *Friendship and social relations in children*, pp. 45–63. New York: John Wiley & Sons.

Mannarino, A. (1978). Friendship patterns and self–concept development in preadolescent males. *Journal of Genetic Psychology, 133*, 105–110.

Mark, E., & Alper, T. (1980). Sex differences in intimacy motivation. *Psychology of Women Quarterly, 5*, 164– 169.

McPartland, J. (1968). *The segregated student in desegregated schools.* (Final report). Baltimore, MD: Johns Hopkins University, Social Organization of Schools. (ERIC Document Reproduction Service No. ED 021 944.)

Miller, N. (1983). Peer relations in desegregated schools. In J. Epstein & N. Karweit (Eds.), *Friends in school: Patterns of selection and influences in secondary schools* (pp. 201–217). New York: Academic Press.

Miller, N., & Gentry, K. (1980). Sociometric indices of children's peer interaction in the school setting. In H. Foot, A. Chapman, & J. Smith (Eds.), *Friendship and social relations in children* (pp. 145–177). New York: Wiley.

Miracle, A. (1981). Factors affecting interracial cooperation: A case study of a high school football team. *Human Organization, 40*, 150–154.

Montemayor, R., & Van Komen, R. (1980). Age segregation of adolescents in and out of school. *Journal of Youth and Adolescence, 9*, 371–381.

Newcomb, A., Brady, J. (1982). Mutuality in boys' friendship relations, *Child Development", 53*, 392–395.

Newcomb, & A., Brady, J., & Hartup, W. (1979). Friendship and incentive condition as determinants of children's task–oriented social behavior. *Child Development, 50*, 878–881.

Newcomb, T. (1961). *The acquaintance process.* New York: Holt, Rinehart & Winston.

Orive, R., & Gerard, H. (1975). Social contact of minority parents and their children's acceptance by classmates. *Sociometry, 38*, 518–524.

Patchen, M., Davidson, J., Hofmann, G., & Brown, W. (1977). Determinants of students' interracial behavior and opinion change. *Sociology of Education, 50*, 55–75.

Patchen, M., Hofmann, G., & Brown, W. (1980). Academic performance of Black high school students under different conditions of contact with White peers. *Sociology of Education, 53*, 33–51.

Pettigrew, T. (1969). The Negro and education: Problems and proposals. In I. Katz & P. Gurin (Eds.), *Race and the Social Sciences* (pp. 49–112). New York: Basic Books.

Putallaz, M., & Gottman, J. (1981). Social skills and group acceptance. In S. Asher & J. Gottman (Eds.), *The development of children's friendships* (pp. 116–149). New York: Cambridge University Press.

Reisman, J., & Shorr, S. (1978). Friendship claims and expectations among children and adults. *Child Development, 49*, 913–916.

Rosenfield, D., Sheehan, D., Marcus, M., & Stephan, W. (1981). Classroom structure and prejudice in desegregated schools. *Journal of Educational Psychology, 73*, 17–26.

Rosenfield, D., & Stephan, W. (1981). Intergroup relations among children. In S. Brehm, S. Kassin, & F. Gibbons (Eds.), *Developmental social psychology: Theory and research* (pp. 271–297). New York: Oxford University Press.

Sagar, H., Schofield, J., & Snyder, H. (1983). Race and gender barriers: Preadolescent peer behavior in academic classrooms. *Child Development, 54*, 1032–1040.

St. John, N. (1975). *School desegregation outcomes for children*. New York: Wiley.

Savin-Williams, R. (1980). Social interactions of adolescent females in natural groups. In H. C. Foot, A. J. Chapman, & J. R. Smith (Eds.), *Friendship and social relations in children* (pp. 343–364). New York: John Wiley & Sons.

Schofield, J. (1982). *Black and White in school: Trust, tension or tolerance?* New York: Praeger.

Schofield, J. (1981). Complementary and conflicting identities: Images and interaction in an interracial school. In S. Asher & J. Gottman (Eds.), *The development of children's friendships* (pp. 53–90). New York: Cambridge University Press.

Schofield, J., & Francis, W. (1982). An observational study of peer interaction in racially-mixed "accelerated classrooms". *Journal of Educational Psychology, 74*, 722–732.

Schofield, J., & Sagar, H. (1977). Peer interaction patterns in an integrated middle school.*Sociometry, 40*, 130–138.

Sebald, H. (1974). Interracial dating and sexual liaison of White and Black college men. *International Journal of Sociology of the Family, 4*, 23–36.

Selman, R. (1977). A structural–developmental model of social cognition: Implications for intervention research. *Counseling Psychologist, 6*, 3–6.

Selman, R. (1980). *The growth of interpersonal understanding: Developmental and clinical analyses*. New York: Academic Press.

Selman, R. (1981). The child as a friendship philosopher. In S. R. Asher & J. M. Gottman (Eds.), *The development of children's friendships* (pp. 242–272). New York: Cambridge University Press.

Selman, R., & Selman, A. (1979). Children's ideas about friendship: A new theory. *Psychology Today, 114*, pp. 70–80, 114.

Shantz, C. (1983). Social cognition. In P. H. Mussen, J. H. Flavell, & E. M. Markman (Eds.), *Handbook of child psychology: Cognitive development* Vol. III; pp. 495–555). New York: John Wiley & Sons.

Sharan, S. (1980). Cooperative learning in small groups: Recent methods and effects on achievement, attitudes, and ethnic relations. *Review of Educational Research, 50,* 241– 271.

Singleton, L., & Asher, S. (1979). Racial integration and children's peer preferences: An investigation of developmental and cohort differences. *Child Development, 50,* 936– 941.

Slavin, R. (1985). Cooperative learning: Applying contact theory in desegregated schools. *Journal of Social Issues, 41,* 45–62.

Slavin, R., & Hansell, S. (1983). Cooperative learning and intergroup relations: Contact theory in the classroom. In J. Epstein & N. Karweit (Eds.), *Friends in school: Patterns of selection and influence in secondary schools* (pp. 93–114). New York: Academic Press.

Smollar, J., & Youniss, J. (1982). Social development through friendship. In K. H. Rubin & H. S. Ross (Eds.), *Peer relationships and social skills in childhood* (pp. 279–298). New York: Springer–Verlag, Inc.

Spurgeon, P., Hicks, C., & Terry, R. (1983). A preliminary investigation into sex differences in reported friendship determinants amongst a group of early adolescents. *British Journal of Social Psychology, 22,* 63–64.

Stephan, W. (1978). School desegregation: An evaluation of predictions made in *Brown v. Board of Education. Psychological Bulletin, 85, 217–238.*

Stimson, S., Stimson, J., Kelton, T., & Carmon, B. (1979). Interracial dating: Willingness to violate a changing norm. *Journal of Social and Behavioral Sciences, 25,* 36–45.

Taylor, D., & Rickel, A. (1981). An analysis of factors affecting school social integration. *Journal of Negro Education, 50,* 122–123.

Thibaut, J., & Kelley, H. (1959). *The social psychology of groups.* New York: Wiley.

Tuma, N., & Hallinan, M. (1979). The effects of sex, race, and achievement on school children's friendships. *Social Forces, 57,* 1265–1285.

Walster, E., Walster, G., & Berscheid, E. (1977). *Equity: Theory and research.* Boston: Allyn and Bacon.

Weigl, R., Wiser, P., & Cook, S. (1975). The impact of cooperative learning experiences on cross–ethnic relations. *Journal of Social Issues, 31,* 219–244.

Wellman, B. (1926). The school children's choice of companions. *Journal of Educational Research, 14,* 126–132.

Willie, C., & Levy, J. (1972, March). Black is lonely on White campuses. *Psychology Today,* pp. 50–52, 76–80.

Youniss, J. (1980). *Parents and peers in social development: A Sullivan–Piaget perspective.* Chicago: University of Chicago Press.

Youniss, J., & Volpe, J. (1978). A relational analysis of children's friendships. In W. Damon (Ed.), *New directions for child development: Social cognition,* pp. 1–22. San Francisco: Jossey–Bass.

Zajonc, R. (1968). Attitudinal effects of more exposure. *Journal of Personality and Social Psychology, 9,* 1– 29.

Part V
Educational Issues and Programs

Educating Black Urban Adolescents: Issues and Programs

Randolf Tobias

This chapter examines four areas related to the education of Black adolescents: (1) socioeconomic factors that impact upon the quality of Black life; (2) contemporary issues of urban secondary public schools that effect learning; (3) examples of traditional and progressive educational programs for Black and disadvantaged youth and (4) strategies for educational improvement of Black adolescents.Development of the chapter represented a struggle from two perspectives. The first perspective is focus. Issues surrounding the education of urban Black youth are many, and complex. Volumes could be written on factors that have set the stage for the educational plight of Black youth. The section on Socioeconomic Factors, for example, provides only a brief overview. The reader is encouraged to read Dubois' (1) Souls of Black Folk (D) (1983), Frazier's (1) The Negro in the United States (D) (1957), and Drake and Cayton's (1) Black Metropolis (D) (1970) for additional information on this topic. The reader also is encouraged to reexamine Chapter 1 of the present volume "Black Adolescents and Youth: An Update on An Endangered Species". In this chapter, Gibbs presents current census data on Black youth with respect to population, age and income, adolescent crime, incarceration and substance abuse, all of which are related to educational issues.

The second perspective involves the need to develop a political frame of reference with respect to the historical development of the American public school system vis–a–vis the Black experience. The reader is reminded that the American public school is Eurocentric in its evolution and that Blacks have always been disenfranchised from the American curriculum development process. My view is that the educational plight of Black adolescents today continues to be a political struggle.

Socioeconomic Factors

Over the past decade, educators and parents have been alarmed over the lack of academic competence among high school graduates. New York State reacted to this problem by initiating its competency testing of high school students (prior to graduation) in 1976. The State of North Carolina initiated its competency testing the following year. Today, most

Educational Issues and Programs

states have competency testing programs to insure academic skill proficiency before a high school diploma is granted. A combination of compounded academic skill deficiency and parental lawsuits (of local school systems that granted high school diplomas to illiterate youth) prompted a national competency testing program. Between 1966 and 1970, the Department of Health, Education and Welfare conducted a nationwide special four–year testing program. The study concluded that a million American youths between the ages of twelve and seventeen could not read, even at the fourth grade level. The results also indicated that illiteracy was more pervasive and severe than ever before, especially among low–income Black males.

Basic academic skills deficiency and illiteracy among Black adolescent youth are symptomatic of larger socioeconomic problems. These problems impact upon the education of urban Black adolescents and can be clearly seen within the context of inner–city living. Inner–city environments were first created as a result of industrial decentralization and middle income groups leaving America's central cities. Industrial flight began to take root during the late forties and early fifties as the American economy began to shift from local to regional areas. Inducements for industrial decentralization were many. Dentler (1968) observes that many northern industrialists who continued to work within old community forms were driven to collapse by the freer–ranging competition of Midwestern and Southern enterprises. Demands for new goods, labor shortages, and an opportunity to increase profits particularly by escaping high industrial taxes being imposed by local governments further uprooted industrial bases. When industry left, jobs left—leaving unskilled Blacks unemployed. Blacks also suffered from the additional plagues of poor housing, poor health, and other urban ills. Unskilled Blacks could not qualify for jobs made available by the remaining service industries.Because of the increasing migration patterns of Blacks from Southern to Northern and Midwestern cities, middle income Whites began to leave central cities for suburban communities. The 1960 census revealed that there was a decrease in population within twelve of the twenty largest American cities between 1950 and 1960. Though middle income Whites left the city, they continued to control institutions, agencies, real estate and other mercantile ventures, thus creating defacto segregated urban communities. The Kerner Commission study (1968) stressed that America was divided into two distinct societies, one White and the other Black. The study was stimulated by the nationwide Black riots of the middle sixties.

Carmichael and Hamilton (1967) and Ogbu (1978) have highlighted broader and more fundamental problems within the infrastructure of the American fabric: institutional racism and caste. Carmichael and Hamilton pointed out that Institutional racism relies on the active and pervasive operation of anti–Black attitudes and practices. A sense of superior group position prevails: Whites are better than Blacks; therefore Blacks should be subordinated to Whites. This is a racist attitude and permeates the society on both the individual and institutional level, covertly and overtly. (p. 5)

Ogbu asserted that lower school performance of Black children lay largely within the American caste system or system of racial stratification. He further stated

> ...The social and economic inequality or gap between Blacks and Whites persists, even though Americans espouse the principles of equality and freedom, and even though public education is believed to be a channel for individual self-improvement. The gap in education is just as wide as the gap in socioeconomic status, and equally persistent. (p. 2)

Anti-Black attitudes are related to the inner-city syndrome which is characterized by (1) the lessening of city services (i.e., police protection, public transportation, sanitation services since the newly arrive Black lacked local political clout), (2) the creation of a purely Black consumer class (since Blacks could not gain access to commercial and personal property ownership and other business ventures, within their communities), (3) non-stabilization within neighborhoods (since unskilled laborers were often laid-off and forced to work in other areas), (4) non-leadership, and control of city institutions that dictate the quality of Black life (i.e., hospitals, banks, police enforcement agencies, educational institutions), (5) poor housing, health care and child care, and (6) unemployment and underemployment resulting in a rise in crime, an increased dependency on welfare, and an increase in social pathology.

Poor health and nutrition also act as deterrents to educational success. Birch and Gussow (1970) provided evidence supporting educational failure as a biological phenomenon resulting from poor eating and the lack of medical attention. They emphasize:

> Good health is a requisite to educational success. A serious program for the abolition of school failure among disadvantaged children must also include improvement of their economic condition, health, and nutritional status. Poor children are exposed to unnourishing food, deficient sanitation, defective housing, and inadequate medical care. The same homes which lack toys and games are the homes in which hunger and disease abound. To be poor in America, and especially to be poor and nonwhite, is to be assailed by a whole range of physical conditions which, by endangering life, growth, and health,depress mental development and educational potential. (p. vi)

Inner-city public schools as examples of de facto segregated institutions controlled by middle income groups reflected and maintained the values of mainstream America. The White teacher-Black student-Black parent dialectic failed during the sixties. This failure was manifested within the context of teacher expectation or the "self-fulfilling prophecy." (See Chapter by Murray and Fairchild in this volume for discussion of this phenomenon).

Throughout the sixties and seventies a combination of events produced an entire movement that resulted in blaming the "victim" rather than analyzing fundamental environmental causes. The Coleman study (1966), for example, concluded that school effects on achievement were much less than family–background. Coleman's "regression analysis" procedure, came under significant criticism. Armor (1972) suggests that the individual student–level correlation and regression analyses were conducted incorrectly. The Coleman procedure underestimated the school input effects on student achievement, since an arbitrary choice was made of first "controlling" for student background, and then introducing school resources into the analysis. Armor pointed out that this underestimation was due to the tendency of higher socioeconomic communities to have better school resources.

Stein (1971) however, labeled efforts for improving the quality of education within the New York City schools during the sixties as "Strategies for Failure." Stein alleged that public officials and educators first "contained" inner school residents through control of school zoning, transfers, new school site selection, and construction. She also stated that departments of teacher education within colleges and universities train teachers to fail through (1) creating a mystique about reading, and spelling out a tangled web of readiness requirements, and (2) the creating a myth of cultural deprivation.

Over the past sixteen years three significant changes have occurred which in turn *should have* made positive changes in the educational plight of Black students: (1) An increase in the number of Black elected and politically appointed officials (locally, statewide, and nationally); (2) an increase in the number of Black educational administrators and supervisors, and (3) an increase in Black participation as members of state and local school boards and professional educational associations and unions. Unfortunately, these changes have not made a *significant difference* in the quality education of Black students, particularly Black adolescents. Gibbs (Chapter I) points out that a surface familiarity with the statistics on the educational attainment of Black youth suggests that there has been *some improvement* in the past 25 years. For example, the proportion of high school dropouts among Black youth in the 14–24 age group steadily declined from 23.8% in 1960 to 13.2% in 1984 and, for 16–17 year olds, from 22.3% to 5.2% in the same period (College Entrance Examination Board, 1985). In recent years, the gap between Black and White overall dropout rates in high school age group has reached parity, in spite of disproportionately high rates for inner–city Black youth. However, national Black student school enrollment has declined since 1977.

Enrollment, however, has dropped since 1970 for Whites, falling from 51.7 million in 1970 to 48.2 million in 1981. The decline for both Blacks and Whites reflects decreases in the population of elementary and high school ages, resulting from a decline in the number of births. High school dropout rates for Black youth however, have continued to decline. In 1981, 10.2 percent of Black youth ages 14–19 were not enrolled in school compared to 8.7 percent of White youth (U.S. Bureau of the Census, July, 1983). In 1984, the overall dropout rate within the New York City public schools alone was 45%, but 78% of Black adolescents did not complete high school (New York Urban Leauge, 1984). Most of the dropouts were Black males. Similar Black male high school dropout percentages are found within the inner–city areas of Detroit, Newark, Chicago, Philadelphia, and Los Angeles. In 1977, 50% of all Black high school graduates enrolled in college, but by 1982 the figure had fallen to 36% (Bastian, et al., 1986).

The quality of Black life within urban areas has continued to diminish. The New York Urban League, for example, released a detailed study in 1984 entitled "Status of Black New York". The study revealed that (1) 1.7 million Blacks who reside in New York City were generally worse off than they were four years ago in areas such as health, housing, education, employment and social services; (2) the 41 percent of all New York City Blacks who live in Brooklyn's seven community districts lost $61.9 million in 1983; (3) during the same period, four heavily Black districts in the Bronx lost $57 million in federal aid—three such districts in Manhattan lost $62 million and one similar district in Queens lost $22.5 million; (4) one out of three Black families in New York City lived in poverty; (5) and for all boroughs the Black median income was well below that of Whites in the same area.

The process of gentrification over the last fifteen years has forced many low–income Blacks out of their neighborhoods and thus worsened their living conditions (since low–income Blacks cannot afford to live in other areas of the city). Due to high taxes of suburban townships coupled with the difficulties of commuting to the central city, middle class families are returning to city areas vacated by their forebears during the 1950's. Whites are vying for living space in areas of Harlem, Brooklyn, Philadelphia, Baltimore and other city areas traditionally inhabited by Blacks. Moreover, it is ironic that some institutions of higher learning are a part of consortia arrangements designed to revitalize inner–city areas, which in turn causes the displacement of many Black families.

The most ominous fallout from the overall economic distress of the Black population, some experts say, is the quality of Black family life (Matney, 1983). Of all Black families living below the officially defined poverty level in 1981, almost three–quarters (70 percent) were maintained by women, substantially higher than the 56 percent in 1970. Moreover, of all Black children living below the poverty line, 75 percent were in households headed by women.

Educational Issues and Programs

Unless significant changes are made in the quality of Black life within our nation's cities, quality education for Black adolescents will not become a reality.

Contemporary Issues of Urban Secondary Public Schools

Although public schools as social institutions mirror the values and problems of society, they have a distinct culture. Rules, regulations, homework and examinations are just a few characteristics of school culture that confront students. Of the many issues that impact on the quality of educational life, particularly for Black adolescents, four issues appear to be fundamental: (1) curriculum relevancy, (2) teacher competence (3) parental involvement, and (4) competent guidance and counseling.

Curriculum Relevancy

The following passage on curriculum relevancy is taken from Goldhammer's *Clinical Supervision* (1969). His comments were geared to the primary grades, but they are relevant to the secondary grades as well.

> Imagine a unit of study, somewhere in the primary grades, on "The Family." And imagine, if you will, the stories in the reader and in materials assembled by the librarian, and the character of classroom dialogue in this context. Even if you are not presently employed in an elementary school, your childhood memories of first grade should provide appropriate images: in this regard, things have not changed very much. How is "family" generally represented in the early grades?
>
> The houses in which families live never, as far as we are told, include toilets. Members of the family never scratch themselves, utter obscenities, cheat on their wives fix traffic tickets, drink beer, play the horses, falsify their tax returns, strike one another, make love, use deodorants, gossip on the telephone, buy on credit, have ulcers, or manifest a million other signs of life that even the most culturally deprived child knows about in the most intimate detail. Indeed, one suspects that children of poverty are at least as knowledgeable about such intimacies of living as their more affluent counterparts.
>
> Certainly at their dinner tables, no textbook fathers talk about having outbargained that New York Jew, about the niggers who are trying to take over the neighborhood, the cops, the Birchers, the hippies, the war, and so on. On the contrary, one may safely expect the textbook family to be disembodied, apolitical, generally without a specific ethnic identity or religious affiliation, free of social prejudice,

innocent of grief, economically secure, vocationally stable, antiseptic and law–abiding straight down the middle. It occupies a universe from which disaffection, divorce, cynicism, loneliness, neurosis, bastardy, atheism, tension, self–doubt, wrecked cars, and cockroaches are inevitably absent.

Unless he is downright dull, it is almost impossible to imagine that at some level of experience the child is not aware of the thundering disparity between the real world and the school's priggish, distorted, emasculated representation of that world. It seems reasonable to suspect that the child's knowledge almost certainly includes the realization that, in plain language, the curriculum is phony, at least in relation to the example we have considered. (p. 3)

Within the secondary school curriculum concepts such as "urban environmental studies," "self–discovery and leadership" and "the Black experience" are a few examples of providing curriculum relevancy.

Urban environmental studies would include such components as applied economics, the local political process, legal aid, the courts and the penal system. What do Black youth really know about the local political process beyond voter registration and voting? What about terms such as "reapportionment," "legislative committees," "lobbying," "caucuses," and "district captains"? These terms are associated with the "nuts and bolts" of power on the local level. Information on the political process should be integrated into the curriculum. Since economically disadvantaged persons are generally without political power, they are usually victimized. High bail, detention, and incarceration confront the poor to a much larger extent that the affluent. Vital information which would increase the sophistication of students in the areas of the legal and judicial process should also be integrated into the curriculum. By employing techniques of field investigation, for example, housing problems can be directly examined by students within their own environment.

Rapid technological change alters the types of skills needed within the labor market. Urban environmental studies would include an investigation of careers and professions that are presently available and probably would enable students to project the types of technical preparation needed for survival in the future world of work.

For many years a variety of thinkers have wrestled with ideas of enabling people to know themselves in relation to their environment. Norman Vincent Peale, Maxwell Maltz, Don Ethan Miller, and others have explored such themes as self–confidence, leadership, conquest over personal handicaps, and mind–body control. For a fee, individuals can attend these seminars to learn how to become more successful. These types of explorations should be available to Black students via the curriculum. Even though many urban Black adolescents live under oppressive conditions, these conditions should not be used as crutches to support failure. By asking fundamental questions such as who am I? Where am I going?-

a self discovery–leadership dialectic could evolve. Such explorations could enable youngsters to accept their strengths and weaknesses, develop self–confidence, build positive self images, and ultimately aspire towards leadership roles.

African–American history, literature, and other approaches to teaching the Black experience are necessary in order to dispel many of the myths about the western experience. Twenty years ago state and local school boards, school administrators and teachers hid behind the excuse that materials and textbooks were unavailable to teach the Black experience. Not any more! With just a "pinch" of initiative, materials and textbooks can be found:

> The world we live in is overwhelmingly nonwhite. By the year 2000, five billion of the six billion people who live on the earth will be nonwhite. Political power is growing in the east and the south. Asia, Africa, South America are the areas of greatest population growth and potential economic development. For the United States these awesome facts mean that we must learn to find an accommodation with the nonwhite world different from that attempted in the past. (The American Association of Colleges for Teacher Education, 1969) (p.)

The fact that many urban Black adolescents are weak in academic skills has been chronicled and thoroughly documented. The mastery of reading, writing, mathematics and science is crucial as well as fundamental. There are now in existence dozens of basic skill programs throughout America's secondary schools geared toward supplementing existing academic curricula. These programs in part may explain why, according to a report issued by the College Board in 1985, the scholastic Aptitude test scores of Black high school students rose at a faster rate in 1984 than the SAT scores of White students. While scores nationwide for all racial groups rose, Black gains were among the largest–three points on the verbal component and four points in mathematics. White students' scores indicated a two point gain on the verbal component and three points in mathematics.

Although these statistics appear to be promising, Black students still score significantly below White students on the SAT. In order to strengthen the College Board's prediction that "the gap is narrowing" Black students must be counseled out of "watery" courses and encouraged to take more English, mathematics and science courses. Simultaneously, testing agencies such as the Educational Testing Service must continue to produce valid instruments that are free of cultural biases.

The teaching of English, mathematics and science and other subjects should extend beyond mere subject–content. "Critical thinking" must emerge as a necessary by–product. Critical thinking emerges as a result of engaging students in a process of inquiry and problem solving. Bruner

(1960) established that inquiry (gathering, reading, and interpreting information) and problem solving (application of acquired knowledge) can be actually introduced in relatively simple forms during the elementary years. Gradual sophistication in these skills can occur in secondary schools as students evolve from mastering simple to more complex tasks.

Curriculum relevancy then is an attempt to make subject matter come alive by presenting concrete examples and making references to real life experiences of students. It is also an attempt to give students the tools needed to survive in a super technological age. For Black students, nothing could be more essential.

Teacher Competence

Over the past twenty years teacher competence has been in the forefront of criticism of inadequate student preparation. Egerton (1967) found that most college departments of teacher education are not concerned with preparing teachers for urban inner school experiences, even though, during the period his observation was made, eighty percent of America's population lived in two hundred metropolitan community areas. Many programs between 1966 and 1976 emerged to address teaching competence in urban inner–city areas i.e., the AACTE–Job Corps Student Teaching Project, Teacher Corps, the Competency–Based Teacher Education Movement. During the present decade, teacher education programs are facing significant reform in the areas of criteria for admission, subject content, quality of student internships, and exiting criteria. Since 1979 for example, the North Carolina State Board of Education and the University of North Carolina Board of Governors have undertaken a joint effort to study and develop a four–tiered Quality Assurance Program in teacher education. When legislation is finalized, this program will address early counseling, screening and evaluation of students considering teaching as a career, changes in the teacher education curriculum, staffing and evaluation of student teaching experience, and procedures for reviewing inservice teachers who seek continuing certification.

As state boards of education along with institutions of higher learning gear up to reexamine and put into place needed changes in preservice teacher training, new inservice teacher training must take place simultaneously. In addition, input is sorely needed from educational professionals, parents, and spokespersons from Black communities.

Parental Involvement

Lightfoot (1978) published a study on the relationship between families and schools. The study, appropriately titled *Worlds Apart* established that since the culture, perceptions, and expectations of families and schools are different, there is a natural and expected conflict between these institutions. Her findings brought to light that educators, social scientists, and policymakers distort and misperceive the true nature of the family–school relationship.

Although the study was conducted within the elementary grades, Lightfoot's conclusions address family–school relationships within secondary schools. A finding of significant importance to parents or guardians of Black adolescents is that although many of the interactional dimensions between families and schools remain constant across grade levels, different issues emerge as children grow older, become more independent of their families, become more identified with the values and perspectives of their peers, and feel less need for parental protection, guidance, and support. Lightfoot also discusses the ritual and contrivance of Parent–Teacher Association meetings, and the fact that parents usually ask for a conference with teachers when they sense their children are unhappy with the school environment or are not learning to read.

These findings are of paramount importance to parents of Black adolescents. Parents, for example, should not diminish their contact with the school because their children are older and have surpassed the elementary grades. Black parents in particular must be proactive rather than reactive in making contact with their children's teachers, and become involved generally with school issues. Black parents must initiate dialogue with teachers, guidance counselors, supervisors and administrators around school policy, homework, tests and actions taken on test scores. They must articulate and demonstrate their willingness to work and cooperate with the school. It is not easy for working parents (especially single working parents) to assume this role. Many Black parents have two jobs in order to provide food, clothing and shelter. Unemployed parents, particularly welfare recipients, are often emotionally distraught. Parental accountability, nonetheless, is sorely needed. Parents and teachers as partners maximize the educational potential and success of students. Parents should also foster student accountability by questioning their adolescent children about their daily school activities. Homework and class work should be examined consistently. Parents can also play a very important role in nurturing and motivating reading activities.

Competent Guidance and Counseling

No research exists on the number of certified Black guidance counselors or Black guidance counselors–to–student ratios in large urban cities across the nation. There are, however, data in New York City that may be indicative of conditions in other urban cities. New York becomes particularly important since this city has the highest concentration of Blacks in the nation; more than 700,000 Blacks live in Brooklyn alone.

New York City Board of Education data (Academic Year 1985–86) reveal that between 940,000 and 945,000 students currently attend its schools. Thirty percent (between 357,000 and 359,000) are Black. Interviews with two New York City administrators of guidance personnel within two different community school districts shed light on guidance problems: (1) there are virtually no guidance vacancies; (2) due to retrenchment (The 1975–76 period, when the New York City economy came close to defaulting) certified counselors were either laid off, sent back to the classroom or were absorbed by the private sector. In one particular school district, the counseling pool was cut back as much as 34%; (3) there are few certified Black counselors to fill positions when positions are available. There are, however, Black personnel who are performing some form of guidance i.e., substance abuse or attendance counseling, but they are not certified. Black counselors who are "provisionals" could be replaced by other persons who become certified; (4) the current New York City Board of Examiners guidance counselor examination is only offered approximately every three years. Since there exists a "rank–order list," a person passing the examination is hired relative to a vacancy and position on the rank order list; (5) the general ratio of certified guidance counselors to students is disproportionate, resulting in less quality time for individual counseling. Available data found in school districts within the boroughs of Queens and Brooklyn, indicate a ratio of about one counselor to every 1,500 students; (6) in predominantly White school districts, there are few to virtually no Black certified guidance counselors to counsel Black students; (7) in predominantly Black school districts, the proportion of Black certified guidance counselors to Black students is small: A Community School District may contain anywhere between eighteen to twenty eight schools excluding high schools. In one predominantly Black school district (Brooklyn) two of ten Black counselors are certified, in another four of fifteen Black counselors are certified.

The contact between parents and guidance counselors is crucial since there is a tendency to counsel Black students out of the college preparatory track. Grouping and tracking based upon standardized test scores are executed as early as the sixth grade. Many guidance counselors use test data to influence Black students to take "watered down" subjects, or subjects that have no relevancy to competitive intellectual development. According to a 1978 survey conducted by the Federal government under the Youth Employment Development Act, idle teenagers expressed many common feelings about school. They include feelings that although they were capable of a better effort, guidance counselors and teachers tacitly encouraged them to take easy credits; that while teachers know their subjects well, they care personally about only a few of the better students; and that the courses in which they were enrolled were impractical and uninteresting.

Guidance counselors must begin to play a stronger role in raising the academic and career expectations of Black adolescents. This point is crucial since many inner-city teenagers live in a state of hopelessness. Their immediate environments are void of cultural activities and centers, i.e., libraries, community centers, movie theaters, parks. Since unemployment and poor housing are found in their neighborhoods, many teenagers notice that quick money can be made through illicit means. Guidance counselors are in an unique position (by virtue of their training, contacts and influence) to make the difference in the lives of hopeless teenagers. Unfortunately, many Black students feel that these professionals have failed them (For additional discussion of these matters see Chapter 15 on counseling Black adolescents and Chapter 16 on therapeutic interventions with Black adolescents, this volume).

Examples of Traditional and Progressive Educational Programs for Black and Disadvantaged Youth

Traditional Programs

Traditional programs are defined here as those programs that receive public funding. Since these programs meet federal and state criteria, they are accepted as safe and void of unusual or radical departures. On the other hand, not all progressive programs have received public funding. From an educational standpoint, many progressive programs contain elements of social reform, individualization, and more creative approaches than are generally found in public funded programs.

In 1965, the Elementary and Secondary Education Act (ESEA) was enacted. This act authorized educational benefits to be directed mostly toward pupils from low-income families. Under Titles I through VIII of this act, educational resource, research, special education, English as a Second Language, and health and nutrition education are all provided.

Black children in both elementary and secondary schools are still receiving supplemental education in reading, writing, mathematics, and computer literacy via ESEA. Although the Economic Opportunity Act of 1965 aided greatly in the development of nursery schools, this legislation enabled Black adolescent high-school juniors and seniors to receive summer instruction on college and university campuses. The Upward Bound program is a good example. During high school, Upward Bound offers placement in a college bound track, field laboratory experiences, and specialized teaching, counseling and tutorial services in the summer and the academic year.

Many secondary schools have developed and implemented a career education curricula. High–tech, and automotive industries, for example, have either funded or directly assisted high schools in providing academic and practical experiences for Black young adults. Many of these career educational experiences are of superior quality; they go beyond career days or career clinics, and some programs include paid internships.

A variety of other public funded programs designed to bridge the gap between high school and college exist. Project Talent Search, for example, is a federally funded program designed to identify talented "disadvantaged" youth enrolled in high school. Based upon aptitudes, interests, and specific talents, this program attempts to find placement and financial assistance in colleges, universities, and career–based programs. Counseling and tutoring are also available.

Most states fund educational opportunities programs within public and private colleges and universities. These programs offer college entrance to "disadvantaged" students who would not be qualified under regular admissions criteria. The basic structure of these programs include proficiency courses in basic skills, as well as counseling, tutoring, and financial assistance. The SEEK programs (Search for Education, Elevation and Knowledge) of the City University of New York are excellent examples of educational opportunity programs. Founded in 1966 for "disadvantaged" Black and Puerto Ricans, SEEK has established a track record for producing outstanding scholars, professionals, and civil servants. A 1984 study of Queens College SEEK graduates (classes 1969 through 1982) revealed (1) approximately 90% of SEEK graduates were employed in viable jobs and careers. (2) approximately two–thirds of SEEK graduates continued on to graduate or professional schools. In addition, a higher proportion of SEEK than non–SEEK students are the first in their immediate families to graduate from college, and SEEK graduates reported their program of study and support services prepared them very well for graduation, post graduate studies, and employment.

Special and Alternative Schools

Most progressive programs still in existence are special or alternative schools. In 1969 several special high schools began to emerge with progressive curricula viz, Metro High School in Chicago, the Parkway School in Philadelphia, John Dewey High School in New York City. The Parkway School, for example, follows a fieldwork curriculum similar to urban environmental studies, discussed earlier. The curriculum of John Dewey was developed around the following progressive principles:

- Wherever feasible, students were enabled to apply academic knowledge to practical situations.
- Students' experiences were respected by encouraging their input in curriculum development.
- Individualization of instruction is encouraged by enabling students to learn at their own rate.
- Students select courses along with field laboratory experiences.

The alternative neighborhood schools founded in the fifties and sixties to address the educational needs of Black children do not receive the exposure and recognition they so richly deserve. These schools embraced different ideologies i.e., Pan–Africanism, Islamic Fundamentalism, Conservatism (basically keeping mainstream American values). A lack of continuous funding, marketing, and community support led to the closure of some of these schools. The Council of Independent Black Institutions based in East Palo Alto, California is still alive. It provides curriculum development and teacher training for its member institutions. CIBI goals, among others, are to develop and implement instructional methodology that will insure maximum academic achievement for Black children, create and sustain independent Black institutions that provide educational, cultural and social development for Black communities, and train and deploy teachers to serve in Black independent institutions. The recently formed Institute for Independent Education Incorporated (IIE) seeks to highlight and support alternative neighborhood schools that are still surviving. Through such initiatives as scholarship services, outreach strategies, research and teacher training, IIE introduces more of these schools to parents, funding sources and education policymakers. Many Black graduates of alternative schools such as Junior Academy (Brooklyn, New York), the Wingate Freedom School (Atlanta, Georgia), the Harlem Preparatory School (New York City) and, Malcolm X Liberation University (Durham, North Carolina), are either enrolled or have graduated from colleges and universities across the nation. Many of these students have emerged as strong individuals armed with a positive self image, and a sense of purpose and direction and have returned to render service to their communities.

Street academies. The street academy movement, founded in 1965 by Dr. Susie Bryant, was created to address underachieving inner–city students, who were either attending public schools or had dropped out. Within a decade of its founding, street academies were established within many cities across the nation. The extent to which street academies exist today is hard to determine. Many academies closed because of a lack of funds. The Urban League was the chief sponsor of academies during the sixties and seventies. When the Urban League withdrew as the chief funding source, academies had to find new sponsors. During the latter seventies, for example, the Union Carbide Corporation sponsored the street academy in Brooklyn, New York.

Under the leadership of Dr. Irving Hamer, formerly Headmaster, Park Heights Street Academy can be seen as a prototype of a progressive alternative school. This academy services high ability adolescents (some having experienced low or limited achievement in other school settings) between the ages of fourteen and twenty–one. Completion of the eighth grade is a prerequisite for entrance. The primary purpose of the academy is to assist students in developing personal attitudes and academic skills which encourage and promote effective participation in higher education, career training and employment. The academy offers a college preparatory curriculum that exceeds the state requirements. The eleven month academic year and the 8:30 a.m. to 4:30 p.m. school day enables students to complete high school in three years. Its rigorous curriculum concentrates on the humanities, social science, and the physical and natural sciences. Examples of specific offerings are Library and Information Science, Latin, Orientation to Life, Business Mathematics, Black American Painters, African–American History, quality instructional software. This shortage is more pronounced within the secondary schools.

When the school opened in 1978 the enrollment was approximately forty students. In 1983 the enrollment doubled. Tuition is calculated on a sliding scale using annual family income and the number of household family members as determinants. The academy's first graduation ceremony was during the Spring of 1980. Ten students graduated at that time. When these students applied for college entrance, they were accepted at a number of prestigious colleges and universities.

Strategies for Educational Improvement of Black Adolescents

Improved socioeconomic conditions are a precursor to improved education for Black adolescents. The basic premise of this chapter is that educational problems are symptomatic of fundamental socioeconomic problems. Solutions, therefore, require long range strategies and benefits may not surface until one or two generations later. However, socioeconomic and educational problems are intertwined, and therefore must be addressed simultaneously.

Robert L. Woodson, President of the National Center for Neighborhood Enterprise calls for a strategy for economic development and the development of an entrepreneurial spirit among the Black underclass through (1) making it possible for low income Black citizens to participate in greater numbers in the mainstream of the American economy, and not by the expansion of a welfare state; (2) development of Black enterprise that will strengthen the economic base of Black neighborhoods and put more money into Black pockets; (3) allowing persons experiencing the problems to play a primary role in designing solutions to them; and (4) disentangling the Black community from the welfare professionals whose objective is to maintain clients.

Although Woodson decries continued traditional civil rights strategies, they are needed. In the past, civil rights strategies were directly responsible for executive orders, legislation, and judicial decisions that directly impacted on the quality of Black life via the political process, affirmative action, and equal educational access. The Woodson model, coupled with civil rights strategies, would provide a rational direction for future improvement of socioeconomic conditions and quality education for urban Blacks.

In April 1983, the National Commission on Excellence in Education released an open letter to the American public entitled "A Nation at Risk: The Imperative for Educational Reform." After documenting that functional illiteracy among minority youth may run as high as 40 percent nationally, the Commission made several recommendations for educational change. These recommendations covered such broad areas as curriculum content, time spent in school, and teacher training. The Commission recommended, for example, that educationally disadvantaged children may require special curriculum materials, smaller classes, and individual tutoring. The commission also recommended for all youth who are generally poor in all academic skills that significantly more time be devoted to learning the new basics. A longer school day or a lengthened school year was recommended to achieve this end. Although the Commission's recommendations were broad and well intended, they did not really address the fundamental issues that will affect educational practices across the board toward the year 2000. At best, these recommendations only addressed the symptoms of fundamental educational problems. The commission's recommendations, then, amounted to short range solutions.

Snyder (1986) addresses fundamental educational problems forthrightly in a report entitled "Learning for Life in Revolutionary Times: Imperatives for American Educators in a Decade of Techno–Economic Change." Originally commissioned by the National Education Association to examine future economic and technological trends that will impact education, Snyders's assessment appears to lay the framework for future strategies to improve the quality of education for Black and, indeed, all youth. Snyder states, for example, that toward the end of the twentieth century one quarter of the American work force will be required to change careers and another twenty five percent will have to be retrained on the job. This fact suggests that career education is paramount in tomorrow's curricula. Snyder states that students will also have to be taught how to shift career directions. The rate of technological change will force

Educating Black Urban Adolescents

individuals to make new career choices. The report also stated that since opportunities for new professional high-tech and skilled craft careers are expected to grow rapidly after the mid-1990's, educators must provide students with the intellectual tools to live such a life effectively and productively. It appears, then, that tomorrow's curricula will have to include coping as well as critical thinking skills. As a futurist, Snyder also compiled a comprehensive review of educational research in order to produce specific recommendations for an action educational agenda for tomorrow's schools. These recommendations included the following:

1. *A wide range of innovative educational delivery arrangements*, since public schools confronted by demands for substantially improved performance will be faced with limited financial and human resources.
2. *Quality instructional materials*, since most instructional materials do not incorporate research-based principles of effective curriculum design.
3. *Experiential learning*—scores on standardized achievement tests indicate that most public schools effectively convey a high percentage of their curriculum content. Schools, however, are much less successful in providing students with the tools to apply learning to real world situations. Assessments of actual post-secondary performance in the work place, and in college consistently reflect declining levels of proficiency among public school graduates. Data suggest that public education has become a series of ritualized activities rather than a practical preparation for adult life.
4. *Improvement in the Quality of Instructional Software*—The relative ineffectiveness of computerized learning has been largely due to the lack of quality instructional software. This shortage is more pronounced within the secondary schools.
5. *Computer Competency*—As life-span learning and sequential careers become a commonplace reality in America, individuals who are unable to use personal computers will be enormously disadvantaged. Public schools must make computer competency a basic educational goal by making them an integral part of student life. Students should be required to use computers for such routine tasks as getting homework assignments, locating and withdrawing library books, or submitting answers to tests.
6. *Teacher Retraining*—Particularly in the areas of computer competency and how to design effective instructional materials.
7. *Precision Teaching*—Precision teaching is a process which involves giving students frequent diagnostic quizzes designed to measure multiple dimensions of learning, in order to identify the specific teacher interventions that will be most effective in aiding each individual student's performance. Studies have shown that

precision teaching typically improves educational effectiveness and student performance by 25% to 50%.
8. *Innovative Evaluation Networks*—Educators must be able to share information about their innovative experiences rapidly and effectively. A means should be established by which evaluations of actual results of specific innovations can be quickly exchanged. Such networks would permit the rapid identification of new teaching technologies and instructional arrangements that have proven productive. (p. 1–6)

Although Snyder was addressing the educational needs of all youth for the purpose of meeting tomorrow's technological demands, his comments are of particular importance to Black students. Black students must be prepared to compete in tomorrow's world. Black Americans, however, from all walks of life have the primary responsibility to caucus around the crisis of providing quality education for Black youths. Black national forums on this issue have been called in the seventies and during this decade. The now defunct African–American Teachers Association sponsored a conference in Brooklyn, New York in April, 1972 which called for a national Black educational system. In May, 1975 the New York Urban League Street Academies convened a conference in New York City entitled "Rethinking Alternatives." A major recommendation of that conference was the establishment of a national organization to provide a network of communication among Street Academies and other alternative locating and withdrawing library books, or submitting answers to tests.

Black national forums like the ones just described must continue on an annual basis. Networking between different forums are essential for continuity and unity of purpose. Naturally, each forum has different purposes and approaches and each desires to maintain a degree of autonomy. The survival of tomorrow's Black adults, however, is the glue that can connect different Black educational ideologies. The NCNE Conference, for example, attempted to coordinate the thinking and philosophies of many independent neighborhood schools. A dialectic emerged between professional community persons and students on the proper course of action for educating poor children.

Forums, however, need follow–through. Educational conferences are held with good intentions. The creative ideas, passion and pledges of these conferences however, seem to die at the end of the "wrap up" session. Follow–through could result in (1) the creation of a national think tank on the subject of quality education for Black adolescents that would sponsor discussions among Black professionals, Black community spokespersons and Black students; (2) the creation of curriculum development strategies and models; (3) the creation of a mechanism to support existing traditional and progressive programs that have helped Black adolescents receive quality education; (4) providing teaching assistance to struggling alternative institutions; and (5) the creation of a mechanism to support agencies and programs such as the Black Child Development Institute, the United Negro College Fund and Educational Opportunity Programs found on predominantly White college campuses.

The possibilities of these endeavors becoming a reality exist more than ever before given the number of trained Black professionals now employed in educational settings. Professionally trained American Blacks hold more degrees and licenses in the field of Education, than any other profession. While this is the case, we must remember, however, that the educational survival of Black children and adolescents, is everyone's business.

References

Armor, D. J. (1972). School and family effects on Black and White achievement: A reexamination of the USOE data. In Mosteller and Moynihan, (Eds.), *On equality of educational opportunity*. New York: Vintage Books.

Bastian, A., Fruchter, N., Gittel, M., Greer, C., and Haskins, K. (1986). *Choosing equality: The case for democratic schooling*. Philadelphia: Temple University Press.

Birch, G. & Gussow, J. D. (1970). *Disadvantaged children: Health, Nutrition, and school failure*. New York: Harcourt, Brace, and World.

Bruner, J. S. (1960). *The process of education*. New York: Vintage Books.

Carmichael, S., & Hamilton, C. V. (1967). *Black power: The politics of liberation in America*. New York: Vintage Books.

Coleman, J. A. et al. (1966). *Equality of educational opportunity*. Washington, D.C. U.S. Department of Health, Education and Welfare, U.S. Government Printing Office.

Costellow, M. J. (1971). The John Dewey high school adventure, *Phi Delta Kappan*, 52(2), 108–110.

Cox, D. W. (1972). *The city as schoolhouse*. Valley Forge, PA: Judson Press.

Dentler, R. A. (1968). *American community problems*. New York: McGraw–Hill Book Company.

Drake, S. C., & Cayton, H. (1970). *Black metropolis*. New York: Harcourt, Brace, and World.

Dubois, W. E. B. (1938). *The souls of Black folk*. Chicago: A. C. McClurg and Co.

Eagle, N. & Modeste, W. (Undated). A follow–up of SEEK Graduates. Queens College, City University of New York.

Egerton, J. (1967). Survey: A lack of preparation in the colleges, *Southern Educational Report*, II, 2–13.

Frazier, E. F. (1957). *The Negro in the United States*. New York: Macmillan.

Gibbs, J. T. (1988). Black adolescents and youth: An update on an endangered species. Chapter 1, this volume.

Goldhammer, R. (1969). *Clinical supervision: Special methods for the supervision of teachers*. New York: Holt, Rinehart and Winston, Inc.

Good, T. L., & Brophy, J. E. (1984). *Looking in classrooms*. New York: Harper and Row.

Hass, G. (1983). *Curriculum planning: A new approach.* Boston: Allyn and Bacon, Inc. (1988). Progress Report 1986–1987. Washington, D.C.: Institute for Independent Education.

Jackson, B. (1975). *Rethinking alternatives: A report on the conference.* Atlanta: Atlanta University, August, 1975.

Lapati, A. D. (1975). *Education in the federal government: A historical record.* New York: Mason–Charter Publishers.

Lightfoot, S. L. (1978). *Worlds apart: Relationships between families and schools.* New York: Basic Books, Inc.

Matney, W. C. Jr. (1986). Black economic plight—A look into the past forecasts challenge to the present. *The Crisis,* 90.

Mitchell, V. (1987). Director of Pupil Personnel Services, Community School District 17, Brooklyn, New York. Interview, April 9, 1987.

Murray, C. B., & Fairchild, H. H. (1988). Models of Black adolescent underachievement. Chapter 12, this volume.

National Alliance of Black School Educators, Inc. (1984). Saving the African American Child. A Report of NABSE, Task Force on Black Academic and Cultural Experience.

National Center for Neighborhood Enterprise (1983). Neighborhood–Based Private Schools: Give a child a choice. Washington, D.C.: National Center for Neighborhood Enterprise.

National Commission on Excellence in Education. (1983). A nation at risk: The imperative for educational reform. A report to the Nation and the United States Department of Education.

New York State Education Department. (1982). From school to work: The youth tightrope. *Inside Education,* Spring/Summer, 6.

New York State Education Department, (1985). SAT scores of Blacks advancing faster than national averages. *Learning in New York.*

New York Urban League. (1984). *Status of Black New York: A study.* New York: New York Urban League.

Ogbu, J. U. (1978). *Minority education and caste: The American system in cross–cultural perspective.* New York: Academic Press.

Park Heights Academy (No date). Park Heights Street Academy, An Informational Brochure. Baltimore, Maryland 21215: Park Heights Academy, 3901 Park Heights Ave.

Quinones, N., & Wagner, R. (1986). Minutes of presentations made to the Mayors' Commission on Black New Yorkers. New York: Mayor's Commission on Black New Yorkers.

Silverman, R. (1987). (District 25, Queens, New York). Interview, March 17, 1987.

Smith, B. O. et al. (1969). *Teachers for the real world.* Washington, D.C.: the American Association of Colleges for Teacher Education.

Snyder, D. P. (1986). Learning for life in revolutionary times: Imperatives for American educators in a decade of techno–economic change. Unpublished paper.

Stein, A. (1971). Strategies for failure. *Harvard Education Review,* XLI, 158–204.

The Chronicle of Higher Education (1985). Scores continued to rise last year on SAT, ACT test. Chronicle of Higher Education, *31(5),* 33, 37.

The Council of Independent Black Institutions (No date). *An informational pamphlet,* 1983. East Palo Alto, CA 94305: CIBI, P.O. Box 50396.

Liaison Committee on the Quality Assurance Program (No date). The Quality Assurance Program: A Report from the Liaison Committee on the Quality Assurance Program to the North Carolina State Board of Education and the Board of Governors of the University of North Carolina.

United States Bureau of the Census Report. (1960). Washington, D.C.: Government Printing Office.

United States Bureau of the Census (1983). Report. Washington, D.C.: Government Printing Office.

United States Riot Commission (1968). Report of the National Advisory Committee on Civil Disorders. New York: E. P. Dutton.

Vogt, D. K. (1973). *Literacy among youth 12–17 years*. U.S.,

Public Health Services Publication No. 131. Washington, D.C.: National Center for Health Statistics.

Woodson, R. (1985). Blacks' self help is salvation. *The Washington Post, Outlook: Commentary and opinion.*

MODELS OF BLACK ADOLESCENT ACADEMIC UNDERACHIEVEMENT

Carolyn B. Murray and Halford H. Fairchild

Introduction

Black American academic underachievement is one of the most pernicious effects of American inequality (see National Commission on Excellence in Education, 1983). It is both a cause and a consequence of historical and contemporary discrimination, and is associated with problems of unemployment, crime, drug abuse, and mortality (Fairchild & Tucker, 1982).

Despite recent progress in educational attainment, racial gaps in academic achievement remain alarming. A suggestive trend is that these achievement gaps increase at older ages and higher grade levels (Holmes, 1983). These effects culminate in adolescence, where Black youth are vocationally tracked, and are reflected in high drop-out rates, poor performance on nationally standardized achievement tests, and generally stiffer challenges in higher education (e.g., Biemiller, 1985).

This chapter critically examines explanations of Black adolescents' educational attainment, including the Genetic Deficit Approach, Cultural Approaches, and Social Cognitive Approaches. We conclude with the development of an alternative approach that synthesizes both macro (i.e., systemic discrimination) and micro (i.e., teacher and student attitudes and behaviors) forces in producing academic underachievement in Black American adolescents.

The Genetic Deficit Approach

The earliest explanation for lower academic and intellectual functioning among Black Americans pointed to "genetic deficits" in the Black population. This hypothesis emerged with the genesis of American psychology (see Guthrie, 1976, 1980), and has been reinvigorated by Jensen (1969, 1985), Herrnstein (1973), Jencks (1980), Shockley (1972), Eysenck (1972) and others. Based on "Social Darwinism", this approach accepted the idea of "survival of the fittest" when applied to human differentiation, and concluded that Whites were a superior race, at least with respect to intellectual functioning.

The Genetic Deficit Model has generated a great deal of controversy (see Fairchild & Gurin, 1978; Williams & Mitchell, 1980). A number of rebuttals have successfully challenged the Genetic Deficit Model on theoretical, methodological, statistical, and ethical grounds (see for example, Baba & Darga, 1981; Kamin, 1974, 1980; Mackenzie, 1980a, 1980b; Persell, 1981; Terrell, Terrell & Taylor, 1980; Vetta, 1980a, 1980b; Williams & Mitchell, 1980). The point, however, is that the Genetic Deficit Model satisfied certain political and ideological objectives, and has remained very much alive in the psychology of the 80's (see Jensen, 1985; Persell, 1981). Contemporary expressions of this model have pointed to differences in the efficiency of the brain and nervous system in processing information (e.g., Jensen, 1980), and to presumed differences in brain hemisphericity (see Reynolds, McBride & Gibson, 1981).

As argued later, the Genetic Deficit Approach has reinforced stereotypes that characterized Black Americans as inferior, and has maintained the comparatively lower teacher expectations that produce academic underachievement. For the current purposes, the Genetic Deficit Approach is criticized because of its failure to adequately define the nature of intelligence, because of the manner in which intelligence has been operationalized (i.e., measured), because of the methodologies for assessing genetic versus environmental determinants of intelligence (or achievement), and because of the ethical issues involved in this area of psychological theory and research.

The nature of intelligence has been debated for decades (cf. Cronbach, 1975). Needless to say, the current discussion will not provide a definitive end to this debate. Most theorists, however, agree that intelligence refers to the ability to learn, or the extent to which one benefits from experience.

If intelligence is concerned with the individual's capacity to learn, then it becomes clear that, at least for biologically "normal" individuals, this capacity is virtually unlimited. Each individual has the capacity to learn a variety of foreign languages, many forms of mathematics, history, geography, science, musical and artistic expression, games, sports, *ad infinitum*. That being the case, it is highly unlikely that psychologists can adequately measure this infinite store of learning potential.

Much of the recent attention on the biological bases of intelligence, and on the more general information processing paradigms, has stemmed from a growing dissatisfaction with the psychometrically–based theories of intelligence that were rooted in traditional paper–and–pencil measures of IQ (Sternberg, 1981). In particular, these psychometric or factor–analytic theories of intelligence have failed to provide an adequate means for hypothesis testing, have failed to identity the *processes* of intellectual functioning, and have failed to provide action implications for training and developing intellectual functioning either for individuals or for the broader society (Sternberg, 1981).

The information processing approaches, in contrast, view the organism as a perceiver, transducer, encoder, processor, and actor in the context of environmental stimuli. This approach has received considerable attention in recent years (e.g., Rafferty, 1980; Sternberg, 1981), and holds some promise for raising the study of intelligence out of its current malaise.

Extrapolating from these new biogenic models of intelligence, Fairchild (1983) suggested that intelligence is reflected in complex sporting events, such as basketball. If the key to intelligence is the ability to accurately perceive the environment, to make decisions about those perceptions, and to act appropriately, then complex decision–based behaviors in sports are clear examples of intelligence at work.

Cultural Approaches

The Cultural Deprivation Model and the Cultural Difference Model were proposed perhaps as by–products of the distaste scholars had for the Genetic Deficit Approach. The Cultural Deprivation Model focused on the "environmental handicaps" confronting Black American families and children (e.g., Hunt, 1964; Moynihan, 1965). This model suggested that economic and social discrimination (including residential isolation) led to self–perpetuating conditions that resulted in the development of dysfunctional personality traits (e.g., low self–concept, a low need for achievement, and an external locus of control) which culminated in lower achievement levels among Black Americans. Although ostensibly pointing to systemic causes, the Cultural Deprivation Model continued to "blame the victim" (see Ryan, 1976) by pointing to "pathological families" and a "culture of poverty" (see Baratz & Baratz, 1970; Valentine, 1971). Most of the compensatory educational programs emerging during the 1960s—including Head Start, Follow Through, and programs designed specifically for adolescents such as Upward Bound and Bridge—were strongly undergirded by the assumptions, goals, and methods of cultural deprivation theorists (Banks, 1982).

More recently, in contrast to the Cultural Deprivation Model, the Cultural Difference Model strongly rejects the assumptions of the cultural deprivation theorists and argues that educational programs for Blacks should be based on the premise of cultural differences. Specifically, proponents of this theory acknowledge that Black students bring unique socio–cultural experiences and psychological dispositions to the educational setting, but they also maintain that these "differences" are not "deficits." Instead, they argue that Blacks have a strong, rich, and diverse culture. For instance, according to the cultural difference theorists, Black English is a dialect that is rich and elaborate (Labov, 1970; Smitherman, 1977; White 1984). Thus, Black American underachievement was the result of a "mismatch" between the culture of the school and the adolescent's cultural expressions at home and in the community. Cultural difference theorists propose that the problem of motivating the Black pupil is essentially one of accommodating the educational goals of the school to the values, goals and learning styles that have been socially transmitted to the child in his or her home and neighborhood environments.

To be sure, both the Cultural Difference and the Deprivation Models diverged on the explanation of why Black students underachieve. However, both also share the normative view generally associated with the Cultural Deprivation Model that Black children suffer from the lack of personality traits that are thought to be necessary for academic success. The most researched and debated of these presumed personality deficits are self–concept, locus of control, and achievement motivation. However, due to methodological inadequacies, erroneous assumptions, biased interpretations, and system inequities which have confounded many of the research conclusions, the relationship between these personality traits and Black student underachievement is still unarticulated, and the currently held cultural explanations are little more than exercises in ethnocentrism (See Chapter 2, by Smith, West, & Murray, this volume, for a discussion of this literature).

The somewhat more liberal ideas of the cultural difference theorists have become less influential during the 1980s since they are unfashionable according to the political neoconservative ideologies of the day. However, Cultural Deprivation Theory, though harshly criticized during the 1970s by many Black scholars, has fared better, gaining more legitimacy during the 1980s because of the heavy emphasis on concepts such as the economic underclass and the female–headed household (Banks, 1982).

By way of comparison, the three models, i.e., *Genetic Deficit*, *Cultural Deprivation*, and *Cultural Difference Models* have commonalities as well as differences. All three models find the cause of the Black youth's achievement problems within the Black adolescent, whether attributing the cause to the Black adolescent's genetic makeup, home environment, or to his or her personality traits.

Social Cognitive Approach

The Social Cognitive Approach, while borrowing much from the personality theorists, discarded the focus on personality traits or situationally defined behavior as determinants of motivation, and instead emphasized individuals' cognitive representation of the environment: perceptions, inferences, and interpretations of social experience.

Most important among these have been the causal attributions, specifically interpretations of achievement outcomes, which occur on three main dimensions: locus (internal vs. external), stability (fixed vs. variable), and controllability (controllable vs. uncontrollable) (Weiner, 1985). Research has demonstrated that maximum pride and security in success were derived from the perception that success was due to the internally stable factor, ability. High achievers tended to attribute their success to both high ability and effort while they perceived failure as due to lack of effort (Kukla, 1972; Weiner, 1979). Low achievers, on the other hand, were less likely to attribute their successes to internal causes, but attributed failure to their low ability (Weiner & Kukla, 1970; Weiner, Frieze, Kukla, Reed, Rest, & Rosenbaum, 1971). The attribution of success to high ability or task ease was found to lead to an anticipation of continued success. Similarly, if a failure was due to these stable causes, continued failure was anticipated. Conversely, unstable causes tended to lead to expectations of change. Failure attributed to bad luck was expected to finally change. Failure attributed to effort by trying harder was expected to lead to future success (Weiner, et al., 1971).

Unfortunately, scant empirical attention has been paid to this intriguing notion to account for achievement patterns of Black American adolescents. Most of the available research has focused on the particular attributions of Blacks and Whites following success or failure at achievement tasks (Graham, 1984; Willig, Harnesch, Hill & Maehr, 1983). In general, Blacks made more external attributions for success and failure than Whites. Blacks were especially likely to attribute their outcome to good or bad luck (e.g., Friend & Neale, 1972; Lefcourt, 1970; Murray & Mednick, 1975). As pointed out by Graham (1986), in terms of the dimensional properties, an attributional self-ascription to bad luck for failure: (1) would identify the cause as external, which would not undermine positive self-esteem; (2) its instability should lead to relatively favorable expectations for future success; and (3) the uncontrollability of this cause should mitigate punishment from one's teacher.

Challenging the earlier finding that Blacks are more external in terms of identifying the causes of their academic outcomes, some research reported no differences between Blacks and Whites on their causal attributions (Willig, et al., 1983), or differences suggesting a more adaptive attributional pattern among Blacks (Graham, 1984). However, several findings suggested that while nonadvantaged Black adolescents made similar attributions as their White counterparts, they tended to have unrealistically high expectations for success, even when achievement outcomes indicated otherwise (Graham, 1986). Furthermore, in contradiction to the underlying assumptions of the theory, and in contrast to the literature on White adolescents, researchers have reported that, for Black adolescents, internal attributions for positive outcomes were negatively associated with grade point average (Belgrave, Johnson, & Carey, 1985).

Attribution researchers have rarely ventured out of experimental settings into actual classrooms. Furthermore, measurement procedures in attribution research have not yet developed an adequate degree of sophistication, and issues such as reliability and construct validity have rarely been considered (Elig & Frieze, 1979; Stipek & Weisz, 1981). These considerations, coupled with the limited amount of research examining the academic outcome attributions of Black adolescents, underscores how little is really known about their attributional strategies. The available data, however, provide the impetus for future research to determine the overall usefulness of this line of investigation.

Rethinking the Problem

Identifying the cause of poor academic achievement as residing solely in the Black adolescent rationalizes all the failures of ghetto schools, and promotes the acceptance of educational inequality in America. Our approach is an integrative one which casts the "victim's role" in this vicious cycle of academic failure within a broader context of inequality in the allocation of educational resources on the macro level, and biased teacher attitudes on the micro level.

Systemic Inequality

The previously discussed traditional approaches to understanding the comparatively lower academic performance of Black adolescents, in contrast to White adolescents, have not considered the collective historical experience of Blacks. Neither have they considered structural barriers of the wider society in general, nor of the public school system in particular. In terms of the collective historical experience, until the end of the Civil War (1865), schooling was limited to the elite White society and, in general, Blacks were systematically excluded by law from formal education. Since the post-Reconstruction era, there has been a set of policies guiding public school education that have consistently sought to maintain the status quo in terms of class and race stratification within the society (Carnoy, 1974). Thus, while it is true that lower-class White education has usually been inferior to that of the White middle and upper-classes, it is equally true that Blacks have been provided still more inferior education as a matter of course (Ogbu, 1981).

Throughout the long period of *de jure* and *de facto* segregation in public schools nationwide, the persistence of the inferior education provided Black youth was insured through mediocre school funding for facilities, supplies, staffing, building maintenance and general operations; through a truncated school year compared to the regular school cycle for White students; and through approved curricula and counseling strategies which stressed manual and vocational training (Ogbu, 1981).

For Blacks in integrated or desegregated schools, the policy to maintain the provision of inferior education has been insured by institutional practices of mandatory administration of culturally-biased standardized testing (Carnoy, 1974; Mercer, 1973), counseling placements, tracking and ability categorization (Oakes, 1985), bigoted textbooks (Khatib & Murray, in press), and inferior curricula (Carnoy, 1974; Oakes, 1985; Ogbu, 1981). To illuminate the endemic nature of these practices, three common school policies especially injurious to Black adolescents' academic achievement are discussed in more detail below. These include public school funding, assignment into remedial and special education classes, and tracking.

The first is public school funding. In the late 19th and through the 20th century, it was axiomatic that Black pupils, particularly those in predominantly Black schools, would receive far less funding support in their schools than would their White counterparts (Carnoy, 1974). In the 1970's and 1980's, however, it is interesting that little has changed in that regard. Washington, D.C., Chicago, and several other large cities have regularly decreased the amount of funding per pupil in several of their public schools as a function of the proportionate increase of the Black student population in those schools (Hughes & Hughes, 1973).

In one empirical report that documented such inequalities in public education, Fairchild (1984) demonstrated that within the Los Angeles Unified School District, large discrepancies were evident in the amount of money spent on instruction in various elementary schools. Moreover, schools varied quite a bit in terms of overall enrollments. More importantly, these resource variable—per-pupil-expenditures and school size—were significantly related to academic achievement in reading and arithmetic scores.

In a test of the *democracy* inherent in public education, Fairchild (1984) then correlated the school resource variables with racial composition indicators, and found that as the percentage of Black students increased, per-pupil-expenditures decreased and school size increased. Similar findings were found for the percentage of Hispanic students. In contrast, as the percentage of White students increased, expenditures increased and school size decreased. Thus, this report offered compelling evidence that the underachievement of Black school children was due, at least in part, to inequalities in educational opportunity. Because elementary school education provides the basis for later educational attainments, such discriminatory policies have clear implications for the academic underachievement of Black American adolescents.

The second policy, the disproportionate assignment of Black pupils into remedial and special education classes, is widespread. This practice, quite obviously, keeps them far afield of mainstream academic endeavors and training, and it also negatively affects the students' chance for securing worthwhile employment. Such large urban areas as San Francisco, New York, Chicago and Los Angeles engaged in this practice since at least the early seventies (Ogbu, 1981). San Francisco was recently found guilty of adversely impacting the education of Black school pupils by its use of IQ tests to assign pupils to special education classes. The plaintiffs demonstrated that in one typical school year, 1976–77, even though Black pupils only made up 31% of the school district's enrollment, over 53% of those assigned into the educable mentally retarded classes were Black pupils. And such a finding was not restricted to San Francisco. During that same time period, the twenty California school districts, which altogether enrolled over 80% of the Black pupils in the state, assigned 62% of those they labeled educable mentally retarded learners from that population, even though Black student enrollment constituted less than 28% of each district (Ogbu, 1981; U.S. District Court, Northern California, 1979).

Tracking, the final common practice to be discussed, is the most widespread and pernicious of all. It is a process of programmatic sorting; a division of students into various academic categories designed to facilitate their placement into classroom groups for fast, average and slow learners. Usually, the "objective" basis for the division is student scores on achievement, ability or placement exams, and/or counselor/teacher selection. Such tracking, however, is not value–free; it is highly political. Students are publicly identified, even targeted, based on high or low teacher perceptions of their intellectual potential, and subsequently placed within an often life–long ability group.

Tracked students come to be identified by peers, staff, teachers, and parents as high or low achievers—bright and smart, or dumb and dimwitted—and the students gain or lose status, privileges and teacher preference as a result of the categorization the students are placed into. Although many public schools deny they track students, many do engage in the practice, notwithstanding the name of the program; it is an entrenched component of public school policy and practice (Oakes, 1985).

In one of the most comprehensive studies of tracking, Oakes (1985) surveyed the practice in twenty–five junior and senior high schools. In analyzing the relationship of race and tracking, Oakes concluded,

> ...It is clear that in our multiracial schools minority students were found in disproportionately small percentages in high–track classes and in disproportionately large percentages in low–track classes. And, as we have seen, this pattern was most consistently found in schools where minority students were also poor. These findings are consistent with virtually every study that has considered the distribution of poor and minority students among track levels in schools. In

academic tracking, then, poor and minority students are most likely to be placed at the lowest levels of the schools' sorting system. (p.67)

Furthermore, according to Oakes, an examination of the curriculum offered in vocational training programs revealed that they provide neither the type nor the scope of education necessary to overcome race and class obstacles to employment.

Thus, Black students disproportionately receive an inferior education which results in a job ceiling far below that of their White counterparts (Ogbu, 1981). In turn, this job ceiling limits Black access (in contrast to White access) to social, economic and political opportunities.

At the macro level, then, there is a striking preponderance of evidence that supports an *a priori* case against rationalizing the cause(s) of poor academic achievement solely or even primarily on the victim's own traits. However, as pointed out by Ogbu, these "structural barriers" make both Whites and Blacks behave in a manner that promotes Black school failure (p. 146). As discussed in the following section, the perceptions and expectations of teachers concerning how Black students ought to perform, often lead them to provide Black students with an inferior education. For Blacks, their own perceptions of these limitations generate attitudes and behaviors that are often not conducive to school success.

Perceptual Biasing Effects

The theoretical models discussed earlier provided the basis for educational policy and reinforced the negative stereotypes inherent in the culture that characterizes Black Americans as intellectually inferior to Whites (Ryan, 1976). Moreover, these explanations legitimized the negative expectations teachers hold for Black children's future success which when translated to the student culminate in a "self–fulfilling prophecy". Thus, the micro forces we propose as responsible for underachievement among Black adolescents are biased teacher and student attitudes and their resulting behaviors.

This process has been coined the Conditioned Failure Model (Bennett, 1979; Murray & Jackson, 1982/83). According to this model, initial teacher perceptions of students' abilities play a precipitating role in their attributions concerning student success and failure. This, in turn, affects the reinforcements that students receive (grades, praise, etc.) and consequently, student motivation, behavior, and achievement.

The major thesis is that the "poor" scholastic performance by Black students may be less a reflection of intellectual abilities or family background than the result of stereotypic conceptions held by their teachers. This phenomena has been generally referred to as the "self–fulfilling prophecy" (Bennett, 1976; Brophy, 1983; Darley & Fazio, 1980; Rosenthal,

1968, 1973, 1976; Harris & Rosenthal, 1985). The Conditioned Failure Model examines the antecedents and consequences of both expectancy congruent and expectancy incongruent student educational performance. Several studies have found that teachers tend to like students who live up (or down) to their expectations regardless of whether those expectations are positive or negative (Brookover, 1973; Coble, 1975; Rubovits & Maehr, 1973;). Due to the lower expectations held by teachers for Black American adolescents, it can be seen that a student will often be rewarded (liked) for failure and punished (disliked) for success. The effects of this type of reinforcement schedule may result in the child perceiving a lack of control over his or her environment and thus may lead to dysfunctional achievement behavior (cf. Coleman, et al., 1966; Katz, 1967).

One form of dysfunctional behavior can be defined as the employment of "self–handicapping strategies", which is "any action or choice of performance setting that enhances the opportunity to externalize (or excuse) failure, thus enabling the individual to avoid or discount negative implications of a performance" (Jones & Berglas, 1978, p. 200). Should failure occur, it is thus more easily attributed to some external impediment rather than to the individual's own lack of ability. Furthermore, in the case of success, the implications for the individual's level of ability are enhanced or augmented (Kelly, 1971) because they occurred in spite of external impediments.

The underachievers are said to be fearful of receiving the unequivocal message that they are unworthy or incompetent. Because Black American adolescents are constantly bombarded with messages of their "basic inferiority" (see Howard & Hammond, 1985), it should come as no surprise that many may only half–heartedly believe in their own competence (Khatib & Murray, in press). The emerging thesis is that such individuals would be motivated to receive equivocal or biased information about their self–worth. Thus, Black adolescents are expected to employ self–handicapping strategies to a greater extent than their White counterparts.

In sum, the interaction between the student and the teacher influences how the student subsequently presents himself or herself. The teacher's tendency to make new information consistent with existing inferences (i.e., stereotypes) has its counterpart in the student's tendency to conform and adapt to the teacher's expectations. Thus, we propose that these micro aspects within the context of inequality in the allocation of resources form the primary mechanism by which the self–fulfilling nature of Black American underachievement occurs.

A Viable Solution

In their popularly published article, "Rumors of Inferiority," Howard and Hammon (1985) contend that the major consequence of Blacks being singled out for the stigma of genetic inferiority is a societal expectancy decrement concerning intellectual development which, when internalized by Blacks themselves, adversely affect Black behavior and cognition. As a move toward neutralizing, even solving this problem, Howard and Hammond call for a nationwide effort to facilitate the construction of a consistent, nurturing environment in which Black youth, in particular, can become free to pursue and fulfill their full intellectual potentials. They identify three basic building blocks of such an effort: attaining deliberate control of expectancy communications; developing strong, consistently positive community attitudes towards intellectual activity; and formulating/implementing some form of effective cognitive training which will encourage young Blacks to attribute their intellectual successes to ability (thereby boosting confidence) and their failures to their own lack of effort. We agree with them. The rest of this article proposes an intervention program specifically designed to help achieve that lofty goal.

The program, entitled "Winners: The Key to Success is Effort," is a comprehensive approach to the psychological treatment of underachievement that deals not only with its behavioral aspects, but places a great deal of stress on its cognitive component. While the underlying theoretical assumptions of the program are drawn heavily from attribution theory, the techniques utilized are adopted with modification from other treatment frameworks. The treatment procedures include attribution therapy (Diener & Dweck, 1978), expectancy training, internal speech as a self–monitoring device elaborated by Meichenbaum and Goodman (1971), social modeling techniques derived from social learning theory (Sarason & Ganzer, 1973) and others. The unique aspects of the program, in addition to integrating several approaches, is that it takes into consideration the fact that Black children's relationship to the important institutions of the society, especially the educational system, is both qualitatively and quantitatively different from that of their White contemporaries.

The major purpose of the Winners program is to equip Black students with cognitive strategies to effectively handle subtle and overt, internal and external, barriers to their academic success. Students are involved in activities which help them to:

1. Identify and understand the cause(s) of their school difficulties
2. Increase confidence in self and their reference group
3. Modify the image of themselves in a healthy direction

4. Understand and learn to analyze subtle messages about their worth
5. Understand the nature and consequence of their own decision–making
6. Understand the nature of time and effort in their products
7. Understand the role which values play in determining decisions and behavior
8. Rearrange their own system of values to perpetuate more effective achievement behavior
9. Reactivate their sense of responsibility in providing rewards for their achievements
10. Plan both short and long range (academic and nonacademic) goals and strategies necessary for their acquisition
11. Realize their long–range goals through academic planning and concentrated effort
12. Develop a mechanism that will enable them to counter or factually interpret communication about their academic performances and abilities
13. Develop an internal reinforcement system, so they gain control over their reinforcements, thus their environment
14. Develop a mechanism by which they will be able to internalize success and externalize or attribute failure to lack of effort
15. Evaluate their own progress
16. Develop a plan to reach their long–term goals

Specifically, 'Winners' consists of a mobile set of workshops conducted within a ten–week period on weekends in predominantly Black middle and senior high schools. Students receive academic credit for participating, along with other incentives. The workshops should be repeated at least twice a year (one run per semester, for example), with the same basic themes reformatted into different presentation packages in order to minimize boredom. Part of the necessity for success in 'Winners' is consistency, repetition (though not redundancy) and creative dynamism. The 'Winners' program will adapt itself to the environmental context of the students themselves, wrapping itself around the hub and flow of student academic life within the participating institutions. Of course, obtaining and maintaining the cooperation of local school administrators and parents is a very necessary ingredient for the programmatic success of 'Winners'.

The workshop topics and activities are structured to get students to increasingly utilize positive self–reinforcement and I–can–do–itism in order to internalize success as the product of qualitative effort, and to attribute failure to lack of effort, while effectively confronting the external barriers (e.g., teacher expectations, peer pressures, inadequate facilities, (etc.,) to their academic success. Furthermore, 'Winners' teaches students to meet the challenges of the accessible future by facilitating their efforts in developing a master plan, teaches them how to successfully and consistently win at the game of academics, and how to keep on winning. These outcomes are accomplished by the student learning to define and control his or her personal academic and professional goals, objectives, and reinforcements.

By Way of Concluding

We emphasize that the solution to the comparatively poorer academic performances of Black American adolescents must begin with the cause, societal racism, before the effects can be rendered curable. The solution should be aimed at the macro (i.e., systemic discrimination) and micro (i.e., teacher and student attitudes and behaviors) forces producing academic underachievement among Black adolescents. Without a twofold solution for changing the present situation, any micro attempts are futile and any macro attempts will impact too late for the present and next generation of Black adolescents.

References

Baba, M. L, & Darga, L. L. (1981). The genetic myth of racial classification. In M. S. Collins, I. W. Wainer, & T. A. Bremmer (Eds.), *Science and the question of human equality*, Banks, J.A. (1982). Education minority youths: An inventory of current theory. *Education and Urban Society, 15(1)*, 88–103. Boulder, CO: Westview Press.

Baratz, S. S., & Baratz, J. C. (1970). Early childhood intervention: The social science base of institutional racism. *Harvard Educational Review, 40(1)*, 29–49.

Belgrave, F. Z., Johnson, R. S., & Carey, C. (1985). Attributional style and its relationship to self-esteem and academic performance in Black students. *The Journal of Black Psychology. 11(2)*, 49–56.

Bennett, C. E. (1976). Student race, class, and academic history as determinants of teacher expectations of student performance. *Journal of Black Psychology, 3*, 71–87.

Bennett, C. E. (1979). The effects of student characteristics and task performance on teacher expectations and attributions. Unpublished Dissertation, University of Michigan.

Biemiller, L. (1985). Black students average aptitude–test scores up seven points in a year. *Chronicle of Higher Education*, p. 17.

Brookover, W. B., Gigliotti, R. J., Henderson, R. D., & Schneider, J. M. (1973). *Elementary school social environment and school achievement*. Cooperative Research Project, No. 1–E–107, 1973.

Brookover, W. B., & Passalacqua, J. (1981). Comparison of aggregate self–concepts for populations with different reference groups. In M. Lynch. A. Noren–Hebeisen, & W. Gergen (Eds.), *Self–concept advances in theory and practice*, Cambridge, MA: Ballinger.

Brophy, J. E. (1983). Research on the self-fulfilling prophecy and teacher expectations. *Journal of Educational Psychology, 75(5),* 631–661.

Carnoy, M. (1974). *Education as cultural imperialism.* New York: David McKay, Inc.

Castenell, L. A. (1983). Achievement motivation: An investigation of adolescents' achievement patterns. *American Educational Research Journal, 20(4),* 503–510.

Coble, J. A. (1975). A study of the relationship between teacher judgment of student ability, student race, and teachers' interaction in the classroom. Unpublished doctoral dissertation, University of Michigan, Ann Arbor, Michigan.

Crandall, V. C., Kathoosky, W., & Crandall, V. J. (1965). Children's beliefs in their control of reinforcement in intellectual academic achievement. *Child Development, 36,* 91–109.

Cronbach, L. J. (1975). Five decades of public controversy over mental testing. *American Psychologist, 30,* 1–14.

Darley, J. M. & Fazio, R. H. (1980). Expectancy confirmation processes arising in the social interaction sequence. *American Psychologist, 35(10),* 867–881.

Diener, C. I. & Dweck, C. S. (1978). Analyses of learned helplessness: Continuous changes in performances, strategy, and achievement cognitions following failure. *Journal of Personality and Social Psychology, 36,* 451–462.

Elig, T. W., & Frieze, I. H. (1979). Measuring causal attributions for success and failure. *Journal of Personality and Social Psychology, 37,* 621–634.

Eysenck, H. J. (1972). *The I.Q. arguement.* Freeport: Library Press.

Fairchild, H. H. (1983). A micro–analysis of the alley–oop with notes on the race and IQ controversy. Paper presented at the 16th Annual Convention of the Association of Black Psychologists, Washington, D.C., August, 1983.

Fairchild, H. H. (1984). School size, per–pupil expenditures, and academic achievement. *Review of Public Data Use, 12,* 221–229.

Fairchild, H. H., & Gurin, P. (1978). Traditions in the social–psychological analysis of race relations. *American Behavioral Scientist, 21(5),* 757–778.

Fairchild, H. H. & Tucker, M. B. (1982). Black residential mobility: Trends and characteristics. *Journal of Social Issues, 38(3),* 51–74.

Friend, R., & Neale, J. (1972). Children's perceptions of success and failure: An attributional analysis of the effects of race and class. *Developmental Psychology, 7,* 124–128.

Gordon, R. A. (1980). Chronometric analysis of intelligence: Comment. *Journal of Biological Structures, 3(2),* 123–124.

Graham, S. (1984). Communicating sympathy and anger to Black and White children: The cognitive (attributional) antecedents of affective cues. *Journal of Personality and Social Psychology, 47,* 40–54.

Graham, S. (in press). An attributional perspective on achievement motivation and Black children. In R. Feldman (Ed.). *Social psychology applied to education.* New York: Cambridge University Press.

Graham, S., & Long, A. (1986). Race, class, and the attributional process. *Journal of Educational Psychology, 78(1),* 4–13.

Gurin, P., & Epps, E. (1975). *Black consciousness, identity, and achievement.* New York: John Wiley & Sons, Inc.

Guthrie, R. V. (1976). *Even the rat was White.* NY: Harper & Row.

Guthrie, R. V. (1980). The psychology of Black Americans: An historical perspective. In R. Jones (ed.), *Black psychology* (2nd ed.), NY: Harper & Row.

Harris, M. J. & Rosenthal, R. (1985). Mediation of interpersonal expectancy effects: 31 meta analyses. *Psychological Bulletin, 97(3),* 363–386.

Heider, F. (1958). *The psychology of interpersonal relations.* New York: Wiley.
Hendrickson, D. E., & Hendrickson, A. E. (1980). The biological basis of individual differences in intelligence. *Personality and Individual Differences, 1(1),* 3–34.
Herrnstein, R. J. (1975). *I.Q. in the meritocracy.* Boston, MA: Little, Brown & Co.
Holmes, B. J. (1982). Black students' performance in the national assessment of science and mathematics. *Journal of Negro Education, 51(4),* 392–405.
Howard, J., & Hammond, R. (1985, September). Rumors of inferiority. *The New Republic,* 17–21.
Hughes, J. & Hughes, A. (1973). *Equal education: A new national strategy.* Bloomington: Indiana University Press.
Hunt, J. McV. (1964). The psychological basis for using pre–school enrichment as an antidote for cultural deprivation. *Merrill–Palmer Quarterly, 10,* 209–248.
Jencks, C. (1980). Heredity, environment, and public policy reconsidered. *American Sociologcial Review, 45,* 723–736.
Jensen, A. R. (1969). Reducing the heredity–environment uncertainty: A reply. *Harvard Educational Review, 39,* 449–483.
Jensen, A. (1980). Chronometric analysis of intelligence. *Journal of Social and Biological Structures, 3(2),* 103–122.
Jensen, A. (1985). The nature of Black–White difference on various psychometric tests: Spearmen's hypothesis. *Behavioral and Brain Sciences, 8,* 193–218.
Jones, E. E., & Berglas, S. (1978). Control of attribution about self through self–handicapping strategies: The appeal of alcohol and the role of underachievement. *Personality and Social Psychology Bulletin, 4(2),* 200–206.
Kagan, J., & Moss, H. A. (1959). Stability and validity of achievement fantasy. *Journal of Abnormal and Social Psychology, 58,* 357–364.
Katz, I. (1969). A critique of personality approaches to Negro performance, with research suggestions. *Journal of Social Issues, 25(3),* 13–27.
Kelley, H. H. Moral evaluation. *American Psychologist,* 1971, *26,* 283–300.
Khatib, S., & Murray, C. B. (in press). Competency and legitimacy as organizing dimensions of the Black self–concept. In R. Jones (Ed.), *Advances in Black psychology,* Richmond, CA: Cobb & Henry.
Kukla, A. (1972). Attributional determinants of achievement–related behavior. *Journal of Personality and Social Psychology, 21,* 166–174.
Labov, W. (1970). *Language in the inner city.* Penn: University of Penn Press Inc.
Lefcourt, H. M. (1970). Recent developments in the study of locus of control. In B. A. Maher (Ed.), *Progress in experimental personality research.* New York: Academic Press.
Mackenzie, B. (1980a). Hypothesized genetic racial differences in IQ: A criticism of three proposed lines of evidence. *Behavior Genetics, 10(2),* 225–234.
Mackenzie, B. (1980b). Fallacious use of regression effects in IQ controversy. *Australian Psychologist, 15(3),* 369–384.
Marsh, H. W., Cairns, L., Relich, J., Barnes, J., & Debus, R. L. (1984). The relationship between dimensions of self–attribution and dimensions of self–concept. *Journal of Educational Psychology, 76(1),* 3–32.
McDill, E., Meyer, E., & Rugby, L. (1966). *Sources of educational climate in high schools.* Baltimore, MD: John Hopkins University.
Meichenbaum, D. H. & Goodman, J. (1971). Training impulsive chidlren to talk to themselves: A means of developing self–control. *Journal of Abnormal Psychology, 77,* 115–126.

Mercer, J. R. (1973). *Labeling the mentally retarded*. Berkeley: University of California Press.

Mingione, A. (1966). Need for achievement in Negro and White children. *Journal of Consulting Psychology, 3*, 45–53.

Moynihan, D. P. (1965). *The Negro family: The case for national action*. Washington, D.C.: U.S. Department of Labor.

Murray, C. B., & Jackson, J. S. (1982/83). The conditioned failure model of Black educational underachievement. *Humboldt Journal of Social Relations, 10(1)*, 276–300.

Murray, S. R., & Mednick, M. T. (1975). Perceiving the causes of success and failure in achievement: Sex, race, and motivational comparisons. *Journal of Consulting and Clinical Psychology, 43*, 881–885.

National Commission on Excellence in Education. (1983). A nation at risk: The imperatives for educational reform. Washington D.C.

Oakes, J. (1985). *Keeping track: How schools structure inequality*. New Haven: Yale University Press.

Obgu, J. U. (1981). Black education: A cultural–ecological perspective. In H. P. McAdoo (Ed.), *Black families*, Beverly Hills: Sage Publications.

Persell, C. H. (1981). Genetic and cultural deficit theories: Two sides of the same racist coin. *Journal of Black Studies, 12(1)*, 19–38.

Porter, J. R., & Washington, R. E. (1979). Black identity and self–esteem: A review of studies on Black self–concept 1968–1978. *Annual Review of Sociology, 5*, 53–74.

Posner, M. I. (1982). Cumulative development of attentional theory. *American Psychologist, 37*, 168–179.

Rafferty, F T. (1980). The problem with intelligence tests. *Psychiatric Annals, 10(10)*, 407–415.

Ramirez, M., & Price–Williams, D. R. (1976). Achievement motivation in chilldren of three ethnic groups in the United States. *Journal of Cross–Cultural Psychology. 7(1)*, 49–60.

Reynolds, C. R., McBride, R. D., & Gibson, L. J. (1981). Black–White IQ discrepancies may be related to differences in hemisphericity. *Contemporary Educational Psychology, 6(2)*, 180–184.

Rosenthal, R. (1976). *Experimenter effects in behavioral research* 2nd. ed.). New York: Irvington.

Rosenthal, R. (September, 1973). The pygmalion effect lives. *Psychology Today*, 56–63.

Rosenthal, R., & Jacobson, L. (1968). *Pygmalion in the classroom: Teacher expectation and pupils intellectual development*. New York: Rinehart, and Winston, Inc.

Rubovits, P. C., & Maehr, M. L. (1973). Pygmalion in Black and White. *Journal of Personality and Social Psychology, 25(2)*, 210, 218.

Ryan, W. (1976). *Blaming the victim*. (2nd ed.). New York: Vintage Books.

Sarason, I. & Ganzer, V. (1973). Modeling and group discussion in the rehabilitation of juvenile delinquents. *Journal of Counseling Psychology, 20(5)*, 442–449.

Shockley, W. (1972). Dysgenics, geneticity, raceology: A challenge to the intellectual responsibility of educators. *Phi Delta Kappan*, 297–307.

Smitherman, G. (1977). *Talkin and testifyin: The language of Black America*. New York: Houghton–Mifflin.

Sternberg, R. J. (1981). Nothing fails like success: The search for an intelligent paradigm for studying intelligence. *Journal of Educational Psychology, 73(2),* 142–155.

Stipek, D. J., & Weisz, J. R. (1981). Perceived personal control and academic achievement. *Review of Educational Research, 51,* 101–137.

Tenhouten, W. (1970). The Black family: Myth and reality. *Psychiatry, 33(2),* 145–172.

Terman, L. M. (1917). Feeble-minded children in the public schools of California. *School and Society, 5,* 161–165.

Terrell, F., Terrell, S. L., & Taylor, J. (1980). Effects of race of examiner and type of reinforcement on the intelligence test performance of lower-class Black children. *Psychology in the Schools, 17(2),* 270–272.

U.S. District Court for Northern California (1979). Opinion: Larry P. vs Riles. San Francisco, California Mimeo.

Valentine, C. A. (1971). Deficit, difference, bi-cultural models of Afro-American behavior. *Harvard Educational Review, 41(2),* 137–157.

Veroff, J. (1966). Measuring the achievement motive in young boys and girls. Unpublished manuscript. Ann Arbor: University of Michigan.

Vetta, A. (1980a). Concepts and issues in the IQ debate. *Bulletin of the British Psychological Society, 33,* 241–243.

Vetta, A. (1980b). Correlation, regression and biased science. *The Behavioral and Brain Sciences, 3,* 357–358.

Weiner, B. (1979). A theory of motivation for some classroom experiences. *Journal of Educational Psychology, 71,* 3–25.

Weiner, B. (1985). An attributional theory of achievement motivation and emotion. *Psychology Review, 92(4),* 548–573.

Weiner, B., Frieze, I., Kula, A., Reed, L., Rest, S., & Rosenbaum, R. M. (1971). Perceiving the causes of success and failure. In E. E. Jones, D. E. Kanouse, H. H. Kelley, R. E. Nisbett, S. Valins, and B. Weiner (Eds.), *Attribution: Perceiving the causes of behavior.* General Learning Press, 95–120.

Weiner, B., & Kukla, A. (1970). An attributional analysis of achievement motivation. *Journal of Personality and Social Psychology, 15,* 1–10.

White, J.L. (1984). *The psychology of Blacks: An Afro-American perspective.* New Jersey: Prentice-Hall, Inc.

Williams, R. L., & Mitchell, H. (1980). The testing game. In R. E. Jones (Ed.), *Black psychology* (2nd ed.), NY: Harper & Row.

Willig, A. C., Harnesch, D. L., Hill, K., & Maehr, M. (1983). Sociocultural and educational correlates of success-failure attributions and evaluation anxiety in the school setting for Black, Hispanic, and Anglo children. *American Educational Research Journal, 20,* 385–410.

Part VI
Career Development and Employment

CAREER AND VOCATIONAL DEVELOPMENT OF BLACK YOUTH

Iris Baly

Between 1960–1980 a body of research was produced whose major thrust was the investigation of factors thought to explain the vocational behavior of Black youth. The major variables investigated included 1) occupational aspirations and expectations, 2) occupational choice/decision–making, 3) vocational self–concept, 4) career maturity, 5) intelligence, 6) reference group perspectives, 7) perception of the opportunity structure, 8) locus of control and 9) sex. In part, the motivation for the research arose from the criticism that vocational development theories and concepts based on middle–class Whites inadequately described the vocational behavior of Blacks.

Vocational development prior to 1957 was viewed as a static concept defined only by the limited dimensions of vocational choice and vocational attainment. Not until the work of Super, Crites, Hummer, Moser, Overstreet & Warnath (1957) was vocational behavior conceived dynamically—as an orderly, ongoing process consisting of vocational developmental tasks. The field witnessed a shift in focus from outcome to process. The process view, however, has its critics (Warnath, 1975; LoCascio, 1967) who argue that *assumptions* about the purpose careers serve in an individual's life and the sequential steps in which careers are selected ignore actual situational determinants and chance factors as they apply to the vocational development process. The use of this framework, in which theories without adequate empirical support are applied to the study of vocational behavior of ethnic minorities, results in spurious research findings and a misunderstanding of the vocational behavior of Black youth. Any investigations directed at understanding the vocational development process in Black youth must be considered within a cultural–pluralistic context in which attention is given to variations in the subjective experience of Black youth which necessarily influence their vocationalization. (Vocationalization is defined as the socialization of individuals to work attitudes, values, and behaviors of the dominant culture.) The dimensions of vocationalization considered in the context of this chapter include 1) aspirations/expectations, 2) perception of the occupational hierarchy, 3) vocational maturity, 4) self–concept, and 5) work values and attitudes.

The Study of Vocational Behavior[1]

Vocational Development Theory: Conceptual Framework

A developmental approach to vocational behavior requires a focus on the evolution of vocationally important traits and on the manner in which a sequence of decisions is approached, clarified, and implemented (Jordaan, in Herr, 1974). A number of theorists and researchers, e.g., Crites (1971), Ginzberg (1951), Gribbons and Lohnes (1968), Jordaan and Heyde (1979), Tiedemann and O'Hara (1963), and Super (1955; 1957; Super & Overstreet, 1960) have followed this approach and have attempted to outline the evolution and direction of specific traits and behaviors.

The major behavioral dimensions along which vocational development has been assumed to proceed are: 1) Realism of Vocational Choice (points to the reality factor as an important variable in explaining the quality of vocational choice through the various life stages [Ginzberg et al., 1951]), 2) Vocational Maturity (a criterion used in the evaluation of vocational behavior and the degree and rate of development [Super, 1955; Super et al., 1957]), and 3) Clarification of the Vocational Self–Concept (the role of the self–concept in mediating between the decision–making tasks and the sociobiological and situational factors which are brought to bear on the developmental stages [Tiedeman & O'Hara, 1963]).

The concepts of vocational life stages and vocational developmental tasks have been borrowed from psychology. The vocational life stages elaborated by Super (1957, 1963) draw on the work of Havighurst's (1953) concept of developmental tasks, Buehler's (1933) life stages and Ginzberg's (1951) study of occupational choice. The stages—Growth, Exploration, Establishment, Maintenance, and Decline—are all defined in terms of the period of their evolution and the vocational developmental tasks salient for each stage. Failure to deal with developmental tasks at the appropriate time, or lack of success in dealing with them are hypothesized to impede the individual's development and to make it difficult to effectively handle the tasks of the next stage (Super et al., 1957).

Vocational Maturity

Introduction of the concept of vocational maturity into the literature by Super (1955) was the first attempt to bring into the discussion of vocational guidance the notion of the maturity of an individual's behavior analogous to the other kinds of maturity—emotional, intellectual, social, etc., found in the literature in developmental psychology. Vocational maturity was "...used to denote the degree of development, the place reached on the continuum of vocational development..." (p. 153).

The study of vocational maturity through various research approaches has generally supported its viability as an important concept in the study of vocational development. Osipow's (1973) review of the research led him to the following conclusion: "In summary, the research evidence in general indicates that vocational maturity is a reasonable and valid concept, and is likely to be of increasing usefulness to our understanding of vocational development." (p. 149).

Research on the Vocational Maturity of Blacks

Several writers, who were concerned that theory and research on vocational maturity have been based on homogeneous White middle-class groups (Calia, 1966; Hall, 1963; Gribbons & Lohnes, 1968; LoCascio, 1974; Smith, 1975; Tyler, 1967), have called for research relevant to lower-class individuals. The thrust of the research has generally been on assessing in minority populations the relationship between a number of psychosocial and environmental variables and vocational maturity (VM). However, inappropriately standardized instruments have been used in studies assessing VM so that conclusions from this line of research generally are of questionable value. LoCascio (1974) suggests that different approaches to the design of vocational behavior instruments should be introduced in order to render them more culture-fair. Palmo and Lutz (1983) agree with LoCascio when they suggest that no further value is served in investigating the CMI scores of Black youth. In studying the vocational behavior patterns of Black youth they recommend examination of variables which influence various aspects of vocationalization, as well as those amenable to change through proactive prevention programs. The following sections cover research which explored relationships among correlates of vocational maturity in Black subjects.

Intelligence and Vocational Maturity

The relationship between intelligence and various measures of vocational maturity has been previously noted. Several studies which employed the CMI (VDI)–Attitude scale in comparing the vocational maturity of lower class students (Black and White) and middle-class students (mainly White) found significant SES differences between the groups (Ansell, 1970; Maynard, 1970; Maynard & Hansen, 1979). However, when intelligence was controlled, the difference between the groups became insignificant, suggesting that ability rather than SES or race was the determining factor in level of VM. In one study (Maynard, 1970), the correlation between intelligence and VDI was .47. The fact that most of the measures of vocational maturity have such a high relationship to tested intelligence led a number of writers to conclude that they are inappropriate for use with low socioeconomic status Black youth (Maynard & Hansen, 1970; McDowell, 1978).

Given the strong relationship between intelligence and vocational maturity implied by past research, it is natural to question whether career maturity is an entity separate from intelligence. The purpose of the Palmo and Lutz (1983) study was to investigate the extent of the relationship between intelligence and career maturity, by examining the relationship of scores on the CMI with those of the Wechsler Adult Intelligence (WAIS) (Wechsler, 1955) for "disadvantaged youngsters". The findings of this study revealed that specific WAIS subtests, namely Vocabulary, Information, and Similarities, related significantly to various CMI subtests. If IQ, as assessed by the WAIS, is in fact a relatively stable construct, then consequently, career maturity is as stable a construct. This hypothesis has far reaching implications for the impact of intensive vocational programs with low socioeconomic status youth between the ages of 16–21 since career maturity may be impervious to such short term interventions. In addition, it may be possible to assess career maturity by investigating a person's school achievement, past vocational successes, or general overall ability. (The reader should note, however, that many scholars believe most extant measures are inappropriate for assessing the intelligence of Black children and youth).

Socioeconomic Status and Vocational Maturity

The issue of whether vocational maturity is related to socioeconomic factors or to race has been variously explored. When lower class Black and White boys are compared to middle–class White boys (a confounded analysis), the lower class groups score lower on both the CMI Attitude and RCP scales than middle–class boys, regardless of race. This is, however, not controlling for intelligence (Ansell, 1970; Ansell & Hansen, 1971; Maynard & Hansen, 1970). Small differences in scores on the CMI Attitude scale were found in Ansel's (1970) study between lower class White and Black boys—with lower class Whites surpassing their Black counterparts. However, these differences were deemed insignificant.

To assess the impact of SES on the development of vocational maturity over a period of time, cross–sectional studies were done on subjects in grades 8–12 (Ansell, 1970; Ansell & Hansen, 1971). It appears that SES is a relatively insignificant determinant of vocational maturity between lower–class and middle–class students in grades 10–12.

The above mentioned studies did not include middle–class Black subjects in their design. Studies which compare lower–class and middle–class Blacks improve over previous studies because the race variable can be controlled and hence give more power to the interpretation of results about the SES variable. Dillard (1976) tested the assumption that levels of vocational maturity are related to SES independent of race. His sample consisted of middle–class and lower–class sixth grade Black males. His findings show that middle–class Black males have significantly higher CMI scores than lower–class Black males and give support to the notion that SES factors rather than race contribute to determining levels of VM. Dillard suggests that the middle–class value orientation toward work which the parents of these subjects share are reflected in their childrearing practices and that these differences reflect differences in the 'vocationalization process' between sixth grade middle and lower class Black males. More potency could have been given to this interpretation if Dillard had included a measure of work value orientation in this design, rather than inferring it from objectively measured SES.

Smith's study went a little further in determining the relationship between SES factors and vocational maturity. Recognizing that SES may be too gross a variable to explain differences in vocational behavior among Black youth, her design focused on a homogeneous sample of lower SES Black male and female high school seniors. In particular, Smith was interested in looking at how Reference Group Perspectives (RGP), "––the shared perspectives of a group toward career goals, and pathways to success—" (p. 322), may explain variations in vocational maturity for students who share the same SES. She developed an instrument, The Survey of Community Opinions (SCO), which assesses two dimensions: 1) Reference Group Perspectives—lower or middle class, and 2) View of the Opportunity Structure—open or closed. The subscores of this measure were correlated with CMI Attitude Scale scores. The findings revealed the following: 1) lower SES Black students with high RGP scores (middle-class orientation) have significantly higher CMI scores than those with low RGP scores; and 2) students who expressed an open view of the opportunity structure (VOP) had middle–class RGPs and also had higher CMI scores than those who expressed an open view of the opportunity structure. Smith suggests that since the CMI is so heavily saturated with items which reflect a middle–class outlook on work and life, it might be measuring career attitudes rather than career maturity. In this way, the negative vocational labeling attributed to individuals from a lower SES can more appropriately be interpreted as vocational attitudes to which they might subscribe rather than to the maturity of their vocational behaviors. Smith comments: "Some lower SES individuals, who, on the basis of their assessment of their life situations and the work world, may be career mature—even though their vocational attitudes are not middle class oriented." (p. 334)

Sex and Vocational Maturity

The studies in which the influence of sex as a predictor of vocational maturity was explored (Lawrence & Brown, 1976; Smith, 1976; Vriend, 1969; Williams, 1977), the consensus is that there are no significant sex differences in vocational maturity ratings.

School Achievement and Vocational Maturity

Jordaan & Heyde, (1979) Smith, (1976) and Vriend, (1969) examined the relationship between school achievement as measured by grade–point average and factors of vocational maturity as measured by various instruments. The findings suggest that students who successfully cope with academic tasks also demonstrate a high degree of competence in dealing with vocational development tasks. These results, which indicate that school achievement is highly correlated with the CMI Attitude scale, suggest that the Attitude scale compares with other standardized achievement assessment instruments, and as such is inappropriate for assessing the attitudinal dispositions of minority groups toward work and careers. Most investigators attest to the value of assessing vocational maturity of lower SES Blacks; however, they do assail the use of the CMI Attitude scale to achieve this aim. LoCascio (1967) suggests that the vocational development of lower SES and lower intelligence groups may follow a different pattern than the one described in the vocational development theory literature for higher SES groups.

Implications of the above suggestions for the direction of future research on assessing vocational maturity in low SES and Black subjects are clear, since none of the previously cited studies examined how unique psychosocial, cultural, and environmental variables are brought to bear upon the structure of vocational development of these subjects.

Vocational development theory, as traditionally espoused, seems to reflect a common cultural expectations approach, e.g., that in order to achieve success and satisfaction vocational development tasks and the sequence of life stages presented should be experienced by all members of society. If it is true that middle–class adults carry the dominant cultural expectations, it follows that in order for the culture to survive, a majority of its members must adhere to these cultural imperatives. However, LoCascio (1974) raises the question of whether the alternate notion of cultural pluralism in vocational development encompassing subjectively different vocational development tasks and a different sequence of vocational stages for "diverse groups" may not also be plausible. If it is appropriate to espouse this cultural pluralistic view, then it would also be appropriate to "...develop different but comparable instruments for each major diverse group.". (p. 132)

Subjective Correlates of Vocational Behavior

A review of the literature on educational and occupational attainment processes of Black and White subjects (Kerchoff & Campbell, 1977; Jencks et al., 1975; Portes & Wilson, 1976; Rosenberg & Simmons, 1972; Smith, 1976; Thomas, 1975) suggests that subjective indicators which require the individual's perception of certain factors and events in the environment, locus of control, significant other influence and support and self–esteem and ambition, etc., have greater predictive power than objective indicators (SES, mental ability) for Black than for White subjects.

The remaining sections of this chapter focus on studies of vocational behavior of Black youth which include subjective variables in their research design. A few investigators attempted to expand the predictive model for career maturity by including more psychosocial predictor variables—Reference Group Perspectives (RGP); View of the Opportunity Structure (VOP); Locus of Control (LOC); and Self–Concept (Lawrence & Brown, 1976; Smith, 1976; Thomas, 1975).

Aspirations and Expectations

Aspirations and Expectations are regarded as principal aspects of vocational behavior in that they represent the incipient tasks in the process of vocational development. The expression of an aspiration by an individual involves the statement of a desired career goal given ideal conditions. Necessarily, inquiries about aspirations tend to encourage fantasy–like responses by the individual (Cosby, 1974). On the other hand, career expectations include an individual's consideration of reality factors which may affect attainment of aspirations. Ginzberg (1951) postulated that the statement of occupational choice proceeds through successive stages from fantasy orientations to more realistic and focused choices.

Occupational choices children express should then be more reality–based as they grow older.

Despite earlier research conclusions to the contrary, current research reveals that Black youth do not set lower aspirations than their White counterparts. In fact, analysis of data from a national panel study (Shapiro & Crowley, 1982) reveals that after controlling for SES, family background and other factors, minority youth of both sexes have consistently higher occupational status aspirations than their White counterparts. Still, level of expectation has to be considered in order to grasp the complexity of career behavior in Black youth. This is so because there is a consistent discrepancy between Black youths' high status occupational aspirations and their level of occupational expectations. Such incongruity is generally observed in low SES Black youth who often feel less optimistic, given the economic reality which surrounds them, about attaining their career aspirations. Cosby (1974) attempted to find an explanation for this discrepancy by looking at changes in expressed levels of occupational expectations over time to see if changes reflect the notion of increasing realism of choice as postulated by Ginzberg (1951). The results of this study on Black and White high school sophomores over a two year period were mixed and therefore offered no real support for increasing realism in choice since seniors as a whole increased their level of occupational expectation. Instead, the results revealed a significant tendency for low SES Black seniors to lower their level of expectations; youth appeared to perceive their aspirations as sharply out of phase with their occupational attainment chances.

The fact that different results were obtained in this study for low SES Black youth than for the rest of the sample population forces alternative formulations of the occupational choice process for Black youth. Thus, indirect support is given to the assertion that traditional vocational developmental theory does not describe the vocational reality of many Black youth. Although there is general empirical support for the finding that the race does not predict aspiration level (Smith, 1976), Cosby and Picuo (1973) sought to clarify the relationship between socioeconomic status (SES) and aspiration/expectation in a survey of Black and White students in the deep South. The results reflect the finding that SES is not an important variable in the expressed aspirations of Black youth as compared to their White counterparts.

The question of which factors affect the expression of aspiration/expectations in Black youth is important to consider. Pallone, Rickard, and Hurley (1970) reported the key influences ranked in first or second position of occupational preference by Black youth and their parents. Although the dominant pattern reflects the same sex parent as the person ranked as the most important, these researchers report that for Black males, the mother is ranked more dominant than the father. This same pattern—of maternal influence greater than paternal influence—was reported by Dillard and Campbell (1981). It appears that the aspirations Black mothers hold for their children contribute strongly to the career expectations of Black adolescents. The strength of parental influence over career attitudes of adolescents is more evident in Blacks than Whites (Lee, 1984). McNair and Brown (1983) speak to the implications of this phenomenon for the development of the career behavior of Black youth. Parents need to be made aware of the impact they have in shaping and determining their children's aspirations and expectations. This is especially significant for low SES Black youth whose career aspirations/expectations would be higher if parental career orientations were also high (Brook, Whiteman, Lukoff, & Gordon, 1979). The studies cited suggest that maternal orientation serves as a link between the social structure and adolescent aspirations/expectations. Structural variables such as race and SES are moderated in the expression of aspirations by parental as well as peer influences.

The concept of anticipatory socialization explains the mobility strivings of individuals who occupy low social status yet espouse middle–class values and seek higher status occupations. Mere contact alone with middle–class peers is not sufficient to foster higher aspirations in lower class Black youth. The concept of reference groups, central to social psychology, explains the modification of behaviors and/or social attitudes when a person moves from one social context to another (Shibutani, 1955). In such situations, the individual designates the group which is different from the group to which he/she objectively belongs as his/her reference group and uses the norms and values shared by its group members as standards for comparison of his/her own behaviors. Low SES Black youth, who express aspirations for attaining high status jobs are, according to this concept, using middle and upper–class norms and values as reference points through which they seek to gain or enhance their status. Smith's (1976) study, cited earlier, rather conclusively supports the application of reference group theory to understanding how low SES Black subjects adopt middle–class orientations which get expressed as high status career aspirations and high career maturity.

Given that identification with and adoption of reference group norms and values mediate between SES and expressed aspirations, it would follow that limiting exposure to middle to high status occupations would result in a restriction of the range of occupational aspirations expressed. The notion of occupational foreclosure (Hauser, 1971) refers to constriction of the range of occupational possibilities a person considers for herself/himself.

Shappell et al. (1971) suggest that the individual's perceptions of the world of work is influenced by socioeconomic status. For Black inner–city students the perceptions of the values and rewards different occupations hold was influenced by the occupational level (Pentecoste, 1975). Ranking of occupational status begins early in children's lives although their conceptions of occupational prestige are more different as they grow older in stage–appropriate ways (Gunn, 1964). Quite naturally, ranking of jobs is influenced by a child's familiarity with different jobs. A study of a sample of 1,917 Black and White children from grades 3–12 from Baltimore City (Simmons, Rosenberg, 1971) reveals that children have a clear awareness of occupational prestige differences and the stratification system of unequal rewards as early as the third grade. The consequence of these perceptions may be reflected in a type of status consciousness that facilitates mobility–striving. The findings also reveal that Black working–class students are less likely than their White middle–class peers to discriminate occupations according to prestige, and to believe that there are barriers to equal opportunity. One possible explanation for the lower status consciousness of Black students may be that they lack exposure to a wide range of jobs within the occupational hierarchy. Despite these findings, results indicate that the majority of low socioeconomic Black youth were optimistically oriented toward upward mobility. A reasonable prediction is that they will exhibit frustration and anger as they enter the world of work and meet barriers to their career aspirations; clearly, the youths' view of the opportunity structure or beliefs about opportunity will be modified.

View of the Opportunity Structure. The question of how the view of the opportunity structure of Black students affects their mobility striving was addressed in Smith's (1976) study which correlated perception of the opportunity structure (open or closed) with career maturity (scores measured by the CMI). The results of the study support other cited research which revealed that optimism about one's chances for occupational attainment is related to the belief that access to the opportunity structure was open to them. A valid question to formulate at this point is what factor(s) influence the perception that access to opportunity is open or closed to an individual. Belief in one's ability to control the rewards for the efforts expended in one's environment is necessarily related to mobility striving. The psychological construct of locus of control identified by Rotter (1966) refers, in its broader meaning, to the degree to which individuals have a sense of efficacy or power and accept personal responsibility for what happens to them. The sense of internal control has been found to be stronger in White subjects than in Blacks, and stronger in middle class than in working class subjects (Battle & Rotter, 1963; Crandall, Katkovsky, Crandall, 1965; Coleman, Campbell, Hobson, McPartland, Mood, Weinfield, & York, 1966).

Thomas (1975) found that subjects with high internal locus of control were more vocationally mature than subjects who had external locus of control. Baly, (1984), who analyzed vocational educational data of low SES Black male high school seniors gathered from a national panel study in 1980, found that sample of subjects to express external locus of control. Dean's (1984) review of the literature, summarizes the prevailing belief among researchers that Black youth who are high on external locus of control are more likely to display a static or regressed career development pattern.

Self-Concept. A number of investigators have attempted to test Super's (1953) hypothesis of the centrality of developing a self-concept in the process of vocational development. Lee's study (1984) explored the role of self-concept in the career choice of a sample of rural adolescents. The results suggest that self-concept has a positive relationship with career choice attitudes for Blacks as well as Whites thereby lending support to Super's (1953) notions regarding the importance of self-concept in the career development process. However, these results contradict other studies (McNair & Brown, 1983; Lawrence & Brown, 1976) which reveal that self–concept has only significant predictive value in the career attitudes of White males, while having little significance in predicting the career behavior of Black males. What most of these studies conclude from results of exploration of related variables (self–concept, parental influence, SES, etc.) to career attitudes/behaviors is that variations arise when these variables interact with race. That is, elaborations of the factors which predict and direct vocational behaviors would more accurately result from different regression equations for White and nonwhite youth (Lee, 1984; McNair & Brown, 1983; Lawrence & Brown, 1976).

Interacting Psychosocial and Subjective Correlates. Numerous indicators point to the importance of considering the interaction of significant psychosocial variables in the elaboration of vocational behaviors of Black (especially low SES) youth. One study which attempted to heed the call for research relevant to the internal frame of reference of Black people was conducted by Baly (1984). The purpose of the study was to develop an alternative approach for assessing vocational behavior patterns of Black youth which directly reflected statements they make about their own vocational behavior choices, values, aspirations, self–appraisal, etc. Data for the study were taken from a nationwide panel study of high school students. An internal measure of vocational behavior patterns which is theoretically related to vocational maturity was derived through factor analysis of questionnaire items. Seven factors which comprised the vocational–Education Decision–Making (VEDM) patterns of low SES Black youth were derived. VEDM patterns of middle and high–income White youth were also derived. In addition, the relationship was determined between VEDM factors for the Black subjects and several psychosocial variables—Locus of Control, Work Orientation, Self–Concept, Significant Other Influence; and Achievement. Results of the study included the following: 1) Low SES Black males display a pattern of VEDM behavior which is significantly different from that of high and medium SES White males. Seven factors on the White sample accounted for more than 70% of the variance, whereas seven factors assessed on low SES Black group accounted for only 56% of the variance. 2) The interrelationships between the factor scores derived from the low SES Black sample and the psychosocial variables yielded a much larger percentage of variance explained than when this same population's factor scores were based on the White population. This outcome supports the previously cited research which suggests that greater explanatory power may be obtained using a research model that has the subject/sample group serving as its own criterion group for the standardization of an instrument. 3) Of the five variables hypothesized as correlates or antecedents of vocational behavior in this study, except for work orientation, all (Achievement, Significant Other Influence, Locus of Control, and Self–Concept) revealed significant correlations with the dimensions of VEDM. The significant correlations of the self–concept variable and four of the seven dimensions of the VEDM gives support to Super's (1955) contention that self–perception plays a role in decisions about career planning.

Baly also found the sample of low SES Black males had a mean score on the Locus of Control variable which reflects an external orientation and that the mother and other significant persons influenced the subject's decisions about post–high school plans to a greater degree than was the case for the medium and high SES White subjects.

The major outcomes of this study resulted in a preliminary description of one aspect of vocational behavior in low SES Black male seniors' Vocational Educational Decision Making patterns. Of the seven dimensions which comprised VEDM, four appear to be dominant: 1) Level of Educational/Vocational Expectation 2) Planning, Knowledge, and Expectation of Resources for Financial Aid 3) Financial Independence and 4) Significant Other Influence. These findings suggest that vocational decision making is influenced by: level of educational/vocational aspiration; an awareness of and expectation of financial support from different resources including those derived from individual work experience; and expectations and other inputs from the parental figures in arriving at vocational and educational plans. Several points and issues which require further exploration are raised by the results of the data anlayses. The seven highly significant differential response patterns of the low SES Black group compared to the medium and high SES White group may indicate that the VEDM construct and its dimensions represent just a partial aspect of a multifaceted process by which low SES Black subjects make decisions about educational and vocational goals.

The question this raises about what other factors enter into the developmental scheme for this population may be answered if the research design used above could be augmented with the inclusion of variables heretofore noted as significant to Black vocational development. These include such factors as the subject's view of 1) actual or perceived racial barriers to opportunities in education and employment, 2) the influence of negative peer pressure which stems from an internalized "sense of fatalism" and 3) the acquired shared reference group perspective which moderates attitudes toward work, vocational and educational aspirations, and, very likely, the feeling of mastery over one's environment.

The test of these hypotheses can only come about as a result of research designs, similar to the one used in this study, which attempt to increase the amount of explained variance among the variables of interest. The call for research relevant to Black youth must be heeded.

Summary

The review of the literature herein included suggests that the process of vocational development for Black adolescents is guided and directed by socioeconomic and (psycho)cultural factors which define their experience and perception. To the extent that such factors deviate from those of the dominant culture, a divergent pattern of vocational development will be revealed for Black subjects. In order to fully elucidate the process of vocational development for Black youth, research attention should be focused on clarifying the full range of 'psycho–socioeconomic' variables relevant to this unique population. This will require both longitudinal and cross–sectional research designs with Black youth, the outcome of which will, in many instances, refute the validity of traditional theoretical constructs such as 'vocational maturity' for explaining the vocational behavior of Black youth.

Notes

1. Vocational behavior is defined as any interaction between an individual and his environment which is significantly related to preparation for, participation in, or retirement from work (Super, Crites, Hummel, Moser, Overstreet, & Warnath, 1957, p. 13).

References

Ansell, E. M. (1970). The assessment of vocational maturity of lower–class Caucasians, lower–class Negroes, and middle–class Caucasians in grades 8–12. Unpublished doctoral dissertation, SUNY at Buffalo.

Ansell, E. M. (1970). Patterns in vocational development of urban youth. *Journal of Counseling Psychology, 17,* 400–404.

Baly, I.E. (1984). *Assessing the vocational-educational decision-making patterns of low ses black male high school seniors: a test of two models.* Unpublished doctoral dissertation, University of California, Berkeley.

Bartlett, W. E. (1971). Vocational maturity: Its past, present, and future development. *Journal of Vocational Behavior, 1,* 217–229.

Battle, E., & Rotter, J. (1966). Children's feelings of personal control of reinforcement. *Psychological Monographs, 80,* 1–28.

Borow, H. (Ed.) (1964). *Man in a world at work.* Boston: Houghton Mifflin.

Borow, H. (Ed.) (1964). *Man in a world at work.* Boston: Houghton Mifflin.

Brook, J. S., Whiteman, M., Lukoff, I. F., and Gordon, A. S. (1979). Maternal and adolescent expectation and aspirations as related to sex, ethnicity, and socioeconomic status. *Journal of Genetic Psychology, 135,* 209–214.

Buehler, C. (1933). *Der menschliche lebenslauf als psychologisches problem*. Leipzig: Hirzel.

Calia, V. F. (1966). Vocational guidance: After the fall. *Personnel and Guidance Journal, 45*, 320–327.

Cattell, R. B. (1978). *The scientific use of factor analysis in behavioral and life sciences*. New York: Plenum.

Cohen, J., & Cohen, P. (1975). *Applied multiple regression/correlation analysis for the behavioral sciences*. New York: John Wiley & Sons.

Coleman, J. S., Campbell, E., Hobson, C., McPartland, J., Mood, A, Weinfield, F., & York, R. (1966). *Equality of education opportunity*. U.S. Dept. of HEW, Washington, D.C.: U.S. Government Printing Office.

Cosby, A. G. (1974). Occupational expectations and the hypothesis of increasing realism of choice. *Journal of Vocational Behavior, 5*, 53–64.

Cosby, A. G. and Picov, J. S. (1973). Structural models and occupational aspirations: Black–white variations among deep–South adolescents. *Journal of Vocational Behavior, 3*, 1–14.

Crandall, V. C., Katkovsky, W., & Crandall, V. J. (1965). Children's beliefs in their own control of reinforcements in intellectual–academic achievement situations. *Child Development, 36*, 91–109.

Crites, J. O. (1961). A model for the measurement of vocational maturity. *Journal of Counseling Psychology, 8*, 255–259.

Crites, J. O. (1965). Measurement of vocational maturity in adolescence. Attitude test of the vocational development inventory. *Psychological Monographs, 79*, No. 2 (Whole No. 595).

Crites, J. O. (1973). *The Career Maturity Inventory*. Monterey, CA: California Test Bureau.

Crites, J. O. (1974). The Career Maturity Inventory. In D. E. Super (Ed.), *Measuring vocational maturity for counseling and evaluation*. Washington, D.C.: National Vocational Guidance Association.

Darlington, R. B., Weinberg, S. L., & Walberg, J. T. (1973). Canonical variate analysis and related techniques. *Review of Educational Research, 43*, 433–454.

Dean, S. A. (1984). External locus of control and career counseling for black youth (1984). *Journal of Non–White Concerns, 12*, 110–116.

Dillard, J. M. & Campbell, N. J. (1981). Influence of Puerto Rican, black, and anglo parents' career behavior on their adolescent children's career development. *Vocational Guidance Quarterly, 30*, 39–48.

Dillard, J. M. (1976). Relationship between career maturity and self–concepts of suburban and urban middle– and urban lower–class preadolescent black males. *Journal of Vocational Behavior, 9*, 311–320.

Forrest, D. J. (1971). The construction and validation of an objective measure of vocational maturity for adolescents. Unpublished doctoral dissertation, Columbia University.

Ginzberg, E. (1972). Toward a theory of occupational choice: a restatement. *Vocational Guidance Quarterly, 21*, 169–176.

Ginzberg, E., Ginzburg, S. W., Axelrad, S., & Herma, J. L. (1951). *Occupational choice: An approach to a general theory*. New York: Columbia University.

Gribbons, W. D., & Lohnes, P. R. (1968). *Emerging careers*. New York: Teachers College Press: Columbia University.

Gribbons, W. D., & Lohnes, P. R. (1969). *Career development from age 13 to age 25*. Career Research Project No. 6–2151 (pp. 193–197). Washington, D.C.: U.S. Office of HEW.

Gunn, B. (1964). Children's conceptions of occupational prestige. *Personnel and Guidance Journal, 42*, 558–563.
Hall, D. W. (1963). The vocational development inventory: A measure of vocational maturity in adolescents. *Personnel and Guidance Journal, 41*, 771–775.
Haller, A. O., & Portes, A. (1973). Status attainment processes. *Sociology of Education, 46*, 51–91.
Hanushek, E. A., & Jackson, J. E. (1977). *Statistical methods for social scientist*. New York: Academic Press.
Hauser, S. T. (1971). *Black and white identity formation: Studies in the psychosocial development of lower socioeconomic class adolescent boys*. New York: Wiley-Interscience.
Havighurst, R. J. (1953). *Human development and education*. New York: Longmans Green.
Jencks, C., Smith, M., Acland, H., Bane, M. J., Cohne, D., Gintis, H., Heyns, B., & Michelson, S. (1973). *Inequality: A reassessment of the effect of family and schooling in America*. New York: Basic Books.
Jennrich, R. I. (1970). An asymptotic chi-square test for the equality of two correlation matrices. *Journal of the American Statistical Association, 65*, 904–912.
Jordaan, J. P., & Heyde, M. B. (1979). *Vocational maturity during the high school years*. New York: Teachers College Press, Columbia University.
Katz, M. R. (1963). *Decision and value*. New York: College Entrance Examination Board.
Kemper, T. D. (1968). Reference groups, socialization and achievement. *American Sociological Review, 33*, 31–45.
Kerchoff, A. C., & Campbell, R. T. (1977). Race and social status differences in the explanation of educational ambition. *Social Forces, 55*, 701–714.
Kim, J., & Mueller, C. W. (1978). *Introduction to factor analysis: What it is and how to do it*. Beverly Hills, CA: Sage Publications.
Kim, J., & Mueller, C. W. (1978). *Factor analysis: Statistical methods and practical issues*. Beverly Hills, CA: Sage Publications.
Knapp, T. R. (1978). Canonical correlation analysis: a general parametric significance–testing system. *Psychological Bulletin*, 410–416.
Lawrence, W., & Brown, D. (1976). An investigation of intelligence, self–concept, socioeconomic status, race, and sex as predictors of career maturity. *Journal of Vocational Behavior 9*, 43–52.
Lee, C. C. (1984). Predicting the career choice attitudes of rural black, white, and Native American high school students. *Vocational Guidance Quarterly, 33*, 177–184.
LoCascio, R. (1967). Continuity and discontinuity in vocational development theory. *Personnel and Guidance Journal, 46*, 32–36.
LoCascio, R. (1974). The vocational maturity of diverse groups: Theory and measurement. In Super, D. E. (Ed.), *Measuring vocational maturity for counseling and evaluation*. National Vocational Guidance Association.
Mangum, G., & Seninger, S. F. (1978). *Coming of age in the ghetto: A dilemma of youth unemployment*. Baltimore: Johns Hopkins University
Marascuiio, L. A., & Levin, J. R. (1983). *Multivariate statistics in the social sciences: A researcher's guide*. Monterey, CA: Brooks/Cole.
Maynard, P. E. (1970). Assessing the vocational maturity of inner–city youths. *Journal of Counseling Psychology, 17*, 400–404.

McDowell, S. L. (1978). Verification of the career maturity inventory attitude scale for use with Oregon twelfth grade students. Unpublished doctoral dissertation, University of Oregon.

McNair, D., & Brown, D. (1983). Predicting the occupational aspirations, occupational expectations, and career maturity of black and white male and female 10th graders. *The Vocational Guidance Quarterly, 32,* 29–36.

Miller, C. H. (1956). Occupational choice and values. *Personnel and Guidance Journal, 35,* 244–246.

Miller, C. H. (1974). Career development theory in perspective. In E. L. Herr (Ed.), *Vocational guidance and human development.* Boston: Houghton Mifflin.

Osipow, S. H. (1968). *Theories of Career development.* New York: Appleton–Century–Crofts.

Osipow, S. H. (1973). *Theories of career development* (2nd ed.). New York: Prentice Hall.

Palmo, A. J., & Lutz, J. G. (1983). The relationship of performance on the CMI to intelligence with disadvantaged youngsters, *Measurement and Evaluation in Guidance, 16,* 139–148.

Pentecoste, J. C. (1975). Occupational levels and perceptions of the world of work in the inner city. *Journal of Counseling Psychology, 22,* No. 5, 437–439.

Picuo, J. W., & Carter, T. M. (1976). Significant other influence and aspirations. *Sociology of Education, 49,* 12–22.

Pindych, R., & Rubenfeld, D. L. (1976). *Econometric models and economic forecasts* (2nd ed.). New York: McGraw–Hill.

Portes, A., & Wilson, K. L. (1976). Black–white differences in educational attainment. *American Sociological Review, 41,* 414–431.

Rotter, J. B. (1966). Generalized expectancies for internal vs. external control of reinforcement. *Psychological Monographs, 80,* Whole No. 609.

Sewell, T. S., Palmo, A. J., & Manni, J. L. (1981). High school dropout: Psychological, academic, and vocational factors. *Urban Education, 16,* 65–76.

Sewell, W. H., Haller, A. O., & Ohlendorf, G. W. (1970). The educational and early occupational status attainment process: Replication and revision. *American Sociological Review, 35,* 1014–1027.

Shapiro, D. & Crowley, J. E. (1982). Aspirations and expectations of youth in the United States. Part 2. Employment activity. *Youth and Society, 14,* 33–58.

Shappel, D. L., Hall, L. G., and Tarrier, R. B. (1971). Perceptions of the world of work: Inner–city versus suburbia. *Journal of Counseling Psychology, 18,* 55–59.

Shibutani, T. (1955). Reference groups as perspectives. *American Journal of Sociology, 60,* 562–569.

Simmons, R. G., & Rosenberg, M. (1971). Functions of children's perceptions of the stratification system. *American Sociological Review, 36,* 235–249.

Simpson, R. L. (1962). Parental influence, anticipatory socialization, and social mobility. *American Sociological Review, 27,* 517–522.

Smith, E. J. (1975). Profile of the black individual in vocational literature. *Journal of Vocational Behavior, 6,* 41–59.

Smith, E. J. (1976). Reference group perspectives and the vocational maturity of lower socioeconomic black youth. *Journal of Vocational Behavior, 8,* 321–336.

Statistical Analysis System (1982). *SAS User's Guide: Basics.* North Carolina: SAS Institute.

Statistical Package for Social Sciences, Inc. (1983). *SPSS–X user's guide.* New York: McGraw–Hill.

Stout, R. T. (1969). Social Class and educational aspiration: A Webanan analysis. *Personnel and Guidance Journal, 47,* 650–654.

Super, D. E. (1955). Dimensions and measurements of vocational maturity. *Teachers' College Record, 7,* 151–163.

Super, D. E. (1962). The structure of work values in relation to status, achievement, interests, and adjustment. *Journal of Applied Psychology, 46,* 234–239.

Super, D. E. (1963). Toward making self–concept theory operational. In D. E. Super et al., *Career development: Self–concept theory.* New York: CEEB Research Monograph, No. 4.

Super, D. E., Crites, J. O., Hummer, R. C., Moser, H. P., Overstreet, P. L., & Warnarth, C. F. (1957). *Vocational development: A framework for research.* New York: Bureau of Publications, Teaches' College, Columbia University.

Super, D. E., & Overstreet, P. L. (1960). *The vocational maturity of ninth grade boys.* New York: Bureau of Publications, Teachers' college, Columbia University.

Super, D. E., Bohn, M. J., Forrest, D. J., Jordaan, J. P., Lindeman, R. H., & Thompson, A. S. (1971). *The career development inventory.* Teachers' College, Columbia University.

Thomas, M. J. (1975). An examination of the relationship between locus of control and vocational maturity, choice realism, and job knowledge among low socioeconomic status black and white male youth. Unpublished doctoral dissertation, New York University.

Tiedeman, D. V., & O'Hara, R. P. (1963). *Career development: Choice and adjustment.* New York: CEEB.

Tyler, L. E. (1967). The encounter with poverty—its effect on vocational psychology. *Rehabilitation Counseling Bulletin, 11,* 61–70.

Vriend, J. (1969). Vocational maturity ratings of inner–city high school seniors. *Journal of Counseling Psychology, 16,* 377–384.

Westbrook, B. W., & Cunningham, J. W. (1970). The development and application of vocational maturity measures. *Vocational Guidance Quarterly, 18,* 171–175.

Westbrook, B. W., Parry-Hill, J. W., & Woodbury, R. W. (1971). The development of a measure of vocational maturity. *Educational and Psychological Measurement, 31,* 541–543.

Westbrook, B. W., & Mastie, M. M. (1974). The cognitive vocational maturity test. In D. E. Super (Ed.), *Measuring vocational maturity for counseling and evaluation.* Washington, D.C.: National Vocational Guidance Association.

Williams, V. (1976). A survey of the career maturity of a select group of black high school students. Unpublished doctoral dissertation, Florida State University.

Zytowski, D. G. (1970). The concept of work values. *Vocational Guidance Quarterly, 18,* 176–186.

TRANSITIONS: THE BLACK ADOLESCENT AND THE LABOR MARKET

Julianne Malveaux

For many Americans, finding and keeping a job is synonymous with being accepted into society. Not only does work provide individuals with income, but it offers many individuals a sense of self-worth. The fact that a job provides so many with a sense of belonging, a sense of future, is communicated by journalist Rechard Louv (1981), who calls a job "the American birthright".

Claiming this birthright may make the difference between success and failure for Black adolescents. The late teens and early twenties represent an exploratory time for young people—a time to think about career options, and to test the feasibility of those options; a time to assert independence, and to claim responsibility by supporting oneself financially; a time to explore the work world and the discipline it imposes, a time to correlate hard work with rewards.

While youth employment is a critical part of the transition of young people from school to work, the labor market may not always welcome young people with open arms. This is especially true when high numbers of adults face joblessness. Unemployment rates have been as high as 11% in the past five years. The American economy has undergone a transformation. Grown men queue up to work for jobs that White teens once scorned. The decline in the manufacturing sector of the economy has left all semi-skilled men vulnerable. And as former auto-workers trade their $15 per hour salaries for lower pay as a computer technician, somebody lower on the totem pole is finding it more difficult to find a job.1

When semi-skilled males seek work, their wives are pulled into the labor force. And so the same kind of competition takes place among women in the labor force. Women with seniority and skills compete favorably against young women of color just entering the labor market. Again, the shifting economy shuffles workers through jobs, and tends to shuffle one group of workers, minority youth, further out of the workplace.

Yet minority youth need jobs to secure their futures. They are less likely than White youth to go to college or to enter training programs, so early jobs provide them with a first glimpse of the workplace. This first glimpse is important because it will shape future perceptions of the work world. And these perceptions may determine whether minority youth will seek work or not.

How bad is the problem? Part One of this paper discusses the labor market status of Black youth. How important is work? Part Two explores Black family resources and explains why work is so very necessary for Black youth. Part Three discusses the educational status of Black youth and its role in determining work status. Part Four highlights public policy initiatives intended to benefit working Black youth.

The Data on Black Adolescents in the Workplace: A Note

This note on data sources provides the reader with sources for further research and explains some of the data limitations of this paper. For the purposes of this paper, Black youth are described as those 16–24 years old. While a technical definition may be broader, this definition is consistent with the way data are reported on employment status.

Labor market data are reported for young people ages 16–19 and 20–24. There were 4.89 million Blacks aged 16–24,2 2.3 million males and 2.5 million females. The data on labor force participation, employment and unemployment and occupational status are reported by the Bureau of Labor Statistics from data gathered in Current Population Reports. CPS tapes and unpublished data also represent a source of information on the labor market status of young people.

Technically, 14–15 year olds would be included in a definition of Black adolescents, and information on their population levels is reported by the Bureau of Census. Detailed data on the labor market status of 13–15 year olds is neither reported by Census, nor by the Bureau of Labor Statistics, and are unaddressed in this paper. (Local school districts sometimes collect data on population levels and employment status of in-school youth, including 13–15 year olds). Research on strategies to improve the employment possibilities of young people, however, sometimes focuses on 13–15 year olds,3 so even though the status of this age group is unaddressed, their problems should not be ignored in a discussion of Black adolescents in the workplace.

It may stretch the definition of "adolescence to include Blacks over age 24 in this paper. But there are hard to employ 25–29 year olds who have not made a successful transition between school and work. The problems they face in the workplace are similar to those of their younger brothers and sisters, but in absence of a work history, it will be costly to prepare these young people for the workplace. The Bureau of Labor Statistics provides as much data on this age group as it does on others, but preliminary research suggests a growing number of young Black men in this age group are totally lacking official work histories, and have been living from a series of underground, semi-official jobs. There are little national data offered to support this premise, but if this problem is a burgeoning one, it too should be part of a discussion on young Blacks and the world of work.

Data on school enrollment and educational status are gathered by both the Census Bureau and the National Center for Educational Statistics. Census data report levels of educational attainment in the population, while NCES data provide enrollment figures as well as information on the number of degrees awarded in different fields.

Finally, data on income, employment, and family status are reported by the Bureau of the Census. These data are reported for persons as young as 15 years old (but usually for 18 to 24 year olds). The employment data included with income data tends to be less complete than that reported by the Bureau of Labor Statistics.

The Employment Status of Black Youth

The Current Employment Status of Black Youth

Though youth may feel that employment is a "birthright", the labor force may be a hostile place for many Black youth. Though data on levels of youth employment may understate the severity of the youth employment problem, the data presented in this section show, alarmingly, that work is more the exception than the rule for Black youth, especially Black teens. Unlike their White counterparts, almost half of whom work, roughly one in four Black teens was employed in 1986. While the employment–population ratios for older youth (20–24) show some improvement, they are lower than the rates for comparable Whites.

Table 1 shows the labor market status of Black youth in 1985.

This table will be used to illustrate some of the labor market definitions discussed in this section, and to highlight reasons why the unemployment rate may be a low estimate of employment problems among Black youth.

The title of the table, "Employment Status of the Civilian Non–Institutional Population", raises the first issue. The "non–institutional" population excludes those in the military, as well as those who are incarcerated. When military employment was added to the "official" unemployment rate in 1983, as a result of soaring unemployment rates, this inclusion lowered the total unemployment rate by a tenth of a percentage point. ("Civilian" employment and unemployment are reported separately for continuity). However, since incarceration disproportionately affects Blacks, an aspect of the "employment" problem is not being dealt with here. A question is raised: to what extent does joblessness

Table 1
Employment Status of the Civilian Non-Institutional Population, 1985

	Black Women 16-19	Black Men 16-19	Black Women 20-24	Black Men 20-24	Black Total 16-24
Population	1,101	1,059	1,447	1,202	4,809
Labor Force	417	471	904	950	2,742
Labor Force Participation Rate	37.9	44.6	62.5	79.0	57.0
Employed	254	278	673	726	1,931
Unemployed	164	193	231	224	812
Unemployment Rate	39.2	41.0	25.6	23.5	29.6
Employment—Population Ratio	23.1	26.3	46.5	60.4	40.2
Not in Labor Force	684	588	543	253	2,068
—Keeping House	106	6	306	11	429
—Going to School	460	455	141	114	1,170
—Can't Work	1	4	5	9	19
—Other	116	124	90	119	449
Not in Labor Force But Want a Job					607
Not Looking Because of:					
—School Attendance					312
—Ill Health, Disability					32
—Home Responsibilities					89
—Think Cannot Get a Job					110
—Other					64

influence rates and levels of incarceration? That answer is beyond the scope of this paper, but remains a critical question to consider in relation to the status of Black adolescents.

The civilian population is divided into those who are part of the labor force and those not part of the labor force. Those in the labor force are those who either hold jobs are who are officially seeking work. Those who have dropped out of the labor force because they cannot find work are not included as part of the labor force, though they may well be eager and anxious for employment.

Transitions: The Black Adolescent and the Labor Market

From Table 1, the majority of Black teens are "not in the labor force". Most of those who are "not in the labor force" are there because they are going to school. Yet school attendance and part–time work are not incompatible. It is likely that the estimate of those in the labor force, working or seeking work, is a low estimate. In fact, 30% of the 2.1 million young Blacks who are not in the labor force say they want jobs. These young Blacks say they are not looking for work because they are in school, or have home responsibilities. But 5% (about 110,000) say they are not looking for work because they think they cannot find it. These workers are called "discouraged workers" because they dropped out of the labor market because they are discouraged about their labor market prospects. As will be discussed later, other workers who want jobs but are not looking might also be considered "discouraged workers".

The labor force participation rate is used as a measure of labor supply. It is seen as a measure of the percentage of the population that is either working or seeking work given current labor market conditions. Low labor force participation rates suggest that few, in a given population, are working or looking for work. The definition of the measure suggests, perhaps, that if more Black adolescents were willing to seek work more of them might find it. As shown in Table 1, labor force participation rates are low. But they would be higher if those who want work (but are not officially seeking it) were included.

The labor force participation rate measures willingness to work, but it says little about existing market conditions and does not measure the ability of the market to absorb these willing workers. We do know that participation rates fluctuate with economic conditions, suggesting that potential workers participate in the market when they think their chances of finding employment are high. But Black youth unemployment rates have been more than twice the level of White youth unemployment rates since the early 1970's, and remain high. During the late 1970's and early 1980's, high youth unemployment rates were the target of many public programs. In fact, youth unemployment rates were so alarming in the 1976–77 period that an Office of Youth Programs was established as part of the Employment and Training Administration of the Department of Labor in 1978. This office was responsible for a "rapid buildup of youth activities" and played a key role in making youth employment a policy priority of the Department of Labor. While youth unemployment rates have not improved considerably, the focus on youth unemployment has been less sharp for several reasons. Firstly, general employment problems have displaced youth employment as a focus of attention. Further, there is discussion about a "shortage" of White youth to take unskilled and semi–skilled jobs. Finally, policy initiatives like job creation, are not likely to be implemented by a fiscally conservative federal government that is committed to "private sector initiatives".

In any case, it is clear that the unemployment rate understates the

Table 2
Labor Force Participation Rates by Age, Race and Sex 1970-1986

	16 to 19					20-24		
	Black Women	Black Men	White Women	White Men	Black Women	Black Men	White Women	White Men
1985	37.9	44.6	55.2	59.7	62.5	79.0	73.8	86.4
1984	35.0	41.7	55.4	59.0	60.7	79.1	72.5	86.5
1983	33.0	39.9	54.5	59.4	59.1	79.4	72.1	86.1
1982	33.5	39.7	55.0	60.0	60.1	78.7	71.8	86.3
1981	34.0	41.6	55.4	62.4	61.1	79.2	71.5	87.0
1980	34.9	43.2	57.4	63.7	60.4	79.8	70.5	87.2
1979	36.8	46.3	57.4	64.8	61.6	80.6	70.5	86.7
1978	37.3	44.9	56.7	65.0	62.8	78.8	69.3	87.2
1977	32.9	43.2	54.5	64.0	59.5	79.3	67.7	86.8
1976	32.9	41.3	52.6	62.3	57.1	79.1	66.2	86.2
1975	34.2	42.6	51.5	61.9	56.0	78.8	65.4	85.5
1974	33.4	46.7	51.7	62.9	58.8	83.5	63.8	86.5
1973	34.2	45.7	50.1	62.0	58.1	83.7	61.6	85.8
1972	32.2	46.3	48.1	60.1	57.1	82.6	59.4	84.3

Source: Handbook of Labor Statistics

extent of Black youth employment problems. If all of those who want work but are not actively seeking it were included in the labor force, the unemployment rate of Black 16–24 year olds would rise from the 29.6% shown in Table 1 to an alarming 42.4%. One might also question how many young Blacks, especially those who are not in the labor force because they are "keeping house", would enter the labor market if affordable child care were available.4 In addition, the fact that many young Blacks work part–time involuntarily (because they cannot find full–time work) further raises questions about accurate measurement of "underemployment".

Because questions have been raised about accuracy in measuring both labor force participation rates and unemployment rates, the employment population ratio is included in Table 1 as a "neutral" measure of employment among Black youth.

This ratio measures the proportion of a population group that is

Table 3
Unemployment Rates by Age, Race and Sex 1970-1986

	16 to 19				20 to 24			
	Black	Black	White	White	Black	Black	White	White
1985	39.2	41.0	14.8	16.5	25.6	23.5	8.5	9.7
1984	42.6	42.7	15.2	16.8	25.6	26.6	8.8	9.8
1983	48.2	48.8	18.3	20.2	31.8	10.3	13.8	
1982	47.1	48.9	19.2	21.7	29.6	31.5	10.9	14.3
1981	42.2	40.7	16.6	17.9	26.4	26.4	9.1	11.6
1980	39.8	37.5	14.8	16.2	23.5	23.7	8.5	11.1
1979	39.1	34.2	14.0	13.9	22.6	18.7	7.8	7.4
1978	40.8	36.7	14.4	13.5	22.7	21.0	8.3	7.6
1977	43.4	39.2	15.9	15.0	25.5	23.0	9.3	9.3
1976	41.6	37.1	16.4	17.3	22.8	22.6	10.4	10.9
1975	41.0	38.1	17.4	18.3	24.3	24.7	11.2	13.2
1974	37.4	33.1	14.5	13.5	19.1	16.2	8.2	7.8
1973	36.1	27.8	13.0	12.3	18.4	13.2	7.0	6.5
1972	40.5	31.7	14.2	14.2	17.9	14.9	8.2	8.5

employed and shows, as mentioned earlier, that work is more the exception than the rule for Black teens, and that low employment levels for Blacks who are 20–24 years old are partly the function of high unemployment rates, not low levels of labor force participation.

Employment Status of Black Adolescents, 1972–1985

Tables 2, 3, and 4 show labor force participation rates, unemployment rates, and employment population ratios by race, sex and age.

These tables show trends in Black youth employment and unemployment, and also compare Black youth with their White counterparts.

Unlike Black teens, whose labor force participation has been relatively constant, White female teens increased their labor force participation by about 8 percentage points since 1972. Young White men increased their participation overall, though it peaked in 1978 and has fallen since. Similarly, Black women in the 20–24 age group increased

Career Development and Employment

Table 4
Employment Population Ratios by Age, Race and Sex 1970-1986

	16 to 29						20-24	
	Black Women	Black Men	White Women	White Men	Black Women	Black Men	White Women	White Men
1985	23.1	26.3	47.1	49.9	46.5	60.4	67.5	78.0
1984	20.1	23.9	47.0	49.1	45.1	58.0	66.1	78.0
1983	17.0	20.4	44.5	47.4	40.3	54.5	64.7	74.3
1982	17.7	20.3	44.6	47.0	42.3	53.9	63.9	73.9
1981	19.7	24.6	46.2	51.3	44.9	58.3	65.0	77.0
1980	21.0	26.9	47.9	53.4	46.2	60.9	64.6	77.5
1979	22.4	28.7	49.4	55.7	47.7	65.5	65.0	81.1
1978	22.1	28.5	48.5	56.3	48.6	62.2	63.6	80.6
1977	18.5	26.4	45.9	54.4	44.3	61.0	61.5	78.7
1976	19.2	25.8	44.2	51.5	44.1	61.2	59.4	76.9
1975	20.2	26.3	42.5	50.6	42.4	59.4	58.1	74.3
1974	20.9	31.4	44.3	54.4	47.6	69.9	58.7	79.8
1973	22.0	32.8	43.6	54.3	47.4	79.6	57.4	80.2
1972	19.2	31.6	41.3	51.5	46.9	70.4	54.6	77.1

Source: Handbook of Labor Statistics

Table 5
Unemployment Rates and Ratios of Youth and Adults
for Selected Years

Year	Overall Rate	16-17	Ratio	18-19	Ratio
1952	3.0	10.0	3.3	7.3	2.4
1960	5.5	15.5	2.8	14.1	2.6
1966	3.8	14.8	3.9	11.3	2.9
1972	5.6	18.5	3.3	14.6	2.6
1978	6.1	19.3	3.2	14.2	2.3
1981	7.6	21.4	2.8	18.4	2.4
1984	7.0	20.2	2.9	16.9	2.4

Source: Employment and Training Report of the President, 1982
Employment and Earnings, January, 1985

Table 6
Family Status by Race, 1984

	Black	Median Income	White	Median Income	Ratio B/W Inc.
Number of Families (in Thousands)	6,778	15,432	54,400	27,686	55.7%
Married Couple Families	3,469	23,418	45,643	30,058	77.9%
Percent of Total Families that are Married Couple Families	51.2%		83.9%		
Excess of Married Couple Income over Total Income (Percent)		51.7%		8.6%	
Number of Families with Wives in the Labor Force	2,221	28,775	23,979	35,176	81.8%
Percent of Married Couple Families with Wives in the labor force	64.04		52.5%		
Excess of Two LF Family Incomes Over married couple Income (Percent)		22.9%		17.0%	
Two LF Families as a Percent of Total Families	32.7%		44.1%		
Excess of two LF Family Income Over total Family Income (Percent)		86.5%		27.1%	
Female Headed Families	2,964	8,648	6,941	15,134	57.1%
Percent of Total Families that are Female Headed	43.7%		12.8%		
Female Headed Family Incomes and a Percent of Total Incomes		56.0%		54.7%	

Source: U.S. Bureau of the Census, Current Population Reports, Series P-60, No. 149, Money Income and Poverty Status of Families and Persons in the United States: 1984. (Washington, D.C.: Government Printing Office, 1985)

their participation rates between 1972 and 1985, but not as rapidly as White women in that age group. Black men had declining participation rates between 1972 and 1985, while White men slightly increased their participation rates.

The ratio between Black and White teen unemployment has worsened for men since 1972, but has remained almost constant among women. But the racial unemployment ratio is greater for those 20–24 years old, and reflects the fact that the overall ratio has been rising since 1972. This suggests that it is harder for young Blacks to successfully enter the labor market, and that while unemployment will drop from its high teen level, it will not drop as rapidly, nor will it reach parity with White unemployment rates.

Low labor force participation rates and high unemployment rates combine to yield low employment population ratios, as shown in Table 4. The gap between Black and White men aged 20–24 is nearly 18 percentage points. The gap between Black and White women is also large, at 11%. These rates, more than unemployment rates and labor force participation rates, give a clear sense of the eroding labor market position of young Black men and the stagnant position of young Black women, all while White employment levels are high and increasing.

How Important Are Youth Employment Problems? Youth unemployment rates have always exceeded those of adults, and for obvious reasons. Young people have higher job turnover because they are not sure about career choices; youth search for jobs longer than do their adult counterparts because of their lack of experience. Thus, the unemployment rates for 16–17 year olds have always been about three times more than overall unemployment rates; unemployment rates for 18–29 year olds have been about two and a half times adult rates (see Table 5).

Levels of youth employment and unemployment have fluctuated over the business cycle. The youth share of jobs, for example, dropped from 7% to 6.5% between 1981 and 1982, as a recession deepened. But concern for youth employment problems may have peaked in 1979, when researchers spent over $1.3 billion in federal resources to study disparities in the unemployment experiences of youth and adults, and of Black and White youth.

While the ratio of youth to overall unemployment has fluctuated steadily, the relationship between White and Black youth unemployment has changed. In 1952, Black 16–17 year olds experienced less unemployment than their White counterparts, while the unemployment rate for Black 18–19 year olds was slightly higher than the rate for White 18–19 year olds. By 1979, Black youth experienced two and a half times as much unemployment as White youth.

Youth unemployment is not a significant problem when youth plan to attend college. But when youth terminate their educations with high

Table 7
Black Family Income for Selected Years in (Constant 1984 Dollars

	1984	1982	1980	1976	1974	1970
Families (Thousands)	6,778	6,530	6,317	5,804	5,491	4,928
Percent	100.0	100.0	100.0	100.0	100.0	100.0
Under $10,000	34.0	35.6	32.1	29.4	28.9	28.4
$10,000-14,999	14.9	15.4	15.4	16.2	16.0	16.2
$15,000-19,999	12.3	11.0	12.2	11.7	13.2	16.5
$20,000-24,999	9.4	10.2	9.8	10.4	10.5	9.3
$25,000-34,999	13.1	14.5	14.7	19.9	20.0	19.0
$35,000-49,999	10.5	9.5	10.9	7.9	7.5	7.0
$50,000 Plus	5.3	3.6	4.9	4.5	3.9	3.6
Median Income	15,432	14,633	15,976	16,863	16,863	16,796
Ratio B/W Income	55.7	55.2	57.9	59.5	59.7	61.3

Source: U.S. Bureau of the Census, Current Population Reports, Series P-60, No. 149, Money Income and Poverty Status of Families and Persons in the United States: 1984. (Washington, D.C.: Government Printing Office)

school and possibly some vocational training, youth unemployment may have scarring effects (Smith, 1980). Black youth are more likely than White youth to terminate their educations at high school, so that the long-term effects of youth employment are more important for White than for Black youth.

Why is Black youth unemployment so much higher than White youth unemployment? Some researchers have controlled for parental status, place of residence (including inner-city residence), job search method, and family background. Such comparisons yield the conclusion that Black and White youth with similar characteristics have different unemployment rates (Malveaux, 1981). What, then, explains the difference? Is discrimination the reason for differences in levels of youth employment? Or are there other reasons why adult Whites and others might be preferred as workers to Black youth in tight labor markets?

Larsen (1986) explores the demand for young Black male workers and confirms that discrimination plays a role in the low employment levels of young Blacks. He further identifies structural employment shifts (from manufacturing to services, and from urban to suburban areas), and a decline in aggregate demand as factors in explaining failing employment rates among young Blacks.

Some explain that Black youth unemployment rates are high because Black youth (or youth in general) are less productive than others. If youth do not produce the same marginal revenue product as their adult counterparts, they represent less value for employers. To make it profitable for employers to hire youth (especially Black youth), this line of reasoning continues, youth wages need to be lowered. The proposal of a youth subminimum (or youth opportunity) wage flows from this premise, and is discussed later in this chapter.

It is also possible to view Black youth unemployment as a problem that flows from the economic underdevelopment of the Black community. Small businesses employ a sizeable number of Black youth, but Blacks own proportionately fewer small businesses than Whites. Further, differences in the occupational status of Black and White parents may mean differences in the number of informal job contacts to which Black youth have access. To the extent that employment (or career development) is seen as part of a high–school curriculum, the impact of some of these differences may be minimized. On the other hand, the elimination of federal youth employment programs has had a negative impact on Black youth employment since a disproportionate number of Black teens worked in government–sponsored programs in the late 1970's.

A number of reasons can explain the fact that Black youth have higher unemployment rates than White youth. And youth unemployment problems may be seen as temporary problems in the sense that as long as youth grow up, their unemployment rates will fall. But Black youth bear a heavier unemployment burden than do others. And youth employment problems are more likely to have a long–term effect on Black youth, many of whom will not go to college, and many of whom will be plagued with the legacy of a spotty youth work history for the rest of their lives.

The Family Status of Black Youth and the Need to Work

The Economic Status of Black Families

The economic status of the families of Black adolescents has an important impact on the economic status of individual adolescents. Family status is a partial determinant of the work expectations of an adolescent, and the impact nonwork will have on an adolescent's future. Family status will also be a determinant of the life chances and access of Black youth, including their access to education, housing, health, and employment. And, importantly, family status may indicate the need for Black youth to contribute to family income.

There were 6.8 million Black families in 1984, 3.5 million of which were married couple families. The majority (64%) of married couple families had working wives. A significant number of Black families (nearly 3 million, or 44%) were female headed. (Table 6 details the status of both Black and White families).

Income varies widely among Black families by family composition. While median income for all Black families was $15,432 in 1984, it was $28,755 in married couple families with the wife in the labor force, but just $8,648 for female–headed households.

An income gap exists between Black and White families regardless of family composition, but the gap is narrowest for married couple families with working wives, where Black families earn almost 82% of what White families earn. Black married couple families are more likely than White married couple families to have wives in the labor force; further, Black married couple families with working wives have median incomes that are nearly double (186%) median incomes of all Black families. In contrast, White married couple families with working wives have median incomes just 27% higher median incomes of all White families. Thus, the work effort of Black women is of more importance in maintaining the income level of Black families than is the work effort of White women. While a more detailed examination of the data will provide a fuller explanation of this phenomenon, the fact that White men earn so much more than Black men partly explains this.

Table 7 shows Black family income for selected years in constant (1984) dollars (the use of constant dollars controls for the effects of inflation). This table does not show information on family composition, but shows detail on the income distribution of Black families. The effects of economic cycles on family income is shown and the economic vulnerability of Black families to recession is illustrated.

For example, the proportion of Black families with incomes over $25,000 (in constant dollars) was higher in 1970 than it was in 1984. Though the proportion of families with such income levels has fluctuated, the decline in the number of families with earnings between $25,000 and $34,999 indicates the fact that some Black families are slipping back into poverty. In contrast, there has been an increase in the number of Black families with incomes above $35,000, suggesting progress for an upper tier of Black families. Much of this progress represents a recapturing of old gains—15.8% of Black families had incomes above $35,000 in 1980; this proportion dropped in 1982, but rose by 1984.

Erosion in the incomes was to be expected between 1980 and 1982, especially given recession and high unemployment rates. But the fact that middle–income Blacks bore a heavier burden of this status than Whites has roots in the "last hired, first fired" concept that makes Blacks more vulnerable during periods of economic fluctuation. Black professionals had a higher concentration in public sector employment during a period

Table 8
Employment Status Civilian Non-Institutional Black Youth, 16-24, by Education, 1985

	Total	LFP	% Unem.	Empop
Black Enrolled	1,707	31.7	32.5	21.4
—High School	1,059	25.3	42.8	14.5
—College	648	42.3	22.5	32.9
Full Time Student	548	35.2	25.6	26.1
Part Time Student	101	82.5	15.3	68.3
Black Unenrolled	3,102	71.0	26.9	48.5
—Not HS Grad	1,000	53.4	42.2	30.9
—High School Grad	2,102	79.3	24.6	59.8
—1-3 Years College	480	64.3	19.4	67.9
—College Grad or More	93	89.7	14.5	76.3

when both the federal and state governments reduced employment levels.5

A corollary to the decrease in the proportion of Black families with incomes of more than $25,000 is the increase in the number of families with low incomes. The proportion of Black families with incomes under $10,000 rose from 1970 to 1984, with a major increase taking place between 1980 and 1982. Though the proportion of Black families with incomes under $10,000 declined between 1982 and 1984, more than a third of all Black families earned less than $10,000 per year in that year.

As stated at the outset, the incomes of Black families are important to adolescents, especially adolescent dependents in these families. High levels of poverty among Black families means that more Black children, and Black adolescents are at risk. While poverty may not make school enrollment or work impossible, family poverty may restrict the access of a Black adolescent. Family poverty may prevent college attendance (or even college application), may limit employment contacts, and may play a major role in the life chances of adolescents.

The increase in the number of Black families with incomes above $25,000 provides a widened set of opportunities for some Black adolescents. These families, though a minority of Black families, tend to be larger than poorer families.6 Still, two in five Black 14 and 15 year olds lives below the poverty level, as do more than one in three 16–21 year olds.7

Family Formation and Black Youth: Potential Losses in Two Generations

Some of the alarm about the status of Black families is focused on issues of Black teen pregnancy and Black male unemployment, underemployment and criminal activity. The alarm has been translated into so many well–publicized "special reports" and "investigations" that it would appear Black teen families make up the majority of all Black families. Nothing could be further from the truth—Black families headed by 15–24 year olds represent 7% of all Black families. Nearly two–thirds of these families are female–headed, and these female headed families represent 10.3% of all Black female headed families. Poverty is disproportionate among families headed by young Blacks, but young Blacks, by no means, represent the majority of Black families8.

Instead, while some aspects of youth lives explain the incidence of poverty among young Black families (such as educational attainment, number of children, and work experience), the incidence of poverty among adult female headed families is equally alarming. Nearly a third (31.8%) of the Black families headed by Black women with some college are families with incomes below the poverty line. So, too, are a third of the Black female headed families where women worked. While rates of poverty are lower when families are not female headed, there is a significant poverty incidence in married couple families where the householder has attended college, where the householder has worked, even full time, and even where there are two workers in a household.

This data on poverty status is not meant to detract from the problems of families headed by young Blacks, but merely to put these families in perspective. Some young Blacks will leave poverty as they age; others, based on data about the current Black population, may remain in poverty even after they are adults.

While the dimensions of the teen pregnancy problem have been overstated, the concern about Black teen parenting and pregnancy are important. But it is notable that Black teen birth rates are falling, while White teen birth rates are rising. The popular media would portray teen pregnancy as a uniquely "Black" problem, while issues of teen sexuality, parenting, and pregnancy are issues that confront the entire population.

Black teen parenting is important because Black teens are less likely than others to marry, and thus will be dependent on their parents, on one income (which is likely to be consumed by child care costs), or on public assistance for survival. Even when young Black men attempt to meet their responsibilities as parents by sharing child care costs, their attempts may be frustrated by the bleak labor market prospects they face.

The fact that so many Black children grow up in poverty is of as much concern as the levels of teen parenting and pregnancy. But all Black children who grow up in poverty are not the sons and daughters of teen parents. More than half of Black children under age three lived in poverty in 1984, as did just half of those between 3 to 5. The older children were, the lower were their poverty rates, but the overall rate of Black child poverty was 33.8% in 1984 (compared to 11.5% for White children).

The Children's Defense Fund (1986) (CDF) has produced voluminous work on the status of children in poverty. Their work has followed patterns in federal budgets, demonstrating losses in levels of funding for education, mental health, welfare services, juvenile justice and other programs. CDF's work on child poverty focuses both on the extent of child poverty and the extent to which government policy has exacerbated levels of child poverty.

CDF reports suggest, in many ways, that two generations are at risk because of policies that exacerbate child poverty. When young girls have children, they are "least likely to receive early and continuous prenatal care". Their children have higher death rates, and lower than average rates of growth. Teen mothers and fathers are at jeopardy because social programs that support them have been eliminated. Their children, too, are at jeopardy, both because of a paucity of programs to support them, and because their parents are placed at risk and often unable to find jobs and provide for them.

Education and the Employment Status of Black Youth

Table 8 shows the positive effect that education has on the current employment status of Black youth. The majority of young Blacks are not enrolled in school. Two-thirds of those not enrolled are high school graduates, and a fraction have attended college or are college graduates. High school graduates and college graduates have higher labor force participation rates and lower unemployment rates than those who did not finish high school or college. Employment–population ratios were highest for Black college graduates, and lowest for high school dropouts.

While those enrolled in school generally had lower employment population ratios than those who were unenrolled, unemployment rates dropped as student seniority rose. High school students had higher unemployment rates than college students. High school students also had lower levels of labor force participation than college students.

Despite the fact that education improves the status of Black youth, gaps between Black and White youth remain, even at the highest levels of educational attainment. Black college graduates had 14.5% unemployment rates, compared to White graduates, whose unemployment rates were 5.5%. Similarly, Black high school graduates had 24.6% unemployment rates, compared to 8.7% rates for Whites.9

Yet the condition of the labor market makes it all the more difficult for Black students to finish their educations, since many find work a condition of education. The majority of Black college students come from families with incomes of less than $12,000 per year. Their parents are frequently unable to make major contributions to their college expenses, meaning that Black adolescents who are enrolled in college have a greater need both for earnings and for financial aid.

Table 8 suggests that Black youth improve their prospects with college educations. But the data show that the proportion of Black students enrolled in colleges and universities has dropped since 1978. In addition, Black students are more likely than White students to be enrolled in two–year programs, and are more likely to drop out of school. As long as such a strong link can be made between education and employment status, it is important that policy be directed to the status of Black students in the educational system, and that resources are directed toward improving that status.

Public Policy and the Labor Market Status of Black Youth

How can public policy improve the labor market status of Black youth? The data reviewed show key differences, and also indicate that labor market data paint a less than complete picture of the employment status of Black youth. While incarceration has been alluded to, it has not been discussed directly in this chapter. Workfare and other programs focused on dependent mothers may have a disproportionate effect on young Black women, and will also impact the status of Black women in the labor force. This topic is left for later investigation.

As incomplete as this discussion has been, it has raised some questions about the race–neutrality of the labor market, especially for Black youth. If young Black college graduates can expect unemployment rates higher than those of White high school graduates, then the market is generating a result that seems to be tainted by race. Thus, affirmative action is an important policy to improve the labor market status of young Blacks.

Education can also play a role in improving the status of Black youth, yet as the federal government moves away from enforcing affirmative action in education, the states may have to play a greater role

(Jaschik, 1986). There remains a need for affirmative action in admissions, but there is also an increasing need for financial aid for Black students, the majority of whom come from poor families.

Job creation is an important way to ensure young Blacks employment opportunities. The programs developed by the Labor Department in the 1978-80 period were successful in providing youth with work experiences, as well as incentives to remain in school. While these programs are costly, their returns may be high enough to warrant their maintenance.

There may be a need to develop different employment enhancement programs for young Blacks based on their gender. Young Black women, especially those who had households, need training opportunities, child care, and programs to move them out of low-wage, part-time "typically female" jobs.10 Young Black men have as great a need for training opportunities as do young women, but they are less likely to need child care and other family-related programs.

Job creation programs have been tried in the past, and with mixed success. They have provided youth with jobs, but critics have questioned the value of the public-sector employment experience. A number of subsidy programs (such as targeted tax credits) have been available in the past for those who have hired the "hard to employ", but these programs have never been fully used by the private sector.

In an attempt to generate youth private sector employment opportunities, the youth subminimum wage was targeted as a policy priority by the Reagan Administration in the early 1980's. The endorsement of the concept by the National Conference of Black Mayors, by former Federal Reserve Governor Andrew Brimmer, and by the predominantly Black National Alliance of Postal and Federal Employees made the concept even more acceptable.11 The Youth Employment Opportunity Wage Act was proposed in 1984. This Act would have allowed employers to pay persons under age twenty an "opportunity" wage of $2.50, or 75% of the minimum wage, during the summers (May through September). The "opportunity wage" was proposed as experimental, and would have been effective only for the three year period between 1984 and 1987.

Development of the Youth Employment Opportunity Wage Act was viewed as a compromise by many who supported the subminimum wage. By restricting the applicable period to summers, the "opportunity wage" is seen as providing an "employment opportunity" for youth, not a labor substitution incentive for employers. By limiting the "opportunity wage" to a three year experiment, proponents of the Youth Employment Opportunity Wage Act allow for the effects of the opportunity wage to be tested, and guard against any permanent erosion in the integrity of the minimum wage. The combination of summer limitations and the three-year restrictions led the National Conference of Black Mayors to conclude that unemployment rates of Black youth are so high that they are willing to try almost "anything", including subminimum wages, to lower rates.

Testimony from the June, 1984 hearings of the Joint Economic Committee and the Senate committee on Labor and Human Resources was interesting, especially because so little proof that the subminimum wage would generate jobs was cited. Some testimony leaned heavily on economic "logic", while other testimony was peppered with anecdotal information and recollections of the very distant past where youth found jobs easily, and accepted jobs gratefully regardless of working conditions.

It is interesting to note that it is currently possible for private sector employers to hire young people at a subminimum wage in certain circumstances. By law, employers can hire a few employees (no more than six, or 10% of all employees) at 85% of the minimum wage. This provision of the law has been effective since 1974, and is designed to facilitate employment of college students. During testimony on the Youth Employment Opportunity Wage Act of 1984, several employers mentioned the current possibility of subminimum wage hiring (Kondor, 1984). Fewer than 2% of the retail grocers in the U.S. used full–time student certificates, and the number had declined since 1981. "Excessive paperwork" was cited as the reason why more would not use full–time student certificates.

Testimony by Bernard Anderson (1984) should be noted since Anderson summarized several studies in his brief comments. He indicated that research by the Minimum Wage Study Commission, as well a experiences under the Youth Incentive Employment Entitlement Program (1978–80) did not support the claim that more youth would be hired in private sector jobs as a result of a wage reduction. Anderson's report that only 18% of those eligible participated in a program to hire youth at a 100% wage subsidy suggests that the implicit 25% subsidy promised by the subminimum may merely erode the wage floor without providing employment opportunities. Finally, Anderson exposes the "opportunity" wage as a youth "opportunity" to be exploited. For while proponents of the subminimum wage say they want to reduce wages because youth are being provided with training "opportunity", "little or no useful training or experience can be obtained in marginal, dead–end jobs".

Pure supply and demand analysis suggests that if the price of a commodity is lowered, then the demand for that commodity increases. If such "simple analysis is extended to the youth labor market, then the concept of a youth subminimum wage can be considered as a potential method for increasing the level of youth employment. However, labor markets are not always analogous to markets for other commodities. And, concepts like equal pay for equal work, have been the cornerstone of our national labor policy. Even if one could guarantee that a youth subminimum wage would generate job opportunities, there might be objections to such wage because it would undercut other policy objectives. Further,

Paul Osterman (1984) notes that all youth do not need the targeted "opportunity" that a youth subminimum would provide.

Given the persistence of high Black youth unemployment rates, it is disappointing that the major public policy initiative to reduce these rates has been the subminimum wage. There is weak evidence that a youth "opportunity" wage would provide opportunities, but implementation of such a policy would trade off obvious negative effects for tenuous and questionable positive effects. As Anderson argued in his June, 1984 testimony, and as Larsen suggests in his research, targeted training and placement programs are a better vehicle than subminimum wages for ensuring the long-term labor market success of Black youth.

Conclusions

Black youth want to work, and family economics dictate that they must, but the labor market, structurally changed and highly competitive, has not welcomed Black youth, and in some cases made underground employment a preferred option to a frustrating, but legal, search for work. Popular images have focused on the pregnant teen, the high school dropout who "hangs out" on the block. But even the Black adolescent college graduate finds unemployment rates nearly thrice those of his White counterparts.

The treatment of Black youth in the labor market is consistent with the treatment of Black adults who also experience high unemployment rates as well. But the promise of the civil rights struggle was that it would be easier for young Blacks to gain equity than it was for their parents. The data belie that promise.

At some point it may be possible for young Blacks to find jobs as easily as young Whites. Until then, intervention in educational and labor markets are important not only to guarantee equity, but even to a fair set of opportunities.

Alfred Camus wrote, "Without work all life goes rotten." Yet work is the exception, not the rule, for Black teens. Black youth between 20 and 24 work much less than White counterparts. Many of these youth have left the labor market because they believe they cannot find work. Others choose education and hope their education will pay off in employment. But one in seven college graduates is unemployed.

"Without work all life goes rotten." Without intervention, the status of Black youth in the labor market is a warning, both about the futures of these young Blacks, and ultimately, about the future of the Black community.

Notes

In addition to the work cited below, this chapter includes a portion of a forthcoming paper, "Two Tier Employment Systems: Wage Attack or Employment Opportunity?" *Urban League Review.*

1. See Paul Flaim and Ellen Sehgala, "Displaced Workers, 1979–83", Bulletin 2240, Bureau of Labor Statistics, July 1985. 5.1 million workers were displaced in the 1979–83 period after three continuous years of full–time employment. Of the 2.8 million workers who were reemployed, nearly half (45.7%) worked in part–time jobs, or at lower earnings than in their last job. See Table 11 for details.
2. In 1985, according to *Employment and earnings, January 1986.*
3. For example, see Julianne Malveaux, "Youth Employment in the San Francisco Bay Area: Data, Perspectives, Programs, Directions," Northern California Grantmakers, 1983.
4. See Julianne Malveaux, No Images: Contemporary Black Women in the labor market (forthcoming, 1987), Chapter One for a discussion of unemployment measures and underestimation.
5. See Julianne Malveaux, "The Economic Status of Black Families" in Harriette McAdoo (ed.), The black family (Beverly Hills: Sage, forthcoming).
6. U.S. Department of Commerce, Bureau of the Census (1986). *Money income of households, families, and persons in the United States, 1984*, Washington, D.C.: Government Printing Office, P–60, No. 151, Table 18, p. 72.
7. U.S. Bureau of the Census, Current population reports, (1984) *Money income and poverty status of families and persons in the United States 1984*, Washington, D.C. Government Printing Office, P–60, No. 149, Table 17, Page 26.
8. U.S. Department of Commerce, Bureau of the Census *Money income of households, families, and persons in the United States, 1984*. P–60, No. 151 (Washington, D.C.: Government Printing Office, 1986). Table 16, p. 61. See also, U.S. Bureau of the Census, Current population reports, Series P–60, No. 149, *Money income and poverty status of families and persons in the United States, 1985.*
9. See *Employment and Earnings*, January, 1986, Table 6 for more detail.
10. See Julianne Malveaux, Similarities and differences in the interests of black and white women, *Review of Black Political Economy*, Summer, 1985; and Low wage black women: Occupational description.
11. Daily Labor Report, June 13, 1985: *Daily Labor Report*, (March 22, 1985).

References

Anderson, B. (1984). Statement to committee on labor and human resources, United States Senate on S. 2687, opportunity wage act of 1984. Washington, D.C.: Government Printing Office.

Children's Defense Fund. (1986). *An analysis of the FY 1987 Federal Budget and children*. Washington, D.C.: Children's Defense Fund.

Jaschik, S. (1986). States called key to college gains for minorities. *Chronicle of Higher Education, 32*, 1.

Kondor, J. (on behalf of the National Grocer's Association). (1984). Statement to committee on labor and human resources, United States Senate on S. 2687, Youth Employment Opportunity Wage Act of 1984. Washington, D.C.: Government Printing Office.

Larson, T. (1986). The demand for young black male workers: 1970–1980. Unpublished paper, Department of Economics, University of California, Berkeley.

Louv, R. (1981). Youth employment: Without work. San Diego: *Diego Union.*

Malveaux, M. (1981). Shifts in the occupational and employment status of black women: Current trends and future implications in Women's Center (Ed.), *Black working women: Debunking the myths, a multidisciplinary approach.* University of California, Berkeley: Women's Resource Center.

Osterman, P. (1984). Statement to committee on labor and human resources, United States Senate on S. 2687, Youth Employment Opportunity Wage Act of 1984. Washington, D.C.: Government Printing Office.

Smith, M. (1980). Early labor market experiences of youth and subsequent wages. Unpublished paper, Western Economics Association.

Appendix A
Percent of Total White and Black Males in the Labor Force by Age Cohort, 1940-80

	1980	1970	1960	1950	1940
65+					
(t)	19.3	80.5	93.4	94.6	95.1
(w)	19.4	81.3	94.0	95.0	95.4
(b)	17.7	72.4	87.6	90.6	92.4
55-64					
(t)	71.3	92.5	95.6	92.1	88.1
(w)	72.2	93.3	96.3	92.8	88.0
(b)	62.3	85.0	89.8	86.2	88.5
45-54					
(t)	90.2	94.8	94.9	81.9	47.8
(w)	91.3	95.6	95.7	82.1	46.4
(b)	81.0	88.1	88.5	80.4	59.5
35-44					
(t)	94.1	93.9	86.2	51.7	—
(w)	95.2	94.7	86.8	51.1	—
(b)	86.3	87.6	82.0	55.8	—
25-34					
(t)	92.8	80.9	50.0	—	—
(w)	94.3	81.6	51.1	—	—
(b)	83.5	76.4	42.4	—	—
20-24					
(t)	82.7	47.2	—	—	—
(w)	84.3	48.9	—	—	—
(b)	73.5	35.8	—	—	—
16-19					
(t)	52.4	—	—	—	—
(w)	55.5	—	—	—	—
(b)	36.5	—	—	—	—

From: U.S. Bureau of Census, Census of Population 1980, General Societal and Economic Characteristics, Table

Part VII
Counseling and Psychotherapy

COUNSELING THE BLACK ADOLESCENT: CRITICAL ROLES AND FUNCTIONS FOR COUNSELING PROFESSIONALS

Courtland C. Lee

There is a tradition of confusion surrounding the role of the school counselor. Counseling professionals continuously grapple with questions regarding their functions within the educational system. School administrators have typically capitalized on such confusion by imposing a myriad of responsibilities upon counselors that have little relation to their professional preparation.

This tradition has received considerable attention from leaders within the counseling profession, stimulating discussion and research on the ideal versus the real role of the school counselor (Carmical and Calvin, 1970; Cook, 1982; Dunlop, 1965; Shumake and Oelke, 1967; Warnath, 1973). Although such scholarly contemplation is important, it often serves to compound the state of confusion for many counselors.

Those counselors who serve the needs of Black adolescents, however, cannot afford the luxury of protracted contemplation, speculation or confusion about the nature of their role. The pressures exerted on the academic, career and personal development of Black youth present a major challenge to counseling professionals. Basic to addressing this challenge must be a definitive notion of the counseling role. Accordingly, school counselors need to develop new perspectives regarding the profession and its place in the educational system. It is important that counselors be a major influence on Black adolescent psychosocial development. A concerted effort is required to develop comprehensive counseling interventions which reflect the needs and realities of contemporary Black youth. Implicit in such interventions must be the concept that counselors are agents of change, with the knowledge and skill to translate dimensions of caring into constructive action. Such action necessitates extending programmed intervention beyond the Black adolescent into the school, home and community.

This chapter offers specific counselor roles and functions considered critical for facilitating the development of Black adolescents. In addition, important counselor functions related to the concerns of school personnel and the educational interests of the Black community are considered. These roles and functions are presented with suggestions for their implementation, as a model for school counseling program development.

The Counselor and the Black Adolescent

The school is the social institution in which adolescents are expected to acquire basic social, intellectual and cultural skills. Through their curricular and extracurricular activities, the junior and senior high schools can help young people strengthen their identities and prepare them to function as responsible citizens (McCandless & Coop, 1979). Unfortunately, the achievement, aspirations and pride of many Black adolescents are stifled by their school experiences. These experiences are often confounded by the complexities of institutional racism inherent in the school as a social system (Washington & Lee, 1981). Given this, counseling professionals must help Black students develop the attitudes, behaviors and skills to meet challenges within the educational system. Additionally, they must help Black youth gain the awareness and competencies necessary to function at optimal levels in the demanding world beyond the school. In order to accomplish these tasks, counselor functions must transcend the traditional boundaries of educational helping. Specific guidance provisions are necessary for heightening awareness, expanding skills and maximizing options on the part of Black adolescents.

A fundamental aspect of counseling interventions for Black youth, however, is understanding the cultural realities of Black people and their importance to development. It has become evident that there are important cathartic, curative and educational aids inherent in Black culture (Pasteur & Toldson, 1982). A primary task for counseling professionals involves finding ways to incorporate African–American cultural dimensions into the helping process (Cross, 1974; Stikes, 1972; Toldson & Pasteur, 1976). Culture–specific approaches to counseling have the potential to transform basic aspects of Black life, generally ignored or perceived as negative in the school setting, into positive psychoeducational experiences.

In order to maximize the effectiveness of cultural specificity in the helping process, emphasis should be placed on group approaches to guidance and counseling with Black youth. On a practical level, group intervention affords service delivery to a greater number of students than individual helping relationships (Irvine, 1968; Wrenn, 1979). The value of group methods as an effective counseling technique has been credibly established over a wide range of experimentation and practice (Corey, 1980; Rosenbaum & Berger, 1963). Outcome studies, which have evaluated various types of counseling groups in schools, have found significant changes in academic achievement (Altman, Conklin & Hughes, 1972), attitude and personality (Finney & Van Dalsem, 1969) and behavior (Lee, 1980) as a result of such interventions. Additionally, during adolescence, peer group interaction is an important means of both social identification and emotional support.

More important for Black adolescents, however, is the fact that group-oriented counseling approaches reflect the communal nature of the African–American experience (Toldson & Pasteur, 1976). Indeed, the dynamics of socialization among Black people emphasize cooperation and group cohesiveness. Group interaction becomes an important means of identity for Black youth. Making use of group intervention in facilitating the personal–social, academic and career development of Black adolescents should be an important goal for counseling professionals.

Personal–Social Development

Facilitating the development of a positive self–identity in Black adolescents is a primary personal–social function confronting counselors. Such a task is often underscored by the failure identity fostered in scores of Black youth through experiences with educational processes predicated on the notion that they are incapable of successful learning. This function need serve as the basis for all others; for it is only when young people accept themselves and their realities with a sense of pride that tangible educational gains are possible.

The following is an example of a comprehensive counseling model designed to promote the Black ego to facilitate personal development on the part of Black youth. The model represents a group counseling approach designed to facilitate behavior modification and promote self–esteem. It is culture–specific counseling approach that transforms basic aspects of Black life, often ignored or perceived as negative in the school setting, into positive educational experiences. Such cultural specificity in counseling has been advocated as a way to facilitate optimal mental health for Black people (Lee, 1983; Lee & Lindsey, 1985; Toldson & Pasteur, 1982). The model is a multisession developmental group counseling or classroom guidance experience for Black students in grades 7 through 12. The model uses selected Black art forms (e.g., music, poetry, folklore, and graphic expression) as educational aids in the counseling process (Toldson & Pasteur, 1976). Using these art forms as a fundamental part of the group intervention, the model stresses an understanding and appreciation of Black culture, development of motivation to achieve, development of positive and responsible behavior, and modeling of positive Black images.

The group participants should be selected to ensure a complementary mix of socioeconomic status, academic skill level, and level of Black awareness. Before the selection of group participants, parents and teachers should be consulted about the nature and purpose of the group, the planned activities, and the expected outcomes. Counselors should be prepared to discuss with parents and school officials the rationale for conducting this segregated group experience in the school setting. If possible, the model should be implemented in conjunction with ongoing Black studies classes. Counselors may want to consult Black studies teachers about conducting the group experience as a guidance activity within the classes.

The model presented here involves 50–minute group sessions, but the time and number may vary according to individual preferences and institutional considerations. The general purpose and the methods of facilitation for each session in the model are discussed below.

"Blackness: A State of Mind, A State of Being"

SESSION I: "BLACK IS "

General Purpose

To have group members begin the process of personalizing their Blackness by thinking about skin color and ethnicity. Particularly, to have students examine negative aspects associated with their Blackness. Additionally to begin to build a sense of community among group members.

Methods of Facilitation

Play "Black Is" by the Last Poets (Hassen, 1976) and have group explore the fundamental question "What is Black?"

DISCUSSION QUESTIONS

1. What does being Black mean in this town?
2. What does being Black mean to you in this school?

SESSION II: "BAD TIMES"

General Purpose

To have group members explore and understand contemporary problems that confront Black people. This includes those problems confronting them as Black students in the school setting. Out of this, participants should become aware of problem–solving strategies and techniques for confronting Black challenges.

Methods of Facilitation

Play "The Message" by Grand Master Flash and the Furious Five (Fletcher, Glover, Robinson & Chase, 1982).

DISCUSSION QUESTIONS

1. When have you felt like you have been pushed to the brink?
2. When have you felt like it is a jungle and you are trying to keep from going under?
3. How has being Black made you feel like this?

Lead a group discussion of personal bad times with a focus on both bad times that students themselves were responsible for and those that were externally caused. As a final activity, have the group participants explore through biographic materials the life of Frederick Douglas, an African–American who overcame bad times.

SESSION III: JOHANNESBURG – "YOUR" BURG

General Purpose

To begin to develop among group members an awareness of Black life in other parts of the world and to instill in them a sense of their place in the world-wide Black experience. In addition, to begin to develop an understanding of world affairs from a Black perspective.

Methods of Facilitation

Play "Johannesburg" by Gil Scott–Heron (Scott–Heron, 1975) or "It's Wrong (Apartheid)" by Stevie Wonder (Wonder, 1985).

DISCUSSION QUESTIONS

1. Where is Johannesburg?
2. What is Apartheid?

3. Where is Soweto?
4. What is happening to Black people in South Africa?
5. Why is it important for you as African–Americans to know what is going on in South Africa?

As a final activity have group members examine through biographical materials the life of a famous historical international Black figure (e.g., Toussaint L'Overture).

SESSION IV: "ROOTS"

General Purpose

To have group members gain a greater understanding of and appreciation for both their African and African–American heritage.

Methods of Facilitation

Play African music and elicit impressions and perceptions of Africa from the group.

DISCUSSION QUESTIONS

1. How many of you have ever thought that your ancestors could have been kings or queens?
2. Do you realize that you probably have cousins living in Africa today? Explore African heritage with group with books, pictures, folktales, etc. Play "Ship Ahoy" by the O'Jays (Gamble & Huff, 1973). Conduct a guided fantasy with the group of the slave voyage from Africa.

DISCUSSION QUESTIONS

1. How does it make you feel to think that your ancestors were slaves?
2. What can you learn about survival from your slave ancestors?

To personalize African and Afro–American history, have each group member attempt to construct a family tree. Have any students who are able to trace their roots back to Africa share their family's history with the group.

SESSION V: "REFLECTIONS"

General Purpose

To have group members personalize group activities experienced thus far, both as young Black people in general, and as Black students in particular.

Methods of Facilitation

Play "Just Got to be Myself" by the Voice of East Harlem (Hutson, Hawkins & Morrison, 1974).

DISCUSSION QUESTIONS

1. What has this group meant to you so far?
   Facilitate a group exploration of three words: *respect, survival, pride*.
1. What do you need to do to get *respect* as a Black student at this school?
2. What things do you need to do to *survive* at this school?
3. What kinds of things can you do to develop *pride* as a Black student at this school?

As a final activity, have group members read biographical material on Malcolm X whose life represents the true development of Black consciousness. After discussing the life of Malcolm X, have students write their own autobiographies as Black people.

SESSION VI: "BLACK IS"

General Purpose

To have group members complete the process of personalizing their Blackness by reflecting on their skin color and ethnicity. In addition, to achieve an affirmation of Blackness among group members.

Play again "Black Is" by the Last Poets. Have group members re-examine the fundamental question, "What is Black?"

Explore with group positive aspects of Blackness related to: skin color, hair texture, lip size, nose shape, etc. Have each group member make a positive statement about their Blackness.

To have group members begin translating experience into positive action, play the recording, "Ain't No Stoppin' Us Now" by McFadden and Whitehead (Whitehead, McFadden & Cohen, 1979). Explore this song and the inspirational meaning it brings to the lives of young Black people.

As a concluding activity, conduct an African/African–American cultural festival including foods, music, dance, and other activities to celebrate the Black experience and to reinforce group activities. Invite parents and community members to participate.

There are four major intended counseling experiences associated with this model. First, to have group members develop an understanding of and appreciation for their Blackness. Second, to have group members delineate positive academic and social roles and begin to assume them. Third, to enable group members to gain a new vantage point on the meaning of their lives. Fourth, to have group members develop appreciation for ethnic and cultural diversity grounded in high self–esteem.

After this group experience, Black students should be involved in group guidance activities with young people of varied ethnic backgrounds. These activities should promote interpersonal appreciation and understanding across ethnic lines.

Academic Development

Guiding the development of motivation and skills for academic achievement among Black adolescents represents a major role for counseling professionals. The school often impedes the academic development of Black adolescents, causing their motivation–to–succeed–educationally to suffer. Frustrated by having experiences perceived as both irrelevant and insensitive, many Black youth give up on the promise of formal education.

The concerned counselor must assume a proactive role in addressing educational alienation among Black youth. Such a role involves helping students work through frustrations and develop attitudes that will promote success within the educational setting.

Multi–session motivational group counseling experiences for junior and senior high school students to increase their motivation for academic achievement would help counselors assume such a proactive role (Lee, 1983). The goal of such group experiences should be to raise consciousness levels, self–expectations and attitudes related to academic achievement. Several important motivational concepts should be learned as a result of participation in such group experiences. First, group members should come to recognize that success in school takes mental strength and stamina. Second, they should begin to understand that they are in control of their responses to challenges and problems within the school setting. Third, participants should develop an awareness of their positive potential and begin channeling it in positive academic directions. Taken together, an understanding of such concepts should contribute significantly to educational motivation.

In conjunction with facilitating the development of positive attitudes toward achievement, counseling for academic development should entail promoting learning skills and competencies among Black youth. Within the context of motivational groups, counselor should plan structured workshops or other experiences that provide students with guidance in the following areas: academic planning, study skills, time management, and test–taking. Importantly, counselors should be active in fostering remedial efforts aimed at overcoming skill deficiencies among Black students.

Career Development

The world of work for the African–American has been landscaped with unfulfilled dreams, wasted potential, dashed hopes and economic struggle. Given this, the issue of career interest and choice becomes a complex dimension in the development of the Black adolescent. Traditionally, it has been the function of counseling professionals to provide vocational guidance in the school setting. However, the committed counselor must consider the social pressures on African–American career development and restructure traditional guidance accordingly.

Such restructuring entails reconceptualizing vocational planning as comprehensive life planning for Black adolescents. While life–planning is important for all young people, it is a complex issue for Black adolescents. This is due, in large measure, to traditions of racism, poverty, and oppression that have often retarded the life progress of Black people (Gary, 1978; Willie, Kramer and Brown, 1973). These traditions have stifled development for thousands of Black youth. Importantly, because Black people often find meeting basic needs on a short–term basis to be a constant challenge, many Black youth do not have an environment conducive to developing long–range planning skills. It has not been unusual to find Black adolescents lagging behind their White counterparts, with respect to critical aspects of life planning and development (Smith, 1975).

Life–planning interventions should be modular in design and implemented over a four to five year period, or the normal course of the adolescent secondary school experience. The modules should consist of counseling, guidance and coordination. The purpose of the counseling module should be to promote life planning among Black students in four ways: by facilitating self–awareness of skills, interests, and values, by facilitating an expansion of options, by facilitating decision–making based on knowledge and experience, and by encouraging students to anticipate future events. To accomplish this, life planning counseling groups should be formed. Group sessions should commence with comprehensive ability, interest, and value assessment and interpretation.

Group experiences should provide participants with opportunities to examine life options and make decisions about future goals. Counselors should begin by having group members reflect on the contemporary state of affairs for many Black people. As an example, have group participants listen to popular recordings that detail the contemporary challenges facing Black people and discuss the importance of planning in their lives.

As the sessions progress, conduct *Life Scenario Exercises* in which participants contemplate educational, occupational, and personal options by answering the question, "What Would You Do If...?" Examples for completing this question might include the following:
- ...you couldn't go to college?
- ...the requirements for your job changed and you didn't have the required skills to keep it?
- ...you could not get into the Armed Forces?

As group members proceed through the process of examining options and making long-range plans, develop a *Peer Counseling Life—Planning Development Network*. This is a system whereby older students who have made important decisions in major areas of their lives (e.g., graduating seniors who have made future educational and/or occupational plans and are beginning to implement them) become involved in counseling group participants about crucial issues in life planning.

Activities in the guidance module should include workshops and experiences related to the mechanics of the world of work and associated life issues. The mechanics of the world of work include how to look for, apply and interview for a job. In the same vein, it is important that counselors provide guidance concerning the proper attire, behavior and attitude for work settings. Related life issues that should be examined in guidance sessions include: money and its management, tax concerns and social security.

In addition to guidance activities, counselors should coordinate educational, community and business resources with the life–planning process of Black adolescents. To accomplish this, counselors should develop a *School–Community–Business Network*. This network is a system in which Black professionals and community representatives are included in life-planning counseling interventions as group facilitators and role models/mentors. It is important that these people represent nontraditional, as well as traditional career areas for Black people (e.g., mathematical/scientific fields, as well as educational/social fields) and present balanced lifestyles (e.g., professional women in nontraditional fields who balance career and family).

As part of such a network, counselors should arrange field trips, career days, and cooperative experiences that allow Black students to get "up close and personal" with role models/mentors and career opportunities in a variety of both traditional and nontraditional occupational fields.

Such proactive counseling with its comprehensive approach to long-range planning is important for Black adolescents, particularly those whose long-range planning skills may be limited by socioeconomic disadvantage. The counseling, guidance and coordination components of this career development approach should provide Black youth with a supportive and relevant context within which to develop skills for life planning.

The Counselor and the Educational System

The anger, frustration and ultimate failure that are the educational reality for scores of Black adolescents have been justification for claims of limited learning potential among African–Americans. The disproportionate numbers of Black youth who fail or become behaviorally labeled, foster the notion of inherent cultural deficits that impede African–American educational progress.

Such thinking however, clouds American educational reality. Traditionally, the educational system has made little allowance for cultural diversity in schooling. School success has been narrowly defined in terms of a White middle–class norm. Within such a context, students whose realities differ from this norm are often required to make important adjustments to ensure a measure of success. These adjustments become critical considering the characteristic lack of sensitivity for diversity on the part of the educational system. Obstacles to school success for the culturally different then, come to be perceived as student inadequacies, rather than considered as originating with institutional insensitivities.

Given such perceptions, the responsibility for problematic school functioning comes to rest solely on the culturally different status of the Black adolescent and its divergence from the educational norm. Little consideration is given to the notion that problematic functioning may in reality be reactive responses by Black students to a system that tolerates little diversity.

The concerned school counselor is faced with a unique dilemma. Charged with facilitating student adjustment to the system, he or she is confronted with the fact that often it is the system that needs adjustment to the student. This is particularly evident when systemic insensitivity negates African–American reality. The solution to this dilemma lies in a redefinition of the counseling role to account for the fact that problems are not always found in students, but often exist in the educational system. Such a redefinition requires an awareness of the systemic barriers to quality education and the development of skills to effectively challenge them (Gunnings and Simpkins, 1972).

The role of student advocate represents such redefinition. In such a role, the concerned counselor can intervene in the educational system on behalf of students in ways designed to eradicate inherent problems and insensitivities. Additionally, a student advocate becomes an important bridge across crucial cultural chasms separating Black youth and the school (Lee, 1982a).

Acting in the role of student advocate, the counselor should function to facilitate an awareness among his or her educational colleagues of the systemic factors that impinge upon the development of Black students. This function can be implemented by conducting individual and group consultations with teachers, administrators and other school personnel to identify racist or alienating factors in their attitudes, behaviors or policies.

Student advocates should also function to promote the professional development of culturally relevant approaches to education. Implementation of this function should involve coordinating professional development experiences for teachers and other educational professionals on ways to incorporate the African–American experience into a total school program. This might include coordinating training sessions related to multicultural curriculum and social planning. Such experiences should focus on increasing awareness of the Black experience among educators. To accomplish this, counselors should include coordinating training sessions related to multicultural curriculum and social planning. Such experiences should focus on increasing awareness of the Black experience among educators. To accomplish this, counselors should include African–American cultural experts and resources in the professional development process.

With challenges and problems inherent in diverse school settings, quality education for Black students often depends upon important changes occurring within the school as a social system. The counseling professional with student advocate skills can function in the vanguard of a thrust for acceptance of ethnic and cultural difference in the educational process.

The Counselor and the Black Community

The Black adolescent brings to the school experience a set of positive behaviors and success expectations fostered both in the home and the African–American community. Traditionally, the Black family and the larger community have placed a high value on education, considering it to be the prime factor in improving socioeconomic status. However, the expectations of Black students, their families and community are often at odds with the realities of contemporary education.

The cultural insensitivities inherent in the educational system tend not to validate the experience of African–American home and community life. More importantly, the system considers such life to have detrimental effects on adolescent development. Because of this, Black parents are often excluded from serious consideration in the education of their children (Lee, 1982b). Recent trends in community control notwithstanding, the educational system has effectively barred the Black community from constructive and knowledgeable participation in the education of its children. It is not unusual therefore, to find that in many instances relations between the school and the Black community are severely strained (Washington and Lee, 1981).

Counseling professionals can and should play an active role in addressing the divergence between the Black community and the educational system. A counselor can serve as an important link between the home, larger Black community and the school. Indeed, the counselor can function to make the system more responsive to the Black community, while at the same time increasing the level of effective participation by the community in the educational process.

Serving as a liaison between the Black community and the school, the counselor should function as a consultant to facilitate the development and incorporation of family and community resources into the adolescent educational process. Consultation activities should include conducting workshops for parents and other significant community people to make them aware of aspects of contemporary education such as standardized testing, grading and placement procedures; conducting constructive parent–teacher conferences; and recent curriculum innovations. The ultimate goal of such consultation should be to make members of the Black community informed consumers of the educational product, so that they can maximize their influence on adolescent academic development.

Another area of consultation should promote the importance of academic and vocational planning during the adolescent years. Counselors should assist parents in developing their decision–making skills as well as help them to improve their communication methods to initiate educational and occupational goal–setting with their adolescent children. This is particularly important since parental influence has been found to be an important variable in educational and occupational goal–setting among Black youth (Lee, 1984, 1986; McNair and Brown, 1983). Workshop sessions and other training experiences should be conducted to inform parents about expanding educational opportunities available to their children and financial aid opportunities for higher education. Counselors conducting these workshops should explore with parents the cumulative effects of education and the value of formal education in dealing with the real world.

In the area of career planning, the workshops should provide parents with employment projections in various occupational areas and understandable information on the changing job market. Counselors should also explain to parents the important stages of career development, particularly career exploration and tentative job choice which characterizes adolescence, and how they can facilitate their childrens' progress through them.

As often as possible, counselors should attempt to conduct such community–school liaison activities in homes and centers of social activity in the Black community. Such outreach efforts would help to promote the school as an institution that is flexible and sensitive to the strengths of the Black community.

Counselors may further facilitate the incorporation of community resources into the educational process by coordinating paraprofessional development programs that involve selected community people in teaching or counseling service delivery. Volunteers from the Black community with unique skills or insights as well as sensitivity to the needs of Black youth can be important extensions of teachers or counselors (Lee, 1980). Counselors should coordinate comprehensive training efforts that will enable those people to offer academic and social guidance in nonformal helping situations.

In conjunction with this, counselors should consult with leaders of community centers of social activity, such as ministers or youth recreation leaders, about establishing supplemental educational programs. These programs could be tutoring, guidance or recreational activities conducted in churches or other community centers. Counseling professionals should play a crucial role in the planning and implementation of such activities.

Conclusions

Innovation for facilitating the academic, career and personal development of Black adolescents such as that discussed here, implies a rejection of many long standing traditions characteristic of the school counseling profession. In assuming these roles and attempting to implement such functions, counselors can no longer commit themselves solely to the task of facilitating Black student adjustment to the educational system. Equally as important, counselors cannot continue passive acceptance of inappropriate role definition. Particularly when such definition is imposed from outside the profession.

Rejection and innovation of the magnitude suggested will inevitably be met with resistance from entrenched forces of racism and conservatism within the educational system. Indeed, counseling professionals must steel themselves against the opposition of significant and powerful others in the system likely to be intimidated by nontraditional, proactive counseling for Black adolescents.

The perennial professional debate concerning the role of the school counselor appears to be useless academic palaver when considered with the educational problems confronting Black adolescents. Such problems preclude the need for counselors who know who they are and what they are about. The academic and social survival of the Black adolescent demands no less.

References

Altman, H. D., Conklin, R. C., & Hughes, D. C. (1972). Group counseling of underachievers. *Canadian Counsellor, 6*, 112–115.
Carmical, L., & Calvin, L. (1979). Functions selected by school counselors. *School Counselor, 17*, 280–285.
Cook, D. R. (1972). The change agent counselor: A conceptual context. *School Counselor, 20*, 9–15.
Corey, G. (1980). *Theory and practice of group counseling* (2nd edition). Chicago: Rand McNally.
Cross, A. (1980). The Black experience: Its importance in the treatment of Black clients. *Child Welfare, 53*, 158–166.
Dunlop, R. S. (1965). Professional educators, parents and students assess the counselor's role. *Personnel and Guidance Journal, 43*, 1024–1028.
Finney, B. C., & Van Dalsem, E. (1969). Group counseling for gifted underachieving high school students. *Journal of Counseling Psychology, 16*, 87–94.
Fletcher, E., Glover, M., Robinson, L., & Chase, J. (Composer). (1982). *The message* from the record album *The message* (Record No. VID–235–A–19). Englewood, NJ: Sugar Hill Records Ltd.
Gambel, K., & Huff, L. (Composers). (1973). *Ship ahoy* from the album, *Ship ahoy* (Record No. AL32408). New York: Philadelphia International Records.
Gary, L. E. (Ed.) (1978). *Mental health: A challenge to the Black community*. Philadelphia: Dorrance & Co.
Gunnings, T. S., & Simpkins, G. A. (1972). A systemic approach to counseling disadvantaged youth. *Journal of Non–White Concerns in Personnel and Guidance, 1*, 4–8.
Hassen, O. B. (Composer). (1976). *Black is* from the record album *Jazzoetry* (Record No. ADLP 6001). New York: Douglas Records.
Hutson, L., Hawkins, P., & Morrison, J. (Composers). (1974). *Just got to be myself* from the record album *Can you feel it* (Record No. JSS–3504). New York: Just Sunshine Records.
Irvine, D. J. (1968). Needed for disadvantaged youth: An expanded concept of counseling. *School counselor, 15*, 176–179.

Lee, C. C. (1980). The homework helper program: Volunteer service for academic and social enrichment in the elementary school. *The School Counselor, 28,* 11–21.

Lee, C. C. (1982). Helping professionals as student advocates: An inservice training model. *The Humanist Educator, 20,* 161–166. (a)

Lee, C. C. (1982). The school counselor and the Black child: Critical roles and functions. *Journal of Non-White Concerns in Personnel and Guidance, 10,* 94–101. (b)

Lee, C. C. (1983). The high risk student: A model for motivation. *The Guidance Clinic, 15,* 13–16.

Lee, C. C. (1984). An investigation of the psychosocial variables in the occupational aspirations and expectations of rural Black and White adolescents: Implications for vocational education. *Journal of Research and Development in Education, 17,* 28–34.

Lee, C. C. (1986). A study of the psychosocial factors in the educational goals of rural and urban Black adolescents. Unpublished manuscript.

Lee, C. C., & Lindsey, C. R. (1985). Black consciousness development: A group counseling model for Black elementary school students. *Elementary School Guidance & Counseling, 19,* 228–236.

McCandless, B. R., & Coop, R. H. (1979). *Adolescence: Behavior and development* (2nd edition). New York: Holt, Rinehart and Winston.

McNair, D., & Brown, D. (1983). Predicting the occupational aspirations, occupational expectations and career maturity of Black and White male and female tenth graders. *Vocational Guidance Quarterly, 32,* 29–36.

Pasteur, A. B., & Tolsdon, I. L. (1982). *Roots of soul: The psychology of Black expressiveness.* Garden City, NY: Anchor Press/Doubleday.

Rosenbaum, M., & Berger, M. (1963). *Group psychotherapy and group function.* NY: Basic Books.

Scott–Heron, G. (Composer). (1975). *Johannesburg* from the record album *From South Africa to South Carolina* (Record No. AL 4044). New York: Arista Records.

Shumake, G. F., & Oelke, M. C. (1967). Counselor Function Inventory. *School Counselor, 15,* 130–133.

Smith, E. J. (1975). Profile of the Black individual in vocational literature. *Journal of Vocational Behavior, 6,* 41–59.

Stikes, C. S. (1972). Culturally specific counseling—the Black client. *Journal of Non-White Concerns in Personnel and Guidance, 1,* 15–23.

Toldson, I. L., & Pasteur, A. B. (1976). Beyond rhetoric: Techniques for using the Black aesthetic in group counseling and guidance. *Journal of Non-White Concerns in Personnel and Guidance, 4,* 142–151.

Warnath, C. F. (1973). The school counselor as institutional agent. *School Counselor, 20,* 202–208.

Washington, V., & Lee, C. C. (1981). Teaching and counseling the Black child: A systemic analysis for the 1980's. *Journal of Non-White Concerns in Personnel and Guidance, 9,* 60–67.

Willie, C. V., Kramer, B. M., & Brown, B. S. (Eds.). (1973). *Racism and mental health.* Pittsburgh: University of Pittsburgh Press.

Wonder, S. (Composer). (1985). *It's wrong (apartheid)* from the record album *In square circle* (Record No. 6134TL). Los Angeles: Motown Record Corp.

Wrenn, C. G. (1979). Proposed changes in counselor attitudes: Toward your job. *School Counselor, 27,* 81–90.

THERAPEUTIC INTERVENTIONS WITH URBAN BLACK ADOLESCENTS

Anderson J. Franklin

The clinical problems presented by Black urban adolescents are on the surface no different from those of any other youth population. They include concerns about self–image, achievement of autonomy, sexuality, peer relationships, school life, and vocational aspirations, to name a few. The difference between the concerns of Black youth from other ethnic peer groups is in the intrapsychic and societal resources available during development. Distinguishing the adolescence of Black youth by race is problematic. Such categorical distinctions can lead to erroneous conclusions about the individual as well as obscure legitimate group references. It is clear that contradictions in research findings on the influence of race supports the need for caution in interpretations. Nevertheless there is sufficient evidence—empirical, clinical and anecdotal—to conclude that growing up Black in America has its unique experiences. The source of Black adolescent distinctiveness is the social environment rather than intrinsically unique differences in the basic processes of development. Therefore understanding Black adolescent development requires comprehending the way growth processes—physical, social, and emotional—respond to characteristics of the social context (e.g., inner city vs. rural small town) and in particular the dynamic impact of racism. The evolution of these psychosocial experiences and the resources available in family and community structures will determine success in personal adjustment and goal attainment.

The Black urban adolescent has all of the concerns that characterize development during this developmental period. In addition, there are unique issues associated with the status of being Black in an urban environment. Life for many urban Black adolescents is rooted in poverty, illiteracy, unemployment, and racism. Adaptive styles for such social circumstances are often not ideal. What confronts the clinician in work with the urban Black adolescent are essentially problems borne out of racism and stressful life conditions masked by common developmental concerns, or vice versa. Given what these youth must cope with, it is not unlikely to find therapists who either disregard the effects of racism on a youth's development or, as noted by Thomas and Sillen (1974), believe that "since social norms cannot be changed overnight the individual must learn to conform to the prevailing scheme of things." (p. 14) The prevailing scheme of things for urban Black residents is abominable. It is worse for adolescents. The consequence of such life conditions is reflected in the high rate of institutionalization (psychiatric and correctional) and poor school performances of Black youth (Kramer, Rosen, & Willis, 1973; Jones, 1973) (See chapter by Myers in this volume for further discussion of Black adolescent mental health). The U.S. ideal of personal success is known by Black youth. It is flaunted daily on television and other forms of mass media. The impact on mental health from the media's conveyance of its embellished form of reality is still controversial (Pierce, 1974). Likewise, the chance of Blacks achieving such a norm is equally known from community referents as well as social statistics. The disparity between the ideal and the actual future life conditions for young Black adults is discouraging. Unfortunately, there is little in the present that foretells better living circumstances in the future. The urban Black adolescent must temper expectations of a better life with that of the average contemporary Black family. When we consider the importance attributed to the relationship between vocational aspirations and identity, the frustrating circumstances of life for the Black adolescent provides another dimension to understanding an already difficult process in development.

The Status of Black Adolescents

According to the 1980 Census there were 10.5 million Black youth under 19 years of age in the United States. Thirty-nine percent of Black youth between the ages of 16–21 were below the poverty level in 1982, and 44% of Black youth between the ages of 14–15. The median family income for Blacks in 1982 was $13,598 in contrast to $24,603 for Whites. For female head of households (no husbands present) the median family income was $7,510 in contrast to $12,510 for a White family in similar circumstances. Unemployment rates for Black males between the ages of 18–19 was 47% in 1982 and 43% in 1983; for White males it was 21% and 18% respectively. For Black females between 18–19 unemployment rates were 40% in 1982 and 56% in 1983 in contrast to White females whose rates were 16% and 15% respectively. In 1980 approximately 70% of Black 18–24 year olds were high school graduates compared to 82% of Whites. Of persons 14–34 years of age in 1981 about 18% of Blacks were high school dropouts compared to 12% of Whites. The high school dropout rates for Blacks in urban areas are projected much higher. (College Board, 1985)

These statistics only partially portray characteristics of the total population of Black youth. Certainly, not every urban Black adolescent can be characterized by these social statistics. Such data, however, provide a description of conditions in which we as professionals might find an urban Black adolescent. None of these statistics captures the social atmosphere or economic stress under which many Black youth live. These discouraging statistics allude to environmental conditions but do not describe adaptive styles these adolescents must employ to cope with such life circumstances.

Developmental and Clinical Problems

The lack of a comprehensive body of knowledge representing the psychological development of the urban Black adolescent makes conclusions in this area difficult. At best, we can draw upon the general literature about adolescence and make inferences about Black adolescents. By following this procedure, we run the risk of misrepresenting development for the Black adolescent. Since the urban Black masses are subject to poor living conditions, the urban Black adolescent's life must be considered within this context. Dohrewend and Dohrenwend (1974) have portrayed the consequences of inner city life as contributing to a high incidence of psychopathology. It is certainly apparent that urban life has many levels of stress, which form particular adaptive behaviors (Clark, 1965; Valentine, 1968). In the category of deviant behaviors, juvenile delinquency has been a popular focus of social and behavioral scientists. An examination of the literature will attest to this preoccupation. A dominant theme within the social science and education literature is the description of the broken or parent–absent family, the welfare dependency of the Black community, the poor school achievement of Black youth, and its overall effects upon the development of Black children (Billingsley, 1968). It is not my intent to critique these assumptions or interpretations but to note that the prevalence of such conditions have not been considered in a systematic analysis of their impact on psychological development of Black adolescents.

The role of the clinician when confronted with the pressing problems of the adolescent is to distinguish between personal concerns that are characteristic of average developmental experiences from those that are markedly deviant and possibly pathological. Since so much of adolescent behavior is viewed as alienation from society's roles and parental authority, deviant behavior is often interpreted in psychopathological terms. It is a period of life during which there is no clear unanimity among professionals about the extent of personal conflicts necessary to justify a diagnosis of psychopathology. Weiner (1970) addresses this confusion amply in his discussion of the different views on normality and abnormality in adolescence:

> ...psychological disturbance is so much a normal concomitant of adolescence that its absence is a cause for concern. Beres (1961) suggests

> that the adolescent who does not experience a state of flux and uncertainty is likely to have suffered a premature crystallization of his response patterns that may presage serious psychopathology. Anna Freud (1958) contends that teenagers who remain "good children" and fail to show outer evidence of inner unrest are displaying deviant development. In her view such children are responding to their impulses with excessive, crippling defenses that impede their normal maturational processes. (p. 42)

The clinician's struggle to determine when adolescent behavior is truly pathological must evolve from a consideration of etiology of symptoms and their developmental history. "It is only when a developmental reconstruction can be made in the course of diagnosis and therapy that a clear distinction between pathology and the normal adolescent process can be attempted." (Sprince, 1964, p. 103). The developmental context becomes extremely important when determining whether or not behavior is pathological. This is a major factor in interpreting the experiences of Black adolescents. Clinicians must be able not only to extract the particulars about early childhood experiences for the Black adolescent but to comprehend the significance of coping with socioeconomic inequities and racism in terms of their impact on psychological development. To compartmentalize the developmental history of the Black adolescent into traditional psychodynamic categories without considering the adaptive forces inherent in the social realities of community life is to forfeit diagnostic precision. Developmental histories must be evaluated within an understanding of the larger social context for proper formulations about behavior. This is a point cogently conveyed by Weiner (1970):

> From the clinical point of view it is unwarranted to automatically interpret model behavior as behavior that does not call for professional assistance.
>
> Yet judgments about normality cannot be completely independent of the context in which behavior occurs. Few would disagree that ritual suicidal behavior has different implications for psychological disturbance in Japan and the United States, primarily because of the different sociocultural values attached to such behavior in the two countries. However it is possible to encompass the import of sociocultural relativism within the normality–as–health perspective. As Romano and others propose, "health" criteria for normality can be defined to include adequate capacity for social interaction which implies that the individual is in relative harmony with his immediate society. At the same time, by focusing on freedom from pain, discomfort, and disability, the health perspective of normality avoids the error of labeling as abnormal an individual who calmly meets an emergency or crisis that is unnerving most of those around him (pp. 49–50).

The importance of this concept to diagnosis is represented by the inclination to formulate pathology when a Black adolescent relates atypi-

Therapeutic Interventions with Black Adolescents

cal family structure or dynamics. For example, clinicians who have no understanding of some harsh realities in urban life may prejudge psychosocial development upon learning a youth shares a bed with siblings. The hardships of some Black families overpower the naive clinician to the point of incomprehension about survival under such conditions and misjudgment about the adaptive styles generated by such an environment (Billingsley, 1968; White, 1980).

The question of when behavior is abnormal and pathological in adolescence is best answered by scrutinizing of the youth's psychosocial history. If there is evidence of patterned maladaptive behavior throughout childhood, there is sufficient reason to conclude that the clinical issue is characterological in substance. On the other hand, if the youth has had a childhood relatively free of psychosocial problems, except for the most recent times, it is likely that current clinical issues are transient, although, simply stated, this judgment is not the easiest to exercise when making a diagnosis. There are problems that seem transient and symptomatic of the developmental experiences for this age but are in fact masking fundamental characterological issues. Truancy is an example of this, where flexibility in schedules, and more permissiveness in high school leads to nonattendance. However the reasons underneath the truancy may be school phobic in substance. Similar to any other age group, there are age–related problems that usually constitute the initial issue for the client. With further clinical interviewing, other issues are exposed. The most common example of this with adolescent patients is the depression associated with the inability to establish affectional ties with peers of the opposite sex. The peer pressure among adolescents to explore sexuality is great. Adolescence is the first time that sexuality becomes a critical conscious concern about the relationship between the sexes (Conger, 1977). Most adolescents are basically naive about the responsible manner in which to integrate the physical, psychological, and emotional demands of this new–found experience. There is very little parental or formal education about sexuality in adolescence. By sexuality I am not limiting this to knowledge about the biological reproductive process. On the contrary, this is only a small part of the dynamics inherent in wholesome heterosexual relationships. We know that in spite of the effort of sex education in the public schools, 11 million teenagers become pregnant every year (Planned Parenthood Federation of American, 1976). Black adolescents have a disproportionate number of teenage pregnancies. When interviewed about the high incidence of pregnancies, teenagers do not profess as much ignorance of the reproductive process, or forms of contraception as they do about the responsibility that goes with heterosexual experiences such as pausing in the moment of passion to use contraceptives, or preventive planning. Very often the dilemma for the adolescent is how to manage the overpowering sex drive within the prevailing social attitudes and sanctions. To some the sex drive is frightening. The complexity of the sex urge is reinforced by peer anecdotes, myths, nocturnal emissions, dreams and fantasies. The anxiety associated with this experience can greatly hamper the development of self–concept. Contributing to this one issue, for example, are such interrelated concerns as parent–child conflicts, management of peer pressure, comprehension of physiological changes, and self–esteem. An adolescent who has managing heterosexual relationships as a primary concern requires the clinician to discern if the issue is developmental and transient or reflective of characterological issues. The following cases are illustrative of this diagnostic issue.

Mary was brought to the clinic by her parents with an expressed concern about her lethargy and her withdrawn and depressed behavior. She was 15 years old, in good health, had no previous history of social or psychological problems, and was an excellent student. In appearance Mary was neat, dressed in peer–appropriate stylish clothes, and adult looking in physical development. Both relatives and peers had commented on her attractiveness, as well as her growing sex appeal. In the initial therapy sessions, Mary denied her depression as "no big thing," saying she just felt "unmotivated" except for school work. She portrayed herself as having several girl friends who felt and acted similar to her, but in recent years she found the number of close friends dwindling as their interest in boys developed. Queried as to her interest in boys, Mary skirted the issue for several sessions, until one day, in a burst of tears, she relayed her confusion about her sexuality. Because Mary had developed at a young age, she attracted suggestive comments and approaches from peers and some adults. Her appearance and experiences caused a change in the way her friends and parents reacted to her. In school, boys hovered around her and tried to persuade her into sexual exploits. She stated that her appearance caused some girl friends to "put her down" and others to associate with her because she attracted boys. These days it seemed like her appearance defined the nature of her relationship with peers. Conflicts with her parents about her manner of dress and attention from boys were frequent. She felt her parents were ashamed of her appearance because they disagreed with the way she dressed. "Tight–fitting jeans or shirts always seemed to set my folks off." Complicating the matter for Mary were her own positive feelings about her manner of dress and the advances of boys. What contributed to her depression was the unresolved frustration from conflicts with her parents and sexual attraction to boys. The "hassles" forced a solution of disengagement from encounters and depression from growing social isolation.

Mary's physiological changes and emerging sexuality at an earlier age than her peers brought increased pressure to assume the consequences of early maturation. As is often the case, Mary had no preparation for the new demands placed on her relationships with others as a consequence of her physical changes. Suddenly, new social rules were

Therapeutic Interventions with Black Adolescents

placed upon her, which became overwhelmingly frustrating to manage. People spent more time responding to her appearance than helping her to gain understanding of how to manage it in a responsible way. In order to minimize the pain and frustration Mary elected to withdraw, thus acquiring new problems from voluntary isolation.

For the clinician treating an adolescent patient such as Mary, the major responsibility is determining whether the manifestation of depression is an historical pattern or situationally specific. Because establishing a trustworthy bond with adolescents can be extremely difficult, learning the basis of adolescent depression can be elusive and misinterpretations can result from the youths' reluctance to explain their behavior. In particular, discussion of sex with an adult therapist can be frustrating because adult reactions are frequently the source of the conflict in the first place. "Sex is just something you don't talk to grown-ups about" is the frequent comment of teenagers. Consequently, unless the therapist can get beyond the implicit adversary tradition of adult-adolescent relationships and establish an open and trusting rapport, the basis of clinical problems can be obscured. In Mary's case, it became clear during the course of therapy that her inability to resolve the management of her experiences in adolescent sexuality was the center of her immediate problems. Her solution to withdraw only compounded the situation. As therapy helped Mary become informed of the naturalness of her sexuality and experiences as well as appropriate ways of managing it, her depression and relationships with others improved. Mary's concerns were indicative of issues presented by passage through a developmental stage. However, if the therapist had been unsuccessful in getting Mary to disclose her true conflicts, it is likely the direction of therapy would have taken a different path. It must be stressed that before clinical formulations become firm about the presenting problems of adolescents, the therapist must be confident that a sufficient bond is established with the youth in order to evaluate the integrity of the disclosures.

In another case concerning adolescent sexuality, preoccupation with achieving the ideal adult male role and the concomitant appropriate social skills in heterosexual relationships obscured a more fundamental issue of sexual identity. A 15 year old Black male was referred to the clinic because of academic difficulties. After six months of therapy, the client reluctantly began to reveal that his school performance was affected by his preoccupation with girls. He had no girl friend and had difficulty establishing any kind of meaningful ties with girls. His naivete about just approaching and talking to girls was indicative of his ineffectual social skills. A high level of enthusiasm to establish relationships with girls led to a treatment plan of discussing boy-girl experiences as well as social skills training. After a short period of working with this treatment plan, it became evident that the client repeatedly sabotaged his own efforts. What emerged was the patient's own ambivalence about girls and a haunting attraction to boys. Once this admission occurred, the issue of sexual identity became the focus of therapy. A suspicion of an identity issue had been formulated early in the initial sessions, but the youth was adamant in asserting his interest in girls. It was only after carefully and slowly confronting the youth about the identity issue and after the youth's failure in social skills assignments mounted that the therapist was to get the youth to acknowledge a basic conflict.

The significance of this case is in the prevalence of the initial problem. Many adolescents present the management of heterosexual relationships during the emergence of their own sexuality as the root of their distress. Peer and societal pressure force certain conforming behaviors upon adolescents that heretofore were not required. In both cases, a therapist can easily succumb to the conclusion that these problems are transient and symptomatic of passage through a developmental phase. In the case of Mary, such an assumption would be appropriate, but with the latter example an apparent incompetence in social skills masked a larger issue of sexual identity.

Sociocultural Implications

Although both of the cited cases involved Black youths, they contain circumstances that could apply to any group of adolescents. The critical variable in synthesizing these experiences for Black youth and making clinical formulations is accurate evaluation of the contribution from their social milieu. In these two examples understanding the cultural emphasis and/or style becomes important. Whereas a therapist may professionally acknowledge that the customs of dress in adolescence are important, its variations by ethnic group or region are equally significant. Likewise it is important to know the ethnic value orientation of parents towards teenage dress and sexuality. Comprehension of the social milieu is essential for the development of an effective treatment plan. According to recent reports on the status of Black adolescents in the United States, these youths are placed in marginal situations and life conditions. Families of Black youth are equally victims of stressful circumstances, in part induced by concerns about economic and educational opportunities for their children (Ogbu, 1978). The stress in Black families today, with deteriorating options, is a context within which problems of Black youth evolve. Hypertension among Black adults and some adolescents is symptomatic of the stress experienced in the Black family and community (Lawson, 1979; Myers & Miles, 1979; Dohrenwend & Dohrenwend, 1974). Likewise, the increasing evidence of physical and mental health problems in the Black community broadens the view of the problems (Kramer, Rosen, & Willis, 1973). To understand the development of Black adolescent self–esteem and adaptive styles, the social milieu of their families must be considered.

Consequently, what may be a suitable clinical judgment for White adolescents may not be appropriate for helping the Black youth.

In Mary's case, an attractive Black adolescent, one of the chief pressures was the encouragement by some peers and school counselors to use her appearance as a vehicle to escape economic hardships through modeling. In spite of her above–average school performance, she was frequently led to believe that her future was dependent upon her physical appearance. On the other hand, her parents were apprehensive that her attractiveness and deportment would get her into trouble. They were brutally frank with community examples of how nice looking girls ended up in trouble with boys. As added pressure, they emphasized the importance of education, not a flaunting of beauty, as a way out of the ghetto. Consequently, in school her beauty was lauded and a feature of her social status, but at home it was devalued and considered an obstacle to upward mobility.

The case of the 15 year old Black male is also an example of how the urban social milieu affects development. He was in a school that reflected many of the problems of contemporary urban high schools. Education and management of the predominantly Black student body was minimal. The school environment was greatly defined by interests of student peer groups rather than teachers and school administrators. At this school education was a laissez–faire proposition for students. Classroom time was frequently consumed with maintaining order. Psychological development in this social context is different from a school environment where educational goals determine the climate. For our male patient, the school environment forced identifying with the social demands of peer groups as the greater priority rather than working toward educational goals. Because the school was so ineffectual in establishing educational demands, no competing alternative existed for the client. The school was at best performing a custodial function. Therefore, for him, negotiating the myriad school demands from peers became the overpowering need when in school.

Guide to Therapy

The Initial Interview

Black adolescents' referrals in urban areas are often from public agencies such as schools or the court system. Seldom do youth come of their own volition, and when they're brought by parents, it usually means that parental control has been lost. Given this circumstance, reluctance to participate in therapy is built–in at the initial contact. This attitude is somewhat molded by the image of psychological services imparted by the schools and the community. Within schools, referral to the guidance counselor is often associated with a discipline problem. As professionally compromising as this position may be, it is frequently the responsibility of the school counselor to remedy a bad situation. This sets up the school counselor as the "bad guy" whose actions can place conditions on the school experience of the youth. When the school counselor cannot help the student, referral and/or suspension can result. School counselors are often the ones who contact parents, monitor attendance and truancy, and handle an assortment of behavior problems. The orientation to therapeutic assistance, therefore, is predetermined. It is not evolving from a self–defined need, but rather from an imposed demand from others.

In addition, the therapist must handle the community image of psychological services as a stigma of defective mental health. Adolescents are just as reluctant as adults to reveal their contact or need of psychological help. Black adolescents indulge in the same patterns of peer deceit about seeing a psychologist as adults. In one instance, I had a youth who repeatedly represented his weekly visits to therapy as special coaching in judo to allay the suspicions of peers and excuse his absence from the regular afternoon of playground basketball.

Heretofore, representatives of traditional professions such as the pastor or physician were the principal source of help for Black families having trouble with their adolescents. Another alternative is to seek the help of the courts. Through a court order, a youth can be placed under the court's authority as a "person in need of supervision" (PINS), which essentially absolves the parent from the responsibility for his child's behavior. Parents who resort to this solution have usually reached their limits of control over the youth. Interviewing such parents often reveals that sufficient signs of problems with the youth were known far enough in advance where if confidence in mental health practitioners had existed, appropriate therapeutic interventions could have stemmed behavioral patterns. For whatever reasons, Black youth are not referred for therapeutic assistance until a problem has become severe.

Further education of the Black community about the utility of mental health services is certainly needed but the reality remains that Black youth come to the attention of therapists only when their behavior is unmanageable. Because youth will rarely see their behavior as problematic and seek therapy of their own volition, and because parents will wait until their authority and control are strained, the circumstances of an initial contact with the therapist are almost uniformly the same: exasperated parents and an unwilling adolescent. This condition, coupled with the Black public attitude toward mental health services, is an issue that a therapist and intake worker must be sensitive to in the development of an adequate initial bond with the adolescent patient.

In the initial contact with the Black adolescent, there is the issue of whether the parent should be included. As a matter of practice, I will see both parent and child during the first session, leaving time to see the adolescent alone. The time alone allows the youth to present his or her interpretation of why he or she is in therapy as well as to ask questions about the process that were unanswered or unclear. It is important to stress the confidential nature of therapy and the benefits that may be gained from the process. Clarifying the therapeutic process becomes an important part of this initial stage. This does not mean that, as therapist, one strives to convince the youth why he or she should be in therapy. Rather, assuring the youth about the advantages of therapy should flow from an exchange of information. However, in some instances in the initial session, the youth will not engage in any meaningful discussion. If silence with occasional monosyllabic responses is the norm, it is sometimes helpful for the therapist to offer reassurances by anticipating the youth's (nonverbalized) concerns.

Trust is at the basis of any therapeutic relationship, but for adolescents it is a major concern. Since they are usually initially brought or referred by other authority figures, there is little to differentiate the therapist from other adults managing their lives. Talking briefly about the therapist's role is an aid to the Black adolescent's understanding of therapy, whether the patient initiates it or not. Another important ingredient of this initial session is the conveyance of the adolescent's responsibility in therapy. Like many patients, the adolescent will expect the therapist to prescribe a quick remedy for the problem. This, of course, has to be dispelled through the educative process on patient responsibility. However, when the youth is brought to therapy based on the motives of others, the youth may vigorously disclaim any reason for why he or she may not agree with it. In fact, the youth may perceive the requirement to see a therapist as a waste of valuable time. Often clinical sessions for adolescents are scheduled in the late afternoon. This frequently conflicts with important after school peer activities from which any absence requires a good reason. Therapy is interpreted as another adult imposition, reinforcing underlying rationalizations for the acting out behavior. Consequently, the therapy session may constitute another area of resistance to adult authority. Trying to overcome such an attitude and to establish a bond is difficult. Yet, that difficulty emphasizes the importance of the initial sessions as a time to build rapport. Without such a tie to the adolescent, therapy will make little progress. Reticence to engage the therapist during the initial sessions may be indicative of all of the above misgivings on the part of the adolescent. This is why the therapist's taking a more active role initially may help the youth to change his or her view of the therapist as another imposing adult figure to that of an empathic and concerned individual.

One advantage of conducting the initial interview with the parents involved is the opportunity to observe the dynamics between parent and child. Because so often the parents are before you in a state of exasperation and possibly desperation, the manner in which they portray issues can be very informative. It is not uncommon for some youths to learn for the first time precisely why their parents are upset with them. In some instances, this can lead to a lively debate between parents and child, affording the therapist a glimpse of the interpersonal dynamics. There are those who cower in the presence of their parents and sit meekly or sullenly while hearing the "charges" against them. Other youths will immediately launch into an argument as to the accuracy of their portrayal. A therapist's pitfall in these exchanges is in appearing to take sides. The parents will seek affirmation of their child–rearing practices from the therapist, and the adolescent will be assessing how much his or her view is valued.

Once an initial understanding of the presenting problem is acquired, the task of developing rapport with the adolescent still remains. An important feature of acquiring fidelity and integrity among adolescents is passing tests of confidence. This can assume numerous forms depending on the circumstances. However, because the adolescent period is a stage during which many adult behaviors are explored and identity is based on sometimes exaggerated or distorted personal notions of adult lifestyles, the sharing of peer exploits is highly guarded. To be privy to such information requires an understanding and trusting person. For an adolescent, this cannot be determined at first contact with anybody, much less an adult. Consequently, various trials to test integrity are presented. Such tests are not restricted to adolescents, but it seems that this age group can devise very creative and provocative forms. There are those who become mummified—a test of strength to endure the stress of silence. You will also encounter the seducer, who seeks validation from you as he or she does from peers; the starer, who will rivet you with continuous eye contact; and the abuser, who will verbally or physically try to intimidate you. The basic dynamic issue in the first sessions of therapy with the adolescent is control. The streetwise kid is very adept at maintaining control over the situation by adopting various roles. This can be deceptive to the naive therapist and lead him or her toward clinical conclusions that are inappropriate. During the early sessions with a streetwise youth, the therapist must be vigilant that he or she is not being misled. Until proven worthwhile, the value of therapy sessions to the coerced Black adolescent is no more than any other forced obligation. The little appeal it may have is its liberation from class time if so scheduled. It will certainly be alienating if therapy sessions interfere with important afterschool peer activities.

There are several types of common behavior seen during the initial sessions of therapy. These take the form of initial resistances to establishing rapport and securing meaningful clinical data. There is the proverbial "reluctant talker". This may be a withdrawn youth whose demeanor may even include physical disengagement (e.g., moving the chair to the other side of the room, turning sideways, and avoiding eye contact by staring at the ceiling or down at the floor.) Such disengagement is not unusual for a youth who objects to being brought to the therapist. Because this form of protest can begin before the youth has reached the therapist's office, it is easy to attribute more psychological disturbance than exists. To help discern whether a ploy is being used by the youth to prevent the therapeutic process, the psychological history can be examined to determine how characteristic is this behavior. In addition, the therapist can consult with significant others such as parents or teachers to learn whether the observed behavior is typical of the youth in other settings. A most common form of marginal participation in therapy that keeps the therapist at bay are monosyllabic responses such as "yes," "no," "maybe," "uh huh," etc. Some youths are very adept at limiting their conversation to such responses no matter how skillfully circumventing questions are devised to open them up to free flowing discussions.

Another type of initial response a therapist might get from a Black adolescent is just the opposite of the withdrawn posture. This type might be termed the "babbler," who discloses everything, dumping every conceivable grievance. Often the tone of this disclosure is bitter, relating how parents, teachers, siblings, or peers have imposed on the youth. One can get the impression that the youngster is the most misunderstood person in the world. The rapidity of issues presented and their lack of focus can keep the therapist from identifying appropriate therapeutic issues. This can be particularly difficult if the youngster repeatedly dominates sessions with complaints and avoids any one issue. Although a therapeutic objective initially may be allowing ventilation of issues of concern, excessive preoccupation may be a veiled tactic to keep the therapist disengaged. For some Black youth who are expansive in this fashion, it is easy to provide embellished stories if the therapist has been caught up in the dramatization. Sometimes the content of the babbler's talk can take the form of convincing the therapist that the youth has everything under control in spite of shocking circumstances. Youngsters who focus their discussion to shock and disarm the therapist I call the "impressors."

It is not uncommon for some urban streetwise Black youth to begin sessions by relating antisocial exploits such as indulgence in drugs, sex, alcohol, or delinquency. These tactics are attempts to force the therapist into making value statements, verbally or nonverbally. Raising eyebrows, furrowing brows, and shifting in one's seat at sensational points in the story are telltale signs to the youngster that he or she has touched judgmental sentiments in the therapist. When urban Black youths meet a White therapist whom they believe is naive and impressionable about street experiences, they may try to employ this offensive tactic either to scare the therapist off and/or test sincerity. It is also a device to measure the therapist's knowledge and empathy for the sociocultural conditions of life for the Black adolescent.

An example that characterizes this dynamic is the experience of two White therapists who were working with a group of Black adolescent girls between the ages of 15 and 18 in a residential group home. Since most of these girls had spent the majority of their lives moving from foster homes to group residential accommodations, they had some sophistication in dealing with the approach of the professional helper. First contacts were received with great indifference on the part of the youngsters. Their indulgence of the administrator's programming of group therapy was met with suffocating apathy and righteous indignation. They were disorderly, assertive, and detached from the therapist's attempts to structure a group. When seen individually in order to obtain more specific intake information, one girl related the "horrors" of her circumstances. Her custody had been shifted from one adult to another throughout her childhood by her mother. To her best recollection she was currently in the custody of her mother's pastor, an elderly woman. She had been in frequent pain over the past year due to a suspected ovarian cyst which could not be treated properly because of confusion over who had authority to permit an operation. She had seen her father shot and killed and was with her best girl friend when the friend overdosed on drugs. Other tidbits along this theme were thrown in for effect. Although these incidents were exaggerated to get a rise out of the therapist, they were basically true. Subsequent sessions and other information revealed that this youth often greeted professional aid in this manner because such services were short term and transient. She did not want to make a personal investment to resolve intrapsychic conflicts under such conditions. But, since she was repeatedly subjected to such transient services by authorities, her only recourse was to disarm the therapists and discourage pursuit of therapeutic objectives by creating a feeling of hopelessness. It was an overwhelming story for the two White therapists, but with supervision and encouragement, they were able to establish rapport with all the girls and work effectively with them.

Establishing Rapport

Being candid, direct, at ease, and engaging with Black adolescents has proven most effective in establishing rapport; whereas shrouding interaction in clinical jargon and deportment tends to alienate and impede the youth's ability to engage the therapeutic process. This does not mean that therapists should discard clinical judgment or responsibility. It does advocate a more assertive role on the part of a therapist when working with adolescents than one might employ with adults. Usually, a significant segment of therapy with Black adolescents is educational, so that the therapist will eventually assume an informative role. Reassuring the patient that the therapist's role is to aid understanding helps to launch the establishment of rapport. Inquiring too early into the rationale of behavior can intimidate and put adolescents on the defensive. It can be perceived as no different from the prying and justifications demanded by parents. Adolescent life is constantly under the scrutiny of adults. The youth's relating of psychosocial experiences are to be encouraged, but deeper exploration should be approached cautiously until such time as rapport is firmly established. A too early exploration of issues in depth can encourage the youth to fabricate information in order to satisfy transparent clinical needs of the therapist. "Giving the therapist what he wants to hear" also fulfills the compliant role expected of youth by adults.

Another therapist's aid in establishing rapport is language. Communication among streetwise urban Black adolescents is sociolinguistically rooted in the use of slang. Knowledge of how youth use language can be valuable to the therapist. When slang is strategically and unpretentiously integrated into the therapist's conversation with the youth, this conveys some understanding of the youth's peer world; it expedites rapport. This ability is often misconstrued by some therapists to mean that they must be facile with "street talk." The biggest error a therapist can make is to try and appear down to earth and fluent in something he or she is not. Such representations out of ignorance appear as inappropriate as errors made when attempting to speak a foreign language. Knowing the slang of Black youth is a helpful but not necessary prerequisite for rapport. The colorful street language of Black youth requires more than knowledge of words. Cadence, tone, timing, and situationally appropriate usage are also essentials for slang fluency. Employing slang words without such cognizance portrays the therapist as unsophisticated. The best solution for therapists' incompetence in the use of slang is to omit it from their conversation, be honest about ignorance of terms, and encourage their patients to educate them about their meanings. Even for therapists who once had facility with street slang but have been out of touch with the world of adolescents, it would be wise to temper the use of dated idioms until acquiring a grasp of contemporary usage.

Physical Appearance and Deportment in Therapy

Physical appearance and deportment in therapy are elements in the bonding process that are given insufficient attention. Dress for Black adolescents is an important dimension of identity. There are instances of Black youth not attending school because they could not afford the clothes required by the peer group dress code. In the Black urban high schools, it is not uncommon to find youth attired in expensive brand-name clothes. How they are acquired is another issue, but the fact is that possession of fine clothes is a status symbol. Although all youth cannot obtain the best, it is an ideal to strive for. It may be the only ostensible means of declaring self-pride, particularly if the family is part of the working poor. Black adolescent attire must be understood within the context of the dress code. Even looking "bummy" has code, that is, the type of sneakers (i.e., gym shoes) one may wear, the type of jeans, tops, etc. Style in adolescent dress runs from head to toe. It is not only what you have to wear but how you wear it that becomes equally important. Therefore it is not just the type of hat, shirt, or show one possesses but the manner in which it is worn that distinguishes one as part of the "pack". There are variations on this fashion, including proper color combinations. Extreme deviation from the style is subject to strong sanctions from the peer group.

Being aware of dress can provide the therapist with an enormous number of nonverbal clues about the Black adolescent. By having some knowledge of the local popular dress codes among adolescent peer groups, the therapist can, from observation, assess how conforming to youth norms the youngster may be. For example, a therapist may plan to determine how genuine or vicarious a youth's identification with his peer culture really is. Observing attire can provide the therapist with clinical hypotheses about that identification. In contrast, attire can impede the establishment of a therapeutic bond if the therapist finds the youngster's manner of dress offensive. The most poignant example that comes to mind is the frequent issue of the "hat" and "coat," Keeping in mind the proposition that attire is frequently an expression of identity or attitude of the youth, a common source of conflict is the manner in which youngsters wear their clothes. A primary issue between Black adolescents and adult authorities is whether adolescents can keep their hats and coats on indoors. For example, a 15 year old Black adolescent male was brought to therapy by his parents because of persistent school failures. During the initial family sessions, the youth sat with his hooded coat on until commanded by one of his parents to remove it. Whenever he was seen alone, the youth kept his coat on throughout all of the early sessions.

How one interprets this simple behavior rests with the emerging clinical data, but it is general knowledge that many adolescents keep outer garments on throughout the day because such garments are part of a uniform. On the other hand, a number of other reasons can exist for this practice. Sometimes Black youth may keep their jackets on because of peer symbolism. For some youths, the outer garment covers other clothes that do not equal the desired quality and value. Sometimes youth keep their coats on through simple habit. Since theft of a good coat from the high school locker is not uncommon, why risk losing a prize possession by hanging it up. Keeping things you prize with and/on you is the law of survival, "its streetwise." On the other hand remaining in their coats during therapeutic session may also reflect a negative attitude toward therapy and the intent to escape as soon as possible.

Although a therapist may find talking to a youngster who is wearing a hat and coat somewhat annoying, the therapist cannot allow this appearance to be overly disconcerting. The therapist must use all behaviors, both verbal and nonverbal, as aids in clinical formulations. One reasonable formulation about why a youth remains wrapped up in outer garments is that it constitutes a form of resistance. Another youth who had remained zippered up with his hood over his head and uncommunicative for several sessions was confronted with the loss in benefits from not using therapy. The therapist emphasized that regardless of how the youth wanted to use the sessions, circumstances required that he attend, so why throw away a unique opportunity to share his concerns confidentially. Once this message was sufficiently conveyed, the young man disclosed how he had successfully frustrated the efforts of another therapist that past year with the same deportment. Although there are possibly other reasons why this youth elected to respond to such overtures from the therapist, the essential point is that use of clothes by Black adolescents can be important clues to intrapsychic dynamics.

Another major example of this phenomenon is the wearing of hats by Black adolescents, especially males. The type of hat a Black youth wears can represent an integral part of his identity. Again, keeping a hat on may be more a part of "the uniform" than an intended disrespect. Careful probing about this behavior can reveal vital information about the character of the peer group the youth identifies with as well as about his self–concept.

The importance of clothes for some Black adolescents extends to the therapist's attire. One Black adolescent who infrequently came to sessions was confronted by his residential counselor about his attendance record. After encouragement, the youth revealed that he was offended by the casual appearance of his therapist. The therapist did not measure up to the youth's perception of how a professional should appear. To this youngster, a stylish dresser even when casual, the therapist's attire was a statement of attitude toward him. Although there were other issues of resistance involved, the therapist's clothes played a part in the dynamics of the bonding process. In general, parents have rarely been free of comments about their clothing from their adolescent children. Because this is a frequent exchange between adolescents and parents (or significant other adults), therapists should be aware of how dress affects youthful attitudes. As a Black therapist working with Black adolescents, I have found that physical appearance and deportment can be intricately linked to the issue of "role model." If a Black therapist is too casual in manner and dress, this creates a paradox with the presumed professional stature. Since clothes are a materialistic symbol of achievement, the youngster may view informality as a contradiction of professional status. It can translate to "he must not be that important nor his job that profitable." Nevertheless, this does not diminish the significance informality can play in the therapeutic process with Black youth.

Individual Therapy for Black Adolescents

Adolescence is a critical period of development in the life–span. Many crises are experienced during this age without the appropriate level of maturity. Many clinical problems found in adults are actually unresolved conflicts stemming from adolescence. The physiological changes that occur during adolescence provide unique demands upon personal adjustment (Katchadourian, 1977). The inadequacy of schooling in urban centers raises issues of personal competence and self–worth. The disillusionment experienced by Black adolescents when confronted with their lack of marketable skills on leaving school is great. Anger, depression, and despair are characteristic symptoms presented by some youth in these circumstances. Acting out behavior for the preservation of a self–image assumes many forms. In some instances, it is the basis for the pursuit of illegitimate careers and/or self–destructive behavior. Black youth want all the trappings of success propagated by the media about the "American dream" (Pierce, 1974). When the reality of unfulfillment is recognized, bitterness ensues.

An example of this is the case of an 18 year old Black male brought to my attention by school authorities for loitering and disruptive behavior. Upon examination of records by the guidance counselor, it was discovered that the youth had been enrolled in the school for four years with accumulated credits equal to two years. This youth was a classic "drop in," one who attends school but not classes with any regularity. School authorities paid little attention to this youth's lack of school progress. At the time of this incident, the youngster was acting out his depression through harassment of younger students. Underneath this behavior was his resentment of the younger students who were attaining a functional level equivalent or better than his. In addition, many of his friends had either dropped out of school or graduated. The loss of his original peer group was increasingly isolating him from the new social order established by a younger student body. To compensate for this loss, he maintained his self–esteem through control and combination of other students. He cultivated a cadre of followers who indulged in various illicit activities. His older appearance and demeanor made him an attractive leader to a number of students following the same pattern. The initial sessions were dominated by attempts to establish rapport and the ventilation of vituperative rage. Depression was exacerbated by family pressures to get a job and/or leave home. Upon discovering that his ability would yield only marginal employment, the youth vacillated between dejection and disparagements. Those of his peers who had left the school were either incarcerated, lost to idle unemployment, in college, or employed. None of these alternatives were either appealing or within the realm of his capability. Frustrated, he sought solace in the security of familiar and negotiable surroundings. The high school was a home away from home. The demeaning lack of opportunities in the world of work was avoided as long as he could remain in school. It was extremely difficult to gain the trust of this youth because of his pattern of resisting assistance from adult authorities. Once confidence was achieved, the youth was slowly guided into recognizing the realities of his circumstances and seeking remedies. While his educational needs were attended to, therapy continued to allow the youth to focus on his anger and channel his energy into constructive goals.

The process of arriving at such an untenable position for this youth is common in urban public schools. Immersed in counterproductive school climates, Black adolescents are lost to neglect. There is little monitoring of academic progress of Black youth. Repeated failure experiences and accumulated skill deficiencies result in frustration and depression. Reconstructing some of the classroom experiences of Black adolescents reveals a combination of contributing factors. Teachers are frequently portrayed by urban Black adolescents in therapy as being disinterested in both them and teaching. In a number of instances, teachers have told classes that they were not fit for an education, or have conveyed the same message through indifferent instruction.

The social disorganization in urban high schools is also at the root of truancy. Truancy cases referred for individual therapy often reveal instances of school phobia. In several cases, Black adolescents were disoriented by the lack of structure in the schools. The impact of the transition from the elementary school structure to the changing classroom schedules of secondary school create an adjustment problem for some youths. Black youths sometimes avoid attending school because they are overwhelmed by a new school plus conformity pressures by older peers. The chaotic lack of decorum of a high school is frightening. Consider the case of Carol.

Carol, an attractive 14 year old, was referred for poor school attendance. School officials also reported that when she did attend, her participation was minimal and she was withdrawn. She was frequently observed sucking her thumb. Carol was very reticent during the first sessions and restricted herself to monosyllabic responses. Her re- sponsibilities at home were great, and she often functioned as a surrogate parent to younger children. Because of poor school performance, authorities placed her in remedial classes, although her prior elementary school record was satisfactory. Although distressed about Carol, both parents were unable to attend to the problem adequately because of inevitable loss of time and money due to job absence. School authorities interpreted this as a sign of disinterest on the parents' part. Although Carol eventually expressed an understanding of her parents' dilemma, she felt torn by the need for their support and the real necessity of maintaining a level of family income necessary for survival. Pressured to be a model for the younger children by her parents, Carol felt an inability to relate her school problems. She reported experiences of sweaty palms, body tremors, racing heart rate and dizziness whenever she had to change classes. Since her first days of high school, the pandemonium of changing classrooms had provoked discomfort. Moreover, the majority of students were complete strangers to her. Carol also frequently went the entire day without using the lavoratory because the toilets were the place where girls frequently congregated to smoke marijuana and coerce others to join them. On one occasion, she actually wet herself; thereafter, she drank little for the entire day. This combination of problems led to an increased withdrawal from school and, subsequently, frequent incidents of truancy.

Carol was taught some relaxation exercises to be employed whenever she experienced anxiety. Some desensitization routines were also used to help reduce her fear of changing classrooms. In addition, role playing to increase social skills for establishing peer contacts was performed. As Carol gained better control over her behavior, it became clear that part of her fear was rooted in the pressure to be a proper role model for her younger siblings. Several sessions with the parents helped to reduce the pressure from home and encouraged a more supportive environment.

The extent to which truancy and disruptive behavior mask school phobia is unknown. For some Black adolescents, the social disorganization that prevails in urban high schools is a source of phobic responses. Fitting into the peer social structure of a school can be a stressful experience for adolescents, especially if the youngster is timid about establishing new relationships. The effect of the urban school environment on personal adjustment is a critical clinical issue to discern during treatment. Frequently, Black youths must manage both pressures from home as well as from school. The therapist must also consider how both of these settings are affected by racism.

Group Therapy with Black Adolescents

Group therapy in counseling Black adolescents is effective because it allows the youngster to learn that problems of adjustment are not unique but shared by many. One of the first realizations acquired by adolescents in group therapy is the commonality of concerns. Although the group session allows shared problems to be exposed, it takes time before admission of adjustment issues are disclosed. This is due to the Black youth's need to protect the image of competency. He will not make self-effacing comments in front of peers. The therapist's ability to get beyond the posturing and bravado to the vulnerability of adolescence is crucial. A therapist must be cognizant of the adolescent's need to maintain and protect a carefully cultivated peer image. The early sessions of group therapy are replete with youngsters playing the roles they are noted for. If the youths are familiar with one another, then their public images are strongly projected. They cannot appear to be any different from when they are outside of the group. If the youths are unfamiliar with each other, then several role possibilities emerge. They can be themselves if basically they are satisfied with the level of acceptance currently given to their image. On the other hand, entering a group with new peers allows an opportunity to alter or modify self-presentation according to the purpose of impression. A scrutiny of psychosocial history and a conference with parents or teachers can determine the discrepancy between projected group therapy image and the image projected in other contexts. There is merit in obtaining this type of clinical data because it discloses the youth's stability and consistency in presentation of self. A youth who is repeatedly changing in character from one type of situational context to another has questionable emotional stability. Although adolescence is a time in which many roles are assumed, something of the basic identity persists. Acquiring an awareness of the consistency of self-presentation in the group in contrast to other social contexts facilitates identification of strengths and weaknesses in the adolescent's identity. One of the objectives of group therapy is to allow the adolescent to feel acceptance by others (MacLennan & Felsenfeld, 1968).

Achieving group therapy goals with adolescents is not the easiest task (Berkovitz, 1972). Although adolescents grow in groups, the formation of new groups is approached with caution. Alliances among friends can inhibit or facilitate the functioning of the group during its early sessions. Likewise, the experience of other adolescents as strangers can produce a variety of coping behaviors, such as wisecracking, incessant laughter, profanity, seat squirming, jostling, bullying, or silence. The range of behaviors is often presented in a dynamic display of expressions in every group. The activity level of adolescents is high. This energy is usually brought into the group situation. A therapist can expect youths to be restive in group sessions.

Because of this usual lack of decorum, I believe that the therapist must be active, engaging the youths, setting limits and goals in the therapy. A therapist who is too passive with the average urban Black youth will encourage group disorganization. Although interpreting the group's response to a passive therapist may have merits, the lack of structure in general is counterproductive. Therapy groups for Black adolescents should be psychoeducational in objective. There should be allowance for disclosing psychological issues and experiencing an educative process in behavior management (Stuart, 1977). With this as an objective, the active therapist must be deliberate in some interventions (Anderson, 1972). In my experience, establishing ground rules in the first session helps to structure the group and makes expectations clear.

The first area of discussion is confidentiality. It is important that youths learn to respect the privacy of others. If this issue is not handled in the initial sessions, it encourages the youths to conceal feelings for fear a breach of confidence will occur. Although no insurance about confidentiality can be given, establishing this as a major agreement allows the therapist and group to handle instances in which confidence is violated. Additional rule settings should be a combination of the therapist's and the group's priorities. For example, some statement about decorum should be made within the context of respecting the participation of others. Youths should learn that as much as they dislike "disrespect,"? so do others. If no control is exercised over the activity level during the group process, youths who want to participate will become discouraged and submit to disruptive behaviors.

The manner in which ground rules are presented and enforced should be consistent with the therapeutic process. Being an active therapist does not mean assuming the role of a severe parent. However, a therapist exhibiting responsible guidance can be a positive role model. Identity achievement is a process that encompasses many role models; therefore, a decisive and responsible therapist–group interaction can be a learning experience. It is particularly important in work with Black youths that a male therapist exhibit strength and empathy. I am aware of several instances in which a passive, easily intimidated male therapist repelled Black male adolescents. His passivity contradicted their notions of "machismo" or masculinity. The therapist's posture must be flexible enough to adapt to whatever arises in the group process.

Handling the assertive Black male in group therapy can be an arduous endeavor. Moreover, when disruptive behavior is the problem, the purpose of the group acquires a special focus. For some youths, being disruptive masks a variety of inner conflicts. It manifests itself as a "camouflaging syndrome" to deceive others about insecurities (Franklin, 1977). Group members with this behavioral manifestation are going to resist strong exposure of inadequacies. There is usually peer support for a youth's deviant behavior. Group therapy can serve as an "alternative peer reference group" to counteract the pressures of buddies. As a youth engages in new forms of behavior, the therapy group can provide support in the face of adversity. Within the nurturing environment of the therapy group, the youth can begin redefining his or her self-image. There is greater freedom to experiment with more constructive roles.

The Psychoeducational Approach

The plight of the urban Black adolescent is poignantly represented by the poor quality of available education. It remains a national concern. Many Black youth referred for therapy have deficiencies in their basic ability to read, write, and execute ordinary arithmetical problems. Many youths are simply functionally illiterate. Because of these circumstances, intrapsychic conflicts are exacerbated. To be effective, therapy must be combined with corrective educational measures. If tutoring is used as an adjunct to therapy, it can enhance the achievement of developmental goals. A more effective and comprehensive approach is a programmatic effort combining a curriculum of instruction and personal development in the therapeutic processes. This is a psychoeducational approach and is represented by the programs offered by alternative schools for adolescents. The development of the Street Academy by the Urban League is an exemplary institutional strategy (National Urban League, 1977). This program services dropouts who voluntarily solicited educational assistance. Subsequently, several urban public school systems have developed programs based on the Street Academy model.

The intent of the alternative school is to reduce the impersonality of education and to increase opportunities for individualized or small group instruction. Curriculum objectives are the improvement of competency in basic skills. The assumption is that the level of basic skill deficiencies is related to the level of self-esteem and deviant behavior. Black youths in such positions have been alienated from formal education. Many students bring with them the self-defeating behavior patterns that disengaged them from school in the first place. The stigma of expulsion, or dropping out, creates resistance in the youth to attempting any corrective efforts. This is particularly the case when youths realize the magnitude of their inabilities.

In the development of a psychoeducational program, therapy and instruction are an integrated experience infused in classroom tutorial and therapy experiences. Youths enrolled in psychoeducational programs must be assessed for both their educational competence and emotional stability. The extent of personal adjustment to this program is linked to the kind of experiences the youth had in the public school. For some youths, the change to a personable environment induces different behaviors. I have had youngsters say that no one had ever paid such attention to them before. Some youths who were thought incorrigible by public schools become task and goal oriented students. On the other hand, there are those who are continually frustrated by their skill dilemma. They may be motivated to improve their skills, but the actions required to achieve this improvement are perceived as overwhelming. The unattractive aspect of the "catch-up" game in remedial work is the humiliation of not being competent. In some instances, a youth's sense of pride would inhibit instruction at levels below self-expectations. For these youths, the input of therapy is critical. The self-concept of the youth must be adjusted to allow him or her to capitalize on the instructional services offered. Because it is recognized that the adolescent population referred to the alternative school is acting out and resistant to program goals, one strategy adopted by a program was to gear the first weeks towards developing "school readiness" (National Urban League, 1977).

Upon entering the program, students were engaged in an agreement to participate fully and obey the ground rules. Persons who felt an inability to comply were free to leave. The youths who remained were exposed to approximately six weeks of intensive personal exploration about their school experiences.

Respect for the views of others was insisted upon and reflected an individual's commitment. Teachers, therapists, administrators, and peer aides all participated in the orientation phase. Each morning, students and staff engaged in a meditation period in a large, hand-linked circle. Afterward, everyone would divide into "rap groups" to discuss personal experiences and attempts at managing school life. Skits were eventually developed to represent the range of scenarios in school life. These were dramatically produced and videotaped by the students for later viewing in group sessions. In one skit, students were encouraged to demonstrate the multitude of ways a disruptive student could control a teacher and the class. Through the group process, students discussed how such behavior was injurious to self and counterproductive. Students were instructed in the positive attributes of assertive behavior; while assertive behavior could be employed to disrupt, it could also be utilized to demand a proper education. Skits were then developed around how assertive behavior could be used constructively and under what circumstances. Group therapy was also videotaped as a source of feedback on interpersonal interactions. Skits were also created around this theme. Encounters with teachers, peers, and family in the students' lives were also developed into a variety of scenarios and videotaped. Videotaping the kinds of experiences the youths would face in the pursuit of their education and the proper management of behavior was the substance of the school readiness phase of the first weeks. During this period, there was very little formal instruction. The assumption was that, until the student learned about his or her own counterproductive behavior and the underlying reasons for that behavior, formal instruction would be ineffective. After the orientation phase, the curriculum was introduced, and the group process integrated into a period of the daily schedule.

The important feature of the psychoeducational approach is the linking of therapy to educational objectives. In this regard, therapy had an explicit goal. Although focused on behavioral management for educational objectives, all of the usual issues raised in therapy were entertained. There was a specific life context—"the schooling process" for the youths to concentrate on, and it provided a unique clarity to other intrapsychic issues. For example, the inability to live harmoniously with parents or siblings was connected to effects on educational achievement. Acquiring a perspective on how to manage behavior in the school context aided students in other domains, such as the home.

The psychoeducational approach blends the goals of formal education and personal development. Several domains in the youth's life are simultaneously treated to maximize self–actualization. A key factor in the effectiveness of the psychoeducational model is the youth's recognition of the interdependence of issues. Intervention was comprehensive. All professional assistance was related to the goals of the program. As an added inducement to attaining program objectives, graduates were employed as paraprofessionals. These youths not only served as role models, but as co–therapists; they could quickly identify the dynamics preventing alienated peers from engaging in this "last chance" opportunity. After a while, graduates conducted most of the school readiness orientation phase of the program, freeing professional staff to concentrate on individual student needs.

A difficulty with this type of psychoeducational approach is the financial cost of implementation. There is a small student–staff ratio and considerable concentration on individualized remedial assistance. In spite of these drawbacks, there is some evidence that suggests that proper programmatic leadership by administrators can overcome the economic obstacles. For example, the school readiness orientation has given some students a sense of individual responsibility that transfers to other settings. Students returning to local schools have made adjustments in behavior management to concentrate on school work.

Summary and Conclusions

The problems of Black adolescents are reflective of their group. However, the dynamics underlying their behavior must be interpreted within the realities of their life conditions. Many of the families of urban Black adolescents exist within marginal socioeconomic circumstances. This creates a social context that contains numerous stressful conditions. Indicative of the situation is the disproportionate incidence of physical and mental health disorders in the Black community. Consequently, in order to understand Black adolescent development and behavior disorders, the conditions of their lives and the management of racism must be an integral part of clinical formulations.

Social statistics reflect the marginal life circumstances for many families of Black adolescents. However, in the diagnosis of behavior disorders the clinician, in spite of the social conditions, must discern if the presenting problem is a by-product of common age-related issues or symptomatic of persistent characterological factors. It is crucial that the clinician, in making this determination, is informed of the social milieu of the Black adolescent. Sensitivity to the adaptive styles generated by the social milieu will facilitate clinical formulations and the therapeutic process. For example, the disruptive behavior of the Black adolescent in school may mask a variety of inadequacies emanating from inequities experienced in an oppressive and racist school environment. A Black adolescent's acting out behavior may directly stem from the stigma of placement in low achieving classes, functional illiteracy and/or no job opportunities. Knowing the parameters of normal and abnormal behavior within the prevailing social context of the Black adolescent refines clinical assessments.

Comprehending the psychosocial background for the average Black adolescent is an important aspect of the initial interview and early therapy sessions. Like many adolescents, Black youth are commonly referred to therapy by educational or judicial institutions. When parents bring adolescents, often such institutions have recommended them. Control of the Black adolescent is a primary reason parents solicit clinical assistance. Because referral is usually based upon one of these circumstances, resistance by the Black youth is often great. The forms resistance takes can be characterized by withdrawal, excessive babbling, monsyllabism, yarn spinning, or aggression. Many times, youths will challenge the clinician to demonstrate trustworthiness. Candor and active confrontation of the Black youth's resistances have proven an effective way of establishing a bond. Until the Black youth's trust is gained, rapport and therapeutic goals cannot be achieved. Therapy for Black adolescents is often an educative as well as a clinical process.

The credibility of mental health services is suspect in the Black community. Black adolescents will reflect this attitude. It is important, therefore, that the advantages of therapy and the ground rules for participation are conveyed early in initial sessions. The therapist's deportment and manner of dress can be important agents in establishing rapport with the Black adolescent. Casual dress and knowledge of slang can be useful so long as it is not superficial. Awareness of dress codes, language usage, and activities of the Black adolescent peer world can also facilitate assessment of the youth's self-concept and peer status.

Individual and group psychotherapy are traditional and appropriate forms of intervention with Black adolescents. In addition, special interventions such as psychoeducational programs can combine many services to focus upon multiple problems. Working with Black adolescents in individual therapy provides several unique pitfalls. The therapist must be cognizant about his or her own feelings about the adolescent experience and those that might be associated with Black adolescents in particular. Equally important for the therapist to be aware of is (un)conscious racism. A by-product of this dynamic is a tendency for the therapist to succumb to stereotypes of Black adolescent life and/or attempt to encourage the youth to accept oppressive life circumstances. When in a group, therapists must be aware that youths will indulge in face-saving behavior in front of peers. Establishing ground rules for the group process is essential in the early sessions. The group experience can provide the Black youth with information about managing interpersonal relations with peers as well as developing strategies for coping with adult authorities. For youth involved with counterproductive peers, the therapy can act as an "alternative reference group" to support disengagement from delinquency and injurious behaviors. Different from the traditional forms of therapy is the psychoeducational approach. An example of such an approach is an alternative high school for dropouts. This program combines services to assist both educational and related psychological need. Black youth who have been disruptive and unproductive in traditional school settings are provided with a concentrated school readiness experience before formal instruction. In the school readiness experience, Black youth and staff examine the dynamics of disruptive behavior or the alienation process. With the aid of group sessions and psychodrama, insight into behavior management is sought. Upon achievement of adequate awareness and control of productive behavior, formal instruction for skill deficiencies is incorporated into the daily activities.

The development of Black adolescents within the context of limited social and economic opportunities is insufficiently understood. There is no comprehensive body of knowledge that clearly delineates the consequences to socioemotional and intellectual growth. A disproportionate number of Black children who are tracked into classes for educable mentally retarded (EMR) classes or low achieving students or who are socially promoted in spite of functional illiteracy must experience devalued self-esteem as well as a substandard overall state of psychological well-being. Likewise, growing up in a community subjected to numerous insufficiencies—social, economic, and political—must have a unique impact on Black adolescent development. Exactly how Black youth internalize the pressures of their life conditions is speculative. There has been no systematic study of the common parameters and processes of mental health development. The social science literature has given much attention to the deviancy in the life of Black youth but little thought to the average developmental experiences of the masses. A paucity of scholarship in this area forces social services for Black youth to evolve from superficial and racist impressions. In order to improve the delivery and effectiveness of services to Black adolescents, it is imperative that more adequate knowledge of average development be obtained.

References

Anderson, R. L. (1972). The importance of an actively involved therapist. In I. H. Berkovitz (Ed.), *Adolescents grow in groups: Experiences in adolescent group psychotherapy*. New York: Brunner/Mazel.
Beres, D. (1961). Character formation. In S. Lorand & H. I. Schneer (Eds.), *Adolescents: Psychoanalytic approach to problems and therapy* (pp. 1–9). New York: Hoeber.
Berkovitz, I. H. (Ed.) (1972). *Adolescents grow in groups: Experiences in adolescent group psychotherapy*. New York: Brunner/Mazel.
Billingsley, A. (1968). *Black families in White America*. Englewood Cliffs, NJ: Prentice-Hall.
Clark, K. B. (1965). *Dark ghetto*. New York: Harper & Row.
Conger, J. J. (1977). *Adolescence and youth* (2nd ed.). New York: Harper & Row.
Crain, R. L., & Mahard, R. E. (1978, Jan.). *The influence of high school racial composition on Black college attendance and test performance*. Washington, D.C.: National Center for Educational Statistics, U.S. Department of HEW.
Dohrenwend, B. P., & Dohrenwend, B. S. (1974). Psychiatric disorders in urban settings. In S. Arieti & G. Capolan (Eds.), *American handbook of psychiatry* Vol. 2 (2nd ed.). New York: Basic Books.
Fanon, F. (21967). *Toward the African revolution*. New York: Grove Press.
Franklin, A. J. (1977, March). Counseling youth in alternative schools. *Personnel and Guidance Journal*, 419–421.
Franklin, A. J. (1979). Ethnocultural considerations in the delivery of mental health services. Unpublished manuscript.
Freud, A. (1958). Adolescence. *Psychoanalytic Study of the Child, 13*, 255–278.
Gartner, A., & Riessman, F. (1974). The performance of the paraprofessional in mental health fields. In S. Arieti & G. Caplan (Eds.), *American handbook of psychiatry*, Vol. 2 (2nd ed.). New York: Basic Books.
Hall, G. S. (1904/1905). *Adolescence* (Vol. 1). Englewood Cliffs, NJ: Prentice-Hall.
Hill, R. B. (1972). *The strengths of Black families*. New York: National Urban League.
Jones, R. L. (1973). Racism, mental health, and the schools. In C. V. Willie, B. M. Kramer, & B. S. Brown (Eds.), *Racism and mental health*. Pittsburgh: University of Pittsburgh Press.
Katchadourian, H. (1977). *The biology of adolescence*. San Francisco: W. H. Freeman.
Kramer, M., Rosen, B. M., & Willis, W. M. (1973). Definitions and distributions of mental disorders in a racist society. In C. V. Willie, B. M. Kramer, & B. S. Brown (Eds.), *Racism and mental health*. Pittsburgh: University of Pittsburgh Press.
Lawson, W. (1979). Hypertension and diabetes mellitus: A challenge for Black behavioral scientists. In A. W. Boykin, A. J. Franklin, & J. F. Yates (Eds.), *Research directions of Black psychologists* (pp. 380–388). New York: Russell Sage.
MacLenna, B. W., & Felsenfeld, N. (1968). *Group counseling and psychotherapy with adolescents*. New York: Columbia University Press.
Moynihan, D. P. (1965, March). *The Negro family: The case for national action*. Washington, D.C.: U.S. Department of Labor, Office of Planning and Research.
Muuss, R. E. (1975). *Theories of adolescence* (3rd ed.). New York: Random House.

Myers, H. F. & Miles, R. E. (1979). Life change stress: Somatization and blood pressure in Blacks. In W. E. Cross, Jr. & A. Harrison (Eds.), *Fourth conference on empirical research in Black psychology* (pp. 7–24). Washington, D.C.: Center for Minority Group Mental Health Programs /NIMH.

National Urban League (1977). *Rethinking alternatives: The New York Urban League Street Academy story–10 years of progress* New York: National Urban League.

National Urban League (1979). *The state of Black America 1979.* New York: National Urban League.

Ogbu, J. U. (1978). *Minority education and caste: The American system in cross–cultural perspective.* New York: Academic Press.

Pierce, C. (1974). Psychiatric problems of the Black minority. In S. Arieti & G. Caplan (Eds.), *American handbook on psychiatry* Vol. 2 (2nd ed.). New York: Basic Books.

Planned Parenthood Federation of America (1976). *11 million teenage pregnancies.* New York: The Allan Guttmacher Institute.

Sprince, M. P. (1964). A contribution to the study of homosexuality in adolescence. *Journal of Child Psychology and Psychiatry, 5,* 103–117.

Stuart, R. B. (Ed.) (1977). *Behavioral self–management.* New York: Brunner/Mazel.

Sue, S., McKinney, H., Allen, D., & Hall, J. (1974). Delivery of community mental health services to Black and White clients. *Journal of Consulting and Clinical Psychology, 42,* 794–801.

The College Board. (1985). *Equality and excellence: The educational status of Black Americans.* New York: College Entrance Examination Board.

Thomas, A., & Sillen, S. (1974). *Racism and psychiatry.* Secaucus, NJ: Citadel Press.

Valentine, C. A. (1968). *Culture and poverty.* Chicago: University of Chicago Press.

Visher, E. B., & Visher, J. S. (1979). *Stepfamilies: A guide to working stepparents and stepchildren.* New York: Brunner/Mazel.

Weiner, I. B. (1970). *Psychological disturbance in adolescence.* New York: John Wiley & Sons.

White, J. L. (1980). Toward a Black psychology. In R. L. Jones (Ed.), *Black psychology* (2nd ed.). New York: Harper & Row.

Yamamoto, J., Quinton, C. J., Bloombaum, M., & Hattem, J. (2967). Racial factors in patient selection. *American Journal of Psychiatry, 124,* 630–636.

Part VIII
Special Topics

ANTECEDENTS AND OUTCOMES OF PREGNANCY IN BLACK ADOLESCENTS

Diane Scott-Jones, E. Joyce Roland, and Anne B. White

Pregnancy in Black adolescents is a troublesome phenomenon documented in recent statistics (Children's Defense Fund, 1988) and widely discussed in the popular press (e.g., Dash, 1986; Haskins, 1984; Height, 1985; Meriwether, 1984). The incidence of unplanned and unwanted pregnancy among adolescents suggests some problems in the development of appropriate, responsible expressions of sexuality. Many emotion–laden issues are associated with adolescent pregnancy: Sexual values, sex education, contraceptive availability, single–parenthood, adoption, and abortion. Consensus on these issues may not be possible or necessary for the amelioration of problems related to teen pregnancy in the Black community. Major tasks are to understand the outcomes of teen pregnancy, in order to provide appropriate services for pregnant teens, and to understand the antecedents of teen pregnancy, so that prevention efforts can be improved.

This chapter begins with a presentation of statistics on the incidence of teen pregnancy. A discussion of the antecedents of adolescent pregnancy follows; a developmental perspective is taken. The outcomes of adolescent pregnancy are then discussed. Attention is given to adolescent fathers and mothers and their offspring. Discussed in the next section are intervention programs aimed at adolescent pregnancy, including programs that provide services for pregnant adolescents and those that attempt to prevent pregnancy or early sexual activity. The chapter ends with suggestions for future research.

Current Statistics

An understanding of the complexities of adolescent pregnancy requires accurate information on the rates of sexual activity, contraceptive use, pregnancies, and births among teens. Each of these rates represents different aspects of the problem and different decision–making points for the Black adolescent. As is true in much research, statistics calculated by race typically have no control for socioeconomic status. Reported race differences, therefore, may be due in part to the substantial socioeconomic differences between Blacks and Whites.

Sexual Activity

The percentage of adolescents who are sexually active has increased over past levels but may have reached a plateau and started to decline somewhat. The percentage of 15- to 19-year-old women having had premarital sexual intercourse increased from 30% in 1971 to 43% in 1976 to 50% in 1979 (Zelnik & Kantner, 1980). Although most of the increase occurred in White females, more Black than White females are sexually active. In 1979, one-half of Black and one-third of White 16-year-old girls had experienced sexual intercourse. An overall decline is suggested in 1982 data from the National Survey of Family Growth, in which 42% of 15- to 19-year-old females had become sexually active (Select Committee on Children, Youth, and Families, 1986). For White teens, there appears to be a slowing of the rate of increase, rather than a decline; for Black teens, there appears to be a small decline in sexual activity (Hofferth, Kahn, & Baldwin, 1987). The decline is limited to older adolescents, however. Both Black and White teens are becoming sexually active at earlier ages (Hofferth et al., 1987).

Studies of sexual activity are not entirely consistent. These studies suggest that Black female teens are more likely to be sexually active but that Black males are much younger when they first become sexually active than are other race/gender groups. The percentage of 19-year-olds who had experienced premarital sex is 65% for White females, 89% for Black females, 77% for White males and 80% for Black males (Moore, 1983). In a sample comprised mainly of 16- and 17-year-olds, White females and males and Black females reported an average age of first intercourse as approximately 15 years. Black males, however, reported an average age of 11.75 years for first intercourse (Cvetkovich & Grote, 1980). Similarly, Finkel and Finkel (1981) report an average age of 12.8 years for first intercourse for males. These statistics may reflect a difference in accuracy of self-report among the four race/gender groups as well as real differences in behavior. In addition, these statistics raise questions regarding the first sexual partners of the very young presumably prepubertal Black males, given that females report a later age of first intercourse.

Contraceptive Use

In spite of the availability of effective contraceptives, adolescents tend not to use them, to use them irregularly, or to use ineffective methods such as withdrawal (Zelnik & Kantner, 1980; Morrison, 1985).

Contraceptive use did increase from 1976 to 1979, however. Because of this increase, the teen pregnancy rate has risen more slowly than has the rate of sexual activity. Without the increase in contraceptive use, the increase in the pregnancy rate would have been even greater. If only sexually active teens are considered, the pregnancy rate actually decreased slightly from 27% in 1973 to 23% in 1978 and 1982 (Alan Guttmacher Institute, 1981; Children's Defense Fund, 1985; Select Committee on Children, Youth, and Families, 1986).

Although the small increase is encouraging, contraceptive use among teens remains quite inadequate. Of sexually active adolescent females, three-fourths used some form of contraception but only one-third reported using contraception regularly. More than half of nonpregnant sexually active Black adolescent females report never using contraceptives. Only one-fourth report always using contraceptives (Rogel, Zuehlke, Petersen, Tobin–Richards, & Shelton, 1980). In addition, younger adolescents are less likely than older ones to use contraceptives (Zabin, Kantner, & Zelnik, 1979; de Anda, 1982).

Pregnancies

Increased sexual activity among adolescents is not accompanied by regular use of effective contraceptives. This fact is reflected in the increased pregnancy rates for adolescents. For 15- to 19-year-old women, the pregnancy rate rose from 9.9% in 1974 to 10.9% in 1979 to 11.2% in 1982 (Select Committee on Children, Youth, and Families, 1986). As mentioned earlier, the pregnancy rate for sexually active 15- to 19-year-old women has actually declined. The overall increase in the pregnancy rate is the result of increases for White teens. The pregnancy rates for Black and White teens are not close to convergence, however. The Black teen pregnancy rate is approximately four times that of White teens (Stewart, 1981). The pregnancy rate remains lower than the birth rate. An increasing percentage of pregnancies ends in abortion (Everett, 1984; Zelnik & Kantner, 1980). In 1980, in addition to females aged 15 to 19 years who gave birth, 3.8% of Whites and 6.6% of minorities had abortions (Moore, 1983). The higher abortion rate for minority teens is a reflection of their higher pregnancy rate. When only pregnant teens are considered, abortion clearly is not chosen as an option by Blacks as frequently as it is by Whites. In 1979, only 26% of pregnant Black teens, in comparison to 41% of pregnant White teens, had abortions (Cummings, 1983). Further, abortion statistics may not be as accurate for Whites as for Blacks. These statistics often are drawn from public health clinics, which a higher proportion of Blacks use, rather than from private physicians, which a higher proportion of Whites use. Statistics may underestimate the actual abortions among Whites. Due to space limitations, the issues surrounding adolescent abortion will not be presented in this chapter. The psychological and legal aspects of adolescent abortion are discussed in Lewis (1987), Melton (1986, 1987), and Melton and Russo (1987).

Births

A common misconception is that the birth rate of adolescents has increased at an alarming rate. Both the number of births and the birth rates of adolescents, however, have declined over the past two decades. The highest birth rates for 16- to 19-year-old women occurred in 1957. The highest rates for 14- and 15-year-olds occurred in 1973. The record high percentages for each successive age from 14 to 19 years were .074%, 2.02%, 4.57%, 8.58%, 13.62%, and 18.4% (Baldwin, 1984). The birth rate has declined for both Black and White teens although the Black rate remains higher than that of White teens. For White teens, the birth rate fell from 5.74% in 1970 to 4.7% in 1980 to 4.36% in 1983. For Black teens, the corresponding birth rates were 14.77%, 10.00%, and 9.55% (Select Committee on Children, Youth, and Families, 1986). Births to teens comprise a small but substantial proportion of total births. In 1980, approximately 16% of all births and 28% of first births were to 14- to 19-year-old mothers (Moore, 1983).

A large proportion of births to Black teens is to unwed teens. The birth rate for unmarried Black teens has decreased, however, and the rate for unmarried White teens has increased (Ventura, 1985). For unmarried Black teens, the birth rate fell from 9.69% in 1970 to 8.64% in 1983. The birth rate for unmarried White teens rose from 1.09% to 1.85 during that same time period. Because of White teens' increase, the overall rate for unwed adolescents has increased. The current birth rate among unwed White teens is in contrast to the 1950s, when many of the relatively high number of teen mothers married and remained in stable families. In 1983, 54% of adolescent mothers were single, compared to only 15% in 1960 (Select Committee on Children, Youth, and Families, 1986). Marriage is an especially difficult issue for the Black teen mother. As a single mother she faces almost certain poverty, although marriage may not enhance her economic status. Black males, particularly teenagers, have very high unemployment rates (Children's Defense Fund, 1985).

The decline in the birth rate has been greater for older than for younger adolescents. Therefore, younger adolescents today have a slightly higher proportion of all births to adolescents than was true in the past. The birth rate still is much higher for the older adolescent. In 1981, for example, the birth rate was 9.21% for 19-year-old females and was 1.41% for 15-year-olds (Baldwin, 1984). It is for the young adolescent, however, that the consequences of pregnancy for her own development and that of her child are likely to be quite negative (Baldwin, 1983). Unfortunately, the young adolescent is more likely than older adolescents to have additional unplanned out-of-wedlock births.

The adolescent birth rate in the United States is higher than that in almost all developed countries and higher than in many developing countries (Alan Guttmacher Institute, 1981), even with the recent declines and with Black teens excluded (Children's Defense Fund, 1985; Jones et al., 1985; Westoff, Calot, & Foster, 1983). The higher birth rate in the United States cannot be explained by the rate of sexual activity. The rates of sexual activity are not greater for American teens than for those in other countries. The major difference appears to be in sex education in other countries (Children's Defense Fund, 1985).

The number of births to adolescents has decreased because of the declining birth rate and also because of the decline in the number of adolescents in the population after 1976, when the largest cohort of World War II "baby boom" children reached 19 years of age (Baldwin, 1984). An examination of the number of births to adolescents also reveals that, contrary to popular perceptions, the majority of teen mothers are White. Black teens tend to be the subject of research, not because of higher absolute numbers of births, but because of their higher birth rates (Brooks-Gunn & Furstenberg, 1986). Race per se may not account for observed birth rate differences between Blacks and Whites, however. No differences between the birth rates of Blacks and Whites are found when the effects of income and basic skills are controlled (Children's Defense Fund, 1986).

Missing in the available statistics is adequate information on the adolescent father. Only recently have researchers begun to direct attention to the adolescent male who fathers a child (Children's Defense Fund, 1985; Hendricks, 1980, 1983; Vaz, Smolen & Miller, 1983). Men older than twenty years, however, father approximately half of the babies born to teenaged women (Children's Defense Fund, 1985; Vaz et al., 1983).

Antecedents of Adolescent Pregnancy

In order to prevent unplanned adolescent pregnancy, information is needed regarding the factors associated with the adolescents' initiation of sexual activity at early ages and with their lack of contraceptive use once they become sexually active. A developmental framework for understanding adolescent sexual activity and contraceptive use is presented below. Some of the factors associated with the adolescents' sexual activity and contraceptive use are then discussed.

Developmental Perspective

The normal developmental tasks of adolescence include the establishment of adult sexuality. Adolescents' developing sexual behavior is influenced by models of adult sexuality and by the adolescents' perceptions of their own future adult roles in the society. The understanding of adolescent pregnancy has been impeded by an emphasis on pathology rather than on the biological and social factors contributing to adolescent pregnancy (Lancaster & Hamburg, 1986). Biological and social aspects of development converge, or perhaps collide, in the phenomenon of adolescent pregnancy. As discussed below, teens reach reproductive maturity at an early age, but American society requires a long period of time during which the adolescent is not expected to take adult roles such as reproduction. Much physical and social change occurs in the prolonged period between early and late adolescence. The antecedents and outcomes of pregnancy may vary with the age of the adolescent.

In a different society or in a different historical period, teen pregnancy might not be associated with the negative outcomes that presently are associated with the phenomenon. Adolescent pregnancy is especially difficult because in contemporary American society it is, like divorce, an unscheduled nonnormative life event. Nonnormative life events are outside the typical course of development for most individuals in the society (Furstenberg & Spanier, 1984). These events pose particular problems because individuals do not prepare for them and social institutions may not provide adequate support.

The Societal Context

Adolescent pregnancy is not an isolated phenomenon but is embedded in societal conditions. Three conditions of note in this regard are trends in nonmarital childbearing for older women, changing and ambiguous adult sexual standards, and employment prospects for Black men.

Childbearing outside marriage has increased for women of all childbearing ages, as well as for adolescents (Ventura, 1985); 62% of nonmarital births are to women over twenty years (Children's Defense Fund, 1985). Births to unmarried women increased by 79% between 1970 and 1982, a period when women could avail themselves of effective contraceptives and legal abortions. During that same period births to married women decreased by 11%. Although many more Black women (7.96%) bear children outside marriage than do White women (1.88%), the birth rate for unmarried Black women actually declined 17% from 1970 to 1982 (Ventura, 1985). The actual number of births outside marriage has increased more than the rates would suggest. Because the children born during the

Antecedents and Outcomes of Pregnancy in Black Adolescents

post World War II baby boom are now 20 to 40 years, there now are many more women of childbearing age (Ventura, 1985). Many of these women, however, are delaying marriage. The number of 20 to 35–year–old unmarried women increased dramatically from 1970 to 1982 (Ventura, 1985). Because these women are likely to be sexually active and may desire to have children before becoming much older, the probability is increased that they will conceive, by choice or chance. Although some unmarried women choose to have and rear children without a spouse (see Eiduson, 1980), unmarried women, both Black and White, both teens and postteens, are more likely to receive inadequate prenatal care and to have low–birth–weight infants than are their married counterparts (Ventura, 1985). An understanding of older women's reasons for remaining unmarried and for bearing children outside marriage may contribute to the understanding of adolescent pregnancy.

The increase in births outside marriage may reflect, in part, a more accepting attitude toward sexual activity outside marriage. Certainly, American society glorifies sexuality, bombarding adolescents at every turn with sexual stimuli. Television, records, books, and radio constantly broadcast the themes of sexuality, premarital sex, and extramarital sex (Ooms, 1981). Youthfulness is especially revered in society's standards of sexual attractiveness. The popular rock–videos readily available on television are replete with explicit, often violent sexual images. Brown (1985), studying the violent and sexual acts in videos and other television programming suggests that the intense, vivid, and often out–of–context act in the video makes it especially compelling. Adolescents may be confused by the conflicting messages they receive about appropriate sexual behavior.

Perhaps more important than the changing and confusing sexual standards are the extremely poor employment prospects for Blacks, especially Black males (see Scott–Jones & Nelson–LeGall, 1986; see also Malveaux & Ogbu, this volume). Black men have high unemployment rates and, when working, low incomes. For Black teenaged males and those in their early twenties, the unemployment rates are even higher than for older Black men. Marriage with little hope of economic security may not seem very attractive. Economic disparities in a society appear to be associated with high rates of adolescent pregnancy. Comparisons of developed countries indicate that in the United States, which has the highest teen pregnancy rate, the percentage of total available income that goes to the low socioeconomic strata is among the lowest (Jones et al., 1985).

In summary, Black adolescents come of age in a society where family structures are in a state of flux, adult standards for sexual behavior are unclear, and employment prospects for Blacks, especially males, are dismal. The societal context strongly affects adolescents. Perceptions of their opportunities and potential roles as adults in the society motivate adolescents' behavior.

Onset of Puberty and Sexual Activity

The onset of puberty marks the biological beginning of adolescence as a stage of development. The average age for the onset of puberty has declined in the twentieth century (Roche, 1979). Currently, girls reach puberty at an average age of 12.5 years. The normal range of onset is 10–15.5 years (Tanner, 1975). Boys reach puberty at an average age of 14 years, with a range of 12–16 years (Tanner, 1970). Further, females in the past experienced a relatively long period of subfertility following menarche (the first menstrual period); the young female could function sexually and socially as an adult without a high likelihood of pregnancy. Because of optimal habitat conditions—a high-calorie diet coupled with a sedentary life style—the average age for both fertility and menarche has declined to possibly the lowest point possible in the range of human variation (Lancaster, 1986).

A concurrent trend has been the delaying of adolescents' achievement of full adult status in the society. The achievement of adult sexuality is a major developmental task of this stage, along with establishing independence from parents, developing a stable identity, acquiring a set of values, and preparing for an occupation (Chilman, 1983). As the age at which children reach puberty has gone down, the age at which we expect adolescents to complete their formal schooling and enter the adult labor force has gone up. The need for advanced schooling conflicts with teens' biological readiness to initiate sexual activity and to have children. There may be a delay of ten years or more between the time adolescents reach biological maturity and the time they are recognized as adults. Because there are no specific rites of passage in American society regarding first sexual activity, the decision to become sexually active may be a difficult one for young people who are biologically mature but have no definitive, realistic guidelines for sexual expression.

The lack of adult guidance may be the most serious problem in the sexuality of adolescents. Many adults are uncomfortable and ambiguous regarding adolescent sexuality. Adults may tell adolescents that premarital sexual activity is unacceptable and that abstinence is the appropriate response to their awakening sexual desires. Merely forbidding sexual activity, however, will not necessarily lead to the development of a positive sexual identity or positive relationships with opposite-sex peers. Much more attention needs to be given to the normal development of same-sex and opposite-sex peer relations in adolescence (for review of adolescent friendships, see Clark, this volume).

There is some suggestion that the age of menarche is related to the age of first intercourse but there is inconsistency regarding whether the relationship holds for Black girls, White girls, or both, and whether the average age for menarche is earlier for Black than for White girls (Jones & Placek, 1981; Kantner & Zelnik, 1972; Westney, Jenkins, Butts, & Williams, 1984). Early dating and a steady relationship are related to sexual activity (Zelnik, Kantner, & Ford. 1981). The majority of Black adolescent females do not consciously plan their first sexual intercourse, however (Rogel, Zuehlke, Petersen, Tobin–Richards, & Shelton, 1980). Their sexual activity tends to be with one partner and is sporadic rather than regular (Rogel et al., 1980). Many will not remain sexually active throughout the teen years.

Contraceptive Use

Although contraceptive use among adolescents increased somewhat from 1976–1979 (Zelknik & Kantner, 1980), effective contraceptives are not widely used by adolescents. Adolescents tend to use the least effective methods, such as withdrawal, rather than more effective methods such as IUDs and oral contraceptives (Zelnik & Kantner, 1980). Although males agree in principle that both males and females share responsibility for contraception, males know less than females about contraceptives (Freeman et al., 1980). In studies of influences on adolescents' contraceptive behavior, parents are not found to be significant (Finkel & Finkel, 1981; Thompson & Spanier, 1978). For males, the sexual partner has the greatest influence. Among females, partners and friends have an influence. More research on males is needed due to the importance of males in the methods of choice for many couples—withdrawal and condoms (Johnson & Staples, 1979; Scott–Jones & White, in press).

Adolescents appear to be woefully ignorant of basic reproductive processes and contraceptive methods (Morrison, 1985). The lack of knowledge about reproduction is not confined to adolescents; 20– to 44–year–old Black women in the National Survey of Family Growth were not substantially more knowledgeable than were teen–aged Black women (Scott–Jones & Turner, in preparation). The majority of teens become sexually active before they seek contraceptive information (Alan Guttmacher Institute, 1981). Zabin and Clark (1981) found that only 14% of teens who visited a family planning clinic had not already become sexually active. The median delay after first intercourse was one year. Unfortunately, pregnancies often occur shortly after sexual activity begins. Findings of various surveys are that 36% of first premarital pregnancies occur within the first three months of sexual activity (Kenney & Orr, 1984); 50% within six months (Zabin, Kantner, & Zelnik, 1979); and 44% within one year (Rogel et al., 1980). The meager data available on the relationship between male initiation of sexual activity and fathering a child suggest a longer delay than that documented for females. A national longitudinal survey indicates that Black fathers aged 22 to 25 years, the majority of whom had become sexually active before age 16 years, had a median time lag of five and six years (for fathers not living and living with their children), respectively (Lerman, 1986).

Some professionals and parents disapprove of contraceptive availability for adolescents (e.g., Schwartz & Ford, 1984), believing that it gives implicit approval to sexual activity among teens and will increase the numbers of teens who are sexually active. When contraceptive information is disseminated, abstinence is sometimes included as an option (Brann et al., 1979). The fear that their parents will learn that they obtained contraceptives is one of the most frequently cited reasons for adolescents' not using them. Other frequent reasons are that they did not know where to get contraceptives, they took a chance without making a conscious decision, they believed available methods were not safe, and they did not expect to have intercourse. Teens also report being embarrassed to buy contraceptives from drugstores and some report thinking they need parental permission to buy these products across the counter (Allen, 1980; Clark, Zabin & Hardy, 1984; Rogel et al., 1980; Morrison, 1985; Taylor, Kagay, & Leichenko, 1986; Zabin & Clark, 1981; Zelnik & Kim, 1982). In much of the research on contraceptive use, Black teens are inadequately represented, samples are not completely identified, and race is confounded with socioeconomic status (Morrison, 1985). In a sample of young teens, Blacks who used contraception were likely to use withdrawal, an ineffective method, and Whites were likely to use condoms (Scott-Jones & White, in preparation). More research is needed on patterns of contraception among Blacks and on the variables associated with effective contraception.

Cognitive Development and Problem-Solving

The decision to become sexually active and to use contraceptives may be related to the adolescent's cognitive development and problem-solving skills. According to Piagetian theory, at the beginning of adolescence the individual is making a transition from concrete to formal operational thought, and is developing the skills that allow consideration of possible consequences of one's actions. The adolescent, especially the early adolescent, may not have skills necessary for making good decisions regarding sexual behavior. Steinlauf (1979), assessing 15–25 year old Black and White women at an abortion clinic and those at a planned parenthood clinic, found a positive relationship between scores on a story-format test of problem-solving skills and number of unplanned pregnancies. Lack of information, in addition to a lack of skills, may affect decision-making. Rogel et al. (1980) hypothesized that adolescents will decide to risk pregnancy if they perceive the risks of contraceptives and the benefits of physical intimacy or pregnancy to be high. Rogel et al. concluded that 12–19 year old Black females lacked information on risks related to contraceptives, especially oral contraceptives, and on the difficulties associated with pregnancy and childrearing. Many girls reported not having planned to have intercourse so they may not have engaged in any rational decision–making process.

School Achievement

Ordinarily, teen pregnancy is thought to be a cause of dropping out of school. The relationship between educational achievement and teen pregnancy is quite complex, and is affected by family socioeconomic status. Many teens who become pregnant or father a child have poor basic skills before the pregnancy occurs. In fact, when income and skills deficits are controlled, the marked difference in teen parenthood rates between Blacks and White disappears (Children's Defense Fund, 1986).

Rates of sexual activity and contraceptive use also appear to be related to adolescents' school achievement. In a study of 13- and 14-year-olds, educational expectations were strongly associated with sexual activity. Teens with high educational expectations were less likely to have become sexually active (Scott–Jones & White, in preparation). A survey of 12- to 17-year olds, which oversampled Blacks and Hispanics, found that teens with low average grades were more likely to have became sexually active. Of sexually active teens those with high grades, as well as those with a specific career aspiration and those involved in sports or other extracurricular activities are more likely to use contraception (Taylor, Kagay, & Leichenko, 1986).

Locus of Control

If many adolescents are not making any conscious decisions regarding contraception, an important factor may be locus of control. Those adolescents with an internal locus of control may take more responsibility for their sexual and contraceptive behavior. Those with an external locus of control may leave the outcome of their sexual behavior to chance or to their partners. Segal and DuCette (1973) found that pregnant White adolescents tended to have an external locus of control and that their nonpregnant counterparts tended to have an internal locus of control. Surprisingly, this finding was reversed for Black pregnant and nonpregnant adolescents. Steinlauf (1979) found that the number of unplanned pregnancies was positively related to external control for both Black and White adolescent girls. Hendricks and Fullilove (1983) report similar findings for Black males.

Related to the adolescent's sense of control is risk–taking. Some adolescents may believe too strongly in their own control of chance events. They know that pregnancy is a possible outcome of sexual activity but may believe that it will not happen to them. Risk–taking in some areas is appropriate for adolescents. They need to test their skills in many situations where failure, as well as success, is a possible outcome. Placing themselves at risk for pregnancy, however, needs to be distinguished from more desirable forms of risk–taking.

Gender Roles

Norms for gender–appropriate behavior may influence the adolescents' developing sexual conduct (Jorgensen & Alexander, 1983). Gender roles, especially regarding the distribution of power between the adolescent female and male in the dyadic relationship, may affect the tendency of the couple to place themselves at risk for pregnancy. If males are viewed as dominant and aggressive, and females as passive and submissive, adolescents are more likely to become sexually active and to fail to use contraceptives than if gender roles are more egalitarian (Cvetkovich, Grote, Leiberman, & Miller, 1978; Hansson, Jones, & Chernovetz, 1979; Jorgensen et al., 1980; MacCorquodale, 1984; Rosen, Martindale, & Griselda, 1976; Scales, 1977). Traditional males and females are less frequent and less effective contraceptors. When adolescents hold traditional views of male and female roles, they may view sexual relations as male conquests and believe that males are not responsible for contraception or for the welfare of their sexual partners. Egalitarian individuals are more likely to believe contraception should be shared (MacCorquodale, 1984). In a sample that was one–third nonWhite, Cvetkovich et al. (1978) found that sexually active adolescent females held more stereotyped sex roles than their nonactive peers. Among the women who were not sexually active, those who said they would never have sex before marriage held more stereotyped sex roles than the sexually active women. Nonactive women who believed that they might be ready to have sex at some point before marriage had the least stereotyped sex roles.

Often the female cites pressure from the male as a reason for beginning sexual activity (Furstenberg, 1976b). Many adolescents want to retain their steady relationship and will become sexually active for that reason. The younger adolescent may find it even more difficult to resist pressure from the male than an older adolescent (de Anda, 1982). In one study, the majority of the boyfriends were very happy about the pregnancy although most of the females had not wanted to become pregnant. Pressure from the male may have been an important deciding factor (DeAmicis, Klorman, Hess, & McAnarney, 1981). Female power, operationalized as participation in decision–making and conflict resolution, is negatively related to frequency of intercourse and positively related to contraceptive use (Jorgensen et al., 1980).

Rogel et al. (1980) provide some information about the gender roles of Black adolescent females, the majority of whom were sexually active and were or had been pregnant. The majority did not equate motherhood with womanhood. Most, however, reported having close teenaged friends and relatives who were pregnant. These pregnant teen relatives and friends may have provided models for the association of pregnancy with adulthood. The majority reported egalitarianism in their sexual relations. They and their boyfriends decided equally about having sex. Most reported positive feelings about their sexual relations although a substantial minority, 40%, reported that sex was forced on them some or all the time. Rogel et al., do not report the relationship of any of these variables to sexual activity or pregnancy.

The strict gender role distinctions of White men and women, which currently are changing, have not existed to the same extent in Black families. A high degree of overlap between male and female roles has been the norm for Blacks, instead of the traditional socialization of males only toward work and achievement and females only toward childrearing and nurturing (see Reid, 1982; Scott–Jones & Nelson–Le Gall, 1986). A problem for Black adolescent males and females, especially those from low–income families, is poor prospects for work roles—the "job ceiling" (Ogbu, 1978) that limits the economic opportunities of Blacks in American society. Black adolescents may see parenthood as a way to achieve maturity and adult status because so many other adult roles are perceived as being closed to them (Gabriel & McAnarney, 1983). Black adolescents are not encouraged to become pregnant but parenthood is valued and is available as an adult role.

Outcomes of Adolescent Pregnancy

Because abortion is not an acceptable resolution of pregnancy for many Black adolescents, they give birth and confront a vast array of problems. An unplanned pregnancy disrupts the development of the adolescent mother and, perhaps to a lesser extent, that of the adolescent father. The development of children born to adolescent parents is also a critical issue.

Teen Mothers

Although most teen mothers do not plan to become pregnant, they are likely to keep their babies rather than place them for adoption. Almost

Special Topics: Pregnancy and Parenting

100% of Black teen mothers, and 90% of White teen mothers, keep their babies (Alan Guttmacher Institute, 1981). Consequently, the adolescent mother faces decisions—whether to marry, how to be a good parent and whether to have additional children—in addition to the more typical adolescent concerns regarding education and occupation.

Marriage. The majority of teen mothers do not marry the child's father (Children's Defense Fund, 1985). Most teen mothers live in a parent's or other relative's household (Select Committee on Children, Youth, and Families, 1986). Those who do marry are likely to have marital difficulties. In Furstenberg's study (1976b), three out of five adolescent couples were separated within five years. The younger the adolescent, the greater the likelihood of separation and divorce. Lack of time for developing a relationship and economic pressures contribute to the breakup of adolescent marriages. Separated and divorced adolescent mothers are less likely than older mothers to receive child support. Only 10% of 14- to 24-year-old and 25% of older mothers receive child support (Children's Defense Fund, 1985). Recently enacted legislation, the 1984 Child Support Amendments of the Social Security Act, requires states to improve child support enforcement but extensive outreach education is necessary in order for teen parents to benefit (Children's Defense Fund, 1987).

Marriage may not be the best solution for the pregnant adolescent female. No clear economic advantage of marriage exists for the Black pregnant teen. Only 20% of Black adolescent males are employed (Children's Defense Fund, 1985). Black adolescent mothers who marry are likely to end their schooling as well as to divorce (Furstenberg, 1976b; McLaughlin, Grady, Billy, Landale, & Winges, 1986). Those who live with their parents for five years after the child's birth have better educational and employment outcomes than those who do not (Baldwin, 1983; Furstenberg & Crawford, 1978).

Parenting and Social Support. The adolescent mother's developing parenting skills are influenced by her own mother, that is, the child's grandmother. A significant correlation exists between Black teen mothers' and grandmothers' knowledge of childrearing (Stevens, 1984). If an adolescent mother receives emotional support from others, particularly a relative or a male partner, she tends to be a more supportive and effective parent (Colletta, 1981; Thompson, 1986). Adolescents who can turn to others for help in solving problems related to early motherhood often have a higher opinion of themselves and less stress in handling problems (Colletta, Hadler, & Gregg, 1981).

In some instances, the social networks available to the adolescent mother may not be entirely positive. In a survey of predominantly Black adolescent mothers, Thompson (1986) found that support from friends and some relatives was associated with high levels of stress in the mothering role. Further, Burton and Bengston (1985) report that the Black grandmother, traditionally the mainstay of the teen mother's support system, may sometimes resent the role she is expected to play. Young Black grandmothers in particular may be unwilling to provide the help needed by the teen mother. Early grandmotherhood, like early motherhood, may require difficult adjustments.

Subsequent Pregnancies. The possibility of additional pregnancies is an issue for the young mother. By age 29, individuals who become parents as adolescents often have more children than their classmates and more children than they had wanted or planned to have (Card & Wise, 1978). The younger the mother is when she first has a child, the greater the likelihood that she will have more children at a faster pace, more unwanted births, and more out-of-wedlock births. Adolescents who have their first births at 15–17 years are likely to have more children than those who have first births at 18–19 years. Both groups have more subsequent births than women who wait until past the age of 20 to start their childbearing (Trussell & Menken, 1978). The idea that teen pregnancy occurs in each subsequent generation in the same family is not supported. In a study of 41 Black family lineage units, only 1 had adolescent pregnancy in three or more subsequent generations (Burton & Bengston, 1985).

Identifying the variables associated with the adolescent's subsequent unwanted pregnancies has been difficult. A two–year study of the subsequent pregnancies of poor, predominantly minority (approximately equal Black and Hispanic) adolescents who were pregnant or were mothers indicated that time was the best predictor. The longer the time since the adolescent's most recent pregnancy, the greater the likelihood of a subsequent pregnancy. Two variables related to school were significantly associated with subsequent pregnancy but these variables accounted for very little variance. The two variables were whether the adolescent was enrolled in school at the beginning of the study and how many times she had dropped out of school. At the end of the study, when the average age was approximately 18 years, 56% of the young mothers had experienced two or more pregnancies (Polit & Kahn, 1986).

Education. The adolescent who becomes pregnant may drop out of school temporarily or permanently. Pregnancy was the reason most frequently cited for dropping out of school for Black, Hispanic, and Indian sophomores (Whalen, 1984). More than one–half of adolescent mothers eventually complete high school (Furstenberg, 1976b). Compared to classmates, though, adolescent parents are behind educationally. The earlier in adolescence the pregnancy occurs, the greater the negative consequences on educational attainment. The very young mother's educational deficits often are not corrected in later years (Card & Wise, 1978; Furstenberg, 1976a, 1976b). Young mothers who become pregnant before the age of 18 often do not reach their own stated educational goals (Furstenberg, 1976b). Comparisons of 21- to 24-year-old women who gave birth during adolescence with those who gave birth during their twenties or who had not given birth indicate differences of from two to three years of schooling (Furstenberg, 1976b; Moore & Waite, 1977.) For Black adolescent mothers, the educational goals of their parents and the amount of help received from parents and teachers are important variables in educational achievement and high school completion (Allen, 1980; Gray & Ramsey, 1986; Moore & Waite, 1977.)

A recently reported 17-year follow-up of Furstenberg's research indicated that the long-term educational outlook for Black teen mothers is not quite as dismal as most previous research suggests. Two-thirds of the mothers had completed high school; one-third of the sample had some education beyond high school; and 5% were college graduates. Some mothers returned to school when their youngest child entered public school (Furstenberg, Brooks-Gunn, & Morgan, 1987).

Occupation. The occupational outlook also is less favorable for adolescent mothers. The majority—85%—of Black single mothers younger than 25 years live in poverty (Children's Defense Fund, 1985). Partly because of lower educational status, adolescent mothers have jobs that pay less than the jobs obtained by women who delay their childbearing until past the teen years (Card & Wise, 1978). In a follow-up study, Furstenberg (1976b) found that one-third of the adolescent mothers but only 4% of their classmates without children were receiving part of their income from welfare. In a 17-year follow-up, Furstenberg et al. (1987) found that slightly less than one-fourth had received public assistance in the past year. Most of the women were not chronic welfare dependents but had relatively brief periods, often associated with a crisis such as divorce or job loss, in which they received public assistance.

Even though adolescent mothers who finish high school may require public aid more often than the mothers who delay childbirth, they still require less help than adolescent mothers who do not finish high school (Moore, 1978). Therefore, programs to help adolescent mothers continue their education would benefit not only the mother but society as well (Moore, 1978). Part of the problem is structural and is related to the "feminization of poverty"; women, particularly Black women, have low earning power in American society.

Teen Fathers

The effect of pregnancy on the adolescent father is sparsely covered in documented research (Hendricks, 1980; 1983; Johnson & Staples, 1979; Pauker, 1971). Demographic profiles of the adolescent father need to be gathered nationally and psychological correlates of adolescent fatherhood need to be examined. The information needs to be obtained from the father rather than from secondary sources. Several studies have begun to provide much needed information about the adolescent father.

In contrast to teen mothers, only half of teen fathers have contact with their child in the first two years after the birth, and a smaller percentage maintains contact after the second year (Barret & Robinson, 1982; Earls & Siegel, 1980). Vaz, Smolen and Miller (1983) found that most (81%) Black fathers in adolescent pregnancies maintained an ongoing relationship with the mother and kept their own families informed about the pregnancy; however, the mean age of the subjects was 18.9 years and at least one–third of the group was between 19 and 28 years of age.

A model prospective longitudinal study by Card and Wise (1978) included the assessment of young Black and White males and females in grades 9, 10, 11, and 12, with an eleven–year follow–up. Consistent with earlier findings of Furstenberg (1976b) and Presser (1980), and a later study by Hendricks, Montgomery, and Fullilove (1984), this study found that the educational achievement level of male and female adolescent childbearers was not as high as their non–childbearing classmates. A direct linear relationship between age at birth of first child and amount of education was found at both five and eleven years past the expected date of high school graduation. At one year post high school, more males who had been adolescent fathers were working than was true of their classmates. At eleven years post high school, when both groups were 29 years old, there were no significant differences between the two groups. More than 9 of 10 men in both groups were employed. The difference was that males who were adolescent fathers were over represented in blue collar jobs and under represented in the professions, reflecting the differences in educational attainment. The adolescent father also was likely to have more children than his agemate who delayed parenthood. Early childbearing limits the number of years an individual, father or mother, would otherwise spend in school, and consequently curtails the level of adult achievement.

Vaz et al. (1983) found that 48% of Black fathers helped with the decision related to pregnancy outcome, 19% discussed the pregnancy with a health professional, and only 9% received contraceptive information. A significant number of males feel social isolation and suffer negative psychosocial consequences that sometimes include depression. Hendricks, Howard and Caesar (1981) investigated the help seeking behaviors of Black teen fathers and found similar results. Services most needed by young fathers were related to parenting, educational and vocational guidance, and psychosocial counseling. An apparent solution to these problems is to involve the male early in his partner's pregnancy. Fathers, to the same extent as mothers, should be provided with psychological support and contraceptive counseling (Barret & Robinson, 1982; Vaz et al., 1983).

Outcomes for Offspring

Prenatal and Infant Development. Compared to older mothers, adolescent mothers are less likely to have health insurance or to obtain adequate prenatal care (Jones & Placek, 1981; McCormick, Shapiro, & Starfield, 1983). Consequently, they have more complications of pregnancy and labor; more low birth weight and handicapped infants, infants with low Apgar scores, and higher infant mortality rates (Jones & Placek, 1981; McCormick et al., 1983; Menken, 1981). Early childbearing is associated with a high number of additional births and short intervals between births (Menken, 1981). Infant mortality rates are substantially higher for 18- to 19-year-olds who have given birth more than once than for same-age mothers having their first child and for mothers over 20 years (McCormick et al., 1983).

Young low-income adolescent mothers are at significantly greater risk of poor health and consequently may begin a pregnancy at a reduced health status (Ventura & Hendershort, 1984). Young mothers in poor general health are more likely to develop toxemia, iron deficiency anemia, and other medical problems associated with pregnancy. Poor health status and late entry into the health care system predispose the poor, Black woman to deliver an infant of low birth weight (Fine, Adams–Taylor, Miller, & Schorr, 1984). In 1982, 6.8% of all infants born in the United States were of low birth weight, compared to 15.5% of births to Black mothers under 15 years, and 13.7% of births to Black mothers between 15 and 19 years (Rosenbaum, 1985). Although it has improved significantly over the last twenty years, the outlook for low birth weight infants is still poor. Low birth weight infants are twenty times more likely to die in the first year of life than are normal weight babies (National Center for Health Statistics, 1982) and are also at greater risk for mental retardation, cerebral palsy, epilepsy, developmental delays, learning disabilities, and visual and hearing defects (Fine et al., 1984).

With good prenatal and follow–up health care, many of the differences in physical health of offspring born to adolescent and older mothers are not found (Chilman, 1980, 1983). The lack of differences in infant outcomes clearly attributable to adolescent childbearing does not mean that adolescent pregnancy is a positive event. Rather, adolescent pregnancy tends to occur in an already precarious situation. Problems of children born to adolescents may be due to poverty and racism rather than to mother's age alone (Chilman, 1980, 1983). The adverse economic conditions of poor minorities exist throughout the childbearing years as well as during the teen years.

Adolescents under the age of 15 years experience more problems than do older adolescents. They have more complications in pregnancy not totally accounted for by lack of or poor prenatal care (Children's Defense Fund, 1985). The physiological immaturity of the very young adolescent may contribute to the higher incidence of certain problems such as toxemia and underdeveloped pelvic growth (Dott & Fort, 1975). Although many studies do not make distinctions within the age range of adolescence, very young adolescents need to be considered separately.

Later Development. With race and socioeconomic status controlled, few differences are found in the later development of children born to adolescent and older mothers (Chilman, 1980, 1983; Morrow, 1979). Lester, Coll and Sepkoski (1982) compared predominantly Black samples of Puerto Rican and mainland adolescent and older mothers to determine the relation between neonatal behavior and maternal age. The behavior of the newborns of adolescent mothers was somewhat different but within normal range.

Although adolescent mothers, especially young ones, may not be prepared for adequate parenting (Simpkins, 1984), family support, particularly among Blacks, may help, so that the child is not raised solely by the teen mother (Baldwin, 1983; Chilman, 1983). In Black families, grandmothers may contribute substantially to the child's development. Black grandmothers are more knowledgeable about childrearing, more responsive and less punitive than are teen mothers in interactions with 13– to 30–month–old infants (Stevens, 1984). The active involvement of the Black grandmother in the child's development may continue throughout childhood when the single mother and grandmother remain in the same household (Wilson, 1984).

Academic achievement of children born to teenaged mothers may not be different from that of children born to older mothers of the same socioeconomic status. In a sample of low–income Black children, Morrrow (1979) found no differences in academic achievement between those born to women 15 years and younger and those born to women 20–24 years. Belmont, Cohen, Dryfoos, Stein and Zayac (1981) found a small linear relationship between maternal age and WISC scores in three large data sets including Black and White subjects. However, the effect of maternal age could be attributed to other factors related to adolescent pregnancy. Broman (1981) found that children born to adolescent mothers were lower on I.Q. scores, motor development and deviant behavior scores than children born to mothers 20 to 29 years old when the children were tested at age four. The effects of socioeconomic status were much greater than the effects of maternal age.

Efforts to document the effects of adolescent childbearing on the social and emotional development of offspring have not yielded results as concise as those on cognitive development. Furstenberg (1976) attempted to measure efficacy, trust, self esteem and ability to delay gratification among children aged 42–60 months. He found no major or consistent effect of having been born to an adolescent mother. Differences emerged when subgroups of the sample were analyzed. Children of adolescents who married the child's father and remained married to him scored higher on the social–emotional development measures than did other children. Children of economically secure families also scored higher on efficacy and trust measures. Children of mothers who went on to finish high school and were not on welfare scored higher than more economically disadvantaged offspring. Furstenburg suggested the factor that most influenced socio–emotional development among intact families was the economic advantage resulting from a two parent family household. Parents in these households seem to be better educated and more regularly employed. Kellam, Ensminger and Turner (1977) reported similar findings in infant outcomes, but attributed the results to presence in the home of a second adult who was not necessarily the father.

Programs and Services

Types of Programs

Most programs for adolescents focus on services during pregnancy, later parenting skills, and contraceptive information, rather than on prevention of the first pregnancy (Badger & Burns, 1980; Block & Block, 1980; Edwards & Steinman, 1980; Everett, 1984; Sloan, 1982). The first federal program specifically for adolescent pregnancy, the Adolescent Health Services and Pregnancy Prevention and Care Act, 1978, was of this type (Everett, 1984). Many programs are multidisciplinary in scope, attempting to meet the perceived physical and psychological needs of mothers and infants. Few programs include the father or the families of the teen mother and father (Barret & Robinson, 1983; Ooms, 1983; Hendricks, 1983; Vaz et al., 1983). A 1985 Wisconsin law required maternal and paternal grandparents to assume financial responsibility for their grandchildren until the teen parents reached 18 years. The law is not viewed as effective and, with the exception of Hawaii, no other state has passed similar legislation (Children's Defense Fund, 1987).

Other programs emphasize the prevention of a first pregnancy. Programs encouraging teenagers to use contraception and to delay pregnancy have existed in this country since at least 1970 (Brann et al., 1979). A federal program, the Adolescent Family Life Act, 1981, emphasizes abstinence as a prevention approach (Everett, 1984). Some programs may provide information about biological functions only or may offer information about contraceptives and alternative solutions to pregnancy.

School-based sex education as a preventive intervention in adolescent pregnancy is a controversial issue. Although some parents fear that sex education leads to more premarital sex among teens, there is no correlation between the two. For sexually active teens, there is a negative correlation between exposure to a sex education program and becoming pregnant (Zelnik & Kim, 1982). Most public opinion polls indicate public support for sex education programs. In their annual survey of public perceptions of schools, Phi Delta Kappa found that 75% of the respondents believed that sex education should be taught in high school. Only 52% of the respondents believed that sex education programs should be taught in fourth through eighth grade (Gallup, 1985). These results were not reported separately for Blacks. A poll sponsored by Planned Parenthood (Harris, Kagay, & Leichenko, 1985), in which Blacks were 11% of the sample, provides separate results for Blacks. In that poll, 91% of Black respondents, compared to 85% of all respondents, thought sex education should be taught in school.

The Planned Parenthood poll suggests some possible reasons for the need to have sex education in the schools. Adults appear not to have strong models for conveying information about sexuality to children. Their own parents frequently were not responsible for providing information about sexuality. Friends were cited as the source of first information about sex by 38% of the Black adults; 22% received first information from mothers, 5% from fathers, and 12% from sex education course. In addition, parents appear to feel uncomfortable providing the full range of information about sexuality. Of Black parents with 6- to 18-year-old children, 65% reported that they talked with their children about sex. Only one-third provided information about birth control. The perception of a lack of parental control of adolescents was prevalent. The majority of Black respondents, 67%, reported the belief that parents have little or no control over adolescents' sexual behavior (Harris et al., 1985). Studies of adolescents suggest that parents do not provide effective sex education (Scott-Jones Turner, in press); adolescents' knowledge and behavior are affected by peers and sexual partners more than by parents (Finkel & Finkel, 1981; Thompson & Spanier, 1978). Schools, then, seem to be an appropriate and needed mechanism for sex education. Parental support of school-based sex education programs is strong.

In spite of adult support, sex education programs are not available to many adolescents. Between 31% and 43% of adolescents have attended formal sex education programs (Alan Guttmacher Institute, 1981). A 1982 survey of approximately 200 school districts in large U.S. cities revealed that sex education is provided in 80% of the districts (Sonenstein & Pittman, 1984), although only 16% of the senior high schools and 11% of junior high schools offered a separate sex education course. Fewer than

Special Topics: Pregnancy and Parenting

10% of students receive information in a formal program lasting more than 40 hours (Kirby, 1984). Of teens who become sexually active by 18 years of age, only one–half have had a sex education course and only two–fifths have had instruction on contraception (Marsiglio & Mott, 1986).

In addition to sex education programs, some communities provide other services for teens. Family planning centers with facilities for counseling and pregnancy testing are found in most major cities. Public health departments encourage teenagers to use their facilities for information on contraception and pregnancy prevention as well as to learn about sexually transmitted diseases. Schools have permitted health clinics to be developed on site for the purpose of improving access to services for teens (Edwards, Steinman, Arnold & Hakanson, 1981). Where these kinds of services have been provided, contraceptive usage has increased and pregnancy rates have dropped. In the Planned Parenthood poll, 76% of Black parents reported the belief that family planning clinics should be housed in public schools (Harris et al., 1985). An exemplary program of this type is the Jackson–Hinds Adolescent Pregnancy Prevention Program in Jackson, Mississippi. In operation since 1979, this program is a collaborative effort of the public school and public health systems. The program provides for the needs of a variety of teens. Counseling in postponing sexual involvement is given to teens not sexually active, contraceptive services are available for sexually active teens, and child care and child health services are provided for parenting teens (Select Committee on Children, Youth, and Families, 1986).

Extensive programs and community efforts are needed to prevent unwanted pregnancy in adolescents. The American Public Health Association has developed policies to guide communities in planning programs to reduce the teenage pregnancy rate (Allen, 1980). Program success seems directly related to the community's acknowledging and responding appropriately to the needs of its own adolescent population. Outreach education, defined as any activity that takes information to the teen, has been suggested as a way to disseminate information (Brann et al., 1979). It includes telephone information lines, follow–up on pregnancy tests and missed appointments, and transmission of information via the mass media. An examination of other Western nations' efforts to combat the adolescent pregnancy problem may be useful (Brown, 1983). In Sweden, strategies include liberalized abortion laws, government subsidies for contraceptives, and a nationally mandated educational curriculum that presents sexuality in the context of personal relationships and their psychological, ethical, and social dimensions.

Evaluation of Programs

Because programs and services related to adolescent pregnancy are diverse and vary from one locale to another, there is little definitive information on their effectiveness. Marsiglio and Mott (1986) found that having taken a sex education course was associated with slightly higher sexual activity among 15– and 16–year-olds, and increased use of effective contraception. They concluded that the overall impact on pregnancy would be quite small. These researchers acknowledge that more information is needed on the quality and quantity of instruction. A study of special services provided to Black and White teens in the first six weeks following their initial visit to a family planning clinic found no significant differences in contraceptive use and pregnancy, 15 months later, from that of controls receiving regular service. The two features of the special services were family counseling sessions and regular follow–up phone calls from the clinic staff (Herceg–Baron, Furstenberg, Shea, & Harris, 1986).

More encouraging results were found in an evaluation of a program in an all–Black inner–city junior high school. The program included a school–based component and also a health clinic in close proximity to but separate from the school. After two years, the following changes were observed in the school population: Increased sexual and contraceptive knowledge; decreased age at first intercourse; greater likelihood of seeing a doctor before or shortly after first intercourse; increased use of effective contraception; and a decrease in pregnancy rates. Critical factors in the success of this program were considered to be the access to free, high–quality services, professional counseling, education, and open communication (Zabin, Hirsch, Smith, Street, & Hardy, 1986).

The Children's Defense Fund (1986) has concluded that programs combining knowledge–based sex education with direct contraceptive services, including counseling, will have a positive effect in reducing pregnancies. In addition, the Children's Defense Fund proposes that teens need assistance in areas such as academic achievement and job preparation. Help in these areas increases teens' "life options" so that they are motivated to avoid pregnancy and work toward their life goals. Both types of interventions appear to be necessary for poor Black teens.

If programs aimed at preventing teen pregnancies are to be effective, more information is needed about the antecedents and correlates of adolescent sexual activity and pregnancy. Current knowledge of the consequences of adolescent pregnancy surpasses knowledge about its antecedents (Jorgensen et al., 1980). Knowledge about antecedents should be placed in the context of normal development during adolescence in this society.

Implications for Future Research

To understand and ameliorate the problems associated with adolescent pregnancy, several demographic and psychological variables are in need of further study. More research is needed on Black adolescents. Researchers (e.g., Allen, 1978; McAdoo, 1981; Ogbu, 1981) strongly urge studying Black populations in context rather than in comparison to other subcultural groups. The factors leading adolescents to place themselves at risk for pregnancy are likely to be different for Black and White adolescents. Pregnancy outcomes also differ for the two groups. A range of socioeconomic levels should be included in research or, at the least, researchers should provide information about the socioeconomic status of their subjects. Some problems related to adolescent pregnancy may be due to poverty rather than the mother's age alone. The effects of race, class, and maternal age are confounded in many studies.

Both males and females need to be included in research and the dyadic relationship between them should be emphasized. The male may play a major role in the contraceptive methods adolescents prefer and most females report a stable male partner. Early, middle, and late adolescence should be studied. Some research has included the entire age range of adolescence without reporting data separately for young adolescents. Because samples often are taken from family planning or abortion clinics, the number of young adolescents is small. Pregnancy in young adolescents is the more serious problem and should be distinguished from pregnancy in older adolescents.

Although recruitment of a sample outside a clinic setting or a college campus may be difficult, more research is needed on less select populations. Prospective longitudinal research is needed that assesses the normal development of sexual and related social behavior during the adolescent years and that allows follow-up comparisons of teens who become pregnant with those who do not. Studying teens who are pregnant or seeking contraceptives misses much of adolescent development. Adolescent pregnancy needs to be understood in the context of the normal developmental tasks of adolescence, including the acquisition of a stable identity as an adult male or female, the development of close relationships with same- and opposite-sex peers, and preparation for career and life goals.

A most difficult task in reducing the negative outcomes of adolescent pregnancy will be for adults to come to terms with standards for sexual behavior. Adolescents need appropriate adult models and clear standards. Changing standards for adult sexual behavior and childbearing, combined with ambiguous standards for adolescent sexual behavior, lead to confusion for the adolescent. If adults could convey more straightforward and realistic guidelines, the socialization of adolescents into responsible expressions of sexuality might proceed in a less conflict–ridden manner.

Teen pregnancy requires problem–solving at many levels: the individual, the dyad, the family, the school, the community. Social–structural change also is required. Adolescents whose future holds only poverty and the most menial work may see little gain in delaying childbearing. Effective contraception and abstinence do not comprise a complete solution. Adolescents need a reason, as well as the capacity, to delay parenthood. Adolescence as a stage of development exists so that young, biologically mature individuals can have a protracted period of preparation for adult roles in a complex, technological society. Some Black adolescents may not foresee legitimate, valued adult roles for themselves. As a major advocacy group (Children's Defense Fund, 1985, p. 3) argues, the "best contraceptive is a real future".

References

Alan Guttmacher Institute (1981). *Teenage pregnancy: The problem that hasn't gone away*. New York: Author.

Allen, W. R. (1978). The search for applicable theories of Black family life. *Journal of Marriage and the Family, 40*, 117-129.

Allen, J. (1980). *Managing teen pregnancy: Access to abortion, contraception, and sex education*. New York: Praeger Press.

Badger, E., & Burns, D. (1980). Impact of a parent education program on the personal development of teen-age mothers. *Journal of Pediatric Psychology, 5*, 415-422.

Baldwin, W. H. (1983). Statement. In U.S. House of Representatives, *Teen parents and their children: Issues and programs*. Hearings before the Select Committee on Children, Youth, and Families, July 20, 1983. Washington: U.S. Government Printing Office.

Baldwin, W. H. (1984). Adolescent pregnancy and childbearing—rates, trends and research findings from the CPR, NICHD. Demographic and Behavioral Sciences Branch, Center for Population Research.

Barret, R., & Robinson, B. (1982). Teenage fathers: neglected too long. *Social Work, 27*, 484-488.

Belmont, L., Cohen, P., Dryfoos, J., Stein, Z., & Zayac, S. (1981). Maternal age and children's intelligence. In K. Scott, T. Field, and E. Robertson (Eds.), *Teenage Parents and Their Offspring* (pp. 177-194). New York: Grune & Stratton.

Block, R., & Block, S. (1980). Outreach education. A possible prevention of teenage pregnancy., *Adolescence, 15*, 657-659.

Brann, E., Edwards, L., Callicott, T., Story, E., Berg, P., Mahoney, J., Stine, J., Hixson, A. (1979). Strategies for the prevention of pregnancy in adolescents. *Advances in Planned Parenthood, 14*, 68-76.

Broman, S. H. (1981). Longterm development of children born to teenagers. In K. Scott, T. Field, and E. Robertson (Eds.), *Teenage Parents and Their Offspring* (195-224). New York: Grune & Stratton.

Brooks-Gunn, J., & F.F. Furstenberg (1986). The children of adolescent mothers: Physical, academic, and psychological outcomes. *Developmental Review,6*, 224-251.

Brown, J. D. (1985). Race and gender in rock video. *Social Science Newsletter* (Available from Institute for Research in Social Science, University of North Carolina, Chapel Hill), *70*, 82-86.

Brown, P. (1983). The Swedish approach to sex education and adolescent pregnancy: Some impressions. *Family Planning Perspectives, 2*, 90-95.

Burton, L. M., & Bengston, V. L. (1985). Black grandmothers: Issues of timing and continuity of roles. In V. L. Bengston & J. F. Robertson (Eds.), *Grandparenthood* (pp. 61-79). Beverly Hills, Ca: Sage.

Card, J., & Wise, L. (1978). Teenage mothers and teenage fathers: The impact of early childbearing on the parents' personal and professional lives. *Family Planning Perspectives, 10*, 199-205.

Children's Defense Fund (1985). *Preventing children having children*. Washington, D. C.: Author.

Children's Defense Fund (1986). *Preventing adolescent pregnancy: What schools can do*. Washington, D.C.: Author.

Children's Defense Fund (1987). *Child support and teen parents*. Washington, D.C.: Author.

Children's Defense Fund (1988). *Teenage pregnancy: An advocate's guide to the numbers*. Washington, D.C.: Author.

Chilman, C. (1980). Social and psychological research concerning adolescent childbearing: 1970-1980. *Journal of Marriage and the Family, 42*, 793-805.

Chilman, C. (1983). *Adolescent Sexuality in a Changing American Society*. New York: John Wiley & Sons.

Clark, S. D., Zabin, L. S., & Hardy, J. B. (1984). Sex, contraception and parenthood: Experience and attitudes among urban Black young men. *Family Planning Perspectives, 16*, 77-82.

Colletta, N. D. (1981). Social support and the risk of maternal rejection by adolescent mothers. *The Journal of Psychology, 109*, 191-197.

Colletta, N. D., Hadler, S., & Gregg, C. H. (1981). How adolescents cope with the problems of early motherhood. *Adolescence 16*, 499-512.

Cummings, J. (1983, November 20). Breakup of Black family imperils gains of decades. *The New York Times*, pp.35-36.

Cvetkovich, G., and Grote, B. (1980). Psychosocial development and the social problem of illegitimacy. In C. S. Chilman (Ed.), *Adolescent Pregnancy and Childbearing: Findings from Research* (pp. 15-41) Washington, D.C.: U.S. Department of Health and Human Services.

Cvetkovich, G., Grote, B., Lieberman, E. J. & Miller, W. (1978). Sex role development and teenage fertility-related behavior. *Adolescence, 13*, 231-236.

Dash, L. (1986, January 26-January 31). At risk: Chronicles of teen-age pregnancy [six-day series]. *Washington Post*.

DeAmicis, L. A., Klorman, R., Hess, D. W., & McAnarney, R. (1981). A comparison of unwed pregnant teenagers and nonpregnant sexually active adolescents seeking contraception. *Adolescence, 16*, 11-20.

de Anda, D. (1982). Pregnancy in early and late adolescence. *Journal of Youth and Adolescence, 12*, 33-43.

Dott, A. B., & Fort, A. T. (1976). Medical and social factors affecting early teenage pregnancy. *American Journal of Obstetrics and Gynecology, 125*, 532-536.

Earls, F., & Siegel, B. (1980). Precocious fathers. *American Journal of Orthopsychiatry, 50,* 469-480.
Edwards, L. E., Steinman, M. E., Arnold, K. A., & Hakanson, E. Y. (1981). Adolescent pregnancy prevention services in high school clinics. In Furstenberg, R. Lincoln, & J. Menken (Eds.) *Teenage sexuality, pregnancy, and childbearing* (pp. 372-381). Philadelphia: Temple University Press.
Eiduson, B. T. (1980). Contemporary single mothers. In L. G. Katz (Ed.), *Current topics in early childhood education.* Norwood, N.J.: Ablex.
Everett, B. (1984). Adolescent pregnancy. *Washington Report: Society for Research in Child Development. 1(2).*
Fine, A., Adams-Taylor, S., Miller, C. A., & Schorr, L. B. (1984). Monitoring the health of America's children. Child Health Outcomes Project, University of North Carolina, Chapel Hill.
Finkel, M. L., & Finkel, D. J. (1981). Sexual and contraceptive knowledge, attitudes, and behavior of male adolescents. In F. Furstenberg, R. Lincoln, & J. Menken (Eds.), *Teenage Sexuality, Pregnancy, and Childbearing* (pp. 327-335). Philadelphia: Temple University Press.
Freeman, W. W., Rickels, K., Huggins, G. R., Mudd, E. H., Garcia, C. R., & Dickens, H. O. (1980). Adolescent contraceptive use: Comparison of male and female attitudes and information. *American Journal of Public Health, 70,* 790-797.
Furstenberg, F. F. (1976a). The social consequences of teenage parenthood. *Family Planning Perspectives, 8,* 148-164.
Furstenberg, F. F. (1976b). *Unplanned parenthood: The social consequences of teenage childbearing.* New York: Free Press.
Furstenberg, F. F., Brooks-Gunn, J., & Morgan, S.P. (1987). *Adolescent mothers in later life.* Cambridge: Cambridge University Press.
Furstenberg, F. F., & Crawford, A. G. (1978). Family support: Helping mothers to cope. *Family Planning Perspectives, 10,* 322-333.
Furstenberg, F. F., & Spanier, G. B. (1984). *Recycling the family: Remarriage after divorce.* Beverly Hills, CA: Sage.
Gabriel, A. & McAnarney, E. R. (1983). Parenthood in two subcultures: White, middle-class couples and Black, low-income adolescents in Rochester, New York. *Adolescence, 18,* 595-608.
Gallup, A. (1985). The 17th annual Gallup poll of the public's attitudes toward the public schools. *Phi Delta Kappan, 67,* 35-47.
Gray, S. W., & Ramsey, B. K. (1986). Adolescent childbearing and high school completion. *Journal of Applied Developmental Psychology, 7,* 167-179.
Hansson, R. O., Jones, W. H., and Chernovetz, M. E. (1979). Contraceptive knowledge: Antecedents and implications. *Family Coordinator, 28,* 29-34.
Haskins, W. J. (1984, November). What about teenage fathers? *Essence, 15,* No. 7.
Harris, L., Kagay, M. R., & Leichenko, S. (1985). *Public attitudes about sex education, family planning, and abortion in the United States* (Study No. 854005). New York: Louis Harris and Associates.
Height, D. I. (1985, March). What must be done about children having children. *Ebony,* pp. 76-84.
Hendricks, L. (1980). Unwed adolescent fathers: Problems they face and their sources of social support. *Adolescence, 15,* 861-869.
Hendricks, L. (1983). Suggestions for reaching unmarried adolescent fathers. *Child Welfare, 62,* 141-146.

Hendricks, L., & Fullilove, R. (1983). Locus of control and the use of contraception among unmarried Black adolescent fathers and their controls: A preliminary report. *Journal of Youth & Adolescence, 12,* 225-233.

Hendricks, L., Howard, C., & Caesar, P. (1981). Help seeking behavior among select population of Black unmarried adolescent fathers: Implications for human service agencies. *American Journal of Public Health, 71,* 733-735.

Hendricks, L., Montgomery, R., & Fullilove, R. (1984). Educational achievement and locus of control among Black adolescent fathers. *Journal of Negro Education, 53,* 182-188.

Herceg-Baron, R., Furstenberg, F. F., Shea, J., & Harris, K. M. (1986). Supporting teenagers' use of contraceptives: A comparison of clinic services. *Family Planning Perspectives, 18,* 61-66.

Hofferth, S. L., Kahn, J. R., & Baldwin, W. (1987). Premarital sexual activity among U.S. teenage women over the past three decades. *Family Planning Perspectives, 19,* 46-53.

Johnson, L. B., & Staples, R. E. (1979). Family planning and the minority male: A pilot project. *The Family Coordinator, 28,* 535-543.

Jones, A. E., & Placek, P. J. (1981). Teenage women in the United States: Sex, contraception, pregnancy, fertility, and maternal and infant health. In T. Ooms (Ed.), *Teenage pregnancy in a family context* (pp. 9-48). Philadelphia: Temple University Press.

Jones, E. F., Forrest, J. D., & Goldman, N., Henshaw, S. K., Lincoln, R., Rosoff, J. I., Westoff, C. F., & Wulf, L. (1985). Teenage pregnancy in developed countries: Determinants and policy implications. *Family Planning Perspectives, 17,* 53-62.

Jorgensen, S. R., & Alexander, S. J. (1983). Research on adolescent pregnancy-risk: Implications for sex education programs. *Theory into Practice, 22,* 125-133.

Jorgensen, S. R., King, S. L., & Torrey, B. A. (1980). Dyadic and social network influencing on adolescent exposure to pregnancy risk. *Journal of Marriage and the Family, 42,* 141-155.

Kantner, J. & Zelnik, (1972). M. Sexual experiences of young unmarried women in the U.S. *Family Planning Perspectives, 4,* 9-17.

Kellam, S., Ensminger, M. A., & Turner, J. (1977). Family structure and mental health of children. *Archives of General Psychiatry, 34,* 1012-1022.

Kenney, A., & Orr, M. T. (1984). Sex education: An overview of current programs, policies, and research. *Phi Delta Kappan, 65,* 491-496.Kirby, D. (1984). *Sexuality Education: An Evaluation of Programs and their Effects, An Executive Summary.* Mathtech, In. Arlington, Virginia.

Lancaster, J. B. (1986). Human adolescence and reproduction: An evolutionary perspective. In J.B. Lancaster & B.A. Hamburg (Eds.), *School-age pregnancy and parenthood: Biosocial dimensions* (pp. 17-38). New York: Aldine de Gruyter.

Lancaster, J. B., & Hamburg, B. A. (1986). The biosocial dimensions of school-age pregnancy and parenthood: An introduction. In J. B. Lancaster and B. A. Hamburg (Eds.), *School-age pregnancy and parenthood: Biosocial dimensions* (pp. 3-16). New York: Aldine de Gruyter.

Lerman, R. I. (1986). Who are the young absent fathers? *Youth and Society, 18,* 3-27.

Lester, B. M., Coll, C. T., & Sepkoski, C. (1983). A cross-cultural study of teenage pregnancy and neonatal behavior. In T. Field & A. Sostek (Eds.), *Infants Born at Risk*(pp. 147-172). New York: Grune & Statton.

Lewis, C. C. (1987). Minors' competence to consent to abortion. *American Psychologist, 42,* 84-88.
Marsiglio, W., & Mott, F. L. (1986). The impact of sex education on sexual activity, contraceptive use, and premarital pregnancy among American teenagers. *Family Planning Perspectives, 18,* 151-162.
McAdoo, H. P. (Ed.) (1981). *Black families.* Beverly Hills, Ca: Sage. McCormick, M. C., Shapiro, S., & Starfield, B. (1983). High-risk young mothers: Infant mortality and morbidity in four areas in the United States, 1973-1978. *American Journal of Public Health, 74,* 18-23.
McLaughlin, S. D., Grady, W. R., Billy, J. G., Landale, N. S., & Winges, L. D. (1986). The effects of the sequencing of marriage and first birth during adolescence. *Family Planning Perspectives, 18,* 12-18.
MacCorquodale, P. L. (1984). Gender roles and premarital contraception. *Journal of Marriage and the Family, 46,* 57-63.
Melton, G. B. (Ed.) (1986). *Adolescent abortion: Psychological and legal issues.* Lincoln: University of Nebraska Press.
Melton, G. B. (1987). Legal regulation of adolescent abortion: Unintended effects. *American Psychologist, 42,* 79-83.
Melton, G. B., & Russo, N. F. (1987). Adolescent abortion: Psychological perspectives on public policy. *American Psychologist, 42,* 69-72.
Menken, J. (1981). Health and social consequences of teenage childbearing. In F. Furstenberg, R. Lincoln, & J. Menken (Eds.), *Teenage sexuality, pregnancy, and childbearing.* Philadelphia: University of Pennsylvania Press.
Meriwether, L. (1984, April). The Black family in crisis: teenage pregnancy. *Essence, 14,* No. 12.
Moore, K. A. (1983). *Facts at a glance.* Washington, D.C.: The Urban Institute (Statistics compiled from the National Center for Health Statistics).
Moore, K. A. (1978). Teenage childbirth and welfare dependency. *Family Planning Perspectives, 10,* 233-235.
Moore, K. A., & Waite, L. J. (1977). Early childbearing and educational attainment. *Family Planning Perspectives, 9,* 220-225.
Morrison, D. M. (1985). Adolescent contraceptive behavior: A review. *Psychological Bulletin, 98,* 538-568.
Morrow, B. H. (1979). Elementary school performance of offspring of young adolescent mothers. *American Educational Research Journal, 16,* 423-429.
National Center for Health Statistics (1982). *Advance Report of Final Natality Statistics,* Vol. 33, No. 6, Supplement. Washington, D.C.: U.S. Dept. of Health and Human Services.
Ogbu, J. U. (1978). *Minority education and caste.* New York: Academic Press.
Ogbu, J. U. (1981). Origins of human competence: A cultural-ecological perspective. *Child Development, 52,* 413-429.
Ooms, T. (Ed.). (1981). *Teenage Pregnancy in a Family Context: Implications for Policy.* Philadelphia: Temple University Press.
Pauker, J. (1971). Fathers of children conceived out of wedlock. *Developmental Psychology, 2,* 215-218.
Polit, D. F., & Kahn, J. R. (1986). Early subsequent pregnancy among economically disadvantaged teenage mothers. *American Journal of Public Health, 76,* 167-171.
Presser, H. B. (1980). Sally's corner: Coping with unmarried motherhood. *Journal of Social Issues, 36,* 107-129.

Special Topics: Pregnancy and Parenting

Reid, P. T. (1982). Socialization of Black female children. In P. Berman & E. Ramey (Eds.), *Women: A developmental perspective*, (pp. 137-155). Washington, D.C.: U.S. Department of Health and Human Services.

Roche, A. F. (1979) Secular trends in human growth, maturation, and development. *Monographs of the Society for Research in Child Development*, 44 (Whole No. 179).

Rogel, M. J., Zuehlke, M., Petersen, A., Tobin-Richards, M. & Shelton, M. (1980). Contraceptive behavior in adolescence: A decision making perspective. *Journal of Youth and Adolescence, 9*, 491-506.

Rosen, R. A., Martindale, L. and Griselda, M. (1976). *Pregnancy Study Report*. Detroit, MI: Wayne State University.

Rosenbaum, S. (1985). A manual: On providing effective prenatal care programs for teens. The Children's Defense Fund's Adolescent Pregnancy Prevention/Prenatal Care Campaign. The Children's Defense Fund, Washington, D.C.

Scales, P. (1977). Males and morals: Teenage contraceptives behavior amid the double standard. *The Family Coordinator, 26*, 211-222.

Scott-Jones, D., & Nelson-Le Gall, S. (1986). Defining Black families: Past and present. In E. Seidman & J. Rappaport (Eds.), *Redefining social problems*, (pp. 83-100). New York: Plenum.

Scott-Jones, D., & Turner, S. L. (in press). Sex education, reproductive knowledge, and contraceptive knowledge among Black adolescent females. *Journal of Adolescent Research*.

Scott-Jones, D., & White, A. B. (in preparation). Correlates of sexual activity in early adolescence.

Segal, S. M. & DuCette, J. (1973). Locus of control and premarital high school pregnancy. *Psychological Reports, 33*, 887-890.

Select Committee on Children, Youth, and Families (U.S. House of Representatives), (1986). *Teen pregnancy: What is being done? A state-by-state look*. Washington, D.C.: U.S. Government Printing Office.

Simpkins, L. (1984). Consequences of teenage pregnancy and motherhood. *Adolescence, 19*, 39-54.

Sloan, L. (1982) Community development strategies for reducing adolescent pregnancy: A case study. *Family and Community Health, 5*, 73-80.

Sonenstein, F. L., and Pittman, K. J. (1984). The availability of sex education in large city school districts. *Family Planning Perspectives, 16*, 19-25.

Steinlauf, B. (1979). Problem-solving skills, locus of control and the contraceptive effectiveness of young women. *Child Development, 50*, 268-271.

Stevens, J. H. (1984). Black grandmothers' and Black adolescent mothers' knowledge about parenting. *Developmental Psychology, 20*, 1017-1025.

Stewart, M. W. (1981). Adolescent pregnancy: Status convergence for the well-socialized adolescent female. *Youth and Society, 12*, 443-464.

Sugar, M. (1980). The epidemic of adolescent motherhood. In Max Sugar, (Ed.) *Responding to adolescent needs* (pp. 199-214). Jamaica, NY: S. P. Scientific & Medical Books, Div. of Spectrum Publications.

Tanner, J. M. (1970). Physical growth. In P. H. Mussen (Ed.) *Carmichael's Manual of Child Psychology*. Vol.1, 3rd. ed. (pp. 77-156). New York: Wiley Publishers.

Tanner, J. M. (1975). Growth and endocrinology of the adolescent. In L. J. Gardner (Ed.), *Endocrine and Genetic Diseases of Childhood and Adolescence*, 2nd ed. (pp. 19-59). Philadelphia: W. B. Saunders.

Taylor, H., Kagay, M., & Leichenko, S. (1986). *American teens speak: Sex, myths, TV, and birth control (Project No. 864012)*. New York: Louis Harris.
Thompson, L. & Spanier, G. B. (1978). Influence of parents, peers, and partners on the contraceptive use of college men and women. *Journal of Marriage and the Family, 40*, 481-492.
Thompson, M. S. (1986). The influence of supportive relations on the psychological well-being of teenage mothers. *Social Forces, 64*, 1006-1024.
Trussell, J. & Menken, J. (1978). Early childbearing and subsequent fertility. *Family Planning Perspectives, 10*, 209-218.
Vaz, R., Smolen, P., & Miller, C. (1983). Adolescent pregnancy: Involvement of the male partner. *Journal of Adolescent Health Care, 4*, 246-250.
Ventura, S. (1985, April). *Recent trends and variations in births to unmarried women*. Paper presented at the meeting of the Society for Research in Child Development. Toronto, Canada.
Ventura, S., & Hendershort, G. (1984). Infant health consequences of childbearing by teenagers and older mothers. *Public Health Reports, 99*, 138-146.
Westney, O. E., Jenkins, R. R., Butts, J. D., & Williams, I. (1984). Sexual development and behavior in Black preadolescents. *Adolescence, 19*, 557-568.
Westoff, C. F., Calot, G., & Foster, A. D. (1983). Teenage fertility in developed nations: 1971-1980. *Family Planning Perspectives, 15*, 105-110.
Whalen, R. E. (1984). Secondary education: Student flows, course participation, and state requirements. In V. W. Plisko (Ed.), *The condition of education* (pp. 149-182). Washington, D.C.: U.S. Government Printing office.
Wilson, M. N. (1984). Mothers' and grandmothers' perceptions of parental behavior in three-generational Black families. *Child Development, 55*, 1333-1339.
Zabin, L. S. & Clark, S. D. (1981). Why they delay: A study of teenage family planning clinic patients. *Family Planning Perspectives, 13*, 205-217.
Zabin, L. S., Hirsch, M. B., Smith, E. A., Streett, R., & Hardy, J. B. (1986). Evaluation of a pregnancy prevention program for urban teenagers. *Family Planning Perspectives, 18*, 119-126.
Zabin, L. S., Kantner, J. F., & Zelnik, M. (1979). The risk of adolescent pregnancy in the first months of intercourse. *Family Planning Perspectives, 11*, 215-222.
Zelnik, M. & Kantner, J. F. (1980). Sexual activity, contraceptive use and pregnancy among metropolitan-area teenagers, 1971-1979. *Family Planning Perspectives, 12*, 230-237.
Zelnik, M., Kantner, J. F. & Ford, K. (1981). *Sex and pregnancy in adolescence*. Beverly Hills, Ca: Sage.
Zelnik, M. & Kim, Y. J. (1982). Sex education and its association with teenage sexual activity, pregnancy and contraceptive use. *Family planning perspectives, 14*, 117-126.

BLACK TEENAGE PARENTING: ISSUES AND CHALLENGES

Lawford L. Goddard and William E. Cavil III

Introduction

The literature on teenage pregnancy has consistently documented the undesirable long-term socioeconomic consequences of early childbearing, such as lower levels of education, arrested career development and greater dependency on public assistance for the teenage parent. In addition the emerging body of literature on the effects of early childbearing on the infants of teenage parents suggests that these infants are an at-risk population, both in terms of socio-emotional development and physical abuse and neglect.

Although little research exists on how prepared the teenage mother is to handle the role of parents, the general conclusion is that the relative disadvantaged status of the teenage parent—lower level of education, less viable socioeconomic status, in association with negative attitudes towards childrearing—produces unfavorable developmental outcomes in their offspring. For example, DeLissovoy (1973) found that teenage parents had limited knowledge and unrealistic expectations regarding developmental milestones. He also indicated that they held punitive childrearing attitudes. These negative parenting styles are said to be associated with low infant intellectual functioning. Furstenberg (1976) in a study of preschoolers born of teenage mothers indicated that these children were unable to complete the preschool inventory because of severe physical and psychological handicaps. In looking at 8th graders, Oppel and Royston (1971) have shown that children of teenage parents were more likely to be delayed in reading grade level and to exhibit more behavioral problems than children of older parents. Other scholars (c.f.: Belmont and Dryfoos, 1979; Bromen, 1979) have also documented the linkage that exists between early maternal age and lower IQ scores in their offspring.

In spite of the overwhelming evidence of the sparse literature, caution should be exercised in the acceptance of the negative perspective of parenting held by teenage parents. Field (1979) in a comparative study of Black teenage and adult parents found that despite the teenage mother's less optimal perception and attitudes, their offsprings did not differ from those of adult members on developmental assessments. In explaining this finding, Field suggests that the nature of the family support system, the availability of substitute caregivers and the infants' exposure to a wide range of playmates might have attenuated some of the developmental differences expected in this group of parents. In a similar vein, Stevens (1980) has documented the mediating role the family support system plays in stimulating infant development of teenage parents. Stevens notes that maternal behavior and the structure of the mothers' social networks were more predictive of how well the infant developed than the teen parents' knowledge of child developmental milestones.

The teenage pregnancy literature clearly indicates that assumption of the mothering role before these young women have completed their education and become integrated into the social structures of the adult world can, and often does, deprive teenage women of the many needed social and educational credentials as well as the social competencies necessary for success as an adult member of this society. In addition, the teenage parent is judged and labelled (in part due to the lack of adult competencies) as a social deviant. It is often implied that the teenage mother is a less fit parent. However, while this general assumption exists there is little information on how these young women raise their children, what parenting skills they have and what values they are imparting to their children.

"Parenting" and "childrearing" are the basic mechanisms humans use to prepare their young to meet the traditional expectations and contemporary challenges of their society as well as to be able to live in accordance with the social and cultural dictates of the time. The family represents the basic unit within which the socialization of the young takes place. It is within this context of human relations that the child is shaped and molded into a societal product. In essence the family unit operates as a system of development and transformation that allows its members to grow and change. In this process of development and transformation the family unit has to satisfy its: (1) Human Imperatives; (2) Cultural Prerequisites; and (3) Relational Essences (c.f., Nobles et al. 1985).

Human Imperatives are those processes and functions which must be performed in order for a people to continue as a social group. These processes are the act of procreation, the provision of sustenance, the provision of shelter and/or protection, the provision of recuperative time and space and developmental guidelines. Cultural Prerequisites are processes, functions and attributes which emerge from a people's "sense of being" and which represent the cultural imprint of that particular cultural group. Some of the African–American cultural prerequisites are the sense of family, the sense of history, spirituality, the significance of names and naming, the importance of signs· and symbols and the use of sound and rhythm. Relational Essences are the dimensions of human functioning characterized by interactive and reciprocal processes and relationships which upon being satisfied result in the sense of human well-being. The relational essences are the sense of biological integrity, the sense of efficacy, the sense of intimacy and the sense of permanence.

In raising their children it should be obvious that teenage parents are faced with the same developmental and transformational task as other parents. However, their situation is aggravated by new and complex social, economic, cultural, legal and political processes that impinge on the teenage parent.

Human Imperatives

In preparing her child to meet the traditional expectations of the society the teenage parent has to satisfy the Human Imperatives and master certain parenting skills. At a minimum the primary Human Imperative facing the teenage parent is to provide basic support for the child. The teenage parent has to provide sustenance (food) and shelter and protection (security) for the child to survive in the first place. That is the teenage parent has to provide for the satisfaction of the physiological needs of the child so that she can grow and develop physically. While catering to the physical development of the child, the teenage parent has to also ensure the social development of the child through the provision of developmental guidelines (education). Social development entails the establishment of a sense of emotional security in the child. Thus, the teenage parent has to provide love, understanding and compassion and has to respond to the call of the child. In this way the child can begin to develop a sense of trust, to know that a familiar and loved one will be there when needed. This initial development of the sense of trust forms the basis for the establishment of bonding ties that ultimately integrate the child into the social space in which she is located. The establishment of the sense of security is related to the broadening of the child's horizons and the development of sociability. That is, the child has to learn how to interact with, and relate to, others on a social level. These social skills represent an integral component of the child's ability to master and manipulate the environment in which he is located. In promoting the social development of the child the teenage parent is also instilling in the child the sense of intimacy and the sense of permanence.

The parent has to address the psychological development of the child. The teenage parent has to help the child to develop his/her mind, to take interest in things around him/her in such a way that learning becomes an integral part of the daily rounds of activities in the world of the parent and the child. At the same time the parent has to help the child to develop a sense of confidence in themselves so that they believe that they can succeed in new and different situations. Thus, the parent has to develop confident and competent children. Parents must also expose children to new and novel situations so that learning can be expanded. These processes instill in the child a sense of efficacy, a belief that she can influence and shape his/her environment.

Cultural Prerequisites

The teenage parent is also faced with the task of imparting the cultural substance of the group to the child. In essence culture is a process that provides people with a general design for living and patterns for interpreting their reality (c.f., Nobles, 1985). It is in the parenting process that the cultural orientation of what is appropriate or not, what is acceptable or not, what is important and of value becomes transmitted to the new generation. Through his process the child comes to acquire the cultural dictates of the society in which she is located. The task of cultural transmission for Black teenage parents becomes complex in that the teenage parent is confronted with two distinct and competing cultural perspectives. On the one hand is the traditional Black culture which stresses values of compassion, cooperation, humaneness, and respect for self and others. Within the Black cultural spectrum the individual self becomes the collective self. On the other hand is contemporary American culture which stresses competition, individualism and survival of the fittest. Within this orientation the individual self is separate and distinct from the other units that comprise the whole. The dilemma for the teenage parent is to make a choice between these two competing orientations. On the one hand she sees the American orientation associated with the material vestiges of success and power, while on the other hand her traditional upbringing suggests that these should not take precedence over human compassion. The result of this dilemma is that the Black teenage parent is often confused about what type of values and cultural orientations to transmit to her child.

The particular manner in which the general issues of parenting are handled is determined by the concrete conditions in which a people is located and the cultural substance of that particular group. For Black teenage parents the issue is confounded by the cultural conflict between traditional Black culture and contemporary American culture.

When one examines the concrete conditions of the overall Black community in America one startling conclusion becomes inescapable. The conclusion is that the so-called "gains of the sixties" are unmistakably illusions. For example in 1983 the Black unemployment rate (17.8%) was more than double the overall unemployment rate (8.1%). The median income for Black families ($13,267) is less than 60% of the median income for White families and one out of every three Black Americans is living below the official government poverty index. A Black child's chances of living in poverty are four times greater than that of a White

Black Teenage Parenting: Issues and Challenges

child and in 1983 41% of all Black families were single–parent female–headed households. While Black babies are twice as likely to be born with low birth weights than White babies and experience an infant mortality rate twice as high as White babies, Black men and women still die at a younger age than their White counterparts. The school dropout rate among young Blacks is 17.3% and as recently as 1980 Blacks comprised 41% of all students labelled as educable mentally retarded.

For a Black teenage parent the concrete condition is even worse. Latest unemployment data indicate that 49% of Black male and 47% of Black female teenagers were unemployed. The Black teenage parent is usually unemployed or works intermittently with low wages and limited chances of occupational mobility. The consequence of this is that the teenage parent is likely to live in poverty. Thus the ability of these parents to provide the basic requirements of food, shelter and clothing is severely limited given their poor economic resources.

Given the overall condition of Black America, the emergent increase in teenage pregnancy and adolescent parenthood only aggravates and intensifies an already deteriorating circumstance. According to Census data 63,000 Black children (6% of all Black children) were living in households maintained by a head under 20 years. Of these 63,000 children 83% were living in female–headed households. Given the general poor economic conditions of teenage parents, these children face a less than auspicious start to their lives in terms of the ability of their parents to satisfy the requirements of family development and transformation.

For example, the ability of the teenage parent to provide a sense of security and stability in the lives of their children is limited by their economic conditions which result in a high degree of residential mobility. In a four–year study of Black Adolescent Familyhood conducted by the Institute for the Advanced Study of Black Family Life and Culture, it was found that in the first year of life of the child the teenage parent had an average of three (3) physical moves, that is change of addresses and six (6) changes of telephone number. Most of the teenage parents in this study could not maintain a telephone in their residence. High residential mobility reflects the high level of stress that the Black teenage parent experiences in the early years of the life of her child. With this condition of stress the requirements of security and stability in the life of the child would be affected and might impair the development of trust and bonding ties in the child. The change and, in most cases, lack of telephone seem to mark the beginning of the social isolation of the teenage parent. In the absence of a telephone the teenage parent seems to be locked into a social world that centers around the child with little or no external social contacts.

In terms of isolation and attenuated development, follow–up studies of teenage pregnancy indicate that one out of every four teenage mothers lives in households where they are the only adult (c.f., Furstenberg and Crawford, 1978). Even more devastating is the fact that teenage parents frequently begin childrearing as the only "adult" at home and are at risk of becoming and remaining the only adult in the household as long as 15 years after the child's birth (Kellum et al., 1982). In fact, Kellum and his associates concluded from their analysis of social involvement that mother aloneness is the long–term common outcome of teenage mothering regardless of the family structure.

The impact of this condition is two–fold. First, a growing body of literature suggests that "social and familial" isolation is related to poorer psychological status and poorer health for individuals so defined. Cutler (1973) and Janowitz (1976) even suggest that the social isolation of individuals also has negative consequences for the stability and social and political order of society. The alone–at–home social isolation of teenage parents can be related to both the poorer psychological and health status of this at-risk population. Secondly, the condition is resulting in the negative evolution of the Black family structure, given the relative youthfulness of the Black population and the increase in teenage parenting. This could ultimately result in the deterioration of the very system which society depends upon to encourage and stimulate the human potential of its member.

Relational Essences

A major difficulty of Black teenage parents is that they are confused as to who they are and where they are going. On the one hand, they seem to have unconsciously accepted the notion that "racism is dead", yet they are being confronted with the same "real" inequality which faced their parents and grandparents. On the one hand there are the myth makers who are popularizing the notion that things have become, and are becoming, better for Black Americans; on the other is the stark reality of unemployment, poverty and inequality. As a result of the real material conditions and the unreal illusions of progress, Black Americans are becoming confused as to what values to transmit to the younger generations. Already there is a subtle shift in value orientations among Black Americans. The Black Adolescent Familyhood Study of the Institute has shown, for example, that Black teenage parents hold a parenting orientation that differed significantly from that of older parents in many critical areas. Although both groups of parents recognized the importance of compassion and a sense of humaneness in governing interpersonal relationships, the older parents placed a heavier emphasis on these than the younger parents. In line with this subtle shift in value orientation more of the teenage parents (70% vs 30%) espoused an individualistic value orientation believing that their own success was more important than helping others. In terms of the mode of social interaction, the older

Black Teenage Parenting: Issues and Challenges

parents placed more emphasis on respect as the dominant mode than the teenage parents. These data indicate that more and more the traditional Black cultural perspective is being eroded and replaced by a more individualistic orientation that has tremendous implication for the way in which children are being raised.

Traditionally Black parenting has been based on an orientation that is geared to develop spontaneity and adaptability in Black children. It is an orientation which places heavy emphasis on compassion, respect for others, cooperation and the recognition of the collective well–being. These values, attitudes and skills represent both the cultural substance of the Black population and the current strategies for mediating and manipulating the material conditions in which we live. Ultimately it is the perception of the nature of the material conditions of the society which results in parents adopting what their own parents did or changing and adapting different parenting techniques to match the perceived "new conditions". For Black teenage parents in particular the misperception of the concrete conditions is leading to the adoption of a different parenting technique that ultimately affects the stability of the family unit.

For example while legally considered an adult, the Black teenage parent is not automatically conferred that status within the Black community. Our data from the Black Adolescent Familyhood Study indicate that the birth of the child did not automatically confer on the teenager the status of adult. In the developmental cycle within Black culture the transition from childhood to adulthood does not occur with the birth of a child. The teenage parent has a new status of parent, but not "grown" (adult). She has to demonstrate to the family and community that she possesses the abilities and skills of an adult before that status is conferred upon her. The implication of this cultural perspective is a complex psycho–social condition for the Black teenage parent of being an adult (in the legal sense) and not an adult (in the cultural sense) at the same time. This status confusion could become the source of tension and conflict within the family, given one's cultural perspective. Within the Black cultural perspective it is common for the teenage parent to "learn to parent" from her own parent; that is the teenage parent relinquishes some control over the raising of her child to her parent or other older relative while she acquires the skills to raise her own child. Ultimately the teenage parent accepts and assumes the responsibilities for raising her child (she now functions as an adult) while the child can grow and develop within the protection of the wider family unit. This process of "parenting by apprenticeship" worked effectively when all members of the family unit accepted the fundamental cultural belief in the oneness or collective nature of the family entity. However, to the extent that the Black teenage parent accepts an alternative cultural perspective that places heavy emphasis on individual rights and comes to believe in her status of adult without the requisite skills of

Special Topics: Pregnancy and Parenting

an adult, then tension and conflict develops within the family unit (Nobles, et al., 1985).

In summary, the data from the Black Adolescent Familyhood Study indicate that the family of origin plays a critical role in easing the transition from childhood to parenthood and ultimately to adulthood; that the male partner represents a critical component of the teenage mother's support system and that he provides valuable psychological and pragmatic support, although he could not undertake the financial responsibility for the rearing of the child; that the teenage parent is often socially isolated with few interpersonal contacts beyond the immediate family; and that the teenage parent experiences a general sense of boredom with lots of free time which is spent mainly watching television. Critical issues identified by the teenage parents were concerns about values and value orientation, knowledge of child developmental milestones, role conflict/confusion and basic life skills (e.g. household management, budgeting, efficient shopping, etc.). Ultimately, this data base indicates that as a result of changes in value orientation, bonds to parents and family can be threatened for the Black teenage parent. The result of this process is that the necessary undertaking of childrearing can be, and is being, seriously damaged.

Toward A Solution

In response to the general problems that the Black teenage parent is confronting and in recognition of the necessity to change and ameliorate the psychosocial problems of Black teenage parents, the Institute for the Advanced Study of Black Family Life and Culture has developed a unique and innovative program for teenage parents. Funded in part by the Rosenberg and Women's Foundations of San Francisco, this effort created a working partnership between the professional staff of the Institute and a subset of teenage parents who were identified as belonging to successfully coping families. In this collaborative effort the task was to take the insights of the teenage parents regarding those processes which they perceived as beneficial to them and to shape them into a form that could be shared with other teenage parents.

Based on this activity the Institute developed a Black Teenage Parenting and Early Childhood Education Curriculum (Nobles et al., 1985) to address the issues identified by the teenage parents and reflected in the general teen pregnancy literature. The Curriculum was developed specifically to advance the state of the art in Black teenage parenting. In so doing we expect to affect teenage pregnancy and parenting by sharing with Black teens the responsibility for shaping what happens to them. In effect this project gave these young women the responsibility for identify-

Black Teenage Parenting: Issues and Challenges

ing and creating solutions to the difficulties of teenage parenthood. In going through the training Curriculum the teenage parent has the novel experience of preparing and planning for issues and concerns associated with their unique position of being Black, young and a parent, all at the same time. This project, in essence, forced the teenage parents to consciously consider the necessary ingredients for raising healthy children and experiencing positive family life (Nobles, et al., 1985).

The Black teen parent training curriculum is delivered in modular form and consists of six distinct modules. The six modules are: (1) Cultural Heritage and Racial Identity; (2) Being a Parent and a Child Simultaneously; (3) Family Interdependence and Self–Reliance; (4) Problem Solving and Decision Making Skills; (5) Capacity Building and Competency Acquisition; and (6) Broadening One's Horizons.

Within each module specific issues of concerns are addressed as units. For example in the Cultural Heritage and Racial Identity module the specific issues of concerns are identified as "Black Family Structures and Cultural Styles" and "Black Parenting Techniques". In the Broadening One's Horizons Module the specific issues addressed are: Maximizing Self, Child and Family Potential, The World of Work and One's Lifestyle and Future. The six modules yield a total of twenty (20) separate issues that are covered in the training curriculum. For each issue a general objective is specified. In addressing the "Black Parenting Techniques" issue, for example, the general objective would be to "provide the teenage parent with the traditional childrearing techniques used by Black parents". Specific objectives are then developed for each general objective, the learning activity is specified, the teaching aids and source materials described and the outcome measures are defined.

The core curriculum was then used to develop a daily lesson plan framework that would guide the training program. The daily lesson plan specifies the actual steps to be taken in the training program and details the process of training in greater detail.

Each module can be given separately and covers a unique aspect of the reality world of the teenage parent. However, the richness and uniqueness of the curriculum lies in its ability to integrate the six modules into a coherent package addressing the unique reality world of the Black teenage parent from a culturally consistent perspective.

The model of the training program calls for the training of a group of teenage parents who would then go into the homes of other teenage parents to train them on the basic curriculum plan. Through this experience the teenage parents acquire skills and expertise around parenting that they in turn impart to other teenage parents. This training process has the potential of ultimately (1) reducing the sense of social isolation experienced by the teenage parent, (2) broadening their horizons by providing new skills, and (3) ultimately reducing the prospects for being "at risk" of child abuse and neglect.

Special Topics: Pregnancy and Parenting

The Institute has completed the first cycle of the Black teenage parent training project. We have trained a select group of teenage parents in the use of the curriculum plan. Their experiences in the training phase has, in fact, greatly enhanced their own parenting skills. In the next phase of the project the teenage trainers will begin to train other teenage parents.

The success of this training program ultimately reflects the fact that Black teenage parents, if given a chance to share in, and become a part of, a positive experience, have the ability to author their own destiny and change their own lives. It is clear that in today's society the teenage parent has a heavy burden to carry and that the odds are stacked against her succeeding. Yet in spite of these conditions some Black teenage parents do succeed and raise healthy, confident and competent Black children. It is our belief that the Black Teenage Parenting and Early Childhood Education Curriculum would provide the framework for most, if not all, Black teenage parents to improve their parenting skills, reduce pregnancy recidivism and become more effective parents.

References

Belmont, L. & Dryfoos, J. (1979). Long term development of children born to New York City teenagers. In R. K. Scott, T. Field, & E. Robertson (Eds.). *Teenage parents and their offspring*. New York: Grune and Stratton.

Bromen, S. (1979). Seven year outcome of 4,000 children born to teenagers in the United States. In R. K. Scott, T. Field, & E. Robertson (Eds.).

Cutler, S. J. (1973). Voluntary association membership and the theory of mass society. In E. V. Lauman (Ed.). *Bonds of pluralism: The form and substance of urban social networks*. New York: Wiley.

DeLissovoy, V. (1973). Childcare by adolescent parents. *Children Today. 2*, 22–25.

Field, T. M. (1979). Teenage lower class, Black mothers and their pre–term infants: An intervention and developmental follow–up. Unpublished manuscript.

Furstenberg, F. F. (1976). The social consequences of teenage pregnancy. *Family Planning Perspectives. 8*, 148–164.

Furstenberg, F. F., & Crawford, A. G. (1978). Family support: Helping teenage mothers to cope. *Family Planning Perspectives. 10*, 322–333.

Janowitz, M. (1976). *Social control of welfare state* New York: Elsevier.

Kellam, S. G., Adams, R. G., Brown, C. H., & Ensminger, M. E. (1982). The long–term evolution of the family structure of teenage and older mothers. *Journal of Marriage and the Family*. 539–554.

Nobles, W. W. (1985). *Africanity and the black family: The development of a theoretical Model*. Oakland: Black Family Institute Publication.

Nobles, W. W., Goddard, L. L. & Cavil, W. E. (1986). *The Km Ebit Husia: Authoritative utterances of exceptional insight for the Black family*. Oakland, Black Family Institute Publication.

Nobles, W. W., Goddard, L. L., & Cavil, W. (1985). Black teenage parenting and early childhood education: Basic Curriculum Plan, Oakland, CA: A Black Family Institute Publication.

Oppel, W., & Royston, A. B. (1971). Teenage births: Some social, psychological and physical sequelae. *American Journal of Public Health, 6,* 751–756.

Stevens, J. H. (1980). Teenage mothers' social network and Black infant development. Paper presented at the Southeastern Conference on Human Development, Alexandria, Virginia.

SUBSTANCE USE AND BLACK YOUTH: IMPLICATIONS OF CULTURAL AND ETHNIC DIFFERENCES IN ADOLESCENT ALCOHOL, CIGARETTE, AND ILLICIT DRUG USE

Edward G. Singleton

Throughout the history of the world people have used drugs for nonmedical reasons. Annual estimates of the extent of substance use in the United States during recent years have shown that history continues to repeat itself (NIAAA, 1982; NIDA, 1979a; Nobles, 1984; USPHS, 1979, 1980b). Two–thirds of the U.S. adult population drinks alcoholic beverages, one–third are cigarette smokers, and at least 68% are occasional users of marijuana. Five million Americans use cocaine, one–half million use heroin and 20% of the population take stimulants, sedatives, or tranquilizers for nonmedical purposes.

Some of the serious consequences linked to substance use (APA, 1980; Gropper, 1985; USPHS, 1979) include incarceration, poor health, family disruption, and impairments in social and occupational functioning. In addition to the severe personal costs of drug use, there are costs to the nation, such as increased crime rates, the economic burden of subsidized medical and mental health care, and the accidental or intentional death of members of American society.

For example, studies have identified cigarette smoking as the largest preventable factor contributing to morbidity, disability, and death in the United States (Telch, Killen, McAllister, Perry, and Maccoby, 1982; USPHS, 1979). Nine to ten million Americans suffer from alcoholism each year, while 16% of the U.S. population experience some problem as the result of alcohol use (APA, 1980; Lachter & Weisman, 1980; Mahoney, 1980). Annually, more than 25,000 traffic fatalities and 35,000 suicides, homicides, and deaths from alcohol–related diseases (e.g., cirrhosis) are attributable to alcohol use. Forty million families each year are affected by alcohol and other drug use, and substance users account for approximately 50% of the five million annual arrests.

Furthermore, Dupont (1978) indicated that approximately 250,000 people per year receive treatment for drug abuse problems in clinics and other facilities in the United States. Two–thirds of the people admitted to these programs are treated for heroin dependence. After heroin, the most frequently reported problems are marijuana, barbituates, and amphetamines. Overall, the annual costs to society for the care of substance–related problems amount to more than $136 billion.

Because of the possibility that the early onset of alcohol and other drug use is associated with problems later in life, substance use in adolescents has become an important area of research. Moreover, adolescent substance use and adult substance use have been viewed as different phenomenona (Bennett, 1983; Varenhorst, 1984). Varenhorst defined the major tasks of adolescence as experiencing sexual maturity, developing one's individuality, forming social commitments, separation and autonomy, outgrowing egocentrism, and reevaluating values. At this stage of development drug use might further disrupt the life situation of youth in the precarious process of moving from childhood to becoming adults.

More importantly, recent estimates of the rates of substance use among youth in America reflected the highest levels of drug use to be found among any industrialized nation in the world (Johnston, O'Malley, & Bachman, 1984). Alcoholic beverages particularly beer and wine, lead the list. They are used by the largest number of youth. (Caplovitz, 1980; Johnston et al., 1984; Lowman, Hubbard, Rachal, & Cavanaugh, 1981). Following alcoholic beverages, the substances most frequently used by adolescents are marijuana, cocaine and other stimulants, hallucinogens, and inhalants (Lowman & NCALI staff, 1982; NIDA, 1979b). Most marijuana users also use cigarettes, alcohol, or both. In fact, polydrug use (i.e., the use of two or more substances is more extensive among youth who drink.

Approximately 4,000 youth also become cigarette smokers each day (USPHS, 1979a). More than 20% of all youth aged 12–17 are regular smokers and, since 1965, the number of girls who initiate smoking has doubled. Additionally, the use of PCP, cocaine, heroin and other opiate use has markedly increased (Johnston et al., 1984).

Substance Use in Black Adolescents

Not surprisingly, substance use among adolescents has come to be considered a major problem for Blacks as well as Whites in the United States. But, is the extent of adolescent substance use different between Blacks and Whites? Behavioral and social scientists have accumulated evidence that the answer is—probably yes (Brunswick, 1977; Myers, 1977; Lowman, Hartford, and Kaelberg, 1983; Lowman, Hubbard, Rachal, & Cavanaugh, 1981; Lowman and NCALI Staff, 1981; Maddahian, Newcomb, and Bentler, 1985; Marel, 1977; Blane and Hewitt, 1977; Rachal, Guess, Hubbard, Maisto, Cavanaugh, Waddell and Benrud, 1980; Klatsky, Friedman, Seigelaub, & Gerard, 1977; Gibbs, 1984; NIDA, 1979b). Some researchers (Lex, 1985; King, 1982; Harper, 1976, 1977, 1979; Harper &

Dawkins, 1976) have, however, cautioned against overinterpreting the findings. Variations in research designs, sampling strategies, and within group differences (e.g., by age or grade, sex, socioeconomic status; or local, regional, and urban–rural differences) have been cited as some of the reasons for rendering the comparisons invalid.

In discussing the potential dangers of racial comparisons, Jenkins (1982) listed three reasons for asking questions about racial differences:
1. To find out where intervention is most needed.
2. To identify ways in which cultural groups respond differently to life situations and thus contribute to an understanding of the human condition.
3. To stigmatize Black people.

Some studies have demonstrated that Blacks have more pathology than Whites. Other studies have shown that Blacks have less pathology than Whites. Jenkins stressed that in either event a pejorative inference may be made. Much of the "literature (in consonance with American society) paints a view of the Black American as being deficient in the mental and emotional qualities that lead to productive and creative living". (pg. ix).

Thus, higher rates of illicit substance use and cigarette smoking among Black adolescents could be taken as evidence that they are "willing to take more risks" than White adolescents. Higher rates of alcohol abstinence might be interpreted as a sign that the "nervous systems of Black youth is less sensitive" than that of their White counterparts.

Conventional Models of Adolescent Substance Use

Models of adolescent substance use were proposed in several investigations of the psychological and social correlates of alcohol and other drug use. Most models focused on identifying patterns of deviance which predicted the initiation, continuation, or progression of adolescent substance use, irrespective of the ethnicity of the user. Three representative models have been selected for review: (a) problem behavior, (b) developmental stages (i.e., "gateway" theory), and (c) relative deviance.

Problem Behavior. The Jessor's (Jessor, 1979, Jessor & Jessor, 1977, 1978, 1980) have viewed substance use within the context of a general social-psychological framework of problem behavior and adolescent development. A model was developed to account for deviant behavior, particularly alcohol use, in a tri–ethnic community (Jessor, Graves, Hanson, & Jessor, 1968), but it was expanded to include other problem behavior among youth in general (e.g., sexual activity, lying, stealing, and aggression). Their model comprised a number of social and psychological concepts located in two major explanatory dimensions, the personality system and the perceived–environmental system.

The single unifying dimension underlying the differences between substance users and nonusers was termed "conventionality–unconventionality". Thus, with respect to the personality system, the adolescent most likely to be involved with alcohol and other substance use was one who was overly concerned with personal autonomy, who lacked interest in the goals of conventional institutions like church and school, who had a jaundiced view of society, and who had a more tolerant view of transgression.

With respect to the perceived environmental system, the perceptions of adolescents most likely to be engaged in substance abuse were: less parental support, less compatibility between the expectations of parents and friends, greater influence of friends not parents, greater approval of peers, and models for substance use from friends.

Gateway Theory. Research conducted by Kandel (1975, 1978, 1980, 1984) has demonstrated that adolescents pass through four stages of substance use: (a) beer or wine, (b) cigarettes or hard liquor, (c) marijuana, and (d) other illicit drugs. Each drug stage acted as a "gateway" or "stepping stone" to the next stage of use, with progression directly related to the intensity of use during the previous stage.

Identification with the beliefs and values of deviant peers, delinquency, and nonconformist ideology were important factors for the initiation of adolescent marijuana use. Poor relations with parents and friends, and exposure to drug–using parents were important factors for the initiation of adolescent marijuana use. Poor relations with parents and friends, and exposure to drug–using parents were important in the transition from marijuana use to the use of other illicit drugs.

Relative Deviance. Dembo and colleagues (Dembo, Blount, Schmeidler, & Burgos, 1985; Dembo, Burgo, Babst, Schmeidler, & LeGrand, 1978; Dembo, Farrow, Des Jarlais, & Burgos, 1981; Dembo, Farrow, Schmeidler, & Burgos, 1979) published several studies of drug use among inner city youth in South Bronx. According to Dembo et al., adolescent substance use was associated with perceptions of higher rates of violence and drug use in the surrounding community, friends use of drugs, time spent "in the streets", and membership in disrupted families. In situations where drug use was acceptable, however, sociocultural norms were more salient. Adolescents who were deviant from the norms of drug use established in their particular sociocultural setting used drugs that were the least acceptable in their environment. This concept of "relative deviance" was, therefore, crucial to an understanding of adolescent drug problems.

Models with Black Adolescents

Most studies of adolescent substance use among Blacks also emphasized psychosocial deficiencies and deviance.

Antisocial Behavior. Kellam and others (Kellam, Ensminger, & Simon, 1980; Ensminger, Brown, & Kellam, 1982; Flemming, Kellam, & Brown, 1984; Ensminger, Brown, & Kellam, 12984) followed–up Black first graders in Chicago at ages 16 and 17 to identify early predictors of adolescent drug use. Aggressiveness, determined by teacher's ratings, was a predictor of alcohol, cigarette, and marijuana use in the teens. Shyness, on the other hand, inhibited the use of cigarettes and marijuana. Shyness and aggression in the first grade, however, increased the risks of marijuana and cigarette use in adolescence.

Early signs of intelligence, namely high I.Q., and school readiness, and signs of trouble with authority in adolescence also predicted substance use. Psychological well–being was not correlated with substance use during adolescence. For boys, attachment to peers and weak school bonds were important contributors to subsequent drug use. For girls, drug use was primarily accounted for by weak bonds to the family and school.

The sex differences were interpreted as an indication that initial shy or aggressive behavior had less impact for girls on social behavior later on in life. The correlations for shyness and aggressions were taken as maladaptive responses by boys to the social demands to interact with others and obey rules. Such antisocial behavior was later attributed to a psychological factor, "the willingness to take risks" (Kellam et al., 1980).

The Natural History of Drug Abuse. Results of investigations involving young Black males and Vietnam veterans, (Robins, 1973, 1978, 1980; Robins, Darvish, & Murphy, 1970; Robins & Murphy, 1967) demonstrated that there is a natural developmental history of illicit drug abuse. In these studies, the earlier drug use began, the more serious it became. Substance use typically started with marijuana use, which itself was associated with early onset of alcohol use and cigarette smoking. Youth who became frequent and heavy users of marijuana exhibited a greatly increased probability of subsequent use of other illicit drugs, although they did not stop using marijuana. Robins (1980) argued against the "stepping stone" or "gateway" hypothesis. Marijuana was a necessary, but not sufficient condition for progression to other illicit substances.

Onset of drug use during adolescence predicted use at ages 23 and 24. Deviant behavior was the most significant predictor of subsequent drug use. Being truant, getting expelled or dropping out of school, getting arrested, fighting, and getting drunk prior to age 15 contributed to substance use. Therefore, the behavior of adolescents prior to the initiation of drug use resembled that of "mild delinquents".

Experimental use was clearly not part of an antisocial personality pattern. *Drug abuse* resembled general adolescent deviance in that it was concentrated in Black males from disrupted family situations, and because it was linked to adolescent delinquency, early dropping out, and drinking. It did not, however, occur, disproportionately in youth from impoverished backgrounds, with below average I.Q.s, or in those with early school failure and acts of truance. Therefore, Robins concluded that the most reasonable explanation seemed to be that drug abuse could be part of antisocial personality, but most users and abusers did not exhibit the syndrome.

Social Stress and Status Incongruency. Brunswick and others (Brunswick, 1977, 1979; Brunswick & Boyle, 1979; Brunswick & Messeri, 1984; Brunswick & Tarica, 1974; Boyle & Brunswick, 1980) conducted a longitudinal health project with Black adolescents in Harlem. The results failed to support Kandel's theory of adolescent substance use. Despite considerable polydrug use in this adolescent group, marijuana use did not increase the probability of future use of illicit substances.

The use of illicit drugs was perceived by Brunswick to be more norm violating for girls than it was for boys. Girls also reported that most of their friends did not use drugs at all. More girls used heroin than boys. Girls lacked social support in their effort to stop using illicit drugs, and they had more serious life outcomes compared to the experiences of boys who used heroin.

Overall, adolescent substance users exhibited more health problems than nonusers. None of the adolescents who used drugs received above average grades, and they were less likely to attend church compared to nonusers. They also had higher occupational aspirations than nonusers, but the discrepancy between these aspirations and expectations was more extreme. Moreover, boys and girls who used drugs stated they felt estranged and lonely, they suffered from depressed attitudes, they worried excessively over future concerns, and most expected to be dead before the age of 60.

Because substance users were concerned with life outcomes (i.e., health, social, and economic outlooks), and because of the sex differential in social norms, Brunswick et al. concluded that social stress and status incongruency had a major role in the etiology of drug use among Black adolescents.

Recently, Brunswick & Messeri (1984) developed an ecological model of cigarette smoking behavior in adolescents. Causal factors included in the model spanned five biopsychosocial domains:

1. Macrosystem: Normative variations by sex, cohort, socioeconomic variables, and geographic region.

2. Microsystem–achievement: Variables that denote the individual in relation to school, such as reading scores, grade point average (GPA), and school placement relative to age.
3. Microsystem–interpersonal: The individual's orientation toward family or peers and involvement in recreation.
4. Ontogenic system: Attitudes toward self and society.
5. Health salience and practices: Health concerns and habits.

Participants were members of the same sample of Harlem youth. One influence on girls' use of cigarettes was recent migration from the South. For boys, absence of a father in the household seemed to influence the onset of smoking. However, none of the socioeconomic measures predicted the initiation of cigarette smoking.

Overall, adolescents who were less academically successful were more likely to start smoking, although the association was stronger for girls. Lower GPAs were the significant indicators for smoking in boys, while girls with lower standardized reading test scores were more likely to smoke than girls with higher reading scores.

Peer involvement increased the likelihood of smoking among boys but not among girls. For girls, spending most of their time with close family members deterred smoking; among boys, having siblings who smoked was a salient factor in the initiation of cigarette use.

Self-esteem had no role in the onset of smoking. Shortened time perspective was a strong predictor of future smoking in girls. Boys were more likely to start smoking if they had a pessimistic attitude toward the likelihood of people making the world any better, if they had low expectations of future success, or if they expressed both views.

Health orientation had a prominent role in the onset of smoking, but some results were counter-intuitive. Boys who reported a greater number of good health practices early in adolescence or boys who did not view themselves as overweight had higher rates of smoking. Minimal concerns about health predicted smoking initiation for girls. A larger appetite and greater food consumption also successfully predicted which girls smoked.

Alternative Models

Some researchers have suggested modifying or discarding conventional approaches to the problem of substance use. Too much attention has been given to defects and deficiencies in Blacks; too little attention has been given to the unique historical and cultural factors exemplified in the Black experience. They have provided descriptive accounts of alternative models of alcohol and substance use in Blacks, that might be appropriate for use with Black adolescents.

King's Conceptual Model. King (1982) has labeled alcoholism the number one problem in Black America; America, however has failed to devote more resources to eradicate the problems of alcohol abuse. King stated that this implies not only a lack of serious consideration to the plight of Blacks, but also the use of alcohol to maintain a particular class relationship. He added that there have been too few attempts to study Black youth or elderly Blacks, to examine multiple causal factors simultaneously, or to examine these factors over some historical time period. He urged that a new research order in the examination of alcohol use in the Black community should be forged. Research should find new methods to allow Blacks to positively recreate themselves and their communities. To this end, King proposed his "conceptual model of alcoholism".

In the conceptual model, the individual Black or Black group is placed at the focal point of four historical and irreducible interactions. Alone, or in combinations, the interactions are believed to produce the behavioral essence of the individual or group. The four interactions—biological (physiological, glandular, metabolic, and central nervous system functions), socioeconomic (class, status, income, education, and role issues), psychological (behavioral indexes and particular personality constructs), and cultural (values, meanings, lifestyles, and worldviews)—are given meaning according to the context of the individual or group environment.

King stated that the status of Black Americans makes them unique. The struggle to surmount oppression resulted in the emergence of Black ethnicity or shared cultural history. King considered alcoholism a cultural artifact, a product of the problems, values, lifestyles, and views of the user. The affects of racism, poverty, social and cultural barriers, and unequal access to health and mental health care are also implicated in the etiology of substance use. Knowledge of alcohol and drug abuse among Blacks might be enhanced if researchers looked at the Black community in ethnic or cultural terms rather than racial terms, and if science placed emphasis on the unique class position occupied by Blacks in American society.

Alcohol and Black Family Features. Lipscomb and Goddard (1984) described the plight of Black adolescents who drop out of school and enter the job market. The affects of racism and lack of appropriate skills make it difficult for them to find work. In America, however, work and status are all important. Work and status are the sole criteria for a sense of personal and social worth. Lacking work, the pathway to success is blocked for these adolescents. This places stress and tension on Black youth who are attempting to find a niche in society.

In the desperate search for a sense of worth, Black adolescents often experience a pervasive sense of alienation leading to feelings of helplessness and perceptions of loss. Alienation and loss, coupled with failure to realize a sense of personal and social worth often provoke profound depression. The overt manifestations of depression are truancy and delinquency; suicides, homicides, and violence in general; and alcohol and other drug use in Black adolescents.

On the other hand, Lipscomb and Goddard stated that social life within the Black community is derived from the cultural features of Black people. These features are based on interrelatedness and mutual dependence of community members and are reflected in the Black family system. The importance of this system is realized in the strong sense of family togetherness, the principal of unconditional love, and familial reciprocity.

Within the context of the Black family, an adolescent achieves personal and social worth based on the characteristics of belonging to the unit. Here work and status are not that significant. Under these circumstances, unconditional love is a blessing for some and a curse to others. It is a blessing in the sense that the adolescent is secure in knowing that family love remains unshaken no matter what she or he does, has, or becomes. It is a curse because the adolescent does not assume responsibility for his or her use of alcohol or other drugs.

Alienation and Human Transformation. Nobles (1984) noted the substance use literature reflects an implicit assumption that the adolescent has a personal "character flaw". He suggested, however, that adolescent alcohol and other drug use is a symptom of the crisis of social alienation permeating the United States. The traditional definition of alienation, nevertheless, is only another means of positing character flaws. Nobles redefined alienation in terms of the "coefficient of alienation" or the degree in which two variables are unrelated. That is, he believed that the degree to which the meaning of "human being" is unrelated to the "experience of human beings" is a measure of alienation in American society.

The philosophical heritage of Western culture is that awareness of self is guided by principles of self-preservation. This uniquely, self-sufficient, independent, competitive, and domineering person is the result of the "gap" between God and the human being. Nobles emphasized that alienation is a crisis of societal meaningness, and the problem of adolescent substance use requires that the problem be raised from the level of character flaw to the level of human meaningness.

Adolescent substance use is a typical response by youth in search of meaningfulness. It is symptomatic of the gap between God and human kind. According to Nobles, African belief systems hold that all things are one with each other and all are one with the Supreme. Therefore, the solution to the problem of adolescent drug use will require the Africanization of America.

Implications for Intervention

Kandel (1980) proposed that adolescent substance use progresses through distinct phases, and that the intensity of use at one level acts as a gateway to more dangerous levels of illicit drug use. Research using samples of Black adolescents, however, has failed to support Kandel's hypothesis (Brunswick et al., 1974, 1977, 1979; Robins, 1980).

Kandel and others (Kandel, 1980; Jessor, 1980; Dembo et al., 1978, 1985) suggested there is also a link between substance use and deviance or pathology, either for individual adolescents or among their family and friends. Although there have been reports of depressive symptoms and delinquent behavior in Black adolescents who use drugs, no serious pathology has been noted (Robins, 1980; Brunswick et al., 1974; Dawkins & Dawkins, 1983). Peers have had little or no influence on the drug use behavior of Black adolescents in several investigations (Brunswick, 1979; Singer, 1983; Dull, 1983; Byram & Fly, 1984: Lowman et al., 1982), but other research has established a relationship between alcohol and other substance use in Black adolescents and the drug use practices of family members (Lipscomb & Goddard, 1984; Singer, 1983; Marel, 1977; Byram & Fly, 1984; Brunswick & Messeri, 1984).

Furthermore, rural and urban differences in the patterns of alcohol and other substance use in Black adolescents have been reported (Globetti, 1970; Globetti, Aliskafe, & Morse, 1977; Harper, 1976; Heath, 1978), and sex differences have been noted in studies by Brunswick et al. (1979, 1984) and Wilsnack (1978). Therefore, in addition to differences in the prevalence of patterns of substance use among Black and White adolescents, differences in the correlates of adolescent drug use among Blacks and Whites, and among various populations of Black youth have been found. Despite these differences, ethnic and cultural variables have been frequently omitted in the consideration of intervention strategies (Smith–Peterson, 1984; Jenkins, Rahaim, Kelly, & Payne, 1982).

Cultural Relevance. Some authors have suggested that drug treatment and prevention efforts should cover a broad range of substance use problems and include both education and drug treatment, as well as provide alternatives to adolescent substance use (Lex, 1985; Gibbs, 1984). More importantly, these authors agreed that all intervention efforts should be targeted to the specific needs and cultural experience of Black youth. Smith–Peterson (1984) emphasized:

> ...past failures to acknowledge important cultural and ethnic differences in substance abuse problems and patterns in the United States have perpetuated problems in stereotyping, misunderstanding, and program ineffectiveness. Intervention and prevention programs must interact in harmony with a client's cultural and ethnic background if they are to be effective. (p. 370)

Suggested approaches for high-risk groups like Black adolescents include social skills, values clarification, decision-analysis, relaxation and meditation techniques (Lex, 1985); and modeling, assertiveness training, systematic desensitization, contingency contracting, and covert sensitization and extinction (Jenkins, et al., 1982). Suggested alternative activities include creative work, physical exercise (Lex. 1985), vocational training, and finishing school (Gibbs, 1984).

Jenkins et al. argued strongly for increased emphasis on a thorough assessment of clients prior to the initiation of drug treatment. The therapist's assessment should include cultural variables which may affect treatment outcome (e.g., How much like this patient am I? Have I developed sufficient rapport with her or him to trust the information this adolescent gives me about using alcohol and other drugs?). They also recommended paying particular attention to the clients cultural milieu. The effectiveness of therapy might be enhanced by using more realistic scenes in imagery techniques and using the client's own language throughout treatment.

It is impossible to evaluate the effectiveness of these suggested interventions. Studies of drug treatment and prevention in Black adolescents are rare. There have been, however, reports of lack of responsiveness in Blacks to alcohol education programs (King, 1984; Globetti et al., 1977; McKirnan, 1978), and Brisbane (1986) had some success using contemporary fiction in bibliotherapy with Black adolescents in alcoholism treatment.

Issues of Access. Gibbs (1984) has pointed out that most drug programs are geared toward the treatment of youth, ages 18 and above. Few federally run or sponsored treatment facilities address adolescent substance use. For the most part, minority drug users do not seek help in majority run treatment centers (Westermeyer, 1984). Taken together, these findings suggest that a large percentage of Black adolescents with substance use problems are not treated. Those Black youth who do seek help, often have no place to go.

Many alternatives have been suggested. One has been to develop minority–run or minority–staffed treatment centers (Westermeyer, 1984). Ethnic programs seem to be as effective as majority programs, and they tend to attract more minorities. Once established, perhaps such programs will attract more Black youth.

Community-based approaches have been mentioned as viable alternatives for drug treatment in Blacks and other high-risk groups (Jenkins et al., 1982; Lex, 1985; Gibbs, 1984). However, too often community-based centers do not serve the people they are designed to serve (Jenkins et al., 1982; Westermeyer, 1976, 1984). It may be necessary to provide outreach services to capture the attention of Black youth.

School-based services have been proposed (Dembo, et al., 1978; Ensminger, et al., 1983). This may be practical because most alcohol and other substance use among Black adolescents appears to take place in school (Brunswick, et al., 1977, 1979).

Lee (1983) preferred to concentrate on the Black family as the primary source in preparing children to handle adolescent pressures like substance use. Gibbs (1984) also acknowledged that parents should be the focal point in the prevention of drug use. Whereas Lee emphasized the family as the primary resource, Gibbs favored a coordinated community strategy with the widespread involvement of parents, schools, churches, peers, local organizations, and community leaders.

Comments and Conclusions

There are apparent differences in the patterns of adolescent substance use among Blacks and Whites. Cigarette smoking and the use of some illicit drugs seems to be more extensive among Black youth. The use of alcohol, hallucinogens and inhalants appears to be greater among White youth. There are also differences between Blacks and Whites in the psychological and social aspects of adolescent drug use. Alcohol and other substance use among Black adolescents also varies according to demographic background.

Differences in the patterns of drug use should not be taken as a sign that the drug *problem* is more severe among adolescents in one group; it only indicates that the use of *specific* substances are disproportionately higher among youth in one group compared to youth in the other group. However, the differences suggest that ethnic and cultural variables should be taken into consideration in developing an understanding of adolescent substance use and eliminating or reducing the use of alcohol and other drugs by youth.

Research using conventional models espouse a *deficit* approach to understanding adolescent substance use. That is, there are defects and deviance in the character of youth, or in their families or peers that somehow account for drug use.

Results from studies of substance use in Black youth sometimes contradict results of conventional research. Nevertheless, these results, for the most part, continue to support the deficit point of view.

The major problem with most deficits research is the lack of clear conceptualization of youthful substance use. Most results are correlational, they are based upon the significance of the association between substance use and demographic, psychological, and social factors. The causal connection between these factors and adolescent drug use is still unclear, and, therefore, knowledge of the problem remains crude and limited in scope.

Despite the shortcomings of research, society depends on the judgement of its experts. Society is free to choose or ignore the advice. To date, American society has either taken the latter alternative or chosen the wrong advice. Failure to acknowledge the importance of ethnic and cultural variations in adolescent substance use has, intentionally or unintentionally, helped reinforce longstanding and comfortable beliefs about the inferiority of Blacks and the deficits in their children. Public concern over the drug problem is irreverent to the difficulties faced by Blacks growing up in America and public policy toward drug prevention and treatment is irrelevant to the needs of Black youth.

Society should begin to pay attention to the advice of other experts who have recognized that America is a mosaic of cultural and ethnic diversity. Some experts suggest increased availability and access to drug treatment and prevention programs that are tailored to the special needs and cultural experience of Black youth. Other experts propose reformulating the issue of substance abuse in terms of historical contexts, familial relations, and the Black adolescent's search for meaningfulness.

Before society begins to listen to the advice of these experts, however, science must first acknowledge the importance of cultural and ethnic differences in substance use. Science must be willing to admit that 100 years of deficits research in the area of drug use has not produced substantive improvements in the position of Black adults or youth. If science listens, then perhaps more would be known about alcohol and other drug use in Black adolescents. Ultimately, more could be done to eradicate this complex phenomenon that threatens all American youth.

NOTES

1. I would like to gratefully acknowledge the assistance of Willa D. Jones in the preparation of this manuscript.

References

American Psychiatric Association (1980). *Diagnostic and statistical manual of mental disorders*. (3rd ed.), Washington, D.C.: Author.

Bennett, G. (1983). Youthful substance abuse. In G. Bennett, C. Vourakis, & D. S. Woolf (Eds.), *Substance abuse: Pharmalogic, developmental, and clinical perspectives*. NY: John Wiley & Sons.

Blane, H. T., & Hewitt, L. E. (1977). *Alcohol and youth: An analysis of the literature, 1960–1975*. Rockville, MD: NIAAA.

Special Topics: Substance Use

Boyle, J. M., & Brunswick, A. F. (1980). What happened in Harlem: An analysis of a decline of heroin use among a generation unit of urban Black youth. *Journal of Drug Issues, 10,* 109–130.

Brisbane, F. L. (1986). Using contemporary fiction with Black children and adolescents in alcoholism treatment. *Alcoholism Treatment Quarterly, 2,* 179–197.

Brunswick, A. F. (1977). Health and drug behavior: A study of urban Black adolescents. *Addictive Disease, 3,* 197–214.

Brunswick, A. F. (1979). Black youths and drug–use behavior. In G.Beschner & A. Friedman (Eds.) (1979). *Youth drug abuse.* Lexington, MA: D.C. Health.

Brunswick, A. F., & Boyle, J. M. (1979). Patterns of drug involvement: Developmental and secular influences on age at initiation. *Youth and Society, 11,* 139–172.

Brunswick, A. F., & Messeri, P. (1984). Causal factors in onset of adolescent's cigarette smoking: A prospective study of urban Black you. In H. Shaffer & B. Stimmel (Eds.), *The addictive behaviors.* NY: The Hayworth Press.

Brunswick, A. & Tarica, C. (1974). Drinking and health: A study of urban Black adolescence. *Addictive Diseases, 10,* 21–42.

Byram, O. W., & Fly, J. W. (1984). Family structure, race, and adolescents' alcohol use: A research note. *American Journal of Drug and Alcohol Abuse, 10,* 467–478.

Caplovitz, D. (1980). *Youngsters experimenting with drugs.* NY: Graduate School and University Center, CUNY.

Dawkins, R. L., & Dawkins, M. P. (1983). Alcohol use and delinquency among Black, White, and Hispanic adolescent offenders. *Adolescence, 18,* 799–809.

Dembo, R., Blount, W. R., Schmeidler, J., and Burgos W. (1985). Methodological and substantive issues involved in using the concept of risk in research into the etiology of drug use among adolescents. *Journal of Drug Issues, 15,* 537–553.

Dembo, R., Burgos, W., Babst, D. V., Schmeidler, J., & LeGrand, L. E. (1978). Neighborhood relationships and drug involvement among inner–city junior high school youths: Implications for drug education and prevention programming. *Journal of Drug Education, 8,* 231–252.

Dembo, R., Farrow, D., Des Jarlais, D. C., Burgos, W., & Schmeidler, J. (1981). Examining a causal model of early drug involvement among inner–city junior high school youths. *Human Relations, 34,* 169–193.

Dembo, R., Farrow, D., Schmeidler, J., & Burgos, W. (1979). Testing a causal model of environmental influences on the early drug involvement of inner–city junior high school youths. *American Journal of Drug and Alcohol Abuse, 6,* 313–336.

Dull, R. T. (1983). Friends' use and adult drug and drinking behavior: A further test of differential association theory. *Journal of Criminal Law and Criminology, 74,* 1608–1619.

DuPont, R. L. (1978). International challenge of drug abuse: A perspective from the United States. In R. C. Peterson (Ed.), *The international challenge of drug abuse.* Washington, D.C.: U.S. Government Printing Office.

Ensimger, M. E., Brown, C. H., & Kellam, S. G. (1982). Sex differences in antecedents of substance use among adolescents. *Journal of Social Issues, 38,* 25–42.

Ensminger, M. E., Brown, C. H., & Kellam, S. G. (1984). Social control as an explanation of sex differences in substance use among adolescents. In NIDA, *Drug abuse treatment*. Rockville, MD: NIDA.

Fleming, J. P., Kellam, S. G., & Brown, C. H. (1982). Early predictors of age at first use of alcohol, marijuana, and cigarettes. *Drug and Alcohol Dependence, 9,* 285–303.

Gibbs, J. T. (1984). Black adolescents and youth: An endangered species. *American Journal of Orthopsychiatry, 64,* 6–21.

Globetti, G. (1970). The drinking patterns of Negro and White high school students in two Mississippi communities. *Journal of Negro Education, 39,* 60–69.

Globetti, G., Alsikafe, M., & Morse, R. J. (1970). Alcohol use among Black youth in a rural community. *Drug and Alcohol Dependence,Negro Education, 39,* 60–69.

Globetti, G., Alsikafe, M., & Morse, R. J. (1977). Alcohol use among Black youth in a rural community. *Drug and Alcohol Dependence. 2,* 255–260.

Gropper, B. A. (1985). Probing the links between drugs and crime. *Research in brief,* Washington, D.C.: NJ.

Harper, F. D. (Ed.) (1976). *Alcohol abuse and Black America.* Alexandria, VA: Douglass Publishers.

Harper, F. D. (1977). Alcohol use among North American Blacks. In Y. Israel, F. B. Glaser, H. Kalant, R. E. Popham, W. S. Schmidt, and R. G. Smart (Eds.). *Research advances in alcohol and drug problems.* Vol. 4. NY: Plenum Press.

Harper, F. D. (Ed.) (1979). *Alcoholism treatment and Black americans.* Rockville, MD: NIAAA.

Harper, F. D., & Dawkins, M. P. (1976). Alcohol and Blacks: Survey of the periodical literature. *British Journal of Addictions, 71,* 327–334.

Heath, D. B. (1798). Ethnicity, class, and alcohol use. *Rhode Island Medical Journal. 61,* 387–388.

Jenkins, A. H. (1982). *The psychology of the Afro–American: A humanistic perspective* NY: Pergamon Press.

Jenkins, J. O., Rahaim, S., Kelly, L. M., & Payne, D. (1982). Substance abuse. In S. M. Turner, & R. T. Jones (Eds.). *Behavior modification in Black populations: Psychosocial issues and empirical findings.* NY: Plenum Press.

Jessor, R. (1979). Marijuana: A review of recent psychosocial research. In R. L. DuPont, A. Goldstein, & J. O'Donnell (Eds.), *Handbook on drug abuse.* Washington, D.C.: U.S. Government Printing Office.

Jessor, R., Graves, T. D., Hanson, R. C. & Jessor, S. L. (1968). *Society, personality, and deviant behavior: A study of a tri–ethnic community.* NY: Holt, Rinehart, and Winston.

Jessor, R., & Jessor, S. L. (1977). *Problem behavior and psychosocial development—A longitudinal study of youth.* NY: Academic Press.

Jessor, R., & Jessor, S. L. (1978). Theory testing in longitudinal research on marijuana use. In D. B. Kandel (Ed.), *Longitudinal research on drug use.* Washington, D.C.: Hemisphere.

Jessor, R., & Jessor, S (1980). A social–psychological framework for studying drug use. In D. J. Lettieri, M. Sayers, & H. W. Peasson(Eds.). *Theories on drug abuse: Selected contemporary perspectives.* Washington, D.C.: U.S. Government Printing Office.

Johnston, L. D., O'Malley, P. M., & Bachman, J. G. (1984). *Highlights from drugs and American high school students 1975–1983.* Washington, D.C.: US. Government Printing Office.

Special Topics: Substance Use

Kandel, D. (1975). Stages in adolescent involvement in drug use. *Science, 190*, 912–914.

Kandel, D. B. (1978). Convergences in prospective longitudinal surveys of drug use in normal populations. In D. B. Kandel (Ed.), *Longitudinal research on drug use*. Washington, D.C.: Hemisphere.

Kandel, D. B. (1980). Developmental stages in adolescent drug involvement. In D. J. Lettieri, M. Sayers, H. W. Pearson (Eds.), *Theories on drug abuse: Selected contemporary perspectives* Washington, D.C.: U.S. Government Printing Office.

Kandel, D. B. (1984). On processes of peer influences in adolescent drug use: A developmental perspective. In H. Shaffer & B. Stimmel (Eds.), *The addictive behaviors*. NY: The Hayworth Press.

Kellam, S. G., Ensminger, M. E., & Simon, M. D. (1980). Mental health in first grade and teenage drug, alcohol, and cigarette use. *Drug and alcohol dependence*, , 273–304.

King, L. M. (1982). Alcoholism: Studies regarding Black Americans. In NIAAA (Eds.), *Special population issues*. Washington, D.C.: U.S. Government Printing Office.

Klatsky, A. L., Friedman, G. D., Seigelaub, A. B., & Gerard, M. J. (1977). Alcohol consumption among White, Black or Oriental men and women: Kaiser–Permanente multiphasic health Examination Data. *American Journal of Epidemiology, 105*, 311–323.

Lachter, S. B., & Weisman, R. (1980). *Let's talk about drug abuse: Some questions and answers*. Washington, D.C.: U.S. Government Printing Office.

Lee, L. J. (1983). Reducing Black adolescents' drug use: Family revisited. *Child and Youth Services, 6*, 57–69.

Lex, B. W. Alcohol problems in special populations. In J. H. Mendelson & N. K. Mello (Eds.) 1985). *The diagnosis and treatment of alcoholism* (2nd ed.). NY: McGraw–Hill.

Lipscomb, W. R., & Goddard, L. L. (1984). Black family features and drinking behavior. *Journal of Drug Issues, 14*, 337–347.

Lowman, C., Harford, T. C. & Kaelberg, C. T. (1983). Alcohol use among Black senior high school students. In NIAAA (Eds.). *Facts for planning; Alcohol and youth*. Rockville, MD: NIAAA.

Lowman, C., Hubbard, R. L. Rachal, J. V., & Cavanaugh, E. R. (1982). Adolescent marijuana and alcohol use. In NIAAA, *Facts for planning: Alcohol and youth*. Rockville, MD: NIAAA.

Lowman, C., & NCALI Staff (1981). Prevalence of alcohol use among U.S. senior high school students. In NIAAA (Eds.), *Facts for planning: Alcohol and youth*. Rockville, MD: NIAAA.

Lowamn, C., & NCALI Staff (1982). Alcohol use as an indicator of psychoactive drug use among the nation's senior high school students. In NIAAA (Eds.), *Facts for planning: Alcohol and youth*. Rockville, MD: NIAAA.

Maddahian, E., Newcomb, M. D., & Bentler, P. M. (1985). Single and multiple patterns of adolescent substance use: Longitudinal comparisons of four ethnic groups. *Journal of Drug Education, 15*, 311–327.

Mahoney, M. J. (1980). *Abnormal psychology: Perspectives on human variance*. San Francisco: Harper & Row.

Marel, R. (1977). *Drug behavior of Black and White adolescents: Patterns, correlates, and predictors of use*. Ph.D. dissertation (abstract). Columbia University, NY.

McKirnan, D. J. (1978). Community perspectives on deviance: Some factors in the definition of alcohol abuse. *American Journal of Community Psychology, 6*, 219–238.

Myers, V. (1977). Drug use among minority youth. *Addictive Diseases, 3,* 187–196.
NIAAA (1982). Physiological effects of alcohol. *Alcohol topics in brief,* Rockville, MD: Author.
NIDA (1979b). (lNational survey on drug abuse, 1979. Washington, D.C.: Author.
NIDA (1979a). *Drug abuse prevention for your community.* Washington, D.C.: U.S. Government Printing Office.
Nobles, W. W. (1984). Alienation, human transformation and adolescent drug use: Toward a reconceptuallization of the problem. *Journal of Drug Issues, 14,* 243–252.
Rachal, J. V., Guess, L. L., Hubbard, R. L., Maisto, E. S., Cavanaugh, E. R., Waddell, R., & Benrud, C. H. (1980). *The extent and nature of adolescent alcohol and drug use: The 1974 and 1978 national sample studies. Adolescent drinking behaviors,* Vol. 1, Rockville, MD: NIAAA.
Robins, L. N. (1973). *Follow–up of Vietnam drug users.* Washington, D.C.: U.S. Government Printing Office.
Robins, L. N. (1978). Study childhood predictors of adult antisocial behavior: Replication from longitudinal studies. *Psychological Medicine, 8,* 611–622.
Robins, L. N. (1980). The natural history of drug abuse. In D. J. Lettieri, M. Sayers, & H. W. Pearson (Eds.).*Theories on drug abuse: Selected contemporary perspectives.* Washington, D.C.: U.S. Government Printing Office.
Robins, L. N., Darvish, H. S., & Murphy, G. E. A. (1970). Follow–up study of 76 users and 146 users. In J. Zubin, & A. Freedman (Eds.), *Psychopathology of adolescence.* NY: Grune & Stratton.
Robins, L. N., & Murphy, G. E. (1967). Drug use in a normal population of young Negro men. *American Journal of Public Health, 57,* 1580–1596.
Singer, M. I. (1983). A bi–racial comparison of adolescent alcohol use. Ph.D. dissertation (abstract), Case Western Reserve University.
Smith–Peterson, C. (1983). Substance abuse treatment and cultural diversity. In G. Bennett, C. Vourakis, & D. S. Woolf (Eds.), *Substance abuse: Pharmacologic, developmental, and clinical perspectives.* NY: John Wiley & Sons.
Telch, M. J., Killen, J. D., McAllister, A. L., Perry, C. L., & Maccoby, N. (1982). Long–term follow–up of a pilot project on smoking prevention with adolescents. *Journal of Behavioral Medicine, 5,* 1–8.
USPHS (1979). *Smoking and Health: A report of the Surgeon General.* Washington, D.C.: U.S. Government Printing Office.
USPHS (1980A).*Smoking, tobacco, & health: A fact book.* U.S. Government Printing Office.
USPHS (1980b). *The health consequences of smoking for women: A report of the Surgeon General.* Washington, D.C.: U.S. Government Printing Office.
Varenhorst, B. (1984). The adolescent society. In *Adolescent peer pressure: Theory, correlates and program implications for drug abuse prevention.* Washington, D.C.: U.S. Government Printing Office.
Westermeyer, J. (1976). Clinical guidelines for the cross–cultural treatment of chemical dependency. *American Journal of Drug and Alcohol Abuse, 3,* 315–322.
Westermeyer, J. (1984). The role of ethnicity in substance abuse. *Advance in alcohol and substance abuse, 4,* 9–18.
Wilsnack, R. W., & Wilsnack, S. C. (1978). Sex roles and drinking among adolescent girls. *Journal of Studies in Alcoholism, 39,* 1855–1874.

BLACK ADOLESCENTS AND THE CRIMINAL JUSTICE SYSTEM

Darnell F. Hawkins and Nolan E. Jones

In both folklore and science the years of adolescence have been associated with heightened social, emotional, and physiological stresses. Such stresses are said to have affected youth during the past and to be recognizable across cultural boundaries. On the other hand, Goodman (1960) has observed that the perils of the adolescence–to–adult transition are particularly devastating for youth in modern, western, highly industrialized societies, such as the United States. Adolescence is marked by higher rates of perceived and actual antisocial/criminal behaviors than are usually found in later adulthood. In the United States one result of such perceptions and/or behavior is that adolescence more so than any other phase of the life course is marked by extremely high rates of contact with the criminal justice system. Thus, in this country the traditional perils of the period are exacerbated for many young people by arrest, conviction and detention within the criminal justice system.[1]

In this essay we consider the particular problems of Black adolescents who have higher rates of involvement with the criminal justice system than any other racial–ethnic/age grouping. We explore the extent of their overrepresentation with that system, from arrest to confinement. We propose that the extensive use of the criminal justice system in an attempt at the social control of Black adolescents has severe negative consequences. Among these consequences is a decrease in the already reduced likelihood that they will be able to find gainful and productive employment as adults. We further propose that the problems that Black youth encounter with the American criminal justice system are similar to those faced by Black adults. That is, the system of racial oppression that has characterized race relations in the United States is a major contributor to high rates of crime and social control for both groups. Before more fully discussing these issues, let us consider recent data on the high rate of involvement by Black adolescents with the American criminal justice system.

Black Youth in Custody

We begin our examination by considering rates of confinement in correctional institutions. A full assessment of confinement rates for adolescents is difficult because persons in the age range typically labeled as adolescence may be confined in juvenile facilities (both public and private), local jails, or state and federal prisons. In addition, during recent years an increasing number of adolescents can be found in mental hospitals and various medical or quasi–medical treatment facilities. In many areas of the country there has also been a trend toward establishing special schools for juvenile delinquents which are a part of the public school system. Given prevailing views that adolescents are more malleable than adults, the formal social control of youth is less retribution–oriented and involves a large number of societal institutions.

Such a wide array of institutions makes extremely laborious the task of documenting precisely the overrepresentation of Black adolescents in the American criminal justice system. For example, private juvenile facilities and many of the more recently established treatment centers house large numbers of middle–class, White youths. The latter facilities are increasingly for–profit operations that are not included in federal juvenile censuses. Black and lower–class White adolescents are likely to be confined in public institutions for which data are available. Nevertheless, available data reveal much about the extent of Black overrepresentation in custodial institutions, especially those designed specifically for social control.

A recent federal document, *The Prevalence of Imprisonment* (U.S. Department of Justice, 1985), provides useful age–, sex– and race–specific data for persons confined in state prisons. Table 1 is taken from that study and reveals the percentage of the population (by sex, age and race) that was confined in prison during a single day in 1974 and 1979. On a given day during 1974 two and one–half percent of all Black males between the ages of 20 and 29 (or 1 in every 39) in the United States were in State prisons. This figure had increased to over 3% (or 1 in 33 during a typical day in 1979. Comparable rates for White males were 0.304 and 0.401, or about 1 in every 330 for 1974 and 1 in every 245 for 1979.

In the more typically adolescent age range, 13–19, nearly four-tenths of a percent of all Black American males were confined in a state prison in 1974. This means that 1 in every 250 Black males in this age range was confined in prison. This compares to a percentage for White males of 0.057, or 1 in every 1,750. At every age range Black males are confined at a rate 7 to 9 times that of White males. It is important to note that Black adolescents (13–19) are confined in state prisons at a rate greater than that for White males in their twenties.

Black females are considerably less likely than Black males to be found in prison, but Table 1 shows that their rate of confinement was considerably higher than the rate for White females across every age range. In addition, while the rate of White female imprisonment stayed relatively stable between 1974 and 1979, the rate for Black females, like that for Black males, increased. During both 1974 and 1979 the prevalence

Black Adolescents and the Criminal Justice System

Table 1
The prevalence of State imprisonment of adults in the United States on a single day in 1974 and 1979, by sex, race and age

Percent of population in State prisons on a single day

Population segment	13-19	20-29	30-39	40-49	50-59	60 and over
1974						
Male						
White	0.057%	0.304%	0.208%	0.106%	0.045%	0.014%
Black	0.396	2.550	1.444	0.753	0.329	0.091
Female						
White	*0.001	0.012	0.010	0.004	*0.001	*0.0001
Black	0.012	0.079	0.040	*0.008	*0.004	*0.001
1979						
Male						
White	0.069	0.410	0.246	0.128	0.043	0.011
Black	0.442	3.027	2.003	0.756	0.390	0.123
Female						
White	0.003	0.016	0.010	0.005	0.002	*0.0001
Black	0.009	0.124	0.094	0.035	0.012	*0.003

Note: Estimates applicable to all other races are not shown because of known inconsistencies between census and survey procedures for designating "other" race. Table percentages are computed from data contained in two sources: estimates of inmates of adult State prisons are from the 1974 and the 1979 nationwide surveys of inmates of State correctional institutions; U.S. population estimates ae from U.S. Bureau of the Census, Current Population Reports, Series P-25, No. 917.

of imprisonment for Black males in a single day was significantly higher (at the 0.05 level) than comparable age–specific estimates for White males, other males, White females, Black females, and other females (*Prevalence of Imprisonment*, p. 3). The study also reported that Black males are more likely than these other groupings to serve a prison sentence during their lifetime. Finally, the study reported significant increases in the rate of imprisonment for Blacks and Whites between 1978 and 1982. The Black adult (18 and over) rate increased from 1.665% of the population to

405

Special Topics: Youth in the Criminal Justice System

2.044% during this period (p. 3). There was a similar rise in the incarceration of Black youth from 1978 to 1982 (Krisberg et al. 1986).

The enormity of the impact of imprisonment on Blacks (males and females) is shown also by the fact that between 1978 and 1982 Blacks made up 47% of all state and federal prisoners in the United States. During this period Blacks made up only 11–12% of the nation's population. The total number of all state and federal inmates ranged between 307,000 and 413,000 during this period. By 1984 this figure had risen to 463,866. Although the rate of increase for the total prison population slowed somewhat due to court intervention between 1982 and 1984, the proportion Black showed a slight increase.[2]

The age–specific data discussed above show that during adolescence and young adulthood Black males and females are *considerably* more likely than White males and female to be confined in prison. As noted above, however, such statistics do not tell the whole story of racial difference in involvement with the criminal justice system. A large number of persons under 20 years of age are confined in local jails. For example, a 1978 survey of inmates of the nation's jails revealed that 24,860, or nearly 16%, of the 158,394 inmates were under 20. Of these youthful jail inmates, 9,533 (38%) were Black. Among Blacks 8,954 were males.[3] The proportion of juveniles confined in the nation's jails decreased between 1970 and 1978 largely because of the implementation of a national policy requiring the segregation of delinquents and adult criminals.[4]

Of course, juvenile facilities house the largest number of youthful offenders, especially those below the age of 18. Table 2 below shows the racial characteristics of residents of public juvenile custody facilities during 1979 and 1982. These figures include juveniles detained for both traditional criminal acts and for status offenses (those acts which are crimes only if committed by juveniles). The courts have, of course, de-emphasized the importance of status offenses in recent years. Ironically, the trend toward decriminalizing status offenses may be one factor contributing to the widening of the gap between Black and White juvenile detention. Status offenses are often ambiguously defined and are consequently more susceptible to racially biased interpretations and enforcement than traditional criminal offenses. Yet, the "save the children" ideology most often associated with the promulgation and enforcement of status offense laws has meant that they have been used to arrest and frequently detain large numbers of White youth. That is, the police and courts have tended to view the enforcement of such laws as a means of preventing White youth, especially those from the middle class, from entering a life of crime.

The data in Table 2 also include a small category of persons held for dependency, neglect, abuse, emotional disturbance, or mental retardation,

Black Adolescents and the Criminal Justice System

Table 2
Race of Residents of Public Juvenile Facilities in the United States, 1979 and 1982

Race	Number(%) in Custody Year	
	1979	1982
White	26,053	27,805
	(60.3)	(57.1)
Black	13,752	18,020
	(31.8)	(37.0)
Other	950	1,104
	(2.2)	(2.3)
Not reported	2,479	1,772
	(5.7)	(3.6)
Total	43,234	48,701

Source: *Sourcebook of Criminal Justice Statistics—1984*, p. 635. Adapted from *Children in Custody: Advance Report on the 1982 Census of Public Juvenile Facilities*, Table 3.

and persons who admitted themselves or were admitted by their parents without ajudication.[5]

The figures in Table 2 do not include a sizeable number of juveniles who were confined to private facilities. Table 3 provides similar statistics for these institutions during the same period.

Like the figures in Table 1, the statistics in Tables 2 and 3 illustrate the disproportionate presence of young Blacks in criminal justice or quasi–criminal justice facilities. In comparison to their numbers in the general population, Black adolescents are more likely than Whites (and other racial groups) to be found in juvenile institutions, local jails, and state prisons. What explains such racial differentials in detention? A major question, of course, is whether the racial differences documented above are the result primarily of the overinvolvement of Black youth in criminal activities. Apart from self–referrals or referrals by family members, which are relatively rare, most of the juveniles held in custody in the United States are held as the result of an ajudication within an adult criminal or juvenile court. And except for status offenses, they are held for offenses that are equivalent to those committed by adults. How substantial are Black–White differences in the level of juvenile arrests and other measures of criminal behavior?

Special Topics: Youth in the Criminal Justice System

Table 3
Race of Residents of Private Juvenile Facilities in the United States, 1979 and 1982

Race	Number (%) in Custody Year	
	1979	1982
White	21,654	22,377
	(75.5)	(71.3)
Black	5,843	7,822
	(20.4)	(24.9)
Other	1,191	916
	(4.2)	(2.9)
Not reported	0	275
		(0.8)
Total	28,688	31,390

Source: Same as Table 2 except p. 636 of *Sourcebook*

Racial Differences in Criminal Behavior

Numerous studies have reported that minority youth are overrepresented at *all* stages of the juvenile justice system as compared to their numbers in the general population (Krisberg et al., 1986; Pope, 1979; Pope and McNeeley, 1981; Velde, 1977). However, research on juvenile delinquency, to a much greater extent than research on adult crime, has shown a substantial discrepancy between levels of *actual* criminal or antisocial behaviors and the rate of official arrests. This research has a long tradition within criminology and has involved comparisons of self–reports of criminal activity with official crime records. Although there have been criticisms of this methodology, the findings from these studies have been widely accepted. Such studies have generally concluded that there are not substantial or consistent differences between racial groups in their level of involvement in delinquency (Bachman et al., 1971, 1978; Elliott and Voss, 1974; Huizinga and Elliott, 1986; Williams and Gold, 1972).

Despite the conclusions reached by these studies, official crime statistics reflect a different reality. Such data are often used to argue against a conclusion that Blacks are discriminated against in the administration of justice. For example, Hindelang (1982) found that Black youth have higher rates of arrest for offenses such as robberies, rapes, aggravated assaults and simple assaults. These are the kinds of offenses that are most likely to result in decisions to detain and later institutionalize offenders (Krisberg et al., 1986). Black over–involvement in these crimes is said to explain their overrepresentation at all stages of the criminal justice process.

The validity of these conclusions can be tested partly by looking at official arrest data for recent years. The Uniform Crime Reports include data on total arrests for persons under 18 during each year. Racial comparisons for the major (index) crimes are shown in Table 4. These are aggregated into two gross violent and property categories.

As in the case of racial comparisons involving adults, there is a substantial racial imbalance in arrests. Blacks under 18 made up between 51 and 54% of all persons arrested for violent offenses for 1975, 1978, and 1980–84. They made up between 25 and 28% of all property offenders. There is little evidence of major change in the racial distribution of arrests during the decade covered by these statistics. While these data do show that Black youth are much more likely than Whites to be arrested for major crimes, they do not necessarily explain the racial differences in rates of custody shown above. For example, most persons confined in prisons or juvenile facilities have committed property crimes rather than crimes against the person. Like Black adults, the rate of confinement in correctional institutions for Black adolescents is generally higher than that expected on the basis of arrests alone.

Huizinga and Elliott (1986) note that studies which control for arrest history (one of the major variables affecting sentencing) commonly find little evidence of racial bias in juvenile justice system processing (Burke and Turk, 1975; Green, 1970; Weiner and Willie, 1971). However, the data collected by Huizinga and Elliott for the period during the late 1970s and early 1980s appear to suggest that minorities are at a greater risk for being charged with more serious offenses than Whites involved in comparable levels of delinquent behavior. This factor, rather than overt racism in post–arrest processing of delinquents, was said to be a factor which may eventually result in higher incarceration rates among minorities (Huizinga and Elliott, 1986:16).

It is beyond the scope of this paper to fully explore the validity of the arguments regarding the presence or absence of bias in the juvenile or adult criminal justice systems. Past studies both support and question the conclusion that racial discrimination plays a significant role in the processing of adults and juveniles within the criminal justice system today. Much depends upon the stage of the criminal justice system that is being evaluated, victim characteristics, type of crime, and a number of other factors often not considered in the numerous studies of racial bias. See Hawkins (1986) for a review and critique of studies of racial bias in the administration of justice.

Special Topics: Youth in the Criminal Justice System

Table 4
Total Arrests by Race, Persons Under 18, 1975, 1978, 1980-84

Offense Category N/%

Year		Whites	Blacks	All Others	Total
1975	Violent[1]	33,142	38,006	1,381	72,529
		(45.7)	(52.4)	(1.9)	
	Property	500,599	186,691	14,472	701,762
		(71.3)	(26.6)	(2.1)	(100)
1978	Violent	42,404	49,596	3,451	94,451
		(44.4)	52.0	3.6)	
	Property	540,465	216,093	23,304	779,862
		(69.3)	(27.7)	(3.0)	
1980	Violent	40,983	44,079	1,050	86,112
		(47.6)	(51.2)	(1.2)	
	Property	502,085	186,864	13,010	701,959
		(71.5)	(26.6)	(1.9)	
1981	Violent	39,108	45,787	901	85,796
		(45.6)	(53.4)	(1.1)	
	Property	484,699	185,063	12,234	681,996
		(71.1)	(27.1)	(1.9)	
1982	Violent	34,243	40,652	1,004	70,899
		(45.1)	(53.6)	(1.4)	
	Property	404,297	168,517	11,550	584,364
		(69.2)	(28.8)	(1.9)	
1983	Violent	32,858	40,835	911	74,604
		(44.0)	(54.7)	(1.2)	
	Property	401,690	165,286	10,868	577,844
		(69.5)	(28.6)	(1.9)	
1984	Violent	29,454	34,084	774	64,312
		(45.8)	(53.0)	1.2)	
	Property	367,544	127,755	10,487	505,787
		(72.7)	(25.3)	(2.1)	

Source: Uniform Crime Reports

There is substantial evidence of discrimination within the American criminal justice system during the past, especially prior to the Civil Rights Movement and the resulting legislation of the 1960s. Further, the current large scale overrepresentation of Blacks among those arrested and imprisoned suggests that we cannot rule out the possibility that racial bias still plays a significant part in the processing of persons charged with crime today. For instance, a recent three–state study by Petersilia (1983) showed significant racial differences in the processing of adult criminal defendants at several stages of the criminal justice process. Further, Petersilia and Turner (1985) have noted that many current methods of determinant or presumptive sentencing are resulting in increased rates of imprisonment for Blacks. This suggests that institutional forms of racism rather than bigotry on the part of criminal justice personnel may play a major role in creating current levels of racial inequality.

But apart from the question of bias, there are other significant social problems that are related to the extremely high rates of arrest and incarceration of Black youth. They are often ignored in the "just deserts" orientation of the arguments surrounding the study of racial bias in the criminal/juvenile justice system. That is, underlying the arguments concerning bias in the administration of justice is a presumption that if it can be shown that Black youth or adults are incarcerated at rates comparable to their rates of committing crime, all is well with the American system of justice. Such a conclusion is made even more likely because in many respects accusations of racial bias have constituted the *major* criticism of the American criminal justice system during the last 25 years.

Advocates of just deserts and retribution approaches to punishment for crime see high rates of incarceration as problematic only if such rates are determined by factors other than the level of criminal involvement (past and present), the characteristics of criminal acts, and other legally relevant considerations. These kinds of arguments are further buttressed by the persistence of the nature–nurture debate on the etiology of crime. Especially in the case of adolescent crime, some researchers prefer to turn their attention to the causes of criminal behavior rather than to the treatment of juvenile offenders. That is, they seek to explain seemingly high rates of serious juvenile crime among Blacks.

Many of these researchers emphasize the part played by economic deprivation and racial oppression in generating high rates of Black adolescent crime. Other scholars and policymakers argue that using environmental or social conditions such as racism, poverty or unemployment to explain anti–social behavior in youth misses the point. This position is argued by James Q. Wilson and Richard J. Herrnstein in their recent work, *Crime and Human Nature* (1985).

In discussing delinquency and other forms of criminal behavior they state that criminal behavior is caused by a combination of factors, some of which are part of the genetically determined "behavioral traits" of certain individuals (constitutional factors). When these predisposed individuals live under certain pathological social conditions they may engage in criminal behavior. These criminogenic circumstances alone, however, do not make everyone a criminal; but the contextual factors produced by these circumstances help create a population that is responsible for much of the crime problem.

These comments suggest that since most Black youth (including nondelinquents) live in criminogenic environments, the delinquent behavior of a portion of that population cannot be attributed solely to these conditions. Rather they must be attributed to other criminogenic factors that are not readily known or currently subject to scientific measurement. But Wilson and Herrnstein (1985:468) argue that we cannot dismiss the possibility that the races differ in the distribution of those constitutional factors that are associated with criminality.

This is not a new argument. Criminal justice researchers during the past have argued, both explicitly and implicitly, that differences in criminal behavior among indiviudals do not appear to be determined solely by environmental conditions. Some have argued that racial differences are partly or mostly biologically determined. The former argument is not without substantial empirical validity. For example, any theory of the etiology of crime among Blacks must account for the fact that despite the supposed criminogenic conditions under which Blacks live, most Blacks do not resort to crime.

Nevertheless, researchers such as Wilson and Herrnstein and many others who advocate less biology–oriented approaches to the question of the Black presence within the nation's criminal justice system ignore or de–emphasize several crucial concerns: (1) Whatever may be its cause, Black youth are disproportionately arrested and confined within correctional facilities in the United States; (2) Apart from questions of fairness, equity or just deserts (as determined by the rate of criminal activity) the extensive use of the American criminal justice system as a mechanism of social control may be questionable on other grounds; (3) The concept of overimprisonment may be useful for describing not only inequitable rates of confinement (e.g., Blacks vs. Whites), it also describes a proclivity in the United States to rely excessively on prisons as a form of social control; and (4) Among other consequences, we must examine the impact of stigmatizing forms of social control such as arrest and imprisonment on the lives of those involved.

Black Youth and Social Control in the United States

The problems that Black adolescents confront in dealing with the American criminal justice system cannot be understood without an appreciation for the extensiveness of formal social control in the United States today. The United States during the last 25 years has come to rely on its formal system of social control (police, courts, prisons, etc.) in an attempt to regulate a number of actual or merely perceived threats to the social order. Such threats include increases in traditional criminal behavior, social unrest, industrial and technological hazards, political and economic misfeasance and malfeasance, as well as the problems produced by prolonged adolescence in an affluent society. The special problems of the Black underclass in urban areas have also increasingly come to be seen as largely a concern for the criminal justice system. The result of this trend is that the United States currently incarcerates a greater proportion of its citizenry than at any other time in its history (Cahalan, 1979) and ranks third behind the Soviet Union and South Africa in per capita rates of confinement.

Cahalan (1979:14) reports that the rate of confinement per 100,000 population increased substantially in the United States between 1850 and the 1970s. Between 1880 and 1977 the rate for state and federal prisons and reformatories increased from 61 to 135. The rate for offenders in jails and other local facilities rose from 44 in 1880 to 68 in 1972. Rates for juvenile facilities moved from 23 in 1880 to 36 in 1974. Rates appear to have increased for all racial/ethnic groups. Especially significant is the increase in the nation's incarceration rate since about 1960.

There are many questions raised by these statistics and trends. Is the increase in the level of criminal and other disorderly behavior in the United States during the last 25 years sufficient to warrant such an increase in rates of formal social control? Or is the increase in the use of imprisonment the result of other factors? Waller notes that there has been a gradual decline over the last century in the use of prisons in countries such as Japan and the Netherlands. What has been their experience with the rate of criminal activity?

Criminologists have frequently noted that increases in the size of the American prison population are not directly related to increases in the crime rate. Is that pattern evident in the United States during the last century? Even if we assume some association between the rates of crime and incarceration, there are additional questions. Are there alternatives to formal social control that might help control criminal behavior? Has the increased reliance on imprisonment helped to reduce the rate of criminal activity in the United States to any significant extent? In confronting these sorts of questions, we again observe the significance of race in shaping the patterns of increased formal social control in this country over the last two decades.

For example, it is the extensive imprisonment of non–Whites in the United States that causes it to rank so high among the major nations of the world. Some data show that the rate of imprisonment for White Americans is comparable to rates found in those countries with relatively low rates of imprisonment, e.g., Canada, Japan and nations in Western Europe. Among non–White populations living within industrialized nations, Blacks in the United States are the most imprisoned people on earth, followed by the Australian aborigines and Blacks in South Africa (Waller, 1982:24).

Cahalan (1979) notes that these racial differences in the use of imprisonment in the United States have not changed substantially since

1880. She reports that in the nineteenth as well as the twentieth century, persons born abroad, Blacks, members of other non–White racial groups, and other non–English– speaking persons have constituted a large percentage of those incarcerated. Declines in the overrepresentation of the foreign born in the country's prisons and jails have been accompanied by increases in the proportion of Black and Spanish–speaking inmates (1979:9)

Considering these facts, we must ask additional questions. Are the rates of imprisonment for Blacks in the United States higher today than they were in the past? Have Blacks to a greater extent than Whites been the targets of increased formal social control in the United States during the last 25 years? If so, to what can we attribute this difference? Unfortunately, these significant questions related to race and criminal justice have not been widely examined by researchers. Two recent studies by Hawkins (1985) and Myers and Sabol (1986) provide useful data on historical trends in Black–White imprisonment. One of the more interesting findings from these two studies and the earlier work of Dunbaugh (1979) and Christianson (1981) is that Black– White differences in rates of incarceration vary considerably from state to state in the United States. Krisberg et al. (1986) reported significant differences across states in the rate of juvenile confinement by race.

Although most of the studies cited above were not concerned with juvenile deliquency, they do suggest that to fully understand the overrepresentation of Black youth within the criminal justice system (especially over time) we must view it from the perspective of the racial/ethnic patterns of social control that characterize much of American history. The institutions of social control that make up what we now call the criminal justice system serve an important function for those groups in power. They have been agencies for class and race control as much as for the control of individual deviant behavior (e.g., see Cox, 1948). Race and class control often have more to do with expanding and contracting job markets than with rising or falling rates of crime. More generally, they are often motivated by economic concerns as much as for a concern to maintain the noneconomic "social order". The detention of Black youth provides a graphic illustration of the interrelations among group social control, the political economy and views of childhood socialization.

Jobs, Socialization and Prisons

Except under conditions of slavery, racial stratification and inequality are associated with high rates of joblessness among members of subordinate groups. This structural unemployment is also a significant factor affecting their entry into and exit from the criminal justice system.

It is not just that joblessness leads to the kind of deprivation that is likely to "cause" individuals to resort to crime. The presence or absence of a job is also taken into account when making post– conviction decisions. In the United States Black youth have been denied access to gainful employment. Their joblessness has also increased the likelihood that they will be detained in the criminal justice system.

Quinney (1977:138) says that prisons in the United States are used mainly for those who commit a select group of crimes—primarily burglary, robbery, larceny and assault. This means that prisons function, for the most part, as institutions for the control of the working class, especially the "surplus" segments of the working class population. Blacks are a significant portion of this surplus population.

This concentration by the criminal justice system on the property–related offenses of the working class population is not primarily a function of a deprivation–caused excess of these crimes among them. Blacks and other members of the American underclass have high rates of involvement in violent crimes against the person, but these are not the crimes that are responsible for the substantial overrepresentation of these groups in the nation's prisons. In fact, since most of such crimes of violence are directed at other members of the same racial or social class group, they are often treated with undue leniency (Johnson, 1941; Garfinkel, 1949, Hawkins, 1983).

Quinney and other conflict theorists suggest that the criminal law in modern capitalist societies is used primarily to protect the "haves" from the "have–nots". Joblessness becomes, therefore, a marker of one's "have–not" status and potential criminality. Consistent with the data presented in the discussion above, Qinney notes that one out of every four Black men in their early twenties spends some time in prison, jail, or on probation. Of course, in large urban areas of the nation the percentage of young Black men who are confined is considerably higher than 25%. In some areas it may be as high as 50–60%. Most often this figure is in the same range as the long–term unemployment and underemployment rates for a given area. Black males are targeted for social control because of the threat they pose to the property interests of middle– and upper–class Americans.

To understand the plight of Black youth does not require that one view American society solely from the kind of conflict perspective advocated by Quinney. Even traditional functionalist–consensus views of society emphasize the linkage between social class status, jobs, and crime. In his Durkheim– inspired theory of anomie and crime, Robert Merton (1968) argued that much of the criminal behavior of the lower class can be attributed to a lack of the means needed to obtain the goals established and recognized by American society. Jobs and other legitimate means of obtaining these goals were said to be routinely denied to members of subordinate groups such as Blacks.

Socialization for Work—Work as Socialization

Traditional conceptions of society's role in the socialization of youth are helpful also for understanding the condition of Black youth in the United States. The adequate socialization of young people is a central task for all societies. Finding and assigning appropriate work for them is a major part of the apparatus of socialization. For juveniles, the process of learning the correct norms and work habits has been made a functional part of several institutions in society. These include, of course, the family, schools, and church. These institutions are usually perceived to be (and often are) less effective for youths from subordinate or peripheral groups such as the lower classes and ethnic and racial minorities. *Hence institutions of social control are often seen as "last resort" methods of socialization for the youth of the dominant group but as primary agencies of socialization for young persons from subordinate groups.*

Cahalan's (1979) observation that American prisons have disproportionately housed various "out" groups over the years supports the idea that such institutions have been viewed as agencies of socialization as well as social control. For example, in the past the youth of various White ethnic groups who had recently immigrated to the United States were seen as especially in need of socialization into the American mainstream. Juvenile institutions were thought to serve this purpose for many of these youth. It is not surprising that the establishment of separate juvenile court facilities and correctional institutions came during the late 1800s and early 1900s after several decades of the immigration in large numbers of previously excluded European ethnics.

The earliest advocates of state–supported prisons in the United States and other industrialized countries stressed the centrality of prison labor in the reformation and socialization of criminals (see Barnes, 1927). Adolescents and young adults have always been seen as the primary targets of such "reformation through work" policies and practices. That is, because of their youth they have been thought to be more likely than older adults to benefit from such work in practical ways (learning job skills, work habits, etc.). For adults, many work requirements have been seen primarily as a form of retribution, or at best penitence.

The Protestant ethic that has been an integral part of American society views work as a means of avoiding a life of crime. Conversely, the commission of crime is seen as evidence of an absence of appropriate work habits. Although American prisons during the late twentieth century are no longer institutions in which labor is a part of the punishment for crime, concern for the work habits of criminals is still evident. For example, the possession of a job or work skills is frequently considered in sentencing and parole decisions. Numerous researchers have noted that much of the post–arrest overrepresentation of Blacks in the criminal justice system may be partly due to Black employment disadvantages.

Black Adolescents and the Criminal Justice System

Black youth are particularly affected by such considerations since they are even more likely than Black adults to be out of work.

There are other perceived linkages between work and youthful crime. It is generally believed that young people have a great deal of "excess energy" which must be guided into correct avenues of conduct. Work during adolescence serves to harness such energies as well as prepare the young person for a life of adult work. But, as Goodman (1960) and others have noted such efforts at guiding adolescent work habits were much more successful in the agrarian economies of the past than they are in modern industrial societies.

In early industrial societies young people were forced to labor in "sweat factories" which presumably served as both outlets for their energies as well as training grounds for later adult work. Of course, the principal motivation for such adolescent work practices was to create larger profits rather than the training of youth. The inhumaneness of such practices and their inappropriateness for purposes of socialization may have been instrumental in helping to produce the conditions that led to excessively large numbers of economically idle young persons in western industrial cities several centuries ago. These same conditions also led to the development of juvenile and young adult correctional institutions during this same period. To a great extent these social conditions have not changed substantially and the lack of appropriate work is a factor contributing to the plight of adolescents today.

Modern economic conditions in the United States have led to several new problems for adolescents, especially Black adolescents. Because of the increasing mechanization of labor and legal restrictions (child labor and minimum wage laws) adolescents have become much more a "surplus population" than during the past. The number of adolescents far surpasses the number of available jobs. The shift toward a service-oriented economy has produced new jobs such as those in fast food restaurants. But these are limited in number and they seldom provide the possibility of job mobility (or continuity) through adulthood. In addition, as the youth of an oppressed racial minority, there is much less interest in the proper socialization of Black youth than there is for majority group youth. This means that available jobs (except the most menial ones) will be reserved for members of more privileged groups. Even the availability of menial labor is being reduced due to the transfer of many industrial operations to Third World countries. Black youth in the United States today, to a greater extent than White youth or Black adults, are a surplus population.

The economic conditions that characterize modern American society are due to major structural changes that are largely irreversible. These conditions pose special problems for the socialization of Black youth. Their age group is twice as likely to be unemployed as Whites (see *The State of Black America*, 1986 report of the National Urban League).

Thus, it is rather difficult for them to be socialized into the work ethic that is so much a part of the ideology of the nation. In addition they are seldom able to obtain the means necessary to achieve even minimally the materialistic goals of American society. To the extent that such an ethic and its rewards are related to criminal behavior (or social control absent criminal behavior), Black youth will continue to make up a disproportionate portion of the nation's prison population.

On the one hand, Black youth are similar to their parents in terms of their status as part of a surplus population. Black adults are also unemployed at levels consistently higher than those for White adults. On the other hand, it appears that economic conditions for Black adolescents have been deteriorating to a much greater extent than those for Black adults over the last thirty years. The 1986 Urban League reported stated: "since 1960, unemployment rates for Blacks have been consistently double those for Whites. Black teenagers have had the highest rates and sharpest increases in these rates among all component groups in both the Black and the White population" (p. 214). Mare and Winship (1984:39) found that "an important exception to the improvements in the relative socioeconomic status of Blacks during recent decades is increased levels of joblessness among Black youths relative to Whites... Although racial convergence on school enrollment and educational attainment has reduced other socioeconomic inequalities between the races, it has widened the employment difference."

The problems of a changing economy combine with persisting racism to further jeopardize the socialization of Black youths. David Milner points out in his recent study, *Children and Race* that racial attitudes still play a tremendous role in the development of children. It is a functional part of their cultural milieu in American society. He says, "While the messages about race which Black and White children receive are the same, the implications are radically different. Whereas White children are encouraged by these images to value and identify with their own ethnic group, and indeed to deem it superior, Black children are confronted with an image of their group which is at worst derogatory and at best ambivalent" (p. 132).

Thus, Black adolescents are confronted with two interrelated sets of conditions that shape their growth and development. First, they are denied work and job opportunities that might provide them with self-esteem, a sense of the future, a work ethic and skills, and economic resources. Second, racism results in the socialization into values that further destroy their perceptions of self. These two sets of conditions combine to lead to a greater likelihood of their involvement with the criminal justice system. One important consequence of such involvement is to create even greater impediments to a successful transition from adolescence-to-adulthood for Black youth than for the youth of other, more privileged groups.

The Effects of Custody: Joblessness and Recidivism

Researchers have noted consistently that recidivism in the criminal justice system is a feedback process. That is, the path from arrest to confinement to re-confinement has been depicted as a circular one for a large number of individuals. The technical aspects of modeling this feedback process have occupied most of the attention of past researchers (e.g., see Belkin, Blumstein and Glass, 1973). Little research has been done on the social dynamics of that process. For example, we still know relatively little about why some individuals within a group of persons with similar sociodemographic characteristics return to the criminal justice system while others do not. Most recidivism researchers propose that it is possible to identify certain traits that distinguish recidivists and non-recidivists despite their similarities.

Critics of recidivism research offer two significant observations. First, they suggest that recidivism is a function not only of the characteristics of individuals, it is also dependent on situational factors (Clarke, 1983). Included among these factors is the post–release employment status of the individual. Second, they propose that recidivism must be seen as partly the result of the crime control efforts of the criminal justice system. That is, confinement itself seems to lead to reconfinement. Reasons ranging from the criminogenic environment of prisons to labeling by criminal justice officials have been offered to explain this finding.

We concur with these criticisms of traditional recidivism research. We offer an additional observation, one that has special significance for understanding the plight of Black adolescents. The tendency to view recidivism as an institutional feedback process has meant that the primary emphasis has been on its impact on the criminal justice system. That is, researchers have been concerned about the impact of recidivism on prison overcrowding and similar organizational problems. A secondary concern has been the failure of correctional institutions to prevent recidivism; but this has been viewed as largely an organizational–management concern.

On the other hand, recidivism is but one of the social consequences of imprisonment and/or its failure. Even absent recidivism, many societal institutions are affected by high rates of imprisonment. The lives of those who are imprisoned are affected in many ways. One major effect is reduced employability. A reduced opportunity for employment is important because it may lead to recidivism. But, even when it does not lead to recidivism, it has a tremendous impact on the lives of those involved. Since adolescence is a period during which there is preparation for employment, the consequences of imprisonment for youth are particularly devastating. We explore some of those consequences below.

Special Topics: Youth in the Criminal Justice System

Socialization for Joblessness

In discussing the worsening employment status of Black youth, Mare and Winship (1984:39, citing U.S. Department of Labor, 1982, statistics) report that in 1954 Black and White unemployment rates for 16 to 24 year olds were 15.8 and 9.9 percent, respectively. This difference of 5.9 percentage points had grown to 8.7 in 1960 and 12.0 in 1970. In 1980 the rates were 26.4 and 12.0 percent respectively, a difference of 14.4 percentage points. The percentage of this age group who were employed declined for Blacks from 47.2 in 1954 to 40.6 in 1980, but increased for Whites from 49.7 in 1954 to 62.0 in 1980.

Mare and Winship note that these trends have not been satisfactorily explained. They suggest that many proposed explanations focus on those social and economic changes believed to hurt Black youths disproportionately. These include the spread of minimum wage legislation, immigrants, changes in job composition and location of industry, the reduced willingness of youths to take low status employment, etc. (p. 40). These are all plausible and likely explanations for the observed trends. However, in an earlier investigation Mare and Winship (1979) observed that these factors appear to alter the employment chances of Black and White youths alike and leave unaffected the race difference. That is, they do not explain why the White youth employment rate has improved since 1954 while that for Blacks has worsened.

Neither the work of Mare and Winship nor the studies they cite consider the potential impact of the criminal justice system on the joblessness of Black and White youth or on the observed race difference. That is, what is the impact on Black youth joblessness of the fact that perhaps a quarter or more of them will serve time in prison during their years of adolescence? Is the decrease in employment for Black youth employment related to the continuing rise in their incarceration rate? If so, what is the connection?

These questions have not been explored in either the criminal justice nor status attainment literatures. During the period between 1954 and the 1980s decreased levels of Black youth employment have been accompanied by large scale increases in the rate of their commitment to correctional institutions. *Researchers have tended to suggest that the economic plight of Black youth is one of the "causes" of their entry into the criminal justice system. Economic deprivation is seen as a catalyst for criminal activity. On the other hand, they have seldom assessed empirically the impact of high rates of detention on levels of employment. That is, to what extent does increased imprisonment reduce the employment potential of Black youth?*

In this paper we do not have the data to provide such an empirical assessment. However, we do suggest the following:

(1) The increased detention of Black youth in correctional facilities

over the last three decades has had a severe negative impact on their chances for employment.
(2) Large numbers of Black youth are confined in correctional institutions during the years traditionally devoted to entry into a career. The years of adolescence for youth from all social classes are devoted to education. For youth from the lowest social classes formal education in institutions of higher learning has been less important than on–the–job training. Confinement in the criminal justice system prevents or delays such career entry, whether it takes the form of additional education or job training.
(3) The criminal record that results from arrest, conviction and confinement further jeopardizes the job potential of Black youth. In contrast to the past, more and more of the low–skilled jobs that offer any chance for advancement are found in services industries. A criminal record is more of a liability for those interested in these jobs than for the less people–oriented work once widely available. In combination with continuing racial prejudice, a criminal record becomes a formidable barrier to finding a reasonably well–paying job for an increasingly large number of Black youth.
(4) Given the absence of meaningful efforts at rehabilitation or job–training within the nation's correctional facilities, these institutions socialize Black youth for joblessness. This results from both the absence of meaningful job training and the presence of "crime laboratories" within such institutions.

Conclusions

We propose that future researchers should assess more systematically the impact on Black youth of confinement in correctional institutions. Beyond issues of just deserts or retribution, the confinement of such large numbers of Black youth is a serious social problem that must be confronted. It is doubtful that Black adolescents are committing crime at a level comparable to their level of incarceration. Even if such were shown to be the case, we must question the benefits to society of a purely retributory correctional policy. Neither juvenile nor adult correctional facilities in the United States offer the kind of rehabilitative environment that could help remedy the employment–related problems caused by incarceration. The trend toward for–profit prisons that is evident in many states today offers some hope of job–training. However, as with convict leasing operations of the past the profit motive may erode the potential for truly rehabilitative efforts in the nation's correctional facilities.

We support Krisberg et al.'s (1986:31) proposal that "A priority should be placed upon raising public awareness about the high incarceration rates of minority youth. This consciousness raising should be focused on stimulating a broad-based community dialogue about both governmental policies and self-help strategies that might change existing incarceration trends". The various alternatives to incarceration that have been so widely discussed during the last decade must become something more than convenient political slogans. Indeed, it is somewhat ironic that major increases in the rate of Black youth and adult incarceration have occurred despite the proven effectiveness of several alternatives to traditional confinement, e.g., restitution and various community-based facilities. Many states are now engaged in the construction of major correctional facilities that will further decrease the likelihood that alternatives to confinement will be chosen. If current trends continue, Black youth and adults will make up more than eighty percent of the prison populations of many states in the nation by 1995, or before.

As we have noted in this paper, to confront the problem of the disproportionate incarceration of Black youth we must also tackle the problem of persisting racism in American society. Racism in both its individual-level and institutional forms has contributed much to the current level of inequality in the rates of incarceration for Blacks and Whites. Neither crime nor punishment occurs within a social vacuum. Racism has been and continues to be a major component of the social milieu wherein justice is administered in the United States.

Notes

1. Of course, we can also ask to what extent the changes brought about by adolescence cause or contribute to antisocial/criminal behavior. Is the period of adolescence in every society one in which there are likely to be challenges to authority, tradition, etc.? Cross cultural studies seem to suggest that there is no uniform pattern of behavior that characterizes adolescence. In some societies the period of transition appears to be more tumultuous than in others. In modern, western societies the period between childhood and adulthood is prolonged in comparison to the past and to that found in nonwestern societies. Many would suggest that it is this postponing of adulthood rather than the process of transition itself that causes so many problems for youth in the United States. On the other hand, we must also explain why the United States in comparison to other highly industrialized societies uses the criminal justice system to a greater extent in efforts to control the behavior of its youth.
2. See *The Prevalence of Imprisonment*, pp. 2–3 and *Prisoners in 1984*.

3. See *Profile of Jail Inmates: Sociodemographic Findings from the 1978 Survey of Inmates of Local Jails*, Table 1, p. 12.
4. See *Profile of Jail Inmates*, p. 2.
5. The number of such persons was relatively small. They numbered 926 or around 2% of all juveniles in 1979 and only 960 of 48,701 delinquents in 1982. See Krisbert et al. (1986) for a more detailed examination of minority youth incarceration in the United States.
6. This is not to say that questions regarding the etiology of crime and the fairness of punishment are not important scholarly and public policy concerns. Rather, we are suggesting that the social consequences of the use of confinement to attempt to control crime have too often been ignored. We also doubt the utility and scientific soundness of sociobiological approaches to the study of Black–White crime differences.

References

Bachman, J. G., O'Malley, P., & Johnston, J. (1978). *Youth in Transition, Volume VI–Adolescence to adulthood: Change and stability in the lives of young men.* Ann Arbor: University of Michigan, Institute for Social Research.

Bachman, J. G., Swayzer, G., & Wirtanen, I. D. (1970, 1971). *Youth in transition, Volumes III and IV.* Ann Arbor: University of Michigan, Institute for Social Research.

Barnes, H. E. (1927). *The evolution of penology in Pennsylvania.* Indianapolis: Bobbs–Merrill.

Belkin, J., Blumstein, A., & Glass, W. (1973). Recidivism as a feedback process: An analytic model and empirical validation. *Journal of Criminal Justice, 1,* 7–26.

Burke, P. J., & Turk, A. T. (1975). Factors affecting post–arrest dispositions: A model for analysis. *Social Problems, 22(3),* 313–331.

Cahalan, M. (1979). Trends in incarceration in the United States since 1880: A summary of reported rates and the distribution of offenses. *Crime and Delinquency, 25* (January), 9–41.

Christianson, S. (1981). Our Black prisons. *Crime and Delinquency, 27,* 364–375.

Clarke, R. V. (1983). Situational crime prevention: Its theoretical basis and practical scope. In *Crime and Justice: An annual review of research.* M. Tonrey and N. Morris (eds.), 4, 225–256. Chicago: University of Chicago Press.

Cox, O. (1948). *Caste, class and race: A study in social dynamics.* New York: Doubleday and Company.

Dunbaugh, F. M. (1979). Racially disproportionate rates of incarceration in the United States. *Prison Law Monitor, 1* (March), 205, 219–222.

Elliott, D. S., & Voss, H. L. (1974). *Delinquency and dropout.* Lexington, MA: D. C. Heath.

Garfinkel, W. (1949). Research note on inter– and intra–racial homicide. *Social Forces, 27,* 369–381.

Goodman, P. (1960). *Growing up absurd.* New York: Random House.

Green, E. (1970). Race, social status and criminal arrest. *American Sociological Review, 35(3),* 476–490.

Hawkins, D. F. (1983). Black and White homicide differentials: Alternatives to an inadequate theory. *Criminal Justice and Behavior*, 10 (December), 407–440.

Hawkins, D. F. (1985). Trends in Black–White imprisonment: Changing conceptions of race or changing patterns of social control? *Crime and Social Justice, Number 24*, 187–209.

Hawkins, D. F. (1986). Beyond anomalies: Rethinking the conflict perspective of race and criminal punishment. Paper presented at the Annual meeting of the Society for the Study of Social Problems, August.

Hindelang, M. J. (1982). Race and crime. In L. D. Savitz & H. Johnson (Eds.), *Contemporary criminology*. New York: Wiley and Sons, pp. 168–184.

Huizinga, D., & Elliot, V. S. (1986). Juvenile offenders: Prevalence, offender incidence and arrest rates by race. Paper presented at the meeting on race and the incarceration of juveniles, Racine, Wisconsin, December.

Johnson, G. B. (1941). The Negro and crime. *Annals of the Academy of Political and Social Science, 217*, 93–104.

Krisberg, B., Schwartz, I., Fishman, G., Eisikovits, Z., & Guttman, E. (1986). The incarceration of minority youth. Working paper prepared at the Hubert H. Humphrey Institute of Public Affairs, University of Minnesota, May.

Mare, R. D., & Winship, C. (1984). The paradox of lessening racial inequality and joblessness among Black youth: Enrollment, enlistment, and employment. *American Sociological Review, 49* (February), 39–55.

McGarrell, E. F., & Flanagan, T. J. (Eds.) (1985). *Sourcebook of criminal justice statistics–1984*. U.S. Department of Justice, Bureau of Justice Statistics. Washington, D.C.: U.S. Government Printing Office.

Merton, R. K. (1968). *Social theory and social structure*. New York: Free Press.

Milner, D. (1983). *Children and Race*. Beverly Hills, CA: Sage Publications.

Myers, S. L. Jr., & Sabol, W. J. (1986). The stability of punishment hypothesis: Regional differences in racially disproportionate prison populations and incarcerations, 1850–1980. Paper presented at the Annual meeting of the Law and Society Association, May 28–June 1.

National Urban League, Inc. (1986). *The state of Black America–1986*. New York.

Petersilia, J. (1983). *Racial Discrimination in the criminal justice system*. Santa Monica, CA: Rand Corporation.

Petersilia, J., & Turner, S. (1985). *Guideline-based justice: Implications for racial minorities*. Santa Monica, CA: Rand Corporation.

Pope, C. E. (1979). Race and crime revisited. *Crime and Delinquency, 25*, 347–357.

Pope, C. E., & McNeeley, R. L. (1981). Race, crime and criminal justice: An overview. In R. L. McNeeley & C. E. Pope (Eds.), *Race, crime and criminal justice*. Beverly Hills, CA: Sage Publications, pp. 9–27.

Quinney, R. (1977). *Class, state and crime: On the theory and practice of criminal justice*. New York: David McKay.

United States Department of Justice. (1985). *The prevalence of imprisonment*, Special Report. Bureau of Justice Statistics. Washington, D.C.: U.S. Government Printing Office.

_____ (1980). *Profile of jail inmates: Sociodemographic findings from the 1978 survey of inmates of local jails*. Bureau of Justice Statistics. Washington, D.C.: U.S. Government Printing Office.

United States Department of Justice (1985). *Prisoners in 1984 Bulletin*. Bureau of Justice Statistics. Washington, D.C.: U.S. Government Printing Office.

United States Department of Labor. 1982. *Labor statistics derived from the current population survey: A databook, Volume 1.* Washington, D.C.: United States Government Printing Office.

Velde, R. W. (1977). *Racial justice: Black judges and defendants in an urban trial court.* Lexington, MA: Lexington Books.

Waller, I. (1982). Canadian crime and justice in comparative perspective: Selected indicators for selected countries, 1900– 1980. Manuscript prepared at the Department of Criminology, The University of Ottawa: Ottawa, Ontario, Canada.

Weiner, N. L., & Charles, V. W. (1971). Decisions by juvenile officers. *American Journal of Sociology, 77(2),* 199–210.

Williams, J. R., & Gold, M. (1972). From delinquent behavior to official delinquency. *Social Problems, 20,* 209–229.

Wilson, J. O., & Herrnstein, R. J. (1985). *Crime and human nature.* New York: Simon and Schuster.

Biographical Sketches and Indexes

Biographical Sketches

IRIS E. BALY, Ph.D. is a Staff Psychologist in the department of psychiatry at Kaiser Permanente Medical Center in Vallejo, California and is in private practice in Oakland, CA.

She has been variously involved in educational institutions as a school counselor, school psychologist, and as an educator at both the secondary and college levels. Family therapy, and work with children and adolescents are particular areas of interest in her clinical practice and research. Dr. Baly earned her Ph.D. in Counseling Psychology from the University of California at Berkeley.

JAMES A. BANKS is Professor of Education at the University of Washington, Seattle. He is also a past President of the National Council for the Social Studies. Professor Banks received his Bachelor's degree in elementary education and social science from Chicago State University and his Master's and Ph.D. degrees in these fields from Michigan State University. He is a specialist in social studies and in multiethnic education, and has written widely in these two fields: over ninety articles, contributions to books and book reviews for professional publications, and more than a dozen books, including *Teaching Strategies for Ethnic Studies* (Fourth Edition, 1987), *Multiethnic Education: Theory and Practice* (Second Edition, 1988), and *March Toward Freedom: A History of Black Americans* (Second Edition Revised, 1978).

His many honors and fellowships include Association of Teacher Educators Distinguished Lecturer, Distinguished scholar/researcher on Minority Education (American Educational Research Association), Spenser Fellowship, and a Rockefeller Fellowship which provided support for a study of Black youth who live in predominantly white suburban communities, the results of which are presented in the present volume.

WILLIAM E. CAVIL III, Associate Director of Development and Dissemination at the Institute for the Advanced Study of Black Family Life and Culture, Inc., Oakland, California, is a communications and media specialist who graduated from San Francisco State University. He is a leading expert on indoctrination methods/techniques and media portrayal of Black family life.

MAXINE L. CLARK is Associate Professor of Psychology at Wake Forest University. She received her doctorate in Developmental Psychology from the University of Illinois and has post–doctoral training at the Institute for Social Research, University of Michigan, National Survey of Black Americans Project. Dr. Clark is a member of the editorial boards of the *Journal of Youth and Adolescence*, the *Journal of Negro Education*, and the *Journal of Genetic Psychology* and is an active reviewer for many other journals. Her research and publications have focused on racial identity and self–identity, social stereotypes, and children's friendships. She is currently conducting research and writing on the friendships and social networks of Black adolescents.

HALFORD H. FAIRCHILD is a Consulting Social Psychologist in Los Angeles, California. He is past President of the Association of Black Psychologists (1986–87) and a Visiting Assistant Professor at California State University, Los Angeles. He has published research on institutional discrimination in housing and education; the creation, production, and evaluation of pro–social television; and Black male/female relationships. Dr. Fairchild received his Ph.D. in Social Psychology in 1977 from the University of Michigan.

ANDERSON J. FRANKLIN is a Professor and Director of the Clinical Psychology Program at the City University of New York. He is also a past coordinator of Child, Adolescent and Family Clinical Training. As a recipient of a post–doctoral fellowship from the Rockefeller Foundation and in collaboration with the Institute for Social Research at the University of Michigan, he has begun a research program studying psychological well–being in Blacks. Dr. Franklin is a member of the New York State Board for Psychology and is particularly interested in issues pertaining to ethnicity and mental health.

JEWELLE TAYLOR GIBBS is currently an Associate Professor and Chairperson of the M.S.W. Curriculum at the School of Social Welfare at the University of California at Berkeley. Her areas of research and teaching are adolescent psychosocial problems, minority mental health, and methods of brief treatment.

Dr. Gibbs, who received her Ph.D. in clinical psychology from the University of California at Berkeley, has served on the Board of Directors of the American Orthopsychiatric Association and the Board of Publications of the National Association of Social Workers. She also served as a member of the Task Panel on Special Populations of President Carter's Commission on Mental Health. In 1985 she was a Fellow at the Mary I. Bunting Institute at Radcliffe College, and is listed in *Who's Who of American Women* and *Who's Who Among Black Americans*. Dr. Gibbs, who was the recipient of the 1987 McCormick Award from the American Association of Suicidology for her scholarly contributions to minority suicide, is the editor of *Young, Black, and Male in America: An Endangered Species*. Dover, MA: Auburn House Publishing Company, 1988.

Biographical Sketches

LAWFORD L. GODDARD is a Sociologist/Demographer who received his doctoral degree from Stanford University and is a leading researcher in the area of Black population studies and family life. He is Associate Director of Education and Training at the Institute for the Advanced Study of Black Family Life and Culture, Inc., Oakland, California, and Senior Research Associate, Alcoholism Studies, Charles R. Drew University of Medicine and Science, Los Angeles.

DARNELL F. HAWKINS is Professor of Black Studies and Sociology at the University of Illinois at Chicago. He received his doctorate in Sociology from the University of Michigan in 1976 and a law degree from the University of North Carolina, Chapel Hill in 1980. His research interests include the study of homicide among Blacks, racial differences in punishment for crime, and the development of state operated prison systems in the United States.

BERTHA GARRETT HOLLIDAY is a community psychologist who has been involved in both scholarly and applied efforts. She has been a member of the faculty at Vanderbilt University, engaged in postdoctoral studies on ecological theories and methods at Cornell University as a Ford Foundation Fellow, conducted legislative and policy analyses in the U.S. Senate as a Congressional Fellow sponsored by the Society for Research in Child Development, and served as manager of evaluation for a national network of dropout prevention projects. Currently, she conducts and supervises policy, legislative, and regulatory analysis activities for the District of Columbia Commission on Mental Health.

Dr. Holliday has published numerous articles and book chapters on the topics of Black family and child socialization, school processes affecting the academic achievement of Black children, and primary prevention strategies. She has served on the Board of Ethnic Minority Affairs of the American Psychological Association and is a member of the Association of Black Psychologists. Dr. Holliday received her B.A. from the University of Chicago, her Ed.M. from Harvard University, and her Ph.D. from the University of Texas at Austin.

NOLAN E. JONES is the Staff Director for the Committee on Justice and Public Safety of the National Governors' Association. Prior to joining the National Governors' staff, he was Assistant Professor of political science at the University of Michigan in Ann Arbor, teaching and researching in the areas of constitutional law, federalism, American policy and race relations. He has published several articles concerning state politics, criminal justice, ethnic politics, and public policy.

Dr. Jones holds a Ph.D. from Washington University in St. Louis, where he was a Woodrow Wilson and an Edna Gelhorn Fellow; and an undergraduate degree, with honors, from Texas Southern University. He has also participated in special studies at Swarthmore College, the University of Wisconsin, the University of Copenhagen, Denmark, and Harvard University.

His many other activities include Advisory board member of Tuskegee Institute and North Carolina Central University's project on Black Institutions of Higher Education, Advisory Council on Career Planning and Placement for the Washington, D.C. Public Schools, Board of Directors of Offender Aid and Restoration, U.S.A., consultant and principal author to the doctoral program in the School of Education at Morgan State University, and consultant to the Department of Justice's project on the "Inequality of Justice: A Report on Crime and the Administration of Justice in the Minority Community."

REGINALD L. JONES is Professor of Afro–American Studies at the University of California at Berkeley. He received the A.B. degree cum laude in psychology from Morehouse College, the M.A. in Clinical Psychology from Wayne State University and the Ph.D. in Psychology from the Ohio State University. He has been a clinical psychologist in military and state hospitals, Professor and Vice Chair, Department of Psychology, The Ohio State University; Professor and Chair, Department of Education, University of California at Riverside, and Professor and Director, University Testing Center, Haile Sellassie I University, Addis Ababa, Ethiopia. He has also taught at U.C.L.A. and at Miami, Fisk, and Indiana Universities.

Dr. Jones has produced 28 instructional videotapes, authored more than 200 chapters, articles, reviews and technical reports, and coauthored or edited more than a dozen books, including *Student Dissent in the Schools* (1971 with I. Hendrick), *Psychoeducational Assessment of Minority Group Children: A Casebook* (1988) and *Black Psychology*, Third Edition (in press).

He received the Citation for Outstanding Achievement from The Ohio State University and, for his work on issues related to assessing and educating Black children, The J.E. Wallace Wallin Award from the Council for Exceptional Children, The Education Award from the American Association on Mental Retardation, and the Loetta Hunt Award from Ohio State. In 1979 and in 1986 he received the Scholarship Award of the Association of Black Psychologists.

COURTLAND C. LEE is an Associate Professor and Director of the Counselor Education Program at the University of Virginia. His areas of research specialization include minority mental health and adolescent development. He has published numerous articles on adolescents and counseling ethnic minorities, particularly Black youth. A major focus of his research has been on the psychosocial development of youth in rural areas.

He is editor of the *Journal of Multicultural Counseling and Development*

Biographical Sketches

and is an active member of the American Association for Counseling and Development. Dr. Lee received his Ph.D. in Counseling from Michigan State University.

JULIANNE MALVEAUX is an Economist and Writer who is currently visiting faculty in the Afro–American Studies Department at the University of California at Berkeley, and an affiliated scholar at the Institute for Research on Women and Gender at Stanford University. Her research focuses on the status of Blacks and women in the labor market and the economy. She was co–editor (with Margaret Simms) of the volume, *Slipping Through the Cracks: The Status of Black Women* (Transactions Publications, 1986), and is currently completing a book on the status of women in the labor market titled *No Images: Contemporary Black Women in the Workplace*. Malveaux received her Ph.D. in economics from M.I.T. in 1980.

CAROLYN BENNETT MURRAY is an Associate Professor in the Psychology Department and Ethnic Studies Program at the University of California, Riverside. She received her doctorate in Social Psychology from the University of Michigan, where she has returned on two separate occasions as a post–doctoral fellow. She has also been a post–doctoral fellow in Aging, Mental Health and Culture at the Institute on Aging, Portland State University, and during the 1985–86 academic year she was a post–doctoral Ford Fellow in the Psychology Department at the University of California, Los Angeles. Her research and published work spans two areas: (1) attribution and affective consequences of negative stereotypic expectations for academic achievement, and (2) social support among the minority elderly.

HECTOR F. MYERS, PH.D. is an Associate Professor of Psychology and Co–Director of the Minority Mental Health Training Program in the Department of Psychology at UCLA, and Director of the Biobehavioral Laboratory at the Charles R. Drew University of Medicine and Science. Dr. Myers is an active researcher with numerous research articles and book chapters on stress and the mental and physical health of Black adults and families to his credit. His most recent research has been on the role of psychosocial stress in the development of essential hypertension in Blacks, and he is a frequent consultant to federal agencies in the development and evaluation of research initiatives on the health status and well being of Black Americans. Dr. Myers is currently involved in a collaborative effort to develop and test a culturally–adapted, behavioral skill based parent training program as a primary prevention tool for Black families.

E. JOYCE ROLAND is Lecturer in Nursing at the University of North Carolina, Chapel Hill, and a doctoral candidate in psychology at North

Carolina State University. She received the B.S. degree in Nursing from Winston–Salem State University, the M.S. in Nursing (Maternal–Child Health) from Seton Hall University, and the M.A. in psychology from North Carolina State University. Ms. Roland has worked on numerous community boards focusing on problems associated with early childbearing. Her Master's thesis examined variables influencing the sexual behaviors and practices of Black adolescent males and her doctoral dissertation (in progress) explores the consequences of early childbearing among Black women.

DIANE SCOTT–JONES is Associate Professor in the Department of Educational Psychology and the Department of Psychology at the University of Illinois. Prior to her present appointment, Dr. Scott–Jones held faculty positions at North Carolina State University and at the University of Pittsburgh. She received the Ph.D. degree in developmental psychology from the University of North Carolina, Chapel Hill. Her research focuses on social development and family processes. She is currently conducting research on adolescent sexuality and pregnancy, and on family influences on cognitive development and school achievement. Her recent publications include "Mother as Teacher in the Families of High and Low Achieving Low Income Black First Graders", in the *Journal of Negro Education*, 1987, and "Families as Educators: The Transition from Informal to Formal School Learning" in *Educational Horizons*, 1987.

EDWARD G. SINGLETON, Ph.D. is a Psychologist in Private Practice in Baltimore, Maryland. He received his doctorate in Personality Psychology from Howard University and his masters degree in Clinical Psychology from Loyola College in Maryland. He is also a Training Consultant for the High Risk Youth (HRY) Project sponsored by Coppin State College in concert with the Juvenile Services Administration of the State of Maryland. HYR's purpose is to implement a model intervention demonstration substance abuse prevention program for youth who are identified as active users and abusers of alcohol and other drugs. Dr. Singleton has conducted research and published several articles and technical reports on substance use and the application of health, educational and correctional policies and programs to youthful populations. He is a member of the American Psychological Association and the Association of Black Psychologists.

SANDRA NOEL SMITH received the Ph.D. degree from The Catholic University and has been on the faculty of Howard University for the past twenty–one years. She has served as Director of Student Teaching, and as a member of the graduate faculty has taught courses in curriculum development, mathematics methodology, methods of college teaching, values analysis and supervision of instruction. She has served as consultant to the Ministries of Education in Indonesia, Bermuda, and Surinam, and to Catholic school systems throughout the United States. On July 1, 1988 she became the first lay principal of Bishop McGuinness High School, the Catholic diocesan high school of Winston–Salem, North Carolina.

BARBARA STAGGERS, M.D., M.PH. is an Adolescent Specialist who is currently Associate Director of Adolescent Medicine at Children's Hospital Medical Center of Northern California. She received the Bachelor of Arts from the University of California at Berkeley and graduated from the University of California at San Francisco with combined Medical and Masters of Public Health degrees. She completed her pediatric residency at Children's Hospital Medical Center of Northern California and her adolescent medicine fellowship at the University of California at San Francisco. Dr. Staggers has designed numerous programs for adolescents and has worked extensively with the Black adolescent population of Northern California.

RONALD L. TAYLOR is Associate Professor (and former Chair) of Sociology at the University of Connecticut. He received his M.A. from Howard University and his Ph.D. in sociology from Boston University. He is the co–editor (with Doris Y. Wilkinson) of the *Black Male in America*, and has published in such journals as the *American Journal of Sociology, American Journal of Orthopsychiatry, Social Science Quarterly, Journal of Black Studies*, and the *Humboldt Journal of Social Relations*. He has served on the editorial board of the *American Journal of Orthopsychiatry, Contemporary Sociology*, University Presses of New England, and is currently guest editor for a special issue of *Youth and Society* on the social and economic status of Black youth in the U.S. and co–editor (with Patricia Bell–Scott) for a special issue of the *Journal of Adolescent Research* on Black adolescents.

RANDOLF A. TOBIAS is an Associate Professor in the Graduate Department of Education and Community Programs at Queens College of the City University of New York. Prior to his present position, he served as Associate Dean for Special Programs, Queens College, CUNY, Director of the Division of Teacher Education at Winston–Salem State University and at Shaw University, and Assistant Professor of Teacher Education, Long Island University, the Brooklyn Center. Prior to his professional career in Higher Education, Dr. Tobias taught secondary and middle school grades within the public and private schools of New York City. As a Mellon Fellow in 1983, Dr. Tobias examined supervisory roles aimed at improving curriculum and teaching in alternative neighborhood schools. His publications include: *Human Issues and Human Values* (1978) a work funded by the North Carolina Endowment for the Humanities, "In Preparation for Pupil Re-assignment" in *Perspectives on Urban Affairs in North Carolina* (1980) Urban Studies Council, University of North Carolina, and "Retention Strategies in Higher Education: A Paradigm" in *Issues in College Learning Centers* (1987) vol. 4, Office of Special Academic Services, Long Island University, the Brooklyn Campus. Dr. Tobias is currently involved in the training of prospective principals and assistant principals within Queens College's School Administration and Supervision Program.

EARLE H. WEST is Associate Dean of the School of Education at Howard University where he has taught for twenty-five years. He received the Ph.D. degree from George Peabody College of Vanderbilt University. His principal areas of teaching and research are the history and philosophy of education.

ANNE BITTINGER WHITE is a Doctoral Candidate in Applied Developmental Psychology at North Carolina State University. She earned the A.B. degree in psychology at Duke University and the M.S. degree in Applied Developmental Psychology at North Carolina State University. Ms. White has worked as a counselor for adolescents in the area of career development. She has served on a number of boards and committees concerned with the development of adolescents. Her primary area of interest is the social development of adolescents, with a focus on the problem of unplanned adolescent pregnancy. Her Master's thesis examined variables associated with sexual activity in early adolescence. She plans to continue her work on the antecedents of adolescent pregnancy, with the aim of developing strategies for prevention.

Author Index

Acland, H., 255, 263
Adams, J., 367
Adams, R., 378, 382
Adams-Taylor, S., 358, 367
Adams, W., 33, 48
Adelson, J., 159, 172, 175, 199
Akbar, N., 145, 149
Alan Guttmacher Institute, 343-345, 349, 354, 361, 365
Alexander, G., 175, 198
Alexander, S., 352, 368
Allen, D., 337
Allen, J., 365
Allen, N., 149
Allen, W., 350, 356, 362, 364-365
Allen, V., 190, 198
Allport, G., 198
Alper, T., 187, 202
Alsikafe, M., 394, 399
Altman, H., 294, 307
American Psychiatric Association, 385, 397
Anderson, B., 287
Anderson, R., 329, 335
Ansell, E., 251-252, 261
Anumonye, A., 150
Antonovsky, A., 145, 149
Aral, S., 104, 106, 117
Armentrout, J., 55, 60
Armor, D., 225
Arnold, K., 362, 367
Asher, S., 176, 185-186, 198, 204
Askenasy, A., 143, 149
Astore, H., 104, 106, 116
Atwater, E., 49, 60
Atwood, J., 47
Auletta, K., 5, 11, 24
Ausubel, D., 90, 93
Ausubel, P., 90, 93
AYC (American Youth Commission), 31-32, 47
Ayers, M., 178, 183, 186, 188, 196, 198, 199

Baba, M., 230, 241
Babst, D., 388, 394, 398
Bachman, J., 53, 60, 139, 150, 386, 399, 408, 423
Back, K., 190, 200
Badger, E., 360, 365
Baker, E., 149
Bailey, M., 368

Baldwin, W., 342, 344-345, 354, 359, 365, 368
Baly, I., 249-261
Bandura, A., 156, 172
Bane, M., 255, 263
Bandura, A., 172
Banks, C., 130, 149
Banks, J., 65-75
Banks, W., 52-53, 60, 74-75
Baratz, J., 241
Baratz, S., 241
Barker, R., 148-149
Barnes, E., 90, 93, 111, 114
Barnes, H., 416, 423
Barnes, J., 243
Baron, R., 179, 193, 198
Barret, R., 24, 357-358, 360, 365
Barth, E., 76
Bartlett, W., 261
Bastian, A., 211, 225
Battle, E., 258, 261
Beardslee, W., 114
Beattie, M., 61, 145, 150
Beatty, L., 60
Bee, H., 370
Belgrave, F., 234, 241
Belkin, J., 419, 423
Belle, D., 146, 149
Belmont, L., 365, 373, 382
Bender, D., 365
Bengston, V., 355, 366
Bennett, C., 237-238, 241
Bennett, G., 386, 397
Benrud, C., 386, 401
Benson, F., 192, 198, 199
Benson, P., 151
Bentler, P., 139, 151, 386, 400
Bereiter, C., 56, 60
Beres, D., 336
Berg, P., 350, 360, 365
Berger, M., 294, 308
Berglas, S., 238, 243
Berkovitz, I., 329, 336
Berndt, T., 187-188, 198
Berscheid, E., 177, 190, 198, 204
Beschner, G., 18, 21, 24
Biemiller, L., 229, 241
Bigelow, B., 180, 182-183, 187, 198
Billingsley, A., 83, 93, 111, 115, 311, 313, 336
Billy, J., 354, 369
Birch, G., 209, 225

Blackman, J., 14, 24
Blane, H., 386, 397
Block, R., 360, 365
Block, S., 360, 365
Blount, W., 388, 394-395, 398
Blumberg, L., 75
Blumstein, A., 419, 423
Bohn, M., 265
Booth, J., 60
Borrow, H., 261
Bowman, P., 111, 115, 124, 143, 151
Boyle, J., 390, 397-398
Bradburn, N., 371
Brady, J., 189, 202
Brand, E., 52, 60
Brann, E., 350, 360, 362, 365 Brenner, H., 143,149
Bridge, R., 14, 24
Bridgett, R., 53, 60
Brigetz, R., 108, 117
Brisbane, F., 398
Bromen, S., 373, 382
Bronfenbrenner, U., 166, 172
Brook, J., 256, 261
Brookover, W., 60, 68, 75, 238, 241
Brooks-Gunn, J., 356, 367
Broman, S., 366
Brophy, J., 226, 238, 242
Broverman, D., 370
Broverman, I., 370
Brown, B., 301, 388
Brown, C., 378, 382, 389, 398-399
Brown, D., 81, 87-88, 93-94, 254-255, 259, 263-264, 305, 308
Brown, G., 146, 149
Brown, J., 366
Brown, P. 362, 366
Brown, S., 4, 24
Brown, W., 203
Bruner, J., 174, 225
Brunswick, A., 8, 24, 102, 115, 139, 149, 386, 390, 394-395, 397-398
Buehler, C., 262
Burgos, W., 388, 394-395, 398
Burke, P., 409, 423
Burns, D., 360, 365
Burton, L., 355, 366
Butts, S., 104, 110, 118, 349, 372
Byram, O., 394, 398
Byrne, D., 176, 198

Caesar, P., 368
Cahalan, M., 413, 423
Cairns, L., 243

Calia, V., 251, 262
Callicot, T., 350, 360, 362, 365
Calot, G., 118, 345, 372
Calvin, L., 293, 307
Campbell, E., 55, 60, 175, 198, 258, 262
Campbell, N., 262
Campbell, R., 255, 263
Caplovitz, D., 386, 398
Card, J., 355-356, 366
Carey, C., 234, 241
Carithers, M., 194, 198
Carlson, E., 65, 76
Carmical, L., 293, 307
Carmichael, S., 225
Carmon, B., 196, 204
Carnoy, M., 234-235, 242
Carter, C., 198
Carter, D., 192, 199
Carter, J., 107, 110-111, 115
Carter, T., 264
Castenell, Jr., L., 56-57, 60, 155, 168, 171, 173, 242
Caton, S., 102, 115
Cattell, R., 262
Cauce, A., 199
Cavanaugh, E., 386, 394, 400
Cavill III, W., 373-382
Cayton, H., 225
Center for Disease Control (1986-1987), 17, 22, 24, 105, 115
Cesaire, A., 148-149
Chacko, M., 108, 115
Charles, V., 425
Chase, J., 297, 307
Cheek, D., 149
Chernovetz, M., 352, 367
Children's Defense Fund (1986), 10, 17, 24, 287, 341, 343-346, 351, 354, 356, 359-360, 365-366
Chilman, C., 10, 16-18, 24, 106, 115, 348, 358-359, 366
Christianson, S., 423
Chronicle of Higher Education the, 226
Cipe, S., 108, 115
Clark, D., 108, 115
Clark, K., 90, 93, 172, 311, 336, 350, 372
Clark, M., 90, 93, 175-199, 348, 366
Clark, R., 172
Clark, S., 105, 115, 350, 366
Clark, T., 76
Clarke, R., 419, 423
Cleary, P., 143, 145, 150
Clore, G., 176, 198
Cloud, O., 66, 76

Author Index

Cloward, R., 57, 60
Coates, D., 199
Coble, J., 238, 242
Cohen, E., 199
Cohen, J., 188-189, 194, 199, 262
Cohen, P., 262, 365
Cohne, D., 255, 263
Coleman, J., 50, 55, 60, 86, 93, 157, 166, 172, 225, 258, 262
Coles, R., 90, 93
Coll, C., 369
College Board, 310, 337
College Entrance Examination Board (1985), 4, 24
Colletta, N., 354, 366
Collins, W., 371
Comer, J., 107, 110-111, 115
Cone, J., 89, 93
Cones, J., 55, 60
Conger, J., 313, 336
Congressional Budget Office (1981), 16, 24
Conklin, R., 294, 307
Connolly, H., 76
Conolley, E., 200
Cook, D., 293, 307
Cook, S., 196, 199
Cook, V., 193, 200
Coop, R., 294, 308
Cooper, H., 179, 193, 198
Copeland, A., 149
Corey, G., 294, 307
Cornoi-Huntley, J., 104, 110, 116
Cosby, A., 87, 93, 255, 262
Costellow, M., 225
Council of Independent Black Institutions the, 226
Cox, O., 225, 414, 423
Craig, G., 199
Crain, R., 196, 199, 336
Crandall, V. C., 57, 60, 242, 258, 262
Crandall, V. J., 57, 60, 242, 258, 262
Crawford, A., 354, 367, 378, 382
Crites, J., 262
Crockett, L., 187, 190, 199
Cronbach, L., 230, 242
Crook, T., 130, 152
Cross, A., 294, 307
Cross, W., 69, 76, 155, 172
Crowley, J., 255, 264
Crowne, D., 54-55, 62
Cummings, S., 165, 170, 172
Cunningham, J., 265
Cutler, S., 382
Cvetkovich, G., 342, 366

CYP (Committee on Youth Commission), 32, 47

Damon, W., 50, 60, 199
Daniel, W., 32, 47
Darga, L., 230-241
Darley, J., 238, 242
Darlington, R., 262
Darvish, H., 389, 401
Dash, L., 341, 366
Davidson, J., 203
Davidson, W., 366
Davis, A., 32, 34-36, 47, 60
Davis, T., 81, 93
Davis, V., 47
Dawkins, M., 394, 398
Dawkins, R., 394, 398
Day, B., 197, 199
Deal, T., 13, 24
DeAmicis L., 352, 366
Dean, S., 262
de Anda, D., 343, 352, 366
Deavers, K., 81, 93
DeBlassie, R., 22, 25
DeBritto, A., 74-75
Debus, R., 243
DeLissovoy, V., 382
DeLongis, A., 150
Dembo, R., 388, 394-395, 398
Dentler, R., 225
DesJarlais, D., 388, 394, 398
Detine-Carter, S., 192, 198-199
DeVries, D., 194, 199
DiCindio, L., 199
Dickens, H., 367
Diehard, A., 108, 118
Diener, C., 239, 242
Dill, J., 50-52, 58, 60
Dillard, J., 262
Doerner, W., 7, 9, 19-20, 26, 103, 118
Dohrenwend, B. P., 143, 145, 149, 316, 366
Dohrenwend, B. S., 143, 145, 149, 316, 336
Dollard, J., 34-36, 47
Douvan, J., 172, 175, 199
Downs, A., 76
Drake, S., 225
Dressler, W., 149
Drewry, D., 185, 196, 199
Dryfoos, J., 365, 373, 382
Dubois, W., 225
DuCette, J., 60, 371
Duck, S., 189, 199
Dull, R., 394, 398
Dunbaugh, F., 423

439

Dunlop, R., 293, 307
DuPont, R., 398
Dweck, C., 200, 239, 242

Eagle, N., 225
Earls, F., 108, 115, 357, 366
Eaton, W., 124, 145, 149
Edelman, M., 46, 48
Eder, D., 189, 200
Edmonds, R., 13, 25
Edwards, K., 194, 199,
Edwards, L., 350, 360, 362, 365, 367
Edwards, P., 117
Egerton, J., 225
Eiduson, B., 347, 367
Eifler, D., 372
Eisenberg, L., 115
Eisenhart, M., 186, 200
Eisikovits, Z., 6-7, 25, 406, 408-409, 424
Eitzen, D., 86, 93
Elder, G., 58, 61
Elig, T., 234, 242
Elliott, D., 25, 408, 423
Elliott, V., 408-409, 424
Ellis, S., 196, 199
Engleman, S., 56, 60
Ensimger, M., 368, 378, 382, 389, 398, 400
Epps, E., 57, 61, 111, 116, 242
Epstein, J., 175, 178-180, 184, 186, 188-191, 194, 200
Epstein, R., 145, 150
Erikson, E., 93, 155, 157, 172
Eveleth, P., 108, 116
Everett, B., 343, 360, 367
Eyler, T., 193, 200
Eysenck, H., 242

Fairchild, H., 210, 226, 229-242
Falk, W., 155, 173
Family Impact Seminar, 25, 106, 115
Fanon, F., 336
Farley, R., 76
Farrow, D., 388, 394, 398
Fazio, R., 238, 242
Felice, M., 116
Felner, R., 199
Felsenfeld, N., 329, 336
Festinger, L, 177, 190, 200
Field, T., 382
Fielding, J., 108-109, 115
Fine, A., 358, 367
Fine, G., 175, 189, 200
Finkel, D., 349, 361, 367
Finkel, M., 349, 361, 367

Finney, B., 294, 307
Fischman, S., 25
Fishman, G., 6-7, 25, 406, 408-409, 424
Fitzpatrick, S., 108, 115
Flanagan, T., 424
Fleming, J., 389, 399
Fletcher, E., 297, 307
Floyd, H., 199
Fly, J., 394, 398
Folkman, S., 143, 150-151
Ford, J., 350, 370
Ford, K., 106, 118, 349, 372
Ford, M., 76
Forrest, D., 262, 265
Forrest, J., 345, 347, 368
Foster, A., 118, 345, 372
Francis, W., 194, 203
Franklin, A., 130, 150, 309-337
Fratoe, F., 81, 85, 93
Frazier, E., 37-39, 48, 89, 93, 225
Freeman, E., 106, 115
Freeman, R., 5, 25
Freeman, W., 367
Freud, A., 336
Frey, W., 76
Friedman, A., 18, 21, 24
Friedman, G., 386, 400
Friend, R., 233, 242
Friesen, D., 86, 93
Frieze, I., 233-234, 242, 245
Fruchter, N., 211-225
Fullilove, R., 363, 368
Fullinwider, S., 33, 48
Furstenberg, F., 10, 16-18, 25, 104-106, 115, 346, 352, 354-356, 363, 367-368, 382
Furth, H., 155, 173

Gaa, J., 61
Gabriel, A., 104, 115, 353, 367
Gallup, A., 361, 367
Gambel, K., 298, 307
Gandossy, R., 9, 25
Ganzer, V., 239, 244
Garcia, C., 106, 115, 367
Gardner, B., 32, 47
Gardner, M., 32, 47
Garfinkel, W., 415, 423
Garn, S., 108, 115
Gartner, A., 336
Gary, L., 301, 307
Gentry, K., 179, 193, 195, 202
Gerard, H., 193, 195, 200, 202
Gerard, M., 386, 400

Author Index

Gibbs, J., 3-25, 55, 61, 100, 102, 105, 108, 115-116, 123, 139, 146, 150, 225, 386, 394-395, 399
Gibson, L., 230, 244
Gigliotti, R., 241
Gintis, H., 255, 263
Ginzberg, E., 250, 262
Glasgow, D., 11, 25, 170, 173
Glass, W., 419, 423
Glidewell, J., 192, 200
Globetti, G., 394-395, 399
Glover, M., 297, 307
Goddard, L., 145, 152, 373-382, 394, 400
Godwin, L., 80, 93
Goethals, G., 155, 157, 173
Gold, M., 6, 25, 408, 425
Goldhammer, R., 212-213, 225
Goldman, N., 345, 347, 368
Good, T., 226
Goodman, J., 243
Goodman, P., 423
Gordon, A., 256, 261
Gordon, M., 76
Gordon, R., 242
Gordon, T., 79, 93
Gottlieb, D., 159, 173
Gottman, J., 176, 185-186, 198, 203
Grady, W., 354, 369
Graham, S., 233, 242
Graves, T., 387, 399
Gray, S., 356, 367
Green, E., 409, 423
Greene, J., 107, 116
Greer, C., 211, 225
Gregg, C., 354, 366
Gribbons, W., 251, 262
Grillo, G., 104, 110, 116
Grimson, R., 108, 117
Griselda, M., 352, 370
Grittel, M., 211, 225
Grizzle, J., 367
Gropper, B., 385, 399
Grote, B., 342, 366
Grueling, J., 22, 25
Gruen, R., 150
Gruskin, A., 108, 116
Guess, L., 386, 401
Gunn, B., 257, 263
Gunnings, T., 303, 307
Gurin, G., 61, 110-111, 116, 124, 143, 145, 150-151
Gurin, P., 57, 61, 111, 116, 230, 242
Gurin, P., 61, 145, 150
Gussow, J., 209, 225

Guthrie, R., 29, 48, 229, 242
Guttentag, M., 145, 150
Guttman, E., 6-7, 25, 406, 408-409, 424

Hadler, S., 354, 366
Hakanson, E., 362, 367
Hall, D., 251, 263
Hall, G., 336
Hall, J., 337
Hall, L., 264
Haller, A., 263-264
Hallinan, M., 175, 178-179, 184-186, 189, 191, 200-201, 204
Hamburg, B., 367
Hamilton, C., 225
Hammond, R., 238, 243
Hampton, P., 13, 25
Hansell, S., 185, 187, 189, 191, 201, 204
Hanson, R., 387, 399
Hansson, R., 352, 367
Hanushek, E., 263
Hardy, J., 105, 115, 350, 363, 366
Hare, B., 61, 155, 168, 171, 173
Harford, T., 386, 394, 400
Harlan, W., 104, 110, 116
Harnesch, D., 233, 245
Harper, F., 386, 394, 399
Harrell, J., 146, 150
Harris, A., 53, 61
Harris, K., 363, 368
Harris, L., 361-362, 367
Harris, M., 238, 242
Harris, T., 146, 149
Harrison, A., 201
Hart, L., 60
Hartup, W., 176, 185, 188-189, 201-202
Harwood, H., 9, 25
Haskins, K., 211, 225
Haskins, W., 341, 367
Hass, G., 226
Hassen, O., 296, 307
Hatcher, R., 367
Hauser, S., 155, 157, 159, 164, 173, 257, 263
Havighurst, R., 80, 93, 159, 173, 263
Hawkins, D., 403-424
Hawkins, P., 299, 307
Heald, F., 108, 115-116
Heath, D., 394, 399
Hediger, M., 108, 116
Heider, F., 201, 243
Height, D., 341, 368
Helmreich, R., 371
Helms, J., 69, 76
Helzer, J., 124, 152

441

Hendershort, G., 358, 372
Henderson, R., 241
Hendricks, L., 345, 356, 360, 363, 368
Hendrickson, A., 243
Hendrickson, D., 243
Herceg-Baron, R., 363, 368
Herman, K., 130, 152
Hernandez, P., 87, 94
Herrnstein, R., 243, 425
Hess, D., 352, 366
Hewitt, L., 386, 397
Heyde, M., 250, 263
Heyns, B., 255, 263
Hicks, C., 189, 204
Hickson, G., 107, 116
Hill, H., 110-111, 115
Hill, K., 233, 245
Hill, R., 83, 94, 336
Hindelang, M., 424
Hirsch, M., 363, 372
Hixson, A., 350, 360, 362, 365
Hobbs, N., 25
Hobson, C., 55, 60, 258, 262
Hofferth, S., 342, 368
Hoffman, L., 368
Hofman, G., 203
Hogan, D., 104, 106, 116
Hogarth, R., 368
Hokada, E., 372
Holinger, P., 11, 25, 101, 116
Holland, D., 186, 200
Holliday, B., 29-48
Hollingshead, A., 368
Holmes, B., 229, 243
Holmes, T., 145, 150
Holzer, C., 111, 115, 368
Homans, G., 176, 201
Howard, C., 111, 115, 368
Howard, J., 13, 25, 238, 243
Hubbard, R., 386, 394, 400-401
Huff, L., 298, 307
Hughes, A., 235, 243
Hughes, D., 294, 307
Hughes, J., 235, 243
Huggins, G., 106, 115, 367
Huizinga, D., 25, 408-409, 424
Hummer, R., 265
Hunt, J., 56, 61, 157, 171, 173, 231, 243
Hunt, L., 157, 171, 173
Hunter, F., 175, 183, 201
Huston-Stein, A., 368
Hutson, L., 299, 307

Ianni, F., 157-158, 166, 173

Ilfeld, F., 146, 150
Irvine, D., 294, 307
Irwin, C., 109, 116

Jackson, B., 226
Jackson, J., 110-111, 116, 124, 143, 150-151, 210, 237, 244, 263
Jackson, T., 200
Jacobson, L., 244
James, J., 7, 9, 19-20, 26, 103, 118
Janowitz, M., 382
Jaschik, S., 284, 288
Jencks, C., 243,255, 263
Jenkins, A., 155, 173, 387, 395, 399
Jenkins, J., 394-395, 399
Jenkins, R., 104, 110, 118, 349, 372
Jennrich, R., 263
Jensen, A., 230, 243
Jessor, R., 387, 394, 399
Jessor, R., 387, 399
Jessor, S., 387, 399
Johnson, C., 39-42, 48, 94
Johnson, F., 108, 116
Johnson, G., 415, 424
Johnson, L., 139, 150, 349, 356, 368
Johnson, R., 102, 109, 116, 234, 241
Johnson, S., 61
Johnston, G., 408, 423
Johnston, L., 386, 399
Jones, A., 349, 358, 368
Jones, E., 155, 173, 238, 243, 345, 347, 368
Jones, K., 101, 116
Jones, J., 52, 57, 60-61
Jones, L., 76, 196, 199
Jones, N., 403-423
Jones, R., 111, 116, 155, 173, 336
Jones, W., 352, 367
Jordaan, J., 250, 263
Jordan, J., 265
Jordan, T., 54, 61
Jorgensen, S., 352-353, 363, 368
Junker, B., 33, 48

Kaelberg, C., 386, 394, 400
Kagan, J., 57, 61, 243
Kagay, M., 350-351, 361-362, 367, 371
Kahn, J., 342, 355, 368, 370
Kandel, D., 9, 21, 26, 102, 115, 117, 186, 188, 201, 388, 394, 399-400
Kantner, J., 16, 27, 104-106, 118, 342-343, 349, 368, 372
Kantor, M., 192, 200
Kaplan, B., 108, 117
Karweit, N., 187, 190-191, 194, 201

Author Index

Katchadourian, H., 326, 336
Katkovsky, W., 57, 60, 242, 258, 262
Katz, I., 51, 61, 238, 243
Katz, M., 263
Katz, S., 108, 116
Katzman, M., 66, 76
Kejaks, S., 108, 116
Kellam, S., 368, 378, 382, 389, 398-400
Kelley, H., 176, 178, 204, 238, 243
Kelly, L., 394-395, 399
Kelton, T., 196, 204
Kemper, T., 263
Ken, J., 143, 152
Keniston, K., 157, 159, 173
Kenney, A., 349, 368
Kerchoff, A., 255, 263
Kessler, R., 143, 145, 150
Khatib, S., 238, 238, 243
Kiev, A., 150
Killen, J., 385, 401
Kilson, M., 168, 173
Kim, J., 263
Kim, Y., 105-106, 118, 350, 361, 372
King, L., 123-124, 150-151, 386, 392, 395, 400
King, S., 352-353, 363, 368
Kirby, D., 362, 368
Kitagawa, E., 104, 106, 116
Klapr, O., 160, 173
Klatsky, A., 386, 400
Klein, I., 145, 150
Klerman, L., 18, 25
Klorman, R., 352, 366
Klos, D., 155, 157, 173
Knapp, T., 263
Knoff, H., 161, 173
Koch, G., 367
Komorita, S., 145, 150
Kondor, J., 285, 288
Konopka, G., 157-158, 173
Kramer, B., 301, 308
Kramer, M., 310, 316, 336
Krammer, M., 124, 152
Krate, R., 157, 164, 166, 173
Krile, D., 189, 202
Krisberg, B., 6-7, 25, 406, 408-409, 424
Korchin, S., 155, 173
Kornblum, W., 166, 174
Kukla, A., 233, 243, 245
Kurdek, L., 189, 202

Labov, W., 232, 243
Lachin, J., 143, 152
Lachter, S., 385, 400

Ladner, J., 10, 16, 25, 65, 76, 106, 116
Ladwig, G., 55, 61
LaGaipa, J., 180, 182-183, 187, 189, 198, 202
Lail, S., 61
Lake, R., 65, 76
Lalli, M., 75
Lamb, M., 369
Lampe, P., 196, 202
Lancaster, J., 348, 367, 369
Landale, N., 354, 369
Lao, R., 61, 145, 150
Lapati, A., 226
Larson, T., 5, 25, 288
Launier, R., 142, 151
Lawrence, L., 107, 111, 117
Lawrence, W., 254-255, 259, 263
Lawson, W., 316, 336
Lazarus, R., 142-143, 145, 150-151
Leaverton, P., 104, 110, 116
Lee, C., 79-93, 256, 259, 263, 293-335
Lee, L., 400
Lefcourt, H., 55, 61, 233, 243
LeGette, H., 53, 62
LeGrand, L., 388, 394, 398
Leichenko, S., 350-351, 361-362, 367, 371
Lemann, N., 36, 46, 48
Lerman, R., 350, 369
Lester, B., 369
Levin, J., 263
Levitan, S., 85, 94
Lewis, C., 369
Lex, B., 386, 394-395, 400
Levy, J., 197, 204
Liaison Committee on the Quality Assurance Program, 227
Lieberman, E., 366
Liem, J., 145, 151
Liem, R., 145, 151
Lightfoot, S., 226
Lincoln, C., 89, 94
Lincoln, R., 10, 16-18, 25, 105-106, 115, 345, 347, 367-368
Lindeman, R., 265
Lindsey, C., 295, 308
Lipscomb, W., 394, 400
Livrant, S., 54-55, 62
LoCascio, R., 249, 251, 254, 263
Lockheed, M., 199
Lohman, M., 199
Lohnes, P., 251, 262
Long, A., 242
Longshore, D., 202
Lonsdale, R., 94
Losoff, M., 187, 190, 199

443

Lott, A., 176-177, 179
Lott, B., 176-177, 179
Louv, R., 267, 288
Lowman, C., 386, 394, 400
Lubin, B., 118
Lukoff, I., 256, 261
Lund, A., 108, 115
Lutz, J., 264
Maccoby, E., 175, 202
Maccoby, N., 385, 401
MacCorquodale, P., 352, 369
Mack, R., 108, 116
MacKenzie, B., 230, 243
MacLenna, B., 329, 336
MacLeod, J., 173
Maddahian, E., 139, 151, 386, 400
Maehr, M., 233, 238, 244-245
Mahard, R., 196, 199, 336
Mahoney, J., 350, 360, 362, 365
Mahoney, M., 385, 400
Maisto, E., 386, 401
Malveaux, J., 267-289
Malveaux, M., 277, 287-288
Manerscheld, R., 151
Mangum, G., 263
Mannarino, A., 175, 184, 202
Manni, J., 264
Marascuilo, L., 263
Marcus, M., 185, 203
Mare, R., 424
Marel, R., 386, 394, 400
Mark, E., 187, 202
Marsh, H., 61, 243
Marshall, H., 76
Marshall, R., 80, 94
Marsiglio, W., 362, 369
Martin, J., 175, 202
Martindale, L., 352, 370
Martinez, A., 369
Mastie, M., 265
Masuda, M., 145, 150
Matney, W., 211, 226
Matteson, D., 369
Maxwell, N., 26
Maynard, P., 251, 263
Mbiti, J., 90, 94
McAdoo, H., 144-145, 151, 201, 364, 369
McAllister, A., 385, 401
McAnarney, R., 104, 115, 352-353, 366-367
McAndrew, G., 25
McBride, R., 230, 244
McCandless, B., 294, 308
McClelland, D., 56, 61
McCormick, M., 358, 369

McCullough, W., 110-111, 116
McDill, E., 53, 61, 243
McDowell, S., 252, 264
McGarrell, E., 424
McGee, E., 26
McGee, M., 370
McKinney, H., 337
McKirnan, D., 395, 400
McLaughlin, S., 354, 369
McLean, F., 108, 117
McNair, D., 87-88, 94, 259, 264, 305, 308
McNeeley, R., 408, 424
McPartland, J., 55, 60, 202, 258, 262
McQuater, G., 74-75
McSeveney, D., 199
McWorter, G., 33, 48
Mecklenburg, M., 369
Mednick, M., 233, 244
Meichenbaum, D., 243
Melton, G., 369
Menken, J., 10, 16-18, 25, 105-106, 115, 355, 358, 369, 372
Mercer, J., 235, 244
Meriwether, L., 341, 369
Merton, R., 424
Merzel, C., 8, 24
Messeri, P., 8, 24, 390, 394, 398
Messin, P., 102, 115
Messner, S., 101, 118
Meyer, E., 53, 61, 243
Michelson, S., 255, 263
Milazzo-Sayre, L., 151
Miles, R., 316, 336
Miller, C., 3, 58, 264, 345, 360, 372
Miller, F., 108, 117
Miller, N., 179, 193, 195, 202
Miller, W., 366
Milner, D., 424
Mingione, A., 56, 61, 244
Miracle, A., 202
Mitchell, C., 117
Mitchell, H., 230, 245
Mitchell, V., 226
Modeste, W., 225
Montemayor, R., 188, 202
Montgomery, R., 363, 368
Mood, A., 55, 60, 258, 262
Moore, K., 343-344, 356, 369
Morbidity & Mortality Weekly Report, 101, 105, 116, 133, 136-137, 150, 152
Morgan, M., 116
Morgan, S., 356, 367
Morland, K., 70, 77
Morrison, D., 342, 349-350, 370

Author Index

Morrison, J., 299, 307
Morrow, B., 359, 370
Morse, R., 394, 399
Moser, H., 265
Moss, H., 57, 61, 243
Mott, F., 26
Moynihan, D., 231, 244, 336
Mudd, E., 17, 26, 367
Mueller, C., 263
Murphy, G., 389, 401
Murray, C., 210, 226, 229-241, 243
Murray, S., 233, 244
Muuss, R., 336
Myers, H., 123-152, 316, 336
Myers, J., 124, 152
Myers, S., 424
Myers, V., 386, 401

Narot, R., 196, 199
National Alliance of Black School Educators, Inc., 226
National Center for Health Statistics, 7, 11, 26, 105, 117, 358, 370
National Center for Neighborhood Enterprise, 226
National Commission on Excellence in Education, 226, 229, 244
National Institute of Drug Abuse (1979), 8, 26, 102, 117
National Institute of Drug Abuse (1980), 8, 26, 102, 117
National Institute of Mental Health, 124, 129, 151
National Urban League Inc, 152, 331-332, 336, 417, 424
NCALI Staff, 386, 394, 400
Neale, J., 233, 242
Neighbors, H., 124, 143, 151
Nelson, S., 9, 21, 26, 108-109, 115
Nelson-Le Gall, S., 347, 353, 371
Neugarten, B., 80, 93
Newcomb, A., 189, 202
Newcomb, M., 139, 151, 386, 400
Newcomb, T., 178, 202
Newsweek, 26
New York State Education Department, 226
New York Urban League, 211, 226
NIAAA, 139, 151, 385, 401
NIDA, 139, 151, 152, 385-386, 401
Nobles, W., 52, 61, 83, 90, 94, 145, 152, 374, 376, 380-382, 385, 401,
Northwood, L., 76
Nowicki, S., Jr., 76

Oakes, J., 235-237, 244
Oberle, W., 155, 173
Oden, S., 176, 185-186, 198
Oelke, M., 293, 308
Offer, D., 25, 101, 116
Ogbu, J., 58-59, 61, 168, 173, 209, 226, 234-237, 244, 316, 337, 353, 364, 370
O'Hara, R., 250, 265
Ohlendorf, G., 87, 93, 264
O'Malley, P., 53, 60, 139, 150, 386, 399, 408, 423
Ooms, T., 347, 360, 370
Oppel, W., 383
Opportunity Wage Act of 1984, 284, 288
O'Reilly, K., 104, 106, 117
Orive, R., 193, 202
Orr, M., 349, 368
Osborne, W., 53, 62
Osipow, S., 264
Osterman, P., 286, 288
Otradovic, C., 108, 115
Overstreet, P., 265
Ozawa, M., 5, 26

Padella, A., 52, 60
Palley, H., 25
Palmo, A., 264
Parham, 69, 76
Park Heights Academy, 226
Paris, B., 22, 26
Park, R., 48
Parker, J., 61
Parry-Hill, J., 265
Passalacqua, J., 60, 238, 241
Pasteur, A., 294-295, 308
Patchen, M., 203
Paterson, A., 68, 75
Paton, S., 9, 21, 26, 117
Pauker, J., 356, 370
Payne, D., 394-395, 399
Pearson, H., 108, 117
Pentecoste, J., 257, 264
Perkins, E., 173
Perry, C., 385, 401
Persell, C., 230, 244
Petersen, A., 187, 190, 199, 343, 349-350, 370
Petersilia, J., 424
Petronio, R., 6, 25
Pettigrew, T., 76, 192, 203
Picou, J., 87, 94, 264
Pierce, C., 310, 326, 337
Pindych, R., 264
Pittman, K., 361, 371
Placek, P., 349, 358, 368

445

Planned Parenthood Federation of
   America, 313, 337
Polit, D., 355, 370
Pope, C., 408, 424
Pope, J., 60
Porter, J., 53, 62, 244
Portes, A., 255, 263-264
Posner, M., 244
Poussaint, A., 111, 115
Powell, G., 117
Presser, H., 370
Price-Williams, D., 51, 62, 244
Primavera, J., 199
Proctor, S., 13, 26
Pumariega, A., 117
Putallaz, M., 176, 203

Quinney, R., 424
Quinones, N., 226

Rabinovitz, F., 76
Rachal, J., 386, 394, 400-401 Rafferty, F., 231, 244
Rahaims, S., 394-395, 399
Rainwater, L., 90, 94, 104, 117
Ramirez, M., 51, 62, 244
Ramsey, B., 356, 367
Randolph, H., 66, 76
Randolph, L, 101-102, 117
Rappaport, J., 148, 152
Raskin, A., 130, 152
Ray, O., 9, 26
Reed, L., 233, 245
Regier, D., 124, 152
Reid, I., 32, 44, 48
Reid, P., 353, 370
Reisman, J., 178, 203
Relich, J., 243
Rest, S., 233, 245
Reynolds, C., 230, 244
Rickel, A., 185, 204
Rickels, K., 106, 115, 367
Riessman, F., 336
Riley, M., 117
Rivers, S., 101-102, 117
Robins, L., 124, 152, 389, 394, 401
Robinson, B., 24, 357-358, 360, 365
Robinson, L., 297, 307
Robinson, S., 25
Rochberg-Halton, E., 159, 161, 173
Roche, A., 348, 370
Roebuck, J., 370
Rogel, M., 343, 349-350, 370Rohrer, J., 37, 48
Roland, J., 1-32

Rose, H., 76
Rosen, B., 56, 62, 310, 316, 336
Rosen, R., 352, 370
Rosenbaum, M., 294, 308
Rosenbaum, R., 233, 245
Rosenbaum, S., 358, 370
Rosenberg, M., 53, 62, 68, 76, 173, 257, 264
Rosenfield, D., 71, 77, 185, 192-193, 203
Rosenkratz, P., 370
Rosenstein, J., 151
Rosenthal, R., 155, 173, 238, 242, 244
Rosoff, J., 345, 347, 368
Ross, C., 372
Rotter, J., 258, 261, 264
Royston, A., 383
Rubenfeld, D., 264
Rubovits, P., 238, 244
Rugby, L., 53, 61, 243
Ruiz, R., 52, 60
Russo, N., 369
Ryan, W., 58, 62, 231, 244
Rychlak, J., 155, 173

Sabol, W., 424
Sagar, H., 186, 194, 203
St. John, N., 193, 203
Sarason, I., 239, 244
Savin-Williams, R., 175, 203
Scales, P., 352, 370
Scanzoni, J., 161, 165, 173
Schachter, S., 190, 200
Schacter, J., 143, 152
Schell, J., 108, 116
Schmeidler, J., 388, 394-395, 398
Schneider, J., 241
Schoenbach, V., 108, 117
Schofield, J., 185-186, 192, 194, 203
Schoggen, P., 149
Schorr, L., 358, 367
Schorr, S., 178, 203
Schroth, M., 56, 62
Schwartz, I., 6-7, 25, 406, 408-409, 424
Schwartz, M., 350, 370
Schwartz, S., 108, 118
Scott-Heron, G., 297, 308
Scott-Jones, D., 1-32, 347, 349-351, 353, 361, 370-371
Sebald, H., 158, 173, 197, 203
Segal, S., 371
Seiden, R., 101, 117, 152
Seigelaub, A., 386, 400
Selavan, I., 125, 152
Select Committee on Children, Youth, and Families, 342-344, 354, 371

Author Index

Selman, A., 180-181, 203
Selman, R., 180-183, 203
Selye, H., 152
Seninger, S., 263
Sepkoski, C., 369
Serafica, F., 201
Severson, R., 145, 152
Sewell, T., 145, 152, 264
Sewell, W., 264
Seyler, H., 80, 94
Shafer, N., 106, 118
Shah, F., 105, 118
Shantz, C., 180, 204
Shapiro, C., 18, 26
Shapiro, D., 255, 264
Shapiro, S., 358, 369
Shappel, D., 264
Sharan, S., 194, 204
Shea, J., 363, 368
Sheehan, D., 185, 203
Shelton, M., 343, 349-350, 370
Shibutani, T., 257, 264
Shiloh, A., 125, 152
Shockley, W., 244
Shumake, G., 293, 308
Sieg, A., 62
Siegel, B., 357, 366
Silber, T., 18, 26
Sillen, A., 130, 152, 309, 337
Silverman, R., 226
Silverstein, B., 157, 164, 166, 173
Simmons, R., 53, 62, 257, 264
Simon, M., 389, 400
Simpkins, G., 303, 307
Simpkins, L., 359, 371
Simpson, R., 264
Singer, M., 394, 401
Singleton, E., 385-401
Singleton, L., 186, 204
Sitkoff, H., 32-33, 48
Slaughter, D., 33, 48
Slavin, R., 194, 199, 201, 204
Sloan, L., 360, 371
Smith, B., 226
Smith, E., 104, 117, 158, 174, 251, 253-256, 264, 301, 308, 363, 372
Smith, F., 108, 115
Smith, L., 192, 200
Smith, M., 159, 174, 255, 263, 277, 288
Smith-Peterson, C., 394, 401
Smitherman, G., 232, 244
Smolen, P., 345, 358, 360, 372
Smollar, J., 180-184, 187, 204
Snyder, D., 223-224, 226

Snyder, H., 194, 203
Sonenstein, F., 361, 371
Spanier, G., 346, 349, 361, 367, 371
Spence, J., 371
Spencer, M., 155, 157, 174
Spero, J., 198
Sprince, M., 312, 337
Sprinthall, N., 371
Spurgeon, P., 189, 204
Spurlock, J., 107, 111, 117
Stack, C., 16, 26, 117, 371
Staggers, B., 99-119
Stahura, J., 76
Staples, R., 79, 83, 94, 101-102, 104, 117, 349, 356, 368
Stapp, J., 371
Starfield, B., 358, 369
Starmer, C., 367
Statistical Analysis System, 264
Statistical Package for Social Sciences, Inc., 264
Statistical Series, Annual Data, 117
Stein, A., 226
Stein, Z., 365
Steinlauf, B., 371
Steinman, M., 362, 367
Stephen, W., 71, 77, 185, 192-193, 196, 203-204
Sternberg, R., 230-231, 245
Stevens, J., 354, 359, 371, 383
Stikes, C., 294, 308
Stimson, J., 196, 204
Stimson, S., 196, 204
Stine, J., 350, 360, 362, 365
Stipek, D., 234, 245
Stokes, R., 53, 61
Story, E., 350, 360, 362, 365
Stout, R., 265
Stowers, K., 155, 173
Streett, R., 363, 372
Strickland, B., 76
Stringer, L., 192, 200
Stuart, R., 329, 337
Stunkard, A., 108, 117
Sudman, S., 371
Sue, S., 337
Sugar, M., 371
Super, D., 250, 265
Sutherland, R., 31, 33, 45, 48
Swayzer, G., 408, 423
Sweet, R., 106, 118

Tanner, J., 109-110, 117, 158, 174, 348, 371
Tardiff, K., 101, 118

Tarica, C., 390, 398
Tarrier, R., 264
Taylor, D., 185, 204
Taylor, H., 350-351, 371
Taylor, J., 69, 77, 230, 245
Taylor, R., 155-174
Telch, M., 385, 401 Tenhouten, W., 245
Terman, L., 245
Terrell, F., 230, 245
Terrell, S., 230, 245
Terry, R., 189, 204
Thibaut, J., 176, 178, 204
Thomas, A., 130, 152, 309, 337
Thomas, M., 255, 265
Thomas, S., 68, 75
Thompson, A., 265
Thompson, J., 107, 116
Thompson, K., 16, 26, 94, 105-106, 118
Thompson, L., 349, 361, 371
Thompson, M., 354, 371
Thompson, P., 369
Thornton, W., 7, 9, 19-20, 26, 103, 118
Tiedeman, D., 250, 265
Till, T., 95
Tobias, R., 207-225
Tobin-Richards, M., 343, 349-350, 370
Toldson, I., 294-295, 308
Tolmach, J., 20, 26
Tom, D., 179, 193, 198
Torrey, B., 352-353, 363, 368
Tower, A., 366
Trussell, J., 355, 372
Tucker, M., 229, 242
Tuma, N., 179, 185-186, 191, 201, 204
Turk, A., 409, 423
Turner, J., 368
Turner, S., 349, 361, 371, 424
Tyler, L., 251, 265

Udry, J., 104, 117
Uniform Crime Reports (1981), 6-8, 26
United States Bureau of the Census (1981), 3-4, 26
United States Bureau of the Census (1983), 79-80, 95
United States Bureau of the Census (N.D.), 105, 118, 211, 227
United States Department of Health and Human Services, 102, 118
United States Department of Health and Human Services (1981), 8, 26
United States Department of Justice, 101, 118, 404-405, 424

United States Department of Labor, 420, 425
United States District Court for Northern California, 236, 245
United States Government Printing Office, 101, 118, 128, 139, 152
United States Riot Commission, 227
USPHS, 385-386, 401

Valentine, C., 52, 62, 231, 245, 311, 337
Van Dalsem, E., 294, 307
Van Komen, R., 188, 202
Varenhorst, B., 386, 401
Vaz, R., 345, 358, 360, 372
Velde, R., 408, 425
Ventura, S., 344, 346-347, 358, 372
Veroff, J., 57, 62, 245
Vetta, A., 230, 245
Vichinsky, E., 118
Vogel, S., 370
Vogt, D., 227
Volpe, J., 204
Von Korff, M., 124, 145, 149
Voss, H., 408, 423
Vriend, J., 254, 265

Waddell, R., 386, 401
Wagne, E., 108, 117
Wagner, R., 226
Waite, L., 356, 369
Walberg, J., 262
Walker, G., 16, 26
Walker, I., 47
Walker, J., 80, 95
Walker, L., 107, 116
Waller, I., 47, 413, 425
Walster, E., 190, 177, 198, 204
Walster, G., 177, 204
Walters, R., 172
Ward, L., 193, 200
Ward, W., 74-75
Warnath, C., 265, 293, 308
Warner, E., 33, 48
Warner, W., 42-43, 48
Washington, A., 106, 118
Washington, D.C. Public Health Services Publication, 227
Washington, R., 53, 62, 244
Washington, V., 294, 305, 308
Watts, G., 145, 152
Webb, H., 109, 118
Webster's Third New International Dictionary, 3, 26
Weigl, R., 204

Author Index

Weinberg, S., 262
Weiner, B., 233, 245
Weiner, I., 135, 152, 311-312, 337
Weiner, N., 425
Weinfield, F., 55, 60, 258, 262
Weisman, R., 385, 400
Weissman, M., 124, 152
Weisz, J., 234, 245
Weitzman, L., 372
Wellman, B., 188, 204
Werner, R., 189, 202
Westbrook, B., 265
Westermeyer, J., 395, 401
Westney, O., 104, 110, 118, 349, 372
Westoff, C., 118, 345, 347, 368, 372
White, A., 1-32, 349-351, 371
White, B., 158, 173
White, J., 111, 118, 155, 174, 232, 245, 337
White, R., 159, 174
Whiteman, M., 256, 261
Wilcox, J., 199
William, R., 61, 104, 108-109, 118, 230, 245
Williams, D., 124, 152
Williams, I., 104, 110
Williams, J., 4, 9-10, 15-16, 25-26, 70, 77, 408, 425
Williams, T., 166, 174
Williams, V., 254, 265
Willie, C., 65, 77, 197, 204, 301, 308
Willig, A., 233, 245
Willis, W., 310, 316, 336
Wilsnack, R., 394, 401
Wilsnack, S., 394, 401
Wilson, J., 425
Wilson, K., 255, 264
Wilson, M., 359, 372
Wilson, W., 65, 77

Winberly, F., 143, 152
Winch, R., 161, 165, 174
Windley, L., 196, 199
Wingard, D., 116
Winges, L., 354, 369
Winship, C., 424
Wirtanen, I., 408, 423
Wise, D., 5, 25
Wise, L., 355-356, 366
Wiser, P., 204
Wolk, S., 60
Wolters, R., 32, 48
Wonder, S., 297, 308
Woodbury, R., 265
Woodson, R., 227
Wrenn, C., 294, 308
Wulf, L., 345, 347, 368
Wyatt, D., 47
Wyatt, G., 143, 152
Wylie, R., 62

Yamamoto, J., 337
Yasuna, A., 366
Yip, R., 108, 118
York, R., 55, 60, 258, 262
Young, J., 33, 48
Youniss, J., 175, 180-184, 187, 201, 204

Zabin, L., 105, 115, 343, 349-350, 363, 366, 372
Zajonc, R., 179, 204
Zayac. S., 365
Zelnik, M., 16, 27, 104-106, 118, 342-343, 349-350, 361, 372
Zschock, D., 66, 77
Zuehlke, M., 343, 349-350, 370
Zytowski, D., 265

Subject Index

Academic underachievement
  program for reducing 239-241
  social cognitive approach to 232-234
Academic underachievement, models of
  Cultural Deprivation Model 231-232
  Cultural Difference Model 231-232
  Genetic Deficit Approach 229-231
  Social Cognitive Approach 232-234
Academic performance, health consequences of 107-108
ACE studies see American Council on Education studies
Achievement motivation
  Black-White differences in 57-58
  Cultural Difference Model and 57
Accidents 101
Adaptation, process of 146-147
Age changes
  developmental models of 50-51
Alcohol use 385-386
Alternative secondary education programs 13-15
Alternative schools 219-221
American Council on Education studies
  findings 34-45
  implications of 46-47
  methodology 33-34
  objectives of 31-32
  significance of 31
  reports
    Children of Bondage 34-37
    Color and Human Nature 42-43
    Growing up in the Black Belt 39-42
    In a Minor Key 43-44
    Negro Youth at the Crossways 37-39
    Thus Be Their Destiny 44
Attributions, underachievement and 232-234
Biethnicity
  definitions of 68-69
  discussion of 72-73
Career development 249-261
Children of Bondage,
  description of 34-37
Cigarette use 385-386
Color and Human Nature,
  description of 42-43
Color, Class and Personality,
  description of 44-45
Conditioned failure model 237-239
Coping, process of 146-147

Correctional institutions, incarceration in 126
Counseling 216-218
Criminal behavior, racial differences in 408-412
Criminal victimization, rates by race 132
Counselor
  Black community and 304-306
  educational system and 303-304
Counseling 293-307
  academic development and 300-301
  career development and 301-303
  cultural specificity and 294-295
  model for 296-300
  personal-social development and 295-296
Criminal justice system, Black youth and 403-422
Custody, Black youth in 403-408
Cultural deprivation model
  underachievement and 231-232
Cultural difference model
  academic underachievement and 231-232
Delinquency and crime
  rates 5-6
  incarceration rates 6-7
Delinquency prevention
  comprehensive programs 20-21
  primary prevention 19-20
  secondary prevention 20
Dropout prevention, programs for 13-15
Drug abuse 102-103
Drug prevention
  community health centers and 21-22
  multi-service programs and 22
  programs for 21-23
  school based clinics and 21-22
  secondary prevention 22
  tertiary prevention 22
Drug use, illicit
  Black adolescents and 386-387
Education
  academic underachievement 234-239
  alternative schools 219-221
  alternative secondary programs 13-15
  counseling in 216-218
  curriculum relevancy and 212-215
  dropouts 4
  guidance in 216-218

451

Black Adolescents

issues 4, 212-218
parental involvement in 215-216
socioeconomic factors and 207-212
street academies 220-221
traditional programs of 218-219
Educational improvement, strategies for 221-225
Employment status
    Black youth and 269-276
    education and 282-283
Ethnic Encapsulation, definition of 68
Ethnic Identity Clarification, definition of 68
Ethnicity typology, stages of 68-70
    suburban Black youth and 68-72
Family formation, Black youth and 281-282
Family planning 16-18
Family status, race and 275
    economics and 278-281
    race and 275
Friendships
    age and 187-188
    cognitive developmental theories and 180-183
    factors influencing 183-189
    friendship proximity and 190-191
    friendship reciprocity and 189-190
    gender and 186-187
    interpersonal attraction theories and 176-180
    personality and attitudes and 188-189
    race and 185-186
Friendship proximity 190-191
Friendship reciprocity 189-190
Genetic deficit approach
    academic underachievement and 229-231
Globalism and global competency, definition of 69
Growing up in the Black Belt, description of 39-42
Guidance 216-218
Health care, issues
    accidents 101
    depression 108
    drug abuse 102
    homicides 101
    hypertension 108
    nutrition 108
    obesity 108
    sexuality-related problems 103-107
    sickle cell disease 109
    stress 107-108
    suicide 101

Homicides 7-8, 101
    deaths and 133
    race and 133
Hospitalization, rates of 124-125
Identity-formation
    psychoanalytic perspective on 156-158
    social learning theory perspective on 158-160
    empirical study of 168
In a Minor Key, description of 43-44
Interracial acceptance 192-193
Interracial contact 193-196
Interracial dating 196-197
Intergroup relations 192-197
Juvenile delinquency, incidence of 131-136
Labor force participation rate,
    definition of 271
    limitations of 271-273
Labor market
    Black adolescents and 267-287
Labor market status
    Black youth and 283-286
    public policy and 283-286
Locus of control
    external 54-56
    internal 54-56
    Black-White differences and 55-56
Medical theory, problems of 109-110
Mental health 123-152
    alternative formulation of 141-142
Morbidity 100
Mortality 100
Multiethnicity and reflective nationalism, definition of 69
Negro Youth at the Crossways, description of 37-39
Parenting, teenage
    cultural prerequisites 376-378
    human imperatives 375-376
    issues 373-373
    program for 380-382
    relational essences 378-380
Personality
    Black-White differences of 49-62
    comparative study of 49-62
    cultural deprivation model of 51
    cultural difference model of 51-52
Preqnancy, Black adolescents and
    antecedents of
    developmental perspective 346
    societal context 346-348
    births 344-
    contraceptive use 342-343, 349-350

Subject Index

current statistics 341-342
outcomes of 353-360
programs 360-362
evaluation of 363
rates of 343-344
research 364-365
sexual activity 342
Property crimes, arrest for by race 132
Psychiatric hospitalization, rates of 125, 127-130
Psychiatric problems, misdiagnosis of 130-131
Psychological captivity, definition of 68
Psychosocial theory, problems of 110-114
Recidivism
   joblessness and 419-420
Role models 155-156
Rural Black America, characteristics of 80-81
Rural Black adolescents 79-95
   aspirations 87-88
   attitudes and values 88-89
   challenges faced by 79
   characteristics of 83
   home and family life 83-85
   psychoeducational intervention with 91-92
   school experiences 85-86
   self-concept 90
   social relationships 86
Self destructive behaviors 136-139
Sex education 16-18
   model programs 17
Sexual activity
   cognitive development and 350
   gender roles and 352-353
   locus of control and 351-352
   onset of 348-349
   problem-solving and 350-351
   school achievement and 351
Self concept
   Black-White differences in 52-53
   SES and 54
Sexuality-related problems 103-107
Social control, Black youth and 412-414
Social indicators 4-11
Social stressors 145-146
Socialization
   for work 416-418
   joblessness and 420-421
   jobs and 414-415
   prisons and 414-415
Special schools 219-221
Street academies 13, 220-221

Substance abuse 8-9, 139-141
   AIDS and 9
Substance use,
   alternative models 391-393
   Black adolescents, models for 389-391
   conventional models of 387-388
   intervention 394-396
Suburban Black youth
   study of 66-77
Suicide 101, 136-139
   incidence of 11
   race and 137
Systemic inequality, underachievement and 234-237
Tanner's stages 110
Teacher competence 215
Teen fathers 356-358
Teen mothers
   education 355-356
   marriage 354
   occupation 356
   offspring of 358-360
   parenting and social support 354-355, 373-382
   subsequent preqnancies 355
Teenage parents
   comprehensive services for 18-19
Therapeutic intervention 309-335
Therapy, Black adolescents and
   clinical problems 311-316
   deportment 323-325
   developmental problems 311-316
   establishing rapport 322-323
   group therapy 328-330
   individual therapy 326-328
   initial interview 317-322
   physical appearance 323-325
   psychoeducational approach 330-333
   role of clinician 311-312
   sociocultural factors in 316-317
Thus Be Their Destiny, description of 44
Tracking 236-237
Unemployment
   rates 5
   work experience and 5
Unwed teen-age pregnancy 9-11
   pschosocial consequences of 10
   children of 10
Urban Black adolescents
   therapeutic interventions with 309-335
Urban stress model 142-146
Violence 131-136
Violent crimes, arrests for by race 132

Black Adolescents

Vocational behavior
    aspirations and expectations and 255
    interacting psychosocial and
        subjective
        correlates and 259-260
    self-concept and 258-259
    view of the opportunity structure
        and 258
Vocational development 249-261
    historical perspective on 249

Vocational development theory 250
Vocational maturity 250-251
    Blacks and 251
    intelligence and 251-252
    school achievement and 254
    sex and 254
    socioeconomic status and 252-253
Work study programs 13
Youth employment programs 15-16
    shortcomings of 15